D1757230

University of Edinburgh
30150 026647153

Venture Capital and Private Equity Contracting

Venture Capital and Private Equity Contracting

An International Perspective

Douglas J. Cumming

Associate Professor and Ontario Research Chair,
York University – Schulich School of Business,
Toronto, Ontario, Canada

Sofia A. Johan

Senior Research Fellow,
Tilburg Law and Economic Centre (TILEC),
Tilburg, The Netherlands

AMSTERDAM • BOSTON • HEIDELBERG • LONDON • NEW YORK • OXFORD
PARIS • SAN DIEGO • SAN FRANCISCO • SINGAPORE • SYDNEY • TOKYO
Academic Press is an imprint of Elsevier

Academic Press is an imprint of Elsevier.
30 Corporate Drive, Suite 400, Burlington, MA 01803, USA
525 B Street, Suite 1900, San Diego, California 92101-4495, USA
84 Theobald's Road, London WC1X 8RR, UK

Library of Congress Cataloging-in-Publication Data
Application submitted

British Library Cataloguing-in-Publication Data
A catalogue record for this book is available from the British Library.

ISBN: 978-0-12-198581-3

For information on all Academic Press publications visit our Web site at www.elsevierdirect.com

Printed in the United States

09 10 11 9 8 7 6 5 4 3 2 1

For
Sasha Adeline
and
Dylan Jedi

Contents

Preface

This book is intended for advanced undergraduate and graduate students in business, economics, law, and management. It is also directed at practitioners with an interest in the venture capital and private equity industries, and it covers several different countries. The definitions of the terms *venture capital* and *private equity* may differ among countries, however, so in the book we define *venture capital* as risk capital for small private entrepreneurial firms and *private equity* as encompassing a broader array of investors, entrepreneurial firms, and transactions, including later-stage investments, turnaround investments, and buyout transactions.

Financial contracting is the common theme that links the topics covered in this book. This book explains the ways these contracts differ across the many types of venture capital and private equity funds, types of institutional investors, types of entrepreneurial firms, and across countries and over time. We will see when and how financial contracts are pertinent to the allocation of risks, incentives, and rewards for investors and investees alike. This book also examines when and how financial contracts have a significant relationship with actual investment outcomes and successes.

Why should we care about financial contracting? Venture capital and private equity funds are financial intermediaries between sources of capital and entrepreneurial firms. Sources of capital typically include large institutional investors, including pension funds, banks, insurance companies, and endowments. These and other sources of capital do not have the time or expertise to invest directly in entrepreneurial firms, particularly high-growth firms in high-tech industries. As such, specialized venture capital and private equity funds facilitate the investment process—at a price, of course. These funds are for all intents and purposes organizations that are established, capitalized, and operated under specific contractual terms and obligations agreed between the investors and the venture capital and private equity funds. A different type of financial contract governs the relationship between venture capital and private equity funds and their investee entrepreneurial firms, how such firms are capitalized, and how they are in turn operated. It is obvious therefore that financial contracting is not only something that venture capital and private equity funds do, but it is also in essence what they are.

Broadly framed questions addressed in this book include, but are not limited to, the following:

- What covenants and compensation terms are used in limited partnership contracts?
- In what ways are limited partnership contracts related to market conditions and fund manager characteristics, and how do these contracts differ across countries?

- What are the cash flow and control rights that are typically assigned in venture capital and private equity contracts with investee firms, and when do fund managers demand more contractual rights?
- Do different contractual rights assigned to different parties influence the effort provided by the investor(s)?
- In what ways are different financial contracts related to the success of venture capital and private equity investments?

By considering venture capital and private equity contracting in an international setting, this book offers an understanding of why venture capital and private equity markets differ with respect to fund governance, investee firm governance, and investee firm performance. This book provides examples of actual contracts that have been used in practice, including a limited partnership agreement, a term sheet, a shareholder agreement, and a subscription agreement. In addition, we provide datasets of venture capital and private equity that include details on a large number of actual contracts. It is important and relevant to review data to distinguish real investment contracts from actual transactions and to explain how financial contracts are central to actual investment decisions and investment outcomes. Without analyzing data, we would at best be limited to our best guesses, which is not our intention. The data considered in this book are international in scope from over 40 countries, with a focus on Canada, Europe, and the United States. It is important to consider data from a multitude of countries to understand how and why venture capital and private equity markets differ around the world. Also, idiosyncratic features of certain countries may distort our understanding of how venture capital and private equity contracts work in practice.

In short, by considering international datasets and not data from only one country, we can gain significant insight into how venture capital and private equity funds operate in relation to their legal and institutional environment. Each chapter in this book, where possible and appropriate, refers to and analyzes data. It is important to keep in mind, however, that venture capital and private equity funds are not compelled to publicly report data, nor are they willing to do so. As such, there are always more data to be collected. This book provides an understanding of how venture capital and private equity funds operate through financial contracts and, it is hoped, will inspire further empirical work in the field so we may better understand the nature and evolution of venture capital and private equity markets in years to come.

A Brief Note on Organization and Data

Part I of this book consists of three chapters. Chapter 1 briefly discusses aggregate industry statistics on venture capital and private equity markets around the world to compare the size of the markets in different countries. Chapter 2 describes agency problems in venture capital and private equity investment and is the only chapter that does not consider data. The intention in Chapter 2 is to provide a framework for understanding various agency problems that are empirically studied in subsequent chapters. Chapter 3 provides an overview of the empirical methods considered in this book. The description of the statistical and econometric techniques used is intended to be user friendly so all readers can follow along each of the chapters regardless of background. Chapter 3 also provides an overview of the institutional and legal settings in the countries considered in the different chapters. A central theme in this book is that differences in venture capital and private equity markets, including but not limited to contracting practices, are attributable to international differences in legal and institutional settings.

Part II (Chapters 4–9) considers venture capital and private equity fundraising and the structure of limited partnerships. Public policy toward fundraising and fund structure are also discussed in Chapter 9. To understand the contractual structure of limited partnerships, this book does not focus exclusively on contracts but rather, by presenting evidence on motivations underlying institutional investment in venture capital and private equity, provides a context through which to understand contracts. Chapter 4 begins with the perspective of institutional investors to reveal the motivations underlying the source of capital: institutional investors. In the United States, many institutional investors have long-standing relationships with venture capital and private equity fund managers that span multiple decades. Internationally, institutional investors have comparatively less experience with investment. Chapters 4, 7, and 8 examine recent data from institutional investors from the Netherlands to study a market that although less developed than that of the United States has significant commitments to venture capital and private equity funds, commitments to funds both domestic and international, and commitments in niche areas such as the socially responsible investment class. Also, regulatory changes make the Netherlands particularly interesting to study from the perspective of institutional investors. Chapters 5 and 6 complement the analysis of data from institutional investors by providing data from venture capital and private equity funds from a multitude of countries (Belgium, Brazil, Canada, Cayman Islands, Finland, Germany, Italy, Luxembourg, Malaysia, Netherlands Antilles, the Netherlands, New Zealand, Philippines, South Africa, Switzerland, the United Kingdom, and the United States). This international comparative evidence highlights the role of legal and institutional differences around the world and the impact on fund governance. Likewise, the data introduced in Chapter 9 on the role of government are examined in several different countries.

While Part II focuses on fund structure and governance, the subsequent sections of this book highlight the role of financial contracts with entrepreneurs (Part III), governance provided to investees (Part IV), and the divestment process (Part V).

Part III (Chapters 10–14) covers material pertaining to financial contracting with entrepreneurs. Chapter 10 summarizes evidence on investment activities in a number of studies from the United States. Chapters 11–13 consider evidence from financial contracting from U.S. and Canadian VCs, with a focus on security design. Chapter 14 considers evidence on financial contracting from Europe. It is worthwhile to compare evidence on financial contracts from the United States, Canada, and Europe to understand how laws and regulations, among other things, influence the design of financial contracts.

Part IV (Chapters 15–18) relates financial contracts and other investment mechanisms to the governance provided to the investee firm. Chapter 15 provides a survey of numerous factors that might influence investee governance. Chapter 16 considers the relation between contracts and actual investor effort in terms of advice and monitoring, as well as disagreement between investors and investees. Chapters 17 and 18 consider noncontractual factors that influence investor effort, particularly the role of geographic proximity and portfolio size.

Part V (Chapters 19–22) studies the exit outcomes of venture capital and private equity–backed companies. Because investees typically do not have cash flows to pay interest on debt or dividends on equity, venture capital and private equity investors invest with a view toward capital gains in an exit event. Chapter 19 provides an overview of the exit decision and summarizes evidence on exits from Australasia, Canada, Europe, and the United States. Chapters 20 and 21 show how exits are significantly related to the governance of the fund (as considered in Chapters 4–9) and contracts between investors and investees (as considered in Chapters 10–14) and the effort provided (Chapters 15–18). Exit outcomes are considered with reference to extensive data from Canada (Chapter 20) and Europe (Chapter 21). Chapter 22 provides evidence on the financial returns to venture capital investment from 39 countries around the world from North and South America, Europe, Africa, and Australasia. The data indicate that financial structures and governance are significantly related to returns. Chapter 22 also discusses evidence on reporting biases of the performance of unexited institutional investors for companies that have not yet had an exit event.

Selected chapters in this book are based on the following previously published materials:

Chapter 5:
Cumming, D., and S.A. Johan, 2006. "Is It the Law or the Lawyers? Investment Covenants Around the World." *European Financial Management*, 12, 553–574.

Chapter 6:
Cumming, D., and S.A. Johan, 2009. "Legality and Venture Capital Fund Manager Compensation." *Venture Capital: An International Journal of Entrepreneurial Finance*, forthcoming.

Chapter 7:
Cumming, D., and S.A. Johan, 2007. "Regulatory Harmonization and the Development of Private Equity Markets." *Journal of Banking and Finance*, 31, 3218–3250.

Chapter 8:
Cumming, D., and S.A. Johan, 2007. "Socially Responsible Institutional Investment in Private Equity." *Journal of Business Ethics*, 75, 395–416.

Chapter 9:
Cumming, D., 2007. "Government Policy towards Entrepreneurial Finance in Canada: Proposals to Move from Labour Sponsored Venture Capital Corporations to More Effective Public Policy." *CD Howe Institute Commentary*, No. 247.

Chapter 11:
Cumming, D., 2005. "Agency Costs, Institutions, Learning and Taxation in Venture Capital Contracting." *Journal of Business Venturing*, 20, 573–622.

Chapter 12:
Cumming, D., 2006. "Adverse Selection and Capital Structure: Evidence from Venture Capital." *Entrepreneurship Theory and Practice*, 30, 155–184.

Chapter 13:
Cumming, D., 2006. "Corporate Venture Capital Contracts." *Journal of Alternative Investments*, Winter 2006, 40–53.

Chapter 14:
Cumming, D., and S.A. Johan, 2008. "Preplanned Exit Strategies in Venture Capital." *European Economic Review*, 52, 1209–1241.

Chapter 16:
Cumming, D., and S.A. Johan, 2007. "Advice and Monitoring in Venture Capital Finance." *Financial Markets and Portfolio Management*, 21, 3–43.

Chapter 17:
Cumming, D., and S.A. Johan, 2006. "Provincial Preferences in Private Equity." *Financial Markets and Portfolio Management*, 20, 369–398.

Chapter 18:
Cumming, D., 2006. "The Determinants of Venture Capital Portfolio Size: Empirical Evidence." *Journal of Business*, 79, 1083–1126.

Chapter 20:
Cumming, D., and S.A. Johan, 2008. "Information Asymmetries, Agency Costs and Venture Capital Exit Outcomes." *Venture Capital: An International Journal of Entrepreneurial Finance*, 10, 197–231.

Chapter 21:
Cumming, D., 2008. "Contracts and Exits in Venture Capital Finance." *Review of Financial Studies*, 21, 1947–1982.

Each chapter of this book begins with a list of learning objectives and ends with a list of key terms and discussion questions. PowerPoint lecture slides for each chapter are available on the Web at http://venturecapitalprivateequity contracting.com. Any comments or questions about the book can be sent to the authors by e-mail at *Douglas.Cumming@gmail.com* and *sofiajohan@ email.com*.

Part One

Introduction

1 Introduction and Overview

These days almost everyone has heard of the terms *venture capital* and *private equity*. The venture capital and private equity markets are frequently discussed in popular media and are often described as "scorching" in the popular press, at least in boom times. The market has direct relevance for entrepreneurs who want to raise money, investors who want to make money from financing entrepreneurs, and individuals who want to work for a fund or set up their own fund. Also, venture capital and private equity are of significant interest to the public sector, as government bodies around the world strive to find ways to promote entrepreneurship and entrepreneurial finance. It is widely believed that venture capital and private equity funds facilitate more innovative activities and thereby improve the well-being of nations. It is thought of as a critical aspect of national growth in the twenty-first century.

The 23 chapters of this book provide an analysis of the issues that venture capital and private equity market participants face during the fundraising process (Part II), investment process (Part III), and divestment process (Part IV). A common theme across all of these issues is agency costs, so agency theory is reviewed in Chapter 2. All of the issues addressed in this book are analyzed from an empirical law and finance perspective, with a focus on financial contracting. Financial contracts are central to the establishment of the relationship between venture capital and private equity funds and their investors. Financial contracts also govern the relationship between venture capital and private equity funds and their investee entrepreneurial firms, as well as determine the efficacy of the divestment process. In most chapters we refer to datasets to grasp the real-world aspects of the venture capital and private equity process. Further, it is important to consider international evidence to grasp the impact of laws and institutions on the respective venture capital and private equity markets. The empirical methods and legal and institutional settings in this book are overviewed in Chapter 3.

1.1 What Are Venture Capital and Private Equity?

At the outset, it is important to discuss the definitions of the terms *venture capital* and *private equity.* Venture capital and private equity funds are financial intermediaries between sources of funds (typically institutional investors) and high-growth and high-tech entrepreneurial firms. Funds are typically established as limited partnerships, but, as we will see, there are other types of funds. A limited partnership is in essence a contract between institutional investors who become limited partners (pension funds, banks, life insurance companies, and endowments who have rights as partners but trade "management" rights over the fund for limited liability) and the fund manager, who is designated the general partner (the partner that takes on the responsibility of the day-to-day operations and management of the fund and assumes total liability in return for negligible buy-in). Chapter 5 examines in detail the structure of limited partnerships and limited partnership contracts. The basic intermediation structure of venture capital and private equity funds is graphically summarized in Figure 1.1.

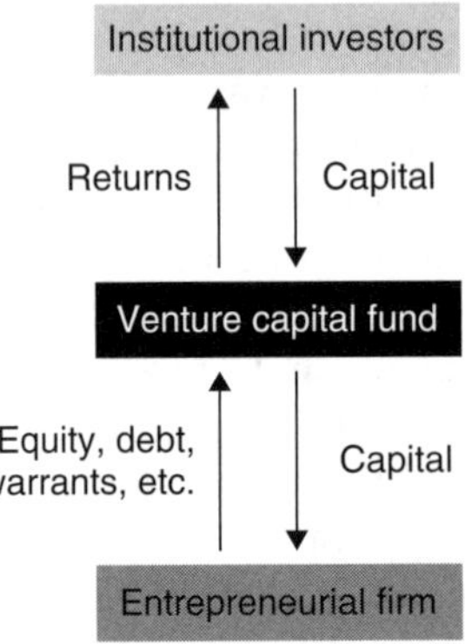

Figure 1.1 Venture Capital Financial Intermediation

Venture capital funds are typically set up with at least US$50 million in capital committed from institutional investors and often exceed US$100 million. Some of the larger private equity funds raised more than US$10 billion in 2006.[1] Fund managers typically receive compensation in the form of a management fee (often 1 to 2% of committed capital, depending on the fund size) and a performance fee or carried interest (20% of capital gains). Chapter 6 discusses factors related to fund manager compensation. Venture capital funds invest in start-up entrepreneurial firms that typically require at least US$1 million and up to US$20 million in capital. Private equity funds invest in more established firms, as discussed further below.

Venture capital is often referred to as the money of invention (see, e.g., Black and Gilson, 1998; Gompers and Lerner, 1999a,b,c, 2001a,b; Kortum and Lerner, 2000) and venture capital fund managers as those who provide value-added resources to entrepreneurial firms. Venture capital fund managers play

[1]See http://www.thomson.com/content/pr/tf/tf_priv_equiconsul/2006_07_17_2Q06_Mega_Funds_Drive.

a significant role in enhancing the value of their entrepreneurial investments as they provide financial, administrative, marketing, and strategic advice to entrepreneurial firms, as well as facilitate a network of support for an entrepreneurial firm with access to accountants, lawyers, investment bankers, and organizations specific to the industry in which the entrepreneurial firm operates (Gompers and Lerner, 1999a,b,c; Leleux and Surlemount, 2003; Manigart, Korsgaard et al., 2002; Manigart, Lockett et al., 2002; Sahlman, 1990; Sapienza et al., 1996; Wright and Lockett, 2003). Academic studies have shown that venture capital–backed entrepreneurial firms are on average significantly more successful than non–venture capital–backed entrepreneurial firms in terms of innovativeness (Kortum and Lerner, 2000), profitability, and share price performance upon going public (Gompers and Lerner, 1999a,b,c, 2001a,b).

Venture capital and private equity investments carried out by a fund typically last over a period of 2 to 6 years. A venture capital limited partnership envisages this extended investment horizon and thus is structured over a 10-year horizon (with an option to continue for an additional 3 years) so the fund manager can select investments over the first few years and then bring those investments to fruition over the remaining life of the fund. Investments are made with a view toward capital gains upon an exit event (a sale transaction), since entrepreneurial firms typically cannot pay interest on debt or dividends on equity. The terms of the investment often give the venture capital fund significant cash flow rights in the form of equity and priority in the event of liquidation. As well, the venture capital fund typically receives significant veto and control rights over decisions made by the management of the entrepreneurial firm.

The terms *venture capital* and *private equity* differ primarily with respect to the stage of development of the entrepreneurial firm in which they invest. Venture capital refers to investments in earlier-stage firms (seed or start-up firms), whereas private equity is a broader term that also encompasses later-stage investments as well as buyouts and turnaround investments. In this book, unless explicitly stated otherwise, for ease of exposition we use the term *private equity* to encompass all private investment stages, including venture capital. The various financing stages are defined as follows.

Seed: Financing provided to research, assess, and develop an initial concept before a business has reached the start-up phase.

Start-up: Financing provided to firms for product development and initial marketing. Firms may be in the process of being set up or may have been in business for a short time but have not sold their product commercially.

Other early stage: Financing to firms that have completed the product development stage and require further funds to initiate commercial manufacturing and sales. They will not yet be generating a profit.

Expansion: Financing provided for the growth and expansion of a firm that is breaking even or trading profitably. Capital may be used to finance increased production capacity or market or product development and/or to provide additional working capital.

Bridge financing: Financing made available to a firm in the period of transition from being privately owned to being publicly quoted.

Secondary purchase/replacement capital: Purchase of existing shares in a firm from another private equity investment organization or from another shareholder or shareholders.
Rescue/turnaround: Financing made available to an existing firm that has experienced trading difficulties—for example, the firm is not earning its weighted average cost of capital (WACC)—with a view to reestablishing prosperity.
Refinancing bank debt: To reduce a firm's level of gearing.
Management buyout: Financing provided to enable current operating management and investors to acquire an existing product line or business.
Management buy in: Financing provided to enable a manager or group of managers from outside the firm to buy in to the firm with the support of private equity investors.
Venture purchase of quoted shares: Purchase of quoted shares with the purpose of delisting the firm.
Other purchase of quoted shares: Purchase of shares on a public stock market.

In practice, sometimes broader categories are used:

Start-up: Sometimes used in practice to refer to start-up and other early stage.
Expansion: Sometimes used in practice to refer to expansion, bridge financing, or rescue/turnaround.
Replacement capital: Sometimes used in practice to refer to secondary purchase/replacement capital or refinancing bank debt.
Buyouts: Sometimes used in practice to refer to management buyout, management buyin, or venture purchase of quoted shares.

Precise definitions of terms vary somewhat depending on the norms in a particular country and the specific individuals surveyed. Because this book uses data from different countries, these terms are defined and explained, along with others, in their specific contexts in each chapter.

Definitions of stages of development in venture capital and private equity are perhaps usefully viewed in the context of a diagram. A common picture used in practice is shown in Figure 1.2. In this picture, venture capital finance is placed in a broader context of other sources of finance. Prior to seeking and obtaining venture capital finance, entrepreneurs who are just starting their venture often obtain capital from *friends*, *family*, and "*fools*" (also known as the 3 Fs or FFF). *Fools* refers to the high risk associated with investment in nascent stage firms, and the "valley of death" depicted in Figure 1.2 is where firms require significant capital inflows but show little or no revenues until subsequent years. Professional individual investors, known as angel investors, are a common source of capital for entrepreneurs prior to obtaining more formal institutionalized venture capital finance (Wong, 2002). Many angel investors are successful entrepreneurs who have, through experience, specialized abilities to recognize talent in other entrepreneurs and their new ventures. A classic example is Andy Bechtolsheim who cofounded Sun Microsystems. He gave \$100,000 to the founders of Google, who could not even cash the check because they had not yet established Google as a legal entity.

A limitation in the study of the market for angel investment, however, is the lack of systematic data.[2] This book will not be considering angel investment.

In Figure 1.2 the term *mezzanine* refers to investment in late-stage firms that are close to an initial public offering (IPO). An IPO is the first time a firm sells its shares for sale in the public market (i.e., lists or floats on a stock exchange). A seasoned equity offering involves additional capital-raising efforts by firms that are already trading on a stock exchange. Chapters 19 to 21 address the issues involved with the exit of venture capital investments through IPOs, mergers and acquisitions, and other exit vehicles.

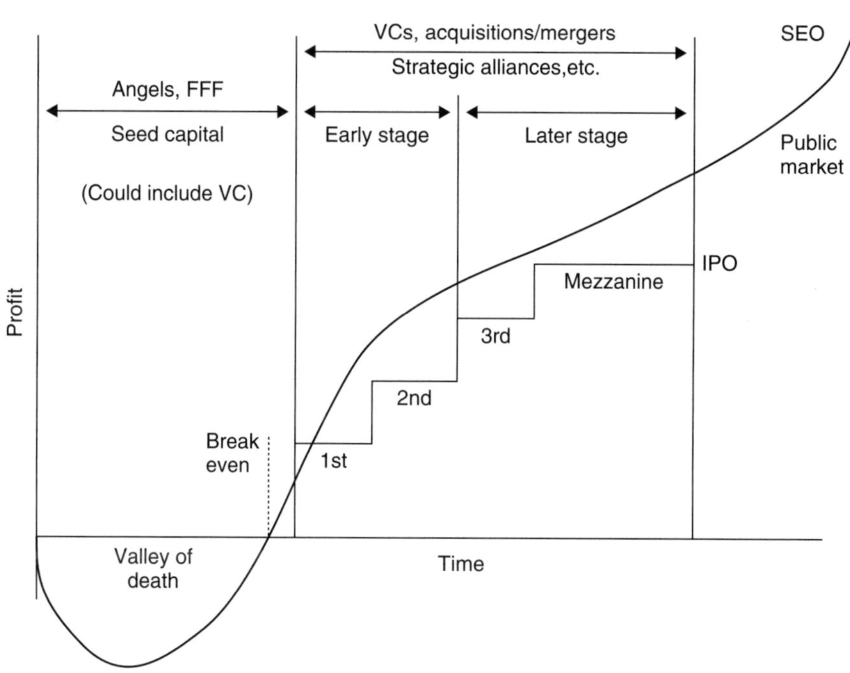

Figure 1.2 Stages of Entrepreneurial Firm Development

1.2 How Do Venture Capital and Private Equity Differ from Alternative Sources of Capital?

A salient point about raising capital for entrepreneurial firms is that there are many different sources of capital. This book considers venture capital and private equity only. But it is worth highlighting at the outset some general characteristics about this type of financing relative to other sources of financing. Table 1.1 provides a helpful, albeit oversimplified, overview of typical characteristics of

[2]Recent efforts spurred by the Kaufmann Foundation have begun to fill this gap, but there is significant work to be done in gathering systematic data.

Table 1.1 Greatly Oversimplified Typical Characteristics of Funds Providers

Source	Investment Motivation	Focus of Attention	Cash Typically Available	Source of Funds	Biggest Drawbacks	Biggest Advantages	Security Required	Subject to Market Conditions?
Internal Operations	Reinvestment	Execution	Unlimited	Earnings	Slow	Nondilutive	None	Some
Founders	Ambition	Varies	$100,000	Savings	Personal Risk	Nondilutive	None	Little
Friends and Family	Relationships	Support	$250,000	Savings	Relationships	Easy Sell	None	Some
Private "Angel" Investors	The Entrepreneur	Varies	$500,000 to $1.5 M	Previous Successes	Varying Commitment	Brings Credibility	None	Considerable
Venture Capital Funds	Business Plan, Team, Market, Trajectory	Contracts, Liquidity Event, Valuation	$1 M to $20 M	Limited Partners, Institutions	Time Consuming, Expensive	Brings Help, Credibility	Contractual Terms and Conditions	Greatly
Private Equity Funds	Mezzanine, Buyout, Turnaround	Contracts, Liquidity Event, Valuation	$20 M to $500 M	Limited Partners, Institutions	Time Consuming, Expensive	Brings Help, Credibility	Contractual Terms and Conditions	Greatly
Commercial Banks (& Venture Banks)	Risk versus Return	Two Repayment Sources	80% of A/R, 50% of inv.	Deposits	Regulatory Agencies	Advice, Clean, Straightforward, Businesslike	A/R, Inventory, IP	Little

Bridge Funds	Risk versus Return	Low Risk	$500K to $5M	Limited Partners, Institutions	Warrants	Speed (5 days to get a loan)	All Assets Including IP	Greatly
Leasing Companies	Risk versus Return	Liquidation Values	80% of Value	Company Treasury	Costly	Cheaper Than Equity	Varies	Little
Factors (buy your A/R)	Risk versus Return	Collections	80% of A/R	Company Treasury	~5% over Prime	Cheaper Than Equity	Varies	Little
Asset Lenders	Risk versus Return	Balance Sheet	80% of A/R, 60% of inv.	Company Treasury	Expensive	Cheaper Than Equity	Personal Guarantee	Little
Partner Companies	What You Can Do for Them	Synergies	Varies	Company Treasury	May Preclude Other Opportunities	2-Way Economics, Low Pricing Pressure	Little	Some
Government Agencies	Mandates	Regulations, Warrants	Varies	Taxes	Paperwork, Oversight	Inexpensive, No Recourse	Little or None	Little
Investment Bankers at IPO	Fees	Stock Market	Unlimited	Public	Costs, Underpricing, Public Disclosure	Advice, Public Exposure	Escrow, Lock-in	Extreme

alternative fund providers for entrepreneurial firms.[3] It shows where venture capital and private equity are positioned within the financing spectrum.

The range of sources of capital enumerated in Table 1.1 is broader than that illustrated in Figure 1.2. Figure 1.2 presented financing sources for start-up firms on a high growth trajectory. But the variety of sources of capital available to firms is much broader than that indicated in Figure 1.2.

Firms may finance their operations internally by reinvesting their profits. Alternatively, for firms that do not have internal finance or sufficient internal finance, they must seek external capital. A well-established literature in finance has established a kind of pecking order of firms' preferences for raising capital. Theoretical and empirical work has shown that firms prefer to finance their growth internally by reinvesting their profits because it is less costly than seeking external finance (Myers and Majluf, 1984; see also Myers, 2000). External capital comes at a cost. The cost of debt finance is the interest payments and the risk of being forced into bankruptcy in the event of nonpayment. The cost of equity finance is the dilution in ownership share associated with the equity sold. Where investors do not provide significant value added to the entrepreneurial firm, equity tends to be a more costly form of finance than debt.[4] In an empirical study of non–publicly traded entrepreneurial firms raising external capital, Cosh et al. (2005) find evidence that is highly consistent with this pecking order.

Different sources of external capital for entrepreneurs include banks, venture capital and private equity funds, leasing firms, factoring firms (that buy your accounts receivable), trade customers and suppliers, partners and working shareholders, angel investors, government agencies, and public stock markets. Cosh et al. (2005) find that firms' ability to access capital from different sources depends primarily on the degree of information asymmetry faced by the investors and their ability to do due diligence to mitigate such information asymmetry. Information asymmetry refers to the fact that the entrepreneur knows more about the project than the external investor does. Information asymmetry is both a risk and a cost to the external investor, and it explains why firms' own profits are a cheaper source of external capital than external debt or equity finance. With internal finance there is no price to pay in terms of compensating a bank or equity investor for carrying out a due diligence review to assess the quality of the firm before investment and for taking on a risk if the investment is carried out. Internal finance also has the advantage that it is nondilutive—that is, the entrepreneur does not have to give up equity ownership to an external investor.

Apart from the founding entrepreneur's (or entrepreneurs') savings, family, friends, and fools are common sources of capital for earliest-stage entrepreneurial firms. An entrepreneur without a track record typically has an easier time raising this type of capital because these investors will have known the entrepreneur for a long time. In other words, information asymmetries faced

[3]Table 1.1 is a slightly modified version of a chart that was circulated at an angel investment forum in Edmonton, Alberta, Canada, in 2003. "A/R" refers to accounts receivable, "inv." refers to inventories, and "IP" refers to intellectual property.
[4]This issue is discussed more extensively in Chapter 11.

by the 3 Fs are lower than that faced by other sources of external capital. As mentioned, angel investors do finance early-stage entrepreneurial firms but in general do not have a prior relationship with the entrepreneur. Angel investors typically look for entrepreneurs with their own "skin the game" (personal wealth invested), in addition to the 3 Fs, as a way to ensure that the entrepreneur is committed to the venture and to make sure that those who know the entrepreneur have faith in his or her abilities.

Venture capital funds tend to finance entrepreneurial firms with significant information asymmetries in terms of not having a lengthy operating history and in high-tech industries with hard-to-value intangible assets. Venture capital funds typically require an equity stake in the firms in which they invest.[5] Venture capital fund managers are specialized investors with the ability to carry out extensive due diligence of suitable projects in which to invest. One explanation for the very existence of venture capital funds is in fact the pronounced information problems associated with financing high-tech start-up entrepreneurial firms (Amit et al., 1998). Because venture capital funds are intermediaries between institutional investors and entrepreneurial firms (Figure 1.1) and there are minimum fund sizes that make the costs of establishing this type of financial intermediary viable, venture capital funds rarely consider projects that require less than US$1 million and almost never consider projects that require less than US$500,000.[6]

There are a variety of sources of external debt capital. Perhaps the most well-known source is the typical commercial banks. Most commercial bank loans require significant collateral and prefer to finance low-risk projects, and bank managers invest with a view solely to ensure that the loan is repaid on time and with interest. Riskier projects such as that considered by venture capital funds typically will not receive bank finance. Some banks, however, do have a strategy of making loans to venture capital–backed entrepreneurial firms. Silicon Valley Bank, which is part of SVB Financial Group, is one well-known example of this type of bank. Other specialized merchant banks undertake riskier projects with terms that compensate for the risk taken.

Bridge funds provide quick short-term sources of capital to firms with significant collateral. Leasing companies, factors (firms that buy your accounts receivable, or A/R), and asset lenders provide terms that are typically less favorable than a typical commercial bank loan, but are often used by entrepreneurial firms that need to ensure cash flow to continue to pay salaries and other ongoing expenses.

Entrepreneurial firms may receive capital from partner firms (such as major suppliers or customers). Costs and benefits depend on the relative bargaining power of the two organizations and the potential for strategic alliances.

Few studies have compared the relative importance of different sources of entrepreneurial capital. Perhaps the most informative data are provided by Cosh et al. (2005), which are based on a sample of 2,520 private firms in

[5]The form of equity taken is discussed in Chapter 11. Occasionally, funds will also invest with debt securities, as shown in Part III.

[6]Unless stated otherwise, dollar amounts in this book refer to 2007 U.S. dollars.

the United Kingdom for capital-raising decisions in 1996–1997. It showed that 37.8% (952 out of 2,520) firms in their data did seek external finance in the 1996–1997 period. The average amount of external finance sought was £467,667, and the median amount sought was £100,000. The average amount obtained was almost 81% of that which was sought, and the median percentage obtained was 100%. Overall, therefore, the data do not suggest a shortage of external capital for firms that make more than a trivial effort in applying for capital. Table 1.2 reports the number of firms in their data that did seek external finance by the type of source of finance, as well as the percentage of all their external capital obtained from the source. Among the firms that did seek external finance, 775 approached banks, 474 approached leasing firms, 151 approached factoring/invoice discounting firms, 138 approached partners/working shareholders, 87 approached venture capital funds, 83 approached private individuals, 53 approached trade customers/suppliers, and 67 approached other sources. It is interesting that outright rejection rates were highest among venture capital funds (46% rejection) and much higher than that for banks (17% outright rejection). The lowest rejection rate was among leasing firms (5%). Banks comprised the median and mean highest percentage of outside finance in terms of which type of source was approached and which type of source provided the finance. In fact, banks comprised the only type of source for which the median percentage of a firm's total external capital was greater than 0% (for banks, the median percentage is 34%; see Table 1.2).

The Cosh et al. (2005) data indicate that there is not a substantial capital gap for the majority of firms seeking entrepreneurial finance; rather, firms seeking capital are able to secure their requisite financing from at least one of the many different available sources. There are, however, differences in firms' abilities to obtain financing in the form they would like. Even after controlling for selection effects, Cosh et al. find that banks are more likely to provide the desired amount of capital to larger firms with more assets. Leasing firms, factor discounting/invoicing firms, trade customers/suppliers, and partners/working shareholders are more likely to provide the desired capital to firms with higher profit margins. Profit margins are not statistically relevant to venture capital funds and private individual investors; smaller firms are more likely to obtain financing from private individuals, whereas young, innovative firms seek external capital from venture capital funds.

Apart from private sources of capital, a variety of different types of government support programs exist to enable access to entrepreneurial finance. The nature and scope of programs varies greatly across different countries. Some of the programs related to venture capital are detailed in Chapter 9.

Finally, entrepreneurial firms may access external capital by listing their firm on a stock exchange in an IPO. This is one of a variety of different ways in which venture capital and private equity funds exit their investments. Part V of this book considers why venture capital and private equity funds exit by IPO versus other forms of exit. Also, Chapter 19 discusses evidence on factors that influence the performance of IPOs.

Table 1.2 Relative Importance of Specific Sources of External Capital in the U.K.

	Banks	Venture Capital Funds	Hire Purchase or Leasing Firms	Factoring/ Invoice Discounting Firms	Trade Customers/ Suppliers	Partners/ Working Shareholders	Other Private Individuals	Other
Number of Firms That Approached This Source for External Capital	775	87	474	151	53	138	83	67
Number of Firms That Did *Not* Approach This Source but Did Seek External Finance Elsewhere	177	865	478	801	899	814	869	885
Number of Firms That Approached This Source but No Finance Offered	133	40	23	29	5	12	20	14
Number of Firms That Approached This Source but Less Than Full Amount Offered	133	8	20	38	10	19	15	15
Number That Approached This Source and Full Amount Offered	509	39	431	84	38	107	48	38

(*continued*)

Table 1.2 *(continued)*

	Banks	Venture Capital Funds	Hire Purchase or Leasing Firms	Factoring/ Invoice Discounting Firms	Trade Customers/ Suppliers	Partners/ Working Shareholders	Other Private Individuals	Other
Mean Percentage of Total External Capital Obtained from This Source	42.749	2.851	23.792	5.892	1.624	5.313	3.910	3.598
Median Percentage of Total External Capital Obtained from This Source	33.580	0.000	0.000	0.000	0.000	0.000	0.000	0.000
Standard Deviation of Percentage Obtained from This Source	39.451	13.948	33.630	18.261	9.069	17.602	16.605	16.224
Minimum Amount Obtained from This Source	0.000	0.000	0.000	0.000	0.000	0.000	0.000	0.000
Maximum Amount Obtained from This Source	100.000	100.000	100.000	100.000	100.000	100.000	100.000	100.000

Source: Cosh et al. (2005).

1.3 How Large Is the Market for Venture Capital and Private Equity?

The market for venture capital and private equity varies significantly in different countries around the world. Data on the amount of venture capital and private equity per GDP for 28 countries are presented in Figure 1.3. Similar data over a longer time horizon are presented in Figure 1.4 and in Table 1.3. Figure 1.4 and Table 1.3 also include information pertaining to the value of exit transactions (sales of investments) and fundraising from institutional and other investors. Table 1.3 presents the sizes of the early stage and the expansion stage, total private equity (including early, expansion, late, buyout, and turnaround stages), fundraising, and dispositions (exits) expressed as a fraction of the gross domestic product (GDP). Values are averaged for the 1990–2003 period.

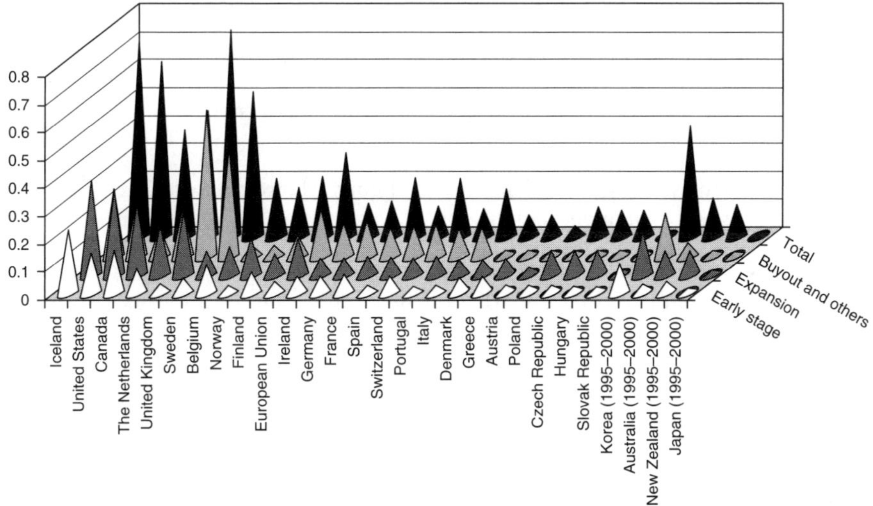

Figure 1.3 Venture Capital Investment by Stages as a Percentage of GDP, 1998–2001
Source: OECD.

The venture capital industry in the United States is the largest in the world in terms of total capital under management. As at 2003 more than US$100 billion in capital was under management by more than 1,000 funds. Funds in the United States are predominantly set up as limited partnerships and are typically very specialized in terms of stage of development and industry focus. There is significant geographic concentration of investment activity. Route 128 in Boston has a high concentration of biotechnology investments, and Silicon Valley in California has a high concentration of electronics and computer-related investments.[7]

[7]http://www.ventureeconomics.com, http://www.vfinance.com, http://www.v1.com, http://www.pwcmoneytree.com/.

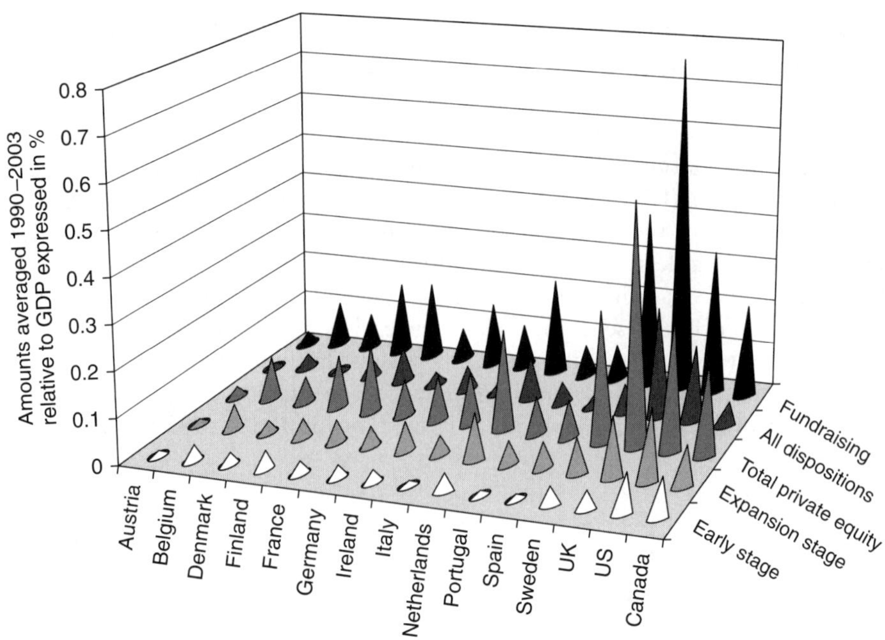

Figure 1.4 Size of Venture Capital and Private Equity Markets Across Countries
Source: Armour and Cumming (2006).

In 2003 Canada had about 130 funds, with US$20 billion in capital under management and approximately 50% of the capital managed by tax-subsidized labor-sponsored venture capital corporations (LSVCCs).[8] LSVCCs are tantamount to a mutual fund that invests in private equity, and they have individual retail-based investors, not institutional investors (discussed further in Chapter 9; see also Cumming and MacIntosh, 2006, 2007). Relative to their U.S. counterparts, funds in Canada tend to be less specialized in terms of stage of development, industry, and geographic focus.

In Australia in 2003 there was approximately US$3 billion in capital under management across 174 funds.[9] Many funds in Australia are quite small, as they are organized as pooled investment vehicles and not traditional limited partnership funds (Cumming et al., 2005b; Cumming, 2007c; Cumming and Johan, 2009b). There was comparatively little early stage investment activity until 1997 when the Government of Australia established the Innovation Investment Fund (IIF) program, which effectively made the government a limited partner in specialized early-stage funds along with other institutional investors that received more favorable terms (Cumming, 2007c).[10]

[8]http://www.cvca.ca, http://www.canadavc.com.
[9]http://www.abs.gov.au/Ausstats/abs@.nsf/0/bffef2819df68ca2ca256b6b007ab94e?OpenDocument.
[10]Technically, these funds were not set up as limited partnerships in Australia because limited partnerships were not permitted until 2005. Funds were established as trusts, which are very similar to limited partnerships. See Cumming et al. (2005b).

Table 1.3 Size of Venture Capital and Private Equity Markets Across Countries

Country	Early Stage	Expansion Stage	Total Private Equity	Fundraising	All Dispositions
Austria	6.06E-03	1.38E-02	2.44E-02	3.72E-02	9.41E-03
Belgium	2.85E-02	5.33E-02	1.03E-01	1.18E-01	4.61E-02
Canada	8.68E-02	9.34E-02	2.01E-01	2.13E-01	4.38E-02
Denmark	1.94E-02	2.79E-02	6.43E-02	9.99E-02	1.16E-02
Finland	3.54E-02	4.40E-02	1.23E-01	1.84E-01	4.26E-02
France	1.92E-02	5.15E-02	1.61E-01	1.91E-01	8.74E-02
Germany	1.92E-02	3.89E-02	8.65E-02	8.60E-02	3.52E-02
Ireland	2.37E-02	5.78E-02	1.05E-01	1.54E-01	6.01E-02
Italy	1.16E-02	4.10E-02	1.19E-01	1.12E-01	1.98E-02
Netherlands	3.17E-02	9.93E-02	2.22E-01	2.26E-01	1.03E-01
Portugal	1.32E-02	4.75E-02	8.16E-02	7.87E-02	4.27E-02
Spain	9.82E-03	5.18E-02	8.42E-02	9.01E-02	2.99E-02
Sweden	3.52E-02	6.98E-02	2.96E-01	4.12E-01	6.13E-02
U.K.	2.96E-02	1.31E-01	5.45E-01	7.70E-01	2.50E-01
U.S.	7.75E-02	1.57E-01	2.96E-01	3.29E-01	1.72E-01

Source: Armour and Cumming (2006).

In Hong Kong in 2003 there were 177 funds that collectively managed US$26 billion in committed capital.[11] In Europe in 2003 there were approximately 700 funds that collectively managed a little more than US$50 billion capital under management.[12]

A number of studies have sought to explain international differences in the size of venture capital and private equity markets. Leleux and Surlemount (2003) focus on differences across Europe and the effect of direct government investment programs in terms of whether they seed or crowd out (displace) private investment. They found that direct government investment programs had little effect. Jeng and Wells (2000) found evidence that favorable legal regimes that encourage pension investment and tax-friendly environments are more likely to stimulate venture capital across countries (consistent with U.S.-based evidence from Poterba, 1989a,b, and Gompers and Lerner, 1998a,b). Black and Gilson (1998), Cumming et al. (2006), and Armour and Cumming (2006) present evidence that public stock markets are important

[11]http://www.hkvca.com.hk/main_about.html.

[12]http://www.evca.com.

for venture capital markets, particularly because they offer an exit vehicle for venture capital funds to sell their investments. Based on the countries listed in Table 1.3, Armour and Cumming (2006) show that laws are just as important, and maybe even more important, and that the more successful venture capital and private equity markets are attributable to entrepreneur-friendly bankruptcy laws, legal environments that have clearly delineated shareholder rights, and low capital gains taxes. The importance of low capital gain taxes is consistent with the empirical work in Poterba (1989a,b); Gompers and Lerner (1998a,b); and Jeng and Wells (2000), and it is also consistent with the theoretical studies of Keuschnigg (2003a,b, 2004a,b), and Keuschnigg and Nielsen (2001, 2003a,b, 2004a,b,c). Armour and Cumming (2006) also found that direct government expenditure programs that create government-subsidized venture capital funds do not play a more pronounced role in stimulating the size of a venture capital market and may even crowd out private investment, particularly in the case of Canada (as discussed by Cumming and MacIntosh, 2006, 2007). A primary problem with the Canadian initiative has been the statutory covenants (essentially a statutory financial contract) governing the operations, or rather hampering the operations, of the LSVCCs. Chapter 9 considers in more detail the relative success of different government initiatives for stimulating venture capital and private equity markets in different countries.

1.4 What Issues Are Relevant to the Study of Venture Capital and Private Equity?

1.4.1 Information Asymmetries and Agency Problems

As we just mentioned, the problems of information asymmetries and agency costs are two of the paramount explanations for the existence of venture capital and private equity funds.[13] If no agency costs or information asymmetries exist, then entrepreneurial firms can simply raise capital from banks or other sources of debt finance. Agency costs and information asymmetries play a central role in shaping the contracts used to set up limited partnerships. Also, agency problems are the primary reason why venture capital and private equity funds use detailed contracts with their investee firms to govern their relationship over the life of the investment. Chapter 2 provides a review of different types of agency problems in entrepreneurial finance, and this material is provided before considering other topics. Agency problems are also defined and discussed in Chapter 2 in the context of different securities utilized by venture capital and private equity investors: debt, convertible debt, preferred equity, convertible preferred equity, common equity, and warrants. Chapter 2 covers agency problems to provide a context for the data that are presented and analyzed in subsequent chapters.

[13]See notes 5 and 6 and accompanying text.

1.4.2 International Institutional and Legal Context, and Empirical Methods

The data considered in this book are international in scope. Consideration of data from just one country might potentially lead to inferences that are not generalizable to other contexts. A classic example of this problem in the related literature on venture capital is the extensive literature on the apparent optimality of one type of security—convertible preferred equity—while the only country in the world where convertible preferred equity is the most frequent financing instrument is the United States. Chapter 3 therefore provides an overview of international differences in institutional and legal settings for the different countries considered, as well as an overview of the statistical and econometric methods presented in this book to help the reader follow all of the chapters regardless of prior training.

1.4.3 How Do You Attract Institutional Investors?

Chapters 4 to 9 focus on the structure of venture capital and private equity funds. Chapter 4 considers factors that influence fund manager fundraising. The underlying factors, both economic and regulatory, that institutional investors consider in making venture capital and private equity investments are examined more closely. The issues involved are illustrated by reference to survey data, which provide a relevant context for understanding the structures of venture capital and private equity and the role of regulation.

1.4.4 How Are Funds Structured?

Chapter 5 analyzes contracts that affect the operation of the fund. Private equity funds are often set up as limited partnerships with the use of very long-term contracts that typically last for 10 to 13 years. The fund investors are the limited partners who are not involved in the day-to-day operation of the fund; the fund manager is the general partner. Fund investors can expect to impose restrictive covenants on the general partners to mitigate the agency problems associated with the investment of the investors' capital. Therefore, to preempt this, the general partners draft the initial contracts that will form the basis of all negotiations. An example of a limited partnership fund contract is provided in Appendix 1 online at http://venturecapitalprivateequitycontracting.com. The initial contracts are also drafted by the general partners for more practical reasons: It allows the general partners to establish and assert their mandate to potential investors, enables the general partners to retain control among the many potential investors during the negotiation process, and minimizes legal costs associated with the setup of the fund. The covenants are then privately negotiated between the investors and general partners in a way that efficiently manages the incentives and controls the potential for opportunistic behavior among the general partners. Chapter 5 investigates how and why private equity fund structures differ internationally and analyzes the frequency of the use of restrictive covenants imposed by investors. In addition, we set out five categories of restrictive covenants used in governing the activities of private equity fund managers in areas pertaining to investment decisions, investment powers, types of investments, fund operations, and limitations on liability. We also analyze the impact of laws and institutions on private equity governance structures. Finally, we investigate the effect of the presence of legally trained fund managers on a fund's contractual governance structure.

1.4.5 How Well Are Fund Managers Compensated?

Chapter 6 considers the issue of fund manager compensation and explains how managerial compensation contracts differ across funds and across countries. We will see that managerial compensation differs depending on legal conditions, economic conditions, institutional investor characteristics, fund characteristics, fund manager education, and experience, among other things. Chapter 6 also examines recent legal debates, such as the taxation of fund managers in 2007. Fund manager carried interest compensation has always been taxed at a lower capital gains tax rate, but recently in both the United States and the United Kingdom (and other countries) efforts to enact higher income tax rates have been initiated.

1.4.6 Does Regulation Matter for Limited Partners and General Partners?

Chapter 7 considers in detail the issue of how to motivate institutional investors to invest in a private equity fund. To answer this question, we build on Chapter 4 with an understanding of the factors that induce institutional investors to allocate capital to private equity. We present data that compare the impact of regulations (as well as the lack of regulation), illiquidity, and other risks and rewards that lead institutional investors to allocate capital allocation to private equity instead of other asset classes. In view of the fact that contracts (discussed in Chapters 5 and 6) are incomplete and cannot possibly cover all eventualities, regulation plays a role in influencing institutional investor commitments to private equity.

1.4.7 Why Are Specialized Investment Mandates Necessary?

Institutional investors invest in private equity funds with the expectation that they will follow a certain investment style or mandate. Chapter 8 first discusses the issue of when institutional investors may be faced with a problem of style drift by the fund managers. We then focus on the central question in the chapter of what draws an institutional investor to a particular type of style: social responsibility. Is there a future in socially responsible private equity investment? What kinds of institutions are looking to invest in this niche? What are the economic, legal, and organizational factors that influence such portfolio allocation decisions? In Chapter 8 we investigate the factors that influence institutional investors to allocate capital to socially responsible private equity investments. Institutional investors' positions regarding their objectives in their strategic asset allocation will be set out and, more significantly, views regarding the perceived risks and hurdles faced by such investors in our attempt to determine the main concerns institutions have in adopting socially responsible investment.

1.4.8 What Role Does Government Play?

Chapter 9 considers government venture capital funds and public policy toward venture capital. Relative to investments in firms that are publicly listed on reputable stock exchanges, private equity investments are significantly more risky and require substantially more screening and monitoring. Given the inherent risks associated with private equity investments, much concern has arisen over the possible existence of an entrepreneurial "capital gap," or a deficiency in the amount of funds available to deserving entrepreneurial firms that are not publicly traded. This potential for a capital gap in private equity is of much concern to academics and policymakers, as it is widely recognized that entrepreneurial firms are key to innovation and economic growth. To mitigate the apparent capital gap, many countries have adopted policies to stimulate private equity investing, particularly venture capital investing. In Chapter 9 we consider how legislative enactments have made a difference to venture capital and private equity markets across the globe.

1.4.9 Time to Invest: The Process

Part III, which consists of Chapters 10 to 14, considers the contractual relationship between venture capital and private equity funds and their investee entrepreneurial firms. Chapter 10 provides an overview of the investment process and explains the role of term sheets (Appendix 2 provides a sample term sheet and is available online at http://venturecapitalprivateequitycontracting.com), shareholders agreements (Appendix 3), and subscription agreements (Appendix 4). An overview of the elements of due diligence, staging, syndication, and contracting are reviewed in Chapter 10. We also review evidence on how the liquidity of exit markets influence venture capital fund managers' investment decisions. Thereafter, Chapters 11 to 14 study contractual terms in much greater detail.

1.4.10 What Security Is Necessary?

Venture capital and private equity fund managers are among the most sophisticated financial intermediaries with abilities to mitigate agency problems. One of the more important steps taken by such sophisticated fund managers to mitigate such problems is the use of appropriate financial instruments to implement their investments and to allocate cash flow and control rights. After all, it would be rather remarkable if all types of entrepreneurial firms were financed with the exact same security, if a unique optimal form of finance for all types of firms existed, and if analogous cash and control rights allocation were used for all investee firms across the board. Rather, more generally, the predominant proposition in the literature since the seminal work of Jensen and Meckling (1976) has been that agency problems differ across different firms, and security design adjusts to appropriately mitigate the set of agency problems that are the most pronounced depending on the characteristics of the firm that is being financed. Chapter 11 investigates the question of whether the probability of use of each form of finance (including debt, common equity, preferred equity, and convertible securities) by private equity fund managers depends on the financing context: agency costs, tax, institutional sophistication and learning, and market conditions. We analyze security design for a variety of types of private equity funds (including limited partnerships, corporate funds, and government funds) and all types of entrepreneurial firms (including early stage, late stage, buyout, and turnaround firms, as well as firms in different industry sectors). Chapter 12 considers in further detail whether security design with different financial instruments "attract" different types of entrepreneurial firms in terms of the adverse selection risks associated with financing low-quality firms in relation to the financial security used.

1.4.11 What Is Distinct about Corporate Venture Capital Investment?

Corporate venture capital funds are widely regarded as having performance results that are inferior to limited partnership venture capital funds. Three explanations for this inferior performance include (1) the comparatively autonomous structure of limited partnership venture capital funds relative to corporate venture capital funds, (2) the greater pay-for-performance sensitivity among limited partnership venture capital funds relative to corporate venture capital funds, and (3) the strategic rationales associated with corporate investing versus the purely financial incentives of limited partnership venture capital funds. Chapter 13 explores a fourth reason: Corporate venture capital funds use contracts with entrepreneurs that are associated with inferior financial returns.

1.4.12 How Do Exit Expectations Influence Financial Contracts?

Chapter 14 empirically considers the role of preplanned exits (the investor's initial strategy to sell the investee company via an acquisition or an IPO at the time of initial contract with the entrepreneur) in influencing the design of venture capital contracts. In addition, a theme in the chapter is that legal conditions and investor versus investee bargaining power influence the allocation of cash flow and control rights in venture capital contracts. The chapter introduces a sample of 223 entrepreneurial investee firms financed by 35 venture capital funds in 11 continental European countries. The data indicate the following.

First, preplanned acquisition exits are associated with stronger investor veto and control rights, a greater probability that convertible securities will be used, and a lower probability that common equity will be used. The converse is observed for preplanned IPOs.

Second, investors take fewer control and veto rights and use common equity in countries of German legal origin, relative to Socialist, Scandinavian, and French legal origin.

Third, more experienced entrepreneurs are more likely to get financed with common equity and less likely to be financed with convertible preferred equity, whereas more experienced investors are more likely to use convertible preferred equity and less likely to use common equity.

1.4.13 What Influences Investor Effort?

By the end of Part III of this book we will have considered the use of formal mechanisms (e.g., actual contracts that specify ownership and control, and the law that governs the enforcement of such contracts) to establish the functions of the private equity fund manager and the entrepreneur within the investee entrepreneurial firm, and to govern the relationship between the parties. Contracts are by definition incomplete, however, since not all eventualities can be anticipated at the time of writing a contract (see, e.g., Hart and Moore, 1994, 1999). For example, while the number of hours to be allocated by each party to the management of the firm can be specified within the contracts, the degree of effort to be contributed during those hours cannot be specified. We therefore expect more "informal" governance mechanisms (e.g., trust, reputation, and management structures) to play a strong role in governing the relationships that are formed by such contracts.

Part IV therefore begins in Chapter 15 with a survey of what is known about factors that influence investor effort. Private equity investors, particularly venture capital funds, are widely regarded as active value-added investors that spend a significant amount of time serving on entrepreneurial firm board of directors, providing strategic, financial, marketing, and administrative advice while also monitoring the actions of the entrepreneurs managing the firm. While this value-added service is an integral aspect of private equity investment, it is the complex contractual structure within which this provision of advice and monitoring can be carried out, which is deemed to be the crux of the success of this form of finance. Various legal and economic factors come into play in laying down the foundations of an investment. Even before the first dollar is collected from investors to make initial investments, fund managers have to ascertain the fund governance structure that sets clear investment patterns and makes clear their investment mandate, such as their financial risk exposure and the extent to which they will be able to provide their services as a resource to the investee firms.

1.4.14 Do Contracts Ensure Effort?

In Chapter 16 we match detailed venture capital contracts to actions taken by venture capital funds in an international context and compare the role of contracts to other more informal governance mechanisms in facilitating participation in firm management by the venture capital fund manager. We provide evidence that the legal framework has a strong impact on each of these closely related areas of governance, and we show how the resolution of each of these issues in turn affects the level of advice and monitoring a fund manager is able to efficiently provide to an investee firm.

1.4.15 Where Should You Invest?

In view of the informational asymmetries and agency problems that characterize private equity investment, it is expected that fund managers will exhibit a "home bias" when investing. Chapter 17 explores home bias by examining the institutional and agency factors that influence geographic proximity in private equity investment.

1.4.16 How Many Investments Should You Have?

Chapter 18 considers how many investments are undertaken in different entrepreneurial firms by venture capital and private equity funds. Unlike mutual funds, venture capital and private equity funds are not well diversified. Venture capital and private equity fund managers are active investors who add value to their investee firms by providing strategic, managerial, financial, marketing, and human resource advice, and they typically sit on the board of directors of their investee firms. Time constraints make it virtually impossible for value-added fund managers to be well diversified. In Chapter 18 we analyze how many investments are carried out by fund managers, and discuss factors that lead to differences across funds.

1.4.17 Time to Divest: The Process

Part V, which consists of Chapters 19 to 22, considers the divestment process. There are five primary types of exits: initial public offerings (IPOs, or new listings on a stock exchange for sale to the general public); acquisitions (in which the venture capital fund and entrepreneur sell to a larger firm); secondary sales (in which the venture capital fund sells to another firm or another investor, but the entrepreneur does not sell); buybacks (in which the entrepreneur repurchases the interest of the venture capital fund); and write-offs (liquidations). Chapter 19 explains the different exit vehicles available to venture capital funds and surveys evidence on the frequency of the mode of exit across countries. In Chapter 19 we illustrate how investment duration varies according to the ability of the venture capital fund manager to provide a sustained competitive advantage to the entrepreneurial firm. Further, we review evidence that considers the performance of venture capital–backed IPOs and acquisitions.

1.4.18 What Exit Vehicle Should You Use?

Exit patterns vary depending on market conditions in the exit year, the characteristics of the private equity investor (private limited partnership, corporate, and government), the characteristics of the investee entrepreneurial firms (industry and stage of development at first investment), and the characteristics of the transaction (capital requirements, syndication, and security design). In Chapters 20 and 21 we analyze the exit profiles of Canadian and European private equity funds, respectively. We explain similarities in factors that influence exit patterns across different countries in reference to contractual terms, among other things.

1.4.19 Valuation and Disclosure

Chapter 22 reviews the mechanics behind valuing venture capital fund investments. An example is provided for the venture capital method of valuation. Thereafter, we review venture capital and private equity performance data for actual investments and relate performance to valuation depending on different financial structures. Finally, we discuss how valuations of un-exited investments are disclosed to institutional investors by venture capital and private equity fund managers. The issue of reporting or disclosure by private equity funds is particularly timely and important. The issue arose in practice in the recent "transparency lawsuits" in which public pension funds such as CalPERS, the largest pension fund in the United States, were forced to publicly disclose the performance results of private equity funds in which CalPERS was invested (an issue that is also addressed in Chapter 7).

The final part of this book provides a summary and concluding remarks. Online at http://venturecapitalprivateequitycontracting.com we provide appendices with sample financial contracts (a limited partnership fund agreement, term sheet, shareholder agreement, and subscription agreement) as well as PowerPoint slides that accompany each chapter.

2 Overview of Agency Theory

2.1 Introduction and Learning Objectives

This chapter provides an overview of the different agency problems in the context of financial contracting. The term *agency cost* generally refers to actions the parties to a contract might do that are in their own self-interest but are against the interest of the other party. If agency problems did not exist, then most details in financial contracts would be immaterial. Much of what venture capital and private equity funds do involves agency costs, and a central mechanism by which agency costs can be mitigated is through financial contracts. Hence, the analysis of venture capital and private equity in this book is focused on financial contracting, and in this analysis it makes sense to begin with a primer on agency costs.

In this chapter we provide an overview of agency costs in the context of different forms of finance (debt, convertible debt, preferred equity, convertible preferred equity, common equity, warrants). Many agency principles can be illustrated within this context. Further, because both venture capital and private equity funds use all of these different forms of finance in practice,[1] it is not an "academic" or trivial exercise to study all forms of finance in the context of either venture capital and/or private equity.

In this chapter we discuss the following:

- What each form of finance (debt, convertible debt, preferred equity, convertible preferred equity, common equity, warrants) actually entails
- How different types of agency problems arise when different forms of finance are used
- How mitigating agency problems can enhance firm value
- How subsequent chapters in this book relate to the topics of how venture capital and private equity fund managers use contracts to mitigate agency problems and enhance firm value

[1]The issue of what forms of finance are used in practice is studied in detail in Chapters 10 to 14. In some countries, such as the United States, a narrower range of different securities are used in early-stage venture capital transactions.

2.2 Forms of Finance

Investments in entrepreneurial firms may take a variety of forms, including debt, convertible debt, preferred equity, convertible preferred equity, common equity and warrants, or any combination of these instruments. Nonconvertible debt and nonconvertible preferred equity are known as fixed claims because they provide the investors with a fixed return on the investment as long as the entrepreneur is able to repay the obligation in full. All of the other securities enable the investor with an equity or ownership stake in the firm and are known as residual claims because the investor shares in the upside as the entrepreneurial firm increases in value. The issue of fixed claims versus residual claims is one of the most fundamental distinctions in terms of different forms of finance.

2.2.1 Debt

Debt claims give the investor higher priority over preferred equity (convertible or otherwise), common equity, and warrant holders. Debt typically comes with stipulated interest payments (typically annual or semiannual), but it is possible to have a "zero-coupon" debt instrument in which there are no interest payments. When interest payments are not made on time and in full, it might be possible for the investor to force the entrepreneurial firm into bankruptcy. If no other debt holders or stakeholders to the firm that have senior claims exist, a debt holder can force the entrepreneurial firm to repay the interest by liquidating the firm's assets, and this may be done formally in bankruptcy proceedings. Debt holders have a higher priority in bankruptcy than preferred equity holders and common equity holders.

Debt may or may not have an option to be converted into common equity. Where such an option exists, the claim is called convertible debt. Convertible debt enables the investor to exercise an option to use the value of the fixed claim to purchase common equity in the company. The value of a common equity claim varies with changes in the value of the entrepreneurial firm. The terms upon which debt can be converted into common equity in a convertible debt claim are prespecified in the initial debt contract. Convertible debt holders will exercise their option to convert when the firm increases in value, and this value increase is expected to continue in the foreseeable future. Once the investor converts the entire debt claim into common equity, the investor loses priority rights in bankruptcy, the stream of interest payments, and the ability to force the firm into bankruptcy. There are, however, payoffs to such sacrifices.

The payoff to a debt holder is illustrated in Figure 2.1. If a debt holder is paid in full, she receives from the entrepreneurial firm the principal (the amount borrowed) and the stream of interest payments. The value of a debt contract is the present value of the interest and principal (accounting for the time value of money).[2] If the entrepreneurial firm is sufficiently successful that

[2]The time value of money is discussed briefly in Chapter 22 in the context of valuation. For an applied discussion on the Internet, see http://en.wikipedia.org/wiki/Time_value_of_money.

it can repay the interest and principal on debt, then increases in the value of the entrepreneurial firm do not have any affect on the value of a debt claim. For this reason, the payoff to debt is a straight horizontal line after the level of the preset value of the principal and interest payments. However, if the entrepreneurial firm is not successful and worth less than the present value of the principal and interest, then the value of the debt claim varies depending on the value of the entrepreneurial firm. In this type of bankruptcy situation, if there are no other claimants to the firm's assets (such as unpaid wages), then the value of the debt claim varies in direct proportion to the value of the entrepreneurial firm. For this reason, we draw a 45% line from the origin in Figure 2.1 up to the level that represents the present value of the interest and principal.

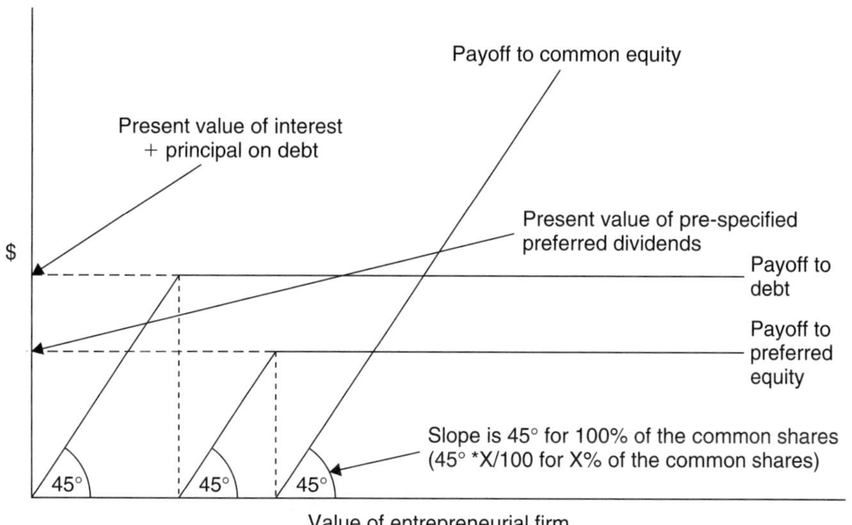

Figure 2.1 Payoff Functions

2.2.2 *Preferred Equity*

Preferred equity investors have the right to a stream of prespecified dividend payments in the preferred equity contract.[3] Preferred equity investors are not the "owners" of the firm. A common misunderstanding among students of entrepreneurial finance is that preferred equity is similar to common equity insofar as equity implies ownership. Preferred equity is a fixed claim that bears much greater similarity to nonconvertible debt than it does to common equity.

[3]Preferred equity shares typically have dividends in perpetuity, and therefore the value of a nonconvertible preferred equity type of claim is simply the prespecified dividend divided by the discount rate. See footnote 2.

The payoff to preferred equity is indicated in Figure 2.1. Preferred equity has value only when the entrepreneurial firm is able to pay principal and interest on debt.

The only way that preferred equity affords rights of ownership is if the preferred equity has a convertibility option (not an obligation) whereby preferred shares can be exchanged for common shares. Terms of conversion are set out in the original preferred equity share. Often, terms of conversion are variable. For example, terms might be specified in a way that enables two preferred shares to be exchanged for one common share if the entrepreneurial firm is below a certain value, but only one preferred share is to be exchanged for one common share if the entrepreneurial firm is above that value. The reasons for these variable conversion terms are discussed later in this chapter.

Preferred equity holders rank behind debt holders but ahead of common equity holders in bankruptcy proceedings. Nonpayment of preferred dividends by the entrepreneurial firm does not enable the preferred equity holder to force the firm into bankruptcy, as in the case of nonpayment of interest on debt. Rather, preferred equity holders only have a right to receive all prespecified preferred dividends in arrears prior to payment of any common equity dividends.

A special type of preferred stock is participating preferred stock. Participating preferred stock gives the investor the right to receive prespecified preferred dividends, as well as additional dividends based on prespecified conditions. Also, participating preferred shareholders may be allocated a pro rata right to the common shareholders' proceeds in the event of liquidation.

2.2.3 Common Equity

Common equity shares enable the investor rights of ownership. Common equity holders are, however, last in priority behind debt and preferred equity holders in the event of bankruptcy. Dividends are not prespecified with common equity, unlike preferred equity. Some firms rarely or almost never pay common equity dividends (e.g., Microsoft Corporation, which was founded in 1975, incorporated in 1981, and floated in 1986, announced its first ever dividend payment on January 16, 2003), whereas other firms more frequently pay dividends. The value of common equity depends on expected dividend payments and capital appreciation. Common equity is a claim to the residual value of the firm: After interest and principal on debt is paid and preferred dividends are paid, capital appreciation of the firm enhances the value of common equity shares. For successful entrepreneurial firms that start small but grow to be large companies, the most valuable security is common equity.

2.2.4 Warrants

Warrants are like option contracts to buy common equity at a prespecified price that is indicated in the contract. The option is typically valid for a few years but might also be valid for an unlimited period of time. Warrants are typically sold at a price that is slightly greater than the current value of common equity.

Unlike options that provide the holder the option to exercise a right to purchase or sell securities already issued by the firm, warrants increase the number of securities issued by the firm when they are exercised. Warrants are also more similar to "American options," which refer to options that enable the option holder to exercise the option anytime between the purchase date and the expiration date; "European options" are options that may be exercised only on the expiration date. Because American options are more flexible, they are more valuable and sell for a premium relative to European options, all else being equal. When a warrant is not exercised and expires past the exercise date, it is worthless.

An investor who purchases a nonconvertible preferred equity claim together with a warrant has a claim that is similar to a convertible preferred equity claim, but these claims are not identical. A convertible preferred equity claim once exercised transforms the entire claim into common equity. An investor with warrants and nonconvertible preferred equity still holds a preferred equity claim after exercising the warrants. Similarly, an investor who purchases nonconvertible debt together with warrants has a claim that is similar but not identical to convertible debt. Payoffs to convertible securities are shown in Figure 2.2.

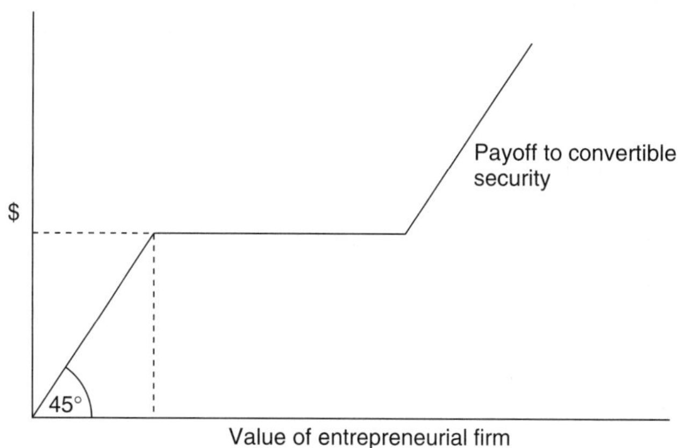

Figure 2.2 Payoff Function for Convertible Security

Investors may purchase any combination of securities issued by an entrepreneurial firm. For example, as we will see in Chapter 11, a venture capital investor may hold a mix of common equity, preferred equity, and debt in the same entrepreneurial firm, with these securities being purchased contemporaneously. While such combinations are quite rare, it is noteworthy that it is not impossible to see such a mix of securities in practice. The lesson is that entrepreneurial firms have the ability to raise capital and issue securities in numerous ways, subject only to their inventiveness and negotiation skills.

Finally, notice that the form of finance in terms of debt, preferred equity, common equity, and so forth is not the only financing term in a contract between an investor and the firm. There are many other contractual clauses that accompany a financing arrangement, and clauses accompanying each security may be varied accordingly. These additional clauses are discussed in Chapters 10, 14, 15, and 21. At this stage, for the purposes of this chapter on introducing agency problems, we focus only on the type of security and not any associated clauses.

2.3 Agency Problems

A principal-agent problem arises when a principal hires an agent under conditions of incomplete and asymmetric information. An agent is responsible for and takes actions that affect the financial returns to the principal. An agent may, however, have either pecuniary or nonpecuniary interests in taking actions that are against the interest of the principal. These potentially adverse actions of the agent are referred to as agency problems. Contracts can be designed to enable a principal to mitigate agency problems, but agency problems can never be fully eliminated (Farmer and Winter, 1986). The central issue considered in this book is how contracts in the context of venture capital and private equity finance can be designed to mitigate agency problems as best possible.

A common example of the principal-agent relationship is the employer-employee relationship. Because it is impossible to continually monitor the activities of an employee, the employee can do many things that are against the interests of his employer. For example, an employee might shirk responsibilities or not work as efficiently as possible when he is not being monitored. Employment contracts can be structured in a way to mitigate agency problems. For example, an employee who is on a fixed salary has a greater incentive to shirk responsibilities than an employee who is working on commission or who receives a performance bonus. Because many actions by employees are observable but not verifiable, it is not possible to write contracts that anticipate and address all aspects of an employer-employee relationship, and therefore agency problems will exist to some extent regardless of the structure of the contract. The key to writing a good contract is to recognize that contracts are by definition incomplete and that although every possible eventuality cannot be foreseen, agency problems that can be anticipated must be addressed while mitigating the capacity for other potential agency problems to develop.

The venture capital and private equity context is particularly interesting for investigating agency problems (Sahlman, 1990). Figure 2.3 illustrates the agency relationships that exist in a typical (albeit simplified) venture capital context. Figure 2.3 considers two limited partnership venture capital funds with two institutional investors (one for each fund). The venture capital funds have invested in the same entrepreneurial firm (a syndicated investment). The agency relationships in Figure 2.3 are presented with the use of arrows whereby the direction of the arrow points to the agent from the principal. The figure actually shows eight distinct agency relationships among different principals and different agents.

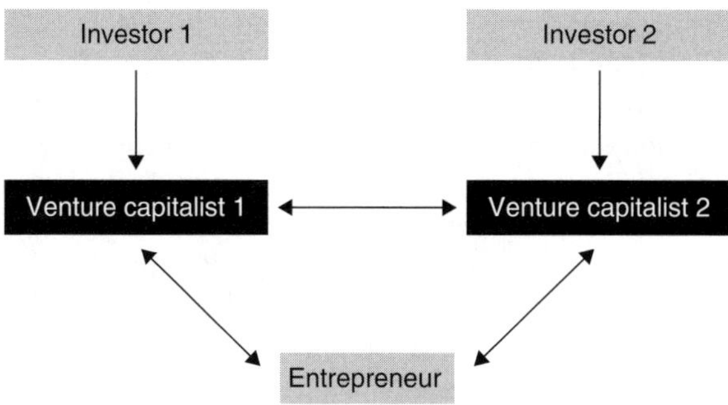

Figure 2.3 Principal ← → Agent Relationships in Venture Capital

	Principal	Agent
1.	Investor 1	Venture Capitalist 1
2.	Investor 2	Venture Capitalist 2
3.	Venture Capitalist 1	Entrepreneur
4.	Venture Capitalist 2	Entrepreneur
5.	Entrepreneur	Venture Capitalist 1
6.	Entrepreneur	Venture Capitalist 2
7.	Venture Capitalist 1	Venture Capitalist 2
8.	Venture Capitalist 2	Venture Capitalist 1

The first agency relationship in Figure 2.3 involves Investor 1 as the principal and Venture Capitalist 1 as the agent. As explained in Chapter 1 (and will be reviewed in more detail in Chapter 5), limited partnership venture capital funds are organized with the venture capital fund manager as the general partner who manages the fund. Investors are the limited partners and by definition do not get involved in the day-to-day operation of the fund activities (otherwise they would lose their limited liability status as limited partners).[4] Therefore, the arrow in Figure 2.3 goes from the direction of Investor 1 to Venture Capitalist 1, and not vice versa. The venture capital fund manager takes steps on behalf of the fund's investors that affect the financial returns to the investors. There are a number of things that a venture capital fund manager might do that are against the interests of its investors, as we will see in Chapter 5. The second agency relationship in Figure 2.3 between Investor 2 and Venture Capitalist 2 is analogous to the first between Investor 1 and Venture Capitalist 1.

[4]In practice, limited partners are known to have some (typically minor) involvement in their funds, and the extent of involvement depends on the fund manager and the limited partners. In legal form, however, the limited partners are not part of the decision making of the fund, which affords them the status of limited liability (Cumming and Johan, 2006a; Gompers and Lerner, 1996).

The third through sixth agency relationships in Figure 2.3 are between Venture Capitalist 1 and the Entrepreneur, and Venture Capitalist 2 and the Entrepreneur. Venture Capitalists 1 and 2 provide capital to the Entrepreneur. The Entrepreneur may act against the interests of Venture Capitalists 1 and 2. Therefore, the Entrepreneur is an agent of the principals Venture Capitalists 1 and 2. At the same time, however, Venture Capitalists 1 and 2 are typically active investors because they provide more than just capital to the Entrepreneur. Venture capitalists sit on boards of directors, and they provide strategic, financial, marketing, administrative, and human resource advice to their investee firms. Some venture capital funds are widely regarded as providing greater value-added advice to their investee firms than others (Hsu, 2004), and venture capitalists might provide significantly different levels of assistance to different investee firms of the same venture capital fund. Hence, the arrows between Venture Capitalists 1 and 2 and the Entrepreneur go in both directions: the Entrepreneur as a principal, and Venture Capitalists 1 and 2 as agents of the Entrepreneur.

The seventh and eighth agency relationships in Figure 2.3 involve Venture Capitalists 1 and 2, which are supposed to be value-added active investors in the syndicated investment. Venture Capitalist 1, however, might "free ride" off the effort of Venture Capitalist 2, or vice versa. The venture capitalists similarly might act against each other's interests. Therefore, there are two additional agency relationships: Venture Capitalist 1 as principal and Venture Capitalist 2 as agent, and Venture Capitalist 2 as agent and Venture Capitalist 1 as principal.

Figure 2.3 highlights the complexity of the agency relationships for typical, very simplified venture capital transactions. For a single transaction there are numerous agency relationships. Many venture capital investments are syndicated,[5] and many involve more than two syndicated investors, so it is common to have even more complex agency relationships in a single transaction. Furthermore, venture capital investments are long-term investments, typically lasting for two to seven years.[6] Amounts invested in an entrepreneurial firm are typically above US$1 million in each transaction. Investment contracts are therefore extremely detailed. The parties have large stakes invested (in terms of financial, effort, and reputational commitment) over lengthy periods of time involving many interested parties, and there is significant scope for the parties to act in ways that are potentially detrimental to one another's interests.

We now highlight some of the common agency problems that arise in venture capital financing arrangements. The different agency problems identified have been developed in the academic literature, particularly since 1970 in the finance literature. The ways in which entrepreneurs and investors can act against one another's interests can be categorized into several areas:[7] moral hazard, bilateral moral hazard, multitask moral hazard, adverse selection, free

[5]Chapter 10 provides statistics on the frequency of syndication in venture capital.

[6]Chapter 19 considers statistics on the duration of venture capital investments.

[7]Practitioners might refer to these terms as academic jargon, but these terms do enable us to identify the particular agency problem at hand.

riding, hold-up, trilateral bargaining, window dressing, underinvestment, asset stripping, and risk shifting.

2.3.1 Moral Hazard

The term *moral hazard* most commonly refers to the prospect of an agent not exerting best effort (against the interest of the principal) in view of his diminished accountability. This effort will in turn affect the expected payoff of the principal. It is not possible to write a contract to enforce effort. Effort is potentially observable but not verifiable and therefore unenforceable (it would generally be implausible to sue someone for "lack of effort"). It is, however, possible to write contracts to incentivize effort. In a venture capital financing context, this is particularly important, as the effort of each party affects the expected value of the entrepreneurial venture.

Recall the different securities discussed earlier in this chapter. An agent's (the entrepreneur's or the venture capitalist's) effort is an increasing function of her residual claim (share in the profits) to the venture.[8] The intuition is straightforward. The entrepreneur and the venture capitalist take unobservable actions that affect the expected payoff to be divided between them. The effort of each agent yields a positive externality on the other party, but such effort is costly to both parties. As such, when bankruptcy is not expected, the entrepreneur's [venture capitalist's] effort into a venture is an increasing [decreasing] function of the relative amount of debt to common equity provided to the venture capitalist. A sharing rule that provides a greater equity share to the venture capitalist yields more [less] VC [entrepreneurial] effort.[9] If the contracting objective is to mitigate moral hazard costs (and abstracting from all other possible contracting objectives and other types of agency problems) and the venture capitalist is not expected to provide effort, it makes sense to provide the venture capitalist with a fixed claim security (nonconvertible debt or nonconvertible preferred equity). If the venture capitalist is expected to provide effort, then it makes sense to provide the venture capitalist with at least some common equity or a convertible security that can be converted into common equity. In short, moral hazard tells us that an agent's incentive to maximize effort is an increasing function of the agent's residual claim to the entrepreneurial venture.

2.3.2 Bilateral Moral Hazard

Situations that involve agency relationships—for example, the contracting parties are both principals and agents—are called bilateral agency relationships.

[8]See, for example, Tirole (1988: 35–36).

[9]The probability of bankruptcy may be nontrivial, in which case a VC that provided debt financing is a residual claimant in bankruptcy states. Therefore, where there is a nontrivial probability of bankruptcy, the VC's effort will be positively related to the total amount of debt financing that the VC contributes to the project. This is in contrast to nonbankruptcy states whereby VC effort is positively related to the equity sharing rule (the VC's ownership stake in the firm).

Figure 2.3 shows a bilateral moral hazard relationship between Venture Capitalist 1 and the Entrepreneur, Venture Capitalist 2 and the Entrepreneur, and Venture Capitalist 1 and Venture Capitalist 2.

2.3.3 Multitask Moral Hazard

Multitask moral hazard refers to situations that involve multiple tasks that the agent may undertake, and only a subset of these tasks benefit the principal (Holmstrom and Milgrom, 1991). A common example of multitask moral hazard involves the entrepreneur as principal and venture capitalist as agent. The venture capitalist will have more than one investee entrepreneurial firm and thus has multiple tasks as an agent for different entrepreneurial firms. The venture capitalist may spend comparatively more time helping a specific entrepreneurial firm in the portfolio. For instance, if the venture capitalist believes a certain investee entrepreneurial firm is going to be far more profitable than the others, he might spend more time ensuring the success of that entrepreneurial firm and less time with other entrepreneurial firms for which he is an agent.

Another common example of multitask moral hazard involves an institutional investor as principal and the venture capitalist as agent. The institutional investor prefers that the venture capitalist works toward maximizing the expected value of the venture capital fund portfolio of entrepreneurial firms in which it has invested on behalf of the institutional investor. As mentioned in Chapter 1, limited partnership funds typically have a lifespan of 10 years. Venture capital fund managers therefore must allocate some of their time fundraising to start another fund before their current fund is wound up to ensure continuity (and employment). The time spent by the venture capital fund manager fundraising does not help increase the value of the existing portfolio investments. Therefore, institutional investors will typically place contractual limits on venture capital fund manager fundraising activities to ensure that sufficient effort is exerted in the portfolio investments. Issues involving limited partnership contracts are discussed further in Chapter 5.

2.3.4 Adverse Selection

Moral hazard, bilateral moral hazard, and multitask moral hazard all refer to agency problems that may arise after a contract is entered into between a principal and an agent (ex post). An agency problem can also exist even before a contract is signed (ex ante). This agency problem is known as adverse selection. The seminal work on adverse selection by George Ackerlof, Michael Spence, and Joseph Stiglitz led to their joint Sveriges Riksbank Prize in Economic Sciences in Memory of Alfred Nobel in 2001 (also known as the Nobel Memorial Prize in Economic Sciences).[10]

[10]See http://nobelprize.org/nobel_prizes/economics/laureates/2001/public.html. Akerlof's (1970) work was in the context of the market for lemons (such as that for used cars). Spence's (1973) work was in the context of job market signaling. Stiglitz's work was largely in the context of contracting (Stiglitz and Weiss, 1981), which is of course primarily our interest in this book.

At a general level in the context of contracting, adverse selection refers to the problem that offers of different types of contracts attract different types of parties to the contract. This problem is usefully illustrated in the context of offers of nonconvertible debt versus common equity finance. An investor that offers debt finance will attract a different type of entrepreneur than an investor that offers equity finance (DeMeza and Webb, 1987, 1992; Stiglitz and Weiss, 1981). We illustrate this proposition by considering two examples. In the first example, we consider entrepreneurs that differ by their level of risk and not their expected mean return. In the second example, we consider entrepreneurs that differ by their expected return, not by their level of risk.

First, let's consider entrepreneurial firms that have the same expected value but different expected risk. In statistics, we would say that the entrepreneurial firms have the same first moment (expect return) but different second moments (expected risk) of the returns distribution. This situation is illustrated in the top part of Figure 2.4, which presents probability distribution functions (graphs of the expected value of the entrepreneurial firm under different states of nature). In Figure 2.4, Entrepreneur 1 is riskier than Entrepreneur 2. There is a high probability that Entrepreneur 1 will be very valuable (a "home run") but also a high probability than Entrepreneur 1 will go bankrupt. Entrepreneur 2, by contrast, has a high probability of a modest value and a low probability of being a home run and a low probability of going bankrupt. Due to the high risk, Entrepreneur 1 is referred to as a "nut" by Stiglitz and Weiss (1981) and other works. In practice, we might think of Entrepreneur 1 as a high-tech firm or an Internet start-up and Entrepreneur 2 as a manufacturing firm for a generic product that has a stable demand from consumers.

Entrepreneur 1 is more likely to be attracted to offers of nonconvertible debt[11] financing than by offers of common equity financing. If Entrepreneur 1's venture turns out to be successful, then Entrepreneur 1 is better off by holding all of the common equity and not sharing common equity with the investor. In Figure 2.4, this is indicated at the point labeled "Heads I win," which is what Entrepreneur 1 says [to himself in reference to the investor] if the project turns out successfully and the investor has nonconvertible debt. If Entrepreneur 1 had common equity financing, Entrepreneur 1 would have to share the upside of the successful project with the investor and thereby significantly dilute the profits that Entrepreneur 1 would enjoy as an owner. In the payoff diagram below the probability distribution functions in Figure 2.4, notice the difference between the value of common equity versus nonconvertible debt.

Now suppose Entrepreneur 1's venture turns out to be unsuccessful. If Entrepreneur 1 is financed by debt, the investor is able to reclaim any value left in the firm in bankruptcy. In Figure 2.4 this point is labeled "Tails you lose," which is what Entrepreneur 1 says [to himself in reference to the investor] if the investor is left with little or no salvage value of the firm's assets in bankruptcy (see the

[11]This example works the same way for nonconvertible debt and nonconvertible preferred equity.

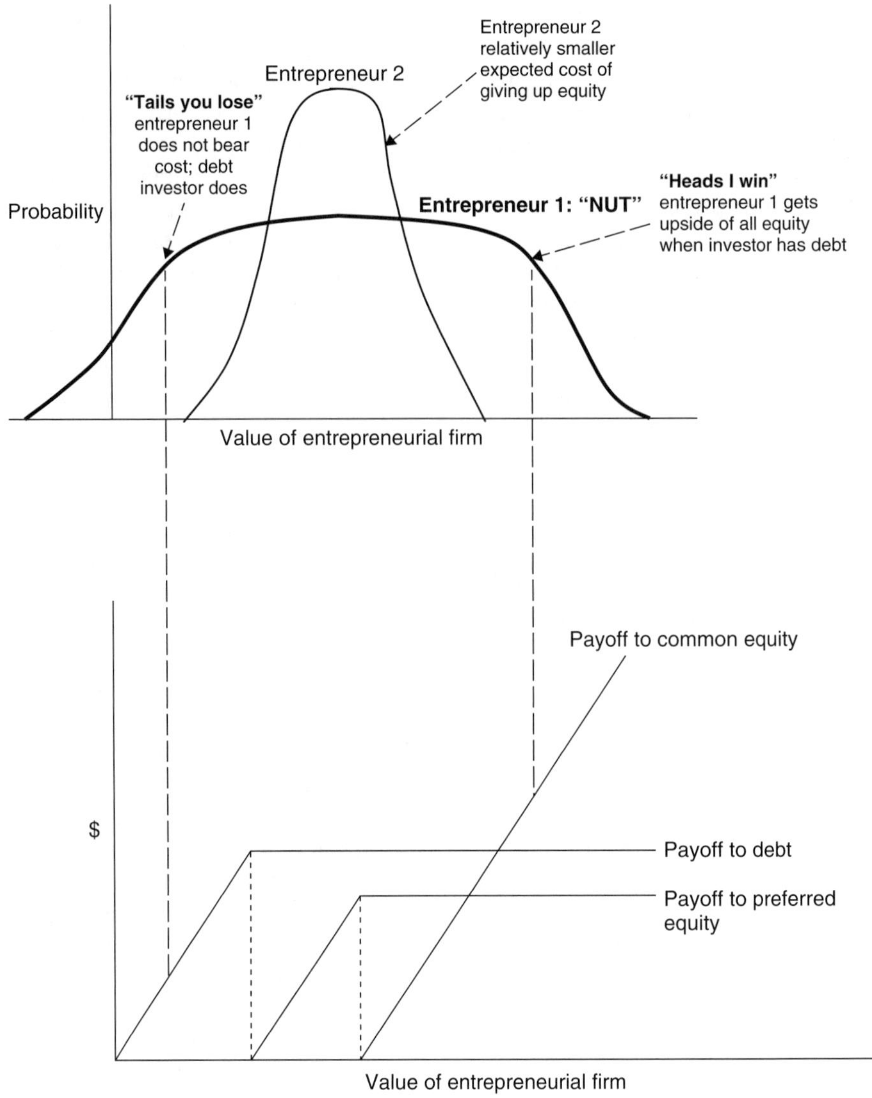

Figure 2.4 "Debt Attracts Nuts"

payoff diagram in the lower part of Figure 2.4). Entrepreneur 1 is not personally liable in bankruptcy and only loses the value of her investment. Discharge from bankruptcy is effective almost immediately in many countries (see Armour and Cumming, 2008, for details across Canada, Europe, and the United States), which means the Entrepreneur is able to quickly start another business.[12]

[12]In part this will involve a reputation cost. However, some venture capitalists have been known to view an entrepreneur's experience with bankruptcy as valuable experience. See Armour and Cumming (2006, 2008).

Entrepreneur 2 has a much lower expected opportunity cost of giving up common equity to the investor than Entrepreneur 1. There is a very low probability than Entrepreneur 2 will be extremely valuable, so Entrepreneur 2 does not lose as much as Entrepreneur 1 from giving up common equity to the investor. If fact, Entrepreneur 2 may have an incentive to sell common equity to the investor to encourage the investor to take steps to increase the expected value of the venture (recall the moral hazard problem with the investor as agent).

In short, an adverse selection problem of offering debt financing is that debt attracts nuts, under conditions in which entrepreneurs differ in terms of their expected risk but not in terms of the expected value. The adverse selection problem is rather different, however, if entrepreneurs diverge in terms of their expected value and not in terms of their risk. This situation is illustrated in Figure 2.5.

In Figure 2.5, Entrepreneur 3 is a "lemon" with a low expected value. Entrepreneur 3 and Entrepreneur 4, however, have the same expected risk in that the second moment of the probability distribution (the width of the probability distribution functions) is the same for Entrepreneurs 3 and 4. In this case, Entrepreneur 4 is relatively more attracted to offers of debt financing, and Entrepreneur 3 is relatively more attracted to offers of equity financing. First, note that at point A in Figure 2.5, Entrepreneur 3 has a comparatively low expected opportunity cost of giving up equity for the probability at Point A relative to the same probability level for Entrepreneur 4 at point B. Conversely, at point C, Entrepreneur 3 is in bankruptcy, and there is a high probability that Entrepreneur 4 is in bankruptcy as well. If the investor holds debt at point C, then Entrepreneur 3 faces a permanent loss in decision rights over the firm in bankruptcy (in terms of a reorganization or complete liquidation) and loses all priority to the investor that holds debt. Overall, therefore, debt is much less attractive to Entrepreneur 3 than to Entrepreneur 4, and the opportunity cost of giving up common equity is much lower for Entrepreneur 3 than Entrepreneur 4. If fact, Entrepreneur 3 may have an incentive to give common equity to the investor to encourage the investor to take steps to increase the expected value of the venture (recall the moral hazard problem with the investor as agent) and shift the probability distribution of Entrepreneur 3 to the right.

In short, an adverse selection problem of offering common equity financing is that common equity attracts lemons under conditions in which entrepreneurs differ in terms of their expected value but not in terms of their risk.

2.3.5 Free Riding

Free riding is an agency problem that exists in the context of ventures in which the effort of different agents is substitutable. For example, in the context of a syndicated venture capital investment, one venture capitalist may free ride off the efforts of another syndicated investor.

2.3.6 Hold-up

Hold-up refers to situations of expropriation in which there is unequal bargaining power between different parties to a contract. The terms of the original

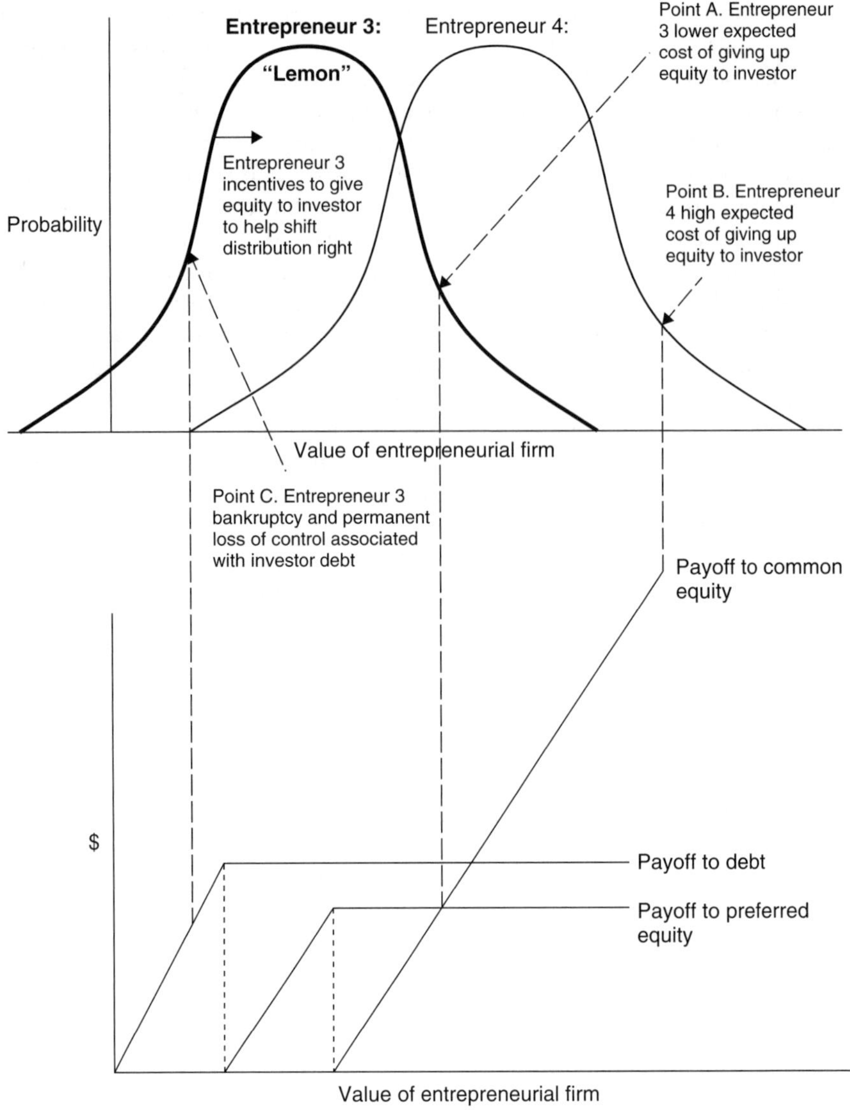

Figure 2.5 "Equity Attracts Lemons"

contract may be renegotiated if the party with the stronger bargaining power decides to "hold up" the other party.

In some situations the entrepreneur may hold up the investor. Suppose the investor contributes a very large amount of capital to finance the venture and that the entrepreneur is the only person capable of ensuring the success of the venture. Suppose the entrepreneur receives an attractive employment offer by another company after receiving financing from the investor. If the entrepreneur accepts the offer, then the venture fails. In this case, the entrepreneur is in a position to renegotiate the initial terms of the investment with the investor. For this reason, many venture capital contracts incorporate terms whereby the entrepreneur's stock options do not become effective until three (or more) years after the initial contract or upon achieving a significant milestone such as public floatation.

In other situations the investor may hold up the entrepreneur.[13] Consider a nonsyndicated investment with one investor. Virtually all venture capital investments are staged, which means that capital is provided periodically (anywhere from a few months to a few years; Gompers, 1995). At the second financing round the investor may ask for significantly less-friendly terms (less friendly to the entrepreneur) relative to that provided in the first round. The entrepreneur might be in a weak position if he is unable to seek external financing from another investor. As well, it is possible that the entrepreneur is subject to contract terms that limit his ability to seek external financing elsewhere (Chapters 10 to 14; see also Cumming, 2005a,b, 2008; Kaplan and Strömberg, 2003). Overall, there is significant potential for venture capitalists to expropriate entrepreneurs, depending on how the contracts are structured.

2.3.7 Trilateral Bargaining

Consider a nonsyndicated venture capital investment. Suppose the entrepreneur has control over the firm and the ability to decide whether to sell the right of control to a different investor (a "third party"). The entrepreneur might consider selling control to a third party in situations where the entrepreneurial firm is approaching the possibility of bankruptcy unless the entrepreneur is able to lower its cost of capital. By selling control to a third party, the entrepreneur is able to obtain cheaper external capital and mitigate the possibility of bankruptcy. By mitigating bankruptcy, the entrepreneur is better off, and by gaining control rights, the third party is better off. (The deal between the entrepreneur and the third party is voluntary, and therefore by definition the entrepreneur and third party are better off.) The initial investor, however, is potentially harmed by this transaction. The initial investor did not undertake the initial investment in the entrepreneur to have decisions made by an unknown third-party investor. It is possible that the third-party investor makes decisions about the future of the firm that are counter to the interests of the initial investor, such as selling assets or investing over a different time horizon than initially contemplated, among other things.

These situations of third-party sales are referred to as trilateral bargaining and have been studied in the theoretical literature in contracting (Aghion and

[13]Although much academic work in venture capital has focused on ways to prevent entrepreneurs holding up investors (e.g., Kaplan and Strömberg, 2003), more recent work has shown it is very important for entrepreneurs to mitigate the possibility of expropriation by their investors (Atanasov et al., 2006). Part III of this book considers strategies from the perspective of both the entrepreneur and the investor.

Bolton, 1992) and specifically in the theoretical literature in venture capital contracting (Berglöf, 1994). Contracts can be written in a way to mitigate the possibility of a trilateral bargaining agency problem arising, as is discussed further in Chapters 10 to 14.

2.3.8 Window Dressing

At a general level, window dressing refers to making one look better on the surface relative to what lies beneath. Much of corporate fraud has been some form of window dressing or another—for example, the accounting scandals ("cooking the books") that led to the demise of Enron and Arthur Anderson (among other things, of course). Window dressing typically has short-term benefits (such as attracting more capital from external investors) but longer-term costs (when investors realize that circumstances are not what they initially appeared to be).

In the context of staged venture capital investments, entrepreneurs have an interest in making their firms look as good as they possibly can to ensure that they will receive the next financing round from their investor(s) and as much money as possible. For instance, some entrepreneurs may exaggerate projected sales, hide expected losses, fake experimental test results for achieving a scientific advancement important to the firm, and/or do anything else that ensures a continued source of capital. In Chapters 10 to 14 we discuss ways in which contracts can be designed to mitigate window dressing problems (see also Cornelli and Yosha, 2003).

Venture capitalists may also engage in window dressing to facilitate their fundraising efforts from institutional investors. For example, as discussed in Chapters 7 and 22 (see also Cumming and Walz, 2004; Cumming and Johan, 2007b), venture capitalists often exaggerate the performance of unrealized investments when they make reports to their institutional investors. As another example, venture capitalists seeking to build a reputation may "grandstand" by taking their investee firms public sooner than that which would otherwise be optimal for the investee. Gompers (1996) shows that grandstanding is quite common among first-time venture capital fund managers who are in the process of fundraising for their subsequent funds.

2.3.9 Underinvestment

Underinvestment does *not* refer to investors providing too little capital. Rather, it refers to entrepreneurs that do not have sufficient incentives to provide the effort to ensure project success. Underinvestment is an agency problem associated with debt finance. In Figure 2.6, consider an entrepreneur financed by debt and currently at point A. An investment opportunity comes along that would enable the value of the firm to increase from point A to point B. The entrepreneur will have to work to ensure that this investment opportunity comes to fruition. Will the entrepreneur undertake the opportunity? Not likely. The entrepreneur's income as a common equity holder is not improved at all by putting forth effort to increase

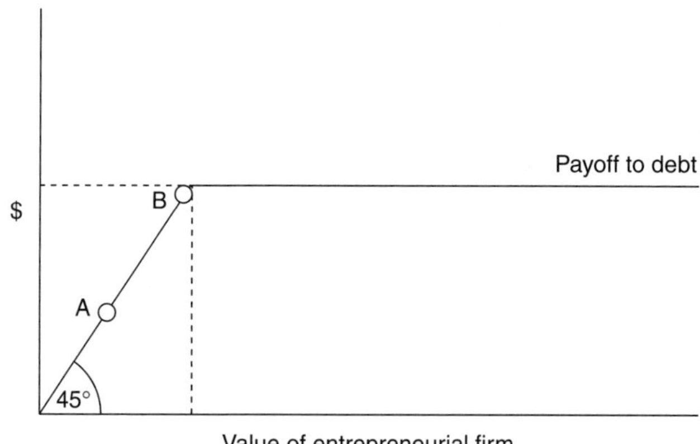

Figure 2.6 Agency Problem of Underinvestment

the value of the firm from A to B. Only the debt holder benefits from the entrepreneur's effort. This is viewed as an agency problem, since the move from A to B is a positive net present value project and is beneficial to the investor (principal) but not carried out by the entrepreneur (agent).

2.3.10 Asset Stripping

Asset stripping is an agency problem that is most pronounced with external debt finance. Suppose in Figure 2.7 that the entrepreneur believes the firm is at point A, but the entrepreneur has better information about the prospects of the firm than the investor does. The entrepreneur tells the investor that the firm is at point C. Thereafter, the entrepreneur starts to remove assets from the firm (e.g., computers, office supplies), travels to unnecessary scientific conferences

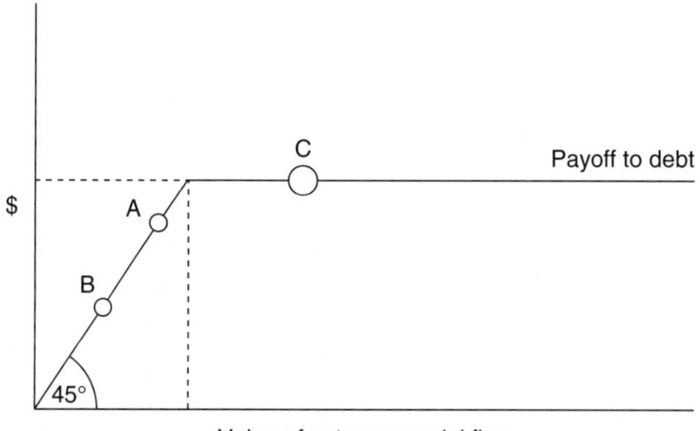

Figure 2.7 Agency Problem of Asset Stripping

in Hawaii and the Caribbean (unnecessary from the perspective of adding value to the entrepreneurial firm) at the firm's expense, and throws an extravagant party for all of the employees (again at the firm's expense). All of these activities are against the interest of the debt investor. Suppose the company goes bankrupt six months after these activities transpire. The firm could have been at point A if these activities had not taken place, but because they did, the firm is now at point B. Essentially, by stripping assets in these different ways, the entrepreneur steals from the investor. But this type of asset stripping is difficult to prove in a court of law because the burden is on the investor to prove not only that the actions were taken outside the course of ordinary business and outside the entrepreneur's authority but also that the entrepreneur knew the firm was facing bankruptcy when these decisions were made.

2.3.11 Risk Shifting

Risk shifting is very similar to the agency problem of adverse selection (discussed previously in this chapter), with the difference being that adverse selection is an ex ante contract agency problem, whereas risk shifting is an ex post contract problem. Risk shifting is most pronounced for firms that are debt financed (Green, 1984). Suppose an entrepreneur has a business plan that fits with the profile of Entrepreneur 2 in Figure 2.4. Then, after obtaining debt financing, the entrepreneur changes the profile of the firm by undertaking projects that have significantly greater risks but potentially greater payoffs. Entrepreneurs that are debt financed capture the increase in expected value associated with the increase in risk because they gain in the expected upside without having to share the proceeds of the gain with the debt investor. Conversely, if the gamble of changing the firm's profile does not work out and the firm goes bankrupt, it is the investor that bears the cost.

By analogy, consider a jockey (who is a good friend) who borrows money from you to buy a stallion. Instead of using the money to buy the stallion, the friend takes the money to Las Vegas and bets it all on a hand of poker. If the friend wins the hand, then you get paid back (but don't expect anything extra in terms of a share of the winnings). If the friend loses, then you don't get paid back.

Examples in entrepreneurial finance are not so extreme but are nevertheless present. Consider for instance a biotechnology firm that seeks to develop additives for foods based on natural (non–genetically modified) processes. After receiving financing, the firm then decides to take on the extra risk of working on engineering genetically modified organisms (GMOs). The production of GMOs is inherently more risky and may give rise to consumer controversies that limit the returns to the investment (increasing the downside risk; Cumming and MacIntosh, 2000a,b). At the same time, however, incorporating GMOs into the product line increases the potential profit margins.

In short, firms that are financed by debt have greater incentives to make decisions that increase the risk profile of the firm to transfer expected wealth from the debt holders (investor) to the equity holders (the entrepreneurs).

2.4 Does Mitigating Agency Problems Enhance Firm Value?

Quite generally outside the context of venture capital and private equity, firms with lower expected agency problems have higher expected values. (For seminal work on this topic, see Jensen and Meckling, 1976, and Jensen, 1986.) The literature on optimal capital structure and firm value originated with Modigliani and Miller (1958), who showed that in an ideal world without taxes and without agency problems, capital structure is irrelevant. The intuition is easily understood with the help of one of Yogi Berra's famous quotes: "You'd better cut the pizza into four pieces because I'm not hungry enough to eat six." In terms of financing a firm, how you divide up the claims between investors does not affect the value. The irrelevance of capital structure is depicted graphically by the horizontal line in Figure 2.8.

Miller and Modigliani (1963) published a correction of their original hypothesis upon recognition that interest on debt is tax deductible. In effect, firms that take on more debt reduce their tax burden, and thus firm value increases. This is depicted graphically by the constant upward sloping line in Figure 2.8.

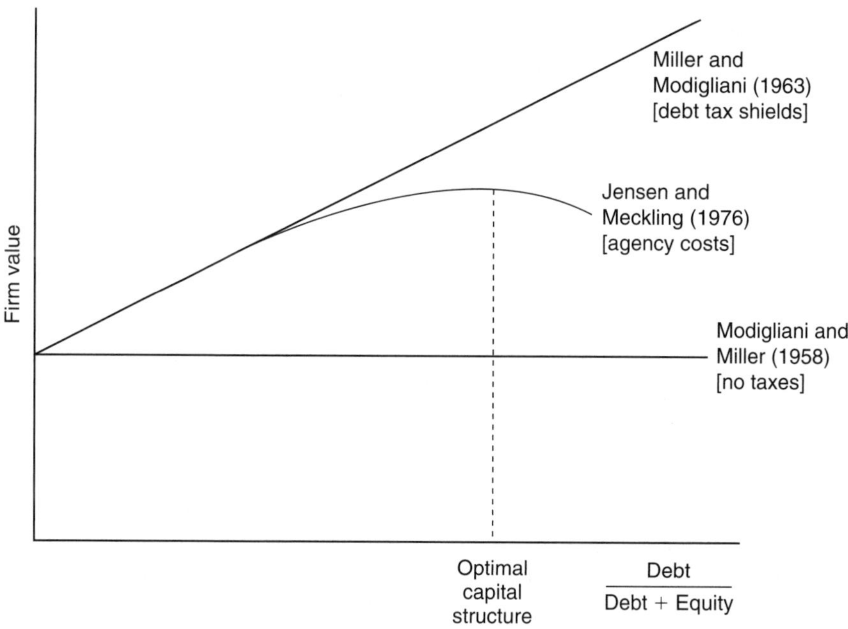

Figure 2.8 Capital Structure and Firm Value

Because firms are almost never financed by 100% debt, the Miller ad Modigliani (1963) story is incomplete. Jensen and Meckling (1976) argue that there are agency costs associated with different capital structures. (Indeed, numerous examples were provided in this chapter.) As agency costs of debt increase (along with risk of bankruptcy), firm value will eventually decline when a firm takes on too much debt. This effect is depicted in Figure 2.8. Numerous empirical studies support the Jensen and Meckling thesis, and as such, their paper is one of the most cited in economics and finance.

In the context of venture capital finance, a large body of literature exists in support of the view that convertible preferred equity is the optimal form of finance for entrepreneurial start-ups. Reasons underlying this view are provided in Chapters 10 to 14. Empirical evidence from U.S. venture capitalists financing U.S.-based entrepreneurs supports this view (Gompers, 1998; Kaplan and Strömberg, 2003). Gilson and Schizer (2003), however, explain that there is a tax bias in favor of the use of convertible preferred equity in the United States. Cumming (2005a,b,c,d, 2006a,b,c, 2007a,b,c, 2008) shows that convertible securities are not used most frequently by Canadian venture capitalists financing Canadian entrepreneurs (Chapter 11), U.S. venture capitalists financing Canadian entrepreneurs (Chapter 11), or European venture capitalists (Chapter 14). The evidence shows that the mix of financing instruments selected by venture capitalists in non-U.S. contexts is consistent with the idea that the different securities used mitigate the set of agency problems that are most pronounced in the particular financing context. (Particular details are provided in Chapters 10 to 14.)

In addition to capital structure choices, there are other mechanisms by which agency problems can be mitigated in the context of venture capital and private equity finance. For example, rarely (possibly never) do venture capital funds finance entrepreneurial firms by providing all of the capital required by the venture up front. Rather, investments are staged with periodic capital provided to the firm subject to benchmarks or milestones being met (Gompers, 1995). Staged capital commitments might occur over the course of six months to two years, depending on the growth path of the firm. More frequent staging is impractical due to the legal and time costs of writing and negotiating contracts and the monitoring required to determine the milestones being met. Less frequent staging is associated with less intensive monitoring but higher agency costs.

The tradeoff between mitigating agency costs and incurring transactions costs with staging is depicted in Figure 2.9. In a world without agency, legal, and monitoring costs, firm value is unaffected by staging frequency. Even if there are no agency costs but only monitoring and legal costs of contracting, then firm value decreases as staging frequency increases. Where both agency costs and monitoring costs are present, we would expect a moderate degree of staging, and optimal staging frequency would depend on the magnitudes of legal and monitoring costs relative to the degree by which staging mitigates agency costs. This tradeoff follows the work of Gompers (1995) and is depicted in Figure 2.9.

In sum, there are ample theory and evidence that support the view that agency problems are paramount in venture capital and private equity finance. It has been argued that venture capital funds exist primarily because of the existence of agency costs (Amit et al., 1998).[14] Without agency costs, start-up

[14]There are other explanations for the existence of venture capital funds, including a risk-sharing argument (Amit et al., 1990) and a "skills learning" story (Chan et al., 1990).

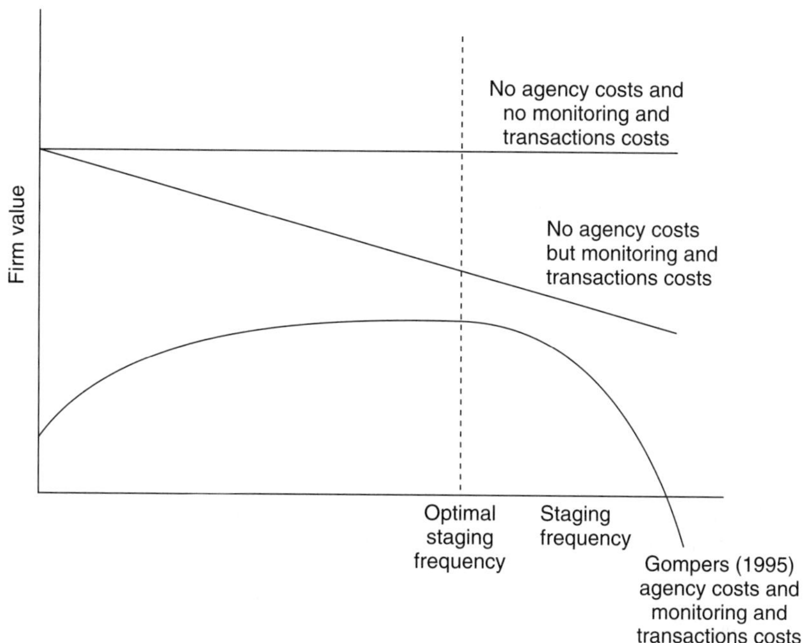

Figure 2.9 Staged Venture Capital Investments and Firm Value

firms would be able to obtain financing from banks. Due to agency costs, start-up firms without a track record and little or no collateral face extreme difficulty obtaining capital from banks. Specialized venture capital funds with managers that have expertise in carrying out due diligence for high-tech entrepreneurial start-ups are able to mitigate problems of adverse selection and write contracts to monitor investments and mitigate moral hazard and other agency problems that might adversely affect firm value.

Agency costs are a highly theoretical concept. Theory can only take us so far, and at the end of the day, we seek to apply theory to practice to see what is relevant in the real world. To this end, this book uses a large amount of data in each of the ensuing chapters. Chapter 3 reviews the statistical and econometric tools used in the data analyses in the subsequent sections of this book.

2.5 Summary and Steps Forward in Remaining Chapters

In this chapter we explained the payoffs to investing with debt, convertible debt, preferred equity, convertible preferred equity, common equity, and warrants. We then reviewed a menu of different agency problems in entrepreneurial finance and used payoffs with different securities to illustrate when these agency problems might be more pronounced. Thereafter, we explained that mitigating agency problems is a central mechanism by which firm value can be enhanced.

A central objective of the remainder of this book is to consider ways in which agency problems in entrepreneurial finance can be mitigated through financial contracts. As well, we will look at the related things that venture capitalists do, such as staging, monitoring, syndication, and portfolio design, among others. We will argue and empirically provide evidence that the effective application of contracts and the ability to implement other mechanisms to mitigate agency problems directly translate into more successful entrepreneurial firms and greater returns to venture capital and private equity funds. To this end, it is important to have a good grasp of the agency problems identified in this chapter before proceeding to the next chapters.

Key Terms

Debt
Convertible debt
Preferred equity
Participating preferred equity
Convertible preferred equity
Common equity
Warrants
Fixed claimant
Residual claimant
Capital structure
Security design
Staging
Syndication
Monitoring
Agency cost
Information asymmetry
Moral hazard
Bilateral moral hazard
Multitask moral hazard
Adverse selection
Lemon
Nut
Free riding
Hold up
Trilateral bargaining
Window dressing
Underinvestment
Asset stripping
Risk shifting

Discussion Questions

2.1. True/False/Uncertain: Agency costs associated with financing entrepreneurial firms can be completely eliminated.

2.2. True/False/Uncertain: Debt holders are always fixed claimants but preferred equity holders are not fixed claimants.

2.3. True/False/Uncertain: Staging and capital structure decisions do not impact expected entrepreneurial firm value.

2.4. Describe and explain the following agency problems in the context of financing an entrepreneurial firm.
   a. Adverse selection
   b. Asset stripping
   c. Free riding
   d. Hold-up

e. Moral hazard
f. Multitask moral hazard
g. Risk shifting
h. Trilateral bargaining
i. Underinvestment
j. Window dressing

Use graphs where appropriate.

3 Overview of Institutional Contexts, Empirical Methods

3.1 Introduction and Learning Objectives

This chapter consists of two main parts. This first part provides an overview of international differences in the institutional and legal settings in different countries around the world from which data are considered in this book. This material provides a basis for understanding potential sources for differences in venture capital and private equity markets across countries. International differences across countries are quantified with the use of indices to reflect differences in legal standards, which enables empirical comparisons of venture capital and private equity markets across countries in subsequent chapters.

The second part summarizes the statistical and econometric methods used in each of the chapters. The statistics and econometrics review is nontechnical and straightforward for all readers, regardless of background, so later chapters should be easy to comprehend. It is important to review large datasets from multiple countries to draw generalizable lessons about venture capital and private equity markets in practice. Without considering data, propositions about the apparent efficient structure of financial contracts in venture capital, for example, might be inaccurate or at least inapplicable to practice. Without considering data from a multitude of countries, inferences drawn might be attributable to the institutional context in a single country and not generalizable to other markets. This chapter provides an overview of the legal and institutional context considered in the different countries studied in the ensuing chapters of this book and reviews basic statistical and econometric methods for empirically studying venture capital and private equity markets.

3.2 An Overview of the International Institutional and Legal Context

Differences in venture capital and private equity markets might be attributable to a variety factors, such as the following:

- *Law*, such as legal origin (English, French, German, Scandinavian), as well as the degree to which a country's courts adhere to the rule of law and the efficiency of courts
- *Culture*, such as differences in the stigma attached to going bankrupt or the extent to which people trust one another

- *Economic conditions*, such as GNP per capita or the size of a country's stock market

Some of the main legal differences across the countries considered in this book are summarized in Table 3.1. There are numerous established indices of law quality around the world. Legal origin is perhaps the most widely recognized benchmark for international legal differences, following La Porta et al. (1997, 1998). The primary legal origins are English, French, German, and Scandinavian. French, German, and Scandinavian legal origin countries follow the civil law tradition, whereas English legal origin countries follow the common law tradition. La Porta et al. (1998) explain that civil law countries afford weaker legal protection than common law countries. Common law countries more often have laws that protect oppressed minorities, require relatively little share capital to call an extraordinary shareholder meeting, and enable stronger enforcement of these and other shareholder rights (La Porta et al., 1998). Similarly, common law countries offer creditors stronger legal protections against managers in terms of being more likely to guarantee priority rules in bankruptcy for secured creditors and precluding managers from unilaterally seeking court protection from creditors (La Porta et al., 1998). Furthermore, common law systems afford greater flexibility and react faster to new developments and governance mechanisms (such as novel contract design instruments used by venture capitalists) relative to civil law systems. This facilitates the set-up of appropriately designed contracts to act as crucial governance devices in venture capital financing (Cumming et al., 2008).

In addition, within and across different legal origins, there is significant variance in law quality on a country-by-country basis. The following are some common measures of law quality:

- Efficiency of the judicial system (the efficiency and integrity of the legal environment)
- The rule of law (the assessment of the law and order tradition in the country)
- Corruption (the extent of government corruption in a country)
- Risk of expropriation (the risk of outright confiscation or forced nationalization)
- Risk of contract repudiation (the risk of contract modification)

These indices are presented in La Porta et al. (1998), who provide more formal definitions for measurement and data sources, and they are briefly summarized in Table 3.1. These indices reflect averages for the years 1982–1995.[1] It is noteworthy that these legal variables are highly correlated and thus impossible to simultaneously use in a regression equation.[2] The Berkowitz et al. (2003) Legality index is a weighted average of the La Porta et al. Indices and is a useful aggregate index of law quality where separate indices are not possible

[1]Legal indices that vary across countries and across time are only available for recent years. As one example, see the World Bank's Doing Business project at http://www.doingbusiness.org/.

[2]See the discussion on collinearity in this chapter.

Table 3.1 Legal Conditions among Countries Considered in This Book

	Legal Origin				Legal Indices							
	English	French	German	Scandinavian	Efficiency of the Judiciary System	Rule of Law	Corruption	Risk of Expropriation	Risk of Contract Repudiation	Legality Index*	GNP per Capita (2005 $US)**	Chapter(s) in Which Data Are from Country in This Book***
Argentina	0	1	0	0	6	5.35	6.02	5.91	4.91	12.34	$4,460	22
Australia	1	0	0	0	10	10	8.52	9.27	8.71	20.44	$33,120	9
Austria	0	0	1	0	9.5	10	8.57	9.69	9.6	20.76	$37,190	14,16,21,22
Belgium	0	1	0	0	9.5	10	8.82	9.63	9.48	20.82	$36,140	5,6,14,16,21,22
Brazil	0	1	0	0	5.75	6.32	6.32	7.62	6.3	14.09	$3,890	4,5,22
Canada	1	0	0	0	9.25	10	10	9.67	8.96	21.13	$32,590	5,6,9,10,11,12,13,17,18, 19,22
Cayman Islands	1	0	0	0							$20,667	5,6
China	0	0	1	0							$1,740	22
Czech	0	0	1	0							$11,150	14,16,21,22
Denmark	0	0	0	1	10	10	10	9.67	9.31	21.55	$48,330	14,16,21,22
Finland	0	0	0	1	10	10	10	9.67	9.15	21.49	$37,530	5,6,22
France	0	1	0	0	8	8.98	9.05	9.65	9.19	19.67	$34,600	14,16,21,22
Germany	0	0	1	0	9	9.23	8.93	9.9	9.77	20.44	$34,870	5,6,14,16,21,22
Greece	0	1	0	0	7	6.18	7.27	7.12	6.62	14.91	$19,840	22
Guatemala											$2,400	22

(continued)

Table 3.1 (*continued*)

	Legal Origin				Legal Indices							
	English	French	German	Scandinavian	Efficiency of the Judiciary System	Rule of Law	Corruption	Risk of Expropriation	Risk of Contract Repudiation	Legality Index*	GNP per Capita (2005 $US)**	Chapter(s) in Which Data Are from Country in This Book***
Hong Kong	1	0	0	0	10	8.22	8.52	8.29	8.82	19.11	$27,690	22
Iceland	0	0	0	1							$48,570	22
India	1	0	0	0	8	4.17	4.58	7.75	6.11	12.8	$730	22
Indonesia	0	1	0	0	2.5	3.98	2.15	7.16	6.09	9.16	$1,260	22
Ireland	1	0	0	0	8.75	7.8	8.52	9.67	8.96	18.92	$41,140	22
Israel	1	0	0	0	10	4.82	8.33	8.25	7.54	16.54	$18,580	9,22
Italy	0	1	0	0	6.75	8.33	6.13	9.35	9.17	17.23	$30,250	5,6,14,16,21,22
Japan	0	0	1	0	10	8.98	8.52	9.67	9.69	20.36	$38,950	22
Luxembourg	0	1	0	0							$68,810	5,6
Malaysia	1	0	0	0	9	6.78	7.38	7.95	7.43	16.67	$4,970	5,6,22
Netherlands	0	1	0	0	10	10	10	9.98	9.35	21.67	$39,340	5,6,7,8,14,16,21,22
New Zealand	1	0	0	0	10	10	10	9.69	9.29	21.55	$25,920	5,6
Norway	0	0	0	1	10	10	10	9.88	9.71	21.78	$60,890	22

Philippines	0	1	0	0	4.75	2.73	2.92	5.22	4.8	8.51	$1,290	5,6,22
Poland											$7,150	14,16,21,22
Portugal	0	1	0	0	5.5	8.68	7.38	8.9	8.57	17.2	$17,190	14,16,21,22
Puerto Rico											$12,221	22
Russia											$4,470	22
Singapore	1	0	0	0	10	8.57	8.22	9.3	8.86	19.53	$26,620	22
South Africa	1	0	0	0	6	4.42	8.92	6.88	7.27	14.51	$4,820	5,6
South Korea	0	0	1	0	6	0	5.3	8.31	8.59	14.23	$15,880	22
Spain	0	1	0	0	6.25	7.8	7.38	9.52	8.4	17.13	$25,250	22
Sweden	0	0	0	1	10	10	10	9.4	9.58	21.56	$40,910	22
Switzerland	0	0	1	0	10	10	10	9.98	9.98	21.91	$55,320	5,6,14,16,21,22
Taiwan	0	0	1	0	6.75	8.52	6.85	9.12	9.16	17.62	$16,764	22
United Kingdom	1	0	0	0	10	8.57	9.1	9.71	9.63	20.41	$37,750	5,6,22
United States	1	0	0	0	10	10	8.63	9.98	9	20.85	$43,560	5,6,7,8,9,10,11,12,13,22

*Legality = .381 *(Efficiency of the Judiciary) + .5778 *(Rule of Law) + .5031 *(Corruption) + .3468 *(Risk of Expropriation) + .3842 (Risk of Contract Repudiation); Berkowitz et al. (2003). Legal indices are not available for some countries.

**Source: World Bank Development Indicators 2007.

***In addition to The Netherlands and the United States, Chapters 7 and 8 consider regions for Asia, Europe outside Netherlands, and Rest of World, without identifying particular countries.

Source: Legal indices data from La Porta et al. (1998).

to consider for reasons of collinearity. A higher Legality index indicates better substantive legal content pertaining to investing, the quality and likelihood of enforcement. For example, with a higher Legality index, the enforcement of contracts and the verifiability of elements of venture capital contracts are much easier, making the implementation of such corporate governance mechanisms in venture capital financing faster and more valuable (Cumming et al., 2008). Notice that Legality appropriately refers to the laws of the country of residence of the entrepreneurial firm.

We will not use the same set of countries in every chapter, primarily for reasons of data availability. Unlike companies that are listed on stock exchanges, venture capital and private equity funds and their investee companies are not compelled to report their information to the public. Some information is available from venture capital associations in different countries, while more detailed information typically must be hand-collected through the use of surveys or other data gathering techniques. (These issues are discussed later in this chapter.) Despite general data limitations in studying venture capital and private equity markets, the data presented in this book represent some of the largest and most detailed venture capital and private equity datasets available from anywhere in the world.

Apart from legal standards, culture may influence international differences in venture capital and private equity markets. For instance, Manigart et al. (2002) report that differences in trust can affect venture capital and private equity contracts, and Guiso et al. (2003) show that international differences in trust affect economic outcomes. In most cases, venture capital and private equity contracts are drafted by expert legal counsels who are obliged to ensure that the venture capitalists are made aware of the potential legal and financial risks of an investment in a company, regardless of the level of trust between the venture capitalists and entrepreneurs, and to take steps to mitigate these risks. The relationship between a venture capitalist and an entrepreneur is at the end of the day a commercially based relationship, and because the venture capitalist is responsible to the investors of the venture capital fund, it is almost a certainty that the venture capitalist will take the necessary steps to contractually protect his financial interest in the relationship in the event the trust is misplaced. Therefore, in accounting for international differences in venture capital and private equity contracts, we believe it is relatively more important to consider international differences in legal standards as opposed to vague measures of trust. Although countries share certain trust indices, these indices are developed to take into account the average individual in a country. There is massive variance in the levels of trust within countries and no reason to believe that the average individual is comparable to a venture capital manager or entrepreneur (or their cynical legal counsel). For these reasons, trust indices are not used in this chapter. By contrast, the legal setting in which the entrepreneurial firm is based is constant for all residents in a country, so legal indices are appropriately considered when accounting for differences in venture capital and private equity markets across countries.

Further, it is noteworthy that cultural attitudes are often reflected in legal standards. For instance, in Europe over the period 1990–2005, bankruptcy laws have been made more lenient, most likely prompted by changing societal attitudes toward failed entrepreneurial ventures. These changes have been found to influence entrepreneurship rates (Armour and Cumming, 2008) and the demand for venture capital (Armour and Cumming, 2006). In short, legal settings do encompass some cultural components for international differences across countries. But without detailed information on the extent to which specific individuals involved in a venture capital or private transaction trust one another, there will always be some element of a "missing variable" that is not realistically obtainable in empirical studies.

Finally, it is important to acknowledge that international differences in venture capital and private equity markets may reflect differences in the country's economic conditions, such as the size of the country's stock market or GNP per capita. Economic conditions and legal conditions are in fact highly positively correlated. Where it is plausible that differences in venture capital and private equity markets may reflect differences in economic conditions and/or legal conditions, it is important to account for both in empirical analyses. For example, Cumming et al. (2006) compare the importance of law versus the size of a country's stock market in explaining venture capital exit outcomes across countries, and Lerner and Schoar (2005), Kaplan et al. (2007), Cumming and Johan (2008b) and Cumming et al. (2008) compare the importance of legal versus economic conditions in explaining differences among transactions in venture capital markets. Now we will examine the techniques for such empirical analyses.

3.3 Statistics and Econometrics Used in This Book

This section summarizes the econometric methods used in each of the chapters in this book. The description of the econometric techniques used is brief and nontechnical for ease of reference. The description is provided here to enable the reader who is unfamiliar with statistics and/or econometrics to follow all of the chapters.

3.3.1 Why Use Statistics and Econometrics and Not Case Studies?

Datasets are collections of cases. In this book we employ statistics and econometrics to study datasets, or collections of cases, and not individual cases. Many books, however, do provide venture capital and private equity case studies that can be used to complement the data analyses in this book.[3] This book focuses on data analyses because we believe it is difficult to draw generalizable lessons from individual cases alone. Individual cases are idiosyncratic, so they

[3]For example, collections of cases are found in Gompers and Sahlman (2001) and Lerner et al. (2005).

do not lend themselves well to forming generalizable principles. Nevertheless, individual cases do highlight the decision-making process in practice and thus are helpful complements to analyses of larger datasets.

Analyses of datasets will enable the reader to study the likely effect of inputs on outputs. For example, to address a generally framed question such as "What is the optimal structure of a venture capital contract?" or a more specifically framed question such as "Is it appropriate for an entrepreneur to give up control rights to a venture capitalist, including the right to replace the entrepreneur as the CEO of the company?," it is worthwhile to examine a large amount of venture capital data from many industries, many different types of venture capitalists, instead of considering one (or a few) specific case study. Further, it is worthwhile to examine data from a multitude of countries because single-country studies can be distorted by institutional or legal factors. Large datasets enable one to assess at the same time a multitude of causal factors that might have influenced the outcome of interest.

3.3.2 What Are the Steps for Analyzing Data?

Data analyses typically have five steps (in this order):

1. An assessment of representativeness
2. A presentation of descriptive statistics of the main variables of interest
3. Comparison tests and univariate correlations
4. Regression analyses
5. Robustness checks

Representativeness

Ideally, data analyses begin with an assessment of representativeness. Analyses of venture capital and private equity markets, however, are plagued with an inability or limited ability to claim representativeness. Unlike companies listed on stock exchanges, privately held companies are not compelled to make information public. Hence, it is difficult to assess the characteristics of the population of venture capital– and private equity–backed companies. Industry associations such as the European Venture Capital Association[4] and the Canadian Venture Capital Association,[5] and data vendors such as Venture Economics Database from Thompson Financial[6] have helped to assess representativeness. However, coverage in datasets is not 100%, and it is difficult to know precisely the extent of coverage. Further, details provided in these datasets are limited. For instance, most of the publicly available datasets from the venture capital and private equity data vendors do not contain details on financial contracts.

[4]http://www.evca.com.
[5]http://www.cvca.ca.
[6]http://www.thomsonfinancial.com.

In view of limitations in publicly available venture capital and private equity data, particularly in respect of financial contracts, it is necessary to hand-collect data. Hand collection involves the use of surveys or proprietary access to information via one's own networks and/or efforts to gather detailed information. Surveys where detailed financial information is solicited most often achieve response rates of less than 20%, and often less than 10% (Brau and Fawcett, 2006; Cumming and Zambelli, 2007; Graham and Harvey, 2001). Where possible, one begins with comparison of the sample with the known population. For whatever dimensions from which the sample can be compared to the population, it is desirable to have minimal discrepancies so the sample considered is representative of the population. If relevant comparisons are not feasible, then at a minimum it is worth qualitatively assessing whether or not response bias is present in data based on the type of information solicited.

Descriptive Statistics

Once data representativeness is assessed, descriptive statistics of the data analyzed is presented. A presentation of means,[7] standard deviations,[8] medians,[9] and minimum and maximum values enables the reader to assess the relevant statistics in the data. The mean is the average value, and the median is the middle value (50% of the observations lie above the median and 50% lie below). The standard deviation measures the dispersion of the values; more disperse values have a greater standard deviation. The mean and median are different for data that have a different degree of dispersion above the median than below the median.

The descriptive statistics enable a characterization of the data. For instance, for an assessment of venture capital contracts, it is worthwhile to know how often different terms are employed in contracts. A presentation of descriptive statistics from a dataset on venture capital contracts enables the reader to understand the frequency of use of different terms.

Comparison Tests and Correlations

Comparison tests are provided in data analyses to assess differences in one subsample of the data relative to another subsample. For instance, to address the question "Are corporate venture capitalists more likely than limited partnership venture capitalists to use contracts with convertible preferred equity?," it is useful to employ a test of the proportion of corporate venture capital contracts that use this security relative to the proportion of limited partnership venture capital contracts that use this security.

Commonly used comparison tests assess the differences in means, medians, and proportions for different groupings of data. These tests are described at

[7]http://en.wikipedia.org/wiki/Mean.
[8]http://en.wikipedia.org/wiki/Standard_deviation.
[9]http://en.wikipedia.org/wiki/Median.

numerous places on the Internet, and some web pages even provide online tests where all you have to do is enter the data.[10] Comparison tests are a useful first step at analyzing relationships among variables. Comparison tests, however, are only indicative and not conclusive. That is, they do not control for "other things being equal." Let's consider an example. Suppose we have a dataset with the following 5 variables and 100 observations in the data.

Data Observation Number	Convertible Preferred Equity	Limited Partnership Venture Cap.	Corporate Venture Capitalist	Investment Year	Legality Index
1	1	1	0	1999	12.34
2	1	1	0	2000	14.09
3	1	0	1	1996	21.55
...					
100	0	0	1	1991	21.78

Notice that the variables "Convertible Preferred Equity," "Limited Partnership VC," and "Corporate VC" are called "dummy variables" in statistics and econometrics because they can only take on two values: 0 or 1. The value 0 means "no" and the value 1 means "yes." For example, for observation #1, convertible preferred equity was used, the VC is a limited partnership, not a corporate VC, and the investment year was 1999. Further, notice that we would refer to the variable "Convertible Preferred Equity" as a "dependent" or an "output" variable, whereas the variables "Limited Partnership VC," "Corporate VC," and "Investment Year" are "independent" or "input" or "explanatory" variables. That is, convertible preferred equity is a contract term that is chosen. Factors that may affect this choice are the characteristics of the investor (such as type of investor, limited partnership, or corporate VC) and investment timing.

In this example, comparing the proportion of limited partnership and corporate venture capital contracts with convertible preferred equity does not conclusively indicate which fund type is more likely to use that type of security because it might be the case that some other factor, such as the market conditions in the year of investment, is more directly linked to the use of contract terms, and corporate venture capitalists and limited partnership venture capitalists tend to invest at different points in time. Nevertheless, it is reasonable and appropriate to begin with comparison tests to get a picture of the tendencies in the data and the plausible relationships among variables.

Similarly with comparison tests, correlation coefficients enable an understanding of the relationships between two variables.[11] Correlation coefficients vary

[10]For instance, see http://www.fon.hum.uva.nl/Service/Statistics.html.
[11]http://en.wikipedia.org/wiki/Correlation.

between +1 and −1. A correlation of 0 implies that the variables are completely unrelated to one another. A correlation of +1 means that the variables move in the same direction at the same time, and a correlation of −1 means that the variables move in the opposite direction at the same time. Correlations cannot exceed +1 and cannot be less than −1. Correlation coefficients are typically presented in a matrix to show the relationships among all the variables of interest in a dataset.

A correlation matrix is useful in two respects. First, it enables an assessment between an outcome variable and an input variable. In the preceding example, useful statistics are the correlation coefficient between the variables for convertible preferred equity and limited partnerships, and between convertible preferred equity and corporate venture capitalists. If the correlation between limited partnerships and convertible preferred equity is greater than the correlation between corporate venture capitalists and convertible preferred equity, then we would infer that limited partnerships tend to use convertible preferred equity more often than corporate venture capitalists. However, as discussed, this is not conclusive, since it is possible that some other variable is more directly attributable to the use of different securities, such as market timing and market conditions in the year of investment.

Second, a correlation matrix enables an assessment of the relationships across different input variables. If different input variables are highly correlated (either close to +1 or −1), then it is difficult to ascertain which of the two input variables is causing the output variables. This second issue is discussed further in this chapter in the context of regression analyses.

Regression Analyses

Regression analyses enable an assessment of causal relations between variables while controlling for other things being equal. Following from the preceding example, a regression equation can be used to assess the likelihood that convertible preferred equity is used in a venture capital contract as per the following hypothetical regression.

$$\begin{aligned}\text{Convertible Preferred Equity} = {} & ß_0 + ß_1 \text{ Limited Partnership VC} \\ & + ß_2 \text{ Corporate VC} + ß_3 \text{ Investment Year} \\ & + ß_4 \text{ Legality Index} + \varepsilon\end{aligned}$$

As discussed, Convertible Preferred Equity is the dependent variable, a choice variable, which is explained by the independent variables Limited Partnership VC, Corporate VC, and Investment Year. The ß terms are coefficients. $ß_0$ is a constant, or the value of the intercept if the equation is viewed as representing a line on a graph. $ß_1$ is a coefficient that indicates the sensitivity (i.e., slope) of the relationship between the variable Limited Partnership VC and Convertible Preferred Equity. $ß_2$ is a coefficient that indicates the sensitivity (i.e., slope) of the relationship between the variable Corporate VC and Convertible Preferred Equity. $ß_3$ is a coefficient that indicates the sensitivity (i.e., slope) of the relationship between the Investment Year and Convertible Preferred Equity. $ß_4$ is a coefficient that indicates the sensitivity (i.e., slope) of the relationship between the Legality Index and Convertible Preferred Equity. *e* represents the error, or "residuals," or the portion of the movement in the Convertible Preferred Equity variable that is unexplained by the variables Limited Partnership VC, Corporate VC, and Investment Year.

The quality of a regression, or its goodness of fit, is often assessed by a statistic known as adjusted R^2. The adjusted R^2 statistic varies between 0 and 1; values closer to 0 mean that the explanatory variables are doing a better job in explaining the movement in the dependent variable.

Statistical software packages (such as Limdep, STATA, SAS, etc.) are used to estimate regression equations. Key items of interest that are estimated include the value of the coefficients and the adjusted R^2 statistic. With respect to the coefficients, it is important to know their sign (positive or negative values) and their size. The coefficients give an indication of the magnitude of the effect that one variable has on another variable; said differently, it indicates "economic significance." Large coefficients are "economically significant"; small ones are "economically insignificant." In addition to the size, econometric programs further assess the probability that the coefficient is estimated accurately. That is, each coefficient has a standard deviation or dispersion measure associated with it. Coefficients that have a relatively high standard error are statistically insignificant.[12] If the coefficient is statistically insignificant, then we would infer that there is no relation between the particular explanatory variable and the dependent variable (regardless of the size of the coefficient). In all regression analyses it is important to assess both statistical and economic significance.

The type of regression employed depends on the nature of the data examined. In particular, depending on the structure of the dependent variable of interest, it is appropriate to use a different type of regression. Perhaps the most commonly used type of regression in practice is known as "ordinary least squares" or OLS for short.[13] OLS is appropriate for dependent variables that can take on an infinite range of value from $-\infty$ to $+\infty$. OLS is used in Chapters 5, 6, 7, and 16.

Where the dependent variable is constricted such that it does not vary between −8 to +8, sometimes it is appropriate to make adjustments. For example, the dependent variable might be a fraction that ranges from 0 to 100%. Fractions are discussed in Chapter 7. At times (albeit not always), making adjustments for fractions or other limited ranges of the dependent variable is material to the coefficient estimates of interest.

Notice that OLS assumes there is a linear relation between the dependent and independent variables. Sometimes theory leads us to expect a nonlinear

[12]t-statistics are used to assess statistical significance. A t-statistic is the coefficient value divided by its standard error. t-statistics that are greater than 1.65 in absolute value are statistically significant at the 10% level. That is, they have a p-value of 10%, or a 10% chance of inferring that the coefficient is statistically significant when in reality it is not. t-statistics that are greater than 1.96 in absolute value are statistically significant at the 5% level, and t-statistics that are greater than 2.59 in absolute value are statistically significant at the 1% level. Regression coefficient estimates are presented with their t-statistics and/or standard errors.

[13]http://en.wikipedia.org/wiki/Least_squares.

relation between the variables of interest. For example, in Chapter 18, we discuss factors that may influence nonlinearities in the determinants of venture capital portfolio size. To empirically assess these nonlinearities, we use Box-Cox regressions,[14] which are explained in detail in Chapter 18.

Often, the dependent variable of interest can take on only a couple of values. In the preceding example, the dependent variable Convertible Preferred Equity can only take on the values 0 and 1; that is, it is a binary dependent variable (a dummy variable). In this case, it is appropriate to use a logit[15] or probit[16] regression.[17] As in OLS regressions, logit and probit regressions yield coefficients, but the economic significance of the coefficients by themselves is difficult to interpret. To assess economic significance, it is necessary to compute the "marginal effects," or the effect of a change in the value of the explanatory variable on the probability that the dependent variable takes the value 1. Logit regression equations are used in Chapters 6, 8, 12, and 14.

It is further possible that the dependent variable of interest can take on a few values. For instance, a venture capitalist can sell an investment by initial public offering, acquisition, secondary sale, buyback, or write-off (see Chapters 19 to 21). It is possible to assess these different choices simultaneously in a multinomial logit model instead of a series of different logit models. The advantage of a multinomial logit model is that it considers the interdependencies between different relevant choices.[18] Multinomial logit regression models are used in Chapters 11, 12, 20, and 21.

Sometimes, a set of discrete choices can be ranked. For instance, it might be of interest to assess the factors that influenced the number of control rights used in a venture capital contract. If so, an ordered logit model is more appropriate than a binomial or multinomial logit model.[19] Ordered logit regression models are used in Chapters 5, 14, 16, and 17.

Robustness Checks

Regression analyses are sensitive to misspecification errors. Indeed, a famous expression indicates there are "lies, damn lies, and statistics."[20] As such, one never considers a single regression equation. Various regressions assessing the same prediction are used to assess robustness to misspecification error.

Common types of misspecification include omitted variables and collinearity. The problem of omitted variables refers to a deficient set of explanatory variables in explaining the dependent variable of interest. Exclusion of relevant explanatory variables may give rise to inappropriate inferences about the effect

[14]http://en.wikipedia.org/wiki/Power_transform.

[15]http://en.wikipedia.org/wiki/Logistic_regression.

[16]http://en.wikipedia.org/wiki/Probit_model.

[17]The use of probit versus logit depends on distribution assumptions of the dependent variable; in practice, the results obtained are extremely similar.

[18]http://en.wikipedia.org/wiki/Multinomial_logit.

[19]http://en.wikipedia.org/wiki/Ordered_logit.

[20]http://en.wikipedia.org/wiki/Lies,_damned_lies,_and_statistics.

of other included variables on the dependent variable of interest. Collinearity, by contrast, refers to the problem of highly correlated explanatory variables being used in the same regression equation. Where variables are overly correlated, the estimated statistical and economic significance may be highly inaccurate. To assess for problems of omitted variables and collinearity, it is appropriate to consider a variety of regressions to explain the same dependent variable with different sets of included explanatory variables.[21] Ideally, the estimated coefficients are not subject to the included set of explanatory variables.

Heteroscedasticity, a nonnormal distribution of residuals in a regression equation, is common in regression equations as well.[22] The resulting statistical significance of the estimated coefficients can be biased when there is pronounced heteroscedasticity. A common approach to correct for this problem is to use White's (1980) robust adjusted estimator, which is done throughout this book. A related issue involves clustering of standard errors (Petersen, 2006) (see, e.g., Chapter 21).

Another problem that can arise in data analysis involves outlier observations (and possibly measurement error). That is, the estimated coefficients may be subject to the presence of only a few observations in the data that are vastly different from all of the other observations. It is appropriate to assess sensitivity to the inclusion/exclusion of outlier observations (see Chapter 5).

The issue of endogeneity is perhaps the most common problem in research corporate finance work, which includes but is not limited to venture capital and private equity. A typical regression equation such as the one just specified involves the right-hand-side (explanatory) variables explaining or causing the left-hand-side (dependent) variable. Endogeneity refers to the problem in a regression equation where the right-hand-side variables are at least in part caused by the left-hand-side variable. The problem of endogeneity arises when the variables on the right-hand-side are "choice" variables, or not exogenously determined. A situation in venture capital research in which endogeneity is a problem involves the relationship between contracts and exits (as we will see in Chapters 20 and 21). Contract terms are clearly choice variables. Exit outcomes (such as an IPO, acquisition, or write-off) typically happen a few years after an initial investment. This timing would lead us to posit a relation such that contract choices cause exit outcomes. But contracts may nevertheless have been written in anticipation of exit, which would suggest an element of endogeneity.

To control for endogeneity, it is customary to use two-step regression methods involving instrumental variables.[23] Instrumental variables are variables that are highly correlated with the potentially endogenous explanatory variable but not correlated with the dependent variable. (In practice, it is typically

[21]Other diagnostic tests are appropriate as well but are beyond the scope of this chapter. Standard econometric textbooks deal with these issues.

[22]http://en.wikipedia.org/wiki/Heteroskedasticity.

[23]http://en.wikipedia.org/wiki/Instrumental_variable.

difficult to find an ideal instrumental variable.) In a two-step regression, first the potentially endogenous variable is regressed on the instruments and then the fitted values from that regression are used as a new variable in place of the potentially endogenous variable in the second regression. This type of two-step regression is used in Chapters 16 and 21.

Sometimes, it is of interest to assess the extent to which variables are endogenous, and this can be done with a Durbin-Wu-Hausman test. This type of test is examined in a venture capital contracting context in Chapter 12.

Another problem that can arise in regression analyses involves selection effects.[24] For example, this issue arises in the context of assessing the determinants of venture capital and private equity returns. Returns are not realized by funds until the fund sells the investee company. At any given point in time for a fund, the sample properties of the realized investments may differ from that of the unrealized investments. For instance, a fund may sell its good investments early in its lifespan and hold onto its bad investments until much later. To account for such selection biases, it is appropriate to use statistical methods developed by Heckman (1976, 1979). This issue is explained in Cochrane (2005) and Cumming and Walz (2004) and in Chapters 8 and 21.

Further details on the econometric methods used in this book are provided in each of the chapters. The statistics and econometrics used are intended to be as user-friendly as possible. Empirical analyses of venture capital and private equity datasets from a multitude of countries are provided to enable generalizable inferences. The data are exciting aspects and a central feature of this book, and we do not wish to detract from the interest with technical details. The data often challenge the conventional wisdom. For example, counter to popular belief, venture capitalists do not *always* use convertible preferred shares! We hope the reader will be drawn toward examining the international data presented herein.

3.4 Summary

In the final part of this chapter, we provide an overview of the international institutional context empirically considered herein, with reference to legal and institutional differences across countries. This background in terms of both the theory and the empirical methods is important for following each of the remaining chapters.

Finally, because a central objective of this book is to empirically examine venture capital and private equity contracts, we provided a brief review of the statistical and econometric techniques used in the ensuing chapters. The data presented in each chapter is intended to be user-friendly. It is important and worthwhile to examine data so readers are familiar with venture capital and private equity contracting in the real world and not just from a theoretical lens. Analyses of large datasets enable generalizable insights, unlike studying one-off

[24] http://en.wikipedia.org/wiki/Selection_bias.

cases. Similarly, analyses of international datasets are useful, since single-country datasets may be attributable to an institutional context that is inapplicable to another country.

Key Terms

Legality index
Common law
Civil law
Efficiency of the judiciary
Rule of law
Corruption
Risk of expropriation
Risk of contract repudiation
Bankruptcy law
Trust
Culture

Key Statistical and Econometric Terms

Mean
Median
Standard deviation
Representativeness
Comparison test
Correlation
Ordinary least squares
Dependent variable
Independent variable
Economic significance
Statistical significance
Probit
Logit
Ordered logit
Multinomial logit
Instrumental variables
Sample selection
Heteroscedasticity
Collinearity
Outliers
Endogeneity

Discussion Questions

3.1. What advantages do common law countries have in terms of facilitating venture capital investment?
3.2. Is a culture index more or less likely to be relevant than a legal index in explaining contract terms used in a venture capital transaction?
3.3. Identify and explain three common hurdles in empirical analyses of venture capital and private equity data.
3.4. What are the advantages/disadvantages of datasets relative to case studies on venture capital?

Part Two

Fund Structure and Governance

4 What Should Fund Managers Care About? Perspectives from Institutional Investors

4.1 Introduction and Learning Objectives

Part II consists of Chapters 4 to 9 and considers the structure and governance of venture capital and private equity funds. Limited partnerships are the most common form of fund structure worldwide and therefore are the focus in Chapters 4 to 8. Chapter 9 considers the role of government policy in stimulating venture capital and private equity activity.

A limited partnership is essentially a contractual arrangement between a group of partners whereby one partner agrees to take on full liability in return for almost full control over the business of the partnership. Unlike the customary partnership, all other partners are limited in potential liability. The profits, however, are shared equally, or on a pro rata basis as per the contract terms. In the case of limited partnership private equity and venture capital funds, the partnership is between institutional investors, who become limited partners (pension funds, banks, life insurance companies, and endowments that have rights as partners but exchange "management" rights over the fund for limited liability), and the fund manager, who is designated the general partner (the partner that takes on the responsibility of the day-to-day operations and management of the fund and assumes total liability in return for negligible buyin). Contracts typically envision a fund lasting for 10 years with an option to continue for an additional 3 years. The 10-year horizon enables fund managers to select investments and bring them to fruition. It typically takes anywhere from 2 to 7 years to bring an investment to fruition (see Chapter 19). Fund managers are typically compensated with a 1 to 2% management fee (as a percentage of the capital committed to the fund) and a 20% performance fee (as a percentage of the profits of the fund and often called the "carried interest"). Fund managers are not given carte blanche and are still bound by restrictive covenants that limit their investment activities to mitigate potential agency costs associated with managing the capital commitments of institutional investors.

Before we delve into limited partnership contractual covenants and compensation terms, there are a few preliminary questions that must be addressed. First, what motivates institutional investors to invest in private equity in the first place, and what are their concerns with private equity investment? These are important questions, as it enables fund managers to consider factors that are relevant for fundraising and managing a fund. These questions are the focus of this chapter. Chapter 5 presents the terms used in limited partnership contracts, and Chapter 6 analyzes compensation in limited partnerships. Chapter 7 shows that because contracts are incomplete (i.e., it is not possible to write detailed enough contracts to address all of the parties' possible concerns, particularly for a 10- to 13-year fund), regulation of fund managers and institutional investors plays an important role for venture capital and private equity fundraising. Issues involving investing in funds with a particular style focus are thereafter addressed in Chapter 8. Finally, government funds are studied in Chapter 9.

To illustrate these issues, Chapters 4, 7, and 8 all use data from institutional investors in The Netherlands and their perspectives with venture capital and private equity investment in continental Europe, the United States, Asia, and the rest of the world. Chapters 5 and 6 use data provided by private equity fund managers from 17 countries around the world. The international perspectives provided by the data highlight the global nature of the market for venture capital and private equity, and show how international differences are related to legal and institutional settings. The data also show a central importance of economic factors and agency costs in venture capital and private equity fund management. Similarly, the data presented in Chapter 9 are from a multitude of countries.[1]

In this chapter we do the following:

- Consider the more common types of institutional investors in venture capital and private equity funds
- Analyze the motivations underlying institutional investment in venture capital and private equity, including both economic and regulatory considerations
- Distinguish between fund commitments and draw downs from capital commitments in limited partnerships
- Distinguish between direct fund investment, direct company investment, and fund-of-funds investment
- Consider expected rates of return from investment in venture capital and private equity
- Consider institutional investor strategies for achieving their risk and return objectives associated with venture capital and private equity investment

In the following section, we explain factors that institutional investors take into account in their decision to allocate capital to private equity. Also, we overview the risks and concerns investors have with respect to allocating capital to private equity funds.

4.2 Institutional Investor Objectives from Investment in Private Equity

Consistent with the empirical theme of this book, in this chapter we use empirical data to introduce and illustrate factors that are relevant to institutional

[1]See Table 3.1, which summarizes the countries from which data are considered in each chapter.

investors, and we discuss how such factors also relate to private equity fund managers. The data in Chapters 4, 7, and 8 are derived from a survey of Dutch institutional investors carried out in 2004 (Cumming and Johan, 2007b,c). Data from The Netherlands during that period, in our opinion, provide an excellent "snapshot" of the dynamic investment climate within Continental Europe in view of the diverse range of institutional investors that invest in private equity both domestically and worldwide and, as you shall see, their reasons for doing so. Further, in this chapter we provide institutional investor perspectives on returns to private equity in Europe and the United States and compare perceptions to historical performance. Additional details and data on venture capital and private equity returns are provided in Chapters 19 to 22.

An overview of the source of data from the Dutch institutional investors is provided in Figure 4.1. The data are from a survey of 100 institutions in The Netherlands in 2004 and are collected with the generous support of Adveq, a worldwide private equity fund-of-funds. Pension funds are the most common type of institutional investor in private equity in The Netherlands, as well as most all other countries around the world (Jeng and Wells, 2000). Private equity managers are usually concerned with the type of institutional investor to target as potential fund investors, as different investors of private equity funds have in mind different investment horizons, liquidity concerns, disclosure requirements, and strategic investment requirements, as detailed in this chapter.

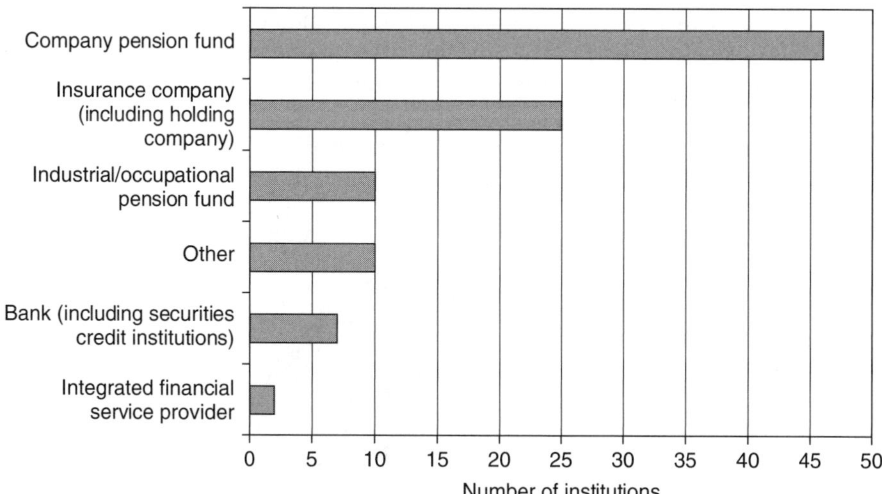

Figure 4.1 Type of Institutional Investor

The range of assets managed by the institutional investors is depicted in Figure 4.2. Most institutions in The Netherlands as of 2005 managed less than €600 million, but a few managed more than €1 billion. The range of assets

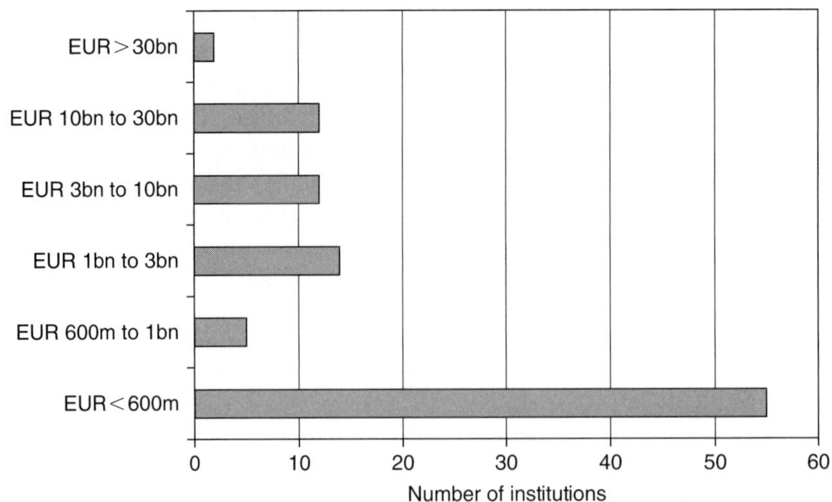

Figure 4.2 Total Assets under Management

managed by institutional investors are taken into account by private equity managers as this will ultimately determine the amount that is available for private equity fund investment as they are in competition with all other forms of traditional and alternative investment instruments. As we will see later in this chapter, larger investors with more capital under management are more likely to invest in private equity funds. Smaller investors do invest in private equity, but by targeting smaller investors, private equity fund managers must include more partners in their limited partnership.

Allocations to private equity as of 2004 are depicted in Figure 4.3. Of the 100 investors in the sample, only 29% had capital allocations to private equity

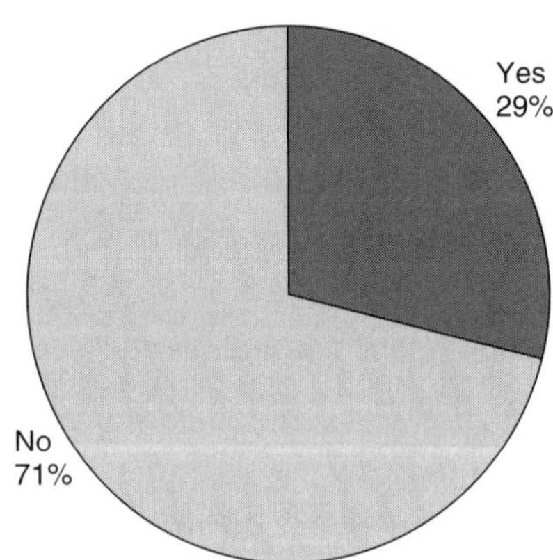

Figure 4.3 Current Allocation to Private Equity

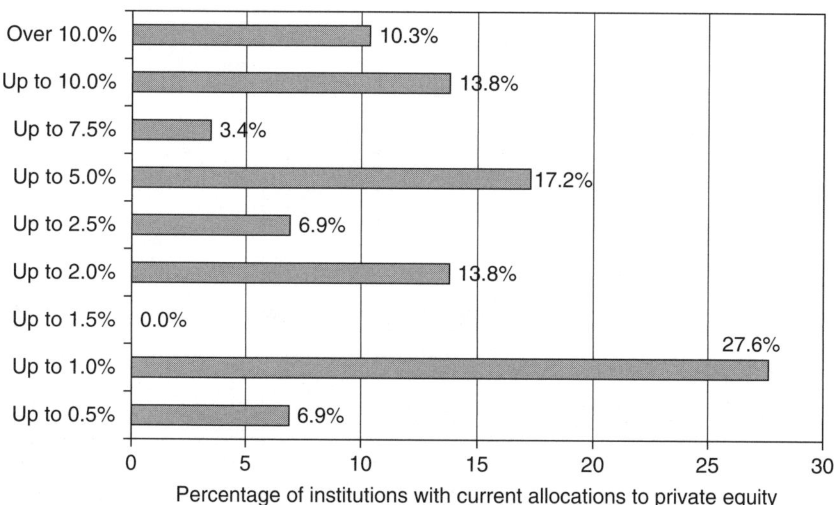

Figure 4.4 Current Committed Allocation to Private Equity by % of Total Assets under Management

funds in 2004. Notice that there is a distinction between capital allocation and capital commitments (depicted in Figure 4.4). Institutional investors set aside a certain percentage of their assets with the intention of investing that amount in private equity, but that amount may not necessarily be invested or committed. What is of concern to private equity fund managers in this case is not only what percentage of the remaining 71% of the noninvestors are interested in private equity investment but have yet to find an appropriate vehicle but also what percentage of that is allocated but not yet committed. This is basically an untapped market.

The capital commitments to private equity relative to assets managed as of 2004 is depicted in Figure 4.4. Institutional investors rarely commit more than 10% of their investment portfolio to private equity funds. Private equity is considered a riskier and more illiquid alternative investment and therefore is not a major part of an institutional investor's investment portfolio. Nevertheless, private equity is viewed as an important part of the portfolio, even for more conservative institutional investors due to the potential to enhance returns, as discussed later in this chapter. Private equity managers find it easier to persuade institutional investors that are already investing in the market to allocate and commit a larger percentage of their assets than to persuade neophyte institutional investors (or rather their investment committees) to take the plunge into this market. Therefore, even within this tapped market, there is still untapped potential to obtain capital for new or follow-on limited partnership funds.

As with the distinction between capital allocations and commitments, the distinction between capital commitments to private equity funds and draw downs of capital commitments is equally important (Cumming et al., 2005b; Ljungqvist

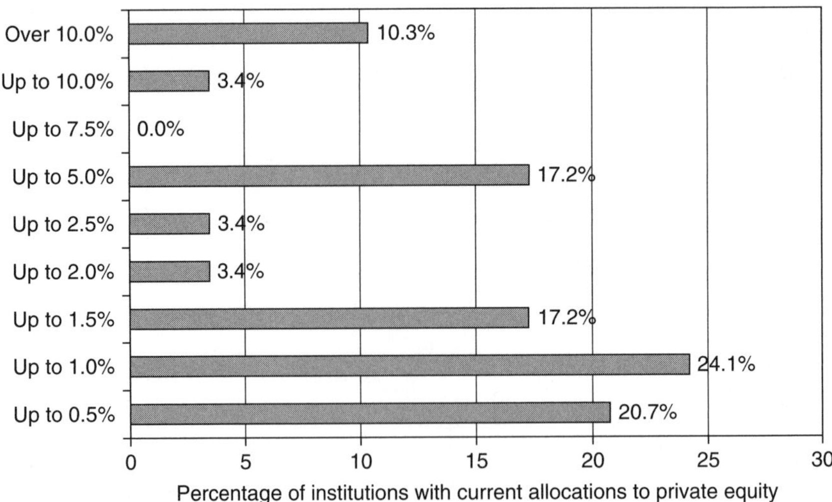

Figure 4.5 Current Actual (Draw Down) Allocation to Private Equity by % of Total Assets under Administration

and Richardson, 2003; Gompers and Lerner, 1998a,b; Poterba, 1989a,b). Draw downs as of 2004 are shown in Figure 4.5. Institutional investors first commit the capital to funds, and the private equity fund(s) to which it has committed subsequently draws down the committed funds over time. The time for an institutional investor to achieve the desired planned exposure to private equity typically takes between three and five years, depending on the rate of commitments and the rate of draw downs by the fund managers. The draw down experience (once a commitment is made) depends on the activities and portfolio characteristics of the private equity fund. In wholesale money management, it is typical for the institutional investors to have monies drawn down on a "just-in-time basis," with the balance of the commitment earning an opportunity cost return (usually in a passive equity benchmark such as a market index). The institutional investor is legally required by contract to pay monies as drawn down by the private equity manager.

As shown in Figure 4.6, there are three ways in which institutional investors can invest in private equity: direct investments in entrepreneurial firms (without any venture capital or private equity intermediaries), through private equity funds, and through private equity fund-of-funds. Whether an institutional investor makes a direct investment in an entrepreneurial firm depends on the level of knowledge she is able to obtain about the prospective investee firm and the skills and resources that are required to manage the investment and bring it to fruition. Investment through a venture capital or private equity fund enables delegation of the due diligence tasks with reviewing and screening potential investees and adding value to investees to help them grow toward potentially becoming a publicly listed company. Given the massive amounts of capital managed by institutional investors, they typically do not have the resources and have not

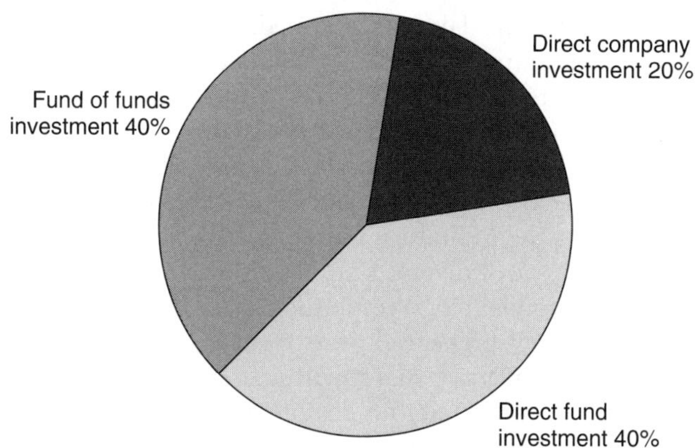

Figure 4.6 Current Private Equity Allocation by Type of Investment

developed the skill and expertise to make small investments in entrepreneurial firms. Private equity and venture capital fund managers, however, have developed the skills and expertise to not only carry out the due diligence and screening of potential investments but also to determine the most efficient method to act as active investors. They are experienced enough to know how difficult such active participation can be, so each private equity and venture capital manager will monitor only a small number of investments. Gorman and Sahlman (1989), for example, find that U.S. venture capital managers spend about half of their time monitoring an average of nine entrepreneurial firms. They report that U.S. venture capital funds that originate investments in entrepreneurial firms spend four to five hours per month in direct contact with entrepreneurs (syndicated venture capitalists that are not the lead investor report spending two to three hours in their visits on average) and extra time helping other venture capitalists when not in direct contact with entrepreneurs. In Chapter 16 we consider the factors that influence the extent of time that venture capital fund managers spend with their entrepreneurial firms in a European context.

A significant difference between direct company investments, direct fund investments, and fund-of-fund investments is the extent to which the institutional investor has control of the selection and management of the investment. Institutional investors have full control over how direct investments are made and managed. There is less control over investments made through limited partnership private equity funds, as the institutional investor has exchanged control over how the fund carried out its investment mandate for limited liability (see Chapters 5 and 6 for how contracts are drafted to mitigate the risk of passing full business control to the private equity fund manager). Institutional investors, however, allocate fewer resources with this form of investment. The final mode of investment that is through a private equity fund-of-fund affords the institutional investors with the least amount of control because there is an additional level of intermediation to contend with.

Fund-of-funds are an extra layer of intermediation. Fund-of-funds accounted for 14% of global commitments made to private equity funds in 2006, according to Private Equity Intelligence Ltd.[2] Fund-of-funds are essentially the capital managers for private equity funds in that they use their network and expertise to raise the capital to be managed by the private equity fund managers free of interference from their diverse set of institutional investors, just as the private equity fund manager provides the capital for entrepreneurs to administer free of interference from their own set of diverse fund investors. Investments made through private equity fund-of-funds may wrestle the last of any potential control over specific investments in entrepreneurial firms from the institutional investors, but in return they enable the institutional investor to diversify risk across a greater range and number of private equity funds. One additional advantage with fund-of-funds is that they potentially enable the institutional investor access to the top quartile performing funds. We know that there is significant persistence in private equity returns (Kaplan and Schoar, 2005).[3] It can be difficult for institutional investors, especially those new to the market, to become invested in the top quartile funds through direct fund investments due to waiting lists (Lerner et al., 2007). Successful private equity fund managers prefer to retain existing partners in follow-up funds, and those institutional investors who have gained sufficient experience with fund investment are willing to wait for an invitation to invest in fund managers with a proven track record. Private equity fund managers would rather have as partners fund-of-funds than neophyte institutional investors because they understand the business and will not seek to supervise the private equity fund managers as some institutional investors tend to do. Similarly, with direct company investments it is harder for institutional investors to get access to the firms with the most potential, since entrepreneurs have incentives to obtain capital from the top quartile venture capital funds (Hsu, 2004). It is important to understand that it is not capital alone that private equity fund managers and entrepreneurs are seeking. They are also looking for industry expertise that the top private equity fund managers can bring to the table, and top private equity fund managers seek capital unbound by unnecessary restrictions that may impede their ability to make and manage investments efficiently. A disadvantage with fund-of-funds, however, is that to obtain access to the best funds, the institutional investor pays for two levels of financial intermediation. A venture capital fund typically has a 1 to 2% fixed fee and a 20% performance fee (see Chapter 6), and the fund-of-funds may have a 1% management fee and a 5% performance fee. With direct company investments, the institutional investor gets the profits "clean" without having to pay fees to anyone.

[2]http://en.wikipedia.org/wiki/Private_Equity. For directories of funds-of-funds, see, for example, http://www.altassets.com/research/rpt_fof2005.php, or http://www.peimedia.com/Product.aspx?cID=5494&pID=166571.

[3]Kaplan and Schoar (2005) estimate that a fund with 1% higher performance in the previous fund is associated with 54 basis point better performance in the current fund. This is in sharp contrast to mutual funds, for example, where there is little or no persistence in returns (Carhart et al., 2002).

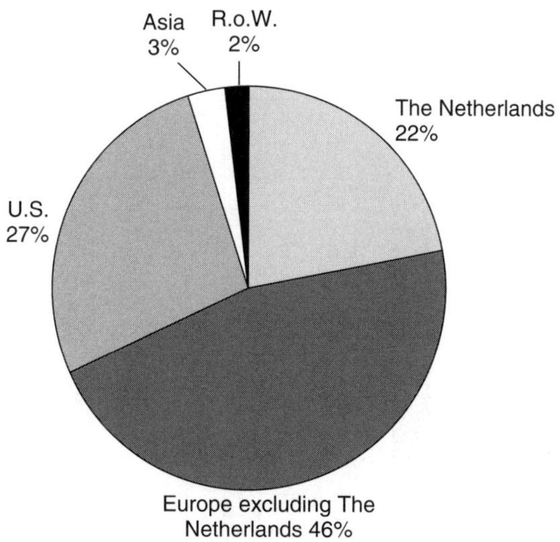

Figure 4.7 Current Private Equity Allocation by Region of Investment

The market for venture capital and private equity is becoming less segmented and increasingly global in scope (Cumming et al., 2004a; Kenney et al., 2007; Manigart et al., 2007; Megginson, 2004). To this end, it is again illustrative to consider the extent to which institutional investors in private equity are internationalized. Allocations of Dutch institutional investors by region of investment are shown in Figure 4.7. Domestic private equity investment accounts for only 22%, while European investment outside The Netherlands accounts for 46% and U.S. investment accounts for 27%. Asia and the rest of the world account for 3% and 2% of private equity allocations, respectively. Figure 4.8 indicates breakdowns by region and type of investment. Direct company investments are more likely to be local, since it is easier for the institutional investor to screen and manage local investees, while direct fund and fund-of-fund investments are more likely to be international.

We noted earlier that only 29% of Dutch institutional investors have allocated a percentage of their assets for private equity in 2004. At 2004, a greater percentage—35%—were expected to be invested in private equity in 2006–2010 (see Figure 4.9).

There are various motivations for the increasing interest in private equity by institutional investors, as indicated in Figure 4.10. On a ranking scale of 1 to 5, with 5 being the most important, portfolio diversification in general regardless of correlations across asset classes is rated the highest, followed closely by an increase in expected rates of return. Some institutional investors seek to diversify risks in the sense that they want to minimize correlations between downside risks. Other institutional investors seek to have a balanced portfolio in terms of minimizing correlations across asset classes (such as publicly traded equities and bonds) as required by law or regulation. Still other institutional investors desire to report yearly positive returns. For venture

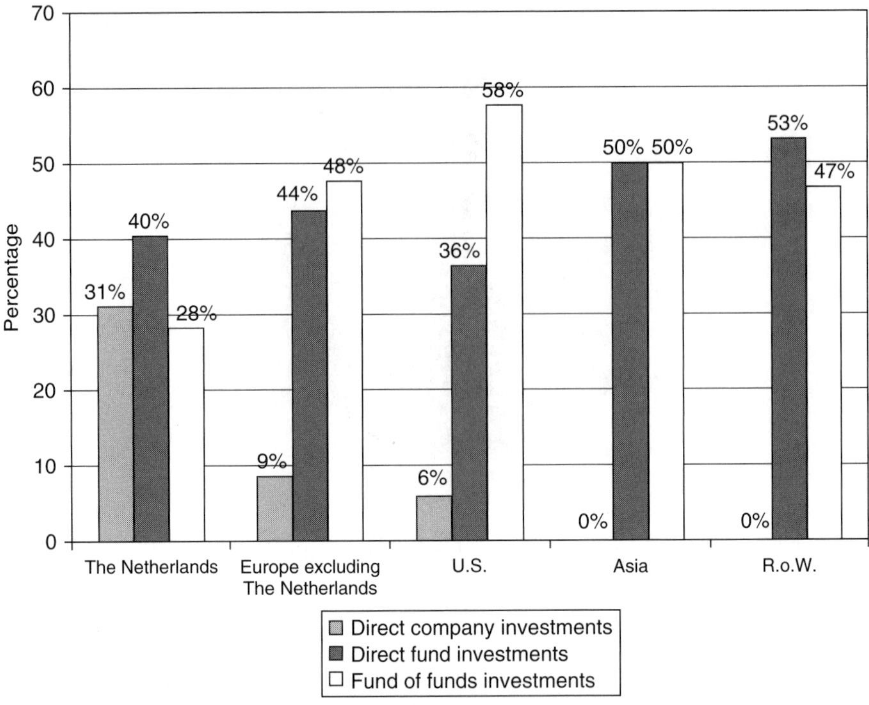

Figure 4.8 Country Breakdown by Type of Investment

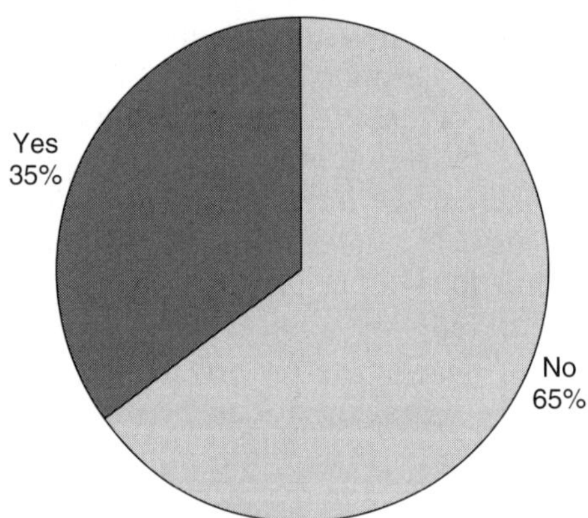

Figure 4.9 Future Allocation to Private Equity (Planned for 2006–2010)

capital and private equity funds, while returns may not be realized each year in terms of sales of entrepreneurial firms, the funds may nevertheless report increases in the value of the portfolio based on expected returns and prior to the realization event. This issue of reporting is discussed further in Chapters 7 and 22. Corporate and other nonfinancial objectives are sometimes relevant

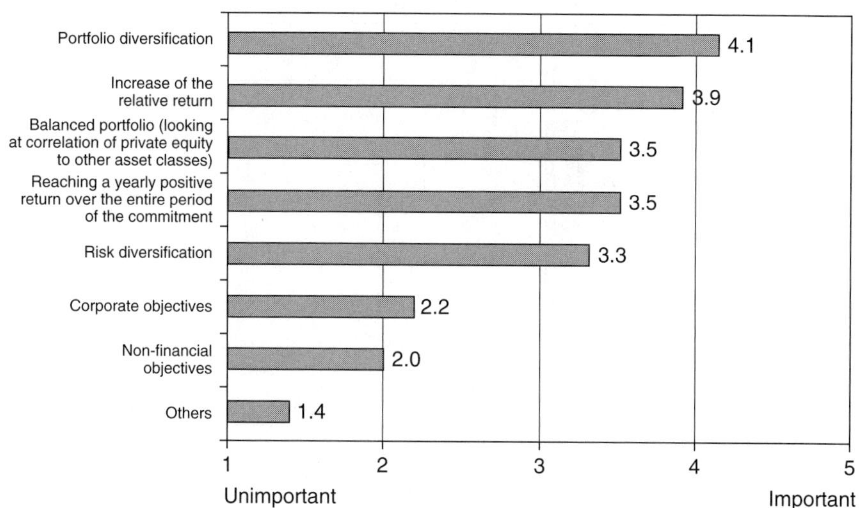

Figure 4.10 Attractiveness of Private Equity Segments within 2006–2010

(albeit on average this is less important) to institutional investors where they seek to invest in entrepreneurial firms with similar strategic goals as that of their own. This rationale is more closely connected with direct company investments. It is a rationale that is also associated with corporate venture capital funds (discussed further in Chapters 11 and 13).

As of 2004, Dutch institutional investors had expected an absolute rate of return (not net of public market returns) of 10% on average from their private equity investments (Table 4.1 and Figure 4.11). Relative to market returns (investments in public equity), they had expected private equity to perform better by 315 basis points (Table 4.1 and Figure 4.12). Different institutional

Table 4.1 Targeted Absolute and Relative Returns, 2006–2010

	In the case of a targeted absolute return, which absolute return is your institution/group seeking to generate from private equity investments?	**In the case of a targeted relative rate of return, what level of over return (in basis points) is your institution/group expecting from private equity in comparison to public equity investments?**
Average	10	315
Median	10	300
Minimum	5	100
Maximum	20	1,000

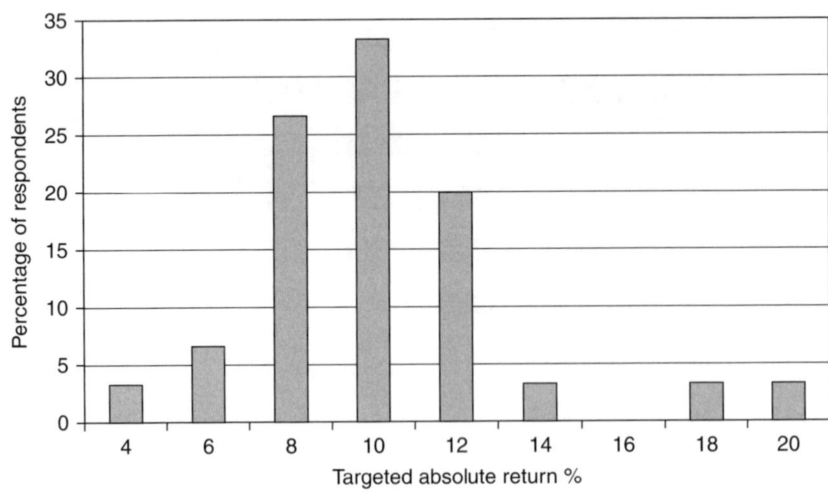

Figure 4.11 Absolute Return Sought from Private Equity Investments

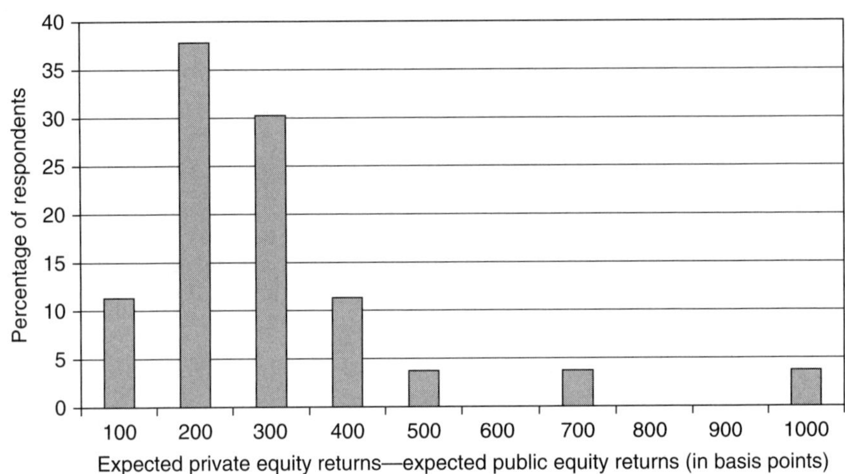

Figure 4.12 Targeted Relative Rate of Return: Private Equity Net of Public Equity Returns (in Basis Points)

investors use different indices to benchmark private equity returns, as indicated in Figure 4.13. Actual performance figures relative to the NASDAQ and S&P 500 for different venture capital and private equity stages for the 20-year horizon up to 2006 are indicated in Table 4.2. With the exception of the mezzanine stage, returns have been consistently above these benchmarks for all venture capital and private equity stages.

Risk diversification is the most important criteria for forming a private equity investment strategy for Dutch institutional investors, as indicated in

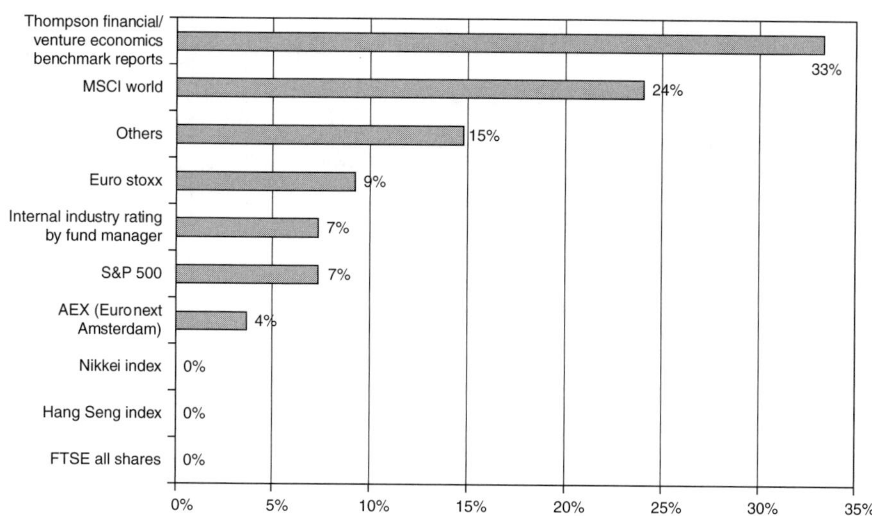

Figure 4.13 Private Equity Benchmarks

Table 4.2 Thomson Financials' U.S. Private Equity Performance Index (PEPI)

Investment Horizon Performance through September 30, 2006 (Expressed in %)					
Fund Type	**1 Yr**	**3 Yr**	**5 Yr**	**10 Yr**	**20 Yr**
Early/Seed VC	2.9	5.5	−5.4	38.3	20.5
Balanced VC	10.7	12.8	1.8	16.8	14.6
Later-Stage VC	27.8	10.5	2.7	9.4	13.9
All Venture	**10.8**	**9.4**	**−1.0**	**20.5**	**16.5**
Small Buyouts	11.3	9.4	5.0	6.0	25.2
Medium Buyouts	37.2	12.3	6.1	10.9	15.3
Large Buyouts	23.1	16.4	8.3	8.3	12.4
Mega Buyouts	23.4	16.2	10.1	8.9	11.6
All Buyouts	**23.6**	**15.6**	**9.2**	**8.8**	**13.2**
Mezzanine	−8.1	4.7	2.9	5.9	8.4
All Private Equity	19.0	13.2	5.9	11.2	14
NASDAQ	**5.5**	**7.8**	**8.7**	**7.1**	**11.4**
S&P 500	**9.7**	**9.9**	**5.2**	**7.5**	**9.7**

Figure 4.14. Institutional investors also seek to match the duration of assets and liabilities. Private equity investments are long term (typically 10 to 13 years, as mentioned), which matches appropriately with, for example, the long-term nature of pension fund liabilities.

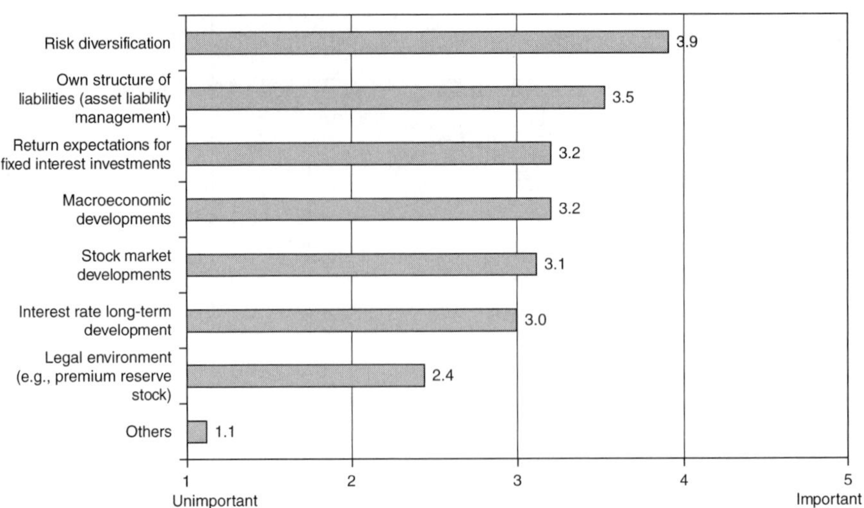

Figure 4.14 Criteria for Private Equity Investment Strategy

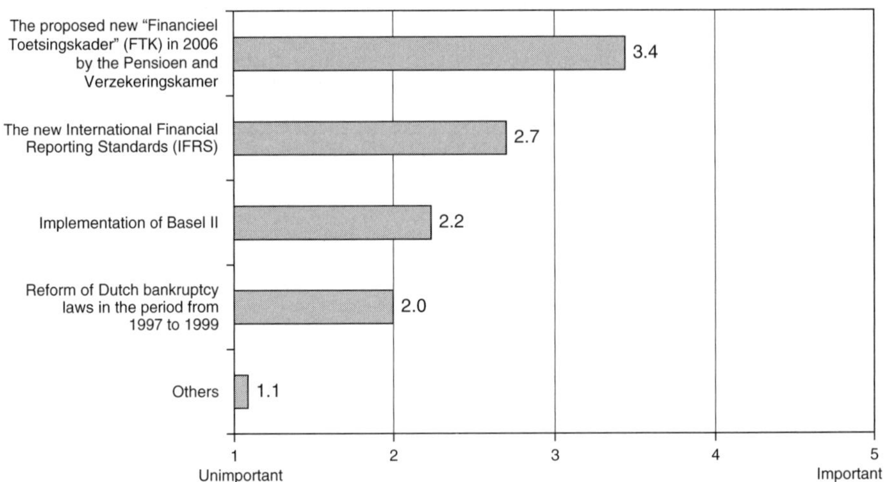

Figure 4.15 Important Changes in the Dutch Legal and Regulatory Environment for Private Equity Investment Strategy

Figure 4.15 indicates regulatory developments are relevant to Dutch institutional investors in private equity funds, particularly the Financieel Toetsingskader (FTK, which involves the regulation of portfolio management standards such as of matching assets and liabilities), the International Financial Reporting Standards (regulation of reporting standards and transparency), and Basel II (regulation of risk management and disclosure standards). These regulations are discussed in more detail in Chapter 7. Private equity fund managers

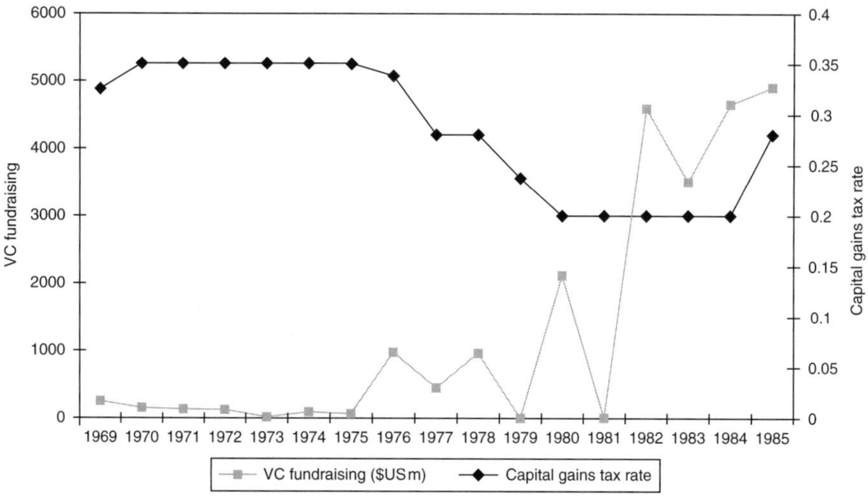

Figure 4.16 Capital Gains Taxes and Fundraising in the United States
Source: Poterba (1989a,b).

are increasingly aware of not only how regulatory changes affect fundraising levels but how their business is carried out. For example, it is noteworthy that the FTK in The Netherlands in 2006 is somewhat similar to changes in the interpretation of the prudent man standards for pension funds in the United States. That is, the U.S. Department of Labor of the Employment Retirement Income Security Act's (ERISA) prudent man rule in 1979 enables diversification in private equity by pension funds to be a "prudent" investment for risk diversification purposes. This change, along with a change in capital gains taxes around that time (Figure 4.16), significantly increased institutional investor capital commitments to private equity funds (Poterba, 1989a,b; Gompers and Lerner, 1998a,b). It is expected that the FTK, which is designed to bring international/European Union directives and standards to The Netherlands, will motivate institutional investment in private equity, just as similar changes in the United States did (this issue, among others, is considered in Chapter 7). Other regulatory changes around this time, including the International Financial Reporting Standards, Basel II, and bankruptcy legislation,[4] are also considered in Chapter 7 (and their comparative ranked importance is indicated in Figure 4.15). While private equity managers may delight in this new development, they are equally aware of the effects the other changes involving regulation of reporting standards, transparency, and risk management will have on their operations. Institutional investors may not desire in the least to administrate the operations of the fund because they have delegated this duty to the fund managers and for all intents and purposes met their

[4]Bankruptcy laws and venture capital are discussed in much greater length in Armour and Cumming (2006, 2008).

fiduciary requirements, but they may be required to be more conscious of the operations of the fund to meet regulatory requirements. This will, for example, affect the scope of reporting required from the private equity fund manager and the level of input expected by the institutional investor at the fund level.

Figure 4.17 indicates that among the Dutch institutional investors with private equity investments, department heads had an average of 4.8 years of experience with private equity (but only an average of 0.6 "exits," or realized investments) and 10.9 years of experience in banking, insurance, or investment management. It is important therefore for private equity fund managers to be aware that during their fundraising exercise that most decision makers have at best minimal experience with the market and at worst absolutely no knowledge of it other than what is reported in the media. Providing sufficient information to enable informed decisions to be made is therefore crucial.

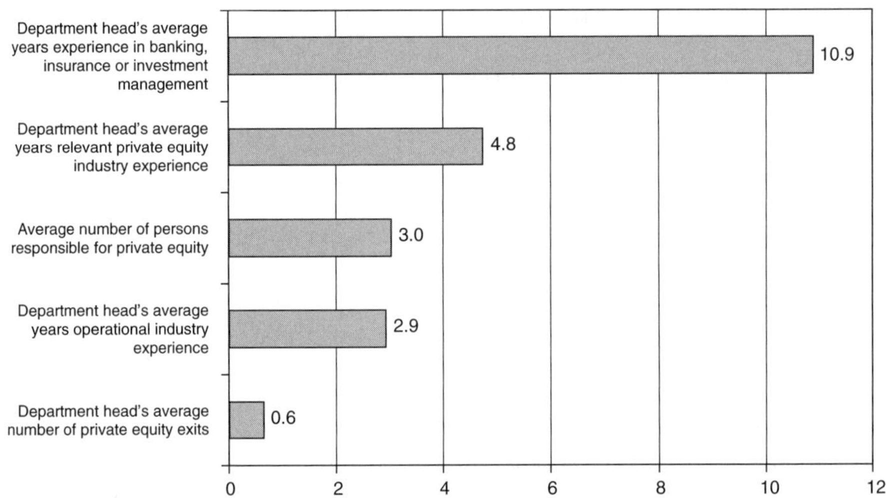

Figure 4.17 Experience among Managers Specifically Assigned Responsibility for Private Equity

It is essential for private equity fund managers to know their potential institutional investors and what criteria are used to select funds. Dutch institutional investors felt that the most important criterion in selecting a private equity fund was the fund manager's track record (Figure 4.18). An oft-repeated mantra in venture capital and private equity is that a superior management team and average business plan and technology are better than a superior business plan and technology and an average management team. It takes skill to evaluate technology and business plans and even greater skill to evaluate management teams successfully. As indicated,[5] there has been significant persistence in private

[5]See footnote 3 and accompanying text.

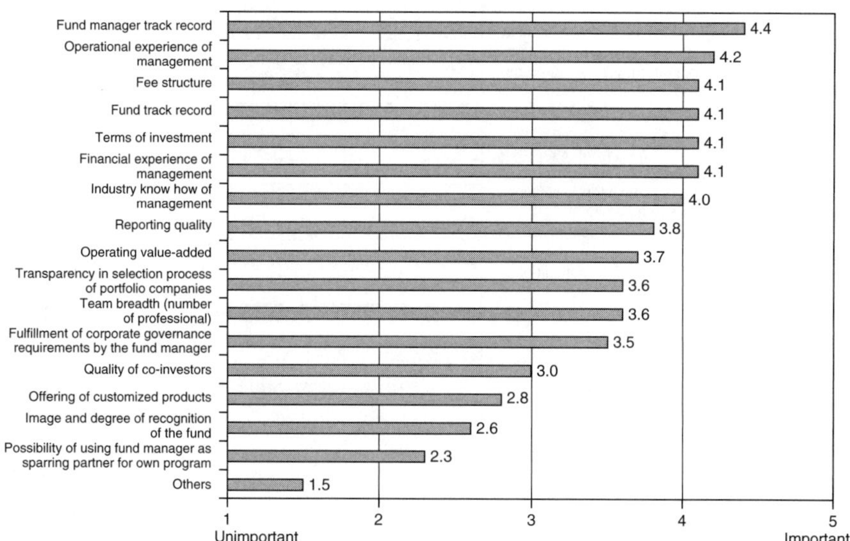

Figure 4.18 Important Selection Criteria for Direct Investments in Private Equity Funds

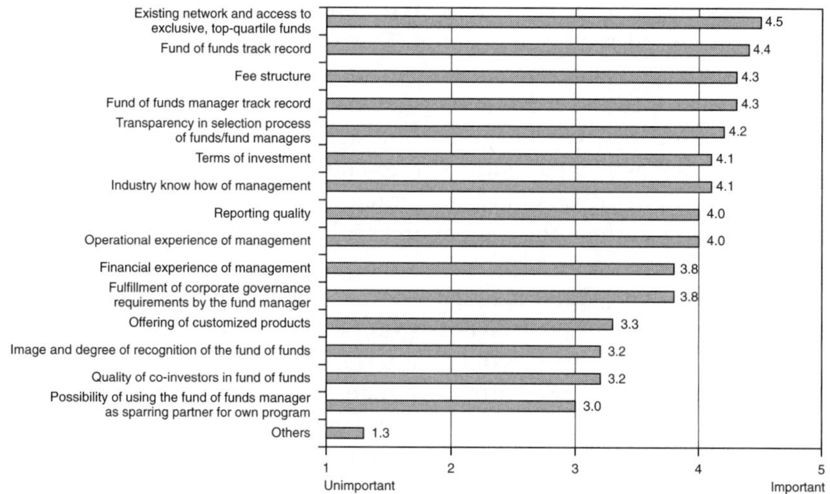

Figure 4.19 Important Selection Criteria for Investments in Fund-of-Funds

equity fund performance, so we can assume that just as the rich get richer, the good get better (and richer, too, of course). Other criteria considered important for direct investment in private equity funds are ranked in Figure 4.19.

Determining the criteria is essential, but in raising funds from potential investors, addressing risk concerns is key. In Figure 4.20 we show the risk concerns taken into consideration by institutional investors. Institutional

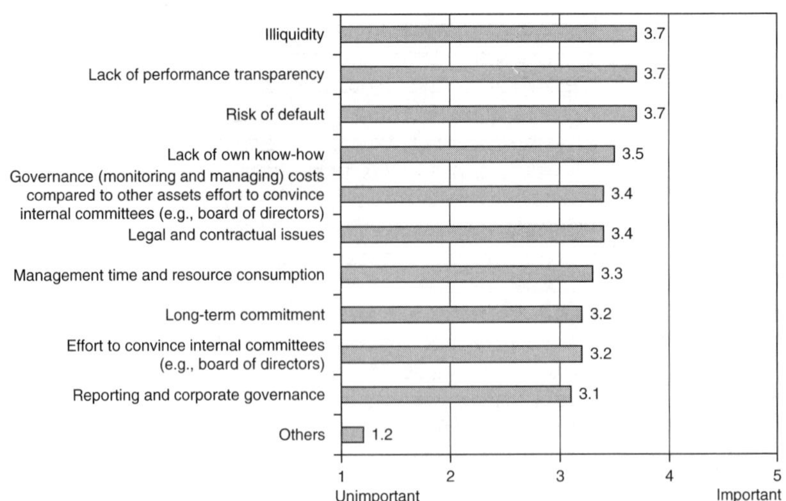

Figure 4.20 Risks and Hurdles Associated with Private Equity Investment

investors view illiquidity as one of the most pronounced risks associated with private equity investment. Risk of default and lack of performance transparency are also considered to be as important on average. The lack of performance transparency is considered in detail in Chapter 7 (and we will further consider performance and transparency in Chapter 22).

Figure 4.21 highlights strategies that institutional investors undertake to mitigate the risks associated with private equity investment as identified in Figure 3.20. Various diversification strategies are more commonly viewed as more important than the use of internal expertise or the expertise of advisors.

Just as private equity fund managers do not consider all institutional investors to be equal, institutional investors do not consider the attractiveness of all private equity funds to be equal. In terms of investment aims, some private equity segments are more attractive than others. As of 2004, Dutch institutional investors considered private equity buyout investments to be more attractive than venture capital investments (Figure 4.22).

Buyouts have in fact attracted a significant amount of capital in recent years, as indicated in Figures 4.23 and 4.24. Returns to top quartile buyout funds have been very high as well, although the major buyout funds that have raised billions in capital may find it difficult to maintain such returns in future years (for a discussion, see Kaplan, 2007). In Chapter 10 we consider factors that lead private equity funds to different stage focus, and in Chapter 8 we consider a relatively new niche segment in the private equity market—socially responsible private equity investments—which were ranked as comparatively less attractive on a pure returns basis (see Figure 4.22), even though demand for such investments is increasing.

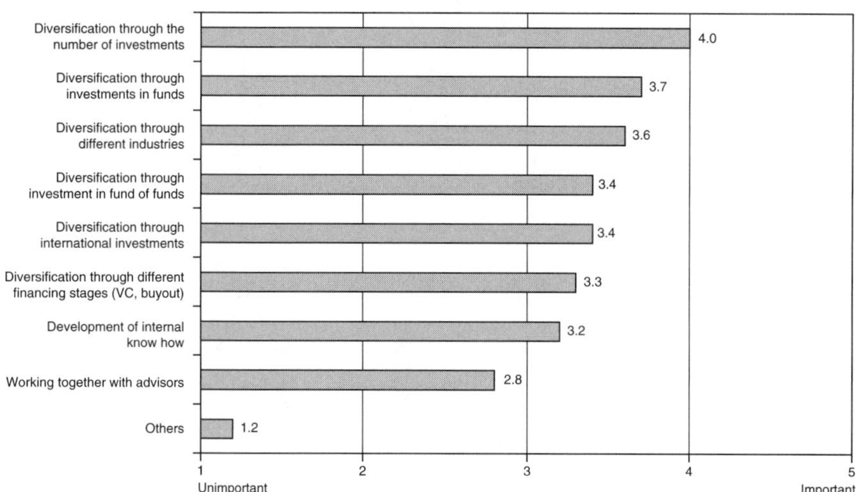

Figure 4.21 Important Approaches to Reduce the Risk of Private Equity Investment

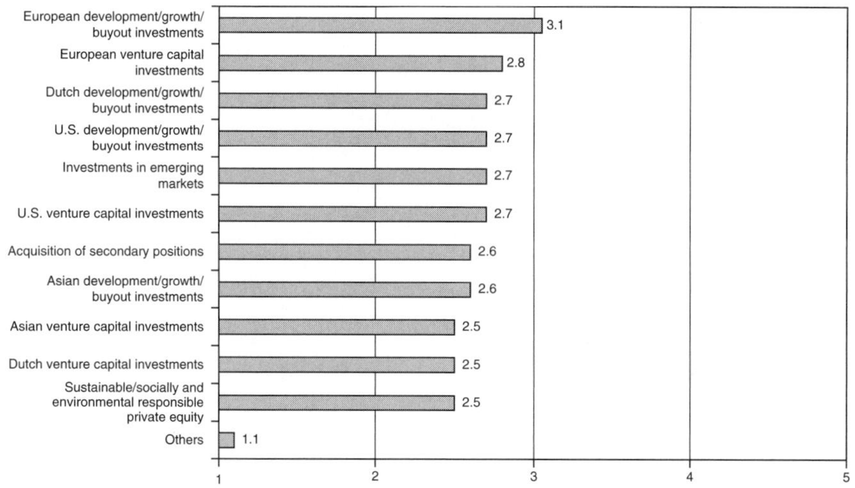

Figure 4.22 Attractiveness of Different Private Equity Segments within 2006–2010

To provide perspective of the recent performance of the U.S. buyout market, Figure 4.25 presents U.S. venture capital performance since 2003 as measured by the Venture Economics Index. From the end of quarter 1 in 1999 to the end of quarter 1 in 2000, annual returns (based on changes in the Venture Economics Index value) peaked at 75%, leading up to the height of the Internet Bubble on April 14, 2000. The high returns and volatility of the venture capital market are contrasted with the performance of the Toronto Stock Exchange 300 Composite Index and the Small Cap Index for publicly traded securities

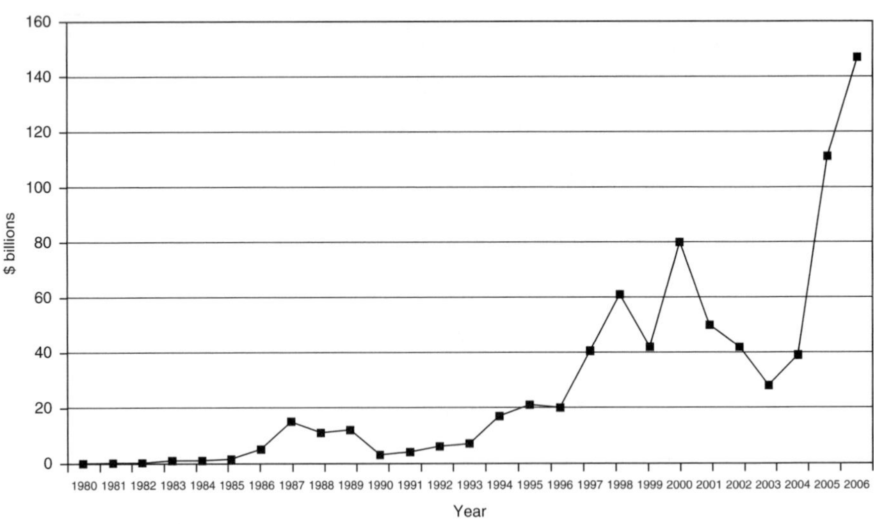

Figure 4.23 Commitments to U.S. Private Equity Partnership 1980–2006
Source: Kaplan (2007).

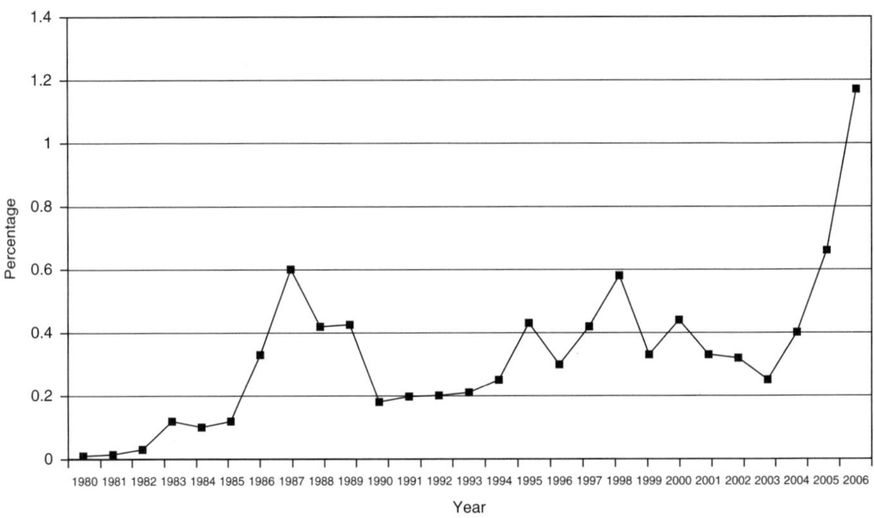

Figure 4.24 Commitments to U.S. Private Equity Partnerships as a Fraction of Total Stock Market Capitalization, 1980–2006
Source: Kaplan (2007).

in Figure 4.26. Figure 4.26 also shows changes in the value of holding risk-free 30-day t-bills. Finally, Figure 4.26 also indicates the performance of Canadian labor-sponsored venture capital corporations (LSVCCs), a tax subsidized venture capital fund in Canada that has clearly underperformed relative to all

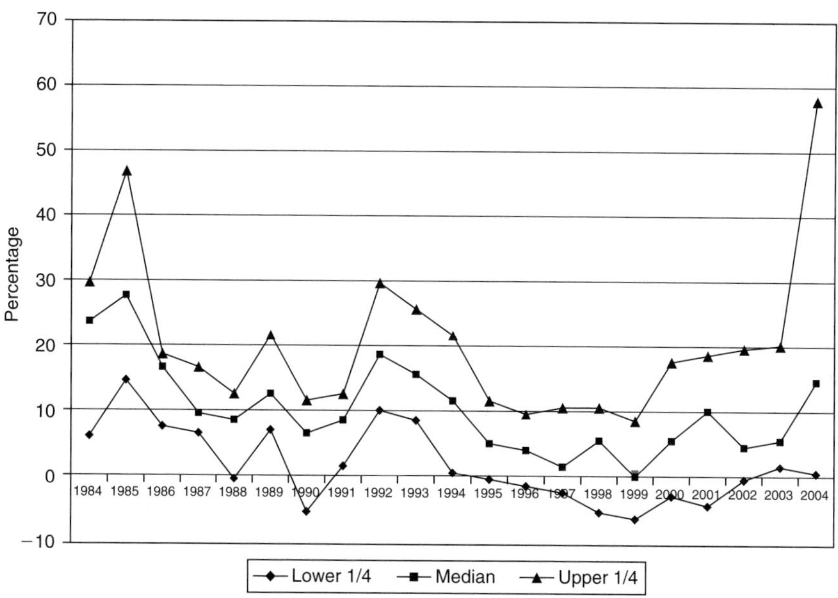

Figure 4.25 U.S. Buyout Returns by Vintage Year Median, Upper, and Lower Quartiles as of December 2006
Source: Kaplan (2007).

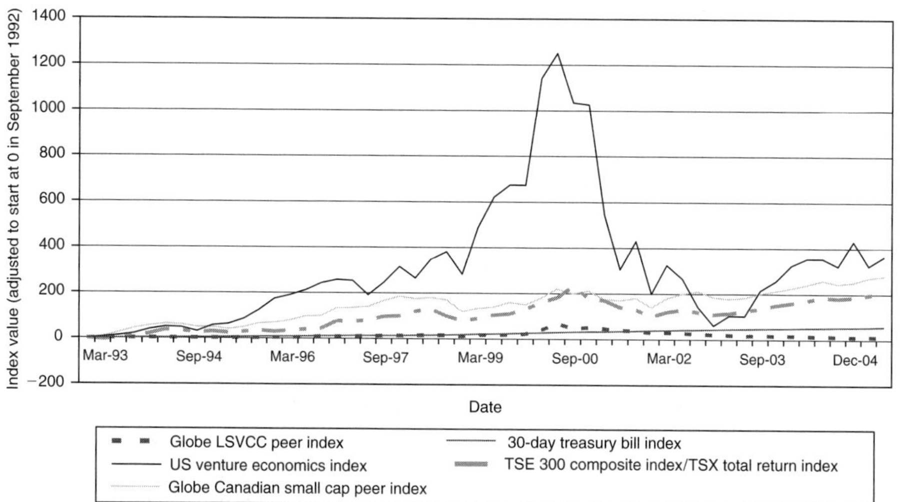

Figure 4.26 Selected Indices 1992–2005
Source: Cumming (2007).

benchmarks. Chapter 9 discusses issues related to these Canadian government funds and other government subsidized funds.

4.3 Summary

This chapter provides an overview of factors that institutional investors deem to be important in venture capital and private equity investment with the aid of survey data from institutional investors in a representative European country. These same issues should be equally influential for private equity fund managers seeking capital from the same investors. Institutional investors of course care most about potential returns. Further investment objectives for institutional investors of private equity funds include strategic objectives, diversification, regulation, and social responsibility. Institutional investors may invest by way of direct company investments, direct fund investments, and fund-of-funds investments. Concerns that institutional investors may have in achieving their private equity investment objectives include fund manager track record (as well as financial and industry expertise); fund track record; operational experience of management; fee structures; the terms of investment, regulation, transparency, and reporting quality; and the fulfillment of corporate governance requirements by the fund management. This chapter also provides insight into institutional investor industry projections and compares them with trends in buyouts and venture capital performance in recent years.

Chapters 5 to 9 discuss further the role of investors and their contractual relations with fund managers. Chapter 5 specifically focuses on the contractual structure of limited partnership funds. Chapter 6 analyzes compensation of fund managers. Chapter 7 considers issues associated with regulation of institutional investors and private equity funds and the associated willingness of institutional investors to contribute capital to private equity fund managers. Chapter 8 investigates specialized fund mandates, particularly those with a focus on socially responsible investment objectives. Chapter 9 considers government involvement in limited partnership funds. Part III examines the contractual relations between fund managers and entrepreneurial firms.

Key Terms

Limited partnership
Institutional investors
Capital commitment
Draw down
Direct company investment
Direct fund investment
Fund-of-funds
Employment Retirement Income Security Act (ERISA)
Prudent man rule
Capital gains tax
Financieel Toetsingskader (FTK)
International Financial Reporting Standards (IFRS)
Basel II
Labor sponsored venture capital corporation (LSVCC)

Discussion Questions

4.1. For what proportion of capital under management do private equity investors typically contribute to private equity? Why? What are some of the benefits/drawbacks associated with investment in private equity for an institutional investor?
4.2. What is the difference between private equity fund capital commitments and draw downs?
4.3. What is the difference between direct company investment, direct private equity fund investment, and fund-of-funds investment? What are the advantages and disadvantages of these different investment strategies?
4.4. How well might an institutional investor expect to do in terms of absolute and relative (to public equity markets) performance by investing in private equity? How well has venture capital and private equity performed in the United States up to 2006? How persistent is performance over time?
4.5. What regulatory impediment existed for U.S. pension fund investment in private equity in the 1970s? What analogous impediment existed in The Netherlands up to 2006?
4.6. What has been the role of capital gains taxes in private equity investment?
4.7. What are the most pronounced risks and hurdles with private equity investment based on perceptions from institutional investors? How might these risks and hurdles vary with regulation, investment strategy, and managerial experience? What might an institutional investor do to mitigate such risks?

5 Limited Partnership Agreements

5.1 Introduction and Learning Objectives

Limited partnerships are the most common form of organization of venture capital and private equity funds in the United States. Because investments in private entrepreneurial firms typically take between 2 and 7 years to bring to fruition in exit (Chapter 19), private equity limited partnerships themselves typically last for 10 years, with an option to continue for an additional 3 years to ensure that the investments have been brought to fruition and the fund can be concluded (Gompers and Lerner, 1996, 1999a,b,c; Sahlman, 1990). Other countries that allow limited partnership structures have also used such structures.[1] Private equity funds that operate in countries that do not allow limited partnership structures have used corporate forms that closely resemble limited partnerships to achieve the same results as the covenants that govern limited partnerships.[2]

The limited partnership structure for venture capital and private equity funds is popular for many reasons. Unlike corporate entities that are formed by articles of incorporation, limited partnerships are established by contracts that are more easily adaptable to fulfill the needs of diverse investors. Limited partnerships enable partners to obtain limited liability while avoiding the additional tax burden of corporate entities. Investors in a private equity fund may be natural persons, foreign corporations, pension funds, and endowments that are exposed to different tax regimes and are able to take advantage of different tax credits and benefits. So while profits of the fund are equally shared by the partners, having the profits directly pass through to the partners may lead to different profit levels as different types of institutions are able to take advantage of exclusive tax benefits.

This chapter discusses the types of covenants found in venture capital and private equity fund limited partnerships. In private equity, the institutional investors are the partners with limited liability not involved in the day-to-day

[1]For example, for funds in Europe, see www.evca.com.

[2]Australia, for example, has only allowed limited partnerships since 2003; prior to that time funds were set up as trusts, but functionally these trusts involved rights and responsibilities that mimicked the limited partnership structure; see Cumming et al. (2005b).

operation of the fund; the fund manager is the general partner that has taken on the administration of the fund with full liability. Institutional investors impose covenants on the general partners to mitigate the agency problems associated with the provision of freedom for the fund managers to invest the institutional investors' capital (Chapter 2). The covenants are privately negotiated between the institutional investors and fund managers in a way that efficiently manages the incentives and controls the potential for opportunistic behavior among the fund managers.

In this chapter we will do the following:

- Identify five main categories of covenants: investment decisions, investment powers, types of investments, fund operations, and limitations on liability
- Consider a dataset involving fund covenants from 17 countries, including developed and emerging markets (Belgium, Brazil, Canada, Cayman Islands, Finland, Germany, Italy, Luxembourg, Malaysia, Netherlands Antilles, the Netherlands, New Zealand, Philippines, South Africa, Switzerland, the United Kingdom, and the United States)
- Evaluate the general proposition that covenants are more likely to be observed when expected agency problems are more pronounced
- Specifically analyze factors that influence the frequency of use of investment covenants imposed by institutional investors in relation to the human capital of the fund managers, legal and institutional conditions in which the funds operate, fund characteristics (such as the type of investments in terms of stage and industry focus), and market conditions

Appendix 1 online at http://venturecapitalprivateequitycontracting.com provides a sample limited partnership agreement. The agreement was used in Europe (and the identity of the parties involved has been kept confidential, as requested by the parties). The terms discussed in this chapter are found in this agreement in Appendix 1 to illustrate how these clauses are implemented in practice.

In this chapter, we first explain the types of restrictive covenants that are found in limited partnership contracts around the world. We then discuss factors that affect the frequency of use of these covenants. Then we examine the dataset to determine the extent to which covenants are implemented in practice. In Chapter 6 we will consider a related issue of compensation contracts that are another mechanism (in addition to restrictive covenants) to mitigate agency costs faced by institutional investors from the actions of fund managers.

5.2 Types of Restrictive Covenants

Venture capital and private equity funds are financial intermediaries between institutional investors (such as banks, endowments, pension funds, life insurance companies, wealthy private individuals) and private entrepreneurial firms. Institutional investors do not have the time and skills to carry out due diligence in selecting worthy entrepreneurial firms for financing and to carry out the monitoring and value-added advice to bring investments in small and medium-sized enterprises to fruition (as is discussed in Chapter 19, the investment process in an entrepreneurial firm can take between 2 to 7 years before an exit event such as an IPO, acquisition, or write-off). Institutional investors therefore commit capital to venture capital and private equity funds so specialized fund managers can manage the investment process in entrepreneurial firms.

Limited partnerships and similar forms of organization involve an assignment of rights and responsibilities in the form of a very long-term contract over a period of 10 or more years. The purpose of this contract is to mitigate the potential for agency problems associated with the venture capital managers' investing institutional investor capital in private entrepreneurial firms. The massive potential for agency problems in the reinvestment of capital (elaborated following) and the long-term nature of the limited partnership contract make extremely important the assignment of rights and obligations in the contract in the form of restrictive covenants. The characteristics of these restrictive covenants among funds in different countries around the world are the focus of this chapter.

In this chapter, we group the venture capital fund restrictive covenants into five categories, four of them based on the innovative work of Gompers and Lerner (1996, 1999a). We have, however, modified those four categories to take into account new types of covenants more commonly used today and to include covenants relating to the limitation of the fund manager's liability. We have also made changes that reflect the structure of funds in countries other than the United States (the only country considered by Gompers and Lerner, 1996, 1999a), where funds may be organized in various legal forms. The changes were made with guidance from a venture capital practitioner (specifically, the head legal advisor of a venture capital fund in Malaysia), and we confirmed the appropriateness of the categorizations based on interviews with six fund managers at nine different funds in three different countries.

5.2.1 Category 1: Authority of Fund Manager Regarding Investment Decisions

The restrictions on investment decisions limit the agency problems associated with the investment of the institutional investor's capital (Gompers and Lerner, 1996). This is important, since the institutional investors cannot interfere with the day-to-day operations of the fund (as limited partners they are legally prohibited from interfering or they may lose their limited liability status). These restrictions include, first, restrictions on the size of investment in any one portfolio firm because otherwise a fund manager might lower her effort costs associated with diversifying the institutional investors' capital across a number of different entrepreneurial firms.[3] Second, there are restrictions on the fund manager's ability to borrow money such as in the form of bank debt and to

[3]Note, however, in some cases funds are set up in a way that enables such restrictions to be waived upon approval of all the investors.

reinvest that borrowed money with the institutional investors' capital. Such an action would increase the leverage of the fund and increase the risks faced by the institutional investors. Third, co-investments by other funds that are managed by the fund manager and co-investments by the fund investors are also restricted. Those restrictions limit the conflicts of interest in the allocation of opportunities to different institutional investors of the fund, as well as limit the incentive by a fund manager to bail out the badly performing investments of a companion fund that is operated by the same manager. Fourth, there are restrictions on the reinvestment of capital gains obtained from investments brought to fruition. Some fund managers might otherwise pursue a strategy of "fame not fortune" in terms of trying to get as many IPO successes as possible, at the risk of losing the profits from one investment in a new, unproven venture. Fifth, there are restrictions on the overall ability and independence of the fund manager to make investment decisions. Finally, there are other less common covenants on other types of investment and divestment decisions (such as limits in terms of timing of investment with draw downs and timing of exits).[4]

5.2.2 Category 2: Restrictions on Fund Manager's Investment Powers

The covenants in the class of restrictions on investment powers also limit the agency problems in the separation of ownership (i.e., by the institutional investors) and control (i.e., by the fund managers) in the investment process. The first restriction in this class involves co-investment of the fund managers themselves. This is similar to co-investment by the fund's institutional investors and co-investment of prior funds (as just described), but instead it involves the personal funds of the fund managers. This restriction limits the incentive problems associated with the allocation of the fund managers' attention to different entrepreneurial firms in the fund portfolio. If the fund manager was permitted to co-invest personal funds, there would be a conflict of interest where the manager might spend a disproportionate amount of time on the firms in which he or she was invested instead of the entire portfolio (as would be expected by institutional investors). Second, there are covenants pertaining to the sale of fund interests by the fund managers, since the institutional investors' financial interest will be compromised by the addition of new institutional investors and, more significantly, the loss of commitment of the fund manager, who is usually also the general partner or the most active fund shareholder. Third, there are key person provisions and limits on the addition of investment principals regarding the fund managers because the contract is made with specific fund managers, and the institutional investors want their money to be managed by

[4]Waiver of these covenants may also be subject to approval of the fund's Board of Advisors, which usually consists of institutional fund investors.

the specific people with whom they have contracted. Finally, there could be other types of restrictions on other actions of fund managers.

5.2.3 Category 3: Covenants Relating to the Types of Investment

Covenants pertaining to the types of investment ensure that the institutional investors' capital is invested in a way that is consistent with their desired risk/ return profile. Restrictions include investments in other venture funds, follow on investments in portfolio companies of other funds of the fund manager,[5] public securities, leveraged buyouts, foreign securities, and bridge financing. Without such restrictions, the fund manager could pursue investment strategies that better suit the interests of the fund managers regardless of the interests of the institutional investors.

5.2.4 Category 4: Fund Operation

Covenants on fund operation are designed to oversee the administrative aspects of a fund, and they include the sale of fund interests by fund investors,[6] restrictions against the fund manager on raising a new fund,[7] public disclosure of fund matters to investors, and provisions to allow fund investors to vote to remove the fund manager without cause (no-fault divorce clauses). The covenant that restricts the sale of fund interest by fund investors (in this category 4) is different from the covenant that restricts the sale of interest by the fund manager (as specified in category 2) because the specific fund manager action of selling pertains to things fund managers cannot do, whereas this category 4 pertains to administrative aspects of all investors. Recall that the fund manager is also the general partner or the most active shareholder of a fund, unlike all other fund investors—hence the different categorizations for seemingly related actions.

5.2.5 Category 5: Limitation of Liability of the Fund Manager

While categories 1 to 4 considered covenants that regulated the activities of fund managers, this last category of covenants pertains to favorable awards of limited liability for the fund managers. Fund manager liability can be limited in the event of disappointing returns from investments made, if the fund manager

[5]This is similar to the co-investment restriction in category 1, but where the category 1 restriction is against another fund managed by the fund manager investing in the fund, this restriction in category 3 is against the fund itself investing in another fund's (usually an earlier fund) portfolio company, also managed by the fund manager.

[6]In category 2, we identified a similar covenant on sale of fund interests by fund managers.

[7]This restriction on fundraising is typically either for a set period of time or hurdle rate.

fails to invest committed capital within the agreed time, and/or if the fund manager is found to be mismanaging the fund.

5.3 What Affects the Frequency of Use of Limited Partnership Covenants?

5.3.1 Human Capital Factors Influencing the Use of Fund Covenants

The frequency of use of venture capital and private equity covenants should be directly related to the human capital of the contracting parties. Because the fund managers unilaterally carry out the day-to-day operations of the fund, and the institutional investors are limited investors who are not involved in the decision making of the fund, it is natural to focus on the human capital of the fund managers and not the institutional investors (refer back to Figures 4.17–4.20). We would expect that more experienced fund managers would have fewer restrictive covenants, and we would also expect more experienced fund managers to have more covenants granting limited liability to fund managers. This prediction is based on the simple reasons that the bargaining power is greater among more experienced fund managers and that institutional investors have less concern among fund managers with a track record.

For the frequency of covenants, we might also be concerned with the fund manager's educational background in addition to experience. Of particular importance is the presence of legally trained fund managers. Each institutional investor contributing capital to a fund will have legal counsel that reviews the covenants pertaining to the set-up of a fund. Likewise, the fund managers will have legal counsel that reviews the covenants. We would expect the marginal impact of the presence of a legally trained fund manager, however, to positively affect the use of covenants, since the manager will be directly attuned to the meaning and importance of each of the fund covenants through his legal training and because these rights and obligations will directly influence the day-to-day job rights and responsibilities of the fund manager.

5.3.2 Legal and Institutional Factors Influencing the Use of Fund Covenants

It is reasonable to expect international differences in law quality to affect the frequency of the use of covenants that govern venture capital and private equity fund managers in different countries. There are two competing hypotheses. On the one hand, we might expect that countries with weaker laws have funds that use more covenants to substitute for the poor legal protections otherwise afforded to the parties. On the other hand, we might expect the legal certainty offered by countries with superior law quality gives rise to a greater benefit/cost of negotiating and implementing covenants governing funds.

Law quality in this chapter is proxied with the use of the Legality index (see Table 3.1), which is a weighted average of the legal index variables introduced by La Porta et al. (1997, 1998). The Legality index is a broad measure based on La Porta et al. (1997, 1998) that is made up of the efficiency of the judicial system, the rule of law, corruption, risk of expropriation, risk of contract repudiation, and shareholder rights (it is a weighted sum of the factors based on Berkowitz et al., 2003). Countries with a higher legality index have stronger laws protecting investors and a greater likelihood of efficient enforcement of such laws. Higher numbers indicate "better" legal systems across each of the factors. Note that legality in the context of fund structure refers to the laws of the country in which the fund was formed.

One component of international differences in laws that is not covered by the Legality index is the civil versus common law difference. We might expect civil law countries to be more formalized about writing contracts in accord with a rule-based legal system, at least relative to common law countries.

Further, an interesting aspect of international differences in investment funds is that sometimes funds are set up "offshore." The institutional investors of such funds invariably come from a diverse array of countries. We therefore expect differences in the frequency of covenants for such funds. Because offshore funds involve institutional investors from a greater number of disparate countries, which implies greater negotiation and contracting costs (i.e., less regulatory harmonization; see Chapter 7 for a further discussion), we expect offshore funds to have fewer covenants.

5.3.3 Fund-specific Factors Influencing the Use of Fund Covenants

A variety of fund-specific factors might influence the frequency of use of limited partnership covenants. First, larger funds might have more covenants if the contracting costs are worth bearing with an increase in the scale of the fund. Second, funds that operate in riskier industries with higher market/book ratios, and among investees in their earlier stage of development, will have more covenants given the risks and scope for opportunistic behavior are more pronounced. Third, the type of institutional investors and the year in which the fund was formed may also be relevant control variables for similar reasons.

5.3.4 Market Conditions and the Use of Fund Covenants

In stronger market conditions, institutional investors might be more likely to accept fewer covenants over fund managers and grant limited liability protection to fund managers if the supply of funds from institutional investors to private equity and venture capital exceeds the talent available in the market for managing these funds. In the next section we shed light on when venture capital and private equity fund managers are more likely to adopt a greater number of fund covenants.

5.4 Survey of Private Equity Funds

5.4.1 Methods and Survey Instrument

For this chapter we surveyed private equity funds across the developed and emerging private equity markets between July 2004 and December 2004. This method of data collection was deemed the most efficient because the covenants used by both fund investors and fund managers to regulate their relationships are almost never made public. Also, because the agreements used to govern the relationship between fund investors and fund managers may not be in English, we felt it best to allow the fund managers themselves to provide the data related to such agreements in a manner that was readable to us. Finally, in view of the fact that the funds surveyed will be subject to different laws, thus affecting the format and literal content of such agreements, we felt it would be far more efficient to allow the fund managers, as those bound by the terms of the agreements, to provide the information regarding the relevant covenants governing or, more specifically, restricting their investment decisions. These publications and other information obtained from respondents' websites were, however, used to verify and enhance the data obtained by the survey. We believe the data we have compiled provide a unique set of variables, which are summarized and defined in Table 5.1.

5.4.2 Potential Sample Selection Bias

One limitation to obtaining data through a survey is the possibility of sample selection bias. While we acknowledge that this is a possibility, we believe from a detailed analysis of the responses received and the data obtained from the responses that this is not a concern in this exercise. First, survey data were gathered for a final sample of 50 funds in 17 countries, as managed by 50 fund managers in 21 countries. We are aware that the seminal work carried out by Gompers and Lerner (1996) used a sample of 140 contracts that were used to establish funds and were obtained from institutional investors (two fund-of-funds and one endowment). Litvak (2004a,b) contains data from 38 funds in the United States. We believe, however, that by obtaining data from funds situated both in and outside the United States, and by having access to data regarding contracts entered into by 21 different fund managers, response bias is mitigated as much as possible. Limitations in our sample size from each country from which we derived data, as well as the limited information about venture capital and private equity funds around the world, however, make reliable statistical comparisons of our sample relative to the population of funds intractable. Our sample of respondent funds includes 8 funds each the Netherlands and the United States; 6 funds each from the United Kingdom and Malaysia; 4 funds from the Netherlands Antilles; 3 funds each from Germany and Belgium; 2 funds each from the Cayman Islands and South Africa; and 1 fund each from the Philippines, Canada, Finland, New Zealand, Luxembourg, Brazil, Switzerland, and Italy

Table 5.1 Definition of Variables

This table defines the variables considered in this chapter. Summary statistics are presented in Tables 5.2 and 5.3.

Variable	Description
Restrictive Covenants	
Investment Decisions	The sum of dummy variables equal to 1 for each of 6 questions regarding the restrictions placed upon fund managers relating to investment decisions in carrying out their duties as manager of the fund. Such restrictions include restrictions on size of investment (either in dollar value or percentage of fund capital) on any one investee firm or portfolio company, restrictions on use of debt instruments, restrictions on co-investment by another fund managed by the fund manager, restrictions on reinvestment of capital gains, and restrictions on the fund manager making investment decisions independently, without fund input.
Investment Powers	The sum of dummy variables equal to 1 for each of the 5 questions regarding the restrictions placed upon fund managers in their carrying out their duties as general partner or most active shareholder of a fund company. Such restrictions include restrictions against the fund manager investing in any of the investee firms, restrictions on the sale of fund interest by the fund manager, and restrictions on investment principal additions to the fund manager. The presence of key person provisions regarding the fund manager and any other important restrictions governing the actions of the fund manager in his capacity as general partner or most active fund shareholder is also indicated.
Types of Investments	The sum of dummy variables equal to 1 for each of the 7 questions regarding the restrictions placed upon fund managers in their making specific types of investments. Such restrictions include restrictions on making investments in other investment funds, restrictions on follow-on investments in an investee firm of which another fund managed by the fund manager has an interest, restrictions on investments in publicly listed securities, restrictions on investments in leveraged buyouts, restrictions on investments in foreign securities, and restrictions on bridge financing. The presence of a minimum percentage of domestic investments is also indicated.

(*continued*)

Table 5.1 *(continued)*

Variable	Description
Fund Operation	The sum of dummy variables equal to 1 for each of the 4 questions regarding the restrictions placed upon fund managers in their administrative operation of the fund. Such restrictions include restrictions on sale of fund interest by any investor, restrictions on the fund manager raising new funds, and restrictions on public disclosure of fund matters. The presence of a no-fault divorce provision that allows fund investors to remove the fund manager without cause is also indicated.
Manager Liability Limited	The sum of dummy variables equal to 1 for each of the 3 questions regarding the limitation of liability of the fund manager. Limitation of liability includes in the event of disappointing returns from investments made, failure to invest committed funds within the agreed investment period, and mismanagement of funds.
Sum of All Covenants (Excluding Limited Liability)	Sum of all covenants deemed to restrict fund manager actions as general partners or most active shareholder, and fund manager investment powers.
Legal and Market Conditions	
Country Legality Index	Weighted average of the following factors (see Table 3.1): efficiency of judicial system, rule of law, corruption, risk of expropriation, risk of contract repudiation, and shareholder rights (as per La Porta et al., 1997, 1998; Berkowitz et al., 2003). Where the weighted average is not available, especially for less developed countries, an approximate index is derived by multiplying the country's GNP per population with a constant variable obtained by carrying out a regression of the legality indices available. Higher numbers indicate "better" legal systems. The log of this variable is used in the empirics to account for a diminishing effect with larger numbers.
Common Law Country	A dummy variable equal to 1 for a fund organized within a common law jurisdiction.
MSCI Index	The country-specific MSCI Index taken for the year prior to that when fundraising commenced. The year prior to fundraising is deemed to be most relevant, as decisions to invest in private equity by institutional investors will be based on available economic indicators. The log of (1+MSCI) is used in the empirics to account for a diminishing effect with larger numbers.

(continued)

Table 5.1 *(continued)*

Variable	Description
Vintage Year of Fund	The year fundraising commences.
Outbound Offshore	A dummy variable equal to 1 for a fund located offshore that obtains its capital from investors from a certain jurisdiction but fund investments are made primarily in assets other than in the jurisdiction of the fund and the fund investors. With reference to U.S. jurisdictional boundaries, a fund will be considered to be an outbound offshore fund if it obtains capital from U.S. investors but it invests outside the United States.
Inbound Offshore	A dummy variable equal to 1 for a fund located offshore that obtains its capital from investors from various jurisdictions but fund investments are made primarily in assets in a certain jurisdiction. With reference to U.S. jurisdictional boundaries, an inbound offshore fund will be a fund located offshore that invests primarily in assets within the United States yet obtains its capital from non-U.S. investors.
Fund Manager Characteristics	
Percentage of Legally Trained Fund Managers	Percentage of principal fund managers with investment-making decisions who are legally trained or are qualified as lawyers. Where managers have some extent of legal training, that fraction of the extent of legal training is also reflected in the data.
Percentage of MBA/CFA Trained Fund Managers	Percentage of principal fund managers with investment-making decisions who have obtained an MBA or CFA qualifications. Where managers have some extent of such training, that fraction is also reflected in the data.
Percentage of Ph.D. (Science) Trained Fund Managers	Percentage of principal fund managers with investment-making decisions who have obtained a Ph.D. in a science-based discipline. Where managers have some extent of formal scientific training, that fraction of training is also reflected in the data.
Percentage of Ph.D. (Nonscience) Trained Fund Managers	Percentage of principal fund managers with investment-making decisions who have obtained a Ph.D. in a nonscience-based discipline. Where managers have some extent of advanced Ph.D. studies, that fraction of training is also reflected in the data.
Average # Years of Relevant Work Experience of Principal Fund Managers	Average number of years relevant work experience of principal fund managers at the time of fundraising. The log of this variable is used in the empirics to account for a diminishing effect with larger numbers.

(continued)

Table 5.1 (*continued*)

Variable	Description
Fund Characteristics	
Funds Raised	The fund size, or amount of funds raised in $US. Where the amount is provided in a local currency, an exchange rate as at December 2003 is used for conversion of such amounts into $US equivalents. The log of this variable is used in the empirics to account for a diminishing effect with larger numbers.
Bank Institutional Investors	The proportion of banks as the fund's institutional investors.
Government Investors	The proportion of government agencies or ministries as institutional investors.
Limited Partnership Funds	A dummy variable equal to 1 for the fund being organized as a limited partnership.
Industry Market/Book	The industry market/book ratio of the industries in which the fund has invested. The industry market/book ratio of 5 general categories—biotechnology and medical, communications and Internet, computers and electronics, manufacturing, and others—is obtained by averaging the total book value of specific industries falling within the general categories. The log of this variable is used in the empirics to account for a diminishing effect with larger numbers.
Early Stage Investee Focus	A dummy variable equal to 1 for funds that indicate a focus on financing provided to firms in their early/ expansion stages of development (not late stages or buyout stages). More specific stages of focus were not tractable due to international differences in the definition of stage focus, as well as style drift that is often observed among different stages of development.

(see Table 5.2). The respondent fund managers include 7 each from Malaysia, the Netherlands, and the Netherlands Antilles; 6 from the United States; 3 each from the United Kingdom and Germany; 2 each from Belgium and South Africa; and 1 each from the Philippines, Canada, Finland, New Zealand, Brazil, Italy, Vietnam, the Czech Republic, Sweden, Norway, France, South Korea, and Uzbekistan. The number of respondents and the fair representation of both funds from developed and emerging private equity markets make a response bias even less likely.

Second, a broad array of respondents replied to the survey. For example, the data show the median respondent fund size of US$39,487,200 and the average being US$103,974,889 (minimum US$263,378; maximum US$482,766,000), indicating respondents were of a variety of fund sizes and of typical size for a sample of non-U.S. countries.[8] The possibility of sample selection bias is further reduced by the presence of (1) both onshore and offshore funds within the final sample; (2) funds organized not only in both common law and civil law jurisdictions but also within jurisdictions in legal systems with English-, French-, Scandinavian-, and German-based legal systems; and (3) funds situated in countries where English is not the primary language.

Finally, a sufficient number of variables regarding both fund and fund manager organization and the relevant features of the fund asset size, fund vintage, investor composition, investment strategy, industry composition of fund investments, and governance structures (the specific covenants provided in the terms within the agreements that govern the relationship between fund investors and fund managers) were collected to minimize the risk of response bias. We unfortunately realize that we cannot absolutely rule out the possibility of a response bias because the data we have compiled here are unique.

5.4.3 Summary Statistics

The summary statistics are presented in Table 5.2 and Figures 5.1 and 5.2. The variables as set out in the Summary Statistics in Table 5.2 that were used to test our hypotheses are broken down into four main categories:

1. Restrictive covenants (investment decisions, investment powers, types of investment, fund operation, limitation of manager liability, and sum of all covenants excluding limitation of manager liability)
2. Legal and market conditions (country legality index, common law country, MSCI index, vintage year of fund, outbound offshore and inbound offshore)
3. Fund manager characteristic (percentage of legally trained fund managers, MBA/CFA trained fund managers, and Ph.D. [science/nonscience-based disciplines] qualified fund managers) within a team, and the average number of years of relevant work experience of principal fund managers)
4. Fund characteristics (amount of funds raised, composition of fund investors (banking institutions and government bodies/agencies), organization as a limited partnership, industry market/book ratio, and early-stage investee focus)

Because the primary variables used to prove our hypotheses are within the first main category, they are further elaborated by Figure 5.1, which sets out the frequency of the use of each of the five subcategories (not including the additional summation category set out in Table 5.2), and Figure 5.2, which sets out the frequency of the use of each specific covenant within each subcategory (not including the summation category set out in Table 5.2). Each variable is presented in 24 rows (28 in total) and 18 separate columns, 1 column representing the total sum or average of the total sum of the rest of the 17 columns, which represent each sample jurisdiction.

[8]For some comparative information on fund sizes among non-U.S. funds, see, for example, www.evca.com.

Table 5.2 Summary

This table summarizes the funds in the data based on the country in which the fund was formed.

	Country of							
	Total	**Belgium**	**Brazil**	**Canada**	**Cayman Islands**	**Finland**	**Germany**	**Italy**
Number of Funds in Our Data	50	3	1	1	2	1	3	1
Restrictive Covenants								
Investment Decisions	3.60	4.00	6.00	4.00	3.50	4.00	3.67	5.00
Investment Powers	3.62	3.00	3.00	4.00	2.00	5.00	3.33	1.00
Types of Investments	4.30	2.33	6.00	6.00	1.50	4.00	3.00	4.00
Fund Operation	2.22	1.67	3.00	4.00	3.50	3.00	1.33	2.00
Manager Liability Limited	1.92	2.67	2.00	3.00	2.00	3.00	2.00	2.00
Sum of All Covenants (Excluding Limited Liability)	13.74	11.00	18.00	18.00	10.50	16.00	11.33	12.00
Legal and Market Conditions								
Country Legality Index	19.82	20.82	14.09	21.13	20.41	21.49	20.44	17.23
Common Law Country		No	No	Yes	Yes	No	No	No
MSCI Index	0.11	0.19	0.62	−0.14	0.01	1.19	0.00	−0.03
Vintage Year of Fund	2000	1999.3	2000.0	2004.0	2000.0	1999.0	1998.0	2002.0
Outbound Offshore	0.28	0.00	0.00	0.00	0.50	0.00	0.00	0.00
Inbound Offshore	0.12	0.00	0.00	0.00	0.50	0.00	0.00	0.00
Fund Manager Characteristics								
Percentage of Legally Trained Fund Managers	5.96	8.33	20.00	33.00	0.00	5.00	3.33	25.00
Percentage of MBA/CFA Trained Fund Managers	75.40	58.33	80.00	67.00	90.00	80.00	86.67	25.00
Percentage of Ph.D. (Science) Trained Fund Managers	8.80	33.33	0.00	0.00	0.00	5.00	3.33	0.00

of the Data

The average values of each category per country are reported.

Fund Formation

Luxembourg	Malaysia	Netherlands Antilles	Netherlands	New Zealand	Philippines	South Africa	Switzerland	U.K.	U.S.
1	6	4	8	1	1	2	1	6	8
3.00	4.33	3.00	3.50	4.00	3.00	3.00	2.00	2.83	3.75
4.00	4.17	5.00	3.38	5.00	3.00	3.50	1.00	3.00	4.38
3.00	3.67	7.00	6.38	5.00	5.00	3.00	1.00	2.67	4.88
0.00	1.50	4.00	2.13	3.00	1.00	0.50	1.00	1.83	3.00
0.00	2.33	2.00	1.75	2.00	0.00	2.00	0.00	1.83	1.88
10.00	13.67	19.00	15.38	17.00	12.00	10.00	5.00	10.33	16.00
21.91	16.67	21.67	21.67	21.55	8.51	14.51	21.91	20.41	20.85
No	Yes	No	No	Yes	No	Yes	No	Yes	Yes
0.01	0.03	0.16	0.18	0.20	−0.63	0.17	−0.08	0.14	0.07
1997.0	2001.5	2000.3	1997.6	2003.0	1998.0	2001.0	2000.0	2000.5	2000.9
1.00	0.17	1.00	0.00	0.00	1.00	0.00	0.00	0.50	0.38
0.00	0.00	0.00	0.13	0.00	0.00	0.00	0.00	0.50	0.13
5.00	4.17	0.00	12.50	5.00	0.00	0.00	0.00	5.00	1.88
80.00	78.33	80.00	63.75	80.00	50.00	83.50	70.00	90.00	77.00
5.00	5.83	5.00	9.38	5.00	50.00	0.00	0.00	10.00	9.38

(continued)

Table 5.2

	Total	Belgium	Brazil	Canada	Cayman Islands	Finland	Germany	Italy
Percentage of Ph.D. (Nonscience) Trained Fund Managers	12.56	33.33	0.00	0.00	0.00	10.00	6.67	0.00
Average # Years of Relevant Work Experience of Principal Fund Managers	14.07	11.33	14.00	18.00	11.00	18.00	11.67	20.00
Fund Characteristics								
Funds Raised	1.04E +08	1.43E +08	1.00E +07	6.79E +07	8.43E +07	3.46E +07	1.49E +08	2.66E +08
Bank Institutional Investors	0.16	0.56	0.00	0.00	0.02	0.00	0.45	0.60
Government Investors	0.15	0.06	0.15	0.00	0.42	0.20	0.03	0.00
Limited Partnership Funds	0.48	0.00	0.00	1.00	0.50	1.00	0.67	0.00
Industry Market/ Book	4.04	3.89	4.84	2.72	2.87	2.48	3.75	2.70
Early Stage Investee Focus	0.50	0.33	1.00	0.00	0.50	1.00	0.67	0.00

The first row in Table 5.2 sets out the sum total of the sample set as 50 funds, with the sample of funds consisting of 8 funds each from the Netherlands and the United States; 6 funds each from the United Kingdom and Malaysia; 4 funds from the Netherlands Antilles; 3 funds each from Germany and Belgium; 2 funds each from the Cayman Islands and South Africa; and 1 fund each from the Philippines, Canada, Finland, New Zealand, Luxembourg, Brazil, Switzerland, and Italy. The sample countries are listed alphabetically.

Rows 3 to 6 in Table 5.2 set out the average frequency of the use of covenants within agreements governing the relationship between fund investors and fund manager, relating to investment decisions, investment powers, types of investment, and fund operation. Row 8 sets out the total average and sum of the 3 types of covenants used across markets. Row 7, although setting out a type of covenant relating to the limitation of liability of fund managers, is not included in the sum of restrictive covenants, since they essentially act to provide more latitude to fund managers in exercising their investment powers. From the data (as summarized in Table 5.2 and Figure 5.2), we can see that

(*continued*)

Luxembourg	Malaysia	Netherlands Antilles	Netherlands	New Zealand	Philippines	South Africa	Switzerland	U.K.	U.S.
10.00	10.00	30.00	15.63	10.00	0.00	0.00	30.00	3.33	15.38
10.00	14.75	14.00	12.13	20.00	10.00	7.00	15.00	15.67	17.25
3.60E+07	3.21E+07	3.04E+08	4.66E+07	2.00E+07	2.30E+07	2.81E+07	2.63E+05	1.63E+08	1.10E+08
0.24	0.17	0.10	0.19	0.00	0.00	0.09	0.00	0.07	0.08
0.00	0.30	0.10	0.25	0.22	0.40	0.10	0.00	0.07	0.08
0.00	0.17	1.00	0.25	0.00	0.00	0.00	0.00	1.00	0.75
4.75	4.42	4.82	3.66	5.79	6.19	5.03	4.10	4.14	3.71
0.00	0.67	0.00	0.38	1.00	1.00	1.00	1.00	0.50	0.50

the most commonly used covenant is that restricting the size of investments made by fund managers, while the least commonly used covenant is that which restricts co-investments by other fund investors. This is possibly due to the fact that investors seek to mitigate the fund's investment risk by ensuring diversification of fund assets, minimizing downside risk. Co-investments by fund investors, on the other hand, will maximize investors' upside potential. We can also see (from Table 5.2 and Figure 5.1) that funds on average do not utilize all of the possible restrictive covenants available to them, although they do utilize a majority of them. It is for this reason that we seek to determine the importance of industry-specific factors in driving the use of covenants.

To carry out our empirical analysis, we use a second category of variables, legal and market conditions, which are compiled primarily from a country legality index (Table 3.1; see also Table 5.1) that is a weighted average of the efficiency of the judicial system, the rule of law, corruption, the risk of expropriation, the risk of contract repudiation, and shareholder rights (as per La Porta et al., 1997, 1998; Berkowitz et al., 2003). Of course, the log of this

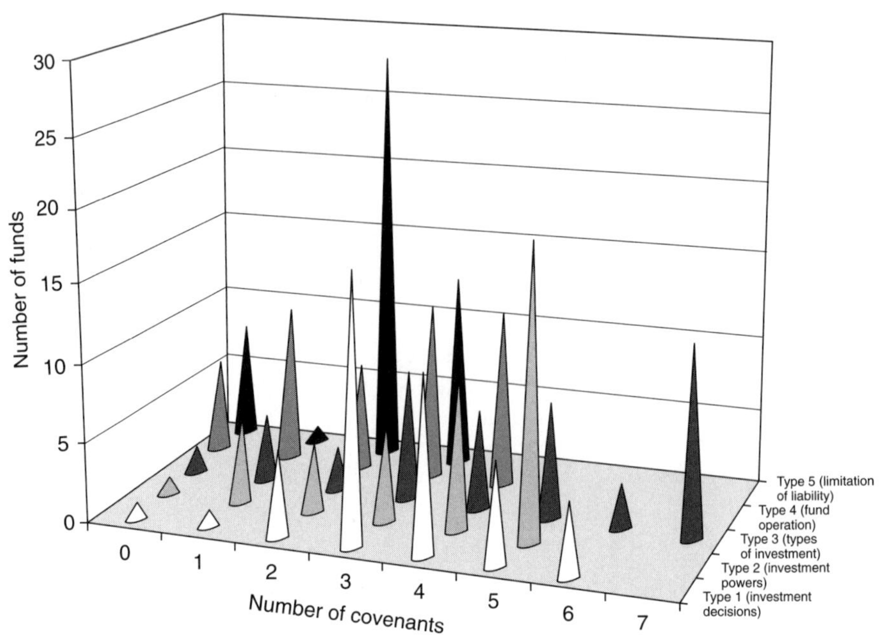

Figure 5.1 Histogram of Different Types of Covenants

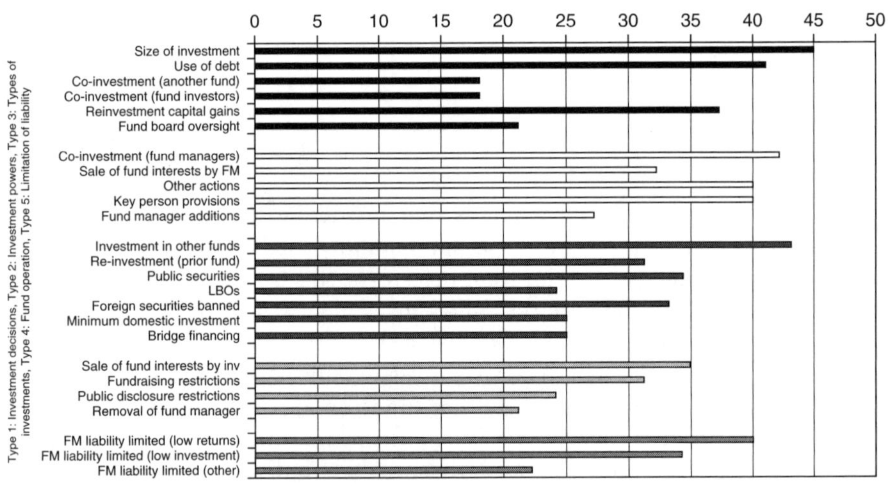

Figure 5.2 Frequency of Use of Each Covenant

variable is used in the empirics to account for a diminishing effect with larger numbers in the multivariate analyses (see following). To test for robustness, we also included variables such as the system of law within each sample country and the MSCI Index of the specific country for the year prior to the vintage year of the fund. The year prior to fundraising is considered the most relevant because decisions to invest in private equity by institutional investors will be based on available economic indicators. Again, the log of (1+MSCI) is used in the empirics to account for a diminishing effect with larger numbers.

To further test our hypotheses, a third category in Table 5.2 that contains variables on fund manager characteristics is provided to determine the extent that the human capital factor affects the use of covenants. The percentage of legally trained fund managers, MBA/CFA trained fund managers, Ph.D. (science/nonscience-based disciplines) qualified fund managers within a team, and the average number of years of relevant work experience of principal fund managers are set out in Rows 17 to 21 of Table 5.2. From this data we are able to observe that a vast majority of fund managers have financial discipline backgrounds, with an MBA/CFA qualification, whereas less than 10% have advanced scientific degrees.

The final category in Table 5.2 provides variables regarding fund organization characteristics, including composition of investors and type of fund. Variables include the average sum of funds raised by all 50 funds and the average of each jurisdiction represented. The proportion of banking institutions and government bodies within each fund, as averaged, is also set out. The proportion of funds organized as limited partnerships, the respective industry market/book ratio, and the proportion of funds with an early-stage investee focus are also included.

Although we have set out the most relevant variables for the purposes of testing our hypotheses, there are other variables within the dataset that serve to confirm and augment the set of variables we have chosen here.

5.4.4 Correlation Matrix

Table 5.3 presents a correlation matrix of the primary variables of interest. The correlations provide preliminary insights into the relations between the hypothesized relations discussed earlier in this chapter. For instance, there are fewer covenants among common law countries but more covenants among countries with higher legality indices. Offshore funds tend to have fewer covenants. Funds with a greater percentage of legally trained fund managers and funds that invest in companies operating in industries with higher market/book ratios both tend to have more covenants. Table 5.3 provides some other insights into the relations between other variables, as well as guidance for the potential for collinearity problems in the multivariate empirical tests provided following.

5.5 Econometric Tests

The econometric tests focus on the counts of the number of different covenants used within the preceding five categories: investment decisions, investment powers, types of investment, fund operation, and limitation of liability. For

Table 5.3

This table presents correlations across the variables defined in Table 5.1. Correlations significant at the 5% level

		(1)	(2)	(3)	(4)	(5)	(6)	(7)	(8)	(9)	(10)	(11)
(1)	Investment Decision Covenants	1.00										
(2)	Investment Power Covenants	0.33	1.00									
(3)	Types of Investment Covenants	0.24	0.26	1.00								
(4)	Fund Operation Covenants	0.08	0.47	0.37	1.00							
(5)	Limitation of Liability Covenants	0.52	0.52	0.04	0.19	1.00						
(6)	Sum of All Covenants (Excl. Liability)	0.56	0.71	0.77	0.68	0.41	1.00					
(7)	Log (Legality)	−0.12	0.08	0.10	0.28	0.11	0.13	1.00				
(8)	Common Law	0.01	0.10	−0.28	0.04	0.13	−0.08	−0.13	1.00			
(9)	Log (1+MSCI)	0.07	0.07	−0.01	0.08	0.36	0.07	0.43	−0.08	1.00		
(10)	GNP/Capita	−0.19	−0.06	0.05	0.18	−0.17	0.00	0.77	−0.33	0.12	1.00	
(11)	Year of Fund Formation	0.03	0.19	−0.08	0.13	0.25	0.08	−0.07	0.32	−0.01	−0.16	1.00
(12)	Outbound Offshore Fund	−0.35	0.25	0.04	0.38	−0.13	0.12	−0.03	0.06	−0.07	0.09	0.03
(13)	Inbound Offshore Fund	−0.22	0.01	−0.34	0.12	0.03	−0.19	0.12	0.23	0.05	0.07	0.07
(14)	Percentage Legal Trained Fund Managers	0.33	−0.06	0.24	−0.06	0.06	0.18	0.05	−0.19	−0.11	0.01	0.12
(15)	Percentage MBA Trained Fund Managers	−0.19	0.05	−0.28	−0.08	−0.01	−0.20	0.09	0.33	0.19	−0.05	0.00
(16)	Percentage Ph.D. (Nonscience) Trained Fund Managers	0.01	0.14	0.32	0.10	−0.01	0.24	0.30	−0.31	−0.06	0.29	−0.04
(17)	Percentage Ph.D. (Science) Trained Fund Managers	−0.19	0.03	−0.13	0.03	−0.17	−0.10	−0.17	−0.14	−0.31	−0.02	−0.03

Correlation Matrix

are highlighted in bold and underline font.

(12)	(13)	(14)	(15)	(16)	(17)	(18)	(19)	(20)	(21)	(22)	(23)	(24)	(25)
1.00													
0.18	1.00												
−0.33	−0.19	1.00											
0.24	0.07	**−0.27**	1.00										
0.10	**−0.27**	0.14	**−0.30**	1.00									
0.22	0.21	0.06	−0.19	0.10	1.00								

(continued)

Table 5.3

		(1)	(2)	(3)	(4)	(5)	(6)	(7)	(8)	(9)	(10)	(11)
(18)	Log (Years Relevant Work Experience)	0.21	0.09	0.08	0.06	0.30	0.15	0.17	0.18	0.21	0.10	0.28
(19)	Log (Funds Raised)	−0.10	0.10	0.22	0.36	0.09	0.22	0.16	0.00	0.17	0.10	0.25
(20)	Bank Institutional Investors	−0.12	−0.25	−0.13	−0.28	0.12	−0.27	0.07	−0.31	0.14	0.11	−0.07
(21)	Government Investors	0.17	0.17	0.16	−0.01	0.15	0.18	−0.19	0.04	−0.15	−0.30	0.00
(22)	Pension Investors	0.01	−0.21	0.07	0.05	0.02	−0.02	−0.12	0.20	0.15	−0.10	0.06
(23)	Endowment Investors	−0.04	0.18	0.24	0.29	−0.01	0.26	0.24	0.08	0.07	0.20	−0.18
(24)	Limited Partnership Fund	−0.13	0.25	0.05	0.37	0.21	0.18	0.33	0.20	0.19	0.27	0.11
(25)	Log (Industry Market/Book)	−0.03	0.13	0.34	0.01	−0.04	0.21	−0.25	−0.03	−0.24	−0.21	0.06
(26)	Early Stage Fund Focus	0.18	−0.04	−0.05	−0.33	0.00	−0.09	−0.30	0.16	−0.20	−0.27	0.08

each of the categories separately, we use ordered logit models to consider the multivariate determinants of the use of covenants. The ordered logits appropriately account for the fact that the dependent variable is ranked and takes a finite number of values. We further consider the determinants of the sum of covenants across the first four categories[9] and use standard OLS regressions for that dependent variable.[10] For each of the six different dependent variables, we present three alternative specifications to show the robustness of the results to the included right-hand-side variables. The explanatory variables include legal and market conditions, fund manager characteristics, and fund characteristics. Overall, there are 18 regression models presented (3 for the first category of fund covenants, 3 for the second, and so on, including the fifth category, and

[9]We exclude the fifth category in the sum of all covenants, since the fifth category is for limited liability and not negative covenants constraining behavior.

[10]Ordered logit models on more than 20 categories in the dependent variable are not tractable for a dataset with 50 observations; hence, OLS was used in this last set of regressions. Other specifications were considered, such as Poisson regression models, but did not improve the properties of the model given the distribution of the use of covenants across the funds (see Figure 5.1).

(*continued*)

(12)	(13)	(14)	(15)	(16)	(17)	(18)	(19)	(20)	(21)	(22)	(23)	(24)	(25)
0.05	0.02	0.13	−0.20	0.09	−0.14	1.00							
0.36	0.04	−0.06	0.00	0.12	−0.16	0.01	1.00						
−0.22	−0.15	0.00	−0.06	0.00	−0.01	−0.06	0.28	1.00					
−0.16	0.13	0.05	−0.34	−0.09	0.07	−0.03	−0.25	−0.23	1.00				
0.08	−0.09	−0.06	−0.09	0.00	−0.22	−0.06	0.24	−0.10	−0.15	1.00			
0.45	0.03	−0.07	0.17	0.16	−0.18	0.07	0.40	−0.18	−0.14	0.21	1.00		
0.47	0.14	−0.12	0.28	0.04	−0.03	0.10	0.40	−0.24	−0.20	0.20	0.54	1.00	
0.21	−0.08	−0.16	−0.07	0.21	0.17	0.06	−0.06	−0.07	0.14	0.03	−0.05	−0.12	1.00
−0.27	0.00	0.12	0.09	−0.08	0.23	−0.03	−0.57	−0.22	0.27	−0.10	−0.27	−0.16	0.34

3 for the sum of categories 1–4 of covenants). The regression results are presented in Table 5.4.

In this section we examine both the statistical and economic significance of the results. The standard logit and OLS regression coefficients are presented. The marginal effects for the economic significance of the logit coefficients were computed separately (using Limdep Econometric Software) and are not reported in the tables for reasons of succinctness and tractability in presentation, but they are discussed following to highlight the economic significance of the results.

The data provide some support for the hypothesized determinants of fund covenants across countries. First, in respect of legality, the data indicate a statistically significant positive relation between the quality of a country's laws and the number of covenants pertaining to fund operations (such as the sale of fund interests, restrictions on fundraising, and matters pertaining to public disclosure; see Models 10–12 in Table 5.4). The legality variable is significant at the 10% level of significance in Models 10 and 12 and at the 5% level in Model 11. However, legality is not a statistically relevant variable for any of the other classes of dependent variables.[11] In Models 10–12, the results indicate

[11]Legality is statistically significant at the 10% level in Model 16, but that result is not robust in Model 17 or 18.

Table 5.4

This table presents OLS and ordered logit regressions of the number of contractual covenants used 1–15, where the dependent variable has up to seven different values; for Models 16–18, the dependent sample consists of 50 funds from 17 countries in Australasia, Europe, and North and South America. *, **, *** Significant at the 10%, 5%, and 1% levels, respectively.

	LHS Variable: Sum of Covenants for Investment				
	Model 1		Model 2		Model
	Coefficient	t-Statistic	Coefficient	t-Statistic	Coefficient
Constant	4.752	1.568	6.762	1.971**	110.821
Legal and Market Conditions					
Log (Country Legality Index)	−0.880	−0.934	−1.427	−1.338	−1.652
Common Law Country			0.202	0.585	−0.016
Log (1+MSCI)			1.273	1.870*	0.712
Vintage Year of Fund					−0.053
Outbound Offshore Fund					−1.099
Inbound Offshore Fund					−0.576
Fund Manager Characteristics					
Percentage of Legally Trained Fund Managers	0.037	2.455***	0.041	2.549**	0.027
Percentage of MBA/CFA Trained Fund Managers			−0.009	−0.960	
Percentage of Ph.D. (Science) Trained Fund Managers					−0.004
Log (Average # Years of Relevant Work Experience of Principal Fund Managers)					0.815
Fund Characteristics					
Log (Funds Raised)	−0.035	−0.368	−0.033	−0.322	0.200
Bank Institutional Investors			−0.398	−0.588	−1.232
Government Investors			0.449	0.561	0.638
Limited Partnership Funds					0.005
Log (Industry Market/Book)	−0.057	−0.112	0.056	0.107	0.036
Early Stage Investee Focus					0.258
Ordered Logit Cut-off Parameters					
μ_1	0.306	1.316	0.320	1.324	0.309
μ_2	1.073	5.115***	1.121	5.113***	1.172
μ_3	2.179	11.565***	2.297	11.724***	2.570
μ_4	2.918	14.269***	3.069	14.545***	3.422
μ_5	3.562	13.457***	3.751	13.602***	4.152
Number of Observations	50		50		50
Pseudo R^2	0.043		0.075		0.139
Log Likelihood	−77.875		−75.197		−70.043
Chi-squared	6.922		12.278		22.588*

to govern the operation of private investment funds. Ordered logit estimates are used for Models
variable can take up to 26 different values, so ordered logits cannot be used and OLS is used. The
The variables are as defined in Table 5.1. White's (1980) HCCME is used in each regression.

Decisions	LHS Variable: Sum of Covenants for Investment Powers					
3	Model 4		Model 5		Model 6	
t-Statistic	Coefficient	t-Statistic	Coefficient	t-Statistic	Coefficient	t-Statistic
1.116	3.058	−0.403	−1.432	−0.424	−112.821	−1.121
−1.379	0.938	0.843	0.713	0.692	0.757	0.660
−0.043			0.035	0.097	0.074	0.183
0.990			0.432	0.637	0.569	0.790
−1.064					0.056	1.110
−2.095**					0.401	0.777
−1.089					−0.456	−0.816
1.466	0.015	−0.782	−0.008	−0.515	−0.009	−0.488
			0.004	0.430		
−0.363					0.004	0.334
1.758*					−0.014	−0.028
1.285	0.099	0.680	0.136	1.253	−0.019	−0.120
−1.547			−1.145	−1.659*	−0.746	−0.936
0.796			0.767	0.977	1.030	1.311
0.011					0.269	0.614
0.057	0.524	1.122	0.620	1.152	0.570	0.872
0.550					−0.279	−0.553
1.264	0.208	4.729***	1.088	4.916***	1.051	4.644***
4.722***	0.191	7.083***	1.498	7.498***	1.477	7.182***
11.952***	0.183	9.615***	1.939	10.314***	1.956	10.123***
15.441***	0.200	11.717***	2.553	12.411***	2.609	12.203***
14.262***						
	50		50		50	
	0.019		0.053		0.075	
	−75.447		−72.848		−71.144	
	2.886		8.084		11.493	

(*continued*)

Table 5.4

	LHS Variable: Sum of Covenants for Types of Investment				
	Model 7		Model 8		Model
	Coefficient	t-Statistic	Coefficient	t-Statistic	Coefficient
Constant	−5.150	−1.709*	−4.488	−1.327	135.031
Legal and Market Conditions					
Log (Country Legality Index)	1.317	1.419	1.420	1.368	1.772
Common Law Country			−0.750	−2.074**	−0.703
Log (1+MSCI Index)			0.302	0.463	−0.016
Vintage Year of Fund					−0.071
Outbound Offshore Fund					−0.041
Inbound Offshore Fund					−1.424
Fund Manager Characteristics					
Percentage of Legally Trained Fund Managers	0.042	2.434**	0.035	1.895*	0.039
Percentage of MBA/CFA Trained Fund Managers			−0.008	−0.858	
Percentage of Ph.D. (Science) Trained Fund Managers					−0.008
Log (Average # Years of Relevant Work Experience of Principal Fund Managers)					0.236
Fund Characteristics					
Log (Funds Raised)	0.171	1.761*	0.279	2.593***	0.403
Bank Institutional Investors			−1.524	−2.221**	−1.825
Government Investors			1.064	1.171	1.798
Limited Partnership Funds					0.042
Log (Industry Market/Book)	1.803	3.540***	1.817	3.466***	1.952
Early Stage Investee Focus					0.106
Ordered Logit Cut-off Parameters					
μ_1	0.723	3.422***	0.810	3.519***	0.932
μ_2	1.018	4.915***	1.141	5.125***	1.339
μ_3	1.726	8.957***	1.913	9.454***	2.252
μ_4	2.177	11.26***	2.399	11.823***	2.803
μ_5	2.687	13.132***	2.977	13.417***	3.456
μ_6	2.893	13.359***	3.231	13.424***	3.736
Number of Observations	50		50		50
Pseudo R^2	0.088		0.147		0.202
Log Likelihood	−87.763		−82.014		−76.757
Chi-squared	16.874***		28.371***		38.866***

(*continued*)

Decisions	LHS Variable: Sum of Covenants for Fund Operations					
9	Model 10		Model 11		Model 12	
t-Statistic	Coefficient	t-Statistic	Coefficient	t-Statistic	Coefficient	t-Statistic
1.286	−5.309	−1.736*	−5.900	−1.712*	−113.999	−1.077
1.522	1.685	1.791*	2.301	2.163**	2.284	1.932*
−1.786*			−0.277	−0.725	−0.318	−0.739
−0.023			−0.279	−0.409	−0.135	−0.186
−1.348					0.054	1.019
−0.078					0.407	0.764
−2.599***					−0.258	−0.471
1.834*	−0.004	−0.236	−0.013	−0.797	−0.003	−0.170
			−0.010	−1.028		
−0.711					0.008	0.698
0.506					−0.115	−0.233
2.564**	0.241	2.431**	0.394	3.492***	0.234	1.479
−2.311**			−2.700	−3.268***	−2.570	−2.679***
1.800*			0.151	0.186	0.766	0.971
0.092					0.042	0.095
3.164***	0.469	0.907	0.278	0.512	0.484	0.762
0.224					−0.785	−1.644
3.579***	0.799	4.727***	0.953	5.055***	0.955	4.945***
5.398***	1.267	7.228***	1.462	7.724***	1.479	7.475***
10.300***	2.009	9.146***	2.314	9.446***	2.403	9.155***
12.962***						
14.655***						
14.544***						
	50		50		50	
	0.064		0.155		0.182	
	−74.291		−66.997		−64.867	
	10.077**		24.665***		28.925***	

(*continued*)

Table 5.4

	LHS Variable: Sum of Covenants for Limited				
	Model 13		Model 14		Model
	Coefficient	t-Statistic	Coefficient	t-Statistic	Coefficient
Constant	−0.027	−0.008	0.494	0.120	−154.758
Legal and Market Conditions					
Log (Country Legality Index)	0.500	0.493	0.178	0.138	−1.573
Common Law Country			0.542	1.351	−0.019
Log (1+MSCI Index)			2.039	2.501**	1.508
Vintage Year of Fund					0.079
Outbound Offshore Fund					−0.927
Inbound Offshore Fund					0.212
Fund Manager Characteristics					
Percentage of Legally Trained Fund Managers	0.001	0.031	0.009	0.513	−0.004
Percentage of MBA/CFA Trained Fund Managers			−0.005	−0.533	
Percentage of Ph.D. (Science) Trained Fund Managers					−0.003
Log (Average # Years of Relevant Work Experience of Principal Fund Managers)					1.059
Fund Characteristics					
Log (Funds Raised)	0.0242	0.236	−0.026	−0.225	−0.205
Bank Institutional Investors			1.136	1.485	1.701
Government Investors			1.173	1.340	1.669
Limited Partnership Funds					1.174
Log (Industry Market/Book)	−0.406	−0.747	−0.164	−0.286	0.112
Early Stage Investee Focus					−0.599
Ordered Logit Cut-off Parameters					
μ_1	0.078	1.043	0.096	1.048	0.104
μ_2	1.656	6.836***	1.913	6.626***	2.200
Number of Observations	50		50		50
Pseudo/Adjusted R^2	0.011		0.119		0.226
Log Likelihood	−51.721		−46.084		−40.488
Akaike Information Criterion	—		—		—
Chi-squared/F-statistic	1.197		12.471		23.663*

(*continued*)

Liability	LHS Variable: Sum of All Types of Covenants (Excl. Limited Liability)					
15	Model 16		Model 17		Model 18	
t-Statistic	Coefficient	t-Statistic	Coefficient	t-Statistic	Coefficient	t-Statistic
−1.110	−7.256	−0.935	−2.703	−0.367	91.172	0.250
−1.115	4.104	1.752*	3.329	1.341	3.364	1.119
−0.042			−0.859	−0.857	−0.816	−0.761
1.772*			2.244	1.184	1.485	0.742
1.132					−0.049	−0.269
−1.586					−0.472	−0.216
0.358					−3.146	−1.164
−0.195	0.102	3.020***	0.086	2.629***	0.074	1.720*
			−0.025	−0.969		
−0.256					−0.001	−0.031
1.817*					0.951	0.703
−1.157	0.637	1.508	0.964	2.283**	0.982	1.675*
1.785*			−6.719	−2.987***	−7.004	−2.680***
1.847*			2.955	1.250	4.685	1.676*
2.241**					0.403	0.274
0.155	4.294	2.245**	3.850	2.194**	3.849	1.904*
−1.085					−0.636	−0.468
1.039						
6.390***						
	50		50		50	
	0.102		0.209		0.146	
	−139.996		−133.885		−131.740	
	5.800		5.755		5.910	
	2.39*		2.44**		1.56	

that the legality variable is also economically significant. For example, an increase in the Legality index from 20 to 21 (a typical improvement among developed nations) increases the probability of an extra covenant pertaining to fund operation by approximately 1%, whereas an increase from 10 to 11 (a typical improvement among emerging markets) increases the probability of an extra covenant pertaining to fund operation by approximately 2%.

Overall, the data indicate support for the proposition that a stronger legal environment is associated with more frequent use of covenants for the category of covenants on fund operations but not the other covenants on the activities of fund managers. Covenants on fund operations such as disclosure and the removal of fund managers are enforced only in conjunction with the corporate laws in the country in which the fund has been set up. This class of covenants is most directly related to the corporate governance of the fund administration. The more specific covenants in the other categories pertain to the day-to-day activities of running the fund itself and may or may not be used independently of the legal environment in which the fund has been set up.

Regarding common versus civil law countries, we conjectured that the propensity to write rules would be more pronounced in rule-based legal systems (civil law countries) as a matter of practice and not as a matter of legal substance. The data do provide some support for this conjecture insofar as civil law countries are approximately 6% more likely to have each additional covenant pertaining to the types of investment (category 3; Models 8 and 9, the common law coefficient is negative and significant at the 5% and 10% levels, respectively). At the same time, however, it is noteworthy that the common/civil law differences are not statistically significant for any other type of covenant.

The data indicate offshore funds are about 10% less likely to have each covenant for the authority of the fund manager (Model 3) and the types of investment (Model 9). This is consistent with our prediction insofar as offshore funds involve a multitude of investors from different jurisdictions and contracting costs are therefore greater. These results might also be related to the fact that offshore funds are set up to be more tax efficient for international investors who want to take advantage of the profits to be made from emerging private equity markets as their own developed ones become oversaturated. These international investors thus have less of a concern with the specific investment decisions made by the fund manager regarding types of investments carried out. For example, a few of the sample funds organized in the Cayman Islands, the Netherlands, Luxembourg, Malaysia (Labuan), and Netherlands Antilles are managed by fund managers situated in Vietnam, Czech Republic, Malaysia, and South Korea.

Note specifically that the results in Table 5.4 indicate that (1) outbound offshore funds have fewer covenants restricting the authority of the fund manager, and (2) inbound offshore funds have fewer restrictions for the types of investments made by the fund manager. An outbound offshore fund obtains its funds primarily from one jurisdiction and invests its funds in a jurisdiction outside that of the fund jurisdiction and that of the primary investors. Conversely, an inbound offshore fund obtains its funds from investors in many jurisdictions and invests its funds in a specific jurisdiction or region, sometimes including that of the fund jurisdiction and that of its investors. We have included the two categories of offshore funds, albeit an overly simplistic categorization, as in practice many funds combine attributes of each of the categories, to take into account the character of investors of offshore funds. By looking at the character of the offshore fund and the direction of investment fund inflow and outflow, we are able to see how they affect the use of covenants. Fewer covenants restricting the authority of the fund manager for outbound offshore funds may be related to the fact that the primary investors are more likely to share a common jurisdiction and have similar levels of contracting costs. It has to be noted that there are numerous factors that fund managers consider in selecting a jurisdiction in which to organize an offshore fund. Given the likely target investor base, not only are the tax laws of the fund's jurisdiction taken into account but also those of the country in which potential investors reside and of the country or region in which the fund may invest. Offshore fund jurisdictions also vary as to the degree of local regulation, the necessity of minimal contacts by the investors with the jurisdiction, the requirement for local fund administrators, forms of available corporate organizations, and quality of available legal and financial advice. When the primary investors are from one jurisdiction, it is easier for the fund manager to select the optimally beneficial jurisdiction for the primary investors, and as such the primary investors will have less issue with the corporate governance of the fund or the authority of the fund manager over the fund. On the other hand, where the investors are dispersed, fund managers have difficulty in selecting an offshore jurisdiction because compromises must be made to achieve some sort of equilibrium among investors. Even factors such as the status and reputation of that potential jurisdiction within the financial community may be crucial as it will determine the number of treaties to which it is a party and thus the withholding taxes payable by investors. This compromise, and the high contracting costs related to reaching an agreement, may be related to our finding that inbound offshore funds have fewer restrictions for the types of investments made by the fund manager. The primary issue during the contract negotiation will not be the powers held by the fund manager in carrying out investments but more the corporate governance issue related to the fund itself, being situated in a jurisdiction probably unfamiliar to many if not most of the investors, as all the investors come to an agreeable compromise.

The data indicate that an increase in one fund manager out of five (a 20% increase) with legal training increases the probability of additional covenants pertaining both to investment decisions (category 1, including factors such as the size of any single investment and co-investment)[12] and types of investment

[12]However, for category 1 in Model 3, the inclusion of the additional right-hand-side variables gives rise to a statistically insignificant coefficient for legally trained fund managers, unlike Models 1 and 2.

(category 3, for different asset classes) by approximately 10%. The presence of legally trained fund managers, however, does not influence the frequency of use of other types of covenants pertaining to investment powers (category 2), fund operation (category 4), and limitation of liability (category 5). The data therefore suggest legally trained fund managers are more sensitive to specifying rules pertaining to their daily activities of investment selection and investment decisions and are neither more nor less sensitive to specifying rules for fund operation relative to nonlegally trained fund managers. Note also that we further control for MBA/CFA training and Ph.D. (scientific versus nonscientific) training and do not find significant differences for these other types of training.

In Model 15, there is evidence that relevant work experience of the fund managers affects the use of covenants (although the coefficient is statistically significant at the 10% level). The economic significance is such that a fund with managers with an average of 30 years of relevant work experience are 20% more likely to have an extra covenant pertaining to limited liability than a fund with managers with an average of 5 years of relevant experience. Note, however, that for the first group of covenants pertaining to investment decisions, Model 3 indicates at the 10% level of significance more covenants with more work experience (counter to our expectations), and the other groups of covenants are unrelated to work experience. One explanation for this result is that it may be that a more relevant variable would be the number of prior funds run by the fund managers; however, that variable was intractable for many of the funds in our data due to the fact that fund managers derived experience from funds other than the group of funds in which they were currently employed.[13]

It is noteworthy that a number of other variables indicate a significant influence on the use of covenants. In particular, Table 5.4 indicates an important relationship among fund covenants and fund size, industry market-book, and the identity of the fund's investors. In particular, larger funds have more covenants; for example, for the third category of covenants on types of investment, an increase in funds raised from US$90 to US$100 million increases the probability of an extra covenant on types of investment by about 0.2%, and an increase from US$10 to US$20 million increases the probability of an extra covenant by about 2% in Model 9. Funds that operate in industries with higher market/book ratios have more covenants. For example, for the third category of covenants on types of investment, an increase in the average industry market/book ratio of investee companies from 2 to 3 increases the probability of an extra covenant on types of investment by about 4%, and an increase from 1

[13]Also, a manager may create a special purpose vehicle for the management of a specific fund, albeit for all intents and purposes that vehicle comprises managers who have managed other funds together before. Proxies for the number of prior funds run by the fund itself did not yield materially different results.

to 2 increases the probability of an extra covenant by about 6% in Model 9. It is also noteworthy that in times of stronger market conditions, institutional investors are more likely to grant limited liability protection to fund managers (see Models 14 and 15); an increase in the MSCI index return from 15 to 20% in the year prior to fundraising increases the probability of an extra limited liability clause by 0.7%, and an increase from 5 to 10% in the year prior to fundraising increases the probability of an extra limited liability clause by 0.8%. Overall, therefore, a number of economic factors influence the frequency of use of covenants alongside the influence of the legal environment and the influence of the lawyers.

5.6 Limitations, Alternate Explanations, and Future Research

This chapter introduces a unique international dataset on private investment fund covenants. Private investment fund covenants are private contractual details that are not widely disclosed and are in fact highly confidential. In short, while the data obtained in this chapter are new and unique and extremely difficult to obtain from private investment funds, there are of course limitations in the number of observations. Further work could consider expanding the data in terms of the number of countries and funds, as well as possibly for different time periods. Nevertheless, as we have already said, we do not have any reason to believe there are biases with regard to sample selection in the data we were able to obtain.

It is noteworthy that we focused on the Legality index (Table 3.1; Berkowitz et al., 2003), which is a weighted average of a number of different legal indices from La Porta et al. (1997, 1998). A limited number of degrees of freedom prevented inclusion of each subcomponent of the Legality index separately. As well, the components of the Legality index themselves are very highly correlated, so collinearity problems prevent simultaneous inclusion of these different variables. Also, the GNP per capita in each country is highly correlated with the Legality index, so it could not be included as a separate variable. While the use of these different variables did not material changes the inferences drawn from the available data, further work with additional data and/or different countries might shed light on the issue of which specific legal index is most pertinent to venture capital fund structures. And although there is as yet no particular theory that would lead one to prefer one legal index over another (or prefer one legal index to the exclusion of another index), further theoretical work might shed additional light on these issues in relation to private investment fund structures and covenants more generally (in the spirit of McCahery and Vermeulen, 2004).

International differences in fund covenants are only one aspect of international differences in fund structures. Further research might also explore international differences in compensation arrangements and investment strategies (in the spirit of Mayer et al., 2005, for example). Numerous related issues on how and why fund structures differ across countries could be considered, as well as the relation between fund structures (as per the covenants studied herein) and contractual arrangements between private investment funds and their investee entrepreneurial firms. This type of research would probably better help us to understand why some private equity and venture capital markets are comparatively more successful than their counterparts in other countries.

5.7 Conclusions

This chapter analyzed the frequency of the use of investment covenants imposed by institutional investors governing the activities of private investment fund managers in areas pertaining to investment decisions, investment powers, types of investments, fund operations, and limitations on liability. We introduced a new dataset that was hand-collected from 50 funds from 17 countries, including developed and emerging markets (Belgium, Brazil, Canada, Cayman Islands, Finland, Germany, Italy, Luxembourg, Malaysia, Netherlands Antilles, the Netherlands, New Zealand, Philippines, South Africa, Switzerland, the United Kingdom, and the United States). Our primary hypotheses considered the role of law versus lawyers in the writing of covenants in contracts establishing private investment funds. Numerous control variables in the new and detailed data were considered in testing the hypotheses developed herein.

The data indicated a statistically significant positive relation between the quality of a country's laws and the number of covenants pertaining to fund operations (such as the sale of fund interests, restrictions on fundraising, and matters pertaining to public disclosure). An increase in the Legality index from 20 to 21 (a typical improvement among developed nations) increases the probability of an extra covenant pertaining to fund operation by approximately 1%, whereas an increase from 10 to 11 (a typical improvement among emerging markets) increases the probability of an extra covenant pertaining to fund operation by approximately 2%. The data further indicate that civil law countries are approximately 6% more likely to have covenants pertaining to the types of investment, but the common/civil law differences were not notable for any other type of covenant.

The data further indicated an important role for the presence of legally trained fund managers in influencing the number of fund covenants. An increase in one fund manager of five with legal training increases the probability of additional covenants pertaining both to investment decisions (such as the size of any single investment and co-investment) and types of investment (in different asset classes) by approximately 10%. Taken together, therefore, while law and lawyers are both important, the data indicated that the presence of lawyers has a more economically significant impact on the use of covenants than the legal environment itself.

Our results have a variety of implications for institutional investors and private equity and venture capital funds. Perhaps most importantly, as private equity and venture capital investment increases internationally, our results indicate that legal practice factors will matter more than the legal setting for the establishment of covenants governing new funds. Moreover, our results provide guidance as to when covenants are more important to put in place for fund governance.

Key Terms

- Limited partnership contracts
- Restrictive covenants
- Investment decisions
  - Restrictions on the size of the investment
  - Restrictions on use of debt instruments
  - Restrictions on co-investment
  - Restrictions on reinvestment of capital gains
  - Restrictions on the fund manager making independent investment decisions
- Investment powers
  - Restrictions against the fund manager investing in any of the investee firms
  - Restrictions on the sale of fund interest by the fund manager
  - Restrictions on investment principal additions to the fund manager
  - Key person provisions
- Types of investment
  - Restrictions on making investments in other investment funds
  - Restrictions on follow-on investments in an investee firm of which another fund managed by the fund manager has an interest
  - Restrictions on investments in public listed securities
  - Restrictions on investments in leveraged buyouts
  - Restrictions on investments in foreign securities
  - Restrictions on bridge financing
- Fund operations
  - Restrictions on sale of fund interest by any investor
  - Restrictions on the fund manager raising new funds
  - Restrictions on public disclosure of fund matters
  - No-fault divorce provision
- Limitations of liability
  - Failure to invest committed funds within the agreed investment period
  - Mismanagement of funds

Discussion Questions

5.1. What are the more commonly observed restrictive covenants used for venture capital and private equity fund limited partnerships? Which covenants are most effective at mitigating agency costs?

5.2. For what types of venture capital and private equity funds are agency costs more pronounced?

5.3. What types of fund characteristics are more likely to be associated with the use of restrictive covenants in venture capital and private equity limited partnerships?
5.4. In what countries are restrictive covenants in venture capital and private equity funds more frequently used?
5.5. How do market conditions influence the frequency of use of restrictive covenants among venture capital and private equity limited partnerships?
5.6. What is an offshore venture capital fund? How is an inbound offshore fund different from an outbound offshore fund? Why do you think some private equity funds are set up offshore? Would you expect agency problems and covenants to be more common among offshore funds? What factors might affect the frequency of use of covenants for offshore funds?

6 Compensation Contracts

6.1 Introduction and Learning Objectives

This chapter empirically investigates venture capital and private equity managerial compensation contracts. Managerial compensation is widely regarded as influential in mitigating agency costs and thus also influencing the performance of corporations (Bebchuk and Fried, 2004), governments (Fisman and Di Tella, 2004), mutual funds (Chevalier and Ellison, 1997, 1999a,b), and private investment funds (Cressy et al., 2007a,b; Dai, 2007; Gompers and Lerner, 1999a,b; Hege et al., 2006; Litvak, 2004a,b; Nikoskelainen and Wright, 2007; Renneboog et al., 2007; Schwienbacher, 2003).[1] Here we focus on compensation contracts for managers of private equity funds. Using a new international dataset, we investigate the relation between fund manager compensation and legal conditions, while controlling for economic conditions, institutional investor characteristics, fund characteristics, fund manager education, and experience, among other factors.

It is important to empirically consider managerial compensation in an international context. Prior theoretical work is consistent with the view that incentive compensation will be stronger, and agency problems therefore less pronounced, in countries with stronger legal standards due to a greater abundance of information (Acemoglu and Zilibotti, 1999). Empirical evidence on the topic, however, is comparatively scant. A recent contemporaneous paper (Khorana et al., 2008) considers international differences in mutual fund compensation, but the mutual fund context involves significantly different institutional considerations than private equity capital (see generally Gompers and Lerner, 1999a,b,c, 2001a,b), which has pronounced incentive compensation schemes. This chapter provides a first look at international differences in compensation contracts for venture capital and private equity fund managers. The topic is timely, as policymakers increasingly consider public policy for venture capital and private equity, particularly in relation to compensation

[1]For related theory and evidence, see also Cressy (2002), Bascha and Walz (2001a,b), and Kanniainen and Keuschnigg (2003, 2004).

(see, e.g., *The Economist*, 2007; for related academic work on topic, see, e.g., Keuschnigg and Neilsen, 2001, 2003a,b, 2004a,b,c).

The dataset used in this chapter is derived from 50 limited partnership funds from 17 countries in Africa, North and South America, Europe, and Australasia (the same dataset introduced in Chapter 5). The data presented show that the structure of compensation contracts depends on the human capital of the fund managers, legal and institutional conditions in which the funds operate, fund characteristics (such as the type of investments in terms of stage and industry focus), and market conditions.

In this chapter we will do the following:

- Study key terms in limited partnership compensation contracts
- Consider different factors that influence the design of limited partnership contracts, including human capital difference across fund managers, legal and institutional conditions across countries, fund-specific differences such as stage and sector focus, and market conditions
- Examine an international dataset on limited partnership compensation
- See which of the factors that might influence compensation are most important in the data
- Draw inferences on how limited partner compensation relates to international differences in venture capital and private equity markets around the world

First we explain the design of limited partnership compensation contracts around the world. We then conjecture factors that affect the structure of compensation contracts. Thereafter we examine the dataset to see how compensation contracts are designed in practice.

6.2 Compensation Contracts in Limited Partnerships

Private equity fund managers are compensated with a two-part fee: a fixed management fee (as a percentage of fund size) and a performance fee (the carried interest percentage). Private equity funds in the United States typically have fixed management fees of around 1 to 3% of the committed capital of the fund (analogous to the case of mutual funds that often have management expense ratios of 1 to 2%), and performance fees of typically 20% (unlike mutual funds; see Gompers and Lerner, 1999a,b,c; Metrick and Yasuda, 2006). The fixed management fee enables fund operations to be carried out prior to fund liquidity events. Private equity funds are typically organized as limited partnerships for a period of 10 to 13 years to facilitate the investment process and exit events (Gompers and Lerner, 1996). Private equity funds, however, invest in firms that are not publicly listed on stock exchanges; these investments are considerably illiquid because liquidity events (such as an initial public offering or an acquisition) typically take 2 to 7 years (Chapter 19). Fixed management fees therefore should sufficiently meet foreseeable overheads arising from the investment and divestment process to be carried out by the fund managers before any profits are earned. Performance fees, on the other hand, align the incentives of fund managers and their institutional investors.

Limited partnership private equity fund managers, however, often face clawback provisions that lower the risk faced by institutional investors in the event of poor performance. From the fund manager's perspective, a clawback is the exact opposite of an incentive performance fee. In this chapter, we compare and contrast the factors that affect the role of legality in "positive" performance incentive fees versus "negative" clawbacks (i.e., "carrots" versus "sticks" in compensation).

It is also important to consider institutional investor compensation because it is somewhat related to fund manager compensation. After an exit event such as an initial public offering, limited partnership funds might either distribute cash proceeds from the sale of the investment to their institutional investors or they may distribute shares in the entrepreneurial firm to their institutional investors. Share distributions to a fund's investors shift the decision of when to liquidate an equity position in an entrepreneurial investee from the fund manager to the funds' investors. The cash versus share distribution decision is important, as it affects the timing of payment via the realization of capital gains among a fund's investors and therefore affects institutional investor compensation. Since they both deal with compensation to opposite parties to a contract, it is worthwhile to consider institutional investor compensation in conjunction with fund manager compensation.

6.3 What Affects the Design of Limited Partnership Compensation Contracts?

6.3.1 Human Capital Factors Influencing the Design of Compensation Contracts

In Chapter 4 we identified fund manager human capital as one of the most important factors that influence institutional investor capital commitments to venture capital and private equity funds. Chapter 5 likewise showed that human capital was a key factor in driving limited partnership covenants. For compensation, we would likewise expect human capital to be a key driver in terms. Gompers and Lerner (1999a,b,c) posit two alternative models of managerial compensation in relation to experience. Under the "signaling model," in which fund managers want to signal their ability to investors, fund managers without experience prefer to trade off lower fixed fees for higher performance fees, consistent with the work of Spence (1973). Under the "learning model," in which risk-adverse fund managers are yet to realize their ability to successfully generate high returns, fund managers prefer to trade off lower performance fees for higher fixed fees. Based on a U.S.-only sample, Gompers and Lerner (1999a,b,c) find support for the learning model but not the signaling model. We would expect the same with the international sample used in this chapter: Fund managers with little relevant work experience are more likely to have higher fixed fees and lower carried interest percentages.

At the same time, however, to the extent that more education is rewarded and considered valuable, it should be reflected in higher compensation generally. We would also expect that fund managers that have a greater number of years of relevant education are more likely to receive both higher fixed and performance fees and less likely to face clawbacks.

6.3.2 Legal and Institutional Factors Influencing the Design of Compensation Contracts

We conjecture that fund managers who operate in legal jurisdictions of poor quality will be more inclined to accept higher fixed fees and lower performance fees. At a general level, information asymmetries are more pronounced in countries with poor legal conditions, and therefore less developed countries are less likely to employ incentive contracts for fund managers and entrepreneurs (Acemoglu and Zilibotti, 1999). Specifically, in the private equity context, prior empirical work is consistent with the view that countries with weaker legal conditions (based on the La Porta et al., 1998, indices) face more uncertain exit markets, whereby it is more difficult to obtain a capital gain and generate fund returns (Cumming et al., 2006; Lerner and Schoar, 2005a,b). As such, we expect risk-adverse fund managers to prefer higher fixed fees in exchange for lower performance fees to garner a more certain income stream.

Partnership profits from limited partnership funds (carried interest) may be taxed at the capital gains tax rate or deemed as business income and taxed at the income tax rate (unlike venture capital firms set up as corporations) (Fleischer, 2005). As such, we control for the difference between income tax and capital gains tax rates for limited partnership funds.

While fund managers benefit from higher fixed fees and lower performance fees in countries with poor legal conditions, institutional investors nevertheless face a particularly pronounced risk of lower profits among funds in countries with inferior laws. Institutional investors may lower the downside costs of low returns with the mechanism of a clawback, which is when institutional investors reduce the compensation paid to fund managers in the event of poor performance. A fund usually distributes cash and other proceeds to the fund manager and other investors upon each liquidating event. The problem of excess distributions may occur when earlier liquidations are profitable, and latter ones are not. This will be further exacerbated if the fund manager accelerates the sale of profitable investments and holds off the liquidation of bad investments. The clawback allows the investors to recover excess distributions upon liquidation of the fund. We therefore expect clawbacks to be more frequently employed in countries with poorer legal conditions.

We further expect legal conditions to influence the mode of distribution of fund profits to institutional investors in terms of cash versus share distributions. Inferior legal conditions increase the financial risk of share positions in entrepreneurial firms; therefore, all else being equal, the greater the uncertainty created by a lower-quality legal environment, the greater the probability of a cash-only distribution policy in the set-up of a private equity fund.

Finally, in an international context, private equity funds can be set up offshore, and doing so typically has significant tax advantages. In the United States, share distributions are common, as the institutional investor can decide the best time to realize capital gains. (There are other reasons for share distributions; see, e.g., Gompers and Lerner, 1997, 1999b.) Since offshore funds are by their very nature tax-lowering entities, the timing of realization of capital gains is a less pronounced concern among institutional investors of offshore funds, and therefore the need for share distributions is less pronounced for offshore funds. Furthermore, aside from concerns relating to taxation, offshore funds commonly consist of various types of institutional investors, such as pension funds, insurance companies, banks, and endowments from a diverse set of countries. Institutional investors from a diverse set of countries typically face nonharmonized legal impediments to acquiring and selling shares in entrepreneurial firms transferred to them from the fund manager. Overall, therefore, offshore funds are expected to mandate cash-only distributions.

6.3.3 Fund Specifics That Influence the Design of Compensation Contracts

Fund characteristics such as fund size, stage focus, and industry focus can affect fees (Gompers and Lerner, 1999a). Larger funds are more likely to have smaller fixed fees simply because the fixed compensation in terms of a percentage of the fund size would be excessive. Funds focused on investing in earlier stages of development and in more high-tech industries are more likely to have higher performance fees to incentivize the fund managers and align their interests with that of the institutional investors (since agency problems and information asymmetries are more pronounced among funds focused in early-stage and high-tech investments).

The type of institutional investor (bank, government, pension fund, etc.) and their respective risk tolerance levels could influence the pay structure of the fund managers in terms of fixed versus managerial fees (for reasons analogous to research in Mayer et al., 2005, and Lerner et al., 2005). As well, the identity of the institutional investors could, of course, affect the probability of use of clawbacks and the mode of distributions in terms of cash versus shares.

6.3.4 Market Factors That Influence the Design of Compensation Contracts

In regards to economic conditions, where the demand for fund managers exceeds supply, fund managers are more likely to be compensated better. For instance, in the boom periods, a phenomenon of "money-chasing deals" (Gompers and Lerner, 2000) typically results, whereby higher quality fund managers are short in supply relative to the institutional investors wanting to contribute to the asset class (Kanniainen and Keuschnigg, 2004). As such, fund managers are more likely to have higher fixed fees and carried interest percentages and are less likely to face clawbacks, in times of boom economic conditions (i.e., in countries with stronger economic environments and at times of better stock market performance).

The data used to test these propositions are described in the next section, after which multivariate empirical tests are provided. Then we will examine limitations, alternative explanation, and future research.

6.4 Data

6.4.1 Data

The data examined in this chapter are from the same source as those used in Chapter 5. An overview of the information collected is summarized in Table 6.1 which defines the primary variables used in this study.

One limitation to obtaining data through a survey is the possibility of sample selection bias. While we acknowledge that this is a possibility, we believe from a detailed analysis of the responses received and the data obtained from the responses that this concern does not arise in this exercise. First, survey data were gathered for a final sample of 50 funds in 17 countries, as managed by 50 fund managers in 21 countries. We are aware that the seminal work carried out by Gompers and Lerner (1996) used a sample of 140 contracts that were used to establish funds, obtained from institutional investors (two fund-of-funds and one endowment). Litvak (2004b) has data from 38 funds in the United States, Metrick and Yasuda (2006) have data from 203 funds in the United States. We believe however that by obtaining data from funds situated both in and outside the United States and by having access to data regarding contracts entered into by 21 different fund managers, response bias is mitigated as much as possible. Limitations in our sample size from each country from which we derived data, as well as the limited information about venture capital and private equity funds around the world, however, makes reliable statistical comparisons of our sample relative to the population of funds intractable. Our sample of respondent funds includes 8 funds each the Netherlands and the United States; 6 funds each from the United Kingdom and Malaysia; 4 funds from the Netherlands Antilles; 3 funds each from Germany and Belgium;

Table 6.1 Definition of Variables

This table defines the variables considered in this chapter. Summary statistics are presented in Tables 6.2 and 6.3.

Variable	Description
Compensation Variables	
Fixed Management Fee %	The fund managers' fixed fee as a percentage of the funds raised from the institutional investors.
Carried Interest Performance Fee %	The fund managers' carried interest performance fees as a percentage of the profits earned by the fund.
Clawbacks	A dummy variable equal to one if the fund allows for clawbacks against the fund managers but not any of the fund investors. A clawback enables the fund investors to lower the fee received by the fund manager in the event of poor performance of the fund.
Cash Distributions	A dummy variable equal to one if the fund managers are required to distribute cash to the institutional investors instead of shares (for realized capital gains from investments in entrepreneurial firms).
Legal and Market Conditions	
Country Legality Index	Weighted average of following factors (based on Berkowitz et al., 2003): civil versus common law systems, efficiency of judicial system, rule of law, corruption, risk of expropriation, risk of contract repudiation, and shareholder rights (as per La Porta et al., 1997, 1998). Where the weighted average is not available, especially for less developed countries, an approximate index is derived by multiplying the country's GNP per population with a constant variable obtained by carrying out a regression of the legality indices available. Higher numbers indicate "better" legal systems. The log of this variable is used in the empirics to account for a diminishing effect with larger numbers.
Legal Origin	Dummy variables equal to 1 for a fund organized in countries of different legal origin, including English, French, German, and Scandinavian.
GNP per Capita	The GNP per capita of the country in which the fund is formed. The log of this variable is used.
MSCI Index	The country-specific MSCI Index taken for the year prior to that when fundraising commenced. The year prior to fundraising is deemed to be most relevant, as decisions to invest in private equity by institutional investors will be based on available economic indicators. The log of (1+MSCI) is used in the empirics to account for a diminishing effect with larger numbers.

(*continued*)

Table 6.1 (*continued*)

Variable	Description
Vintage Year of Fund	The year fundraising commences
Outbound Offshore	A dummy variable equal to 1 for a fund located offshore that obtains its capital from investors from a certain jurisdiction but fund investments are made primarily in assets other than in the jurisdiction of the fund and the fund investors. With reference to U.S. jurisdictional boundaries, a fund will be considered to be an outbound offshore fund if it obtains capital from U.S. investors, but it invests outside the United States.
Inbound Offshore	A dummy variable equal to 1 for a fund located offshore that obtains its capital from investors from various jurisdictions but fund investments are made primarily in assets in a certain jurisdiction. With reference to U.S. jurisdictional boundaries, an inbound offshore fund will be a fund located offshore which invests primarily in assets within the United States yet obtains its capital from non-U.S. investors.
Tax Difference	A variable equal to, for top marginal tax rates, (Income Tax Rate – Capital Gains Tax Rate) * (Limited Partnership Dummy Variable), for partnerships for which carried interest is taxed at the capital gains rate, and fixed management fees are taxed at the income tax rate.
Fund Manager Characteristics	
Percentage of Legally Trained Fund Managers	Percentage of principal fund managers with investment-making decisions who are legally trained or are qualified as lawyers. Where managers have some extent of legal training, that fraction of the extent of legal training is also reflected in the data.
Percentage of MBA/CFA Trained Fund Managers	Percentage of principal fund managers with investment-making decisions who have obtained an MBA or CFA qualifications. Where managers have some extent of such training, that fraction is also reflected in the data.
Percentage of Ph.D. (Science) Trained Fund Managers	Percentage of principal fund managers with investment-making decisions who have obtained a Ph.D. in a science-based discipline. Where managers have some extent of formal scientific training, that fraction of training is also reflected in the data.
Percentage of Ph.D. (Nonscience) Trained Fund Managers	Percentage of principal fund managers with investment-making decisions who have obtained a Ph.D. in a nonscience-based discipline. Where managers have some extent of advanced Ph.D. studies, that fraction of training is also reflected in the data.

(*continued*)

Table 6.1 (*continued*)

Variable	Description
Average # Years of Relevant Work Experience of Principal Fund Managers	Average number of years relevant work experience of principal fund managers at the time of fundraising. The log of this variable is used in the empirics to account for a diminishing effect with larger numbers.
Fund Characteristics	
Funds Raised	The fund size, or amount of funds raised in $US. Where the amount is provided in a local currency, an exchange rate as of December 2003 is used for conversion of such amounts into $US equivalents. The log of this variable is used in the empirics to account for a diminishing effect with larger numbers.
Bank Institutional Investors	The proportion of banks as the fund's institutional investors.
Government Investors	The proportion of government agencies or ministries as institutional investors.
Limited Partnership Funds	A dummy variable equal to 1 for the fund being organized as a limited partnership.
Industry Market/ Book	The industry market/book ratio of the industries for which the fund has invested in. The industry market/book ratio of five general categories—biotechnology and medical, communications and Internet, computers and electronics, and manufacturing and others—is obtained by averaging the total book value of specific industries falling within the general categories. The log of this variable is used in the empirics to account for a diminishing effect with larger numbers.
Early-stage Investee Focus	A dummy variable equal to 1 for funds that indicate a focus on financing provided to firms in their early/expansion stages of development (not late stages or buyout stages). More specific stages of focus were not tractable due to international differences in the definition of stage focus, as well as style drift that is often observed among different stages of development.

2 funds each from the Cayman Islands and South Africa; and 1 fund each from the Philippines, Canada, Finland, New Zealand, Luxembourg, Brazil, Switzerland, and Italy (see Table 6.2). The respondent fund managers include 7 each from Malaysia, the Netherlands, and the Netherlands Antilles; 6 from the United States; 3 each from the United Kingdom and Germany; 2 each from Belgium and South Africa; and 1 each from the Philippines, Canada, Finland, New Zealand, Brazil, Italy, Vietnam, the Czech Republic, Sweden, Norway, France, South Korea, and Uzbekistan. The number of respondents, and the fair

Table 6.2 Summary

This table summarizes the funds in the data based on the country in which the fund was formed.
distributions, where the number of funds is reported). The variables are as defined in Table 6.1.

							Country of Fund	
	Total	**Belgium**	**Brazil**	**Canada**	**Cayman Islands**	**Finland**	**Germany**	**Italy**
Number of Funds in Our Data	50	3	1	1	2	1	3	1
Compensation								
Fixed Management Fee %	2.22	2.33	3.00	2.00	2.50	2.50	2.50	2.50
Carried Interest Performance Fee %	18.07	20.00	10.00	20.00	20.00	20.00	20.00	20.00
Clawbacks	13	0	1	1	0	0	0	0
Cash Distributions	20	1	1	0	1	1	0	1
Legal and Market Conditions								
Country Legality Index	19.82	20.82	14.09	21.13	20.41	21.49	20.44	17.23
GNP per Capita	18024.80	21650	2930	19970	18060	19300	23560	19840
MSCI Index	0.11	0.19	0.62	−0.14	0.01	1.19	0.00	−0.03
Vintage Year of Fund	1999.96	1999.33	2000.00	2004.00	2000.00	1999.00	1998.00	2002.00
Outbound Offshore	0.28	0.00	0.00	0.00	0.50	0.00	0.00	0.00
Inbound Offshore	0.12	0.00	0.00	0.00	0.50	0.00	0.00	0.00
Fund Manager Characteristics								
Proportion of Legally Trained Fund Managers	5.96	8.33	20.00	33.00	0.00	5.00	3.33	25.00
Proportion of MBA/CFA Trained Fund Managers	75.40	58.33	80.00	67.00	90.00	80.00	86.67	25.00
Proportion of Ph.D. (Science) Trained Fund Managers	8.80	33.33	0.00	0.00	0.00	5.00	3.33	0.00

of the Data

The average values of each category per country are reported (except for clawbacks and cash

Formation									
Luxembourg	Malaysia	Netherlands Antilles	Netherlands	New Zealand	Philippines	South Africa	Switzerland	U.K.	U.S.
1	6	4	8	1	1	2	1	6	8
2.00	2.25	0.80	2.44	2.50	4.60	2.13	2.50	2.25	2.01
20.00	20.00	15.00	20.00	20.00	10.00	11.25	20.00	17.50	17.00
0	4	0	1	0	1	1	0	1	3
1	1	4	1	0	1	0	0	3	4
21.91	16.67	21.67	21.67	21.55	8.51	14.51	21.91	20.41	20.85
35760	3140	20950	20950	12600	850	2980	35760	18060	24740
0.01	0.03	0.16	0.18	0.20	−0.63	0.17	−0.08	0.14	0.07
1997.00	2001.50	2000.25	1997.63	2003.00	1998.00	2001.00	2000.00	2000.50	2000.88
1.00	0.17	1.00	0.00	0.00	1.00	0.00	0.00	0.50	0.38
0.00	0.00	0.00	0.13	0.00	0.00	0.00	0.00	0.50	0.13
5.00	4.17	0.00	12.50	5.00	0.00	0.00	0.00	5.00	1.88
80.00	78.33	80.00	63.75	80.00	50.00	83.50	70.00	90.00	77.00
5.00	5.83	5.00	9.38	5.00	50.00	0.00	0.00	10.00	9.38

(*continued*)

Table 6.2

	Country of Fund							
	Total	Belgium	Brazil	Canada	Cayman Islands	Finland	Germany	Italy
Proportion of Ph.D. (Nonscience) Trained Fund Managers	12.56	33.33	0.00	0.00	0.00	10.00	6.67	0.00
Average # Years of Relevant Work Experience of Principal Fund Managers	14.07	11.33	14.00	18.00	11.00	18.00	11.67	20.00
Fund Characteristics								
Funds Raised	1.04E +08	1.43E +08	1.00E +07	6.79E +07	8.43E +07	3.46E +07	1.49E +08	2.66E +08
Bank Institutional Investors	0.16	0.56	0.00	0.00	0.02	0.00	0.45	0.60
Government Investors	0.15	0.06	0.15	0.00	0.42	0.20	0.03	0.00
Limited Partnership Funds	0.48	0.00	0.00	1.00	0.50	1.00	0.67	0.00
Industry Market/Book	4.04	3.89	4.84	2.72	2.87	2.48	3.75	2.70
Early-stage Investee Focus	0.50	0.33	1.00	0.00	0.50	1.00	0.67	0.00

representation of both funds from developed and emerging private equity markets, make a response bias even less likely.

Second, a broad array of respondents replied to the survey. For example, the data show a median respondent fund size of US$39,487,200, with the average being US$103,974,889 (minimum US$263,378; maximum US$482,766,000), indicating that respondents were of a variety of fund sizes and of typical size for a sample of non-U.S. countries. The possibility of sample selection bias is further reduced by the presence of both onshore and offshore funds within the final sample, the presence of funds organized not only in both common law and civil law jurisdictions but also within jurisdictions in legal systems with English-, French-, Scandinavian-, and German-based legal systems, and the presence of funds situated in countries where English is not the primary language.

Finally, a sufficient number of variables regarding both fund and fund manager organization and the relevant features of the fund asset size, fund vintage,

(continued)

Formation									
Luxembourg	Malaysia	Netherlands Antilles	Netherlands	New Zealand	Philippines	South Africa	Switzerland	U.K.	U.S.
10.00	10.00	30.00	15.63	10.00	0.00	0.00	30.00	3.33	15.38
10.00	14.75	14.00	12.13	20.00	10.00	7.00	15.00	15.67	17.25
3.60E +07	3.21E +07	3.04E +08	4.66E +07	2.00E +07	2.30E +07	2.81E +07	2.63E +05	1.63E +08	1.10E +08
0.24	0.17	0.10	0.19	0.00	0.00	0.09	0.00	0.07	0.08
0.00	0.30	0.10	0.25	0.22	0.40	0.10	0.00	0.07	0.08
0.00	0.17	1.00	0.25	0.00	0.00	0.00	0.00	1.00	0.75
4.75	4.42	4.82	3.66	5.79	6.19	5.03	4.10	4.14	3.71
0.00	0.67	0.00	0.38	1.00	1.00	1.00	1.00	0.50	0.50

investor composition, investment strategy, industry composition of fund investments, and governance structures—more specifically the particular covenants provided in the terms within the agreements that govern the relationship between fund investors and fund manager—were collected to minimize the risk of response bias. We also sought information on the method of calculating management fees, the treatment of other fees such as consulting and monitoring fees, and profit sharing and distribution terms. We accept that we cannot absolutely rule out the possibility of a response bias, as the data we have collected here are unique.

6.4.2 Summary Statistics

The summary statistics are presented in Table 6.2. In the data, the average performance fee is 18.1%, and the median performance fee is 20%. The average fixed fee is 2.2%, and the median fixed fee is 2.5%. Of the 50 funds, 13 imposed clawbacks against fund managers in the event of poor performance; the extent of these clawbacks was most often 20% of the fund manager fees. Cash-only distributions were mandated by 20 of the 50 funds.

The level of the Legality index for each country is indicated in Table 6.2. The Legality index is a weighted average of the legal index variables introduced by La Porta et al. (1997, 1998), as defined by Berkowitz et al. (2003). Each of the components of the Legality index is highly pertinent to private equity finance, and they consist of the efficiency of the judicial system, the rule of law, corruption, risk of expropriation, risk of contract repudiation, and shareholder rights. The Legality index is an appropriate focus of our analysis in view of the fact that the components of the Legality index are very highly correlated, and focusing on a subset of indices within the component of legality to avoid the collinearity problem might look like data mining. Moreover, as we have a relatively small number of observations, a focus on a weighted average legal index suitably mitigates the possibility of incorrect statistical inferences with outlier observations and the inclusion or exclusion of certain countries in the data.[2] A higher Legality index indicates better substantive legal content pertaining to investing and the quality and likelihood of enforcement. Higher numbers indicate "better" legal systems across each of the factors.

Of the funds in the data, 28% are outbound-offshore funds, and 12% are inbound-offshore funds. As indicated in Table 6.1, an outbound-offshore fund is one that obtains its capital from investors from a certain jurisdiction but fund investments are made primarily in assets other than in the jurisdiction of the fund and the fund investors. With reference to U.S. jurisdictional boundaries, a fund will be considered to be an outbound-offshore fund if it obtains capital from U.S. investors, but it invests outside the United States. An inbound-offshore fund is one that obtains its capital from investors from various jurisdictions, but fund investments are made primarily in assets in a certain jurisdiction. With reference to U.S. jurisdictional boundaries, an inbound-offshore fund will be a fund located offshore that invests primarily in assets within the United States yet obtains its capital from non-U.S. investors. As these distinctions appear to be important in practice for private investment fund management in an international setting, we control for these variables in our empirical analyses.

A majority of funds are managed by MBA graduates, and a typical fund has relevant work experience of about 14 years. Science and law graduates exist among some of the funds in the data, and some fund managers had partial training (i.e., some nondegree courses) in law and/or the sciences (and this partial training is reflected in our data by recording the proportionate number of years

[2] We did consider specific components of the Legality index, and the results pertaining to statistical significance and signs were not materially different (although in some cases there were differences in economic significance).

of training). We control for the specific training of the fund managers in our empirical tests. This control is carried out for reasons set out in Armour (2004).

The average fund in the data had raised US$108 million in capital commitments. Of the 50 funds, 24 were set up as limited partnerships, and the remainder were set up as limited liability companies or trusts (see, e.g., Cumming and Walz, 2004; Cumming et al., 2005b; and Chapter 5 on limited partnerships versus other types of fund structures). Fifty percent had a pure venture capital (early-stage focus), and most had significant exposure to high-tech industries (as reflected by the industry market/book ratio of the investee firms in which the funds had invested). The range across each of the different funds and countries for these and the other variables is detailed in Table 6.2.

6.4.3 Correlation Matrix

A correlation matrix for many of the variables in the data is provided in Table 6.3. The correlations are suggestive of the main factors that drive fixed and performance fees, as well as clawbacks and cash-only distributions. Higher Legality indices are significantly positively correlated with performance fees and negatively correlated with fixed fees (these relations are also graphically depicted in Figure 6.1). Higher legal indices are also negatively related to the use of clawbacks. Legality is not significantly related to cash-only distributions, but offshore funds are more likely to have cash-only distributions.

Table 6.3 also provides insight as to areas of potential problems in respect of collinearity across the funds in the data. Most notably, GNP per capita and Legality are highly positively correlated. As such, in the multivariate analyses following, we assess the robustness of the statistical and economic significance to the inclusion/exclusion of a variety of different explanatory variables.

6.5 Econometric Tests

6.5.1 Econometric Methods

We analyze four different dependent variables in this section: fixed fees (Table 6.4), performance fees (Table 6.5), clawbacks (Table 6.6), and cash-only distributions (Table 6.7). The various right-hand-side explanatory variables were identified previously in this chapter and defined in Table 6.1. For each dependent variable, we provide five alternative sets of regressions to show robustness (for a total of 20 different models, consecutively numbered across Tables 6.4 to 6.7). Tables 6.4 and 6.5 use standard OLS regression methods corrected for heteroskedasticity with White's estimator (1980). The dependent variable in Tables 6.4 and 6.5 are bounded below by zero and above by one; we considered different methods of estimating fractions (Bierens, 2003) but did not find any material differences to the conclusions drawn. Alternative specifications are available upon request. The dependent variables in Tables 6.6 and 6.7

Table 6.3

This table presents correlations across the variables defined in Table 6.1. Correlations significant at the 5% level are

	(1)	(2)	(3)	(4)	(5)	(6)	(7)	(8)	(9)	(10)	(11)
(1) Fixed Management Fee %	1.00										
(2) Carried Interest Performance Fee %	−0.07	1.00									
(3) Clawbacks	**0.37**	−0.24	1.00								
(4) Cash Distributions	−0.26	−0.24	−0.20	1.00							
(5) Legality of Country of Formation	**−0.44**	**0.43**	**−0.46**	−0.06	1.00						
(6) English Legal Origin	−0.05	−0.07	**0.30**	−0.11	−0.13	1.00					
(7) French Legal Origin	−0.01	−0.06	−0.16	0.15	0.03	**−0.78**	1.00				
(8) German Legal Origin	0.08	0.18	−0.20	−0.14	0.14	**−0.35**	−0.25	1.00			
(9) Scandinavian Legal Origin	0.06	0.08	−0.08	0.17	0.08	−0.15	−0.11	−0.05	1.00		
(10) GNP of Country of Formation	**−0.31**	**0.30**	**−0.49**	0.06	**0.90**	−0.26	0.09	0.26	0.05	1.00	
(11) MSCI Year of Fund Formation	−0.24	0.08	**−0.31**	0.08	**0.43**	−0.08	0.04	−0.12	**0.39**	0.26	1.00
(12) Year of Fund Formation	−0.06	0.01	0.20	0.03	−0.07	**0.32**	−0.22	−0.16	−0.04	−0.12	−0.01
(13) Outbound Offshore Fund	**−0.42**	−0.16	**−0.27**	**0.58**	−0.03	0.06	0.00	−0.06	−0.09	0.04	−0.07
(14) Inbound Offshore Fund	−0.03	0.03	−0.08	**0.45**	0.12	0.23	−0.15	−0.12	−0.05	0.14	0.05
(15) Proportion of Ph.D. (Science) Trained Fund Managers	0.05	0.05	−0.10	0.15	−0.17	−0.14	0.23	−0.12	−0.03	−0.07	**−0.31**
(16) Proportion of Ph.D. (Nonscience) Trained Fund Managers	**−0.39**	0.08	**−0.32**	0.15	**0.30**	**−0.31**	**0.33**	−0.01	−0.02	**0.27**	−0.06
(17) Proportion of Legally Trained Fund Managers	0.05	0.18	0.12	−0.22	0.05	−0.19	0.26	−0.10	−0.01	0.06	−0.11

Correlations

highlighted in bold and underline font.

(12)	(13)	(14)	(15)	(16)	(17)	(18)	(19)	(20)	(21)	(22)	(23)	(24)	(25)	(26)
1.00														
0.03	1.00													
0.07	0.18	1.00												
−0.03	0.22	0.21	1.00											
−0.04	0.10	**−0.27**	0.10	1.00										
0.12	**−0.33**	−0.19	0.06	0.14	1.00									

(*continued*)

Table 6.3

		(1)	(2)	(3)	(4)	(5)	(6)	(7)	(8)	(9)	(10)	(11)
(18)	Proportion of MBA Trained Fund Managers	**−0.25**	0.02	−0.14	−0.13	0.09	**0.33**	**−0.42**	0.11	0.03	−0.01	0.19
(19)	Years Relevant Work Experience	0.01	−0.06	0.08	0.09	0.17	0.18	−0.16	−0.10	0.12	0.14	0.21
(20)	Funds Raised	**−0.35**	−0.07	−0.18	**0.37**	0.16	0.00	0.19	**−0.29**	−0.02	0.19	0.17
(21)	Bank Institutional Investors	−0.05	0.11	−0.22	−0.15	0.07	**−0.31**	0.22	0.21	−0.09	0.12	0.14
(22)	Government Investors	**0.27**	−0.03	0.24	−0.03	−0.19	0.04	0.08	−0.20	0.03	**−0.29**	−0.15
(23)	Pension Investors	−0.17	−0.13	−0.18	0.01	−0.12	0.20	−0.10	−0.13	−0.08	−0.08	0.15
(24)	Endowment Investors	**−0.41**	−0.13	−0.11	0.18	0.24	0.08	−0.02	−0.06	−0.08	**0.26**	0.07
(25)	Limited Partnership Fund	**−0.40**	0.01	−0.20	0.20	**0.33**	0.20	−0.22	−0.05	0.15	**0.35**	0.19
(26)	Industry Market/Book	−0.15	−0.13	−0.02	0.04	−0.25	−0.03	0.08	0.03	−0.21	**−0.27**	−0.24
(27)	Early-stage Fund Focus	0.21	0.06	0.14	**−0.33**	**−0.30**	0.16	−0.25	0.07	0.14	**−0.31**	−0.20

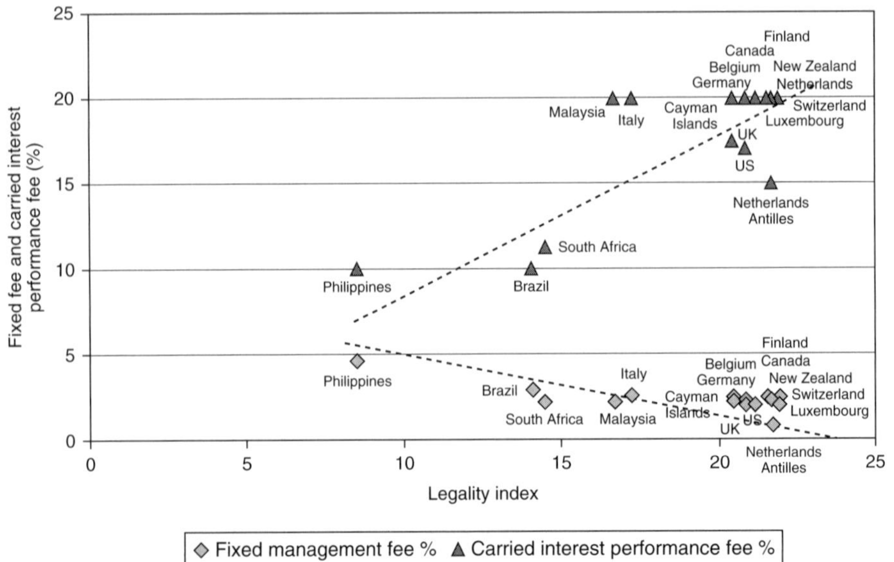

Figure 6.1 Graphical Depiction of the Relation between Fees and Legal Conditions

(*continued*)

(12)	(13)	(14)	(15)	(16)	(17)	(18)	(19)	(20)	(21)	(22)	(23)	(24)	(25)	(26)
0.00	0.24	0.07	−0.19	−0.30	−0.27	1.00								
0.28	0.05	0.02	−0.14	0.09	0.13	−0.20	1.00							
0.25	0.36	0.04	−0.16	0.12	−0.06	0.00	0.01	1.00						
−0.07	−0.22	−0.15	−0.01	0.00	0.00	−0.06	−0.06	0.28	1.00					
0.00	−0.16	0.13	0.07	−0.09	0.05	−0.34	−0.03	−0.25	−0.23	1.00				
0.06	0.08	−0.09	−0.22	0.00	−0.06	−0.09	−0.06	0.24	−0.10	−0.15	1.00			
−0.18	0.45	0.03	−0.18	0.16	−0.07	0.17	0.07	0.40	−0.18	−0.14	0.21	1.00		
0.11	0.47	0.14	−0.03	0.04	−0.12	0.28	0.10	0.40	−0.24	−0.20	0.20	0.54	1.00	
0.06	0.21	−0.08	0.17	0.21	−0.16	−0.07	0.06	−0.06	−0.07	0.14	0.03	−0.05	−0.12	1.00
0.08	−0.27	0.00	0.23	−0.08	0.12	0.09	−0.03	−0.57	−0.22	0.27	−0.10	−0.27	−0.16	0.34

are binary variables; as such, we use simple logit regressions and again correct for heteroskedicity. Marginal effects for the logit models were computed using Limdep Econometric Software (see Greene, 2002, 2003). Alternative specifications (e.g., probit models) did not materially affect the results, but they are available upon request. The results are also robust to inclusion/exclusion of most of the countries in the data and potential outliers.[3] We use logs of the right-hand-side variables (except the dummy variables) to reduce the weight of outlier observations and account for diminishing effects. Again, the results are quite robust and alternative specifications are available upon request.

6.5.2 Regression Results

The regression results in Tables 6.4 and 6.5 indicate that legal conditions by far have the most statistically and economically significant effect on fixed fees and performance compensation. Table 6.4 indicates fixed fees are significantly

[3]One exception to the robustness of results to exclusion of countries is that where the number of observations is significantly reduced by excluding countries, some of the results reported are not robust. Excluding countries with just one fund did not affect the primary results reported.

Table 6.4 Regression Analyses

This table presents OLS regressions of the fixed management fee % for the private Africa, Australasia, Europe, and North and South America. The variables are as defined Significant at the 10%, 5%, and 1% levels, respectively.

	Model 1		Model 2	
	Coefficient	**t-Statistic**	**Coefficient**	**t-Statistic**
Constant	9.644	4.361***	11.273	5.582***
Legal and Market Conditions				
Country Legality Index	−2.021	−2.913***	−3.993	−3.622***
English Legal Origin				
French Legal Origin				
German Legal Origin				
GNP per Capita			0.442	2.204**
MSCI Index				
Vintage Year of Fund				
Outbound-offshore Fund				
Inbound-offshore Fund				
Tax Difference			−0.003	−0.531
Fund Manager Characteristics				
Proportion of Ph.D. (Science) Trained Fund Managers	−0.001	−0.257	−0.004	−0.867
Proportion of Legally Trained Fund Managers				
Proportion of MBA/CFA Trained Fund Managers				
Average # Years of Relevant Work Experience of Principal Fund Managers				
Fund Characteristics				
Funds Raised	−0.133	−2.863***	−0.144	−2.834***
Bank Institutional Investors				
Government Investors				
Limited Partnership Funds				
Industry Market/Book	−0.667	−2.580**	−0.598	−2.338**
Early-stage Investee Focus				
Number of Observations	50		50	
Adjusted R^2	0.296		0.321	
f-Statistic	6.15***		4.87***	
LogLikelihood	−43.060		−41.013	
Akaike Information Statistic	1.922		1.921	

of Fund Fixed Management Fees

investment fund managers. The sample comprises 50 funds from 17 countries in in Table 6.1. White's (1980) HCCME is used in each regression. *, **, ***

Model 3		Model 4		Model 5	
Coefficient	t-Statistic	Coefficient	t-Statistic	Coefficient	t-Statistic
8.446	4.548***	11.071	6.133***	21.211	0.708
−1.857	−3.250***	−3.883	−3.342***	−2.107	−2.561**
		−0.196	−0.711		
		−0.132	−0.376		
		−0.074	−0.151		
		0.416	1.731		
−0.320	−1.066	−0.086	−0.241		
				−0.006	−0.413
				−0.684	−3.264***
				0.258	1.506
−0.002	−0.399	−0.004	−1.045		
		−0.004	−0.721		
		−0.004	−0.950		
0.268	1.322	0.213	1.016		
−0.121	−2.394**	−0.131	−2.230**	−0.096	−1.522
0.272	0.527	0.130	0.274		
0.600	2.796***	0.667	2.172**		
				0.021	0.161
−0.765	−3.092***	−0.700	−2.607***		
				−0.238	−1.017
50		50		50	
0.293		0.271		0.336	
3.53***		2.30**		4.54***	
−40.855		−37.652		−39.882	
1.994		2.106		1.915	

Table 6.5 Regression Analyses of Fund

This table presents OLS regressions of the carried interest performance fee % for the private Africa, Australasia, Europe, and North and South America. The variables are as defined Significant at the 10%, 5%, and 1% levels, respectively.

	Model 6		Model 7	
	Coefficient	**t-Statistic**	**Coefficient**	**t-Statistic**
Constant	−9.378	−1.106	−18.584	−1.904*
Legal and Market Conditions				
Country Legality Index	9.764	4.121***	19.086	3.433***
English Legal Origin				
French Legal Origin				
German Legal Origin				
GNP per Capita			−1.921	−1.645
MSCI Index				
Vintage Year of Fund				
Outbound-offshore Fund				
Inbound-offshore Fund				
Tax Difference			−0.025	−0.623
Fund Manager Characteristics				
Proportion of Ph.D. (Science) Trained Fund Managers	0.028	1.757*	0.040	2.116**
Proportion of Legally Trained Fund Managers				
Proportion of MBA/CFA Trained Fund Managers				
Average # Years of Relevant Work Experience of Principal Fund Managers				
Fund Characteristics				
Funds Raised	−0.288	−0.923	−0.179	−0.543
Bank Institutional Investors				
Government Investors				
Limited Partnership Funds				
Industry Market/Book	−0.562	−0.311	−0.894	−0.543
Early-stage Investee Focus				
Number of Observations	50		50	
Adjusted R^2	0.146		0.160	
f-Statistic	3.09***		2.55**	
LogLikelihood	−128.652		−127.104	
Akaike Information Statistic	5.346		5.364	

Carried Interest Performance Fees

investment fund managers. The sample comprises 50 funds from 17 countries in
in Table 6.1. White's (1980) HCCME is used in each regression. *, **, ***

Model 8		Model 9		Model 10	
Coefficient	**t-Statistic**	**Coefficient**	**t-Statistic**	**Coefficient**	**t-Statistic**
−10.426	−0.971	−19.208	−1.705*	−116.463	−0.503
10.913	4.237***	25.427	3.935***	11.224	4.158***
		−2.754	−1.440		
		−3.723	−1.953*		
		−0.734	−0.321		
		−3.202	−2.544**		
−1.261	−0.780	−2.095	−1.219		
				0.050	0.433
				−0.325	−0.262
				−0.193	−0.120
0.019	1.121	0.039	1.372		
		0.063	1.405		
		−0.018	−0.855		
−0.971	−0.377	−1.383	−0.602		
−0.337	−1.039	−0.024	−0.057	0.002	0.004
1.800	0.915	1.638	0.803		
0.691	0.393	−0.595	−0.301		
				−0.800	−0.934
−0.490	−0.236	−0.453	−0.248		
				1.338	0.867
50		50		50	
0.101		0.123		0.113	
1.69		1.49		1.89*	
−127.602		−123.025		−127.875	
5.464		5.521		5.435	

Table 6.6 Regression Analyses of

This table presents logit regressions of the probability that a fund has a clawback against investors). The sample comprises 50 funds from 17 countries in Africa, Australasia, White's (1980) HCCME is used in each regression. The standard logit coefficients are Significant at the 10%, 5%, and 1% levels, respectively.

	Model 11		Model 12	
	Coefficient	**t-Statistic**	**Coefficient**	**t-Statistic**
Constant	25.662	2.737***	22.344	2.262***
Legal and Market Conditions				
Country Legality Index	−8.172	−2.836***	−4.762	−0.933
English Legal Origin				
GNP per Capita			−0.702	−0.765
MSCI Index				
Vintage Year of Fund				
Offshore Fund (Inbound Offshore or Outbound Offshore)	−1.234	−1.121	−1.266	−1.139
Fund Manager Characteristics				
Proportion of Ph.D. (Science) Trained Fund Managers	−0.053	−0.935	−0.043	−0.831
Proportion of Legally Trained Fund Managers				
Proportion of MBA/CFA Trained Fund Managers				
Average # Years of Relevant Work Experience of Principal Fund Managers				
Fund Characteristics				
Funds Raised	−0.087	−0.342	−0.060	−0.223
Bank Institutional Investors				
Government Investors				
Limited Partnership Funds				
Industry Market/Book	−1.227	−0.945	−1.4418	−1.067
Early-stage Investee Focus				
Number of Observations	50		50	
Pseudo R^2	0.286		0.296	
Chi-squared	16.363***		16.954***	
LogLikelihood	−20.471		−20.176	

Clawbacks against Fund Managers

the private investment fund manager (and without clawbacks against any of the fund
Europe, and North and South America. The variables are as defined in Table 6.1.
reported in the table; the marginal effects are discussed in the text. *, **, ***

Model 13		Model 14		Model 15	
Coefficient	t-Statistic	Coefficient	t-Statistic	Coefficient	t-Statistic
27.365	2.411***	34.319	2.209**	−731.895	−1.636
−10.657	−2.701***	−11.313	−2.559**	−8.076	−2.666***
		−0.327	−0.151		
−5.065	−1.984**	−5.638	−1.714*		
				0.378	1.689*
−2.882	−1.836*	−3.225	−1.581	−1.951	−1.480
−0.163	−1.685*	−0.205	−1.587		
		−0.034	−0.486		
		−0.036	−0.824		
2.308	1.686*	2.131	1.335		
0.581	1.175	0.636	0.968	−0.424	−1.241
−7.590	−1.683*	−11.000	−1.506		
4.300	1.638	3.678	1.133		
				0.882	0.835
−2.487	−1.316	−3.266	−1.330		
				−0.961	−0.944
50		50		50	
0.523		0.542		0.337	
29.993***		31.082***		19.320***	
−13.656		−13.112		−18.993	

Table 6.7 Regression Analyses of

This table presents logit regressions of the probability that a fund mandates cash distributions opportunity to distribute shares. The sample comprises 50 funds from 17 countries in defined in Table 6.1. White's (1980) HCCME is used in each regression. The standard text. *, **, *** Significant at the 10%, 5%, and 1% levels, respectively.

	Model 16		Model 17	
	Coefficient	**t-Statistic**	**Coefficient**	**t-Statistic**
Constant	11.796	1.000	24.809	1.533
Legal and Market Conditions				
Country Legality Index	−4.650	−1.193	−16.041	−1.615
English Legal Origin				
French Legal Origin				
German Legal Origin				
GNP per Capita			2.195	1.310
MSCI Index				
Vintage Year of Fund				
Offshore Fund (Inbound Offshore or Outbound Offshore)	3.478	3.141***	3.729	3.205***
Fund Manager Characteristics				
Proportion of Ph.D. (Science) Trained Fund Managers	0.019	0.584	0.019	0.610
Proportion of Legally Trained Fund Managers				
Proportion of MBA/CFA Trained Fund Managers				
Average # Years of Relevant Work Experience of Principal Fund Managers				
Fund Characteristics				
Funds Raised	0.494	1.329	0.328	0.896
Bank Institutional Investors				
Government Investors				
Limited Partnership Funds				
Industry Market/Book	−1.327	−0.846	−0.9942	−0.617
Early-stage Investee Focus				
Number of Observations	50		50	
Pseudo R^2	0.466		0.497	
Chi-squared	31.378***		33.471***	
LogLikelihood	−17.962		−16.915	

Cash versus Share Distributions

to institutional investors, such that the fund manager does not have the
Africa, Australasia, Europe, and North and South America. The variables are as
logit coefficients are reported in the table; the marginal effects are discussed in the

Model 18		Model 19		Model 20	
Coefficient	t-Statistic	Coefficient	t-Statistic	Coefficient	t-Statistic
12.533	0.965	67.108	1.700*	16.609	0.060
−5.923	−1.428	−16.467	−1.728*	−3.859	−0.965
		−4.548	−1.413		
2.835	1.383	0.334	0.076		
				−0.004	−0.029
3.895	2.715***	7.261	2.121**	3.835	3.268***
0.040	1.074	−0.019	−0.196		
		−0.147	−0.884		
		−0.162	−1.274		
0.917	0.703	0.695	0.296		
0.531	1.102	0.589	0.914	0.529	1.152
−0.263	−0.141	−11.131	−0.982		
0.776	0.308	−3.516	−0.633		
				−1.783	−1.241
−1.452	−0.850	−6.243	−1.485		
				−1.217	−1.034
50		50		50	
0.512		0.702		0.505	
34.466***		47.278***		34.018***	
−16.417		−10.011		−16.642	

lower in countries with stronger legal conditions, and this result is robust to any of the different specifications in Models 1 to 5, among others not presented. (This strongly supports our prediction earlier in this chapter.) Further, Table 6.5 indicates that Legality is the most economically and statistically significant variable in explaining performance fees. In regards to the economic significance, based on the legal numbers indicated in Table 6.2, the data indicate that a move from the Philippines to the United States (one of the most extreme improvements in legal conditions in our data) gives rise to a reduction in fixed fees by approximately 1.5% and an increase in performance fees by approximately 10%. A more modest improvement in legal conditions from the Philippines to South Africa, for example, gives rise to a reduction in fixed fees by approximately 0.9% and an increase in performance fees by 6.9%.

These results are robust to the inclusion and/or exclusion of controls for a variety of factors, including market conditions, institutional investor, and fund manager characteristics such as education and experience, as well as fund factors such as stage and industry focus, among other control variables available shown explicitly in the tables (among others considered in one dataset but excluded for reasons of conciseness).

Some of the control variables are significant in Tables 6.4 and 6.5 in ways that are expected. Larger funds have lower fixed fees (Table 6.4). Ph.D.'s in science are more likely to have higher performance fees (Table 6.5, but this effect is significant only in Models 6 and 7). The presence of government investors gives rise to larger fixed fees, and funds focused in high-tech industries (with higher market/book ratios) are more likely to have smaller fixed fees. The other variables, however, are generally insignificant and/or not robust. For example, differences between income and capital gains tax rates do not affect fixed fees versus performance fees. Overall, therefore, the most robust variable is Legality for explaining international differences in fixed and performance fees.

As in Tables 6.4 and 6.5, Table 6.6 indicates that the legal environment is the most statistically and economically significant determinant of clawbacks among private equity funds across countries. In terms of the economic significance, a reduction in the quality of legal conditions increases the probability clawbacks by approximately 26.8% for a move from South Africa to the Philippines and approximately 44.9% for a move from the United States to the Philippines.

It is important to stress the asymmetric relation between Legality and fund manager compensation. Fund managers have higher fixed fees and lower performance fees in countries with weak legal conditions (see Tables 6.4 and 6.5). But in regards to penalty clauses, fund managers in countries with weak legal conditions are more likely to face the downside risk of a clawback on their fees (see Table 6.6). The intuition underlying this asymmetric result is possibly explained by the fact that risk-averse fund managers trade off a higher fixed fee for a lower performance fee when legal conditions are weak, whereas risk-averse institutional investors are more likely to require clawbacks to protect against downside risk in countries with poor laws.

The only other significant and robust variable in Table 6.6 to explain the frequency of clawbacks is the MSCI index. In better market conditions across time, fund managers are less likely to face clawbacks. This is consistent with results in previous work (see, e.g., Gompers and Lerner, 1999a,b, 2000, for empirical work; Kanniainen and Keuschnigg, 2004, for theoretical work) that shows demand and supply conditions affect fees. When money is chasing deals (excess capital flowing from institutional investors to private equity funds for the given inelastic supply of private equity fund managers), fund managers receive more favorable deal terms from their institutional investors.

With regard to the economic significance of Legality in Tables 6.4 and 6.5, notice that when GNP per capita is included alongside the Legality index, the statistical significance of Legality is not affected, but the economic significance is. The reason for this change is the high correlation between Legality and GNP per capita (see Table 6.3). Given the bias introduced by simultaneously including both Legality and GNP per capita, we feel much more confident with the economic significance associated with only including the Legality index without the GNP per capita variable. Notice as well in Table 6.6 that the simultaneous inclusion of GNP per capita and Legality gives rise to a statistically insignificant relation between Legality and the probability of use of clawbacks. Again, this is due to the high correlation between Legality and GNP per capita (Table 6.3).

Table 6.7 analyzes the relation between Legality and payment terms to a fund's institutional investors in terms of cash versus share distributions from realized investments in entrepreneurial firms. The data do indicate a weak (not robust) relation between Legality and cash distributions in Model 19 (which therefore only weakly supports our prediction earlier in this chapter): Cash-only distributions are more likely in countries with weak legal conditions.

Much more significantly in Table 6.7, however, is the result that institutional investors mandate cash-only distributions for offshore funds. The estimates coefficients for Legality in Models 16 to 20 provide very strong support for our prediction. In regards to the economic significance, institutional investors are approximately 83.3% more likely to require cash-only distributions when the fund is established as an offshore fund. This finding is consistent with the view that share distributions for tax reasons are less meaningful, since offshore funds are already tax pass-through entities. Furthermore, institutional investors in an offshore fund are commonly from a diverse set of countries, and they typically face nonharmonized legal impediments to selling shares in entrepreneurial firms transferred to them from the fund manager. Hence, it is much more efficient for liquidity reasons to have cash-only distributions among offshore fund structures.

The fact that none of the other variables is significant in Models 16 to 20 further supports the importance of a distinction between offshore and onshore funds. In Table 6.7, because all of the outbound-offshore funds used cash-only distributions (and most of the inbound-offshore funds did as well), we cannot estimate the logit model with outbound-offshore and inbound-offshore funds as separate variables. Nevertheless, the correlation matrix in Table 6.3 does indicate the comparative importance of these two variables. Outbound-offshore funds are slightly more likely to have clawbacks than inbound-offshore funds, as the correlation with clawbacks is 0.58 for outbound offshore versus 0.45 for inbound offshore (see Table 6.3).

6.6 Limitations, Alternate Explanations, and Future Research

An international comparison of fee structures among private equity funds involves a number of inherent limitations. First, and perhaps most notably, the funds' reports are by definition private, which creates difficulty in assembling a large sample. In fact, the details regarding fees are highly sensitive and confidential.[4] Many fund managers in most countries around the world are loathe to discuss personal finances, let alone disclose their fees. Garnering an international sample of comparable details across countries around the world required a significant effort. Our data are comparable to other international venture capital datasets (see, e.g., Hege et al., 2006; Kaplan et al., 2007; Lerner and Schoar, 2005). We have described the representativeness of the data as fully as possible, while recognizing that this study is the first of its kind. Further research may discover new insights from obtaining more data and/or a broader set of countries.

Second, we have not explicitly reported certain details in the data. For example, most funds have graduated fixed fees for different asset sizes. We used the starting fixed fee percentages for the lowest amounts of capital among those funds that graduate their fees; alternative definitions of this variable in the data did not materially influence the results. As another example, we used the number of years of work experience of the fund managers as opposed to the number of prior funds as a proxy for relevant work experience; the different ways of specifying this variable and alternatives did not materially influence the results. Likewise, the other additional details in the data did not materially impact the inferences drawn and reported previously; additional details are available upon request.

Third, there are a host of legal indices that we could have focused on from La Porta et al. (1997, 1998) instead of the overall "Legality" index (Table 3.1) from Berkowitz et al. (2003; see also Allen and Song, 2003; Black, 2001; Gilson, 2003; McCahery and Vermeulen, 2004). The different Legality indices are highly correlated with each other; alternatives did not materially affect the results. We reported the results with legal origin variables as well to consider robustness, and other specifications with other legal indices are available upon request.

Fourth, there exists international differences in taxation. In the United States and Canada, for example, tax issues comprise both federal and state differences in taxation; federal versus state differences do not exist in many of the other

[4]Most respondents indicated that restrictions on public disclosure of fund matters, even to investors, were provided in the terms within the agreements that govern their relationship.

countries in our data. Also, the treatment of carried interest varies across countries, as partnership profits may be taxed at either a capital gains tax rate or an income tax rate. Prior work in the U.S. context has shown that tax matters for the structure of venture capital contracts with entrepreneurs, particularly in respect to stock options (Gilson and Schizer, 2003). Similarly, empirical and theoretical work has shown the importance of capital gains tax in affecting venture capital fundraising and investing (see, e.g., Gompers and Lerner, 1998a,b; Jeng and Wells, 2000; Armour and Cumming, 2006; Kanniainen and Keuschnigg, 2003, 2004; Keuschnigg, 2003, 2004a,b; Keuschnigg and Nielsen, 2004a,b; Poterba, 1989a,b). In our discussions with the fund managers that provided the data, we learned that taxation was not a driving force behind the structuring of the manager's fixed management fees versus carried interest, as the managers are more concerned with balancing the different tax, legal, and operational concerns in regards to potential investors (each with potentially conflicting objectives) during the set-up of the fund. Likewise, there is no relation between taxation and the use of clawbacks. We nevertheless controlled for tax but did not find this to be a significant variable (this is also consistent with our conversations with the fund managers). There are, however, tax implications for cash versus share distributions for onshore versus offshore funds, and this tax aspect was discussed and control variables in our data were employed in our tests. We do note that a fund manager's personal tax management/avoidance strategies could impact the desired timing of receipt of income from the fund (e.g., it could be advantageous for tax reasons to defer income to later years by having lower fixed fees and higher carried interest), but again our discussions with fund managers indicated this was not a pronounced concern that was driving the choice of fixed versus management fees among the managers at any of the funds in our data. Overall, therefore, while it is possible that unknown and/or hidden tax factors exist with some funds, our anecdotal and empirical evidence suggests that tax is not a systematic driving factor behind the compensation variables studied herein.

There are a number of implications for future work from the results in this study. For instance, future work could study the relation between Legality, fees, and fund performance. Consistent with our findings of a positive relation between incentive compensation and Legality, prior work has shown that countries with better laws have higher private equity fund returns (Cumming and Walz, 2004; Hege et al., 2006; Lockett et al., 2002; Manigart et al., 2002a) and a greater probability of IPO exits (Cumming et al., 2006). However, what remains unknown is the comparative importance of Legality for facilitating higher performance fee percentages as reported herein versus the importance for Legality for mitigating information problems in exit transactions. Said differently, whether law quality provides more "bang for the buck" in facilitating incentive contracts (thereby indirectly facilitating better exits) versus directly facilitating certainty in private equity exit transactions is an unresolved empirical issue. Future work could also examine the ways incentive compensation among private equity fund managers in different countries impacts incentives of fund managers to carry out investment in early-stage versus late-stage and high-tech versus non-high-tech investments, as well as the structure of those investments (see also Bascha and Walz, 2001a,b; Casamatta, 2003; Cumming et al., 2006; Hsu, 2004; Kaplan et al., 2007; Kirilenko, 2001; Klausner and Litvak, 2001; Lerner and Schoar, 2005; Schmidt, 2003). The role of Legality in influencing the compensation contracts for entrepreneurs and rates of innovation among venture-back companies across countries could also be examined in future work (see Gilson and Schizer, 2003, for an analysis of entrepreneurial compensation in relation to U.S. tax laws; and also Kortum and Lerner, 2000). In the spirit of research on other aspects of private equity financial intermediation (see, e.g., Gompers and Lerner, 1996, 1999b, 2001a,b; Sahlman, 1990; Litvak, 2004a,b; Schmidt and Wahrenburg, 2003), future work could investigate a variety of international differences in other forms of financial intermediation in relation to legal and institutional structures.

Policy-oriented work could examine the tax implications of carried interest performance fees. At the time of this writing, policymakers in many countries have been debating the appropriateness of taxing carried interest at capital gains tax rates instead of at the regular (and higher) income tax rates.[5] Fleischer (2008) has pointed out that taxation of carried interest at capital gains rates does not seem altogether consistent with the rationale for lower capital gains tax rates. Capital gains taxes are lower than income taxes because investors that receive a capital gain put their own capital at risk and should be rewarded with a lower capital gains tax rate. In the case of venture capital and private equity fund managers, however, the capital being risked is the capital of the institutional investors and not that of the fund managers, and the carried interest performance fee more closely resembles a performance bonus than a capital gain for the fund managers.

In the following discussion questions, we provide a few questions relating fixed fees and carried interest to total fund manager compensation over the life of the fund. Additional questions and examples along these lines are found in Metrick (2006) and Metrick and Yasuda (2006).

6.7 Conclusions

This chapter considered for the first time international differences in managerial compensation for private equity funds. The data provided evidence of the view that poor legal conditions gave rise to higher fixed fees and lower performance fees. Consistent with the theoretical work of Acemoglu and Zilibotti (1999), risk-averse private fund managers substitute fixed compensation for performance compensation as legal conditions worsen. The data in fact indicated that legal conditions by far have the most statistically and economically significant effect on compensation, even in comparison to the role of the managers'

[5]For a U.S.-based discussion, see, for example, http://www.money.cnn.com/2007/03/29/markets/pe_taxes/index.htm. For a U.K.-based discussion, see, for example, http://www.taxresearch.org.uk/Blog/2007/07/12/tax-private-equity-carried-interest- as-income/.

education and experience, as well as a variety of other fund characteristics including fund size and industry and stage focus.

While risk-averse fund managers trade off performance fees for fixed fees in countries with inferior laws, risk-averse institutional investors are also more likely to require clawbacks of fund manager fees in the event of poor fund performance. In other words, there is an asymmetry in fund manager compensation in relation to legal conditions: Fund managers have higher fixed fees and lower incentive fees in countries with weak legal conditions, but fund managers in countries with weak legal conditions are also more likely to face the downside risk of a clawback on their fees.

Finally, to complement the analysis of how fund managers are compensated, we further show that legal conditions influence the mode of payment to institutional investors in terms of cash versus share distributions from realized investments in entrepreneurial firms. Institutional investors are much more likely to mandate cash-only distributions (and do not allow for share distributions) for offshore funds. Institutional investors in an offshore fund are commonly from a diverse set of countries, and they typically face nonharmonized legal impediments to selling shares in entrepreneurial firms transferred to them from the fund manager. It is therefore more efficient for liquidity reasons, among other things, to have cash-only distributions among offshore fund structures.

That legal conditions affect the payment conditions of fund managers and institutional investors across countries has a number of implications for future research. Legal conditions influence fund manager compensation, which in turn could have implications for fund investment selection, returns, and the development of private equity markets across countries. The comparative importance for law in compensation contracts versus the role of law directly in other aspects of fund management could be a fruitful avenue for future research.

Key Terms

Fixed fee or management fee
Performance fee or carried interest
Clawback
Cash distribution
Share distribution
Learning model of compensation
Signaling model of compensation

Discussion Questions

6.1. What are the typical compensation terms for private equity limited partnership fund managers? How would you expect compensation terms to vary across different countries?
6.2. For what types of private equity funds are agency costs more pronounced? For what types of funds would you expect fund manager compensation contracts to have higher performance fees and lower fixed fees?
6.3. What is a clawback? When are clawbacks more commonly observed?
6.4. What is the difference between cash versus share distributions? When would institutional investors seek distribution clauses in their limited partnership contracts?

6.5. Consider a U.S. private equity fund that raised $200,000,000 under terms of management fees of 1.5% of *committed* capital for years 1–5 of the fund, 1.5% of *invested* capital (draw downs) for years 6–10 of the fund, and performance fees of 20%. Suppose the fund is fully invested by year 5. Suppose the fund generates exit proceeds of $300,000,000 at the end of its 10-year lifetime. How much did the fund managers earn in total fixed fees and total performance fees at the end of the 10-year life of the fund?

6.6. Consider a Philippines private equity fund that raised $200,000,000 under terms of management fees of 4% of *committed* capital for years 1–5 of the fund, 4% of *invested* capital (draw downs) for years 6–10 of the fund, and performance fees of 10%. Suppose the fund is fully invested by year 5. Suppose the fund generates exit proceeds of $300,000,000 at the end of its 10-year lifetime. How much did the fund managers earn in total fixed fees and total performance fees at the end of the 10-year life of the fund?

6.7. Under the assumptions in questions 6.5 and 6.6 and perfect foresight, would the overall fee differences lead you to prefer to be a fund manager in the United States or in the Philippines? With conditions of uncertain returns, how might returns expectations and clawbacks affect your answer?

6.8. Do you think fund manager–carried interest should be taxed at income tax rates or capital gains tax rates? Explain your answer with reference to the underlying rationale for the existence of differences in income and capital gains tax rates. If carried interest were taxed at the income tax rate, how do you think this would impact the markets for venture capital and private equity?

7 Fundraising and Regulation

7.1 Introduction and Learning Objectives

The purpose of this chapter is to improve our empirical understanding of the factors that motivate institutional investors to allocate capital to private equity. Chapters 5 and 6 analyzed limited partnership agreements in detail with data from 17 countries around the world. This chapter shows that because contracts are incomplete (i.e., it is not possible to write contracts that cover all contingencies, particularly for a 10- to 13-year fund), contractual agreements are by themselves not sufficient to address all of the concerns that institutional investors have when investing in venture capital and private equity funds. As such, regulation plays a strong role in influencing institutional investor capital commitments to private equity funds.

Like Chapter 4, in this chapter we empirically study institutional investors in the Netherlands and the investment decisions as of 2004 for the period 2006 to 2010. The consideration of Dutch institutional investors at this time is of interest to enable an assessment of the role of regulation versus market forces in driving institutional investor capital allocation decisions to private equity funds. More broadly, it is of interest to study regulations in the context of private equity contracting in view of their effect on contracts entered into by the institutional investors and the private equity fund managers. The general theme of this book is that proper financial contracting is a key ingredient for private equity investment, and in this regard regulations and laws matter a great deal.

Of particular interest in this chapter is the fact that institutional investors face significant regulatory oversight, unlike the private equity funds they invest in. We explain in this chapter that both the heavy regulation of institutional investors and the dearth of regulation for private equity funds have an effect on institutional investor capital commitments to private equity funds. In addition, we show how market conditions and other factors influence capital allocation decision to private equity funds.

In this chapter we will do the following:

- Consider the ways in which institutional investors are regulated
- Explain the dearth of regulation of private equity funds
- Empirically consider the effect of regulation of institutional investors and private equity funds relative to market factors, among other things, on institutional investor capital allocations to private equity funds

In this chapter we empirically study institutional investors in the Netherlands and the investment decisions as at 2004 for the period 2006–2010. The consideration of Dutch institutional investors is of interest due to regulatory changes at that time that enable an empirical assessment of the role of regulation versus market forces in driving institutional investor capital allocation decisions to private equity funds. Recall in Chapter 4 that one of the Dutch regulatory changes in 2006, the Financieel Toetsingskader (FTK), closely resembles the U.S. Department of Labor's Employment Retirement Income Security Act's (ERISA) change to the prudent man rule in 1979. Regulation of this type better enables pension fund managers to invest in venture capital and private equity funds, since it is viewed as being consistent with the objectives of pension fund beneficiaries.

In the first part of this chapter we explain the regulation of institutional investors and private equity fund managers. Then we go on to examine the regulation of institutional investors and private equity fund managers and outline the theoretical propositions and testable hypotheses. Then we look at the multivariate empirical analyses of private equity allocations by Dutch institutional investors and regulations. We consider the issue of why incumbent private equity funds may oppose disclosure despite the evidence that greater disclosure would bring more capital into the private equity industry, as well as extension and future research.

7.2 Regulation of Institutional Investors and Fund Managers

Our particular interest in this chapter is assessing the role of the institutional investors' *perceived* importance of law versus economics in driving institutional investor capital allocation decisions to private equity. First, we study the effect of a comparative dearth of regulations of private equity funds on institutional investor allocations to private equity. The lack of regulations in private equity to which we refer is related to the fact that investors in private equity funds are institutional investors and high-net-worth individuals (not the so-called unsophisticated retail investors), and therefore these funds do not receive the same degree of scrutiny as other types of retail-based funds, such as mutual funds. Private equity funds regularly justify their opaque or less than transparent disclosure of their activities and returns (particularly unrealized returns on unexited investments not yet sold in an IPO or acquisition)[1] to their institutional investors as necessary in the interest of their private investee firms. The only actual oversight that private equity funds face includes the fact that private equity funds, if structured

[1]Private equity funds invest for reasons of capital gain, and investment duration is typically 2 to 7 years before an exit event and capital gain is realized (Chapter 19). Prior to the exit event, each year private equity funds make disclosures on their anticipated returns for unexited investments to their institutional investors. Cumming and Walz (2004) find evidence that these disclosures on unexited investments tend to be grossly exaggerated, as discussed in Chapter 22. Phillapou and Zollo (2005) confirm this finding.

as a corporate body or limited partnership, are subject to the requirements of all other like institutions, and if registered with a government ministry for tax purposes (tax deductions for subsidizing R&D and the like), are also subject to the ministry's requirements. In every practical sense, therefore, the operations of private equity funds are not regulated above and beyond that of any corporate body. This is in sharp contrast to mutual funds, for example.

In the second major component of this empirical chapter, we consider the extent to which the changes in regulation of institutional investors by regulators seeking to "harmonize" the existing regulations affecting different types of financial institutions are important to institutional investors' decisions to allocate capital to private equity. We examine three primary regulatory changes: the new International Financial Reporting Standards ("IFRS") in 2005, the proposed new Financieel Toetsingskader ("FTK") for 2006, and the new Basel II regulations in 2004. Harmonization of regulations faced directly by institutional investors facilitates investment in private equity by enabling different types of institutional investors (pension funds, banks, and insurance companies) to act as limited partners for the same private equity fund and by enabling different institutions in different countries to act as limited partners in private equity funds. This is expected to affect institutional investors' asset allocation decisions in private equity, the geographic region in which institutional investors invest, and the mode of private equity investment (direct private company, direct fund, and fund-of-fund investments).

This chapter is in part motivated by the fact that prior work has shown that financial market regulation and harmonization affect investment volume and portfolio allocations in areas other than private equity, such as stock exchanges (e.g., Charemza and Majerowska, 2000; Errunza, 2001; more generally, see La Porta et al., 1997, 1998). It is natural to consider whether regulation and harmonization impact private equity markets, particularly in a European setting. Practitioner reports of venture capital markets around the world are consistent with the view that regulation is one of the most important factors hindering the development and internationalization of private equity markets (Deloitte Touche Tohmatsu, 2006).

This chapter is also inspired by prior work on venture capital and private equity fundraising. Gompers and Lerner (1998b) have shown that private equity fundraising is facilitated by economic (stock market conditions and real GDP growth) and legal conditions (taxation and the prudent man rule), based on data from the United States (see Poterba, 1989a,b; see also theory in Keuschnigg and Nielsen, 2003a,b). Subsequent evidence has documented international differences in private equity fundraising using aggregate industry datasets (Allen and Song, 2003; Armour and Cumming, 2006; Jeng and Wells, 2000; Leleux and Surlemount, 2003).[2] Our study differs from these prior papers in that rather than

[2]See also Mayer et al. (2005), Lerner et al. (2005), and Nielsen (2006) for related work on the role of sources of funds from types of institutional investors in venture capitalist activities. Other studies on international differences in private equity and venture capital markets include Hege et al. (2006), Lerner and Schoar (2005), Black and Gilson (1998), Gilson (2003), Bascha and Walz (2001b), Bigus (2006), Gilson and Schizer (2003), Manigart et al. (2002a), and Schwienbacher (2003).

examining data from a private equity fund as in Gompers and Lerner (1998b) or international aggregate industry-wide datasets, we instead focus on data from institutional investors that contribute capital to private equity funds. We study for the first time the effect of (1) institutional investors' perceived importance of the comparative dearth of regulations pertaining to private equity funds for capital commitments to private equity and (2) institutional investors' perceived importance of harmonization of regulations pertaining to institutional investors on institutional investors' allocations to private equity.

To empirically study the two primary issues addressed in this chapter, we use a dataset from a survey of Dutch institutional investors that was carried out in 2005 (see also Chapter 4). The survey data contain information from 100 Dutch institutions, 29 of which are currently investing in private equity and 35 of which plan on investing in private equity over the period 2006 to 2010. The data comprise extremely specific details on the institutions' portfolio management practices, as well as their perceptions of the importance of various economic, legal, and institutional factors that influence portfolio allocations.

7.3 Legal and Institutional Details and Testable Hypotheses

Private equity limited partnerships typically last for 10 years with an option to continue for a further 3 years as the investments of the private equity fund are wound down. Private equity investments also take time (often a few years) to reach the desired level of exposure, as fund managers must themselves screen potential investees (Gompers and Lerner, 1998a,b, 1999). Investment in private equity is therefore extremely illiquid. Institutional investors—typically pension funds, insurance companies, and banks—are limited partners, while the general partner is a professional private equity fund manager that earns a fixed fee based on contributed assets from institutional investors (typically 1 to 3%) and a carried interest that is commonly around 20% (at least for riskier venture capital investments). Limited partners are legally prohibited from being involved in the day-to-day operation of a private equity fund, or they risk losing their limited liability status as a limited partner.

Institutional investors are subject to stringent regulatory oversight in view of the nature of the products they offer and their customer demographics. Institutional investors' commitments to private equity funds are regulated in terms of the proportion of assets that institutional investors can contribute to private equity. Customers of pension funds, insurance companies, and banks are more vulnerable, as they entrust a significant fraction of their income and accumulated wealth to these institutions. Regulations are therefore in place to address the funding of these institutions to ensure that the institutions do not take advantage of the customers and provide the proper products that are not only appropriate for each type of customer but also structured properly to meet their expectations. Laws also regulate solvency requirements to ensure that the contractual liabilities of these institutions are met, especially in view of the vulnerable nature of their customers. Assets have to be protected in some manner, as institutions such as pension funds and insurance companies only meet their contractual obligations to their beneficiaries in the distant future. The allocation of assets must be balanced in terms of risk, return, and ability to meet expected and unexpected liabilities.

7.3.1 Regulatory Harmonization of Institutional Investors

Regulatory harmonization can facilitate institutional investor investment in private equity in at least two direct ways. First, where different types of institutional investors have the same regulatory constraints, different types of institutions (such as a pension fund and an insurance company) can act as a limited partner on the same private equity fund. Second, where regulations are harmonized across countries, institutional investors from different countries are better able to act as institutional investors for the same private equity limited partnership. There are two issues that are central to every asset allocation strategy: (1) The strategy must be able to stand up to regulatory scrutiny pursuant to stringent regulations that address funding and solvency requirements, and (2) the strategy must achieve a balanced portfolio with risk diversification as the objective. An institutional investor needs to account for its unique features and client or beneficiary demographics in the development of the institutions' strategic asset allocation techniques (such as matching its assets and liabilities). Long-term plans also need measures to make specific adjustments to cater for market movements and regulatory modifications.

The empirical analyses in this chapter center on regulatory harmonization in Europe, with a focus on the Netherlands. Relevant regulatory harmonization measures include three primary regulatory changes: the new Basel II regulations, the IFRS, and the FTK. Basel II directly relates to the credit risk management practices of banks and indirectly relates to insurance companies and pension funds in respect to institutions generally adopting best practices and standards for risk management and capital adequacy (in line with comparable retail client-based financial institutions). Overall, we may hypothesize that Basel II will enhance institutional investor participation in private equity for many reasons. An institutional investor will look at its asset allocation strategy to determine its efficiency. Diversification is required, which should increase in private equity, which will provide better returns than the stock markets. Caution will be taken during the decision-making process, as the internal processes are increasingly scrutinized, if not by Basel II, then by those customers who agree with Basel II objectives. This additional cautionary behavior will follow through not only from that initial decision but also with a view of the nature of information that will have to be disclosed to the public under the Basel II (as well as under the IFRS, discussed following). Even if the institution is not obliged by Basel II, its clients and beneficiaries who agree with the Basel II objectives will expect to see similar practices within other comparable financial institutions (it is more likely for a person to be a client of a bank than a client or beneficiary of a pension fund or insurance company).

The IFRS pertains to accounting practices and reporting standards, providing clarity for private equity reporting practices among institutional investors and across countries. The objective of the IFRS is to ensure that the financial statements of all listed companies adequately reflect the losses that are incurred at the balance sheet date. From January 1, 2005, all listed companies in the European Union (EU) are required to apply the IFRS when preparing their consolidated financial statements. The Dutch went one step further and in February 2005, the Lower House of the Dutch Parliament approved a bill encouraging Dutch *unlisted* companies to apply the IFRS. Differences in accounting practices can occur for a number of reasons. For example, many private equity funds are conservative in their assessments and value investments at cost until the investments are realized. Other funds—particularly first-time funds—may be aggressive in their valuations by not writing down poorly performing companies or even overstating the value of ongoing ones, especially in difficult times (see Blaydon and Wainwright, 2005; Gompers, 1996). These differences in assessed values induce little confidence in the reported values and the Internal Rates of Return (IRRs) of private equity funds (Gompers and Lerner, 1998a). So with standardized accounting for both listed and unlisted companies, institutions will have to fairly report private equity investments, and private equity fund managers will in turn be incentivized to report their positions fairly. The IFRS therefore potentially facilitates private equity investment by harmonizing reporting standards in private equity, particularly for the reporting of investments in unexited private investee companies (see also EVCA/PriceWaterhouseCoopers, 2005).

The FTK is perhaps the most directly relevant regulatory change for institutional investors in the Netherlands. The FTK is designed to bring international/EU standards to the Netherlands. The FTK requires for the first time that the risk of asset classes not be assessed individually; rather, risk models must consider the *entire* portfolio of a financial institution.[3] Therefore, portfolio diversification is more important under the FTK. This will also stimulate demand for alternative investments (such as private equity) that have a low correlation with traditional asset categories. Moreover, for pension funds and insurance companies, alternative assets (such as private equity) will enable a better matching of the present value of assets and liabilities.

7.3.2 The Dearth of Private Equity Fund Regulation

Institutional investors' commitments to private equity are influenced in terms of the reports that institutional investors receive from private equity funds with

[3]Similarly, in the United States, changes in the interpretation of the prudent man standards for pension funds significantly increased pension fund capital allocations to private equity funds (Gompers and Lerner, 1998b).

regard to fund performance and in terms of institutional investors' ability to in turn disclose such reports to their own clients and beneficiaries (e.g., pensioners in the case of pension plans, etc.). Prior to the CalPERS lawsuit in California, private equity funds enjoyed complete secrecy in terms of their disclosure of their performance to the public generally, and reports by private equity funds to their institutional investors were not regulated. The effect of a comparative dearth of regulations in private equity on the flow of funds into the private equity market cannot be known without empirical scrutiny, particularly in light of the debate surrounding the topic. On the one hand, the lack of regulations in private equity may facilitate the flow of funds into private equity as it enables needed flexibility for the funds to carry out their investment activities without interference from regulatory oversight and reporting requirements. Private equity funds and commentators often put forward this view in the popular press.[4] Private equity funds have been vigorously opposed to disclosing their performance figures to the public, and to standardized setting of reports that they provide to their institutional investors.[5] On the other hand, the comparative dearth of regulations in private equity and lack of reporting standards may disincentivize institutional investors to contribute capital to private equity funds. Institutional investors often put forward this view,[6] and some pension funds have been forced to rethink their investment strategy into private equity funds.[7] In the following sections, we assess these competing conjectures of the effect of a comparative dearth of

[4]See, for example, "Capital Ideas" in The Monitor Blue Skies Capital Ideas 4/09/2005 at http://www.epolitix.com/EN/Publications/Blue+Skies+Monitor/; accessed August 1, 2005 (arguing that money flow into private equity is hampered by regulations in the United Kingdom (U.K.) and facilitated by a dearth of regulations in continental Europe). It has also been argued that new U.K. disclosure laws are making private equity groups uncomfortable by Henry Tricks, "Throwing Open a Secretive World" (*Financial Times*, page 20, January 17, 2005), and by John Mackie, "Private Equity: An Open-and-Shut Case for Transparency Complaints about the Secretiveness of the Private Equity Industry Are at Odds with Its Regulatory Procedures" (*Financial Times*, page 10, April 18, 2005), and by Martin Dickson, "UK: Time for Faceless Face of Capitalism to Grow Up" (*Financial Times*, page 18, August 24, 2005). See also Andrew Hill, "Blurred Distinctions in the Fund Industry" (*Financial Times*, page 6, September 12, 2005) arguing that overstrict regulations hampers the expansion of investments in other alternative asset classes.

[5]For example, see, http://www.ventureeconomics.com/vec/1031550742742.html; accessed January 11, 2004. The CalPERS lawsuit forced private equity funds in the United States to disclose returns among public institutional investors; as a result, some private equity funds have restricted participation from such public limited partners—for example, Sequoia Capital rejected the University of Michigan as an institutional investor in its funds. See also http://www.mercurynews.com/mld/mercurynews/business/6390139.htm; accessed January 11, 2004.

[6]The Institutional Limited Partners Association in the United States, for example, has been working toward setting standards for reports from venture capital and private equity funds. The National Venture Capital Association (NVCA) in the United States recently (as of March 3, 2004) rejected a proposal by the Private Equity Industry Guidelines Group regarding valuation guidelines, creating controversies among the Institutional Limited Partners Association and other industry associations. See http://www.privateequityonline.com/TopStory.asp?ID=4498&strType=1; accessed March 4, 2004.

[7]For example, CalPERS has been forced to reconsider its private equity allocations and in ways that differ relative to what it might otherwise have done but for the public disclosure. See http://www.ventureeconomics.com/vcj/protected/1070549534318.html; accessed January 11, 2004.

regulation of private equity funds on the flow of funds into the private equity market.

7.4 Data

7.4.1 Methods and Survey Instrument

The data assembled for this chapter are derived primarily from a survey of Dutch institutional investors carried out between February 2005 and May 2005. This use of surveys was necessary for the nature of information analyzed in this chapter. Data on past and current institutional asset allocation and investment levels in private equity do exist from some venture capital associations and annual financial reports,[8] but other information, such as projected or future asset allocation, investment objectives, and private equity investment selection criteria, are not available in the public domain. More significantly, we sought to determine the effect that perceived risks and hurdles in private equity investing had on institutional investment behavior. The relative importance of such perceived risks and hurdles, including poor product knowledge, complex terms and conditions, long time horizons, limited liquidity, lack of transparency, and lack of market-wide accepted performance benchmarks, could, in our opinion, only be obtained by survey. To verify and enhance data obtained by the survey, follow-up interviews were carried out, and, where possible, reference was made to institutions' websites and publications.

The instrument we used to obtain the detailed data required about current and projected Dutch institutional investor asset allocation, particularly private equity participation, is a 13-page questionnaire consisting of 32 questions. Robustness is achieved chiefly by framing questions in a way that calls for numeric responses or a simple "yes" or "no" response. In view of the fact that the potential respondents, although financial institutions, are from different branches of finance, a glossary of terms was provided in the survey to ensure uniformity in defining terms that may not necessarily be used in the same manner across sectors. The investment officers that provided the data were familiar with the existing regulations and any impending amendments and additions to such regulations. It is their primary responsibility to know these regulations, regardless of whether or not they are invested in private equity. As well, with the changes in the regulations and surrounding media attention (particularly for the FTK in the Netherlands), these regulations in particular were very well known. An overview of the information collected is summarized in Table 7.1, which defines the primary variables used in this study.

7.4.2 Potential Sample Selection Bias

The potential respondents—the population of institutional investors in the Netherlands—were identified from various sources including but not limited

[8]See, for example, www.evca.com for European data and www.nvp.nl for Dutch data.

Table 7.1 Variable Definitions and Summary Statistics

This table presents selected variables and descriptive statistics in the dataset of 100 Dutch institutional investors based on data from 2005. There were 22 institutions that planned on increasing their total allocations to private equity, 7 institutions that planned on decreasing their total allocations to private equity (and 71 without any change), and 35 planning on being invested in private equity in 2006–2010 and 29 invested in private equity in 2005. The expected returns variable and the legal variables are summarized for the subsample of funds expected to be invested in private equity in 2006–2010.

Variable Name	Definition	Mean	Standard Deviation	Median	Minimum	Maximum	Number of Observations
Institutional Investor Characteristics							
Pension Fund	A dummy variable equal to 1 for a pension fund institutional investor	0.56	0.50	1	0	1	100
Insurance Company	A dummy variable equal to 1 for an insurance company institutional investor	0.25	0.44	0	0	1	100
Bank/Financial Institution	A dummy variable equal to one for a bank/financial institutional investor	0.19	0.39	0	0	1	100
Assets (Millions of Euros)	The total assets managed by the institutional investor (in millions of 2005 euros)	4,753.00	9,060.41	800	300	50,000	100
Private Equity Allocations in 2006–2010							
All Private Equity 2006–2010 (Full Sample Including Non-PE-investors)	The percentage of the institutions' total assets invested in private equity expected for 2006–2010	1.44	2.76	0	0	11.25	100

(continued)

Table 7.1 *(continued)*

Variable Name	Definition	Mean	Standard Deviation	Median	Minimum	Maximum	Number of Observations
All Private Equity 2006–2010 (Subsample Excluding Non-PE-investors)	The percentage of the institutions' total assets invested in private equity expected for 2006–2010	4.12	3.29	3.75	0.25	11.25	35
Dutch Private Equity 2006–2010	The percentage of the institutions' private equity investments in the Netherlands expected for 2006–2010	17.49	33.61	0	0	100	35
European Private Equity 2006–2010	The percentage of the institutions' private equity investments in Europe excluding the Netherlands expected for 2006–2010	46.89	28.79	50	0	100	35
U.S. Private Equity 2006–2010	The percentage of the institutions' private equity investments in the United States expected for 2006–2010	28.94	24.81	30	0	100	35
Asia Private Equity 2006–2010	The percentage of the institutions' private equity investments in Asia expected for 2006–2010	2.17	6.02	0	0	33	35
Rest of World Private Equity 2006–2010 (excluding the preceding categories of regions)	The percentage of the institutions' private equity investments in the rest of the world expected for 2006–2010	1.66	5.10	0	0	25	35

Direct Company Investment 2006–2010	The percentage of the institutions' direct entrepreneurial investee company private equity investments expected for 2006–2010	18.09	36.23	0	0	100	35
Direct Fund Investment 2006–2010	The percentage of the institutions' direct private equity fund investments expected for 2006–2010	32.34	38.29	10	0	100	35
Fund-of-funds Investment 2006–2010	The percentage of the institutions' direct private equity fund-of-funds investments expected for 2006–2010	46.71	41.80	40	0	100	35
Change in Private Equity Allocations from 2005 to 2006–2010							
Change in Private Equity from 2005 to 2006–2010 (Full Sample Including Investors without Changed PE Allocations)	The percentage of the institutions' total assets invested in private equity expected for 2006–2010 less the percentage allocated in 2005	0.35	1.38	0.00	−6.5	5	100
Change in Private Equity from 2005 to 2006–2010 (Subsample Excluding Investors without Changed PE Allocations)	The percentage of the institutions' total assets invested in private equity expected for 2006–2010 less the percentage allocated in 2005	1.21	2.39	1.75	−6.5	5	29

(continued)

Table 7.1 *(continued)*

Variable Name	Definition	Mean	Standard Deviation	Median	Minimum	Maximum	Number of Observations
Change in Dutch Private Equity from 2005 to 2006–2010	The percentage of the institutions' private equity investments in the Netherlands as expected for 2006–2010 less the percentage allocated in 2005	−0.24	27.71	0	−100	100	29
Change in European Private Equity from 2005 to 2006–2010	The percentage of the institutions' private equity investments in Europe excluding the Netherlands expected for 2006–2010 less the percentage allocated in 2005	11.55	39.56	0	−100	75	29
Change in U.S. Private Equity from 2005 to 2006–2010	The percentage of the institutions' private equity investments in the United States expected for 2006–2010 less the percentage allocated in 2005	8.72	22.21	0	−52	50	29
Change in Asia Private Equity from 2005 to 2006–2010	The percentage of the institutions' private equity investments in Asia expected for 2006–2010 less the percentage allocated in 2005	−0.07	3.84	0	−17	10	29
Change in Rest of World Private Equity from 2005 to 2006–2010 (excluding the above categories of regions)	The percentage of the institutions' private equity investments in the rest of the world expected for 2006–2010 less the percentage allocated in 2005	0.72	4.77	0	−5	25	29

Change in Direct Company Investment from 2005 to 2006–2010	The percentage of the institutions' direct entrepreneurial investee company private equity investments expected for 2006–2010 less the percentage allocated in 2005	1.66	20.70	0	−45	100	29
Change in Direct Fund Investment from 2005 to 2006–2010	The percentage of the institutions' direct private equity fund investments expected for 2006–2010 less the percentage allocated in 2005	0.17	43.22	0	−100	100	29
Change in Fund-of-funds Investment from 2005 to 2006–2010	The percentage of the institutions' direct private equity fund-of-funds investments expected for 2006–2010 less the percentage allocated in 2005	18.86	40.33	0	−50	100	29
Expected Private Equity Returns Relative to Public Equity Returns							
Excess Expected Basis Points for Private Equity	The number of basis points expected from private equity investments in excess of publicly listed equities in 2005 and over the period 2006–2010	120	156.61	55	0	1,000	100
Legal Variables							
Rank Dearth of Legal Restrictions	The institutional investor's rank (1 = low and 5 = high) of the importance of the comparatively fewer legal restrictions in private equity for the decision to invest	2.93	0.70	3	1	5	100

(*continued*)

Table 7.1 *(continued)*

Variable Name	Definition	Mean	Standard Deviation	Median	Minimum	Maximum	Number of Observations
FTK 2006	The institutional investor's rank (1 = low and 5 = high) of the importance of the new "Financieel Toetingkader" (FTK) in 2006 by the Pensioen & Verzekeringskamer for the decision to invest	2.60	0.99	2	1	5	100
IFRS 2005	The institutional investor's rank (1 = low and 5 = high) of the importance of the new International Financial Reporting Standards (IFRS, 2005) for the decision to invest	2.23	0.92	2	1	5	100
Basel II 2004	The institutional investor's rank (1 = low and 5 = high) of the importance of the new Basel II (2004) for the decision to invest	1.58	0.91	1	1	5	100

to the Pensioen & Verzekeringskamer (pensions and insurance supervisory authority of the Netherlands, PVK), De Nederlandsche Bank (Dutch Central Bank, DNB), Autoriteit Financiële Markten (the Netherlands Authority for the Financial Markets, AFM), the Dutch Private Equity and Venture Capital Association (NVP), and the EVCA; websites of Dutch financial institutions were also researched. Pursuant to identifying the appropriate contact persons, the survey instrument was sent to approximately 1,114 Dutch institutions, consisting of 797 pension funds,[9] including company pension funds, industrial pension funds, and occupational pension funds; 205 insurance companies;[10] and 112 banks,[11] including universal banks, securities credit institutions, savings banks, and mortgage banks. Participation was chiefly solicited with the promise that the aggregated survey results would be disseminated to respondents. Only one questionnaire was disseminated in hard copy by mail to each institution and addressed specifically to the institution's chief investment officer or an equivalent manager of private equity investments for an institution where such contact details are available.

One limitation to obtaining data through a survey is the possibility of sample selection bias. While we acknowledge that this is a possibility, we believe from a detailed analysis of the responses received and the data obtained from the responses that this concern does not arise in this exercise. First, survey data were gathered for a final sample of 100 institutional investors consisting of company pension funds, industrial pension funds, occupational pension funds, life and nonlife insurance companies, banks, and other financial service providers. Our sample of respondent institutions includes 56 pension funds, 25 insurance companies, and 19 banks and other types of financial service providers (see Table 7.2). Limitations in our sample size from each sector of the finance industry from which we derived data, as well as the limited information about comparable academic work on institutional investor behavior in private equity,

[9]All types of pension funds were included to mitigate response bias. As of 2004, all pension funds in the Netherlands had assets at €442 billion, with Dutch company pensions having assets of over €141 billion. Pension funds with assets below €1 million have, however, been excluded (954 in total) primarily because the possibility of sample selection bias is mitigated by the breadth of asset size of the pension funds that were sent survey questionnaires. Of the 797 pension funds surveyed, 524 have assets between €10 million to €1 billion. A majority of those have assets less than €100 million. Thirty four pension funds control assets between €1 billion and €5 billion, while 12 have more than €5 billion within their control.

[10]Those institutions within this category but described as institutions with an office in the Netherlands or with unrestricted services to the Netherlands and mutual benefit companies have not been included. While their inclusion will increase the approximate figure provided to 1,916, they are not deemed as Dutch institutions for the purposes of this study. As in the case of the target pension funds, we believe that the breadth of asset size of the insurance companies that were sent survey questionnaires mitigate any possible sample selection bias. Of the number surveyed, 32 have assets between €100 million and €1 billion, 27 have more than €1 billion, and 29 have less than €100 million.

[11]Non-EU and EU bank branches have not been included.

Table 7.2 Summary

This table summarizes the data by the characteristics of the institutional investors in terms future asset allocations (Panel B), and their current and expected future private equity

Panel A. Characteristics of the		
Type of Financial Institution	**Number of Institutions in the Dataset**	**Average Assets (Millions of Euros)**
Pension Fund	56	€2,942.86
Insurance Company	25	€5,008.00
Bank/Financial Services	19	€9,752.63
All Types of Institutional Investors	100	€4,753.00

Panel B. Asset Allocations (Percentage of		
Type of Financial Institution	**Publicly Traded Equities**	**Bonds**
Pension Fund	33.38	50.89
Insurance Company	23.80	55.72
Bank/Financial Services	27.32	48.43
All Types of Institutional Investors	29.83	51.63

. . . Planned (for the		
Type of Financial Institution	**Publicly Traded Equities**	**Bonds**
Pension Fund	31.51	51.73
Insurance Company	24.71	59.02
Bank/Financial Services	24.95	47.59
All Types of Institutional Investors	28.56	52.77

Statistics

of assets and expected rates of return in private equity (Panel A), their current and investments (Panel C).

Institutional Investors in the Dataset	
Average Targeted Absolute Rate of Return for Private Equity Investments (%) (as at 2005) for Institutions That Will Invest in Private Equity 2006–2010	**Average Targeted Relative Rate of Return for Private Equity Investments Relative to Public Equity (Basis Points) (as at 2005) for Institutions That Will Invest in Private Equity 2006–2010**
10.35	286.11
8.14	287.50
13.17	440.00
10.40	314.81

Assets Invested in Different Asset Classes)

Cash/Currencies	Index Funds	Private Equity	Other Types of Alternative Investments	Other
4.32	1.60	1.17	7.43	1.21
9.56	0.48	0.73	6.23	3.48
5.11	0.58	1.36	16.05	1.16
5.78	1.13	1.09	8.77	1.77

period 2006–2010)

Cash/Currencies	Index Funds	Private Equity	Other Types of Alternative Investments	Other
2.86	1.97	1.67	9.53	0.73
2.52	2.16	0.62	8.37	2.60
2.68	1.05	1.86	21.34	0.53
2.74	1.85	1.44	11.48	1.16

(*continued*)

Table 7.2

Panel C. Private

...Current

Type of Financial Institution	Number of Institutions Investing in Private Equity (All Regions)	Percentage of Private Equity Investments in the Netherlands	Percentage of Private Equity Investments in Europe outside the Netherlands	Percentage of Private Equity Investments in the United States
Pension Fund	14	23.00	43.43	25.71
Insurance Company	7	26.71	49.43	23.86
Bank/ Financial Services	8	13.38	44.75	28.13
All Types of Institutional Investors	29	21.24	45.24	25.93

...Planned (for the

Type of Financial Institution	Number of Institutions Investing in Private Equity (All Regions)	Percentage of Private Equity Investments in the Netherlands	Percentage of Private Equity Investments in Europe outside the Netherlands	Percentage of Private Equity Investments in the United States
Pension Fund	19	13.00	52.42	28.58
Insurance Company	8	35.00	40.00	23.75
Bank/ Financial Services	8	10.63	40.63	35.00
All Types of Institutional Investors	35	17.49	46.89	28.94

(*continued*)

Equity Investments (as at 2005)				
Percentage of Private Equity Investments in Asia	Percentage of Private Equity Investments in Rest of World	Percentage of Direct Company Investments	Percentage of Direct Fund Investments	Percentage of Fund-of-funds Investments
4.86	3.00	8.57	41.86	49.57
0.00	0.00	23.57	52.86	23.57
0.63	0.63	36.88	19.00	31.63
2.52	1.62	20.00	38.21	38.34

period 2006–2010)				
Percentage of Private Equity Investments in Asia	Percentage of Private Equity Investments in Rest of World	Percentage of Direct Company Investments	Percentage of Direct Fund Investments	Percentage of Fund-of-funds Investments
3.21	2.79	6.32	36.58	57.11
1.25	0.00	32.25	31.50	36.25
0.63	0.63	31.88	23.13	32.50
2.17	1.66	18.09	32.34	46.71

however, makes reliable statistical comparisons of our sample relative to the population of other types of investors in private equity intractable.

Second, a broad array of respondents replied to the survey. For example, the data show the median respondent asset size of €800,000,000, with the average being €4,665,000,000, indicating respondents were of a variety of asset sizes. We did not find a statistically significant difference between average assets of respondents versus nonrespondents. The possibility of sample selection bias is further reduced by the presence of institutions that do not currently allocate any of their assets to private equity and do not plan to allocate any up to 2010, institutions that plan to increase current allocations in the near future, and institutions that plan to reduce allocations by 2010.

We unfortunately realize that we cannot absolutely rule out the possibility of a response bias due to the unique nature of the data collection. The survey design and motivation for the survey was initially to determine which Dutch institutions currently allocate, and plan to allocate, capital to private equity. In this regard, the survey instrument also had to provide for allocations to all other types of assets to enable us to determine which asset classes would "lose out" to any future proposed reallocations to private equity. Notice that questions pertaining to regulation (among other things) were added at the end of the survey to the more primary questions regarding asset allocation. Therefore, we believe our sample does not contain *only* those institutions interested in private equity regulations.

7.4.3 Summary Statistics

The data indicate that the 100 institutional investors consisting of pension funds, insurance companies, banks, and other financial institutions invested on average 1.09% of their assets in private equity as at 2005 and planned on investing 1.44% of their assets in private equity over the period 2006–2010 (Table 7.2, Panel B). Of these 100 institutions, 19 plan on (over the range 2006–2010) investing on average more than 2.5% of their assets in private equity, 10 plan on investing more than 5% of their assets in private equity, and 6 plan on investing more than 7.5% of their assets in private equity. The private equity disbursed to funds amounted to €3.1 billion as at 2005, or 2.3% of the worldwide total for private equity funds raised in 2005. The private equity disbursed in the Netherlands amounted to approximately €1.9 billion, or 59% of the total funds raised in the Netherlands in 2005.[12]

The data also enable consideration of investment direction in respect to which regions the institutions will be investing in the future and by how much

[12]Industry statistics for total funds raised worldwide are available from PriceWaterhouseCoopers (2005). These summary figures for amounts in 2005 are for commitments from the institutional investors to the private equity funds, excluding direct company investments. Notice as well that there is a distinction between amounts committed and draw downs of the committed funds (for a related discussion and analysis of Australian evidence on fundraising and draw downs, see Cumming et al., 2005b).

and what mode (direct company investment, direct fund investment, and fund-of-funds investment; see Tables 7.1 and 7.2, Panel C). It should be noted that some large Dutch funds appear to invest a significant fraction of their private equity allocation outside the Netherlands. Of these, three institutions plan to allocate all of their private equity investments in Europe (outside of the Netherlands), one institution plans on allocating all of its private equity investments in the United States, and another institution plans on allocating one-third of its private equity investments in Asia.

Table 7.3 elaborates on the risks and hurdles faced by institutional investors in private equity. Rankings are provided for all types of institutions (pension funds, insurance companies, and banks) in the data in Table 7.3. It is interesting to note that Table 7.3, Panel A, indicates banks on average rank the importance of Basel II to be most important. The banks in the sample also tend to rank the other regulatory changes higher than the rankings provided by pension funds and insurance companies; however, pension funds and insurance companies are relatively more likely to give the FTK and the IFRS higher rankings than Basel II, which is expected given that the FTK and the IFRS are more directly relevant to pension funds and insurance companies than Basel II. The institutions expecting to be invested in private equity in 2006 to 2010 in the sample ranked the FTK as the most important regulatory development for their participation in private equity markets (an average ranking of 3.4 based on a scale of 1 to 5, where 5 is the most important). By contrast, the comparative dearth of regulations in private equity received an average ranking of 2.8, the IFRS received an average rank of 2.7, and Basel II received an average rank of 2.2.

Table 7.3, Panel B, depicts the risks and hurdles perceived by those institutions that will be invested in private equity in 2006–2010. On average, the most important risk faced by institutional investors is the illiquidity of the investment (ranked an average of 3.7 on a scale of 1 to 5, where 5 is the highest). Private equity investments can take many years to bring to fruition (typically at least 7 years) in an exit event. Other important risks associated with private equity investment include lack of performance transparency, risk of default, lack of know-how, and governance costs. There are legal and contractual issues with establishing limited partnership private equity funds (see Gompers and Lerner, 1996, 1999a,b,c; Sahlman, 1990), and writing these contracts is viewed as a major hurdle to private equity investment (ranked an average of 3.4 on a scale of 1 to 5). Table 7.3, Panel C, shows the relative importance of the regulatory issues (Panel A) to the other perceived economic risks and hurdles to investing in private equity. Notice that the comparative rankings for the FTK (2006), the IFRS (2005), and Basel II (2004) have trends corresponding to the timing of the regulatory change (the FTK has the highest rank and occurred more recently in 2006), and this may overstate the relative importance of the FTK regulatory change. This comparative ranking is nevertheless a useful benchmark for the empirical analysis of the survey data and will be used as a robustness check in the empirical analyses following.

Table 7.3 Descriptive Statistics for Rankings for

This table summarizes the data by the characteristics of the institutional investors in terms private equity investment (Panel B), and legal factors affecting investment in private equity expecting to invest in private equity in 2006–2010. Rankings are based on the scale relative rankings (i.e., if the FTK was ranked as the most important factor relative to the least important. Both the absolute rankings (Panel A) and the relative rankings (Panel C)

Panel A. Average Rankings of Importance Changes in the Dutch Legal and

Type of Financial Institution	The New "Financieel Toetingkader" (FTK) in 2006 by the Pensioen & Verzekeringskamer	The New International Financial Reporting Standards (IFRS) in 2005
Pension Fund	3.42	2.37
Insurance Company	3.25	2.88
Bank/ Financial Services	3.50	3.38
All Types of Institutional Investors	3.40	2.71

Panel B. Average Rankings of Other Perceived Risks

Type of Financial Institution	Illiquidity	Lack of Performance Transparency	Risk of Default	Lack of Own Know-how	Governance (Monitoring and Managing) Costs Compared to Other Assets
Pension Fund	3.63	3.74	3.58	3.16	3.16
Insurance Company	3.50	3.25	3.13	2.75	3.13
Bank/ Financial Services	3.38	3.13	3.25	2.88	3.38
All Types of Institutional Investors	3.54	3.49	3.40	3.00	3.20

Factors Associated with Investing in Private Equity

of rankings of factors leading to investment in private equity (Panel A), objectives for (Panel C). The rankings are summarized in this table for the 35 institutions that are where 1 = low and 5 = high in Panels A and B. Panel C presents the average values of other factors, then the number 15 was recorded, and 1 if the factor was indicated as ıre used in the regression analyses in the subsequent tables.

Regulatory Environment for the Institution's Private Equity Investment Strategy	
Implementation of Basel II in 2004	**Dearth of Regulations in Private Equity**
1.74	2.79
2.63	2.75
2.88	2.75
2.20	2.77

and Hurdles Associated with Investment in Private Equity

Legal and Contractual Issues	Management Time and Resource Consumption	Long-Term Commitment	Effort to Convince Internal Committees (e.g., Board of Directors)	Reporting and Corporate Governance	Others
3.26	3.11	2.89	3.11	2.89	1.21
3.25	3.13	3.38	3.00	2.63	1.38
3.25	3.00	3.00	2.63	3.50	1.50
3.26	3.09	3.03	2.97	2.97	1.31

(continued)

Table 7.3

Panel C. Average Comparative Rankings of Importance Changes in the Dutch Legal and Relative to Other Ranked Variables in Panels A–C	
Type of Financial Institution	**The New "Financieel Toetingkader" (FTK) in 2006 by the Pensioen & Verzekeringskamer**
Pension Fund	10.95
Insurance Company	10.62
Bank/Financial Services	10.25
All Types of Institutional Investors	10.71

7.4.4 Difference of Means and Medians Tests and Correlation Matrix

Table 7.4 presents difference of means and medians tests for the subsample of institutional investors that do plan (as at 2005) to invest in private equity in 2006–2010 versus those that do not plan on making such investments. The comparison tests are a useful preliminary look at the data to understand how the characteristics of the two populations of institutional investors differ. The following section considers the robustness of these differences while controlling for other factors in a multivariate setting with sensitivity to robustness checks.

The data indicate a number of statistically significant differences between investors that do and do not plan on investing in private equity. First, the mean and median level of assets is much higher among those institutional investors that do plan on investing in private equity. This result is expected because smaller institutions are required to adhere to capital adequacy ratios such that the contract and monitoring costs of investing in private equity may outweigh benefits for smaller-scale investments. Moreover, smaller institutions are less likely to have access to the top performing funds (Lerner et al., 2005). As well, as would be expected, Table 7.4 indicates that those institutions that expect a higher return from investing in private equity are more likely to invest in private equity.

Second, the institutions' rankings of the degree of the importance of a comparative dearth of regulations in private equity are higher for those institutions that do not plan on investing in private equity than those institutions that do plan on investing in private equity. The mean difference is marginally insignificant at the 10% level of significance, while the median difference is statistically significant (however, the relative ranking based on the information provided in Table 7.3 is statistically insignificant). This is somewhat suggestive that the dearth of regulation of private equity funds somewhat discourages institutional investors to invest in private equity.

Third, the introduction of legislation designed to bring about clarity and harmonization in the ways institutional investors are regulated (via the FTK, the IFRS, and Basel II) all increase the likelihood that an institutional investor

(continued)

Regulatory Environment for the Institution's Private Equity Investment Strategy		
The New International Financial Reporting Standards (IFRS) in 2005	**Implementation of Basel II in 2004**	**Dearth of Regulations in Private Equity**
4.32	6.84	7.89
8.75	9.37	8.62
7.25	11.00	8.25
6.00	8.37	8.14

will invest in private equity. More specifically, the data indicate that institutions that place greater importance on such regulations generally are more likely to invest in private equity. These results show a greater extent of robustness relative to the dearth of regulations ranking. Regardless, further multivariate analyses are provided following.

A potential concern with regard to the ranking variables and the decision to invest in private equity is the direction of causality. To deal with this issue, we asked the respondents to rank their perception of the importance of the dearth of regulations, the FTK, the IFRS, and Basel II, and asked other information about their asset allocation strategies. We also presented a counterfactual to the respondents: We asked if they would change their ranking (to any of the ranked factors) if they altered their allocations to private equity and other asset classes (by altering the allocation to private equity by +/− 1%, and 2%—that is, both increasing and decreasing where possible). The respondents did not indicate a change in their rankings associated with these counterfactuals; rather, they offered rankings based on how important they felt those issues were, and their perception was not contingent on their investment allocations. As such, consistent with the data source, we take the view that rankings are not endogenous to investment allocations.

Table 7.5 provides a correlation matrix across a number of different variables to shed further light on the univariate relations in the data. Generally speaking, the correlations provide further support for the comparison tests presented in Table 7.4, as well as provide insights into factors related to the change in private equity allocations from 2005 to 2006 to 2010. Larger institutions—institutions that expect relatively greater returns to private equity, institutions that rank FTK, IFRS, and Basel II higher, and institutions that rank the dearth of regulations of private equity funds lower—are all more likely to invest in private equity. Also, it is noteworthy in Table 7.5 that pension funds rank the importance of Basel II and the IFRS as being less important, while banks rank them as being more important. The other correlations provide insight into the relations between the variables.

Table 7.4 Difference of Means and Medians Tests

This table presents difference of means and medians tests as well as asset sizes and expected returns to private equity relative to public equity, as well as for the rank of the importance of the dearth of legal restrictions for the decision to invest in private equity. As indicated in Tables 7.1–7.3, this absolute ranking value is based on a 1–5 scale. Ranks are also provided relative to other ranked variables indicated in Table 7.3. *, **, *** Statistically significant at the 10%, 5%, and 1% levels, respectively. The medians test is the two-sample equivalent of the one-sample Sign-Test and this test is just as crude and insensitive; however, because there are so few assumptions, a statistically significant result is very convincing; see http://www.fon.hum.uva.nl/Service/Statistics/Median_Test.html for details on the calculations. The medians test result in this table for the absolute values of the rankings indicates that the median rank of the importance of the dearth of legal restrictions for the decision of whether or not to invest in private equity is higssher for those institutions not planning on investing in private equity.

	Planning on Investing in Private Equity in 2006–2010			Not Planning on Investing in Private Equity in 2006–2010			Difference of Means Test	Difference of Medians Test
	Number of Observations	Mean	Median	Number of Observations	Mean	Median		
Assets (Million Euros)	35	10,114.29	2000	65	1,866.15	500	3.70***	p <= 0.000***
Expected Return on Private Equity in Excess of Public Equity (Basis Points)	35	252.57	250	65	48.62	50	5.91***	p <= 0.000***

Absolute Rankings of Legal Variables								
Rank of Importance of Dearth of Legal Restrictions	35	2.77	3	65	3.02	3	−1.55	p <= 0.014**
FTK (2006)	35	3.40	4	65	2.17	2	5.77***	p <= 0.003***
IFRS (2005)	35	2.71	3	65	1.97	2	3.68***	p <= 0.546
Basel II (2004)	35	2.20	2	65	1.25	1	4.58***	p <= 0.008***
Relative Rankings of Legal Variables (Relative to Other Factors Indicated in Table 7.3)								
Rank of Importance of Dearth of Legal Restrictions	35	8.14	9	65	8.72	9	−0.79	p <= 0.748
FTK (2006)	35	10.71	12	65	5.06	5	7.90***	p <= 0.052*
IFRS (2005)	35	6.00	5	65	2.15	2	4.81***	p <= 0.181
Basel II (2004)	35	8.37	9	65	4.62	4	4.70***	p <= 0.084*

Table 7.5 Correlation

This table presents correlation coefficients across selected variables as defined in Table 7.1. Correlations sample of 100 Dutch institutions.

		(1)	(2)	(3)	(4)	(5)	(6)	(7)	(8)	(9)
(1)	All PE 2006–2010	1.00								
(2)	All PE 2006–2010 Less All PE 2005	0.39	1.00							
(3)	Dutch PE 2006–2010	0.28	0.02	1.00						
(4)	Dutch PE 2006–2010 Less Dutch PE 2005	−0.08	−0.08	0.30	1.00					
(5)	European PE 2006–2010	0.60	0.35	−0.02	−0.17	1.00				
(6)	European PE 2006–2010 Less European PE 2005	0.08	0.29	0.01	**−0.21**	0.42	1.00			
(7)	U.S. PE 2006–2010	0.49	0.32	−0.08	−0.10	0.49	0.11	1.00		
(8)	U.S. PE 2006–2010 Less U.S. PE 2005	0.16	0.46	−0.05	−0.13	0.21	0.13	0.42	1.00	
(9)	Asia PE 2006–2010	0.41	0.29	−0.02	−0.02	0.17	−0.10	0.28	0.19	1.00
(10)	Asia PE 2006–2010 less Asian PE 2005	0.05	−0.13	0.03	−0.03	0.05	0.06	0.04	**−0.22**	**−0.51**
(11)	Rest of World PE 2006–2010	0.22	0.08	−0.04	0.00	0.25	0.26	0.15	−0.03	0.06
(12)	Rest of World PE 2006–2010 Less Rest of World PE 2005	−0.11	0.08	−0.01	0.00	0.16	0.29	−0.17	0.01	−0.03

Matrix

significant at the 5% level are highlighted in bold and underline font. Correlations are for the full

(10)	(11)	(12)	(13)	(14)	(15)	(16)	(17)	(18)	(19)	(20)
1.00										
−0.03	1.00									
−0.12	**0.65**	1.00								

(continued)

Table 7.5

		(1)	(2)	(3)	(4)	(5)	(6)	(7)	(8)	(9)
(13)	Rank Dearth of Legal Restrictions	−0.23	−0.12	−0.36	−0.19	−0.01	−0.01	0.00	0.05	−0.02
(14)	FTK	0.44	0.27	0.24	−0.08	0.56	0.25	0.36	0.25	0.15
(15)	IFRS	0.30	0.12	0.08	−0.03	0.34	0.02	0.35	0.13	−0.09
(16)	Basel II	0.38	−0.07	0.11	0.12	0.49	0.06	0.41	−0.04	0.01
(17)	Pension Fund	0.09	0.13	−0.09	−0.10	0.06	0.19	−0.02	0.06	0.10
(18)	Insurance Company	−0.17	−0.19	0.14	0.15	−0.07	−0.12	−0.07	−0.08	−0.06
(19)	Bank/ Financial Institution	0.07	0.05	−0.04	−0.04	0.01	−0.11	0.11	0.01	−0.07
(20)	Log (Assets)	0.29	0.18	0.14	−0.02	0.38	−0.07	0.46	0.10	0.14
(21)	Log (Excess Expected Basis Points for PE)	0.30	0.14	0.11	−0.01	0.35	0.07	0.26	0.06	0.16

For conciseness, we excluded from Table 7.5 variables for the mode of investment (direct company investments, direct fund investments, and fund-of-funds investments). Among those excluded variables, it is most noteworthy that the different types of regulatory harmonization efforts are all positively associated with higher percentages of fund-of-funds investments. With the level of fund-of-funds investments in 2006 to 2010, the correlations are 0.70 for FTK, 0.36 for IFRS, and 0.29 for Basel II, and all significant at the 5% level. With the change in levels from 2005 to 2006 to 2010, the correlation with FTK is 0.45 and significant at the 5% level, but the IFRS and Basel II correlations are statistically insignificant.

7.5 Multivariate Analyses

This section examines a number of regressions that are presented in Table 7.6. Table 7.6, Panel A, presents logit analyses of the probability that an institutional investor will allocate capital to private equity in 2006–2010. Also, Panel A presents OLS regression analyses of the planned percentage of capital to be allocated to private equity funds in 2006–2010, as well as a specification with

(*continued*)

(10)	(11)	(12)	(13)	(14)	(15)	(16)	(17)	(18)	(19)	(20)
0.04	−0.03	0.00	1.00							
−0.08	0.09	0.11	−0.07	1.00						
0.16	−0.05	−0.07	0.12	0.47	1.00					
0.10	0.03	−0.03	0.02	0.44	0.44	1.00				
−0.08	0.13	0.04	−0.09	−0.03	−0.26	−0.25	1.00			
0.10	−0.11	−0.02	0.16	−0.05	0.11	0.11	−0.65	1.00		
−0.01	−0.05	−0.02	−0.06	0.09	0.21	0.20	−0.55	−0.28	1.00	
0.11	0.08	−0.18	0.09	0.37	0.37	0.28	−0.33	0.09	0.33	1.00
0.01	0.11	0.01	−0.04	0.29	0.16	0.15	−0.10	−0.04	0.17	0.36

a dependent variable measured as the change in percentage allocations from 2005 to 2006–2010. Notice that the benchmark year is 2005 (the year of data collection), while 2006–2010 is used as the comparison horizon because it takes at least a few years for institutional investors to reach desired allocations in private equity through draw downs of committed capital (Cumming et al., 2005; Gompers and Lerner, 1999). Panel B presents ordered logit estimates for changes to private equity allocations from 2005 to 2006–2010. In Panel B, the left-hand-side (LHS) variable is equal to 0 if there is a reduction in the allocation, 1 if there is no change in the allocation, and 2 if there is an increase in the allocation. Panel C presents regressions that explain regional differences in private equity allocations (Europe and the United States) and the mode of investment (by fund-of-funds). In total, 16 different regressions are presented in Panels A–C. Alternative specifications were also considered.[13]

[13]One type of alternative specification reported in an earlier draft was a set of Heckman (1976, 1979) regressions. That is, we first considered the probability that the institutional investor invests in private equity and then considered the fraction of investment in private equity and in a specific region. The results were quite robust to alternative specifications, but the use of different variables in the first and second step regressions was difficult to rationalize. Other types of alternative specifications used alternative right-hand-side variables (such as those summarized in Tables 4.1–4.3). These alternative specifications yielded very similar regression results and are available upon request.

Table 7.6 Logit, Ordered Logit, and OLS

This table presents, in Panel A Models 1–2, logit regression estimates of the probability of investment in OLS estimates of the percentage of the amount invested in PE investment relative to assets managed for the were invested in PE in 2005 or 2006–2010. Panel B Models 6–10 present ordered logit regression estimates 2006–2010 from 2005. Panel C Models 11–16 consider the extent of allocations for fund-of-funds PE United States. The dependent variable in Models 3–5 and 11–16 is ln(Y/(1 – Y)), where Y is the percentage unbiased estimates associated with percentages bounded below by zero or bounded above by 100%.For from 2005, = 1 if allocation to PE did not change in 2006–2010 from 2005 or if no allocation to PE, are as defined in Table 7.1. The logit models in Panel A present the marginal effects, not the standard logit significance. The total sample of firms comprises 100 Dutch institutional investors described in Tables 7.1–7.3. significant at the 10%, 5%, and 1% levels, respectively.

Panel A. Logit and OLS Analyses

	Mean of RHS Variable (Marginal Effects Are Computed at Means)	Model 1		Model 2	
		Logit Probability of PE Allocation in 2006–2010		Logit Probability of PE Allocation in 2006–2010	
		Marginal Effect	t-Statistic	Marginal Effect	t-Statistic
Constant		−2.468	−3.483***	−0.897	−2.564**
Log (Assets)	7.12	0.199	3.231***	0.088	1.794*
Log (Excess Expected Return on PE)	3.20	0.058	1.732*	0.100	2.806***
Pension Fund	0.56	0.513	2.921***	0.136	0.992
Insurance Company	0.25	0.378	1.281	0.099	0.556
Degree of Importance of Dearth of Regulations in PE	2.93	−0.323	−2.597***		
Dearth of Regulations Relative Rank	8.52			−0.014	−0.854
FTK	2.60	0.199	2.108**		
FTK Relative Rank	7.04			0.059	2.730***
IFRS	2.23	0.046	0.466		
Basel II	1.58	0.370	2.601***		
Model Diagnostics					
Number of Observations		100		100	
Number of Observations Where LHS = 1		35		35	
Pseudo R^2 (Adjusted R^2 for Models 3–5)		0.605		0.547	
Log Likehood Function		−25.547		−29.330	
Chi-square Statistic (f-Statistic for Models 3–5)		78.395***		70.829***	

Estimates of Private Equity (PE) Allocations

PE by a Dutch institutional investor in the period 2006–2010. Panel A Models 3–4 present full sample of 100 institutions, while Model 5 uses the subsample of 37 institutions that of the probability of PE investments increasing, staying the same, or decreasing in investments, PE investments in Europe outside the Netherlands, and PE investments in the value for the respective model. This transformation of the dependent variable enables Models 6–10, the dependent variable = 2 if allocations to PE increased in 2006–2010 and = 0 if allocation to PE decreased in 2006–2010 from 2005. The independent variables coefficients, in order to explicitly show the economic significance alongside the statistical White's (1980) HCCME estimator is used in all regressions. *, **, *** Statistically

Allocation to Private Equity (PE)

For Models 3–5, the LHS Percentage Variable Is Transformed as ln (Y/(1 − Y)).					
Model 3		Model 4		Model 5	
OLS of % PE Allocation in 2006–2010		**OLS of % PE Allocation in 2006–2010**		**OLS of % PE Allocation in 2006–2010 for Subsample That Was in PE in 2005 and/or Will Allocate to PE in 2006–2010**	
Coefficient	**t-Statistic**	**Coefficient**	**t-Statistic**	**Coefficient**	**t-Statistic**
−5.914	−11.766***	−5.759	−11.524***	−3.731	−5.594***
0.132	2.414**	0.121	2.442**	0.026	0.409
0.029	1.991**	0.022	1.428	−0.020	−0.429
0.472	2.660***	0.293	1.306	0.755	3.120***
0.065	0.364	−0.057	−0.275	−0.295	−1.061
−0.216	−1.787*			−0.260	−1.885*
		−0.019	−0.913		
0.214	2.616***			0.222	2.257**
		0.106	5.956***		
0.089	1.109			−0.031	−0.355
0.246	2.587***			0.152	1.333
100		100		37	
0.469		0.471		0.248	
−84.170		−85.072		−31.241	
11.94***		15.70***		2.49**	

(continued)

Table 7.6

	Mean of RHS Variable (Marginal Effects Are Computed at Means)	Panel B. Ordered Logit Analyses of the Change in For Models 6–10, the LHS variable = 2 if Allocations to Private from 2005 or if No Allocation to PE, and = 0 if Allocation to PE				
		Model 6				
		Coefficient	t-Statistic	Marginal Effect LHS = 0	Marginal Effect LHS = 1	Marginal Effect LHS = 2
Constant		0.570	1.237			
Log (Assets)	7.12					
Log (Excess Expected Return on PE)	3.20					
Pension Fund	0.56	0.063	0.190	−0.007	−0.010	0.018
Insurance Company	0.25	−0.433	−1.134	0.059	0.051	−0.110
Degree of Importance of Dearth of Regulations in PE	2.93					
Dearth of Regulations Relative Rank	8.52					
FTK	2.60	0.418	3.314***	−0.048***	−0.070***	0.117***
FTK Relative Rank	7.04					
IFRS	2.23					
Basel II	1.58					
Ordered Logit Cutoff Parameter		2.427	10.145***			
Model Diagnostics						
Number of Observations	100					
Number of Observations Where LHS = 0	7					
Number of Observations Where LHS = 1	71					
Number of Observations Where LHS = 2	22					
Pseudo R^2	0.094					
Log Likehood Function	−69.046					
Chi-square Statistic	14.392***					

(*continued*)

Allocations to Private Equity (PE) in 2006–2010 Relative to 2005

Equity (PE) Increased in 2006–2010 from 2005, = 1 if Allocation to PE Did Not Change in 2006–2010
Decreased in 2006–2010 from 2005.

Model 7		Model 8		Model 9		Model 10	
Coefficient	t-Statistic	Coefficient	t-Statistic	Coefficient	t-Statistic	Coefficient	t-Statistic
0.947	5.880***	−0.011	−0.013	1.347	1.453	0.018	0.020
		0.107	1.158	0.110	1.200	0.103	1.094
		0.003	0.067	0.002	0.037	0.003	0.067
0.081	0.244	0.208	0.587	0.201	0.562	0.185	0.503
−0.478	−1.263	−0.363	−0.925	−0.404	−1.037	−0.370	−0.937
		−0.043	−0.232			−0.059	−0.319
				−0.021	−0.532		
		0.359	2.634***			0.374	2.332**
0.101	3.228***			0.086	2.555**		
						0.151	0.878
						−0.178	−1.094
2.438	10.086***	2.453	10.108***	2.466	10.043***	2.487	10.029***
100		100		100		100	
7		7		7		7	
71		71		71		71	
22		22		22		22	
0.091		0.104		0.103		0.115	
−69.323		68.293		−68.403		−67.492	
13.839***		15.900***		15.678***		17.500***	

(*continued*)

Table 7.6

Panel C. OLS Estimates of the Change in Percentage

	Mean of RHS Variable in Full Sample	For Models 11–16, the LHS Percentage					
		Model 11		Model 12		Model 13	
		OLS of % PE Allocation in 2006–2010 to Fund-of funds		OLS of Change in % PE Allocation in 2006–2010 from 2005 for Fund-of-funds		OLS of % PE Allocation in 2006–2010 to Europe Outside the Netherlands	
		Coefficient	t-Statistic	Coefficient	t-Statistic	Coefficient	t-Statistic
Constant		−6.232	−24.885***	−0.968	−3.706***	−5.668	−17.557***
Log (Assets)	7.12	0.082	3.272***	−0.027	−1.410	0.084	2.290**
Log (Excess Expected Return on PE)	3.20	0.021	2.682***	0.005	1.418	0.023	2.123**
Pension Fund	0.56	0.386	3.583***	0.075	1.079	0.284	2.110**
Insurance Company	0.25	0.092	0.884	0.091	1.062	−0.011	−0.071
Degree of Importance of Dearth of Regulations in PE	2.93	0.044	0.661	0.027	0.408	−0.059	−0.736
FTK	2.60	0.307	4.701***	0.201	3.364***	0.131	2.002**
IFRS	2.23	0.028	0.477	−0.033	−0.813	0.016	0.322
Basel II	1.58	0.014	0.285	−0.028	−0.755	0.225	2.248**
Model Diagnostics							
Number of Observations		100		100		100	
Adjusted R^2		0.541		0.184		0.424	
Log Likehood Function		−40.631		−23.048		−52.570	
f-Statistic		15.57***		3.79***		10.11***	

Notice that the regression with the dependent variable is a percentage term (Panels A and C of Table 7.6), the left-hand-side variable is transformed so that it is not bound between 0% and 100%, in a standard way of modeling fractions (see, e.g., Bierens, 2003) so the residuals and estimates have properties consistent with assumptions underlying OLS. Specifically, if Y is a dependent variable that is bound between 0 and 1 (i.e., a fraction), then a possible way to

(continued)

Allocation to PE in 2005 to 2006–2010					
Variable Is Transformed as ln(Y/(1 – Y)).					
Model 14		Model 15		Model 16	
OLS of Change in % PE Allocation in 2006–2010 from 2005 for Europe outside the Netherlands		OLS of % PE Allocation in 2006–2010 to the United States		OLS of Change in % PE Allocation in 2006–2010 from 2005 for the United States	
Coefficient	t-Statistic	Coefficient	t-Statistic	Coefficient	t-Statistic
−0.041	−0.615	−5.449	−12.445***	−0.795	−7.015***
−0.009	−1.400	0.124	3.183***	0.008	1.081
0.001	0.221	0.007	0.712	−0.004	−0.666
0.039	1.868*	0.252	1.803*	0.009	0.248
0.011	0.385	0.015	0.125	−0.019	−0.359
0.005	0.318	−0.085	−1.056	0.012	0.506
0.044	1.968**	0.015	0.290	0.055	2.218**
−0.009	−0.545	0.047	0.857	0.012	0.541
0.001	0.039	0.072	1.270	−0.029	−1.191
100		100		100	
0.062		0.258		0.058	
78.752		−41.592		49.898	
1.82*		5.30***		1.76*	

model the distribution of Y conditional on a vector X of predetermined variables, including 1 for the constant term, is to assume that

$$Y = \frac{\exp(\beta' X + U)}{1 + \exp(\beta' X + U)} = \frac{1}{1 + \exp(-\beta' X - U)}$$

where U is an unobserved error term. Then

$$\ln(Y/(1 - Y)) = \beta'X + U$$

which, under standard assumptions on the error term U, can be estimated by OLS.[14]

Following, we first describe the impact of harmonization of regulations on institutional investors on allocations to private equity and then the impact of a dearth of regulations on private equity funds. Thereafter, we discuss the effect of nonregulatory factors on private equity allocations.

7.5.1 The Impact of Institutional Investor Regulatory Harmonization on Institutional Investor Allocations to Private Equity

The evidence strongly supports the view that the FTK has facilitated Dutch institutional investor participation in private equity. Model 1 in Table 7.6, Panel A, indicates an increase in the ranking of the FTK by 1 on a scale of 1 to 5 indicates Dutch institutional investors are 19.9% more likely to participate in private equity, and this effect is statistically significant at the 5% level. For the alternative specification of the FTK relative rank variable (for which 15 means the highest ranked factor, while 1 means the lowest ranked factor of the 15 factors ranked in Table 7.3), Model 2 indicates an increase in the relative ranking of the FTK by 1 increases the probability of investment in private equity by 5.9%.[15]

In addition to the effect of the FTK, Model 1 indicates Basel II significantly increases the probability of institutional investment in private equity, but the IFRS has not had an impact. The economic significance of Basel II in Model 1 is such that an increase in the ranking by 1 on a scale of 1 to 5 increases the probability of participation by 37.0%, and this effect is statistically significant at the 1% level. The IFRS variable, by contrast, is statistically insignificant in Model 1. The significance and magnitude of the FTK and Basel II variables are quite robust to inclusion/exclusion of the other ranking variables, unlike the IFRS variable. For instance, in specifications (not reported for reasons of conciseness) where the FTK and Basel II variables are excluded and the other variables in Model 1 are included, the IFRS variable is statistically significant at the 5% level, and the economic significance is such that an increase

[14]For some regressions, some of the fractions for the left-hand-side variables are exactly equal to 0, which makes the ratio ln(Y/(1 − Y)) undefined. We deal with this by adding 0.01 to Y to avoid cases where Y is equal to 0. The results are quite robust to alternative magnitudes of this "correction" term. For further robustness checks, we considered OLS and tobit regressions on the nontransformed dependent variable (although those specifications are not ideal since the left-hand-side variable is not bounded in the OLS case, and not bounded above for the tobit case). While neither solution is perfect, the results pertaining to the effect of the legal variables of interest were not materially different relative to that reported herein.

[15]This effect was similar for regressions for the relative rank of the FTK and Basel II but not presented for reasons of conciseness. Notice that the rankings of the FTK, Basel II, and the IFRS are not presented in the same regressions due to the high collinearity between these variables (Table 4.5).

in the ranking by 1 increases the probability of investment in private equity by 13.4%. However, the IFRS is statistically insignificant in the specifications where FTK and Basel II are also included.

The FTK rank is significantly related to the percentage allocated to private equity in each of Models 3 and 4 in Panel A (for the dependent variable in percentage levels in 2006–2010) and Model 5 in Panel A (for the dependent variable in percentage levels for the subsample that has been invested in private equity in 2005 and/or will be invested in 2006–2010). Relative to the mean values, an increase in the ranking by 1 on a scale of 1 to 5 (a 1 standard deviation change) is associated with approximately 0.4% more private equity investment in Model 3 with all institutions considered. The economic significance is greater at 0.9% in Model 5 for the subsample of institutional investors that are in private equity in 2005 and/or plan to be in private equity in 2006–2010.[16] Also, there is statistically significant evidence that Basel II facilitates investment in private equity in Model 3 with an economic significance that is slightly greater than that for the FTK variable. For the alternative specifications with the FTK relative rank variable in Model 4, an increase in the relative ranking by 1 is significantly associated with an approximately 0.2% increase in the level of private equity investment in 2006–2010.

The ordered logit models (Models 6–10 in Panel B) show similar significance of the FTK rank variable (Models 6, 8, and 10) and the FTK relative rank variable (Models 7 and 9). The economic significance is explicitly shown in Model 6 and shows higher rankings by 1 on the scale of 1 to 5 are 11.7% more likely to increase their allocations to private equity, 7.0% less likely to keep constant their allocations to private equity, and 6.8% less likely to reduce their allocations to private equity.[17] These effects are all statistically significant at the 1% level of significance.

In Panel C, the data indicate the FTK rank is statistically associated with fund-of-funds allocations (Models 11 and 12), as well as international allocations in Europe outside the Netherlands (Models 13 and 14) and in the United States (Models 15 and 16). The level of private equity fund-of-funds investment in 2006–2010 is approximately 0.5% higher among funds that rank the FTK higher by 1 on the scale of 1 to 5 (Models 11 and 12). The level of international private equity investment in Europe outside the Netherlands in 2006–2010 is approximately 0.2% higher among funds that rank the FTK higher by 1 (Model 13). Also, Model 13 shows Basel II facilitates international investment in Europe outside the Netherlands, and the statistical and economic significance is twice as large relative to the effect of the FTK in Model 13.

[16]The economic significance for the OLS regressions in Table 4.6, Panels A and C, is calculated by transforming the regression $\ln(Y/(1 - Y)) = X\beta$ to $Y = eX\beta/(1 + eX\beta)$. The economic significance is easily calculated by using the estimated coefficients and mean values of the variables reported in Table 4.6 and then adjusting the variable of interest (in this case the FTK) by 1 and comparing the value of Y in both cases.

[17]The economic significance is presented for Model 5 and not for the other ordered logit models in Table 4.6, Panel B, for reasons of conciseness. The economic significance was not materially different in the different specifications.

Finally, Models 14 and 16 show an increase in the rank of the FTK by 1 gives rise to an increase in European PE investment and U.S. PE investment by approximately 1% in 2006 to 2010 relative to 2005.

7.5.2 The Impact of a Dearth of Private Equity Fund Regulations on Institutional Investor Allocations to Private Equity

The regression estimates in Table 7.6, Panels A–C, indicate evidence consistent with the view that the comparative dearth of regulations in private equity is a barrier to Dutch institutional investor private equity investment. Perhaps most notably, for the logit specification in Model 1 in Table 7.6, Panel A, the data indicate that an increase in the ranking of the importance of a comparative dearth of regulations in private equity by 1 on a scale of 1 to 5 reduces the probability that an institutional investor will invest in private equity by 32.3%. It is worth pointing out, however, that the economic significance of this result is estimated to be lower at 14 to 20% for alternative specifications (not reported for reasons of conciseness) when only one of the ranking variables for FTK, IFRS, and Basel II is included in the regression. Further, note that the statistical significance of the estimates for the dearth of regulations are not perfectly robust, since the logit specification in Model 2 shows the dearth of regulations variable is statistically insignificant when it is specified as a relative ranking.

The regressions for the percentage invested in Panel A also provide some support to the hypothesis that the dearth of regulations inhibits investment in private equity. Model 3 indicates an increase in the ranking by 1 reduces the percentage invested in private equity by 0.3% for all institutional investors in the dataset; similarly, for the full subsample of institutional investors that have been invested in private equity in 2005 or will invest in 2006–2010, Model 5 indicates an increase in the ranking by 1 reduces the percentage invested in private equity by 0.8% for the subsample of institutions that were invested in private equity in 2005 and/or will be invested in 2006–2010. Notice, however, that while these effects are consistent with the univariate trends in the data indicated in Tables 7.4 and 7.5, these effects are not robust to the particular econometric specification in Table 7.6. The alternative specification using the relative rank variable presented in Model 4 indicates the effect is statistically insignificant. As well, the variable for the dearth of regulations variable is not significant in Panel B for the ordered ranking dependent variable, and the evidence in Panel C indicates no statistical relation between the dearth of regulations variable and the mode of PE investment or the location of PE investment.

7.5.3 The Impact of Nonregulatory Factors on Institutional Investor Private Equity Allocations

The regression evidence in Table 7.6, Panels A–C, indicates that nonregulatory factors affect allocations to private equity, including the type of institution, the institutions' asset size, and returns expectations.[18] The data indicate that larger institutional investors invest a greater percentage of assets in private equity (and this is modeled at a diminishing rate with the use of logs): An increase in the assets managed by an institutional investor from €1 billion to €2 billion increases the probability that an institutional investor will invest in private equity by 6.0%, while an increase in assets from €10 billion to €11 billion increases the probability that an institutional investor will invest in private equity by 0.8% (based on Model 1). Larger institutions and higher returns expectations for private equity relative to publicly traded stocks give rise to larger percentages invested (at a diminishing rate based on the log specifications; see Models 3 to 5). Larger institutions are also more likely to invest in private equity fund-of-funds and invest internationally (Models 11, 13, and 15). Higher return expectations for private equity relative to publicly traded stocks are also related to fund-of-funds investments (Model 11) and international investments (Model 13). There is also some evidence that pension funds are 51.3% more likely to invest in private equity than banks and insurance companies (Model 1). The data further indicate pension funds will invest a greater proportion of their assets in private equity than insurance companies and banks (Models 3 and 5), and are more likely to invest this money in fund-of-funds (Model 11), as well as internationally in Europe (outside the Netherlands; see Models 13 and 14) and in the United States (see Model 15).

7.5.4 Summary

Overall, the regression evidence indicated the most robust support for the view that the FTK facilitates private equity investment, fund-of-funds private equity investment, and cross-border private equity investment. The regressions provided some mixed evidence that Basel II was important for private equity investment and no evidence that the IFRS was important for private equity investment. There was significant evidence that the perceived dearth of regulations in private equity to a large degree inhibits private equity investment. The statistical significance of this effect, however, was in some cases contingent on the specification of the regression model. The data also show larger institutions, pension funds, and funds with higher return expectations for private relative to public equity are more likely to invest in private equity and to a greater degree in fund-of-funds and internationally.

7.6 Extensions and Future Research

The data from institutional investors offered in this chapter support the view that more disclosure would bring in more money into private equity. Regardless,

[18]In an earlier draft of this chapter, we also reported evidence that corporate objectives, portfolio diversification objectives, and views on the importance of achieving a yearly rate of return to report to their own beneficiaries were also significant determinants. However, inclusion/exclusion of these variables did not materially affect the legal variables of interest; therefore, we excluded these extraneous variables for reasons of conciseness. Alternative specifications are available upon request.

private equity fund managers vigorously oppose higher disclosure standards. This gives rise to an important question for future work: If private equity funds realized these results, then would they not want to voluntarily disclose? While this question is beyond the scope of our empirical analyses, we nevertheless suggest several issues to consider for future research. First, disclosure imposes additional administrative costs of reporting, and such costs may exceed the benefits of additional deal flow (the number of deals referred to private equity fund managers by entrepreneurs). Disclosure may discourage deal flow from entrepreneurial firms seeking capital, as entrepreneurial firms may not want public reporting of their financing terms (and performance) by their private equity investors. The benefits of disclosure by private equity funds in terms of raising additional capital from their institutional investors may be outweighed by the costs in terms of the quantity and quality of deal flow from entrepreneurs. This study is the first attempt to empirically assess the benefits of increased disclosure in terms of facilitating greater capital commitments from institutional investors to private equity funds (although the costs of increased disclosure have not been empirically quantified).

Second, disclosure may disproportionately benefit nascent private equity fund managers relative to more established private equity fund managers. It is well established that there is persistence in the performance of venture capital and private equity fund returns (past performance is the best predictor of future performance). Established funds with a successful track record do not have problems raising additional capital for follow-on funds; in fact, established funds typically have long wait lists among institutional investors that would like to invest. Hence, greater disclosure disproportionately benefits newly established private equity funds relative to established funds. Existing well-established private equity funds have an entrenched interest to avoid disclosure as a way to enforce a barrier to entry against new private equity fund managers.

While a full accounting of the costs and benefits has yet to be undertaken, the new evidence in this chapter suggests that there are significant social benefits that warrant further consideration of government intervention mandating greater disclosure. Our analysis strictly focuses on the positive question as to how regulatory changes (specifically, institutions' perceptions of these regulatory changes) influence institutional investor allocations to private equity, and whether the comparative dearth of regulations in private equity influenced institutional investors' attitudes towards investing in private equity. The data herein also do not address the question as to whether there could exist better regulatory harmonization measures that would facilitate private equity investment (other than the FTK, the IFRS, or Basel II). These topics are beyond the scope of our chapter, and further work on this topic is warranted.

7.7 Conclusions

In this chapter we considered the relation between regulation and institutional investment in private equity, including the level of investment, geographic concentration, and vehicle for investment. We introduced a new detailed dataset from a survey of Dutch institutional investors. The data indicated evidence consistent with the view that Dutch institutional investor participation in private equity is negatively affected by the comparative dearth of regulations in private equity. This effect is attributable to an increase in screening, search, and monitoring costs associated with low disclosure standards for private equity investment.

Further, the data showed regulatory harmonization of institutional investors facilitates investment in private equity, as well as international investment in private equity. In particular, the data supported the propositions that harmonization of standards from the FTK (regulation of portfolio management standards such as matching of assets and liabilities) has facilitated clarity and certainty for institutions that desired to invest in private equity. While our data do not enable an examination of the question as to whether there could exist better regulatory harmonization measures that would better facilitate private equity investment, our data are nevertheless consistent with the view that the FTK has had a more robust and pronounced effect than Basel II, which in turn has had a more robust and pronounced effect than the IFRS. The FTK has clearly had the greatest impact for Dutch institutional investors investing in private equity within the Netherlands and abroad.

In sum, the data in this chapter support the view that harmonized regulatory standards for institutional investors enable different types of institutional investors and institutional investors in different countries to contribute capital to private equity fund managers. Further, the dearth of regulations surrounding private equity fund managers discourages institutional investors from contributing capital to private equity funds. One particular concern, for example, surrounds the reporting standards on valuations of unexited investments (an issue addressed further in Chapter 22). It appears that interest in improving disclosure standards for private equity funds is of interest to some but not all market participants. Market participants themselves have had difficulties resolving this debate on disclosure standards.[19]

Key Terms

Limited partnership
Institutional investors
Capital commitment
Draw down
Direct company investment
Direct fund investment
Fund-of-funds
Financieel Toetsingskader (FTK)
Employment Retirement Income Security Act (ERISA)
International Financial Reporting Standards (IFRS)
Basel II

[19]See footnotes 4 to 7 and accompanying text.

Discussion Questions

7.1. How might private equity fund managers distort returns reported to institutional investors, and what are the advantages and disadvantages to such misreporting?
7.2. Why is private equity fund disclosure of returns relevant to institutional investors, and how might returns disclosures affect capital commitments to private equity?
7.3. Would you expect misreports of returns to have a differential impact on institutional investors that have never committed capital to private equity funds relative to investors that have for many years committed capital to private equity funds?
7.4. Why do you think the private equity industry associations and limited partner associations had such difficulty in agreeing on performance reporting standards? Do you think these standards should be formal rules for auditing or merely guidelines?
7.5. Why is regulatory harmonization important for private equity fundraising? Do you think regulatory harmonization is more important for different types of institutional investors within the same country or for different institutional investors across countries? Do you think your perspective will be the same in 10 or 20 years from now?
7.6. How are the FTK, Basel II, and IFRS relevant for private equity? Which is relatively more important for private equity?
7.7. Is the dearth of regulation of private equity funds more important than the design of institutional investor regulation for facilitating investment in private equity? Explain why or why not.

8 Specialized Investment Mandates

8.1 Introduction and Learning Objectives

Private equity funds are established with stated objectives in terms of the focus for investments. Part of the fund objectives may include the stage of entrepreneurial firm development and/or industry. Fund objectives are set out in the contract establishing the limited partnership to ensure that every partner is clear about what the objectives are (see Chapter 4). Fund managers, however, may deviate from the stated objective. This type of deviation is known as a style drift. Fund managers may style drift to increase their pool of investment opportunities, diversify the fund to minimize risks, and seek better investments as opportunities change over time (indeed, funds last for 10 to 13 years). However, fund managers that do style drift risk the loss of reputational capital for not following their stated objectives, as well as potential litigation for breach of contract. A style drift may also increase the risk faced by a fund where managers invest outside their area(s) of expertise. At a minimum, an already risky investment is further exacerbated by this added complexity in the sense that institutional investors face a deviation from their planned risk/return profile for their private equity investment allocations.

Cumming et al. (2004b) study style drift among a sample of U.S. private equity funds in terms of the stage firm development of focus of the fund (recall the stages identified in Chapter 1). They find, first, that style drift is more common among older private equity fund managers (here we refer to the organization): An increase in the age of the private equity fund manager by five years increases the probability of style drift by 1%, and similarly, each successive private equity fund managed by that organization is 0.5% more likely to experience style drift. Hence, for example, an experience fund manager like Kleiner Perkins with over 30 years is approximately 6% more likely to style drift than a first-time fund manager. Second, Cumming et al. (2004b) show that changes in market conditions from the time of fund formation to the time of investment significantly affect the propensity to style drift. Specifically, a 20% increase in NASDAQ from the time of fundraising to the time of investment gives rise to a 4% reduction in the probability of a style drift by funds committed to early-stage investments but a 5% increase in the probability of a style drift by funds committed to later-stage investments. Relatedly, the Internet Bubble period was associated with a 4% lower probability of a style drift among funds committed to an earlier-stage focus and a 0.5% higher probability of a style drift among funds committed to a later-stage focus. The intuition is that earlier-stage investments are more attractive to early-stage– and late-stage–focused funds in times of better market conditions, since there are greater investment opportunities. Third, they show style drifts are associated with a 4% increase in the probability of an IPO exit, controlling for other factors that might affect exit outcomes. This suggests that due to the potential reputation costs associated with style drifts just discussed, private equity funds will style drift only for investments that are more likely to yield favorable realizations.

While style drift is a risk faced by many institutional investors, as they become more aware of this potential risk of deviation, institutional investors are paying more attention to fund investment mandates and the compliance of such mandates by private equity fund managers. With this recent attention, private equity fund managers have found an avenue to differentiate themselves from the pack, so to speak. Not only are they voluntarily including restrictive covenants related to investment mandates and investment styles in their contracts to restore confidence, they are also seeking new areas of specialized investments to differentiate themselves.

In this chapter, we examine a particular way in which private equity fund managers have begun to differentiate themselves and to restore confidence in the industry: the area of social responsibility. The focus of socially responsible investment in private equity is particularly timely. For example, Kleiner Perkins, one of Silicon Valley's leading venture capital fund managers, hired Nobel Peace Prize winner Al Gore in 2007 to assist them in their focus on socially responsible investment.[1] We will not focus on *when* fund managers deviate from the socially responsible investment goal, but rather we examine the preliminary question as to *why* institutional investors and private equity fund managers are paying an increasing amount of attention to this rather specialized area of socially responsible investment.

In particular, we empirically investigate the factors that influence institutional investors to allocate capital to socially responsible private equity investments. Private equity fund managers act as financial intermediaries between institutional investors and entrepreneurial firms. Private equity is a viable and important asset class for institutional investors,[2] and there has been a growing trend toward socially responsible investment practices.[3] While prior work has examined the role of business ethics in entrepreneurship (see Hannafey, 2003, for a literature review; see also Miles et al., 2004; Spence et al., 2003; Wempe, 2005), no prior study has considered an empirical analysis of the direct intersection

[1]http://money.cnn.com/2007/11/11/news/newsmakers/gore_kleiner.fortune/.

[2]For recent literature on private equity and venture capital, see, for example, Black and Gilson (1998); Cumming and Johan (2006a,b); Gompers and Lerner (1999); Lockett et al. (2002); Manigart et al. (2000); Mayer et al. (2005); Sapienza et al., (1996); and Wright and Lockett (2003).

[3]For recent literature on corporate social responsibility and socially responsible investment, see, for example, Cowton (2002, 2004); Dillenburg et al. (2003); Sparkes and Cowton (2004); Waring and Lewer (2004); Guay et al. (2004); Mill (2006); and Lockett et al. (2006).

between socially responsible investment and private equity (although there has been related work).[4] This issue is nevertheless important for institutional investor capital allocation, as well as for private equity funds and companies seeking capital to undertake socially responsible entrepreneurial activities.

In this chapter we will do the following:

- Consider what motivates an institutional investor to consider investing in a fund with a socially responsible investment mandate
- Empirically compare the importance of an institution's internal organization structure versus legal and economic factors driving socially responsible investment

In this chapter we propose that two elements influence socially responsible institutional investment in private equity: institutional organizational structure and internationalization. In the spirit of research on corporate governance and institutional investors (e.g., Mallin, 2001; Mallin et al., 2005), we introduce in this chapter a new dataset from a survey of Dutch institutional investors that was carried out in 2005. The survey data consist of information from 100 Dutch institutions, 24 of which currently have a socially responsible investment program (of these, 14 include socially responsible private equity investment programs), and 19 plan on adopting a socially responsible investment program over the period 2006–2010 (of these, 5 include socially responsible private equity investment programs). The data contain extremely specific details on the institutions' portfolio management practices, as well as their perceptions of the importance of various economic, legal, and institutional factors that influence their portfolio allocation decisions. Institutional investors' positions regarding their objectives in their strategic asset allocation were sought. More significantly, views regarding the perceived risks and hurdles faced by such investors were sought to determine main concerns in adopting socially responsible investment. The data enable an empirical assessment of institutional investor allocations to socially responsible investment with consideration to controls for a variety of factors potentially pertinent to asset allocation.

The next section outlines the theoretical propositions and testable hypotheses. The data are then introduced alongside summary statistics and multivariate empirical analyses of socially responsible asset allocations by Dutch institutional investors. Limitations are discussed, and suggestions for future research are outlined after the multivariate analyses.

8.2 Why Socially Responsible Investments in Private Equity? Testable Hypotheses

Institutional investors have various motivations in their investment strategies when deciding to allocate capital to equities, bonds, derivatives, and alternative

[4]Most notably, see Maula et al. (2003) for an analysis of social capital and knowledge acquisition in the context of corporate venture capital.

investments, such as private equity. Portfolios are specifically designed to optimally trade off risk and return by allocation of the portfolio to appropriately diversified combinations of assets, with consideration to institutional and regulatory factors, and possibly behavioral biases and decision-making processes. Following up the potential effect that behavioral biases and decision-making processes may have on an institution that is determining current and projected levels of asset allocation, this study seeks to ascertain a potential trend toward investing in a more specialized form of private equity—socially responsible private equity—also sometimes referred to as sustainable private equity.

We propose that two central elements influence socially responsible institutional investment in private equity: the institutions' internal organizational structure and the institutions' external environment in terms of internationalization. The intuition underlying our two main hypotheses applies not only to socially responsible investment in private equity but also other asset classes. However, we focus on socially responsible investment in private equity because it is a new "alternative" asset class that is now being closely scrutinized internally by institutions' decision makers as well as externally by media for its diversification properties and consistent annual returns. Some of the factors discussed following, however, are more directly pertinent only to socially responsible investment in private equity.

First, in regards to internal organizational structure, institutions (or rather their human resource) will have to balance the conflicting needs of their stakeholders. The practice of socially responsible investment does not mean that returns must be sacrificed (Geczy et al., 2003), even though some may hold this perception (for recent survey evidence, see Guyatt, 2005).[5] An effective socially responsible investment program should incorporate the objective to gain the maximum possible return for stakeholders in the institution, at an acceptable risk, with the idea of combining social, moral, legal, and environmental concerns. Any decision made by management or the board of directors will affect each stakeholder differently. As such, decisions on important policies regarding investment and asset allocation, which will directly affect the returns of the institution, are not taken lightly. In an institution where there is decentralized investment decision making, where a general investment team consisting of employees who compete with one another, each employee is more likely to seek to maximize expected returns, as this is the most obvious performance indicator to the management and less likely to risk adopting potentially less profitable socially responsible investment. In an organization where investment decisions are centralized through a chief investment officer (CIO),

[5]In our data (described in the next section), some of the institutional investors ranked socially responsible investment returns quite highly and to be comparable with other asset classes, consistent with recent empirical evidence (see, e.g., Doweell et al., 2000; Schroder, 2003; Ali and Gold, 2002; Geczy et al., 2003; Derwall and Koedijk, 2005; Plantinga and Scholtens, 2001). As well, note that recent evidence indicates socially responsible investments provide significant diversification benefits (Guyatt, 2005; although see also Bello, 2005, for a less optimistic view of the diversification benefits associated with a sample of socially responsible investment funds).

who is not only a member of management but also on the board of directors, it is more probable that innovative (thus untested and risky) socially responsible investment policies be formulated, approved, and implemented. The board of directors, in the exercise of their discretion, will deem their reliance on the CIO's advice sufficient to meet their duty of care to stakeholders, regardless of the outcome of the implementation of the program. This suggests that the presence of a CIO who will take "ownership" and responsibility for the program can facilitate a socially responsible investment policy.[6]

Guyatt (2005, 2006) argues that an impediment to nonstandard investment approaches is the need to justify decisions to those above one in the organizational hierarchy, using "conventional" arguments. Thus, even if socially responsible investment does not lose money, there is a disincentive to invest that way because you have to "stick your neck out" and do without recourse to conventional justifications of investment decisions. This problem is removed or reduced when investment decision making is centralized.

Moreover, there are reputation incentives for compliance with norms of corporate social responsibility that institutions are more likely to comply with when decisions are made centrally. It has also been argued that corporations will adopt corporate social responsibility when they recognize their stakeholders prefer such policies (thereby increasing firm value); corporations will be more likely to recognize and implement the corporate social responsibility preferences of their stakeholders and implement such preferences when decisions about socially responsible investment are made centrally (Small and Zivin, 2002).

Overall, our first primary hypothesis is that socially responsible investment programs are more likely to be adopted by institutions that centralize investment decision making. Our second primary hypothesis relates to the extent to which an institution internationalizes its investments. On the one hand, we may expect socially responsible investment to be more common domestically in view of the fact that institutional investors' stakeholders are primarily based within the country in which they reside, particularly for the Netherlands. Socially responsible investments are not only on the rise as a result of increasing social awareness by institutions but primarily as a result of the increasing public (beneficiary) interest in social responsibility. Thus, the public perception is that institutions need to "return to society," a sense of social responsibility that has been given to them by their stakeholders. And, because charity begins at home, domestic stakeholders likely want to enjoy the benefits that increased corporate social responsibility brings, such as increased adherence to labor and environmental laws by local companies.

On the other hand, there are two primary factors that may lead to a greater focus on socially responsible investment policies among institutions with an international investment focus (Dowell et al., 2000; Dunning, 2003). First,

[6]A related argument could be that more socially responsible people go to work for corporations with centralized decision making (Montgomery and Ramus, 2003).

larger corporations and those with an international or multinational presence typically face public scrutiny with regard to their socially responsible investment policies (Dunning, 2003). Second, long-term returns to socially responsible investments, particularly for international investments over the long run, are reported as being viewed as being very favorable by a significant number of institutional investors in a recent survey (for details, see Guyatt, 2005). Third, it may be easier for Dutch institutions to find viable socially responsible investment opportunities outside the Netherlands in view of its size and a dearth of suitable local socially responsible investments (with the caveat that they may prefer to buy locally because they have greater knowledge of local conditions).

Different regions around the world have different legal standards and social norms in regards to socially responsible investment policies. Most notably, in Asia (Dunning, 2003; Hanna, 2004) and less-well-developed countries with high levels of corruption (Doh et al., 2003), there is comparatively weaker spirit toward socially responsible investments as well as weaker legal standards compared to Europe and North America (Dunning, 2003; Hanna, 2004). Corporate accountability standards tend to be more lax in some countries (particularly less-developed countries) as a way to encourage foreign direct investment. While there is some evidence (e.g., Angel and Rock, 2005) that global corporations often operate at higher standards than those required by local regulation, this has traditionally not been observed in Asia. Therefore, we expect international institutional investments to be less socially responsible in Asia.

In sum, there may be different reasons for investing outside the Netherlands and finding a difference between Europe outside the Netherlands, North America, and Asia. First, sustainable private equity opportunities will be limited in any one country, especially a relatively small one such as the Netherlands. This will tend to make sustainable investments more international than conventional investments, ceteris paribus. Second, it may not just be a question of where other sustainable opportunities are actually located; information about those opportunities is critical. Linguistic, cultural, geographical, and transparency factors are likely to be more favorable to the discovery and take-up of opportunities in Europe outside the Netherlands and North America versus Asia and less-developed countries. Both these issues are discussed with respect to empirical evidence in Cowton (2004).

Thus, our second primary hypothesis is that socially responsible investment opportunities are likely to be limited in the Netherlands, which will tend to make such investments more international than conventional investments, ceteris paribus. Institutional investors are more likely to invest in socially responsible investment in Europe (outside the Netherlands) and North America than in Asia and less-developed countries.

8.2.1 Other Factors Relevant to Socially Responsible Private Equity Investments

The primary objective of institutional investors' asset allocation is to achieve the most optimal trade-off of risk and return. The achievement of this objective, however, will differ in accordance with specific institutional characteristics. For example, a pension fund and a bank will have different funding and solvency requirements, assets and liabilities, and extent of regulatory oversight. Different institutions may exhibit differences in corporate objectives, contributor/stakeholder/beneficiary demographics, and sensitivity to regulatory oversight and accounting rules. Hence, our empirical analyses control for the type of institutional investor (pension funds, insurance companies, and banks/financial institutions).

Private equity fund managers are financial intermediaries between institutional investors and entrepreneurial firms. Institutional investors do not have the time and specialized skill set to carry out due diligence in screening potential private entrepreneurial firms in which to invest, nor do they have the time and skills to efficiently monitor and add value to the investee entrepreneurial firms. The pronounced risks, information asymmetries, and agency problems associated with investments in small, illiquid, and high-tech entrepreneurial firms are the primary explanations for the existence of private investment funds with specialized skill sets to mitigate such problems. We conjecture that institutional investors with larger asset bases are more inclined to invest in private equity and in socially responsible investments that require more extensive due diligence.

Investments in private equity can be carried out as direct fund investments, direct company investments, or fund-of-funds investments. Private equity fund-of-funds allocate their institutional investors' assets in what they perceive to be the top private equity funds; therefore, fund-of-funds remove the decision to invest in a socially responsible manner from the institutional investor. As such, fund-of-funds investments are less likely to be socially responsible because they need to balance the needs of many institutional investors and do so by following a strict profit-maximizing objective. We control for fund-of-funds investments in our empirical tests.

Socially responsible private equity investment decisions may further be influenced by the extent to which institutions are concerned about reporting standards. We may expect increased transparency of investment decisions via International Financial Reporting Standards (IFRS, adopted in 2005, and relevant for reports of private equity investments) increased vulnerability to public perception and pressure, to lead to a greater tendency toward socially responsible investments (consistent with Hillman and Kleim, 2004; Kolk, 2005; Kolk and Tulder, 2001; Kolk et al., 1999; Mallin et al., 2005; McInerney, 2006; and Shaffer, 1995).

We consider other control variables in the empirical analyses. For instance, we control for the expected return on socially responsible investments relative to that of other investments. This expectation is a qualitative ranking of socially responsible investment returns relative to other returns (returns are based on the institutions' self-formed reported ranking of the risk-adjusted return on a simple 1 [low] to 5 [high] scale). The higher the relative expected return for socially responsible investments, the greater the allocation to socially responsible investments. As a qualitative matter, in our interviews most investors felt that socially responsible investment opportunities were lower risk–sustainable investments than most other asset classes (see Guyatt, 2005, for consistent evidence). But we do not separately quantitatively rank risk and return,[7] and we just use the risk-adjusted return ranking. The survey data and summary statistics are described in the next section. Thereafter, multivariate empirical tests are provided and followed by a discussion of future research.

8.3 Data

8.3.1 Methods and Survey Instrument

We introduce in this chapter a new dataset from 100 Dutch institutional investors. The data assembled for this chapter are derived primarily from a survey of Dutch institutional investors carried out between February 2005 and May 2005.[8] This use of surveys was necessary for the research questions considered in this chapter. Data on past and current institutional asset allocation and investment levels in private equity do exist from some venture capital/private equity associations and annual financial reports,[9] but other information, such as projected or future asset allocation, investment objectives, and current and projected socially responsible investment activity, are not available in the public domain and, in our opinion, could only be obtained by survey. Our survey instrument also enabled us to determine the perceived effect the IFRS had on socially responsible investment activity. To verify and enhance data obtained by the survey, follow-up interviews were carried out, and, where possible, reference was made to the institutions' websites and publications.

Notice that there is no clear industry definition of socially responsible investment programs. Institutions, while provided with general guidelines by both regulators and stakeholders, are not as yet bound by any legislation, rules, or regulations, and instead create their own internal policies.[10] Alternative definitions provided in our survey include "negative screens" (e.g., excluding investments

[7]Investors felt that risk was more difficult to rank, since the benchmark against which risk is ranked could vary drastically, and differ at different points in time. As a matter of implementation, we were only able to obtain one ranking for risk-adjusted returns expectations.

[8]Pursuant to identifying the appropriate contact persons, the survey instrument was sent to approximately 1,114 Dutch institutions including 797 pension funds (company pension funds, industrial pension funds, and occupational pension funds); 205 insurance companies; and 112 banks, including universal banks, securities credit institutions, savings banks, mortgage banks, and other financial service providers.

[9]See, for example, www.evca.com for European data and www.nvp.nl for Dutch data.

[10]Public pressure may eventually result in institutional investors being forced to declare to what extent social and environmental criteria are factors in their investment decisions. In some countries (e.g., the United Kingdom) some institutional investors already have to make a declaration.

in areas or industries where moral and/or legal rights are violated, or environmental standards are not met, or firms involved in the production of weapons); "positive screens" (e.g., including investments in alternative fuel industries or educational industries); and "best in class" (an extension of positive screens for investments that demonstrate socially responsible leadership within specific areas or industries). The examples we have listed here are of course not exhaustive but are intended only to illustrate the "ingredients" of a socially responsible investment program to guide the survey respondents. The institutions surveyed in this study were left to decide if their socially responsible investment policies and practices, if any, fell within the scope of an integrated socially responsible investment program that is consistent with industry definitions (Social Investment Forum, 2003).[11]

The instrument we used to obtain the detailed data required about domestic and international socially responsible investment activity by Dutch institutions is a 13-page questionnaire consisting of 32 questions. Robustness is achieved chiefly by framing questions in a way that calls for numeric responses, or a simple "yes" or "no" response. In view of the fact that the potential respondents, while financial institutions, are from different branches of finance, a glossary of terms was provided in the survey to ensure uniformity in defining terms that may not necessarily be used in the same manner across sectors. An overview of the information collected is summarized in Table 8.1, which defines the primary variables used in this study.

While it is easy to see why institutions are moving toward socially responsible investment, we have to acknowledge that the majority of institutional investors do not currently have socially responsible investment programs. Of the 100 institutions surveyed, only 24 currently have a socially responsible investment program for any asset class (of these, 14 include socially responsible private equity investment programs). However, 19 institutions plan on adopting a socially responsible investment program over the period

[11]The Social Investment Forum (2003, page 9) defines socially responsible investing as follows: "Socially responsible investing (SRI) is an investment process that considers the social and environmental consequences of investments, both positive and negative, within the context of rigorous financial analysis. It is a process of identifying and investing in companies that meet certain standards of Corporate Social Responsibility (CSR) and is increasingly practiced internationally. As the Prince of Wales Business Leaders Forum explains: 'Corporate Social Responsibility means open and transparent business practices that are based on ethical values and respect for employees, communities, and the environment. It is designed to deliver sustainable value to society at large, as well as to shareholders.' Whether described as social investing, ethical investing, mission-based investing, or socially aware investing, SRI reflects an investing approach that integrates social and environmental concerns into investment decisions. Social investors include individuals, businesses, universities, hospitals, foundations, pension funds, corporations, religious institutions, and other nonprofit organizations. Social investors consciously put their money to work in ways designed to achieve specific financial goals while building a better, more just and sustainable economy. Social investing requires investment managers to overlay a qualitative analysis of corporate policies, practices, and impacts onto the traditional quantitative analysis of profit potential."

Table 8.1 Variable Definitions and Summary Statistics

This table presents selected variables and descriptive statistics in the dataset of 100 Dutch institutional investors based on data collected in 2005. Dummy variables have minimum values 0 and maximum values of 1, and the mean reflects the percentage of observations that take the value 1.

Variable Name	Definition	Mean	Median	Standard Deviation	Minimum	Maximum	Number of Observations
Socially Responsible Investment Program 2005–2010	A dummy variable equal to 1 for institutions that currently have a socially responsible investment program as at 2005, or plan on adopting one in 2006–2010.	0.43	0	0.50	0.00	1.00	100
Socially Responsible Investment Program 2005	A dummy variable equal to 1 for institutions that currently have a socially responsible investment program as at 2005.	0.24	0	0.46	0.00	1.00	100
Socially Responsible Private Equity Investment Program 2005–2010	A dummy variable equal to 1 for institutions that currently have a socially responsible private equity investment program as at 2005, or plan on adopting one in 2006–2010.	0.19	0	0.39	0.00	1.00	100
Socially Responsible Private Equity Investment Program 2005	A dummy variable equal to 1 for institutions that currently have a socially responsible private equity investment program as at 2005.	0.14	0	0.35	0.00	1.00	100
The Netherlands Domestic Private Equity Investment	The percentage of the institutions' total assets invested in private equity in the Netherlands expected for 2006–2010.	0.25	0	1.27	0.00	9.00	100

European (outside the Netherlands) Private Equity Investment	The percentage of the institutions' total assets invested in private equity in Europe excluding the Netherlands expected for 2006–2010.	0.69	0	1.58	0.00	11.25	100
U.S. Private Equity Investment	The percentage of the institutions' total assets invested in private equity in the United States expected for 2006–2010.	0.41	0	1.00	0.00	5.63	100
Asia Private Equity Investment	The percentage of the institutions' total assets invested in private equity in Asia expected for 2006–2010.	0.05	0	0.25	0.00	2.06	100
Fund-of-fund Investment 2006–2010	The percentage of the institutions' total assets invested in private equity fund-of-fund investments expected for 2006–2010.	0.62	0	1.49	0.00	8.00	100
International Financial Reporting Standards	The institutional investor's rank (1 = low and 5 = high) of the importance of the new International Financial Reporting Standards (IFRS) (2005) for the decision to invest.	2.23	2	0.92	1.00	5.00	100
Rank of Attractiveness of Returns to Sustainable Investment	The institutional investor's rank (1 = low and 5 = high) of the comparative attractiveness of the returns (relative to the risk) of adopting a socially responsible investment program relative to not adopting such a program.	2.49	3	1.16	1.00	5.00	100

(*continued*)

Table 8.1 *(continued)*

Variable Name	Definition	Mean	Median	Standard Deviation	Minimum	Maximum	Number of Observations
Chief Investment Officer Responsibility	A dummy variable equal to 1 for institutions that allocate the responsibility to adopting a socially responsible investment program to a single chief investment officer.	0.08	0	0.27	0.00	1.00	100
Assets (Millions of Euros)	The total assets managed by the institutional investor (in millions of 2005 euros).	4,753.00	800	9,060.41	300	50,000	100
Pension Fund	A dummy variable equal to 1 for a pension fund institutional investor.	0.56	1	0.50	0	1	100
Insurance Company	A dummy variable equal to 1 for an insurance company institutional investor.	0.25	0	0.44	0	1	100
Bank/Financial Institution	A dummy variable equal to 1 for a bank/financial institutional investor.	0.19	0	0.39	0	1	100

2006–2010 (of these, 5 include socially responsible private equity investment programs). Reasons for the hesitance on the part of institutions to enter the socially responsible investment arena may include the perception that with corporate social responsibility, optimal returns may be forfeited. Institutions, at the end of the day, have the main goal of creating and maintaining stakeholder value. While some stakeholders deem social responsibility to be an important factor, others may see it as separate from their main aim of obtaining the best financial returns. The ability to balance stakeholder needs may be more easily achieved by some institutions (or rather the managers and board of directors of these institutions) than by others. The human resource factor in formulating and implementing socially responsible investment programs is also analyzed in this study. Also, many institutions are able to hide behind the cloak of confidentiality to evade calls by their stakeholders to increase social responsibility. They can easily justify their secrecy about policies by the need to protect the same stakeholders who seek increased transparency. This cloak of confidentiality is also the main reason why in this study we have relied on survey responses provided confidentially by respondents.

8.3.2 Potential Sample Selection Bias

One limitation to obtaining data through a survey is the possibility of sample selection bias. While we acknowledge that this is a possibility, we believe from a detailed analysis of the responses received, and the data obtained from the responses, that this concern does not arise in this exercise. First, survey data were gathered for a final sample of 100 institutional investors that consisted of company pension funds, industrial pension funds, occupational pension funds, life and nonlife insurance companies, banks, and other financial service providers. Our sample of respondent institutions includes 56 pension funds, 25 insurance companies, and 19 banks (see Table 8.2). Limitations in our sample size from each sector of the finance industry from which we derived data, as well as the limited information about comparable academic work on institutional investor behavior in private equity, however, make reliable statistical comparisons of our sample relative to the population of other types of investors in private equity intractable.

Second, a broad array of respondents replied to the survey. For example, the data show the median respondent asset size of €800,000,000, with the average being €4,665,000,000, indicating respondents were of a variety of asset sizes. The possibility of sample selection bias is further reduced by the presence of institutions that do not currently allocate any of their assets to private equity and do not plan to allocate any up to 2010, institutions that plan to increase current allocations in the near future, and institutions that plan to reduce allocations by 2010. We further did not find a statistically significant difference between average assets of respondents versus nonrespondents. However, we accept that we cannot absolutely rule out the possibility of a response bias due to the unique nature of the data.

Table 8.2 Summary Statistics

This table summarizes the data by the characteristics of the institutional investors in terms of assets and number of institutions with a socially responsible investment program (Panel A), and their current and future asset allocations (Panel B). Other types of alternative investments primarily encompass hedge funds and real estate.

Panel A. Characteristics of the Institutional Investors in the Dataset

Type of Financial Institution	Number of Institutions in the Dataset	Average Assets (Millions of Euros)	Number of Institutions with a Socially Responsible Investment Program	Number of Institutions with a Socially Responsible Investment Program in 2005 or Planning to Adopt One in 2006–2010
Pension Fund	56	€2,942.86	14	23
Insurance Company	25	€5,008.00	10	13
Bank	19	€9,752.63	5	7
All Types of Institutional Investors	100	€4,753.00	29	43

Panel B. Asset Allocations (Percentage of Assets Invested in Different Asset Classes)
...Current (as at 2005)

Type of Financial Institution	Publicly Traded Equities	Bonds	Cash/ Currencies	Index Funds	Private Equity	Other Types of Alternative Investments	Other
Pension Fund	33.38	50.89	4.32	1.60	1.17	7.43	1.21
Insurance Company	23.80	55.72	9.56	0.48	0.73	6.23	3.48

Bank	27.32	48.43	5.11	0.58	1.36	16.05	1.16
All Types of Institutional Investors	29.83	51.63	5.78	1.13	1.09	8.77	1.77

…Planned (for the period 2006–2010)

Type of Financial Institution	Publicly Traded Equities	Bonds	Cash/ Currencies	Index Funds	Private Equity	Other Types of Alternative Investments	Other
Pension Fund	31.51	51.73	2.86	1.97	1.67	9.53	0.73
Insurance Company	24.71	59.02	2.52	2.16	0.62	8.37	2.60
Bank	24.95	47.59	2.68	1.05	1.86	21.34	0.53
All Types of Institutional Investors	28.56	52.77	2.74	1.85	1.44	11.48	1.16

8.3.3 Summary Statistics

The data indicate that the 100 institutional investors consisting of pension funds, insurance companies, banks, and other financial institutions invested on average 1.09% of their assets in private equity as at 2005 and plan on investing 1.44% of their assets in private equity over the period 2006–2010 (Table 8.2, Panel B). Out of these 100 institutions, 19 plan on (over the period 2006–2010) investing on average more than 2.5% of their assets in private equity, 10 plan on investing more than 5% of their assets in private equity, and 6 plan on investing more than 7.5% of their assets in private equity. Total private equity investment accounted for approximately €10.5 billion as of 2005. The proportional allocations to private equity in the Netherlands are consistent with institutional investor allocations to private equity funds in the United States (see, e.g., Gompers and Lerner, 1999a,b,c) and Australia (see, e.g., Cumming et al., 2005b).

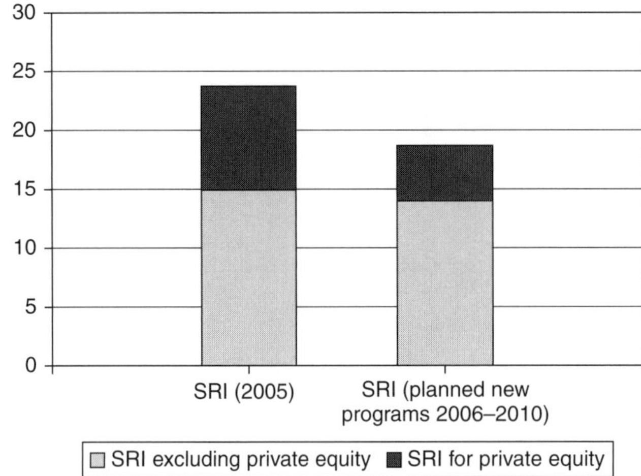

Figure 8.1 Socially Responsible Investment (SRI) Programs for Private Equity and Other Asset Classes among 100 Dutch Institutional Investors

Figure 8.1 indicates 24 (of 100) institutions currently have a socially responsible investment program (of these, 14 include socially responsible private equity investment programs), and 19 that plan on adopting a socially responsible investment program over the period 2006–2010 (of these, 5 include socially responsible private equity investment programs). Figure 8.2 shows the investment in socially responsible investment programs by type of institutional investor (pension fund, insurance company, and bank). The picture in Figure 8.2 does not suggest there is a material difference in the propensity to invest in socially responsible investments across different types of Dutch institutions.

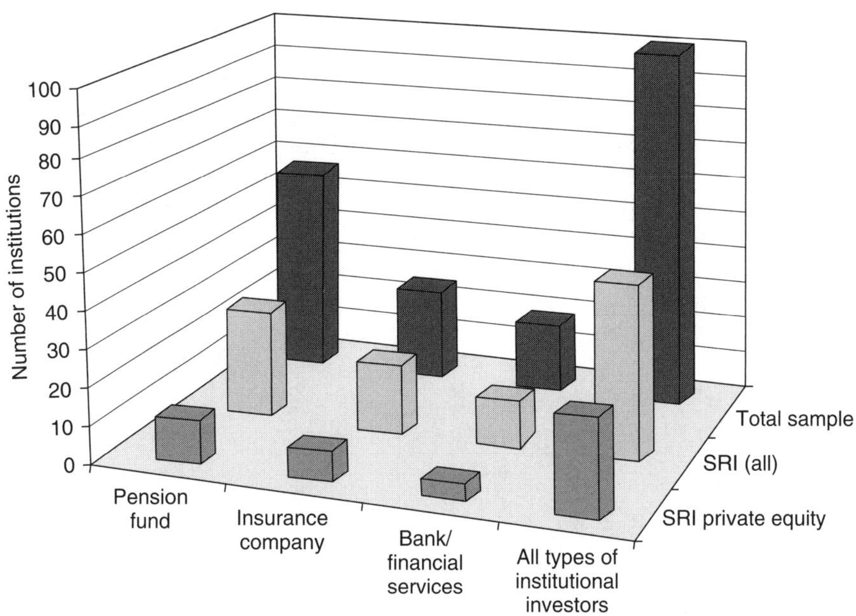

Figure 8.2 Socially Responsible Investment (SRI) Programs by Type of Institution (Current as of 2005 or Planned for 2006–2010)

Tables 8.3 and 8.4 provide comparison tests and a correlation matrix, respectively. These univariate tests indicate relations between the variables without simultaneously controlling for other factors. The univariate summary statistics and tests in Tables 8.3 and 8.4 indicate that socially responsible private equity investment is observed more often for European investments (outside the Netherlands) and investments in the United States from Dutch institutional investors. Socially responsible investment is observed more often when institutional investors rank the importance of the IFRS as being more important. Socially responsible investment is also observed more often among larger institutions and among institutions that centralize decision-making responsibility via a CIO. Notice as well that socially responsible private equity investment is observed more often for fund-of-funds investments, but fund-of-funds investments are also correlated with size (and hence the effect is shown to be different in the multivariate tests that follow). In the next section we provide multivariate analyses of the determinants of socially responsible investment in private equity (and other asset classes) that simultaneously control for a wide range of variables.

Tables 8.3 and 8.4 provide useful preliminary insights into the relations between the variables. These summary statistics also enable assessment of potential problems with the multivariate empirical tests in regards to, for example, collinearity across explanatory variables or some other type of misspecification error. For example, due to the high correlation between the

Table 8.3 Difference of Means, Proportions, and Medians Tests

This table presents difference of means, proportions, and medians tests for the population of institutional investors that do and do not have as at 2005 (or plan on having for 2006–2010) a socially responsible private equity investment program. *, **, *** Statistically significant at the 10%, 5%, and 1% levels, respectively.

	Socially Responsible Private Equity Investment Program (Current at 2005 or Planned for 2006–2010)			No Socially Responsible Private Equity Investment Program (Current at 2005 or Planned for 2006–2010)			Difference of Means Test	Difference of Medians Test (or Difference of Proportions Test for Dummy Variables)
	Number of Observations	Mean	Median	Number of Observations	Mean	Median		
The Netherlands Domestic Private Equity Investment	19	0.34	0.00	81	0.2353	0.00	0.52	$p \leq 0.146$
European (outside the Netherlands) Private Equity Investment	19	2.39	1.88	81	0.30	0.00	3.55***	$p \leq 0.000$***
U.S. Private Equity Investment	19	1.67	1.13	81	0.12	0.00	3.98***	$p \leq 0.000$***
Asia Private Equity Investment	19	0.16	0.00	81	0.03	0.00	1.92*	$p \leq 0.213$

Fund-of-funds Private Equity Investment	19	1.35	0.88	81	0.45	0.00	2.35**	$p \leq 0.000$***
International Financial Reporting Standards	19	2.63	3.00	81	2.14	2.00	1.89*	$p \leq 0.677$
Rank of Attractiveness of Returns to Sustainable Investment	19	2.89	3.00	81	2.40	3.00	1.76*	$p \leq 0.171$
Chief Investment Officer Responsibility	19	0.32	0.00	81	0.02	0.00	2.62**	4.21***
Log (Assets)	19	12,336.84	6,500.00	81	2,974.07	800.00	3.10***	$p \leq 0.001$***
Pension Fund	19	0.47	1.00	81	0.58	1.00	−0.82	−0.84
Insurance Company	19	0.32	0.00	81	0.23	0.00	0.72	0.77
Bank	19	0.21	0.00	81	0.19	0.00	0.24	0.25

Table 8.4 Correlation

This table presents correlation coefficients across selected variables as defined inTable 8.1.

		(1)	(2)	(3)	(4)	(5)
(1)	Socially Responsible Investment Program 2005–2010	1.00				
(2)	Socially Responsible Investment Program 2005	0.74	1.00			
(3)	Socially Responsible Private Equity Investment Program 2005–2010	0.56	0.48	1.00		
(4)	Socially Responsible Private Equity Investment Program 2005	0.46	0.63	0.83	1.00	
(5)	The Netherlands Domestic Private Equity Investment	−0.07	−0.07	0.03	−0.01	1.00
(6)	European (outside the Netherlands) Private Equity Investment	0.20	0.19	0.52	0.44	0.03
(7)	U.S. Private Equity Investment	0.28	0.25	0.61	0.50	0.00
(8)	Asia Private Equity Investment	0.07	0.00	0.22	0.09	0.02
(9)	Fund-of-funds Private Equity Investment	−0.01	−0.01	0.24	0.16	0.34
(10)	International Financial Reporting Standards	0.07	0.22	0.21	0.25	0.19
(11)	Rank of Attractiveness of Returns to Sustainable Investment	0.26	0.05	0.17	0.05	−0.14
(12)	Chief Investment Officer Responsibility	0.19	0.06	0.42	0.20	0.00
(13)	Log (Assets)	0.17	0.18	0.46	0.40	−0.02
(14)	Pension Fund	−0.04	−0.10	−0.08	−0.05	0.09
(15)	Insurance Company	0.10	0.14	0.07	0.03	−0.06

Matrix

Correlations significant at the 5% level are highlighted in bold and underline font.

(6)	(7)	(8)	(9)	(10)	(11)	(12)	(13)	(14)
1.00								
0.50	1.00							
0.32	**0.53**	1.00						
0.45	**0.32**	**0.41**	1.00					
0.25	**0.23**	−0.10	**0.29**	1.00				
0.04	0.08	0.05	−0.09	−0.14	1.00			
0.17	**0.21**	**0.26**	**0.37**	0.13	0.07	1.00		
0.26	**0.36**	0.12	**0.31**	**0.37**	−0.17	**0.27**	1.00	
0.02	0.07	0.11	0.18	**−0.26**	0.18	−0.11	**−0.33**	1.00
−0.14	−0.14	−0.09	−0.16	0.11	−0.07	0.09	0.09	**−0.65**

regional variables, such variables are not included simultaneously in the multivariate regressions presented in the next section. Alternative multivariate models are presented and discussed following.

8.4 Multivariate Empirical Analyses

The multivariate empirical tests in this section focus on logit regression analyses of the probability that an institutional investor has a socially responsible private equity investment program. In Table 8.5, Panel A, we consider all 100 institutional investors in the dataset, regardless of whether or not they invest in private equity of any type. In Table 8.5, Panel B, we consider logit regression analyses of the subset of 35 institutional investors that are (2005) or expect to be (2006–2010) invested in private equity. Table 8.5, Panel B, also considers in Model 11 bivariate logit analyses involving two steps: the probability that an institutional investor invests in private equity and the probability that an institutional investor is invested in socially responsible private equity. The Model 11 specification is a useful robustness check to ascertain whether there are statistical differences in the subset of firms that invest in private equity versus those that do not and to econometrically correct for those potential differences in the spirit of Heckman (1976, 1979). Table 8.6 considers logit regression analyses of the probability that an institutional investor invests in social responsibility for any asset class, not only private equity. Each of the regression models (17 in total) is provided to show robustness to alternative subsets in the sample, alternative definitions of the dependent variable, and alternative explanatory variables. The variables are as defined previously (see also Table 8.1). The structure of the data in terms of the questions put to the institutional investors in the survey was also designed to mitigate any concern with potential endogeneity in the relations studied, as indicated by the variable definitions in Table 8.1. The alternative specifications across the 17 regression models provide further robustness checks for potential collinearity across the variables, and other specifications not explicitly reported are available upon request from the authors.

Table 8.5 provides interesting evidence in respect to the three primary hypotheses outlined previously. In regards to our first hypothesis, notice that regression evidence indicates that socially responsible private equity investment is more common when the decision to implement such an investment plan is placed in the hands of a CIO as opposed to a broader investment team. When a CIO is in charge, a socially responsible private equity investment program is approximately 40 to 50% more likely to be adopted. Socially responsible investments may be perceived to involve a sacrifice in expected returns by some investors, and when investment personnel within an organization compete with each other on the basis of their returns performance, they are less likely to invest in socially responsible investments. By contrast, when a CIO takes responsibility for the type of investments to be carried out, socially responsible investment programs are much more likely to be adopted.

In regards to our second hypothesis, the regressions indicate that socially responsible private equity investments are more common among institutional investors that invest internationally. In particular, socially responsible investment is approximately 1 to 2% more common among institutional investors, with a 10% greater international investment focus in Europe (outside the Netherlands; see Models 2, 5, 6, 8, and 11 in Table 8.5, Panels A and B).[12] The economic significance of a 10% change is as low as 0.4% in Model 6 and as high as 2.7% in Model 11. All of these estimates are statistically significant at the 10% or higher level of significance, and robust to control variables for other factors that influence institutional investor investment allocations.

Table 8.5, Model 3, indicates that socially responsible private equity investment is not statistically different for private equity investments in the United States by Dutch institutional investors when all 100 Dutch institutional investors are considered together regardless of whether or not they invest in private equity. However, when we consider the subsample of Dutch institutional investors that invest in private equity separately, the data indicate that socially responsible private equity investment is approximately 5 to 6% more common among institutional investors, with a 10% greater international investment focus in the United States. By contrast, there is no evidence from any specification that socially responsible private equity investment is statistically related to cross-border investment decisions in Asia and/or for domestic investments in the Netherlands.

In regards to the control variables, recall in the preceding description of the data that there was univariate correlation evidence that socially responsible investment is more common among institutional investors that are more sensitive to the IFRS. However, it appears that other factors independently affect the association between the importance of the IFRS to an institution and the propensity to invest in socially responsible private equity investments: The relation between these variables is not robust in a multivariate context with controls for other factors in Table 8.5, Panels A and B. As such, the data offer suggestive but not conclusive evidence that institutions are sensitive to reporting standards and public perception of their socially responsible private equity investment activities. It is nevertheless noteworthy that Model 17 in Table 8.6 (for all types of investment, including public stock markets and not just private equity) that the IFRS is statistically related (at the 10% level of significance) to the propensity to invest in socially responsible investments. Model 17 indicates that an increase in the ranking of the importance of the IFRS by 1 (on a scale 1 to 5, where 5 is the most important) increases the likelihood that an institutional investor will adopt a socially responsible investment program by 1.1%.

[12]The 10% change is simply hypothetical and is selected merely to illustrate the economic significance (the size) of the effect. The effect is modeled as linear in the econometric specification. Diagnostic tests (such as likelihood ratio tests) did not suggest a preference for a nonlinear specification, and the linear specification seemed most appropriate for the data. Alternative specifications are available upon request.

Table 8.5 Logit Regression Analyses for Sustainable/

This table presents logit regression estimates of the probability adoption of a sustainable and socially all 100 institutional investors in the sample regardless of whether or not they are or plan on investing in policy means either adoption has taken place as at 2005, or the institution plans to adopt such a practice as at 2005. Panel B considers the subsample of institutional investors that will be invested bivariate regression in the spirit of Heckman (1976, 1979) whereby in the first step the probability that the institution makes socially responsible private equity investments is estimated. The independent potential problems associated with collinearity of included and excluded variables. The total The values presented are not the standard logit coefficients; rather, they are the marginal effects so difference for the sample of all other firms in the group at the 10%, 5%, and 1% levels, respectively.

Panel A. Full Sample of

	Model 1		Model 2		Model 3
	Marginal Effect	t-Statistic	Marginal Effect	t-Statistic	Marginal Effect
Constant	−0.966	−4.144***	−0.824	−2.821***	−0.741
The Netherlands Domestic Private Equity Investment	0.015	0.632			
European (outside the Netherlands) Private Equity Investment			0.111	2.180**	
U.S. Private Equity Investment					0.262
Asia Private Equity Investment					
Fund-of-funds Private Equity Investment	−0.014	−0.577	−0.069	−1.685*	−0.095
International Financial Reporting Standards	0.015	0.386	−0.006	−0.172	0.021
Rank of Attractiveness of Returns to Sustainable Investment					
Chief Investment Officer Responsibility	0.496	2.044**	0.661	2.423**	0.621
Log (Assets)	0.085	3.454***	0.069	2.591***	0.049
Pension Fund	0.137	1.376	0.130	1.167	0.072
Insurance Company	0.110	0.798	0.201	1.041	0.173
Model Diagnostics					
Number of Observations	100		100		100
Number of Observations Where Dependent Variable = 1	19		19		19
Adjusted R^2 (Pseudo R^2 for Model 1)	0.314		0.541		0.530
Log Likehood Function	−33.348		−22.318		−22.837
Chi-square Statistic	30.549***		52.608***		51.570***

responsible investment policy in private equity by a Dutch institutional investor. Panel A considers
private equity. In Models 1–5, adoption of a sustainable and socially responsible investment
policy sometime within the period 2006–2010. In Model 6 adoption only refers to the current
in private equity in the period 2006–2010 in Models 7–10. Model 11 in Panel B involves a 2-step
that the institution invests in private equity is estimated, while in the second step the probability
variables are as defined in Table 8.1. The coefficients on the independent variables are robust to
population of firms comprises 100 Dutch institutional investors described in Tables 8.1 and 8.2.
that the economic significance is shown alongside the statistical significance. *, **, *** Significant

100 Dutch Institutions

	Model 4		Model 5		Model 6	
t-Statistic	Marginal Effect	t-Statistic	Marginal Effect	t-Statistic	Marginal Effect	t-Statistic
−2.626***	−0.969	−4.083***	−0.794	−2.421**	−0.661	−2.868***
			0.075	1.710*	0.040	1.818*
1.549						
	0.145	0.998				
−1.303	−0.025	−0.788	−0.042	−1.302	−0.028	−1.322
0.475	0.034	0.823	0.005	0.178	0.027	1.117
			0.046	1.875*	0.020	1.096
2.190**	0.459	1.893*	0.512	1.414	0.096	0.817
1.692*	0.080	3.356***	0.056	2.164**	0.044	2.464**
0.590	0.136	1.361	0.097	1.086	0.101	1.348
0.992	0.107	0.793	0.154	0.887	0.088	0.818
	100		100		100	
	19		19		14	
	0.323		0.596		0.393	
	−32.906		−19.633		−24.596	
	31.434***		57.978***		31.801***	

(*continued*)

Table 8.5

	Panel B. Subsample of Private Equity Investments (Models 7–10)				
	Model 7		Model 8		Model 9
	Subsample of Institutions in Private Equity		Subsample of Institutions in Private Equity		Subsample in Private
	Marginal Effect	t-Statistic	Marginal Effect	t-Statistic	Marginal Effect
Constant	−0.716	−1.155	−2.477	−2.207**	−1.349
The Netherlands Domestic Investment	−0.025	−0.339			
European (outside the Netherlands) Investment			0.204	1.764*	
U.S. Investment					0.574
Asia Investment					
Fund-of-funds Investment	−0.113	−1.481	−0.188	−1.950*	−0.271
International Financial Reporting Standards	−0.088	−0.711	−0.063	−0.392	0.002
Rank of Attractiveness of Returns to Sustainable Investment	0.375	1.851*	0.207	1.621	0.245
Attractiveness of Returns to Private Equity versus Public Equity					
Chief Investment Officer Responsibility			0.470	2.506**	0.404
Log (Assets)	0.122	1.566	0.211	2.018**	0.060
Pension Fund	0.151	0.528	0.324	0.962	0.037
Insurance Company	0.159	0.579	0.289	1.064	0.194
Model Diagnostics					
Number of Observations	35		35		35
Number of Observations where Dependent Variable = 1	19		19		19
Adjusted R^2 (pseudo R^2 for Model 1)	0.193		0.406		0.440
Log Likehood Function	−19.466		−14.323		−13.520
Chi-square Statistic	9.331		19.618**		21.223***

(continued)

and Bivariate Logit Estimates with Sample Selection (Model 11)

	Model 10		Model 11			
of Institutions Equity	Subsample of Institutions in Private Equity		Step 1: Probability of Investment in Private Equity		Step 2: Probability of Socially Responsible Private Equity	
t-Statistic	Marginal Effect	t-Statistic	Marginal Effect	t-Statistic	Marginal Effect	t-Statistic
−1.376	−2.173	−2.103**	−3.490	−3.315***	−4.451	−2.786***
					0.274	2.039**
2.227**						
	0.217	0.680				
−1.983**	−0.173	−1.574				
0.016	0.011	0.067			−0.380	−1.622
1.837*	0.237	1.955*				
			0.013	3.506***		
2.125**	0.450	1.983**			0.700	1.448
0.567	0.188	1.944*	0.243	1.587	0.290	2.883***
0.110	0.279	0.920				
0.862	0.083	0.256				
	35		100		35	
	19		35		19	
	0.296					
	−16.990		−46.219			
	14.282*					

Table 8.6 Logit Regression Analyses for

This table presents logit regression estimates of the probability adoption of a sustainable and investor. In Models 12–16, adoption of a sustainable and socially responsible investment policy to adopt such a policy sometime within the period 2006–2010. In Model 17 adoption only defined in Table 8.1. The coefficients on the independent variables are robust to potential total population of firms comprises 100 Dutch institutional investors described in Tables 8.1 are the marginal effects so that the economic significance is shown alongside the statistical the group at the 10%, 5%, and 1% levels, respectively.

	Model 12		Model 13		Model 14	
	Marginal Effect	**t-Statistic**	**Marginal Effect**	**t-Statistic**	**Marginal Effect**	**t-Statistic**
Constant	−0.819	−2.280**	−0.840	−2.142**	−0.622	−1.451
The Netherlands Domestic Investment	−0.021	−0.373				
European (outside the Netherlands) Investment			0.156	1.975**		
U.S. Investment					0.412	1.717*
Asia Investment						
Fund-of-funds Investment	−0.073	−1.363	−0.173	−2.191**	−0.229	−1.809*
International Financial Reporting Standards	0.033	0.504	0.014	0.201	0.021	0.294
Rank of Attractiveness of Returns to Sustainable Investment						
Chief Investment Officer Responsibility	0.406	2.327**	0.476	3.219***	0.459	2.957***
Log (Assets)	0.071	1.740*	0.066	1.531	0.038	0.776
Pension Fund	0.227	1.481	0.269	1.631	0.210	1.195
Insurance Company	0.219	1.341	0.286	1.726*	0.257	1.555
Model Diagnostics						
Number of Observations	100		100		100	

Sustainable/Socially Responsible Investment

socially responsible investment policy in any asset class by a Dutch institutional
means either adoption has taken place as at 2005, or the institution plans
refers to the current practice as at 2005. The independent variables are as
problems associated with collinearity of included and excluded variables. The
and 8.2. The values presented are not the standard logit coefficients; rather, they
significance. *, **, *** Significant difference for the sample of all other firms in

Model 15		Model 16		Model 17	
Marginal Effect	t-Statistic	Marginal Effect	t-Statistic	Marginal Effect	t-Statistic
−0.871	−2.361**	−1.185	−2.755***	−1.029	−3.014***
		0.144	1.698*	0.071	1.598
0.229	0.867				
−0.102	−1.575	−0.157	−1.962**	−0.088	−1.631
0.048	0.688	0.018	0.247	0.113	1.915*
		0.121	2.344**	0.027	0.648
0.400	2.252**	0.441	2.415**	0.047	0.233
0.073	1.793*	0.077	1.707*	0.048	1.409
0.233	1.516	0.203	1.143	0.189	1.313
0.220	1.353	0.262	1.480	0.275	1.566
100		100		100	

(*continued*)

Table 8.6

	Model 12		Model 13		Model 14	
	Marginal Effect	t-Statistic	Marginal Effect	t-Statistic	Marginal Effect	t-Statistic
Number of Observations Where Dependent Variable = 1	43		43		43	
Adjusted R^2 (Pseudo R^2 for Model 1)	0.072		0.124		0.143	
Log Likehood Function	−63.440		−59.866		−58.559	
Chi-square Statistic	9.783		16.930**		19.545***	

The data therefore suggest that reporting standards are more closely connected to public investments as opposed to private investments, but again, these statistical differences are not very pronounced in the data.

Many of the other control variables in the regression models are statistically significant and worth mentioning. Socially responsible private equity investment programs are more common among larger institutional investors and those institutions in the data expecting greater economic risk-adjusted returns from socially responsible investments. An increase in the rank of the relative returns to socially responsible investments by 1 (on a scale of 1 to 5, where 1 is the lowest) increases the probability of a socially responsible investment by 1 to 3% depending on the specification of the model (see Models 5 and 7–10). We find no statistically significant differences in the propensity to carry out socially responsible investments depending on the type of investor (pension fund, insurance company, or bank/financial institution) in any specification in Tables 8.5 and 8.6. We do find evidence that socially responsible investment is approximately 1 to 3% less common among institutional investors that invest a 10% greater proportion in fund-of-funds (see Models 8–9 and 13–16, but the statistical significance of this evidence is not robust in some of the other specifications), which is expected as fund-of-funds remove the decision making from the institutional investors to the fund-of-funds managers.

Finally, note by comparison of Table 8.6 to Table 8.5 that the evidence that the factors that give rise to socially responsible investment decisions for private equity are quite similar to those for other asset classes. This is a somewhat unexpected result, as private equity is widely viewed as a distinctive asset class.[13] We did make note of the fact that the IFRS appears to be somewhat

[13]See references supra note 1.

(*continued*)

Model 15		Model 16		Model 17	
Marginal Effect	t-Statistic	Marginal Effect	t-Statistic	Marginal Effect	t-Statistic
43		43		29	
0.076		0.167		0.120	
−63.120		−56.929		−52.994	
10.424***		22.805***		14.442***	

more closely related to investments other than private equity, but these differences were not statistically pronounced in the data. It is possible that regulatory factors not captured by the data could better explain differences across asset classes, but that issue is beyond the scope of this chapter and the new dataset used herein. This issue, along with other related issues, is discussed further in the next section.

8.5 Extensions and Future Research

This chapter introduced the first international dataset on socially responsible private equity investments. Because the data obtained in this chapter are new and unique and extremely difficult to obtain from institutional investors, there are of course limitations in the number of observations. We nevertheless gathered sufficient details in the data to control for a variety of factors that could affect institutional investor allocations to different asset classes and to socially responsible investments. And as we have discussed in the chapter, we do not have any reason to believe there are biases with regard to sample selection in the data we were able to obtain.

Our analysis focused on Dutch institutional investor allocations to socially responsible private equity investment in the Netherlands, Europe (outside the Netherlands; our data cannot distinguish between specific countries in Europe due to the confidential nature of the data considered), the United States, and Asia (again, we cannot distinguish between specific regions). We provided suggestive evidence, although not conclusive, that regulations may have different effects for different asset classes in regards to social responsibility. Further work could consider expanding the data in terms of more closely investigating different asset classes, as well as possibly for different time periods and different countries (in the spirit of Manignan and Ralston, 2002; see also Mayer et al., 2005, for a discussion of differences in institutional investor decisions in the United Kingdom versus the United States).

Given the increase in institutional investor propensity to adopt socially responsible investment programs in private equity (and other asset classes), further research could also investigate the factors that give rise to private equity fund managers to themselves offer such investment alternatives to their institutional investors. The data introduced in this chapter suggest there is an increasing demand by institutional investors to invest responsibly, and as such it is natural to expect the market to be more sensitive to the socially responsible asset class. There is ample scope for further research to consider when, why, and how private fund managers implement such programs.

8.6 Conclusions

The study investigated for the first time the factors that influence institutional investors to allocate capital to sustainable socially responsible private equity investments. We introduced a new detailed dataset from a survey of Dutch institutional investors. Perhaps most important, there was very strong evidence in the data introduced herein that socially responsible investments are more likely among institutions that centralize decision making in the hands of a CIO. Institutions that make use of an internal competitive model among investment personnel are 40 to 50% less likely to consider social responsibility in their decisions.

The data indicated strong evidence that Dutch institutional investors are more likely to invest in socially responsible private equity investments in Europe (outside the Netherlands) and in the United States, in contrast to domestic Dutch investments and Asian investments. That socially responsible investment is more likely in Europe (outside the Netherlands) and the United States relative to within the Netherlands likely reflects investment opportunities. Similarly, prior work has shown that socially responsible investment is less widely regarded generally among Asian countries.

Finally, the data indicated socially responsible investment is more common among larger institutional investors and those investors expecting greater risk-adjusted returns from such investments. There was also some, albeit less robust, support for the view that socially responsible investment was more likely among institutions that consider adherence to the IFRS to be more important.

Overall, we did not find pronounced differences across factors that lead to socially responsible investing in private equity versus other asset classes. Further empirical research on other asset classes and/or institutional investors from different countries would shed more light on the topic. It would also be worthwhile to investigate deviations or style drifts from stated objectives of social responsibility in the context of private equity and other asset classes.

Key Terms

Style drift
Socially responsible investment
Negative screens
Positive screens
Best in class
International Financial Reporting Standards (IFRS)
Chief investment officer
Corporate social responsibility

Discussion Questions

8.1. What is style drift? Why is it important? Do you think style drift is a more pronounced concern in private equity or mutual fund investment? Why?
8.2. What is socially responsible investment? What factors motivate institutional investors to invest in socially responsible private equity investment? Are these factors different for other asset classes outside the private equity context?
8.3. Is an institution's internal structure more important than external influences for driving institutional investor allocations to socially responsible private equity investment?
8.4. Would you recommend to a prospective venture capital fund manager to establish a new fund with a socially responsible investment mandate? Or would it be better for the fund to consider only a portion of its investments in socially responsible asset classes?
8.5. Do you think socially responsible private equity investment will be more profitable or less profitable in the coming years? How do you perceive Kleiner Perkins' hiring of Al Gore to assist them in their socially responsible initiatives?
8.6. Should institutional investors centralize or coordinate decision making through a chief investment officer for deciding asset allocations to socially responsible investment classes?

9 The Role of Government and Alternative Policy Options

9.1 Introduction and Learning Objectives

The Organisation for Economic Co-operation and Development (OECD, 1996) has argued that the financing of entrepreneurship and innovative ideas will facilitate economic growth and the competitive advantage of nations in the twenty-first century. Much evidence, albeit not all, indicates small high-tech firms contribute disproportionately to innovation and economic growth (the World Bank, 1994, 2002, 2004; see also Industry Canada, 2002, 2006). The primary source of capital for these small growth-oriented high-tech start-up firms is venture capital, and venture capital facilitates the success of firms that eventually list on stock exchanges. For example, while venture capital averaged less than 3% of corporate R&D in the period 1983 to 1992, it was nevertheless responsible for more than 8% of the U.S. industrial innovations in that decade (Kortum and Lerner, 2000).

There is a widely held perception that there exists a capital gap in the financing of entrepreneurial firms in that entrepreneurial firms are not able to raise all of the capital that they need and that good firms are not getting funded.[1] In theory, we may expect a capital gap because investment in privately held entrepreneurial firms that are not listed on stock exchanges is typically highly illiquid and riskier than most other investments due to information asymmetries and potential investors' inability to assess the value of the nascent technologies such firms are developing. Also, it is often stated that the returns to innovation are not fully captured by the innovating entrepreneurs and their investors because there are broader returns to the development of an innovative society; that is, it is believed that the social rate of return to financing entrepreneurial start-up high-tech firms is greater than the private rate of return. As an empirical matter, however, it is difficult to measure capital gaps, and there is little consensus as

[1]On the apparent capital gap, see, for example, http://strategis.ic.gc.ca/epic/internet/insbrp-rppe.nsf/en/rd01918e.html. Some commentators on an earlier edition of this book suggested that there are capital gaps in Canada for late-stage venture capital, and as such Canadian firms must seek capital from U.S. investors to get suitable financing. In one recent empirical study, however, data show that entrepreneurs are typically able to raise the capital they want, although not always in the form that they would like (Cosh et al., 2005). More data collection and further empirical analyses are warranted.

to the extent of capital gaps for entrepreneurial firms (Industry Canada, 2002). Regardless, given the perceived capital gap for such potential entrepreneurial firms, a major strategic focus of policymakers around the world has been to get directly involved in promoting the high-tech sectors and the stimulation of venture capital markets through direct government investment programs and laws that are appropriately designed to facilitate entrepreneurship and entrepreneurial finance. For example, the World Bank spent more than $US10 billion from 2001 to 2005 to promote small enterprises (Beck et al., 2005).

In this chapter we concentrate on venture capital, as it is mainly start-up high-tech entrepreneurial firms that are becoming victims of this capital gap. Broadly classified, public policies toward venture capital come in one of two primary forms: (1) law, which can be categorized further into taxation, securities law, and other types of laws for facilitating entrepreneurship and entrepreneurial finance, and (2) direct government investment schemes. Table 9.1 provides an overview of a wide range of policy alternatives that fit within each of these two categories.[2] In this chapter we briefly review the properties, benefits, and drawbacks of these different policies, with a focus on the following topics that are reviewed in this order:

- Taxation
- Securities regulation
- Other regulations pertaining to the demand for venture capital
- Other regulations pertaining to the supply of venture capital
- Direct government investment programs, with reference to examples from the United States, Israel, Canada, the United Kingdom, and Australia

9.2 Taxation

There are at least four important types of tax incentives that enable entrepreneurial finance around the world, as summarized in Panel A of Table 9.1. The first tax mechanism, capital gains tax, is perhaps the most well known. Capital gains tax is widely recognized as being one of the most important legal instruments for stimulating venture capital markets, and both theory and empirical evidence show a direct causality from lower capital gains taxation to more venture capital.[3] U.S. venture capital fundraising increased from US$68.2 million in 1977 to US$2.1 billion in 1982, as there was a reduction in the capital gains tax rate from 35% in 1977 to 20% in 1982 (see Figure 4.16 in Chapter 4).

[2]Jääskeläinen et al. (2007) provide a similar table that outlines some of the different government incentive programs and policy options listed in Table 9.1.

[3]See Poterba (1989a,b); Gompers and Lerner (1998); Jeng and Wells (2000); Keuschnigg (2003, 2004); Keuschnigg and Nielsen (2001, 2003a,b, 2004a,b,c); and Armour and Cumming (2006). We do not address tax neutrality issues in this chapter, but this issue is worth considering by policymakers.

Table 9.1 Summary of Alternative Public Policy Initiatives for Providing Venture Capital Support

Feature	Description	Potential Benefits	Potential Drawbacks	Examples	Related Research
Panel A. Taxation					
Capital Gains Taxes	Government charges low rates on capital gains taxes	Incentives for private investors to contribute capital to venture capital funds and entrepreneurial companies	Lower tax revenues	United States 1975–1980	Poterba (1989a,b); Gompers and Lerner (1998); Keuschnigg, (2004); Keuschnigg and Nielsen (2001, 2003a,b); Armour and Cumming (2006)
R&D Tax Policy	Government provides special tax incentives for R&D	Increases R&D expenses, which benefit society generally due to spillovers	Costly forgone tax revenues	Adopted in various forms in most developed countries around the world	Bloom et al. (2002); Cumming (2006b)
Taxation of Stock Options	Government does not scrutinize low valuations of stock options provided to entrepreneurial companies	Incentives for entrepreneurs to start their own companies	Lower tax revenues	United States	Sandler (2001); Gilson and Schizer (2003)
Offshore Tax Haven Double Taxation Treaties	Government enters into double taxation treaties and allows private investors to set up funds offshore	Incentives for private fund managers to establish venture capital funds	Lower tax revenues	Bermuda; Cayman Islands; Labuan (Malaysia); Luxembourg	Cumming and Johan (2006a)

(*continued*)

Table 9.1 *(continued)*

Feature	Description	Potential Benefits	Potential Drawbacks	Examples	Related Research
Taxation of Venture Capital and Private Equity Carried Interest	Taxed at capital gains rates, could be raised to income tax rates	Higher tax revenues; equity	Diminished incentive to become a venture capital or private equity manager	Policy debates in 2007 in United States, among other countries	Fleischer (2008)
Panel B. Securities Laws					
Minimal Prospectus Requirements/ Maximum Prospectus Exemptions for Companies	Lower cost of preparing a prospectus; do not require prospectus for small companies—greater scope of prospectus exemptions	Incentives for individuals to start companies and greater access to capital	Fraud	Canada versus United States comparisons	MacIntosh (1994)
IPO Hold Periods and Escrow Requirements	Low cost of going public	Lower costs of going public facilitate capital raising for small companies	Fraud	Canada versus United States comparisons	MacIntosh (1994)
Foreign Ownership of Majority Shares in Companies	Majority foreign ownership is permitted	Foreign ownership is a substitute for bad laws as the foreign owner is subject to the higher standard	Transfer of knowledge and wealth abroad, particularly for high-tech industries, which the countries want to keep internally	Korean limits to foreign ownership; U.S. limits to foreign ownership for certain industries	Denis and Huizinga (2004)

Panel C. Miscellaneous Laws					
Bankruptcy Law	Government minimizes time to discharge in personal bankruptcy	Encourages entrepreneurial activity and people to start their own companies, thereby increasing self-employment and the size of venture capital markets	Default and fraud	The Netherlands and Germany introduced discharge from personal bankruptcy in 1997 and 1999, respectively	Armour and Cumming (2006, 2008)
Labor Laws	The ease with which labor laws enable employees to be fired	Regulatory barriers inhibit company size and growth, and hamper the entry of new companies	Employment security and social welfare	United States versus Europe versus less developed countries	Klapper et al. (2006)
Incorporation	The number of procedures to start a company	Regulatory barriers inhibit company size and growth, and hamper the entry of new companies	Fraud	United States versus Europe versus less developed countries	Klapper et al. (2006)
Institutional Investor (e.g., Pension Fund) Regulation	Prudent man rules enabling institutional investors to invest in venture capital	Increases flow of funds to entrepreneurial companies	Risk pension plan and insurance firms' (beneficiaries') assets	ERISA (United States, 1979) FTK (the Netherlands, 2006)	Gompers and Lerner (1998); Cumming and Johan (2006a)

(*continued*)

Table 9.1 *(continued)*

Feature	Description	Potential Benefits	Potential Drawbacks	Examples	Related Research
Venture Capital Fund Reporting Requirements	Dearth of reporting standards of venture capital funds discourages participation of institutional investors	Increased disclosure increases flow of funds	Costs of reporting and disclosing sensitive materials	CalPERs lawsuit (2002) in United States	Cumming and Johan (2007b); Cumming and Walz (2004)
Regulatory Harmonization	Harmonization of laws governing institutional investors	Facilitates venture capital investment with different types of institutions (or institutions in different countries) acting with same regulatory guidelines within the same limited partnership	Lack of regulatory competition	The Netherlands (2006) FTK; Basel II; IFRS	Cumming and Johan (2007b)
Patent Policy	The extent to which intellectual property is protected	Rewards innovators	Creates a monopoly; and "patent trolls" that acquire patents only for suing	BlackBerry lawsuit	Jaffe and Lerner (2004)

Panel D. Direct Government Venture Capital Programs and Other Incentives

Tax Subsidies for One Type of Venture Capital Fund	Government provides tax breaks to individuals that invest in one type of venture capital fund	Greater fundraising (at least for one type of venture capital fund)	Crowds out other types of funds; lowers returns in the market	Canadian LSVCCs; United Kingdom VCTs	Cumming (2003); Cumming and MacIntosh (2001, 2003a,b, 2006, 2007)
Government Research Grants	Government provides 100% of the funding needed for a particular project	Encourages entrepreneurial activity and people to start their own companies, thereby increasing self-employment and the size of venture capital markets	Direct costs of providing the grants; scientists using funds on noncommercializable projects, or excessive risk taking	United States SBIR	Lerner (1999, 2002)
Government Subsidies for Operating Costs	Government subsidizes the venture capital management firm to partly cover operating costs	Lowers fixed costs and thereby increases the returns to operating a fund	Venture capital fund managers do not have the same incentives to invest in new projects in a timely manner; may also give rise to excess staff or unnecessary operating expenses	European Seed Capital Scheme	Jääskeläinen et al. (2007)

(*continued*)

Table 9.1 *(continued)*

Feature	Description	Potential Benefits	Potential Drawbacks	Examples	Related Research
Government Loans	Government provides a loan with interest	Maximum incentives for the investee entrepreneurial company to work towards success as the investee does not have to give up equity	Entrepreneur has an incentive to risk shift—that is, take on excessively risky projects	United States SBIC	Lerner (1999, 2002)
Government Participation in a Venture Capital Fund as a Limited Partner	Government matching the investments by private investors	Increased fundraising opportunities for venture capital funds; sometimes structured with limited upside potential for the government	Costly; uncertain politicized selection process of fund managers; possible lack of independence in selection of investee entrepreneurial companies	Australia Innovation Investment Fund (IIF); Australian Pre-Seed Fund (PSF) has limited upside for government	Cumming (2007); Cumming and Johan (2009b)
Government Lower Priority	Government investor is last to get paid	Increases the expected rate of return for private investors	Venture capital fund managers have an incentive to risk shift—that is, to take on excessively risky projects	United Kingdom Regional Venture Capital Funds	Jääskeläinen et al. (2007)

Government Guarantees in Downside	Government incurs losses of the fund	Increases the expected rate of return for private investors	Venture capital fund managers have an incentive to risk shift—that is, to take on excessively risky projects	Germany WFG; France SOFARIS; Denmark Equity Guarantee Program	Jääskeläinen et al. (2007)
Private Investor Option to Buyout Government	Private investors are given the option to buy the government's shares at predetermined rates and over a preset period	Government capital is more liquid and can be reinvested; private investors' returns potentially enhanced	Timing constraints may distort incentives to do things that are in the best interest of the entrepreneurial company	Israel Yozama; New Zealand Venture Investment Fund	Jääskeläinen et al. (2007)
100% Owned Government Venture Capital Fund	Government run and funded venture capital fund	Finances companies that would otherwise not receive capital, such as regionally isolated companies; provision of trade education, consulting services	Depending on how it is structured and operated, it can be costly; uncertain politicized selection process of fund managers; possible lack of independence in selection of investee entrepreneurial companies; inefficient projects if private investors would not finance such projects; possible competition with private venture capital	Many provincial and federal sources; e.g., Canada Community Investment Plan	Bates (2002); Lerner (2002)

(*continued*)

Table 9.1 *(continued)*

Feature	Description	Potential Benefits	Potential Drawbacks	Examples	Related Research
Privatization of Government Entities	Privatization of government companies and assets; particularly for developing countries and transition economies	Increases the scale and scope of viable projects for venture capitalists to consider as investment opportunities	Politicized process in terms of who gets to buy the company; conflicts of interest	Russia, Eastern Europe	Megginson et al. (2004)
Export Financing	Financing companies with exports and assisting the actual exports of companies; pre-shipment financing, equity investments, note payables, credit, contract, and political insurance	Encourages exports and enables companies to be more competitive internationally	Potentially induces reliance on government for assistance; potentially politicized process with selection of companies that receive assistance	Export Development Corporation	Industry Canada (2006)

As entrepreneurial firms typically do not have the positive cash flows to pay interest on debt and dividends on equity, venture capitalists invariably invest with a view toward an exit and the ensuing capital gains. Therefore, tax policy in the area of capital gains taxation is particularly important for venture capital finance.

Second, many countries around the world adopt tax incentives for R&D expenditures (see, e.g., Bloom et al., 2002). In Australia, for example, prior to 2001, there was a flat R&D tax concession of 125% for all firms with eligible R&D expenses in Australia. In 2001 there was a policy change that introduced a 125% rebate ("offset") for firms with R&D expenses between AU$20,000 and AU$1 million and turnover of less than AU$5 million. The 2001 policy change also introduced a premium 175% R&D tax concession (called the Premium Concession). The Premium Concession is perhaps the most unique feature of the policy change, as it provides incentives to accelerate R&D expenses: The premium 175% rate is only available for incremental R&D above the firm's most recent three-year history of average R&D expenditures. Cumming (2006b) examined the inducement rate, or the amount of additional R&D expenditure made for every dollar of benefit from tax concessions given to a firm, for different designs in the Australian R&D tax policy. The inducement rate for the tax offset (which applies to financially constrained firms) is not greater than 100%. By contrast, the inducement rate in Australia is estimated by Cumming (2006b) to be significantly greater than 100% for the Premium Concession with incentive hurdles to spend more on R&D relative to prior years and is estimated to be much higher than that for countries without special hurdles (as estimated by Bloom et al., 2002, among others). Hence, the Australian R&D tax policy design with financial incentives with hurdles for increasing R&D expenses significantly induces more R&D in a cost-effective manner. The Australian experience with its 2001 policy change is suggestive that tax policy toward R&D[4] in other countries might benefit from implementing Premium Concessions as in Australia.

Third, taxation of stock options has been another important mechanism for facilitating entrepreneurship in the United States. The Internal Revenue Service passive acquiesces to valuations of employee stock options that motivate people to start companies, as explained in section 10.8 in Chapter 10.

It is unknown whether this type of tax incentive applies in *practice* (it is the practice of tax law and not a special rule) in other countries, but evidence to date indicates its application is much less prevalent than in the United States relative to, for example, Canada.[5] This issue is discussed further in Part III, Chapters 10–14.

Fourth, there are tax incentives for venture capital fund managers to establish offshore funds in tax havens. Tax-favorable jurisdictions include, for

[4]See http://www.parl.gc.ca/information/library/PRBpubs/899-e.htm for details.

example, Bermuda, the Cayman Islands, and Labuan (Malaysia). The structure and governance of these venture capital funds is discussed studied in Chapter 5 (see also Cumming and Johan, 2006a). In Chapter 5 we explained that there are both inbound offshore funds (that are established by institutional investors from potentially a variety of countries and the fund invests specifically in one country) and outbound offshore funds (that are established by institutional investors from one country for the fund to invest in potentially a variety of different countries). We saw that, from a sample of 50 funds from 17 countries around the world, 28% of funds were outbound offshore and 12% of funds were inbound offshore. Overall, the data in Chapter 5 suggested that there are significant incentives for venture capital funds to be established in offshore jurisdictions, as the investors are able to take advantage of double taxation agreements when they repatriate their profits from the various jurisdictions in which the fund has invested. Governments need to be careful to monitor offshore funds that invest within their jurisdiction to ensure the investment is not facilitating tax evasion.

Analogous to offshore tax haven funds, many European venture capital funds invest in German entities through an intermediate holding company that is resident in Luxembourg. This enables the fund to obtain more favorable tax rules in Luxembourg. Industry commentators believe this is an important incentive for venture capital investment in Germany, and proposals to curb this tax incentive have been criticized (despite the loss in tax revenues to Germany).[6] The lesson from the Luxembourg-Germany example is that there needs to be an important balance for favorable tax treatment to facilitate investment versus collecting tax revenues.

The final issue involving taxation has been the tax treatment of carried interest for venture capital and private equity fund managers. Fund managers currently (as of 2007) enjoy carried interest taxation at the lower capital gains tax rates. Capital gains tax rates are lower than income tax rates to compensate entrepreneurs for risking their own capital. But for lower capital gains tax rates, there would be deficient incentives to risk capital. One reason why policymakers are revisiting the tax treatment of carried interest of venture capital and private equity funds is that the capital being risked is not the capital of the fund managers but rather the capital of the institutional investors. Hence, on one view, fund managers are unjustly taxed at low rates. Whether or not there will be any changes to tax treatment of carried interest remains to be seen.[7] There are various counterarguments to making any changes to the tax treatment of carried interest, such as disproportionate value added provided by the industry to economic growth, and the concern that a tax change would be harmful to the industry.

[5]Sandler (2001) discusses the Canadian tax treatment of employee stock options.
[6]Private equity comment from S.J. Berwin, www.sjberwin.com, September 8, 2006.
[7]http://money.cnn.com/2007/03/29/markets/pe_taxes/index.htm.

9.3 Securities Laws

Securities laws facilitate entrepreneurial finance in two primary ways that are related to the costs of preparing a prospectus (see Panel B of Table 9.1). First, where exemptions from prospectus requirements are more readily available for entrepreneurs seeking to raise capital, costs of raising funds are lower. In Canada for example, it has been argued that prospectus requirements are too onerous and prospectus exemptions are too narrow, thereby making entrepreneurial capital relatively more costly than in other countries such as the United States.[8] Second, for companies seeking an IPO, hold period and prospectus requirements are overly onerous, thereby increasing the costs of IPOs, particularly for smaller companies. The risk with less onerous prospectus requirements, however, is fraudulent behavior (e.g., as in the infamous 1997 case of Bre-X).[9]

An additional item that can facilitate entrepreneurial finance is in relation to foreign majority ownership restrictions implemented by protectionist governments. For example, there are foreign ownership restrictions in Canada in selected industries, and lifting such ownership restrictions in Canada would directly facilitate increased foreign investment and increase the supply of capital in Canada. This would benefit entrepreneurs in Canada by providing greater access to capital. Similarly, Canadian investors would benefit from the lifting of foreign ownership restrictions abroad and potentially repatriate benefits of such investment back to Canada. A lifting of foreign ownership restrictions in other countries would also benefit foreign firms. Especially for countries with weak standards for minority shareholders, firms are made better off by majority foreign ownership, since the majority foreign owner is held to the higher standard of the foreign country in regards to protecting the rights of minority shareholders. Therefore, it follows that lifting ownership restrictions on foreign majority ownership will facilitate entrepreneurial finance, especially since most venture capital funds operating in developing countries are foreign funds.

9.4 Regulation Pertaining to the Demand for Entrepreneurial Capital

In Panel C of Table 9.1, we set out a variety of other laws that are pertinent to entrepreneurial finance. Entrepreneurship and the demand for entrepreneurial capital are facilitated by laws that minimize penalties associated with bankruptcy, minimize the costs associated with starting a business, and make changes to staffing decisions. Perhaps the most salient item that explains

[8]See MacIntosh (1994). Notice that post June 2002 after Sarbanes Oxley, it is less clear whether capital costs are cheaper in Canada or the United States. Further research is warranted.
[9]http://en.wikipedia.org/wiki/Bre-X.

international differences in rates of entrepreneurship and venture capital around the world is bankruptcy law. There is ample empirical evidence that more entrepreneur-friendly bankruptcy laws facilitate self-employment, risk taking, and entrepreneurship, thereby spurring the demand for venture capital.[10] Similarly, labor laws that facilitate ease of firing and incorporation laws with fewer procedures for starting a business also spur entrepreneurship around the world (Klapper et al., 2006).

Another potentially important legislative instrument for facilitating entrepreneurship and entrepreneurial finance is patent law. Conventional wisdom suggests patent laws encourage entrepreneurial activity by rewarding innovators. But there has been academic debate regarding the suitability of patents. Some papers by Aghion and Howitt (2006), and somewhat more controversial papers by Boldrin and Levine (2002), argue that there are private incentives to invest in R&D and there should not only be reliance on government.[11] Patents create monopolies and reduce competitive pressures, but competitive pressures to innovate may be as important as patents (for an extended discussion, see Gallini, 2002). Perhaps less controversial is the idea that patents encourage disclosure and technology transfer (Gallini, 2002).

A well-accepted problem with patent law and policy in the United States concerns "patent trolls" (Jaffe and Lerner, 2004). Patent trolls are firms and/or individuals that acquire patents not for the purpose of furthering entrepreneurial activity but rather for the purpose of suing (some say blackmail) others that invent similar technologies. The most illustrative example is the case of RIM and BlackBerry, in which patent trolls obtain patents relevant to BlackBerry but did not use any of them and successfully sued RIM for a majority of the profits.[12] Patent trolls clearly dissuade entrepreneurial activities, but the law as it currently stands offers ample support to patent trolls. Legislative changes are clearly warranted (Jaffe and Lerner, 2004).

9.5 Regulations Pertaining to the Supply of Entrepreneurial Capital

In addition to laws that favor entrepreneurial activities, there are supply-side regulations that encourage investment in venture capital and private equity. Various regulations governing investments of institutional investors in different countries around the world have been empirically shown to facilitate

[10]Armour and Cumming (2006, 2008). Entrepreneur-friendly bankruptcy laws directly benefit entrepreneurs. They also indirectly benefit investors to the extent that investors capture part of the returns to more risk-taking entrepreneurs (with the potential costs associated with excessive risk taking, as reviewed in Chapter 2).

[11]See, for example, Aghion and Howitt (2005) and Boldrin and Levine (2002).

[12]See, for example, http://cliffreeves.typepad.com/dyermaker/2005/12/rim_blackberry_.html.

investment in entrepreneurial companies. In the United States, the Employee Retirement Income Security Act (ERISA) established prudent man standards that enabled pension fund investment in venture capital, since it established the validity of venture capital as an appropriate investment for part of a pension fund's portfolio.[13] Similarly, the Netherlands in 2006 introduced the Financieel Toetsingskader (FTK), which changed pension fund portfolio management standards to enable a closer matching of assets and liabilities, thereby facilitating investment in venture capital (Chapters 4 and 7). Similar regulations that harmonize the regulations faced by European institutional investors (including the International Financial Reporting Standards, Basel II, and the FTK) also facilitate institutional investor investment in venture capital, as it better enables different types of institutions (such as banks, insurance companies, and pension funds), as well as institutional investors from different countries to act as limited partners for venture capital funds. As a related example, there is evidence that dissimilar regulations in Quebec exacerbate the fragmentation of Canada's venture capital market (Chapter 17).

Unlike their institutional investors, venture capital fund managers face few regulations. The dearth of regulations faced by venture capital funds has been shown to hinder institutional investment in venture capital. Institutional investors' commitments to venture capital are influenced by the fund performance reports that institutional investors receive from venture capital funds and also the institutional investors' ability to in turn disclose such performance reports to their own clients and beneficiaries (e.g., pensioners in the case of pension plans, etc.). Prior to the CalPERS lawsuit in California, venture capital funds enjoyed complete secrecy in terms of their disclosure of their performance to the public generally, and reports by venture capital funds to their institutional investors were not regulated. The effect of a comparative dearth of regulation of venture capital funds on the flow of funds into the venture capital market was discussed in Chapter 7, where we saw that the dearth of regulations of venture capital funds discourages institutional investors from investing in venture capital (see also Cumming and Johan, 2007b). Hence, rules (or at least formal guidelines) that increase transparency of investment in venture capital for institutional investors would facilitate institutional investment in venture capital. The lack of well-accepted reporting standards for reporting returns on unexited venture capital investments in the past has discouraged institutional investors from investing in venture capital, since venture capital managers have a tendency to overreport returns on unexited investments (see Chapter 22; see also Cumming and Walz, 2004). But there have been reforms to curb this problem, including new GAAP (Generally Accepted Accounting Principles) rules introduced in 2006 and clearly described industry standards for valuation by the Canadian Venture Capital Association (as well as similar

[13]Gompers and Lerner (1998). These standards have evolved as a benchmark for other countries around the world.

associations around the world).[14] Further research could assess the impact of these reforms.

9.6 Direct Government Investment Programs

Aside from legal incentive structures to facilitate entrepreneurship and entrepreneurial finance, the second main form of government support is via direct government created or subsidized venture capital funds. The range of alternative programs is summarized in Panel D of Table 9.1. Lerner, Cressy, and Cumming and MacIntosh, among others, have all discussed the ways in which government funds can be successfully implemented to work alongside private venture capitalists.[15] One of the most important items is the need for government funds to partner with, and not compete with, other types of venture capital funds. It is also important for government funds to bridge the gap in the market where there exists a clear and identifiable market failure in the financing of firms due to, for example, structural impediments in the market that have given rise to a comparative dearth of capital. Further, it is useful for government funds to be structured in ways that minimize agency costs associated with the financing of small high-tech firms.

9.6.1 United States

The U.S. Small Business Innovation Company (SBIC) Program, administered by the U.S. Small Business Administration (SBA) is the largest government support program for venture capital in the world. SBICs have invested over US$21 billion in nearly 120,000 financings to U.S. small businesses since the 1960s. Investee firms include such successes as Intel Corporation, Apple Computer, Federal Express, and America Online.[16] The SBIC program invested US$7 billion between 1983 and 1997. The SBIC does not distinguish between types of businesses, although investments in buyouts, real estate, and oil exploration are prohibited. In 1998, the SBIC invested US$3.4 billion in 3,470 ventures, approximately 40% by number and 20% by dollar value of all venture capital financings.

SBICs are operated like private independent limited partnership venture capital funds and are operated by private investment managers. The difference between a private independent limited partnership venture capital fund and an SBIC is that the SBIC is subject to statutory terms and conditions in respect to

[14]See, for example, http://www.privateequityvaluation.com/documents/IPEV_Press_Release_15.11.2006.pdf.

[15]Lerner (1999, 2002); Cressy (2002); Cumming and MacIntosh (2006, 2007).

[16]http://www.sebi.gov.in/commreport/venrep10.html.

the types of investments and the manner in which the investments are carried out.[17] For example, there is a minimum period of investment of one year, and a maximum period of seven years for which the SBIR can indirectly or directly control the investee firm. The SBIC does not distinguish between types of businesses, although investments in buyouts, real estate, and oil exploration are prohibited. Investee firms are required to be small (as defined by the SBA), which, generally speaking, is smaller than those firms that would be considered for private independent limited partnership venture capital financing. SBICs also face restrictions as to the types of investment in which they may invest. Capital is provided by the SBA to an SBIC at a lower required rate of return than typical institutional investors in private independent limited partnership venture capital funds. Excess returns to the SBIR flows to the other nongovernmental private investors and fund managers, thereby increasing or leveraging their returns. Empirical evidence shows early stage firms financed by the SBIR have substantially higher growth rates than non-SBIR financed firms.[18] This program has been quite effective in spurring venture capital investment and creating sustainable companies. A key feature of this program is that it complements and partners with, and does not compete with, private sector venture capital investment.

Lerner (1999) shows that early-stage firms financed by the SBIC have substantially higher growth rates than non-SBIC-financed firms. Overall, the SBIC program has been quite successful; however, as Lerner (1999) notes, welfare implication of the program in relation to SBIC program expenditures have not been fully studied.

9.6.2 Israel

The government of Israel supports venture capital through international cooperation with governmental bodies in other countries. The most successful of these ventures has been the Bilateral Industrial Research and Development Foundation (BIRD). BIRD started in 1977 as an equal partnership with the U.S. government. The BIRD Foundation was seeded with US$110 million to fund joint ventures between Israeli and U.S. firms. BIRD provides 50% of a firm's R&D expenses, with equal amounts going to each partner. Its return comes from the royalties it charges on the firm's revenue. A similar partnership, started in 1994 between Canada and Israel, is the Canada Israel Industrial Research and Development Foundation (CIIRDF).

Any pair of firms, one from each country, may jointly apply for BIRD support if between them they have the capability and infrastructure to define, develop, manufacture, sell, and support an innovative product based on industrial R&D. BIRD and CIIRDF often play a proactive role in bringing potential strategic partners together.

[17]These terms and conditions are summarized at http://www.sba.gov/INV/overview.html.
[18]Lerner (1999).

In practice, only 25% of the BIRD-funded projects have been successful. This success rate is comparable to private venture capital funds (Cochrane, 2005; Cumming and MacIntosh, 2003a,b; Cumming and Walz, 2004; Gompers and Lerner, 1997). Israel's small high-tech companies and Israel's high-tech economy have been tremendously successful over the past 20 years. Israel's investment in R&D has been among the highest in the world over the past few years (approximately 3% of GDP), and Israel has more than 3,000 technology-based firms.

It is noteworthy that Israel has been particularly successful in creating successful high-tech firms that eventually list on NASDAQ (Rock, 2001). One explanation for the Israeli success story is that its governmental support body has created successful international partnerships and networks (although there exist other explanations related to legal conditions, education, training, culture, and the like; see Rock, 2001).

9.6.3 Canada

The primary government support mechanism for venture capital in most jurisdictions in Canada since the 1980s has been the labor sponsored venture capital corporation (LSVCC) program. One estimate places the cost of the LSVCC program between 1992 and 2002 to be at least Can$3 billion (Cumming and MacIntosh, 2004). Many recent academic studies offer empirical analyses of the LSVCC program and the data point to a lack of success.[19] We will now review the reasons why the LSVCC program has not been successful. The data indicate there are differences in the quality of LSVCCs, and there is anecdotal evidence that not all labor-sponsored funds have been failures. Strictly based on the data, however, there are reasons to question the utility of the governmental LSVCC expenditures. The LSVCC program is described in detail herein because of its "memorable" and illustrative results as to how program design impacts real outcomes.

LSVCCs are tax-subsidized investment funds designed like mutual funds. Unlike mutual funds that invest in firms listed on stock exchanges, LSVCCs invest in privately held firms not listed on a stock exchange and typically high-growth firms in the technology sectors. As described following, in exchange for their tax subsidies, LSVCCs face statutory covenants that restrict their investment activity. LSVCCs have a three-pronged mandate: maximize employment, shareholder value, and economic development in the jurisdiction in which they are based. Most LSVCCs, however, state publicly that their only interest is in maximizing shareholder value (Cumming and MacIntosh, 2007; Halpern, 1997; MacIntosh, 1994, 1997). LSVCCs must have a labor union sponsor, but

[19]This first part draws on a number of recent studies on Canada's venture capital market, including for the most part work that the author has prepared with Professor Jeffrey MacIntosh of the University of Toronto Faculty of Law; see Cumming and MacIntosh (2003a,b, 2004, 2006, 2007). For other related studies of Canada's venture capital market, see also MacIntosh (1994, 1997); Cumming (2005a,b; 2006); Brander et al. (2002); Amit et al. (1998); and Halpern (1997).

it is often stated that labor unions merely rent their name to LSVCCs without providing any additional governance over the fund's operations.[20]

LSVCCs were first introduced in Quebec, Canada, in 1983. Thereafter, the federal government adopted LSVCC legislation in 1987; British Columbia in 1989; Manitoba in 1991; Ontario, Saskatchewan, and Prince Edward Island in 1992; New Brunswick in 1993; and Nova Scotia in 1994. Newfoundland and Alberta have not adopted LSVCC legislation. In 2005 there were 125 funds operated by LSVCCs in Canada,[21] including 16 federal funds, 67 Ontario funds, 7 British Columbia funds, 2 funds each in Saskatchewan and Manitoba, 3 funds in Quebec, and 28 in the Atlantic Provinces. Ontario revoked the tax subsidies to LSVCCs in August 2005, and one LSVCC in Manitoba was shut down due to a misuse of funds in 2005.

LSVCC investors are individuals (retail investors), as only individuals may invest in a LSVCC. Individuals are not restricted on their investment based on their wealth. Tax subsidies are provided to LSVCC investors as long as the LSVCC follows the statutory covenants that govern the fund. Investors are, however, subject to an eight-year lock-in period. Cumming and MacIntosh (2006, 2007) argue that this lock-in period limits investors' ability to vote with their feet by moving their capital out of poorly performing funds and thereby limits competition across LSVCCs. That only individuals may invest in LSVCCs clearly means that no one has the ability or incentive to collectively control managers; by contrast, pension funds with large holdings in a firm have incentives to have a "chat" with managers.

Most individuals invest in LSVCCs due to the tax savings provided through individual registered retirement savings plans (RRSPs). LSVCCs typically advertise the tax savings as the most advantageous reason for investment (Cumming and MacIntosh, 2007). Table 9.2 summarizes the tax position of a LSVCC investor in Ontario (prior to August 2005). The tax benefits vary depending on the tax bracket of the individual investor and are more favorable for investors in higher tax brackets (see Table 9.2 for details). For the highest tax bracket in Ontario, the initial tax generated return on a Can$5,000 investment was over 323% (see Table 9.2).

LSVCCs are bound by a number of statutory constraints, which are similar across the different Canadian provinces and are described in detail in Cumming and MacIntosh (2004). These constraints include limits on the geographical range of investment opportunities to within the sponsoring jurisdiction, constraints on the size and nature of investment in any given entrepreneurial firm, and requirements to reinvest fixed percentages of contributed capital in private entrepreneurial firms within a stated period of time (typically one to three years, depending

[20]Testimony before the Manitoba legislature in 1997 (six years after the Manitoba LSVCC legislation), for example, is consistent with this view. See http://www.gov.mb.ca/legislature/hansard/3rd-36th/vol_061a/h061a_4.html.

[21]Some LSVCCs have investment managers that manage more than one LSVCF, such as GrowthWorks and the Canadian Medical Discoveries Fund.

Table 9.2 Labor Sponsored Venture Capital Fund (LSVCF) Tax Savings Chart

This table presents the tax savings associated with an individual LSVCF investment of $Can 5,000. The table shows that returns vary from at least 109.21% to up to 323.73% from the tax savings only, before any gains or losses on the net asset value of the LSVCF.

Taxable Income ($Can):	**Up to $20,753**	**$30,754–$30,813**	**$30,813–$53,811**	**$53,812–$61,508**	**$61,509–$61,628**	**$61,629–$63,505**	**$63,505–$100,000**	**Over $100,000**
Registered Retirement Savings Plan (RRSP) Investment	$5,000	$5,000	$5,000	$5,000	$5,000	$5,000	$5,000	$5,000
Federal Tax Credit	$750	$750	$750	$750	$750	$750	$750	$750
Provincial Tax Credit*	$750	$750	$750	$750	$750	$750	$750	$750
Combined Federal and Provincial Tax Credit	$1,500	$1,500	$1,500	$1,500	$1,500	$1,500	$1,500	$1,500
RRSP Tax Savings	$1,110	$1,410	$1,560	$1,655	$1,855	$1,970	$2,170	$2,320
Combined Federal and Provincial Income Tax Rates	Up to 22.20%	28.20%	31.20%	33.10%	37.10%	39.40%	43.40%	46.40%
Total Tax Credits and Tax Savings	Up to $2,610	$2,910	$3,060	$3,155	$3,355	$3,470	$3,670	$3,820
Net Out of Pocket Cost on $5,000 Investment	At least $2,390	$2,090	$1,940	$1,845	$1,645	$1,530	$1,330	$1,180
Initial Return** = ($5,000 − Out of Pocket Cost)/Out of Pocket Cost	109.21%	139.23%	157.73%	171.00%	203.95%	226.80%	275.94%	323.73%

Sources: http://www.bestcapital.ca/why_invest.htm; accessed June 1, 2002; Department of Finance, Canada; and Cumming and MacIntosh (2007)

*Ontario provincial rates are used in this chart. For other provincial rates, see http://www.bestcapital.ca/why_invest.htm; accessed June 1, 2002; and Department of Finance, Canada.

**Initial return calculation does not account for any returns (losses) that may or may not be generated by a LSVCF's investment activities.

on the jurisdiction). It has been argued in prior work (Cumming and MacIntosh, 2006, 2007) that these constraints are extremely inefficient because they limit the investment opportunities and at times force LSVCCs to make investments in inferior firms and/or without adequate due diligence. Private independent limited partnership venture capital funds also have constraints or restrictive covenants imposed by their institutional investors, but these covenants are significantly different from those used by LSVCCs. For instance, private independent limited partnership venture capital fund covenants include restrictions on the use of debt (to prevent the fund managers from leveraging the fund and increasing the risk to the institutional investors), time restrictions on fundraising by fund managers for their subsequent funds (so that the fund managers spend their time pursuing and nurturing investments that further the interests of the current fund beneficiaries), among other things.[22] These covenants also vary depending on the agreed-upon needs of the fund investors and fund manager. This is important because it enables the limited partners and the general partner to best design covenants that are suited to the particular objectives of the fund. LSVCC constraints are invariant across funds and only change over time with statutory change.

Figure 9.1 indicates the growth of LSVCC capital over the 1992 to 2005 period relative to all other types of venture capital. These data are based on figures provided by the Canadian Venture Capital Association (CVCA)

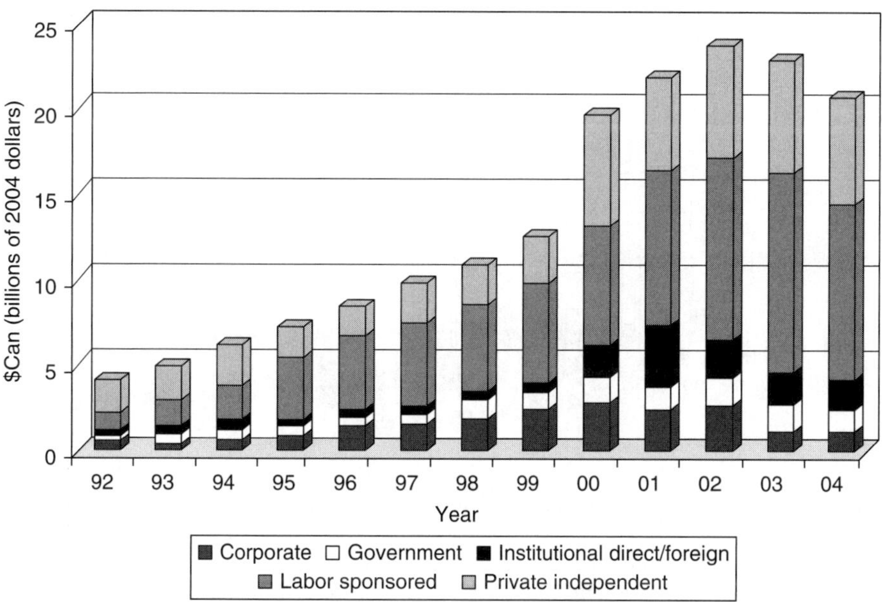

Figure 9.1 Venture Capital under Management by Investor Type in Canada: 1992–2004

[22]See Chapter 5.

and Macdonald and Associates, Limited (Toronto), and have been presented in prior work (e.g., Amit et al., 1998; Cumming and MacIntosh, 2006, 2007, among others). By 2005, LSVCCs comprised roughly 50% of the aggregate of all venture capital under management in Canada. LSVCCs started 2005 with more than Can$10 billion of capital under management (in 2005 dollars).

Figure 9.2 presents CVCA data for aggregate capital under management in the venture capital industry, capital available for investment, and new capital contributions in each year from 1992 to 2005 (see Cumming and MacIntosh, 2006, 2007). "Capital available for investment" indicates uninvested contributions to venture capital funds (capital allocated by institutional investors but not yet invested). Much of this uninvested capital has been accumulated in the LSVCCs. Some LSVCCs in the past (e.g., Working Ventures in 1997; Fonds de Solidarité in 2002 to 2003) had an excess of capital available for investment and thereby had to limit their capital contributions from individual investors, since they could not reinvest the money on time; that is, they did not want to face the statutory penalties for not reinvesting the contributed money within the time constraint.

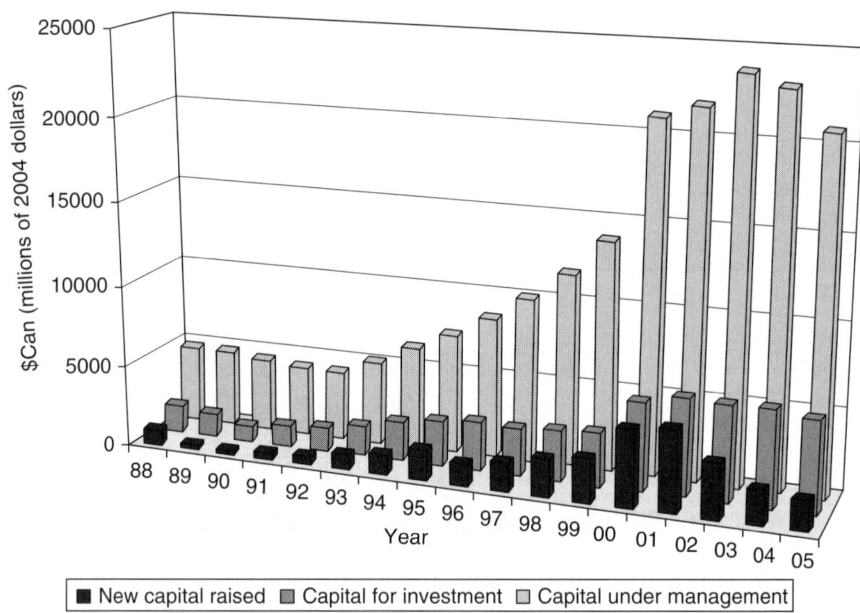

Figure 9.2 Capital for Investment in Canada: 1988–2004
Source: CVCA and Macdonald and Associates, Limited (Toronto).

Figure 9.3 presents the performance of LSVCCs over the past 10 years (Cumming and MacIntosh, 2006, 2007). Figure 9.4 shows that most LSVCCs are

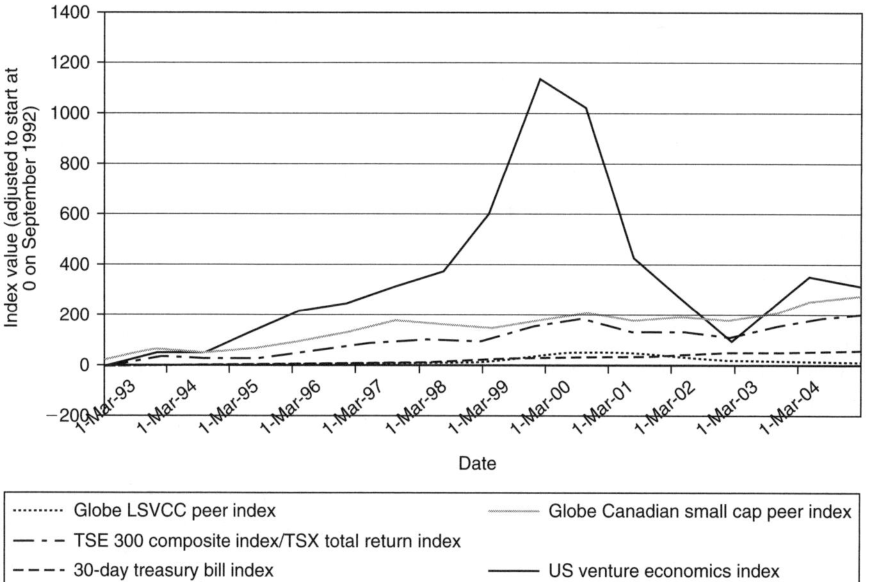

Figure 9.3 Selected Indices 1992–2005
Source: www.Morningstar.ca.

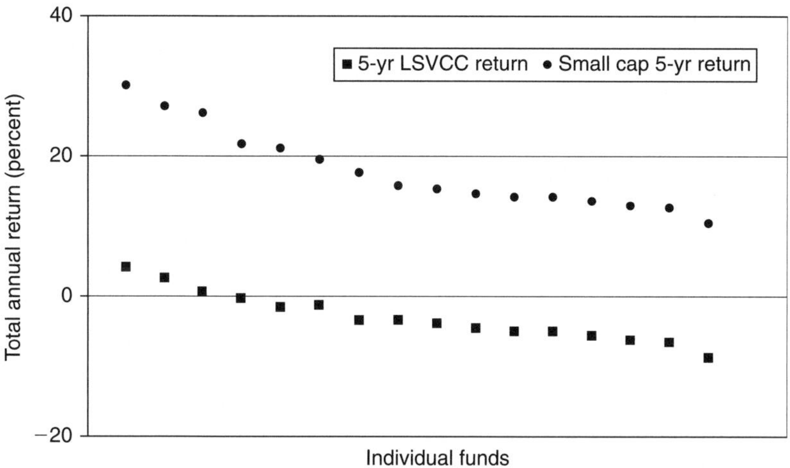

Figure 9.4 Ranked Scatter Plot of LSVCC Returns (All Funds) versus Canadian Small-cap Equity Mutual Fund Returns (Sample)
Source: Prepared by Finn Poschmann of the C.D. Howe Institute, based on data from www.Morningstar.ca as at 2005.

incurring economic losses (not including the tax-generated return for investors).[23] LSVCC returns do not even outperform risk-free 30-day t-bills. There are not even outlier LSVCCs that have had notably better performance than their counterparts (Figure 9.4). Most LSVCCs are barely breaking even with an economic rate of return of 0 over the past five years (Figure 9.4). In fact, Figure 9.4 shows that only 3 LSVCCs have earned a positive economic rate of return over the last five years, and even the best LSVCCs do not earn rates of return that are comparable to the contemporaneous worst performers that fit within Morningstar's small-cap categorization.

An oft-repeated excuse for poor LSVCC performance is that not all LSVCCs are earning losses and that their low returns are due to the fact that they are not pure profit maximizers. Figure 9.4 does indicate that three LSVCCs have earned a modest positive return. When viewed in conjunction with their multifaceted statutory objectives (profit maximization, labor growth, regional development, etc.), some commentators believe that certain funds are doing a good job based on anecdotal evidence. For example, an anonymous commentator on an earlier draft of this chapter indicated that the Quebec LSVCCs are different from those operating in the rest of Canada, and labor unions in Quebec play a stronger role in governance of labor fund manager activities relative to labor unions in other provinces. Despite the lack of data that precisely evaluate this anecdotal evidence, it is natural to expect differences across funds, and the characteristics of the people involved with the funds clearly will play a significant role in eventual outcomes. It is also possible that the people involved may have done an even better job if the statutory constraints of the LSVCC program were designed differently. For the overall evaluation of the LSVCC asset class, Figures 9.3 and 9.4 indicate there is ample room for improvement in the program design (regardless of whether some funds have done worse than others).

It is particularly noteworthy that the average LSVCC management expense ratio (management expenses/assets, or MER) is over 4%, which is substantially higher than that for all other types of mutual funds in Canada and the United States (Cumming and MacIntosh, 2007; Ruckman, 2003). Given that the economic rate of return for LSVCCs (Figures 9.3 and 9.4) is not net of MERs at 4%, most LSVCCs are negative value-added investment vehicles, since the returns do not cover management expenses. In the absence of tax subsidies, it would not be rational for an investor to contribute capital to LSVCCs. There is a mismatch between the massive capital accumulation among the LSVCCs (Figure 9.1) alongside the poor LSVCC performance (Figure 9.3), which can only be explained by the massive tax subsidies to LSVCCs (Table 9.2). Venture capital has been inefficiently allocated in Canada due to the tax breaks accorded to LSVCCs.

In relation to the very poor performance of LSVCCs, it is noteworthy that LSVCCs have massive portfolios per investment manager. Normally, venture

[23]Canadian data sources for Figure 9.3: www.globefunds.com, www.morningstar.ca (as reported in Cumming and MacIntosh, 2006, 2007).

capital managers only undertake the supervision of a few investee firms so as to be able to spend time adding value to their investees by sitting on the board of directors and providing strategic, finance, marketing, and human resource advice. LSVCCs have on average 6.5 investee firms per investment manager, compared with 2.5 investee firms per investment manager for private independent limited partnership venture capital funds (Cumming, 2006a). Other evidence indicates that LSVCCs are much less likely to have successful exit outcomes than private independent limited partnership venture capital funds in Canada. LSVCCs are much more likely to have unsuccessful buyback exits and secondary sales than IPOs and acquisitions.[24]

It is worth pointing out that much academic work is consistent with the view that a major hurdle in creating sustainable venture capital markets involves developing skilled venture capital managers (see, e.g., Gompers and Lerner, 1999; Keuschnigg and Nielsen, 2004c). There is a learning curve associated with venture capital investing. Some commentators on an earlier version of this chapter indicated that this was the biggest hurdle in Canada. The empirical evidence in Cumming and MacIntosh (2007), however, shows no evidence of older LSVCCs systematically performing better than more recently formed LSVCCs. One possible explanation is the massive portfolios per fund manager among LSVCCs, such that there is little or no time for LSVCC fund managers to get involved in the management of their investee firms. Of course, many LSVCC managers are likely highly capable individuals; but policymakers might consider alternative mechanisms to facilitate improved training of younger fund managers other than the environment offered by the typical LSVCC.

There are significant costs associated with the inefficient allocation of venture capital in Canada. First, there are direct costs of the tax subsidies, which have been estimated to be in excess of Can$3 billion over the period 1992 to 2002 (Cumming and MacIntosh, 2004). Second, there are indirect costs of LSVCCs crowding out private venture capital funds. The crowding out effect is due to the fact that LSVCCs compete directly with other types of venture capital funds. LSVCC tax subsidies enable LSVCCs to outbid other types of venture capital funds for investee firms, thereby discouraging institutional investors and private fund managers from starting private venture capital funds, since LSVCCs inefficiently drive up deal prices and lower returns in the market. Risk-averse institutional investors commit capital prior to knowing the increase in LSVCC fundraising in any given year. Risk-averse institutional investors are thereby likely to overestimate the extent of LSVCC funding and reduce their commitments to private venture capital funds. In effect, LSVCCs may even reduce the size of the venture capital market if the crowding out is pronounced. Empirical evidence is highly consistent with LSVCCs crowding out private venture capital in Canada (Cumming and MacIntosh, 2006).

[24]See Chapter 20; see MacIntosh (1997) and Cumming and MacIntosh (2003a,b) for earlier work.

In sum, studies of venture capital in Canada are consistent with the view that LSVCCs have fallen short of achieving their intended objectives for bolstering the Canadian venture capital market. The Provincial Governments in Canada have only recently shown signs of actively reforming the public subsidization of LSVCCs. For example, since 2004, Nova Scotia has placed their funds under a year-to-year watch to see if the tax credit should continue.[25] On August 29, 2005, the Province of Ontario completely dropped the tax credits afforded to LSVCCs.[26] In 2005 Manitoba shut down one of the province's two LSVCCs due to poor governance and scandals in misuse of public funds.[27] The poor structure and governance of LSVCCs (Cumming and MacIntosh, 2007) and the evidence that LSVCCs crowd out private venture capital investment in Canada (Cumming and MacIntosh, 2006) suggest that Ontario's taking the lead in abandoning LSVCCs is timely. To the extent that LSVCCs have been or should be abandoned in Canada, are there better policy options? The next part of this chapter considers this issue by outlining alternative policy options.

9.6.4 United Kingdom

In the autumn of 1995, Venture Capital Trusts (VCTs) were introduced to increase the pool of venture capital in the United Kingdom. VCTs are publicly traded companies (listed on the London Stock Exchange) that invest in small private firms and firms listed on the U.K. Alternative Investment Market (AIM). The VCT investment vehicle is similar in structure to that of other U.K. investment trusts. The main difference is that the individuals who invest in VCTs receive special tax breaks (detailed in Table 9.3; see also Cumming, 2003). In exchange for their tax status, VCTs face a number of statutory restrictions on their investment activities (these covenants are explained in detail by Cumming, 2003).

Overall, the United Kingdom's VCTs are extremely similar to Canadian LSVCCs. VCTs and LSVCCs are government-created funds that exist because of generous tax incentives offered to investors. Investors are individuals, but VCTs and LSVCCs are mutual funds that invest in private equity. VCTs and LSVCCs face statutory covenants governing their behavior in exchange for their tax subsidies. There are differences in the statutory governing mechanisms between VCTs and LSVCCs. Broadly speaking, LSVCCs' covenants do tend to be more onerous than VCT covenants (for details see Cumming, 2003), but the general effect is similar. The tax incentives to invest are also slightly different: LSVCCs have a smaller limit for tax-deductible investments, but the tax breaks are larger (as outlined in Table 9.3). The British Venture Capital

[25]http://www.gov.ns.ca/finance/taxpolicy/taxcredits/LSVCCreview2002.pdf.

[26]http://www.fin.gov.on.ca/english/media/2005/nr08-LSVCC.html.

[27]http://www.cbc.ca/news/background/personalfinance/labour_investmentfunds.html.

Table 9.3 Comparison between Canadian LSIFs and U.K. VCTs

This table presents a comparison of risk and returns to the Canadian Labour Sponsored Investment Funds (LSIFs) (also known as Labor sponsored venture capital corporations, or LSVCCs) and the U.K. Venture Capital Trusts (VCTs). Figures are for the period ending March 1, 2005. LSIF sources: http://www.globefund.com and http://www.morningstar.ca; VCT data source: http://www.trustnet.com/vct/ <all accessed 1 March 2005>. Both U.K. VCTs and Canadian LSIFs are among the class of mutual funds that invest in private equity. U.K. VCTs are regulated slightly differently than LSIFs (for specific details, see Cumming, 2003). The pseudo-beta measure for LSIFs is as defined in Table 9.2. The Riskmetrics™ Risk-Grades Rank for VCTs is defined at http://www.trustnet.com/vct/, and is a standardized measure of volatility; for comparison, U.S. t-bills have a Risk Grade of approximately 40, the S&P 500 has a Risk Grade of approximately 110, and NASDAQ has a Risk Grade measure of approximately 210. The low risk for VCTs and similarly the low beta for LSIFs reflect the periodic valuations of the underlying portfolio of investee firms. An untrained investor might be confused as to why risk measures are so low for LSIFs and VCTs based on information provided on various web pages, including the data sources, among others (as discussed in the text).

	U.K. VCTs				Canadian LSIFs			
	Riskmetrics Risk-Grades Rank	1-Year Return	3-Year Return	5-Year Return	Pseudo-beta	1-Year Return	3-Year Return	5-Year Return
Mean	59.019	9.027	−6.175	−34.395	0.097	−3.664	−6.915	−6.968
Median	54.390	5.800	−10.000	−40.300	0.090	−4.130	−6.370	−5.010
Standard Deviation	53.879	21.613	42.791	39.038	0.081	9.880	7.701	6.738
Minimum	1.360	−43.600	−70.100	−82.900	−0.030	−34.640	−26.010	−23.840
Maximum	381.280	86.200	191.100	95.200	0.340	26.200	5.460	1.660
Number of Funds for Which Data Exist in Column	72	78	69	38	47	111	44	23
Total Number of Funds as at March 2005	99				123			

(*continued*)

Table 9.3 (*continued*)

	U.K. VCTs				Canadian LSIFs			
	Riskmetrics Risk-Grades Rank	1-Year Return	3-Year Return	5-Year Return	Pseudo-beta	1-Year Return	3-Year Return	5-Year Return
Year of Legislation Allowing First Fund	1995				1983 Quebec, 1988 Federal Canada, 1989–1994 Other Canadian Provinces			
Aggregate Pool of Capital in Asset Class Managed as at March 2005	£1.6 Billion				£4.3 Billion			
Broadly Described Tax Incentives for Investors to Invest	40% Tax relief on individual investments of up to £200,000 (after Finance Act 2004); 20% tax relief on individual investments of up to £100,000 (before Finance Act 2004)				The maximum tax subsidized investment in any year is Can$5,000 (£2,164). The after-tax cost of a $5,000 LSIF investment made through the vehicle of an RRSP (see Section 9.6.4) ranges from $1,180 to $2,390, or roughly 27 to 48% of the nominal dollar cost of the investment (see Table 1)			

Association (BVCA) successfully lobbied the U.K. government regulators in 2002 to further facilitate VCT fundraising efforts through the expansion of tax subsidies and tax-exempt contributions (again, see Table 9.3).

From the comparable data available (summarized in Table 9.3), two things are immediately apparent. First, as with LSVCCs, VCTs appear to have very smooth earnings streams. The Riskmetrics risk ranking for VCTs (described in Table 9.3) shows VCTs as having a level of risk that is comparable to a government bond. This low-risk ranking is attributable to the valuation of VCT portfolios, which is quite similar to the LSVCC portfolio. LSVCC share prices are not determined in the market, but by periodic evaluations of net asset values per share as determined by the board of directors (for interim reporting periods) and by an independent valuer (for year-end reporting), with some variation in the frequency of these valuations. Therefore, LSVCC returns are not driven by CAPM-type assumptions. For this reason, Cumming and MacIntosh (2007) refer to LSVCC betas as "pseudo-betas." While LSVCC pseudo-betas are measured in the way betas on all stocks are measured [beta = covariance (market return, fund return)/variance (market return)], the LSVCC pseudo-betas are not an accurate measure of systematic risk but at best constitute a measure of the relative risk across the different LSVCCs, because the valuations of LSVCCs only change a few times per year. These valuations that give rise to the appearance of low risk among mutual funds that invest in private equity is completely artificial, and has adverse consequences, as described in Cumming and MacIntosh (2007).

Second, with the exception of the average U.K. VCT returns in the one-year horizon to March 2005, both VCT and LSVCC returns have been extremely low. In the five-year horizon to March 2005, median VCT returns were –40.3%, and median LSVCC returns were –5% (Table 9.3). In the one-year horizon to March 2005, median VCT returns were +5.8% and median LSVCC returns were –4.1%. The more recent improved one-year VCT performance appears to be directly attributable to an improvement in portfolio valuations from the years immediately prior to the March 2004 to March 2005 period (i.e., portfolio valuations were reduced immediately prior to the most recent year, so the improvement in returns may or may not be persistent in coming years).

Given the policy objective of stimulating venture capital investment, have LSVCCs and/or VCTs achieved their mandate? The similarity of evidence of VCTs and LSVCCs indicates that if policymakers adopt LSVCCs and/or VCTs in other countries, the effect is likely to be the same. The tax expenditure is extremely large, and the economic benefits from such expenditures do not appear to match the costs. The weak statutory governance structure is consistent with underperformance (see Cumming and MacIntosh, 2006, 2007, for LSVCCs; and see Cumming, 2003, for VCTs). Further, the tax subsidization to just one type of venture capital fund in the market creates distortions in the market that have the tendency to displace other forms of private venture capital, at least in the Canadian case (Cumming and MacIntosh, 2006; see Armour and

Cumming, 2006, for evidence from Europe).[28] Other forms of private venture capital finance foster sustainable and successful entrepreneurial firms that contribute to innovation and economic growth (Gompers and Lerner, 1999, 2001); the evidence from the tax-subsidized funds examined here does not show the existence of such benefits. The social benefits of using tax monies to create governmental venture capital funds of the form described in this paper are wanting.

We do note that further insights about VCTs may be gleaned from additional years of data, with a more in-depth analysis of fund-specific VCT details and an evaluation of the effect of the recent 2004 tax changes expanding their scope. Further research on this issue is warranted.

9.6.5 Australia

The government of Australia adopted the Innovation Investment Fund (IIF) program in 1997. As in the U.S. SBIR program, a key feature of the Australian IIF program is that it operates like a private independent limited partnership venture capital fund. The IIF program is one of eight related programs in Australia; other initiatives include the Renewable Energy Equity Fund (REEF) program, the Pre-Seed Fund (PSF) program, the Pooled Development Funds (PDF) program, the Venture Capital Limited Partnerships (VCLP) program, the Commercial Ready Program, the Commercializing Emerging Technologies (COMET) program, and the R&D Tax Concession. These related initiatives are summarized by the Department of Industry, Tourism, and Resources (2004).

In this brief summary of Australia's programs, we focus on the IIF program because it has been in existence for a comparatively longer period of time and has had a salient impact on the market.

The IIF was established in 1997 to stimulate the financing of small high-tech firms in Australia. The IIF fund had the following objectives:

- By addressing capital and management constraints, to encourage the development of new technology firms that are commercializing research and development
- To develop a self-sustaining Australian early-stage, technology-based venture capital industry
- To establish in the medium term a "revolving" or self-funding program
- To develop fund managers with experience in the early-stage venture capital industry

The IIF program operates in a manner that is most similar to the U.S. SBIC program. The Australian government held two competitive selection rounds in 1997 and 2000, which led to five IIFs being established in late 1997 (and early 1998) and another four being established in 2001. In total, 10-year licenses to nine private sector fund managers were awarded on a competitive basis. The first round of the program was announced in the Government's Small

[28]See also Leleux and Surlemount (2003).

Business Statement in March 1997 and provided AU$130 million, which has been matched on the basis of a Government to private sector capital ratio of up to 2:1. In round one, five licensed funds were established (A&B, AMWIN, Momentum, GBS—formerly Rothschild, and Coates Myer) and became operational during 1998. The second round of the IIF program enabled funding of AU$90.7 million and also matched by private sector capital on the basis of a Government to private ratio of up to 2:1. The Government to private capital ratio was a competitive element in the selection of the round two funds. Under round two, four funds wee licensed (Foundation, Nanyang, Neo—formerly Newport, and Start-up) and became operational in 2001. In total, the nine licensed funds have total capital of AU$385.05 million, of which the Australian government is contributing AU$220.7 million and the private sector AU$137.35 million.

Annual management fees were fixed at 3% of committed capital for the five round one funds and range from 2.5 to 2.8% among the four round two funds. Management fee levels, like government to private capital ratios, were a competitive element in the selection of the round two funds.

As with the U.S. SBICs, the Australian IIFs are administered by licensed private sector fund managers who make all investment decisions, subject to the terms of their license agreements with the Australian government and other governing documents.

These are the key elements of the IIF program's operating requirements:

- The ratio of Government to privately sourced capital must not exceed 2:1.
- Investments will generally be in the form of equity and must only be in small, new-technology firms.
- At least 60% of each fund's committed capital must be invested within five years.
- Unless specifically approved by the Industry Research and Development (IR&D) Board, an investee firm must not receive funds in excess of AU$4 million or 10% of the fund's committed capital, whichever is the smaller.
- Distribution arrangements provide for the following:
    - Both the Government and the private investors to receive an amount equivalent to their subscribed capital and interest on that capital.
    - Any further amounts are to be then shared on a 10:90 basis between the Government and private investors.

      The private investors' component is to be shared with the fund manager as a performance incentive.
    - The funds established under the IIF program will have a term of 10 years, after which they will be closed in a commercially prudent manner.

To be eligible for support under the IIF program, investee firms must do the following:

- Be commercializing the outcomes of R&D activities (as defined by the IR&D Act).
- Be at the seed, start-up, early, or expansion stage of development.
- Have a majority of its employees (by number) and assets (by value) inside Australia at the time a licensed fund first invests in the firm.

- Have an annual average revenue over the previous two years of income that does not exceed AU$4 million per year and revenue in either of those years that does not exceed AU$5 million.

A time series of all first-round investments (excluding staged financing rounds) is provided in Figure 9.5. Data for this section are provided by the Australian Venture Capital Association (AVCAL) and the Thompson Financial Venture Economics Database (the AVCAL data), which consists of 280 Australian venture capital and private equity funds and their investments in 845 entrepreneurial firms. For a statistical and econometric analysis of the Australian venture capital market and the impact of the IIF program, see Cumming (2007). While the extent of coverage for all venture capital and private equity investments in the AVCAL data is unknown, the AVCAL data provide the most comprehensive look at the history of the Australian venture capital and private equity industry. For example, it is known (Department of Industry, Tourism, and Resources, 2004) that the IIFs had financed 66 firms as of June 30, 2004, and the AVCAL data contain 55 of those 66 firms as of June 30, 2004 (and 57 investments in total including investments up to 2005 [Q1]; the difference is due to incomplete reporting to AVCAL). Moreover, the AVCAL database contains investments from all of the nine IIF funds and the vast majority of private equity and venture capital funds in Australia. The profile of Australian investments over time is quite consistent with patterns observed in the United States (Lerner, 2002), Canada (Cumming and MacIntosh, 2005), and Europe (Armour and Cumming, 2006). Venture capital and private equity investments around the world showed

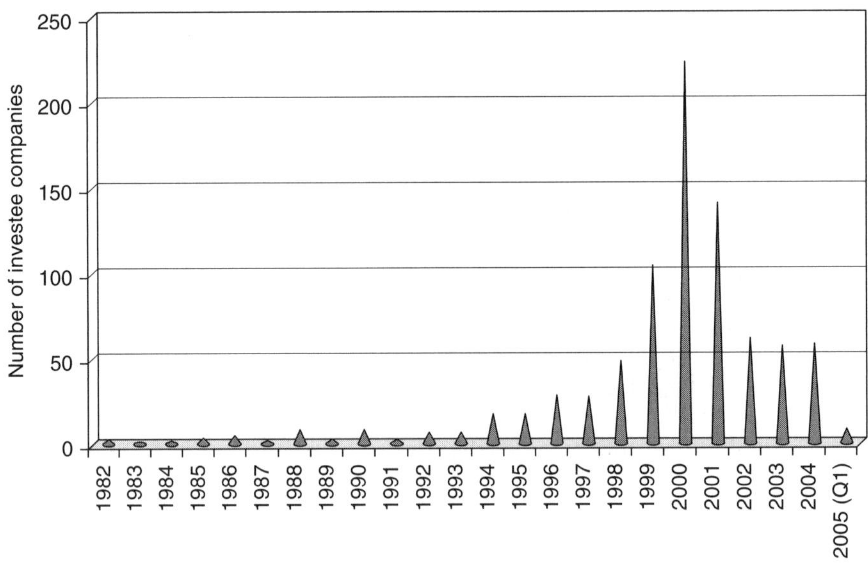

Figure 9.5 Australian Venture Capital and Private Equity Investments, All Stages, 1982–2005 (Q1)

a drastic increase in 1999 and 2000 leading up the beginning of the end of the bubble in April 2000.

Figure 9.6 provides further details about the stage of investment at the time of first investment for the time series of all venture capital and private equity investments. Figure 9.6 highlights as well the start date of the IIF investments in the two rounds. It is very noteworthy from Figure 9.6 that hardly any start-up and early-stage investments existed in Australia prior to the introduction of the IIF program.

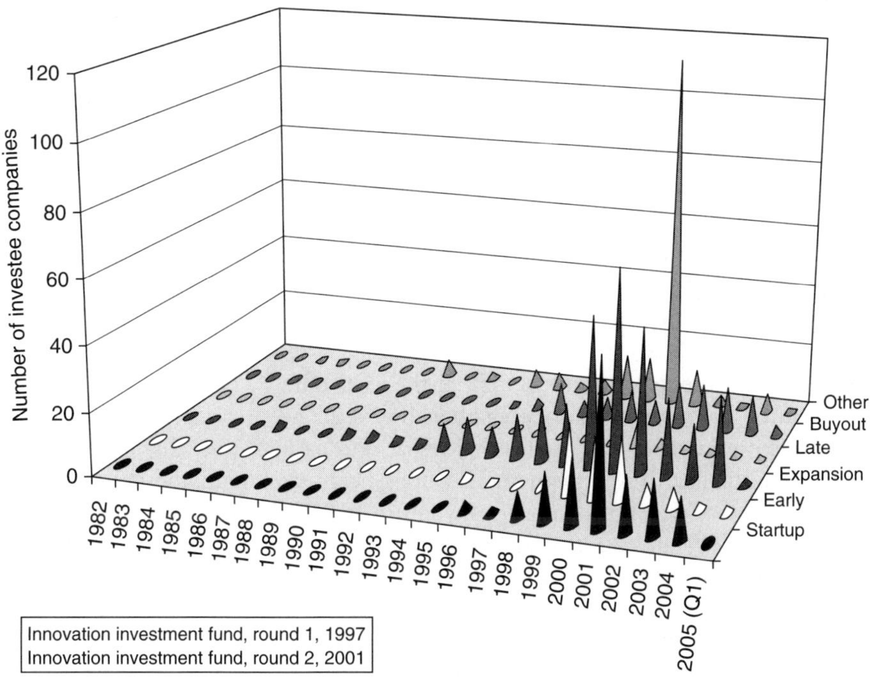

Figure 9.6 Australian Venture Capital and Private Equity Investments, by Stage, 1982–2005 (Q1)

Figure 9.7 provides a time series profile of the start-up and early-stage investments by the identity of the investors. Investor types of four categories are indicated in Figure 9.7: IIFs, private funds part of venture capital organizations that are associated with IIFs, other governmental program funds, and nongovernmental associated funds. This graphical presentation of the data shows nongovernmental funds hardly invested in start-up and early-stage companies prior to the IIFs. Nongovernmental IIF investments were, however, quite a significant portion of the market in 2001. A more rigorous assessment of the type of fund more likely to invest in start-up and early-stage firms is also provided.

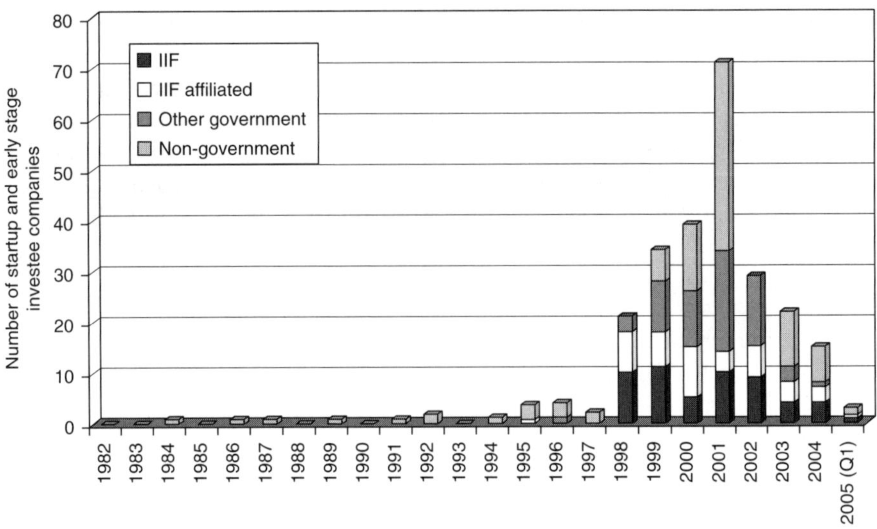

Figure 9.7 Australian Start-up and Early-stage Venture Capital Investments, by Investor, 1982–2005 (Q1)

Figure 9.8 presents a graphical look at the exits data by exit type. A clear limitation of the data is that exits other than IPO exits are not represented prior to 2002. It is noteworthy that the time series of IPO exits is quite dissimilar to that observed in the North American and European venture capital and private equity markets. In other developed countries, venture capital IPO exits were much more common in 1999 and 2000 than the period following the crash of the bubble (Lerner, 2002). By contrast, the AVCAL data indicate that the Australian venture capital market was not sufficiently developed to have as pronounced a boom in IPO exits in the period leading up to the peak of the Internet bubble and that the drop-off in VC-backed IPOs was only observed in 2001.

Figure 9.9 shows the time series of venture capital–backed IPOs by investor type. As in Figure 9.9, four categories of investor types are indicated in Figure 9.9: IIFs, private funds associated with IIFs, other governmental program funds, and nongovernmental associated funds. The majority of IPO exits appear to have been derived from nongovernmental funds. This is expected, as the primary governmental funds (such as the IIFs) were introduced in the recent past, governmental investments are in earlier stage firms (which take longer to bring to fruition in an exit), and many investments have yet to be exited.

Figure 9.10 presents the average share price returns of the venture capital–backed IPOs. It is important to point out that these returns are not the returns to the investors from taking the company public. Rather, these returns are the share price returns from the end of the first day of trading until June 30, 2004. As well, notice that 12 of the 55 IPOs were delisted. The returns calculations have been done on the basis that the returns to delisting have been −100%

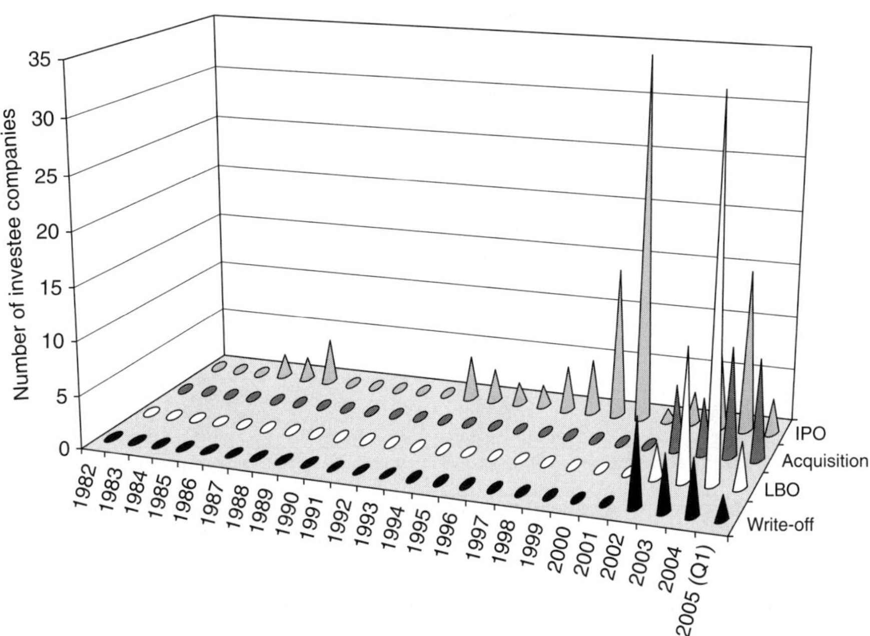

Figure 9.8 Australian Venture Capital and Private Equity Exits by Exit Vehicle, 1982–2005 (Q1)

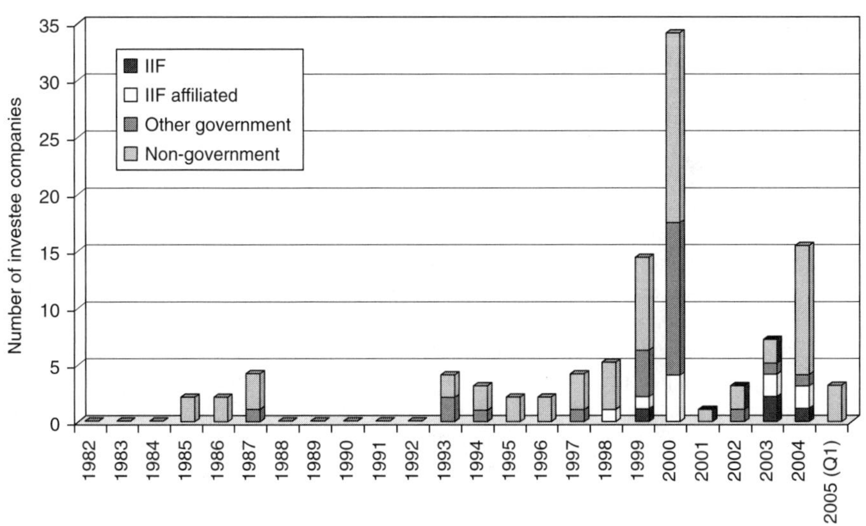

Figure 9.9 Australian IPO Exits by Investor Type, 1982–2005 (Q1)

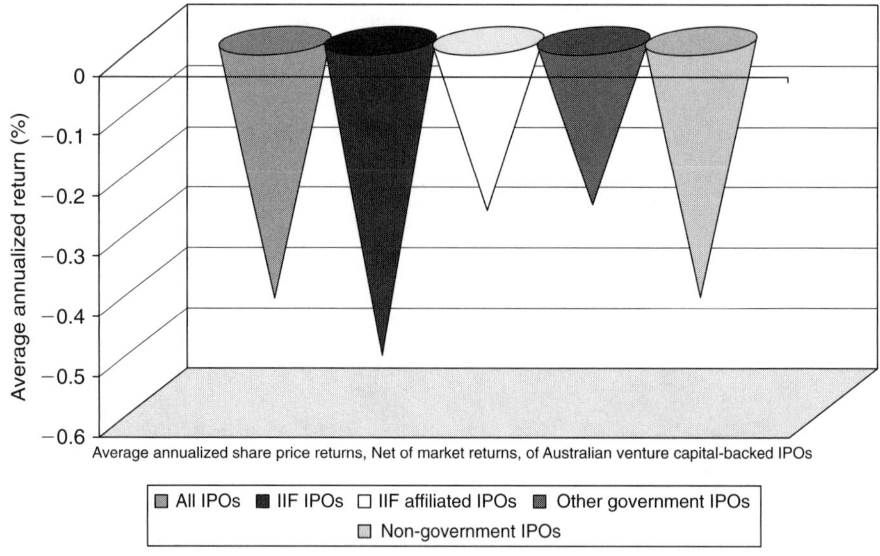

Figure 9.10 IPO Share Price Returns, Net of Market Returns, by Type of Venture Capital Backing

(which may overstate the degree of poor performance, as investors may have been compensated with some value prior to delisting). On average, returns performance is quite negative for all types of funds, and there are not statistically significant differences across different fund types. The negative performance is expected and similar to IPOs in other countries that went public over contemporaneous periods. IPO performance is discussed further in Part IV.

In sum, the evidence on IIFs up to 2005 indicates the following (see Cumming, 2007, for additional details):

- The IIF program has significantly contributed to the financing of start-up and early-stage firms, as well as high-tech firms, in Australia. Prior to the establishment of the IIF program, there was a comparative dearth of such investments in Australia. The IIF program is meeting its stated objective of encouraging the development of new technology companies that are commercializing R&D.
- IIF fund managers are also more likely to stage and syndicate investments and invest in fewer portfolio firms per fund manager. More frequent staging and syndication are consistent with the notion of better screening and value-added advice provided to the investee firms, as established in prior research in venture capital finance. Similarly, fewer portfolio firms per manager are also consistent with the notion of greater value-added advice provided to each investee. As such, the evidence on each of these dimensions is consistent with the view that IIF managers on average add more value to their investees than their counterparts.
- The IIFs are part of organizations with managers that have privately raised companion funds. These companion funds are also more likely finance start-up and early-stage entrepreneurial firms and those in high-technology industries. As such,

the data are consistent with the view that the IIF program is facilitating the training or professionalization of venture capital fund managers with experience in early-stage investing. Overall, this is a long-term benefit for the development of a self-sustaining Australian early-stage, technology-based venture capital industry.

- It is not possible to ascertain whether the IIF program will eventually be a "revolving" or self-funding program, since the majority of investments have yet to come to fruition. To fully address this question, a reevaluation of the program at the time when all IIF investments have been exited would be warranted. The IIFs have had to "weather the storm" of the Internet bubble crash, which has made exiting existing investments comparatively more difficult since April 2000. The available data to date indicate that exit performance of IIFs and non-IIFs alike have been equally flat to date. The evidence that IIFs are providing suitable governance to their investee firms is suggestive that the IIFs will achieve better than average performance results and successful exits. To date, however, the available data from AVCAL do not indicate any statistical difference in performance across the funds. Further research is warranted as additional exit and performance data become available.

9.6.6 Summary and Other Possible Design Mechanisms for Government Venture Capital Funds

In sum, international evidence indicates it is quite a challenge to design a successful government venture capital program. Government policy toward venture capital in the United States and Israel in the form of private/public partnerships and international partnerships appears to have been quite successful. By contrast, the available evidence indicates substantially fewer social benefits of using tax monies to create governmental venture capital funds of the form of mutual funds that invest in private equity, as done in Canada and the United Kingdom. As indicated, there are other governmental policy programs in these other countries that have not been mentioned here (primarily for reasons of conciseness); only the primary programs in these other countries have been reviewed.

There are other specific support mechanisms that governments can provide to venture capital markets summarized in Panel D of Table 9.1, including government loans, priority reversals for the government as an investor, and bailouts for losses (listed in Table 9.1).[29] These provisions naturally facilitate incentives for investors to start and invest in venture capital funds. But they also create potentially distortionary incentives as well. It is well known that there are significant agency problems associated with debt, such as underinvestment, risk shifting, and asset stripping.[30] Empirical evidence in regards to security design in Canada and Europe is consistent with the view that debt is not used when these agency costs associated with debt are expected to be pronounced (see Chapters 11 and 14, respectively). Similarly, we may conjecture

[29]See also Jääskeläinen et al. (2007) for an extended discussion.
[30]These terms were defined in Chapter 2.

that if these problems are expected to be pronounced among venture capital fund managers supported by the government, then these schemes will not be as valuable as one might think.

Governments have also delved into creating 100% government owned venture capital organizations, such as the Canada Community Investment Plan (CCIP).[31] Academic work on the topic indicates such programs are more likely to finance firms that might not otherwise receive capital, such as entrepreneurial firms in regionally isolated communities (Bates, 2002; Lerner, 2002). Some government programs focus on increasing the export intensity of their domestic firms, such as the Export Development Corporation (Industry Canada). In some countries other than Canada, government programs have focused efforts on privatizing firms and thereby increase the scope of viable projects for venture capitalists to consider as investment opportunities.[32] The success of these various policy strategies depends on a wide range of structural, political, and economic aspects of the country in which they are adopted, as well as the manner in which the policy is implemented. It is not always clear that the incentives are well aligned in any of these cases. Further research is warranted.

9.7 Summary

This chapter surveyed a variety of alternative ways to promote entrepreneurship and efficient venture capital investment. The evidence reviewed in this chapter indicated appropriate legal changes could include more entrepreneur-friendly bankruptcy laws, lower capital gains taxes, and less onerous securities regulation, among other mechanisms detailed in Table 9.1.

This chapter also highlighted the Canadian case as an example of extreme outcomes with different policy options. We explained that LSVCCs are an inefficient statutory tax-subsidized type of venture capital fund in Canada. LSVCCs manifest poor governance mechanisms, charge very high fees, and earn economic returns that lag behind 30-day risk-free t-bills. Expenditures by the government on LSVCCs have not resulted in value-added venture capital investment and appear to have crowded out private venture investment in Canada. The tax subsidies to LSVCCs were removed in the Province of Ontario in Canada in 2005. Empirical studies of Canada's venture capital market are consistent with the view that all jurisdictions in Canada should follow Ontario's lead. As regards to other direct government programs, the most successful program in the world has been the U.S. SBIR program. A somewhat similar program that appears to be successful is the Australian IIF program. A common feature of successful programs is that they partner with the private sector and do not compete with private funds.

[31]http://strategis.ic.gc.ca/epic/internet/inccip-picc.nsf/en/h_cw01102e.html.

[32]See Megginson et al. (2004) for related work on privatizations.

In sum, empirical evidence is quite consistent with the view that successful government subsidization of venture capital and private equity markets involves favorable tax laws and legal structures that accommodate entrepreneurial activities and the establishment of venture capital and private equity funds, liberal bankruptcy laws that provide little or no time to discharge for entrepreneurs, and a small scope for direct government investment programs that partner and do not compete with private investors.

Key Terms

Securities regulation
Initial public offering (IPO)
Hold period
Prospectus
Stock option
Patent policy
Venture Capital Trust (VCT)
Labor sponsored venture capital corporation (LSVCC)
Labour Sponsored Investment Fund (LSIF)
Small Business Investment Company (SBIC)
Bilateral Industrial Research and Development Foundation (BIRD)

Discussion Questions

9.1. What are the two main ways in which governments may subsidize venture capital and private equity markets? What does existing empirical evidence suggest about the relative success of these different approaches?

9.2. Compare and contrast direct government expenditure programs for venture capital in Australia, Canada, Israel, the United Kingdom, and the United States. Which program has been most successful, and why?

9.3. Among different regulatory policy options, which is comparatively more important for venture capital markets: patent policy, bankruptcy law, capital gains taxation, or securities regulation? Why?

9.4. Discuss the benefits and drawbacks toward government loans and downside guarantees to venture capital fund managers provided by governments. How do you think government programs of this type might influence different agency problems associated with fund management?

Part Three

Financial Contracting between Funds and Entrepreneurs

10 The Investment Process

10.1 Introduction and Learning Objectives

Part III contains Chapters 10 to 14 and considers the structure and governance of venture capital and private equity fund investments in entrepreneurial firms. The investment process may be viewed as involving the following issues:

1. Due diligence (screening potential investee firms)
2. Selecting the stage of entrepreneurial firm development at which to invest (the various stages were indicated in Chapter 1) and industry in which to invest (e.g., biotech, computers, etc.)
3. Staging (number of financing rounds)
4. Valuation
5. Syndication (number of investors)
6. Board seats
7. Contracts between the fund and its investee firms, which includes decisions over matters that include, but are not limited to the following:
   a. Security (debt, preferred equity, common equity, etc.)
   b. Control rights (such as the right to replace the founding entrepreneur as the CEO, among other rights)
   c. Veto rights (such as over asset sales and purchases)

The purpose of this chapter is to provide a brief overview of the issues pertaining to each of the preceding items. Further, in this chapter we provide a road map of items considered in more detail in Chapters 11 to 14. Part IV (Chapters 15–18) considers related issues of investor value-added advice, including issues pertaining to location, portfolio size, and advice and monitoring provided by the investor.

10.2 Due Diligence

The process of due diligence is a natural place to start because it involves the screening of potential investee firms. Academic evidence indicates that a typical venture capital fund will receive more than 1,000 business plans per year, but many will not even seriously consider business plans unless they are referred by someone known to the fund manager. Fund managers may look at 50 of these plans but seriously consider only about 25 of them. Of these, venture capitalists may carry out in-depth due diligence at significant financial and time cost on 10 business plans and then only end up financing 1 or 2 of these ventures (Sahlman, 1990). The costs incurred by the fund manager during the due diligence process may include external consultant cost to review the technology, external legal and financial advice, and of course the time and resources of the fund manager herself. It is for this reason that prior to commencing an in-depth due diligence review, the fund managers will draft what is called a term sheet that will set out the general terms and conditions of the investment as anticipated by the fund manager based on what he knows of the deal at that time (and the fund manager will ask the entrepreneurial firm to agree to the terms; see Appendix 2, which provides a sample term sheet). Sometimes the term sheet will require that in the event that a deal is found unviable as a result of the exposure of a critical omission on the part of the entrepreneurial firm during the due diligence, then the entrepreneurial firm will bear part of the cost. This is to ensure that the entrepreneurial firm acts sincerely and legitimately during the process.

It is noteworthy that business plans accompanied by a nondisclosure agreement (NDA) are typically not read by a fund manager. Fund managers review a large number of different process, technological, and other ideas for firms, many of which are somewhat related and do not have time to consider potential litigation associated with business plans that are potentially related to one another in ways they may not have considered. As well, fund managers receive many business plans without such nondisclosure conditions attached. And it is noteworthy that entrepreneurs are protected by common law in ways that are similar to nondisclosure agreements. If a fund manager read a proposal and then used the information strictly from the proposal in ways that were detrimental to the entrepreneur (even when they are not in a contractual relationship), then there is common law that supports the view that the entrepreneur has rights to seek compensation for the harmed caused. In Canada, for example, this issue was considered by the Supreme Court in a context outside venture capital finance but nevertheless in an analogous context. In the case *Lac Minerals*,[1] Corona Resources proposed a mining site to Lac Minerals with the view toward developing the site jointly. After Corona revealed the location to Lac Minerals, Lac Minerals went ahead with the plan without including Corona. Corona sought damages and was successful in gaining a judgment against Lac Minerals. The Supreme Court of Canada thereby established the position that the party in receipt of the information has a duty to the provider of information, even before they are in a contractual relationship. It is noteworthy, however, that on the facts of this case that the information was offered in reasonable expectation of forming a contractual relationship. An entrepreneur that simply mails a business plan to a fund manager may not be able to use the same argument. But an entrepreneur that reveals specific material details to a fund manager in the process of negotiations over deal terms might owe a duty to the entrepreneur to not use that information even if no contractual

[1]*Lac Minerals Ltd. v. International Corona Resources Ltd.* [1989] 2 S.C.R. 574.

relationship emerged between the entrepreneur and fund manager, even without a nondisclosure agreement.[2] Note also that a fund manager is only as good as his deal flow, so any hint of inappropriate behavior on his part may affect his chances of getting good deals in the future.

There is much anecdotal evidence that the due diligence carried out by fund managers differs significantly in different countries. For example, entrepreneurs in the city of Toronto, Canada, have mentioned to the authors that the extent of due diligence by some fund managers in Canada is much less thorough than that carried out by fund managers in the United States. Anecdotally, for example, U.S. fund managers are more likely to involve the opinion of Ph.D.'s in biotechnology and active researchers in biotechnology before making an investment in a biotech start-up company, while some Canadian fund managers might be less likely to be as rigorous in their screening process (for instance, even if the opinion of someone with a Ph.D. is involved, that person is less likely to be the leading expert in the relevant subject matter). However, this may be related to the resources availed to the respective fund managers during the due diligence process and the costs involved, and there is not empirical evidence to date measuring these differences.

Nevertheless, there is evidence from Kaplan and Strömberg (2004) on due diligence from a sample of 67 U.S. venture capital investments by 11 limited partnerships. Internal factors influencing the investment decision include the quality of management, performance to date, funds at risk/downside, influence of other investors, VC portfolio fit and monitoring cost, and valuation. External factors influencing the decision to invest include market size and growth, competition and barriers to entry, the likelihood of customer adoption, and financial and exit market conditions. Finally, difficulty of execution influences the decision to invest, including the product and/or technology as well as the business strategy/model.

In Chapter 2, we introduced the concept of "adverse selection." Adverse selection is the risk of attracting a low-quality or high-risk entrepreneurial firm by virtue of the nature of the contract that is offered. In Chapter 12 we examine cases in which adverse selection risks are more pronounced and thereby provide practical guidance as to when fund managers need to be relatively more concerned about carrying out due diligence. In Chapter 16 we consider how investment risks along these lines relate to the advice and monitoring provided by the fund manager post investment.

10.3 Stage of Development and Industry

It goes without saying that central elements of the investment process are the choice of stage of entrepreneurial firm development and industry in which to

[2]Of course, whether or not the entrepreneur has the resources to pursue legal action is another matter altogether.

invest. As discussed in Chapter 5, limited partnership private equity funds are established with contracts that set out expectations as to the stage of entrepreneurial firm development in which the fund will invest. Also, we mentioned in Chapter 8 that often funds style drift from their objective investment stage. For instance, in the boom of the Internet bubble, some late-stage funds may have found it irresistible to venture into computer-related dotcom firms with the lure of potentially higher returns relative to their designated fund focus. Hence, while investment stage and industry are set out in contracts that establish private equity funds, investment decisions sometimes deviate from the stated objectives in ways that reflect changes in market conditions (Cumming et al., 2004b).

In a recent paper, Cumming et al. (2005a) show that the nature of investments in private equity varies with different cycles in the stock market, and in particular the IPO market.[3] Based on a sample of 18,774 U.S. private equity financings between 1985 and 2004, they show that in times of expected illiquidity of exit markets (high liquidity risk), fund managers invest proportionately more in new high-tech and early-stage projects (high-tech risk) to postpone exit requirements. When exit markets are liquid, fund managers rush to exit by investing more in later-stage projects. Cumming et al.'s estimations indicate that an increase of liquidity by 100 IPOs in a year reduces the likelihood of investing in new early-stage projects (as compared to new investments in other development stages) by approximately 1.5 to 2.3%, depending on the econometric specification. This effect is graphically depicted in Figure 10.1.

10.4 Staging

Staging is an important aspect of private equity investment, as staging facilitates monitoring and thereby mitigates agency costs (see Figure 2.9 and accompanying text in Chapter 2). Essentially fund managers are able to minimize their financial risk and keep the entrepreneurial firms on track with their business plan with staging the capital provided. The stages of capital infusion are usually agreed upon between the fund manager and the entrepreneurial firm with reference to the business plan and forecasts provided. If the benchmarks agreed upon at the outset cannot be met by the entrepreneurial firm, it does not necessarily mean that the investment is aborted but that future capital infusion will be revalued and the entrepreneurial firm can expect significantly increased monitoring. Gompers (1995) provides examples of staging of some of the better-known U.S. firms today:

Federal Express

US$12,250,000 September 1973 US$204.17/share
US$6,400,000 March 1974 US$7.34 per share

[3]Gompers et al. (2008) find the same result.

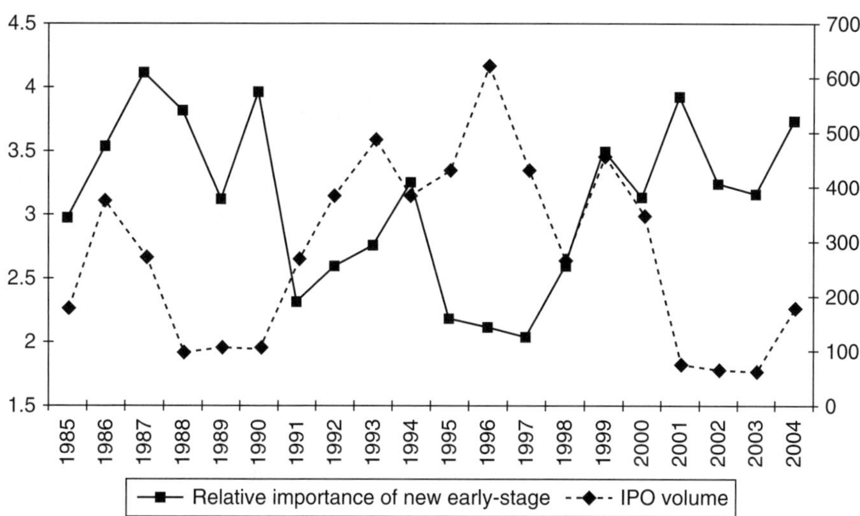

Figure 10.1 Importance of New Early-stage Investments and IPO Volume in the United States from 1985 to 2004. The bold line (with left-hand Y-axis) gives the ratio of new early-stage investments over all new expansion-stage and later-stage investments in each year. The IPO volume (right-hand Y-axis) is shown by the dashed line and represents the number of initial public offerings (IPOs) as reported by Ritter and Welch (2002). It refers to IPOs on the NASDAQ, NYSE, and AMEX.
Source: Cumming et al. (2005a).

US$3,800,000 September 1974 US$0.63 per share
Firm went public in 1978 at US$6 per share

Apple Computer
US$518,000 January 1978 US$0.09/share
US$704,000 September 1978 US$0.28/share
US$2,331,000 December 1980 US$0.97/share

Gompers shows that staging is more frequent when expected agency costs are more pronounced. That is, fund managers more frequently stage the earlier-stage entrepreneurial firms in high-tech industries. Also, for industries with greater asset specificity (high industry-specific and firm-specific value and few alternative uses and hence smaller liquidation values), there is a shorter investment duration between investment rounds and more frequent staging of investments.

Cumming et al. (2005a) further show that conditions of exit market liquidity impact the decision to invest in new projects versus follow-on investment in continuing projects pursuant to staged financing (in the spirit of Gompers, 1995). An increase in IPO volume by 100 increases the probability of investment in a new project (as opposed to a follow-on project) by approximately 1.2 to 4.1%, depending on the econometric specification. This effect is graphically depicted in Figure 10.2.

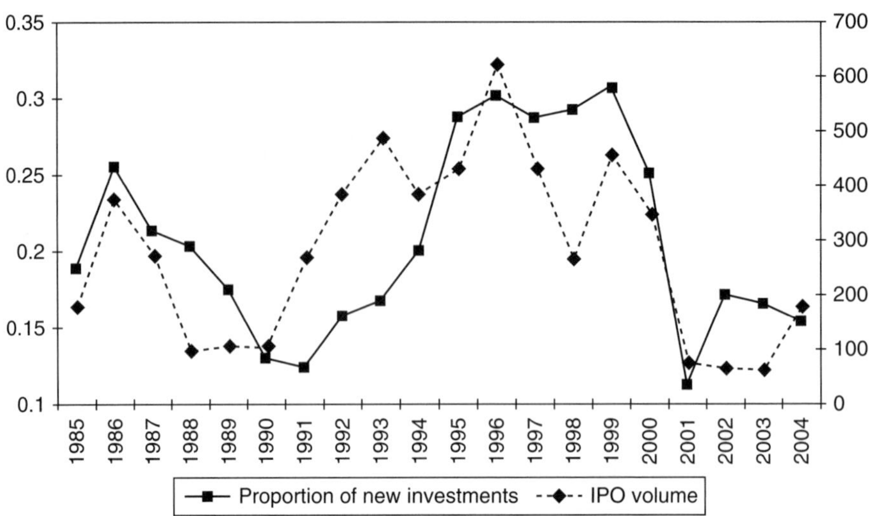

Figure 10.2 Importance of New Investments Compared to Follow-on Investments. The bold line (left-hand Y-axis) gives the proportion of new investments from all investments (new and follow-on) in each year. The dashed line (right-hand Y-axis) gives again the number of IPOs in each given year (IPO volume).
Source: Cumming et al. (2005a).

10.5 Fund Flows and Valuations

The pricing of a deal or the amount of capital the fund manager will provide to the entrepreneurial firm will of course depend on the amount sought by the entrepreneurial firm. Some firms will ask for far too much, and others will surprisingly ask for too little. At the end of the day, the final amount will be determined by the fund manager depending on what he values the investment to be or, rather, the potential of the investment. Also, as just noted, the valuation may change over the course of the investment. It is noteworthy that public market cycles also impact the pricing of venture capital deals. Gompers and Lerner (2000) show that capital inflows into the venture capital market positively affect the pricing of venture capital deals based on 4,000 U.S. venture capital financings between 1987 and 1997 (a phenomenon known as money chasing deals). A doubling of the fund inflows into venture capital funds causes an increase in valuations by 7 to 21%, and a doubling of public market values causes an increase in value of private equity by 15 to 35%. This effect is graphically depicted in Figure 10.3, where the inflows are normalized at 1 for 1987, and the average pre-money valuations are in millions of U.S. dollars. Gompers and Lerner interpret these results as consistent with the demand pressure interpretation: Values are higher because of money flowing into the VC market and not due to an improvement in investment opportunities, and success rates (IPO or acquisition) did not differ from the early 1990s (bad market) and late 1980s (hot market).

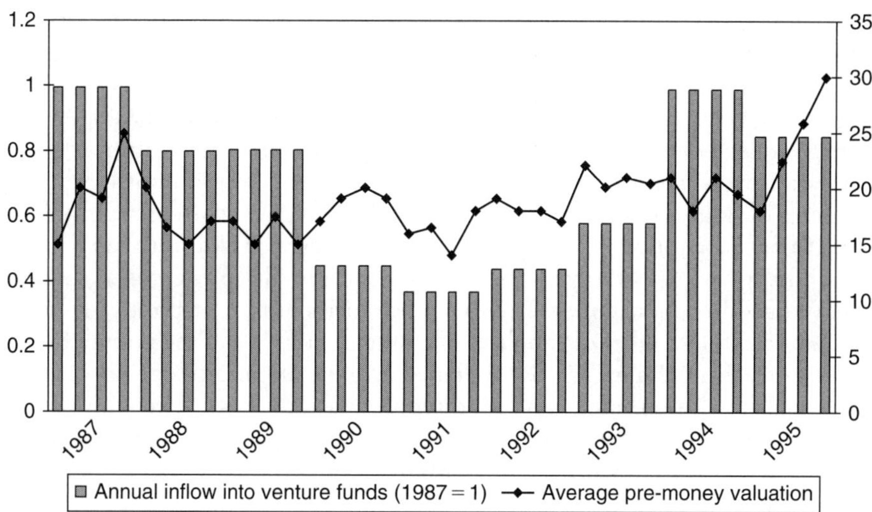

Figure 10.3 Relation between Pre-money Valuation and Annual Fund Inflows into Venture Capital
Source: Gompers and Lerner (2000).

Chapter 22 considers issues pertaining to valuations of venture capital and private equity investments. This material follows after a discussion of exiting investments and returns.

10.6 Syndication

Private equity funds typically syndicate their investments. Lerner (1994), Lockett and Wright (1999, 2001), and Wright and Lockett (2003), among others, have reviewed various reasons why fund managers syndicate their investments. One explanation is that syndication facilitates better decision making as to whether to invest (Sah and Stiglitz, 1986). It is akin to having another fund manager corroborate your evaluation of a firm's potential. If so, syndicated investments would perform better, according to Lerner (1994).[4] Cumming and Walz (2004) provide a sample of more than 5,000 private equity investments from 39 countries around the world and find evidence consistent with the view that syndicated investments perform better; this evidence is discussed further in Chapter 22. Another reason for syndication is that syndicated fund managers might collude to overstate the value of the entrepreneurial investment upon exit

[4]Brander et al. (2002) interpret better-performing investments as consistent with the hypothesis that syndication facilitates value-added help provided by venture capital fund managers to the investee firm and inconsistent with the better screening hypothesis. The intuition is that if the investee firm were of very high quality, then the investor would not invite syndicated partners.

(Lakonishok et al., 1991). As such, we would expect fund managers to offer the best deals to those that are able to reciprocate the favor (other well-established private equity firms; see Lerner, 1994). Syndication also facilitates diversification through risk sharing or sharing of possible losses (Wilson, 1968). A fund manager does not want to underperform his peers and risk not attracting new capital for investment (Lerner, 1994). Finally, syndication also mitigates agency problems of hold up (as defined in Chapter 2). That is, an entrepreneur is more likely to have a contract renegotiated by a nonsyndicated investor than a syndicated one. In the case of a syndicated investment, the entrepreneur is more likely to have outside opportunities. Theory and empirics indicate a positive relationship between the number of suppliers of capital to a firm and the growth opportunities of a firm (Rajan, 1992). Reliance on one supplier of capital provides that supplier with an information monopoly that adversely affects investment incentives because of potential hold-up problems. Such hold-up problems will be particularly acute for firms with substantial growth opportunities because a single supplier has too much control over liquidation (exit) decisions.[5]

Lerner (1994) provides interesting evidence on syndication from 271 biotechnology firms financed in 651 investment rounds by venture capitalists over

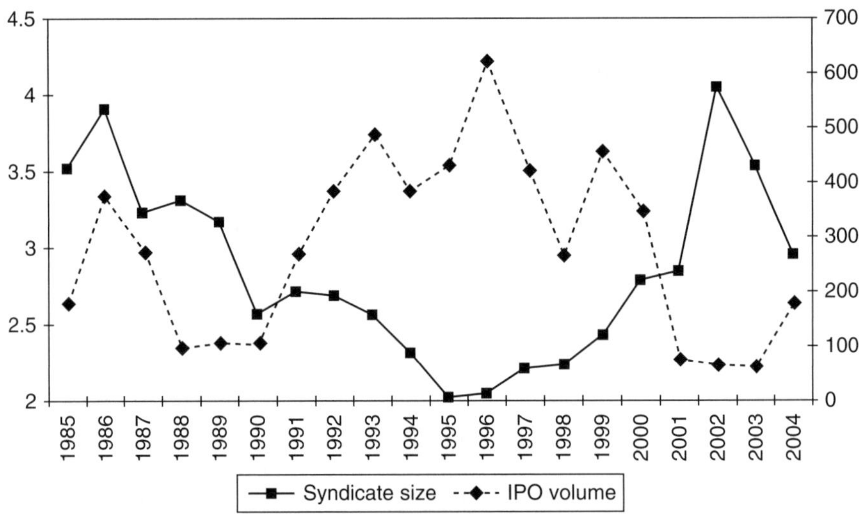

Figure 10.4 Syndicate Size for New (First-round) Investments and IPO Volume in the United States from 1985 to 2004. The bold line (left-hand Y-axis) gives the average number of syndicate partners involved in new investments in each year. The dashed line (right-hand Y-axis) gives again the number of IPOs in each given year (IPO volume). *Source:* Cumming et al. (2005a).

[5]This issue is also discussed in Chapter 11. As well, the Appendix in Chapter 11 reviews other theories of syndication in the context of financial contracting.

the years 1978–1989. Lerner finds evidence in support of these rationales for syndication. It is noteworthy that the mean number of venture capitalists per investment round increases with each staged investment: In Round 1 there are 2.2 investors on average; in Round 2 there are 3.3 on average; and in Round 3 there are 4.2 investors on average. Lerner also shows that experienced venture capitalists do not invest with inexperienced venture capitalists in the first round. Also, experienced venture capitalists do not invest with inexperienced venture capitalists in later rounds where inexperienced venture capitalists initiated the first-round financing. Lerner finds equity holdings are relatively constant across investment rounds. Further, there are later-round syndications of investments in promising firms, which is consistent with the theory of collusion to overstate the value of the portfolio firm upon exit.

Cumming et al. (2005a) found evidence that venture capital syndicate size is highly variable across different investment cycles. At times of illiquid IPO markets, syndicate size is larger on average, while in times of hot IPO markets syndicate size is much smaller. This effect is depicted in Figure 10.4. In their econometric specifications, Cumming et al. found that an increase in IPO volume by 100 gives rise to approximately 0.2 fewer syndicated partners.

10.7 Board Seats

Fund managers are active investors that typically sit on the board of directors of their investee firms to monitor the activities of the firm and to essentially protect their investment. Lerner (1995) investigates fund manager board membership based on a U.S. sample of 271 biotechnology firms over the period 1978 to 1989. Lerner finds that venture capitalist board membership generally increases with each financing round, but so does membership from other outsiders and other insiders. The important difference between fund manager representation on boards is related to the level of oversight required and the likelihood that the firm's managers might deviate from value-maximizing decisions. In particular, Lerner studies CEO turnover in entrepreneurial firms. When there are problems with the firm, the CEO is terminated and replaced by a new CEO. Lerner shows that there is an increase in venture capital board membership around the time of CEO turnover and no significant change in the number of other outsiders on the board around the time of CEO turnover. As well, Lerner provides evidence that more than 50% of the entrepreneurial firms in his sample have a venture capitalist director within 60 miles of headquarters, and more than 25% have a venture capitalist director within 7 miles. There is a 22% chance that a venture capitalist director is within 5 miles of the entrepreneurial firm. Lerner finds the importance of the venture capitalist director and location is robust even after controlling for the equity held by the venture capitalist, the size, and the age of the venture capitalist fund, among other things.

10.8 Contract Terms

The contracting process is probably the most critical part of the investment process, as the contracts will be the basis of the understanding and relationship between the entrepreneurial firm and the fund manager. The contracts that are usually tabled and negotiated during the investment process include the term sheet (see Appendix 2), the shareholders agreement (see Appendix 3), and the subscription agreement (see Appendix 4). These appendices are available online at http://venturecapitalprivateequitycontracting.com.

A term sheet sets out the prospective terms of the deal,[6] and it is not necessarily a legally binding contract. Rather, it is used to establish areas of agreement before the parties have their lawyers work on the formal binding agreement. The use of a term sheet not only enables the entrepreneur to have a clear understanding of what the eventual terms will be to enable the parties to continue with negotiations but more important, it saves the parties legal fees (it is expensive to formally draft contracts), as the main terms are presumed to be acceptable to both parties as thus less billable hours spent on redrafting contracts. A shareholders agreement, by contrast, is the legally binding contract among shareholders of a company that sets out the "new" terms of the relationship among shareholders with the inclusion of the venture capital shareholder.[7] A shareholders agreement includes terms such as rights of first refusal and tag along and drag along clauses (see Chapter 14 for details). A subscription agreement is the agreement between the venture capital shareholder and the company (as distinct from the shareholder agreement, which is an agreement among the shareholders of a company). The subscription agreement sets out terms of subscription: Shareholders subscribe to shares, and the subscription agreement sets out the type of shares, the rights obtained as a result of ownership, and terms of payment. The terms of these contracts are usually incorporated into the entrepreneurial firm's memorandum and articles of incorporation, and where necessary the share structure itself as different classes of shares with unique modified terms may have to be created. Chapter 14 reviews the different terms that commonly exist in venture capital contracts around the world. Contract terms generally include cash flow (payoffs to the entrepreneur and the investors) and control rights (decision rights).

Gompers (1998) and Kaplan and Strömberg (2003) examine specific details in U.S. venture capital contracts based on hand-collected samples of 50 and 213 investments, respectively (see also Hart, 2001, for a summary of this and related work). More specifically, the Kaplan and Strömberg study consists of 213 investments in 119 U.S. portfolio companies by 14 limited partnerships. Based on U.S.-only datasets, both Gompers (1998) and Kaplan and Strömberg (2003) show that venture capitalists separately allocate cash flow rights, voting rights, board rights, liquidation rights, and other control rights. They

[6]http://en.wikipedia.org/wiki/Term_sheet.
[7]http://en.wikipedia.org/wiki/Shareholders'_agreement.

find that convertible preferred equity is used and that cash flow rights, voting rights, control rights, and future financings are often contingent on observable measures of financial and nonfinancial performance. As well, venture capitalists often include clauses to mitigate the potential hold-up between the entrepreneur and the investor. Kaplan and Strömberg show that venture capitalists retain control of the management of the firm if the firm performs poorly. If firm performance improves, then entrepreneurs regain control and also additional cash flow rights. Venture capitalists relinquish control and liquidation rights as firm performance improves but for the most part retain their cash flow rights. In Chapter 14 we investigate in more detail factors that affect the allocation of each of these rights.

Kaplan and Strömberg's (2003) sample is derived entirely from U.S. venture capitalists financing U.S. entrepreneurial firms. In their influential paper, Gilson and Schizer (2003) show that U.S. tax law biases venture capitalists' and entrepreneurs' incentives to use convertible preferred shares. This tax bias has been shown to be absent in other countries such as Canada (see, e.g., Sandler, 2001). Gilson and Schizer explain this tax advantage as follows:[8]

> *[Venture capital] portfolio companies [in the U.S.] issue convertible preferred stock to achieve more "favourable" tax treatment for the entrepreneur and other portfolio company employees. The goal is to shield incentive compensation from current tax at ordinary income rates so managers can enjoy tax deferral (until incentive compensation is sold, or longer) and a preferential tax rate ... [by assigning an artificially low value to the entrepreneurs' common equity claim at the time of investment].*
>
> *Our analysis suggests the difficulty of financial modeling for activities in which low-visibility, "practice"-level patterns are of first-order significance. Unless informed by institutional knowledge deep enough to reveal such patterns, models will miss a significant factor that is influencing behavior.*
>
> *(Gilson and Schizer, 2003, pp. 876–878)*

Unfortunately, and rather surprisingly, most academic studies in the area of venture capital and private equity contracting do not acknowledge the possibility of a tax bias in favor of convertible preferred securities for fund managers and entrepreneurs in the United States.

The vast majority of theoretical work in venture capital and private equity contracting is based on empirical data from the United States, and U.S. tax laws significantly bias the choice of contract structure toward convertible preferred equity (Gilson and Schizer, 2003).[9] Therefore, it is worthwhile to examine data outside the United States to see ways in which contracts are written absent of such tax biases.

The importance of this issue as to whether or not convertible preferred equity is the optimal form of venture capital finance cannot be understated.

[8]See also Fried and Ganor (2006).

[9]Sahlman (1990) also recognized this tax bias.

There has been two decades' worth of academic research that has repeated the mantra that convertible preferred equity is the optimal form of finance leading up to the evidence produced by Gompers (1998) and Kaplan and Strömberg (2003).[10] All of the evidence in support of the proposition that convertible preferred equity is optimal has been from one country and one country alone. Triantis (2001) even characterized the use of convertible preferred equity as the one central distinguishing feature of venture capital investment relative to other types of investment. Cumming (1999) demonstrated with non-U.S. data that venture capitalists use a variety of securities (and this work was subsequently published in Cumming, 2005a,b,c, 2006, 2007). Contemporaneous work by Bascha and Walz (2007), Cumming (2008), Cumming and Johan (2008), Schwienbacher (2003), Hege et al. (2003), and Kaplan et al. (2007), among others, showed convertible preferred equity as not being the most frequently used security in Europe. Cumming et al. (2004) and Lerner and Schoar (2005) show convertible securities are less frequently used in developing countries. Chapters 11–14 investigate security design in both venture capital and private equity investments in more detail.

Given the pronounced differences in security design in the U.S. venture capital market and other countries around the world, Chapters 11–14 investigate issues involving security design (common equity, warrants, preferred equity, convertible preferred equity, debt, and convertible debt). We investigate Canadian data in Chapters 11–13 due to the fact that it is the largest dataset in the world with information on venture capital and private equity security design (the Canadian Venture Capital Association collects data on securities used in transactions, unlike other venture capital associations in other countries). Chapters 11–13 contain information from investors resident in both Canada and the United States and from entrepreneurial firms resident in Canada (we do not consider security design for entrepreneurial firms resident in the United States given the tax bias in favor of convertible securities just mentioned). Chapter 14 thereafter considers security design alongside other details in contracts in the European context. Thereafter in Part IV (Chapters 15–18), we investigate the issue of whether cash flow and control rights influence the advice and monitoring of the venture capitalist.

10.9 Summary

This chapter summarized evidence in venture capital and private equity related to due diligence, investment stages, industry, staging, valuation, syndication, board seats, and contracts. In brief, ample data and empirical evidence from a multitude of studies indicate venture capital and private equity fund managers are specialized investors that carry out extensive due diligence, invest in ways that vary significantly with changes in stock market conditions (particularly

[10]See Chapter 11 for further details.

IPO markets), frequently stage and syndicate their investments, sit on board of directors particularly in times where entrepreneurial firms are in financial distress, and write detailed contracts with contingent control rights.

In the remaining chapters in Part III, we examine in more detail security design (Chapter 11), adverse selection and security design (Chapter 12), corporate venture capital contracts (Chapter 13), and the role of preplanned exits in influencing the use of specific contractual clauses (Chapter 14). Then Part IV (Chapters 15–18) addresses issues of investor value-added advice, and Part V (Chapters 19–22) addresses issues involving exits and returns.

Key Terms

Due diligence
Nondisclosure agreement
Staging
Syndication
Board seats
Money chasing deals
Term sheet
Shareholders agreement
Subscription agreement

Discussion Questions

10.1. What are some of the things venture capital and private equity fund managers consider when they carry out due diligence?

10.2. How does the stage of private equity investment vary with market conditions? Why?

10.3. Why do venture capitalists syndicate their investments? What is the typical number of syndicated partners in a venture capital transaction? How does the propensity of venture capitalists to stage and syndicate their investment vary with market conditions?

10.4. True/False/Uncertain (and explain why): "Convertible preferred equity is the optimal form of venture capital finance."

10.5. In what ways do taxes potentially influence venture capital contracts for entrepreneurs resident in the United States?

10.6. When are venture capitalists more likely to sit on the board of directors of entrepreneurial firms? Why?

10.7. Explain and describe the functional difference between a term sheet, a shareholders agreement, and a subscription agreement. What are the main contractual clauses that you observe in these sample agreements? Explain why the clauses you identified might be important to the expected success of the financing arrangement and to the contracting parties.

11 Security Design

11.1 Introduction and Learning Objectives

The academic venture capital literature is dominated by the view that convertible securities are the optimal form of venture capital finance (see, e.g., Bascha and Walz, 2001a; Berglöf, 1994; Bergmann and Hege, 1998; Casamatta, 2003; Cornelli and Yosha, 2003; Gompers, 1998; Gompers and Lerner, 2001; Hellmann, 2006; Kaplan and Strömberg, 2003; Marx, 1998; Sahlman, 1990; Schmidt, 2003; Trester, 1998; and others). The *only* empirical support for this proposition around the world is found in U.S.-based research comprising hand-collected datasets with up to 213 observations from U.S. venture capital funds (Bergmann and Hege, 1998; Gompers, 1998; Kaplan and Strömberg, 2003; Sahlman, 1990).

There are a number of theoretical "agency cost" explanations as to why convertible preferred equity are "optimal" in that the use of that security mitigates a set of agency problems under a set of conditions assumed in theoretical frameworks (see Chapter 2 for a description of these agency costs). For example, Cornelli and Yosha (2003) show that convertible securities mitigate window-dressing problems in staged financing. Berglöf (1994) shows that convertible securities mitigate trilateral bargaining problems associated with sales of the firm (in the spirit of the seminal work of Aghion and Bolton, 1992; see also Bascha and Walz, 2001a). Casamatta (2003), Schmidt (2003), Trester (1998), Marx (1998), and others argue that convertible securities provide appropriate incentives in a bilateral moral hazard context, such that both the venture capital fund manager and the entrepreneur have incentives to add value to the venture.

In view of the fact that convertible preferred equity is deemed to be the crux of venture capital finance, it is worth considering the issue as to whether non-U.S. venture capital funds and U.S. venture capital funds that are financing non-U.S. firms use convertible preferred equity. If so, then this would greatly enhance the credence to the claim that convertible securities are truly the optimal form of finance for all types of venture capital investments. After all, it would be rather remarkable for all types of entrepreneurial firms to be financed with the exact same security in view of the fact that the capital structure literature (outside the realm of the narrowly defined venture capital literature) has never suggested that there exists a unique optimal form of finance for firms across the board. Rather, more generally, the predominant proposition in the literature since the seminal work of Jensen and Meckling (1976) has been that agency problems differ across different firms, and security design adjusts to appropriately mitigate the set of agency problems that are the most pronounced depending on the characteristics of the firm that is being financed. Furthermore, other theoretical venture capital research has suggested that convertible securities are not uniquely optimal (see, e.g., Garmaise, 2007; Yung, 2002; and De Bettignes, 2007, for a behavioral finance perspective on venture capital contracts; see Manigart et al., 2002a; see also Barney et al., 1994, and Landström et al., 1998).

In this chapter we will do the following:

- Consider reasons why different securities might be used by venture capital fund managers financing different types of entrepreneurs, such as in different stages of development and different industries
- Consider reasons why different types of venture capital funds (such as corporate, limited partnership, government) might use different securities
- Consider reasons why security design might be influenced by legal and institutional factors such as taxation
- Consider reasons why security design might change over time
- Examine a very large dataset of securities used in 12,363 transactions involving both U.S. and Canadian venture capital fund managers financing Canadian entrepreneurial firms
- Investigate whether the data fit the theoretical reasons as to how security design varies by type of entrepreneur, type of investor, tax, and other factors

This chapter presents data from Canadian venture capital funds spanning the years 1991 (Q1) to 2003 (Q3) and consisting of 12,363 transactions. The data clearly indicate that convertible preferred equity is not the dominant security. For all types of venture capital funds and entrepreneurial firms, common equity has been the most frequently used security (in 28.66% of all transactions), followed by straight debt (15.34%), convertible debt (14.63%), convertible preferred equity (10.77%), straight (nonconvertible) preferred equity (9.25%), mixes of common equity and straight debt (4.90%), and mixes of straight preferred equity and common (1.82%); other combinations comprise 14.64% of all transactions. The Canadian data considered are rich in both breadth and depth. The data comprise a variety of types of venture capital funds (including limited partnerships, corporate fund, government funds, LSVCCs, institutional funds) and all types of entrepreneurial firms (including early-stage, late-stage, buyout, and turnaround firms, as well as firms in different industry sectors). We show that a variety of securities are used, not just convertible preferred equity, and it does not depend on the definition of the term *venture capital*.[1] We extend prior work by showing that there have been changes in the intensity of use of different forms of finance over time, and we relate these changes not only to agency problems but to institutional venture capital fund structures, learning,

[1]This observation has also been reported in other work in different non-U.S. contexts, including Bascha and Walz (2001b), Cumming (2005a,b,c, 2006a,c, 2008), Hege et al. (2003), Schwienbacher (2003), and Cumming et al. (2008).

market conditions, and taxation. We further extend prior work by providing a theory as to why securities other than convertible preferred equity might be optimal in certain contexts and relate the new theory to the data.

We conjecture four main explanations for the patterns of forms of finance observed in the data: (1) economic agency costs explanations; (2) tax explanations; (3) institutional, sophistication, and learning explanations; and (4) market conditions. The first category, agency costs, is based on the view that different expected agency problems will be more pronounced depending on the characteristics of the transacting parties, and therefore the security selected is designed to mitigate the expected agency problems. The theoretical explanations for the optimality of convertible preferred equity in the venture capital finance literature are in fact derived from this perspective: Convertible preferred equity has been shown to optimally incentivize the entrepreneur and venture capital fund manager to provide effort and to mitigate agency problems surrounding exit decisions.

The second category, tax explanations, purports that the selected security is a response to taxation and primarily capital gains taxation in view of the fact that the majority of venture capital fund returns are derived upon exiting the investment (typically in an IPO or acquisition exit). In the U.S. context, Gilson and Schizer (2003) have shown that there exists a significant tax advantage with the use of convertible preferred equity. In brief, entrepreneurs receive incentive compensation in the form of stock options, and the use of convertible securities enables the venture capital funds' equity to be valued higher than the entrepreneurs' common equity; therefore, the strike price of the entrepreneurs' stock options can be undervalued. This enables a high-powered form of entrepreneurial incentive compensation that is uniquely attributable to the use of convertible preferred securities. While this "tax practice" has evolved in the United States and is not scrutinized by the Internal Revenue Service (IRS), it is less clear as to whether Revenue Canada (the Canadian equivalent to the IRS) would permit this to be carried out in Canada (Sandler, 2001). We nevertheless consider changes in taxation over the period considered to see if such changes have materially affected the security choice in ways that are consistent with Gilson and Schizer's explanation.

The third category—institutional, sophistication, and learning explanations—is studied by considering differences in the selected securities over time and by different types of investors. Consistent with the theoretical literature, we consider the proposition that Canadian investors are becoming more sophisticated in the sense that they use convertible securities more frequently over time. We also consider the impact of U.S. venture capital funds operating in Canada to test whether U.S. venture capital funds are more sophisticated than their Canadian counterparts (in the academic venture capital sense that they might be more inclined to use convertible preferred equity).

The last category, market explanations, considers the effect of stock market conditions on the selected security. We may conjecture that unfavorable stock market conditions increase the venture capital funds' interest in the use of securities with downside protection, as well as affect entrepreneurs' incentives to acquiesce priority in bankruptcy.

More important, we should point out that other recent papers have identified the existence of different securities used in venture capital investments outside the United States, and in ways that are consistent with the Canadian data. This means that the outlier country in terms of financial contracts in venture capital is not Canada but rather the United States. Schwienbacher (2002), Hege et al. (2003), Cumming (2008), Bascha and Walz (2001b), Kaplan et al. (2007), and Cumming et al. (2004), for example, all identify the existence of a variety of securities used by venture capital funds in Europe, and Lerner and Schoar (2005) identify the use of a variety of securities by venture capital funds in developing countries (see also Lerner, 2000, and Songtao, 2000, for a discussion of Asian evidence). Those studies differ from the study at hand in several ways. First, those studies have a tendency to ignore even the possibility of a tax bias in favor of the use of convertible preferred securities in the United States (see, e.g., Kaplan et al., 2007), which would render prior work on tests of financial contracting in the United States less generalizable than previously thought (see, e.g., Kaplan and Strömberg, 2003). Acknowledgment of the work of Gilson and Schizer (2003) on the U.S. tax bias in fact renders that majority of academic work on financial contracting in venture capital to be less generalizable than that which was previously believed to be the "truth."[2] Second, those studies are based on hand-collected samples consisting of at most a few hundred observations, and they lack a completeness of the majority of transactions in a country.[3] Third, and related to the second point, those studies do not account for the possibility that different syndicated partners may select different securities. Fourth, those studies lack time series variation in the data, which could be important if there is an evolution in the design of securities and/or if the selected security is related to market conditions. Of course, this is not to say that those studies are without merit. As well, it does not mean that the data offered in this chapter enable a complete characterization of financial contracting in venture capital (the limitations with the current data are clearly documented later in this chapter). However, it does mean that there is much to be gleaned from the current dataset, and there is ample scope for further work in the area of financial contracting in venture capital.

[2]The work of Gilson and Schizer (2003) is completely counter to the larger body of work on financial contracting in venture capital. The response in the academic venture capital community has typically been to simply not acknowledge Gilson and Schizer (2003), which the authors believe to be extremely unfortunate.

[3]A complaint of the current dataset among those authors that hand-collect their own venture capital contract data is that this chapter is contingent on the accuracy of the firm Macdonald & Associates, Ltd., for recording the data (of course, this complaint would equally apply to Venture Economics databases, which are more often used in academic venture capital research, but do not comprise information on the selected security). Macdonald and Associates, Ltd., certifies the accuracy of these data and is the only firm worldwide to have collected data on securities used by venture capital funds. The fact that the Canadian data are quite consistent with all other non-U.S. hand-collected datasets is comforting, and the volume of the data (12,363 transactions; industry-wide over 13 years) is highly attractive (particularly relative to prior studies based on datasets with up to 213 transactions; see, e.g., Kaplan and Strömberg, 2003).

11.2 Theory and Hypotheses

This section analyzes agency costs and considers the role of tax. The roles of institutional factors, learning, and market conditions are also examined.

11.2.1 Agency Costs

Particular agency costs (including moral hazard, adverse selection, hold-up, free-riding, window-dressing, and trilateral bargaining) are more pronounced depending on the structure and stage of investment and the characteristics of the entrepreneurial firm. We will first examine the buyout stage, as it provides a useful analytical benchmark. Then we will look at turnaround stage firms, start-up and expansion stage financing, first-time and syndicated investments, high-tech entrepreneurial firms, and agency issues associated with venture capital fund characteristics and governance.

Buyouts

Buyout financings ("buyouts") provide the entrepreneurial firm with capital to acquire a product line, a division, or another firm (on buyouts generally, see, e.g., Wright et al., 2001). Firms obtaining buyout financing have a relatively more established track record than their counterpart firms in the start and expansion stage of development. In general, venture capital fund managers are active investors that closely monitor and provide managerial input into their investments (in areas of managing, finding suitable legal advisors, strategic partners, underwriters, suppliers, marketing, and so forth, see, e.g., Sahlman, 1990). In the general case, therefore, the venture capital fund manager can increase the expected returns from the project through greater effort. The venture capital fund manager's effort will depend on the extent of financial commitment relative to the entrepreneur and the form of investment. Because the returns to the venture depend on the effort of both the venture capital fund manager and the entrepreneur, there is a bilateral moral hazard problem. In the case of buyouts, however, the moral hazard problem could be considered to be more unilateral. Buyouts require a significant amount of effort on behalf of the entrepreneur to buy out the particular product line or firm but relatively little effort by the venture capital fund manager. The role of the venture capital fund manager in a typical buyout transaction is to provide the capital needed by the entrepreneur so the entrepreneur, as the established expert in this enterprise and area of business with inside knowledge, can carry out his intended transaction without the venture capital fund manager's involvement other than the capital (Macdonald, 1992).

A well-known result from moral hazard theory[4] is that an agent's (the entrepreneur's or the venture capital fund manager's) effort is an increasing function

[4]See, for example, Tirole (1988: 35–36).

of her residual claim (share in the profits) to the venture. The intuition is straightforward. The risk-averse parties (the entrepreneur and the venture capital fund manager) take unobservable actions that affect the stochastic distribution of the size of the pie to be divided between them. The effort of each party yields a positive externality on the other party, but such effort is costly to both parties. As such, where the probability of bankruptcy is trivial, the entrepreneur's [venture capital fund manager's] effort into a venture is an increasing [decreasing] function of the relative amount of debt to equity provided to the venture capital fund. A sharing rule that provides a greater equity share to the venture capital fund yields more [less] venture capital fund manager [entrepreneurial] effort.[5] In view of the fact that buyouts require entrepreneurial effort, not venture capital fund manager effort, debt appears a priori to be a relatively more attractive form of finance than equity. A mix of debt and common equity might also be observed where the venture capital fund's capital contribution is significant (Noe and Rebello, 1996).[6] Furthermore, because buyout firms have an established track record, unsystematic risk is low relative to systematic risk. Adverse selection costs of debt are therefore not as significant for buyout investments relative to other investments. Buyouts, therefore, are normally highly leveraged.

Hypothesis 11.1: *A greater proportion of contracts with at least some debt will be observed among buyout stage venture capital investments.*

Turnaround Investments

Turnaround firms ("turnarounds") are defined as those that were once profitable but are now earning less than their cost of capital (Macdonald, 1992). Turnarounds tend to have a high failure rate and high variability in returns. A unique menu of agency costs arises within the context of turnarounds. Costs of entrepreneurial incompetence and the risk of asset stripping are significant for turnarounds. Risk shifting problems are also characteristic of turnarounds. As turnarounds approach bankruptcy, inside equity holders (entrepreneurs) will not have the incentive to adopt all positive NPV projects because such

[5]The probability of bankruptcy may be nontrivial, in which case a venture capital fund that provided debt financing is a residual claimant in bankruptcy states. Therefore, where there is a nontrivial probability of bankruptcy, the venture capital fund manager's effort will be positively related to the total amount of debt financing that the venture capital fund contributes to the project. This is in contrast to nonbankruptcy states whereby venture capital fund manager effort is positively related to the equity-sharing rule (the venture capital fund's ownership stake in the firm).

[6]Aghion and Bolton (1992) also show that straight debt and common equity have complementary roles in that the fixed payment of debt reduces managerial compensation in bad states and limits investment in takeover defenses, whereas equity enables efficiency-enhancing takeovers. Berglöf (1994) shows that a combined debt and common equity contract limits potential trilateral bargaining conflicts (in the sense of Aghion and Bolton, 1992) associated with the sale of the firm because the entrepreneur has control in good states of nature and the venture capital fund has control in bad states of nature. However, in Berglöf's (1994) set-up, the combined debt-equity contract is inferior to a convertible contract; see infra subsection 10.3.2.

projects only (or mostly) benefit debt holders. Inside equity holders will adopt excessively risky projects to transfer expected wealth from debt holders to equity holders (Green, 1984; Jensen and Meckling, 1976). Convertible debt mitigates risk-shifting problems because the venture capital fund shares in any increase in equity value associated with risk shifting (Green, 1984).

One of the most significant agency problems in the context of a turnaround investment arises from *trilateral bargaining* (Berglöf, 1994). As described in Aghion and Bolton's (1992) seminal paper, trilateral bargaining problems arise when a third party (an outside investor) contracts with the entrepreneur (after the initial venture capital fund and the entrepreneur contract) such that the entrepreneur and the third party extract surplus from the initial venture capital fund. Trilateral bargaining problems are particularly acute when the entrepreneurial firm is experiencing financial distress because the entrepreneur has a pronounced incentive to give up control of the firm to lower the cost of outside financing. The cost of outside financing from a third-party investor is lower where the third-party investor acquires control over the firm and the outside party attaches value to the control rights. The arrival of a third-party investor can therefore improve the situation of the entrepreneur and worsen the situation of the initial venture capital fund (Berglöf, 1994). The entrepreneurial firm is better off when it no longer faces bankruptcy as a result of the low-cost additional financing provided by the third-party investor. The third-party investor is better off after gaining effective control over the firm's assets. The situation of the initial venture capital fund may be worsened after the arrival of the third-party investor that acquires control of the firm and strips the firm's assets without paying full value (the value of an entrepreneurial firm's assets is often difficult to ascertain in court; see Berglöf, 1994).

Berglöf (1994) shows that convertible preferred equity and convertible debt mitigate trilateral bargaining problems during times of financial distress.[7] The reason is that the option to convert allows the parties to contract on the state of nature. The option to convert will be exercised upon a favorable realization of market uncertainty, and the control of the firm's assets will change after the securities have been converted. A state contingent allocation of control protects against the incentives of two parties contracting to extract surplus from a third party. The convertibility option in securities held by the venture capital fund enables the venture capital fund to retain effective control over the decision to sell the firm regardless of the state of nature. In the event of good economic times, the venture capital fund converts its securities into common equity to capture the upside potential of the firm's value. (The venture capital fund may or may not have effective control after conversion, depending on the

[7]A contract that combines straight debt and straight common equity also mitigates trilateral bargaining but is inferior to a convertible contract (Berglöf, 1994, Proposition 5). The least-effective contract is one that uses only straight debt or only straight common equity (Berglöf, 1994). Other research has suggested that the high agency costs associated with turnaround investments make leverage less valuable and monitoring more valuable (Harris and Raviv, 1991).

terms of conversion. In the event that the venture capital fund is a minority equity holder after conversion, the venture capital fund still benefits as a residual claimant capturing the upside value of the firm.) In bad states, however, the venture capital fund retains effective control and can prevent the entrepreneur from contracting with a third party to extract surplus from and worsen his situation as the initial venture capital fund. As a result, convertible contracts will be more frequently employed among investments in entrepreneurial firms that are not earning their cost of capital. Note that Berglöf (1994) derives this result generally, irrespective of whether the firm was at the turnaround stage. The argument here is that relative to other development stages, an entrepreneur's incentive to lower the cost of outside finance will be more pronounced at the turnaround stage.

In addition to mitigating the perverse incentives associated with trilateral bargaining, when an entrepreneurial firm is doing poorly, there may be another reason for employing convertible securities. Marx (1998; see also Casamatta, 2003, and Schmidt, 2003) argues that convertible preferred equity dominates both straight common equity financing and straight debt financing by generating the right incentives for a risk-averse venture capital fund to intervene in the project as a response to poor performance. Marx assumed that the venture capital fund could increase the return to a poorly performing project but not one that is performing moderately well or better. Intervention is not cost-free (the venture capital fund manager must exert effort and the entrepreneur loses the benefit of control), but intervention does increase the expected value of the project in the first-order dominant sense. Given Marx's assumptions, straight debt is not optimal. There will be excessive intervention by the venture capital fund because the venture capital fund is the sole residual claimant under a debt contract when the entrepreneurial firm is doing poorly. The venture capital fund only considers its benefit and the cost of intervention without taking into account the entrepreneur's benefits/costs. Similarly, a straight common equity contract is suboptimal because there will be too little intervention. When the entrepreneurial firm is doing poorly, the venture capital fund bears the full cost of the effort associated with the intervention but shares the benefit of the intervention with the entrepreneur. In contrast, under a convertible contract, the venture capital fund's payoff contains a fixed part and a proportional part. By choosing appropriate parameters, the convertible preferred equity contract could induce the venture capital fund to choose the efficient intervention strategy.

In sum, convertible contracts mitigate against problems of risk shifting (Green, 1984) and trilateral bargaining (Berglöf, 1994) and may provide desirable incentives for venture capital fund intervention (Marx, 1998) when the entrepreneurial firm is doing poorly. As a result, it is expected that venture capital fund investments in firms that are earning less than their cost of capital, turnaround stage firms, will be financed with convertible securities.

Hypothesis 11.2: *A greater proportion of contracts with convertible securities will be observed for turnaround stage venture capital fund investments.*

Start-up and Expansion Stage Investments

Start-up firms ("start-ups") are in their early stages of development. The firm may merely be based on a concept without a product or any marketing efforts, or it may have a product being developed but not yet sold commercially. Start-ups generally require a moderate amount of capital, but venture capital funds generally tend to have to invest more effort in start-ups for a relatively longer time to bring the firm to fruition.

Three factors characterize start-ups. First, start-ups have significant *systematic risk* (the returns to start-up investments are highly dependent on the state of the economy). Their inherent systematic risk arises from the fact that R&D, product development, and market research comprise their entire expenditures. In effect, start-ups have significant operating leverage (fixed to variable costs), which makes their success contingent on the state of the economy. Second, start-ups have a high degree of *unsystematic risk* and *informational asymmetry* for the following reasons. They have, by definition, little or no track record; start-ups typically have not been incorporated for more than one year (Macdonald, 1992, pp. 8–9). Start-ups generally have a single product (or no product at all) without a demonstrated market potential. The difficulties faced by start-ups generally make their success highly dependent on the abilities and perseverance of the entrepreneur. It is difficult to assess the entrepreneur's risk preferences, nonpecuniary preferences, and work/leisure preferences, and it is therefore difficult for the venture capital fund manager to evaluate the investment. As a result, adverse selection costs will be significant for start-up investments. A third characteristic of start-ups is that they tend to have significant *moral hazard costs* (in which the venture capital fund is the principal and the entrepreneur is the agent). The malleable nature of their assets provides entrepreneurs of start-up firms with greater discretion to invest in personally beneficial strategies. If financing is in the form of equity, then entrepreneurs may not invest in risky projects; if financing is in the form of debt, then entrepreneurs may invest in projects that are too risky to transfer expected wealth from debtholders to equity holders.

Expansion stage investments ("expansion investments") provide the entrepreneurial firm with significant capital for plant expansion, marketing, and initiation of full commercial production and sales (Macdonald, 1992, pp. 8–9). Expansion investments are typically made for about four years, and venture capital funds tend to contribute quite a large amount of capital to the project relative to entrepreneurs at the start-up stage. As with start-ups, expansion investments have nontrivial levels of systematic and unsystematic risk and a variety of growth options, and they require a significant amount of effort to ensure their success.

The significant growth options available to start-ups and expansion investments give rise to a number of agency costs and a role for staging (periodic capital flows, rather than a lump-sum investment) to facilitate monitoring (Gompers, 1995). Syndication of early-stage investments typically involves an arrangement with a lead "inside" investor(s) (involved in earlier financing rounds) and a number of "outside" investors involved at latter financing rounds (Admati and Pfleiderer, 1994; Lerner, 1994; Sahlman, 1990). Theory and empirics indicate a positive relationship between the number of suppliers of capital to a firm and the growth opportunities of a firm (Rajan, 1992). Reliance on one supplier of capital provides that supplier with an information monopoly that adversely affects investment incentives because of potential hold-up problems. Such hold-up problems will be particularly acute for firms with substantial growth opportunities because a single supplier has too much control over liquidation (exit) decisions. As a result, an early-stage entrepreneurial firm with significant growth opportunities that is financed by an inside venture capital fund will require (as part of the contract with the inside investor[s]) additional outside syndicated investors at latter investment rounds to avoid renegotiation hold-up problems.

A financial contract in a staged and syndicated investment relationship seeks to minimize agency costs among the entrepreneurial firm and its syndicated investors (Admati and Pfleiderer, 1994; Lerner, 1994). In particular, the interdependent financial contracting objectives are to (1) limit free riding on the effort between the outside and inside venture capital funds, (2) minimize overstatement/understatement of capital requirements by the inside venture capital fund to the outside venture capital funds, and (3) facilitate optimal continuation decisions (all positive NPV projects). In their seminal work on this issue, Admati and Pfleiderer (1994) show that the objectives are met when the payoff to the inside venture capital fund is independent of the financing provided by the outside venture capital funds. In particular, Admati and Pfleiderer argue "fixed-fraction" contracts are optimal. Admati and Pfleiderer (1994: 385) define a fixed-fraction contract as one in which the inside venture capital fund ["VC_1"] provides the same fraction of future capital required by the firm and VC_1 receives the same fraction of the firm's total payoffs. Admati and Pfleiderer (1994: Proposition 2 at 385) claim that fixed-fraction contracts induce optimal continuation decisions. Admati and Pfleiderer's (1994: 385–386) intuition for the result that fixed-fraction contracts induce optimal continuation is as follows. VC_1's initial investment provides VC_1 with a fixed fraction of the firm's payoff, and VC_1 is solely responsible for providing the same fraction of capital required by the firm. If VC_1 was required to invest a greater fraction than the fraction of payoffs received, then there may exist some positive NPV projects that VC_1 will not finance. Similarly, some negative NPV projects will be financed if VC_1 receives a greater fraction of the payoffs than the fraction of capital provided.

Fixed-fraction contracts necessarily require outside investors ["VC_2"] to be involved at latter financing rounds because VC_1 only finances a fraction of future capital requirements. Admati and Pfleiderer (1994: 387) explain that the fixed-fraction contract resolves the information advantage that VC_1 has over VC_2. Because VC_1 receives a fixed fraction of the firm's payoff (and VC_1 provides the same fraction of required capital), VC_1's payoff is independent of the pricing of all securities issued at latter financing rounds. The pricing of

VC_2's securities simply determines the division of surplus between VC_2 and the entrepreneur. Given the independence of VC_1's and VC_2's payoffs, VC_1 has no incentive to misrepresent information to VC_2; in fact, VC_1's concern over her reputation mitigates information asymmetry between the entrepreneur and the outside syndicate(s). Admati and Pfleiderer (1994: 387) note that their model does not predict the type of securities issued to later-stage investors if managers are not risk neutral. Admati and Pfleiderer (1994: sections V and VI), however, do suggest that risk aversion and effort incentives may lead outside investors to employ options and/or warrants (consistent with the large volume of literature on convertible preferred equity being optimal in venture capital finance).

In the Appendix to this chapter, we provide a syndication example and simple theoretical framework that shows that fixed-fraction contracts are not robust to consideration of entrepreneurial moral hazard. In the context of the example in the Appendix, we further show that there are other security choices that facilitate independent payoffs to the different syndicated investors, thereby solving the continuation problem identified by Admati and Pfleiderer. For example, one investor could use straight preferred equity and another could use convertible debt. But the obvious limitation with the use of straight preferred equity is that there are few effort incentives for the VC_1. If the moral hazard costs of VC_1 qua agent outweigh the importance of VC_1 to act as an unbiased intermediary between the entrepreneur and VC_2, then a VC_1 may select a contract with upside potential so that VC_1 is a residual claimant. Other nonmutually exclusive firm characteristics may give rise to more pronounced agency problems and the use of other forms of finance. In sum, convertible preferred equity securities optimally incentivize the entrepreneur and venture capital fund manager to provide effort in the financing of start-up and expansion stage firms. A venture capital fund partner of a syndicate may hold a straight preferred claim for start-ups to mitigate agency problems between syndicated investors.

Hypothesis 11.3: *A greater proportion of contracts with convertible preferred equity (for "inside" venture capital funds) will be observed for start-up and expansion stage venture capital fund investments.*

Hypothesis 11.4: *A greater proportion of contracts with straight preferred equity (for "inside" venture capital funds) will be observed for start-up investments if agency problems between syndicated investors are pronounced. (See the Appendix to this chapter.)*

So far, we have reviewed the role of alternative forms of financing in reducing moral hazard and adverse selection costs of buyouts, turnarounds, and start-ups and expansion investments. These investment stages are *mutually exclusive*. We now consider other characteristics (that are *not* mutually exclusive) of the investment transaction and entrepreneurial firm that may affect the selected form of finance. In particular, we contrast first-time financing with follow-on investments, discuss high-tech entrepreneurial firms, and examine investor characteristics.

Syndicated Investments, Amounts Invested Relative to Deal Sizes, and Staged Rounds

Syndication was just discussed in the context of firm development stages. For start-ups and expansion investments, straight preferred equity and convertible debt were noted to have a role in mitigating informational asymmetries and inducing truth telling from inside investor(s) to outside investor(s). In this subsection, syndication does not distinguish between inside and outside investors but rather describes a group of investors investing at the same time (e.g., a group of inside investors or a group of outside investors). In the econometric analysis following, syndication is included as a separate independent variable. A group of investors (e.g., a group of inside and/or a group of outside investors) may share screening abilities to mitigate adverse selection costs (and therefore reduce the associated costs of debt finance). Syndication is a valuable part of the venture capital screening process in the initial investment stage (Lerner, 1994; Lockett and Wright, 1999, 2001; Wright and Lockett, 2003). Syndication also enables risk avoidance through risk sharing, and it may enable greater value added (Brander et al., 2002), as well as enable venture capital funds to exploit informational asymmetries and collude to overstate their performance to potential investors upon exit, which can increase the attractiveness of common equity finance (or securities that enable at least some equity participation).[8]

A variable that is highly correlated with contemporaneous syndication is the amount invested relative to the deal size (which is of course larger for non-syndicated deals). Noe and Rebello (1996, Propositions 3 and 4) intuitively show that increases in the amount invested relative to the deal size would be expected to be related to the use of less debt and more equity for the investor.

Hypothesis 11.5: *A greater proportion of contracts with debt (where adverse selection costs are lower) and contracts with common equity participation (where performance can be overstated and to facilitate value-added) will be observed for contemporaneously syndicated venture capital fund investments. Relatedly, larger amounts invested relative to the total deal size are expected to be associated with a greater probability of venture capital fund equity participation.*

In contrast to syndicated investments, first-time financing, or "new" investments, which will generally have a more uncertain quality than "follow-on" investments (i.e., investments in firms that have previously received venture capital fund finance as in the case of a staged investment), will impart higher adverse selection costs than follow-on investments (Gompers, 1995). New

[8]As these rationales for syndication may lead to an established investor syndicate, and are independent of the hold-up rationales for syndicating start-up and expansion investments, a separate dummy variable in the econometric analysis in section 10.4 is included for the firm development stages and for contemporaneous investments made by syndicated investors. Collinearity was not present with this specification in the econometric analysis. Akaike and Schwartz information criteria were used to confirm the appropriateness of this specification; see section 10.4.

investments are a distinguishable characteristic in a venture capital fund transaction that will be relevant to the selected form of finance. A new investment can be made at any stage of entrepreneurial firm development (start-up, expansion, buyout, or turnaround). New investments are distinct from start-ups, for example, because *new* investments are characterized by the pronounced adverse selection costs faced by venture capital funds, whereas start-ups are characterized by moral hazard and adverse selection costs between venture capital funds and entrepreneurs, as well as among syndicated venture capital funds. It is therefore expected that a greater proportion of common equity contracts will be observed for newer investments to mitigate adverse selection costs. In addition, because of the relative insensitivity of convertible securities to the risk of the issuing firm, it is easier for the entrepreneur and the venture capital fund to agree on the value of the securities (Brennan and Kraus, 1987). Therefore, convertible securities are also expected for new investments.

Hypothesis 11.6: *A greater proportion of contracts with common equity participation will be observed for earlier round staged venture capital fund investments.*

It is important to reiterate the fact that when an investment is new or syndicated, it does not in and of itself suggest the use of a particular form of finance, but it does suggest an independent rationale for employing a particular security. As already discussed, an investment can also be characterized by the firm's stage of development (e.g., a new investment may be made at the start-up, expansion, buyout, *or* turnaround stage of development), and the agency costs associated with different investment stages may be relatively more important in certain transactions. An investment may also be a high-tech enterprise, which may bear relevance on the selected form of finance, as discussed following.

High-tech Entrepreneurial Firms

Technology financing ("tech firms") encompasses the financing of firms in the biotechnology, communications, computers, electronics, energy, environmental technology, medical, and other high-tech industries. Tech firms have a greater degree of information asymmetry than nontech firms (Noe and Rebello, 1996). A significant percentage of tech firms' assets are intangible (such as human capital), so tech firms may be difficult to value. As such, there may be significant adverse selection costs with tech firms, especially smaller tech firms, and therefore such firms will carry less debt (Noe and Rebello, 1996). The tangible assets of tech firms also have a high degree of specificity (i.e., few alternative uses), which impairs the collateral value of tech-sunk investments, reduces the benefits of financial leverage, and reduces liquidation values. Tech firms are therefore unlikely to be financed by debt.

Hart and Moore (1994) argue that greater managerial rents exist with the intangible assets in tech firms because they are harder to replace. If moral hazard costs (with the entrepreneur qua agent) are perceived to be significant by the venture capital fund manager, and because adverse selection costs are nontrivial for tech firms, neither straight debt nor straight common equity will be employed. Rather, the venture capital fund manager will stage the capital contributions. Staging facilitates a reduction in agency costs by enabling the venture capital fund manager to monitor the entrepreneur and discontinue funding if the venture capital fund manager receives negative information about the entrepreneur's performance and the firm's prospects (Cornelli and Yosha, 2003; Gompers, 1995). Cornelli and Yosha (2003) show that convertible contracts mitigate informational (window-dressing) and overinvestment problems in sequential financing. Bilateral moral hazard is also mitigated (but not eliminated) because the venture capital fund's payoff is greater when the project does better, thereby providing the venture capital fund manager with an incentive to put forth optimal effort and continue to fund the project. The entrepreneur's payoff also depends on the performance of the project so she has sufficient incentive to work.

Hypothesis 11.7: *A greater proportion of contracts with convertible preferred equity will be observed for high-tech venture capital fund investments.*

Venture Capital Fund Characteristics

The Canadian Venture Capital Association and Macdonald & Associates, Ltd.,[9] classify venture capital funds in Canada into one of seven categories: private independent, corporate, labor-sponsored, institutional, government, foreign (U.S. venture capital funds financing Canadian entrepreneurs), and other. Each of these types of funds in Canada has been described in previous research (Amit et al., 1998; Halpern, 1997; Macdonald, 1992; MacIntosh, 1994). Private independent funds are those most similar to limited partnerships in the United States, and corporate funds in Canada are analogous to the U.S. corporate funds (Gompers and Lerner, 1999; MacIntosh, 1994). Federal or provincial governments run government funds through employing professional venture capital fund managers. Institutional funds consist of institutional investors that make direct investments in entrepreneurial firms. Government and hybrid funds have profit-maximizing objectives analogous to private funds in Canada (but there are exceptions among a few funds; see MacIntosh, 1994, and Halpern, 1997, for Canadian research; more generally, see Lerner, 1999, 2002; Kanniainen and Keuschnigg, 2003, 2004; and Keuschnigg and Nielsen, 2001, 2003a,b, 2004a,b). The category of "other" encompasses nontraditional institutional funds that do not fit within the other categories. All funds employ expert fund managers (Halpern, 1997; Macdonald, 1992; MacIntosh, 1994).

Prior work is consistent with the view that limited partnerships provide greater value-added than corporate and government funds (Gompers and Lerner, 1999; Lerner, 1999). As such, we expect limited partnerships to use securities with equity participation more frequently than corporate and government venture capital funds.

[9]See www.cvca.ca and www.canadavc.com, respectively.

Hypothesis 11.8: *Limited partnerships are more likely to use securities with equity participation than other types of venture capital funds.*

The type of fund in Canada with the most capital under management in recent years is the labor sponsored venture capital corporation (LSVCC). LSVCC legislation was introduced in most Canadian jurisdictions around the late 1980s to facilitate business and employment growth (see Halpern, 1997; Macdonald, 1992; MacIntosh, 1994). LSVCCs manage over Can$4 billion (more than half of the industry total), and over 60% of new venture capital came from LSVCCs in the late 1990s (Cumming and MacIntosh, 2006). Unlike private venture capital corporations that purely invest for profit, statutes governing LSVCCs require that they mix the goal of profit maximization with that of job creation (but many publicly state that their goal is nevertheless profit maximization; see Halpern, 1997; MacIntosh, 1994). In addition, LSVCC legislation imposes a number of constraints on the manner in which funds can be invested, including a requirement that 60% (under the federal legislation) of new funds received must be invested within a certain amount of time after receipt (otherwise a penalty is imposed)[10] in small firms, and the remaining assets must be invested in more liquid securities. Some LSVCCs have received more funds than they have been able to invest. Cash windfalls attract less-experienced entrants that may overinvest (greater liquidity leads to more and larger investments; Jensen, 1986) and monitor less efficiently than experienced venture capital fund managers (Blanchard et al., 1994). In net, moral hazard is problematic (with the LSVCC's managers qua agents), and investment is inefficient.

LSVCC legislation further requires that 60% be invested in nondebt securities (see Gompers and Lerner, 1999, for similar restrictive covenants used among U.S. limited partnerships). For the remaining 40%, LSVCCs have an incentive to use debt-type securities for three reasons. First, LSVCCs are Registered Retirement Savings Plan (RRSP) eligible investments, and therefore LSVCCs prefer interest payments (deductible by a corporate player and nontaxable to the recipient) to dividends (which bear nonrefundable tax at the corporate level). Second, LSVCCs can only invest the lesser of Can$10 million or 10% of the equity capital in any one firm; under this limited capital contribution, debt is more likely to be employed than equity (Noe and Rebello, 1996, Propositions 3 and 4). Third, LSVCCs have been subject to much public scrutiny because they have received excessive amounts of capital and have achieved mediocre returns. To enhance the book value of returns, some LSVCCs have been noted to use debt instruments so that the annual accrued interest makes their performance appear to be relatively better on an annual basis.[11] These three factors suggest Hypothesis 11.9.

[10]Under the Ontario and Canadian federal legislation, for example, the LSVCC may have to pay a 20% deficiency tax and additional penalties (including possible revocation of the fund's registration) depending on the circumstances.

[11]This observation was made by Mary Macdonald of Macdonald & Associates, Limited (the firm that collects data for the Canadian VC Association) during a lecture at the University of Toronto Law School in February 1998.

Hypothesis 11.9: *LSVCCs have an incentive to employ at least some debt, irrespective of the financial instruments that would minimize the agency costs associated with their entrepreneurial firms.*

11.2.2 Taxation

In the U.S. context, Gilson and Schizer (2003) have shown that there exists a significant tax advantage with the use of convertible preferred equity. In brief, entrepreneurs receive incentive compensation in the form of stock options, and the use of convertible securities enables the venture capital funds' equity to be valued higher than the entrepreneurs' common equity, so the strike price of the entrepreneurs' stock options can be undervalued. This enables a high-powered form of entrepreneurial incentive compensation that is uniquely attributable to the use of convertible preferred securities. While this "tax practice" has evolved in the United States and is not scrutinized by the Internal Revenue Service (IRS), it is less clear as to whether Revenue Canada (the Canadian equivalent to the IRS) would permit this to operate in Canada (Sandler, 2001). We nevertheless consider changes in taxation over the period considered to see if such changes have materially affected the security choice in ways that are consistent with Gilson and Schizer's explanation. The most significant capital gains tax rate change occurred in 2000, where the effective capital gains tax rate was lowered from 36.6 to 23.2%.[12] Based on Gilson and Schizer's (2003) theory, we would expect convertible equity to be more frequently used when capital gains tax rates are comparatively lower relative to income taxes because it exacerbates the high-powered incentive compensation associated with undervaluing common equity.

Hypothesis 11.10: *Reductions in capital gains taxes are associated with more frequent use of convertible preferred equity.*

11.2.3 Sophistication and Learning

We consider differences in the selected securities over time and by different types of investors. In the spirit of the preceding discussion on the optimality of convertible preferred securities, we consider the proposition that Canadian investors are becoming more sophisticated in the sense that they use convertible securities more

[12]Canada's corporate and income tax rates have been comparatively stable over the period considered; see http://www.taxpolicycenter.org/taxfacts/international/..%5Ctables%5CInternational%5CPDF%5Chistorical_corporate.PDF; see also http://www.taxpolicycenter.org/taxfacts/international/..%5Ctables%5CInternational%5CPDF%5Chistorical_income.PDF. For the most recent Canadian tax information, see http://www.fin.gc.ca/fin-eng.html; http://www.ccra-adrc.gc.ca/menu-e.html; http://www.ccra-adrc.gc.ca/tax/individuals/faq/2003_rate-e.html; and http://www.ccra-adrc.gc.ca/tax/individuals/faq/2000_rate-e.html. Note, however, that there are some differences, depending on the provinces, as taxes comprise both a federal and provincial portion. As well, there are differences depending on the income levels. These various details in tax considerations were empirically intractable with our dataset. Nevertheless, the most drastic changes relevant to our analysis were with respect to capital gains, and these changes have been controlled for in the empirics. Alternative specifications were considered (but did not materially change the substantive econometric results), and are available upon request.

frequently over time. In the same spirit, we further expect U.S. venture capital funds financing Canadian firms to more often use convertible securities if such investors are more sophisticated than their Canadian counterparts.

Hypothesis 11.11: *Canadian venture capital funds are becoming more sophisticated over time in that they are more frequently using convertible preferred equity. U.S. investors financing Canadian firms will also more often use convertible preferred equity.*

11.2.4 Economic Conditions

Unfavorable stock market conditions increase venture capital funds' interest in the use of securities with downside protection, as well as affect capital constrained entrepreneurs' incentives to acquiesce priority in bankruptcy to their investors to secure financing.

Hypothesis 11.12: *Less favorable market conditions are associated with a greater probability that venture capital funds will obtain securities with downside protection in bankruptcy (either with some form of debt or preferred equity).*

11.2.5 Summary

In sum, the mix of financing instruments and the structure of venture capital contracts are a response to conditions of asymmetric information. Problems of moral hazard and adverse selection are more pronounced at the (mutually exclusive) stages of the entrepreneurial firm's development, and other nonmutually exclusive characteristics. Further, market conditions, taxes, institutional factors such as sophistication and learning, and the type of venture capital fund can all affect the selected security. The hypotheses are summarized in Table 11.1. Tests of these hypotheses are provided in the next sections.

11.3 Data

The data in this chapter were obtained from Macdonald & Associates, Ltd. (Toronto). The data consist of information on a disaggregated basis (12,363 financings of privately held firms) from 1991 (Q1) to 2003 (Q3).[13] The details of these transactions by type of venture capital fund and type of entrepreneurial firm are reported in Tables 11.2a to 11.2f, and in Figures 11.1 and 11.2. For all types of venture capital funds and entrepreneurial firms, common

[13]There are 2,064 transactions in publicly traded companies in the data that were excluded from the database, primarily because such investments are outside the realm of the interest of the research questions considered herein. Gompers and Lerner (1999) note that many venture capital funds are prohibited from investing in public securities by restrictive covenants from their institutional partners. Cumming (2005a, 2006c) presents data over a subset of funds considered herein and up to 1998, and presents results on some publicly listed buyout and turnaround firms. The inclusion/exclusion of the later-stage publicly listed firms is immaterial to our results.

Table 11.1 Summary of Testable Hypotheses

This table summarizes the predicted effects, for the entrepreneurial firm characteristics, deal-specific characteristics, VC fund characteristics, and institutional and market factors. The predictions are outlined in the text and the Appendix.

	Hypothesis #	Explanatory Variables	Dominant Expected Agency Problem(s)	Predicted Security	Alternative or Secondary Prediction
Entrepreneurial Firm Characteristics	11.1	Buyout	Entrepreneur as agent	Debt	VC may have equity stake if expected to provide value-added
	11.2	Turnaround	Trilateral bargaining	Convertible preferred equity	
	11.3, 11.4	Start-up	(1) Entrepreneur as agent;	Convertible preferred equity for agency problems (1) and (2)	Straight preferred equity for agency problem (3) for start-up
			(2) VC as agent;		
	11.3, 11.4	Expansion	(3) Agency problems between investors		
	11.7	High-tech	(1) Window-dressing	Convertible Preferred Equity	Less likely to use any form of debt; check robustness with Life Sciences
			(2) Trilateral bargaining		
Deal Characteristics	11.5	$ Invested/$ Deal Size	VC better negotiation position for more equity when larger $ invested/deal size	Less debt for higher values	Correlated with the syndication; see Hypotheses 11.3 and 11.4 for agency problems between investors

	11.6	Round Number	Adverse selection and window-dressing problems in earlier rounds	Convertible preferred equity for earlier rounds	First round (new) financing: alternative variable used to check robustness
VC Characteristics	11.8	Limited Partnership VC	Greater VC value-added; more likely to have at least some equity share	Convertible preferred equity	Common equity
	11.8	Corporate VC	Greater VC value-added; more likely to have at least some equity share	Convertible preferred equity	Some use of debt, if add less value relative to other VCs
	11.8	Government VC	Less incentive to take equity stakes with upside (ownership)	Less ownership equity	
	11.9	LSVCC	Incentives to use at least some debt to show book value returns	At least some debt	
	11.11	U.S. VC	Experience using convertible preferred equity as for domestic U.S. financings	Convertible preferred equity	
Institutional and Market Factors	11.10	Capital Gains Tax Rate		Higher capital gains tax lowers likelihood of convertible preferred equity (Gilson and Schizer, 2003)	Higher values make equity less valuable
	11.11	Trend (Learning Variable)		Expect to converge to convertible preferred equity, as in the United States	
	11.12	TSX Index		Lower index more debt and preferred (downside protection)	

Table 11.2 Summary of Securities Used by Canadian and U.S.

This table presents a summary of the total number of securities used by Canadian and U.S. venture fund and the type of entrepreneurial firm. The data are presented for private independent limited Canadian government VCs in Panel D; U.S. VCs in Panel E; and institutional investors in Panel F. stage of entrepreneurial firm development (start-up, expansion, buyout, and turnaround); column 6 column 1 less the number of tech investments in column 6); column 7 presents data on syndicated number of syndicated investments in column 7); and new (first round) investments are in column 8 round investments in column 8). The average financing round number is reported in column 9; the is reported in column 10; the average amount invested divided by the total amount of all syndicated average TSX index is reported in column 12; the average capital gains tax rate across different investment year (1991 = 1, 1992 = 2, etc.) is reported in column 14. Sample period: 1991 (Q1) to 2003 (Q3).

Panel A. Private Independent Limited

Forms of Finance	(1) Total # Investments	(2) # Inv. Start-up	(3) # Inv. Expansion	(4) # Inv. Buyout	(5) # Inv. Turnaround	(6) # Inv. High-tech
Common	971	600	281	43	19	731
Preferred	302	231	65	3	1	268
Convertible Preferred	373	250	109	4	9	330
Preferred and Warrants	12	10	2	0	0	10
Convertible Debt	471	254	188	13	10	365
Straight Debt and Warrants	30	11	19	0	0	29
Straight Debt	303	138	106	15	15	190
Warrants	9	6	2	0	0	9
Common and Straight Debt	77	23	28	11	4	28
Common and Preferred and Debt	9	1	5	0	2	2
Preferred and Debt	6	3	1	0	1	4
Preferred and Common	56	35	14	7	0	40
Common and Warrants	17	16	1	0	0	17
Other Combinations	328	220	93	9	5	280
Total	2964	1798	914	105	66	2303

Venture Capitalists for Canadian Entrepreneurial Firms

capitalists (VCs) for Canadian entrepreneurial firms, categorized by the type of venture capital partnerships VCs in Panel A; corporate VCs in Panel B; labor-sponsored VCs in Panel C; Column 1 presents data on the total number of investments; columns 2–5 present data for each presents the data for the high-tech investments (nontech investments are equal to the total number in investments (nonsyndicated investments are equal to the total number in column 1 less the (follow-on staged investments are equal to the total number in column 1 less the number of first average amount invested with each security (in thousands of real 1992 Canadian dollars) VC financing provided to the firm (at the time of investment) is reported in column 11; the years associated with the different securities is reported in column 13; and the average investment Total number of observations: 12,363.

Partnership Venture Capitalists

(7)	(8)	(9)	(10)	(11)	(12)	(13)	(14)
# Inv. Syndication	**# Inv. New**	**Average Round #**	**Average $Can Invested Real 1992 ('000)**	**Average $ Invested/ $ Deal Size**	**Average TSX Index**	**Average Capital Gains Tax**	**Average Year Number Trend (1991 = 1)**
511	393	2.59	904.67	0.61	6573.97	0.36	7.65
235	90	2.70	1152.68	0.40	7265.32	0.31	9.63
286	111	2.70	1001.90	0.40	7385.29	0.32	9.51
10	3	2.08	2260.03	0.38	7870.14	0.28	10.67
252	174	2.67	629.28	0.59	6727.11	0.34	8.45
15	5	3.80	2206.59	0.58	7469.07	0.24	11.80
126	110	2.70	746.96	0.71	6202.50	0.35	7.18
3	5	1.78	468.66	0.81	7339.72	0.23	11.67
33	41	1.87	921.93	0.73	5127.49	0.37	5.61
3	3	2.89	1552.35	0.78	5081.26	0.36	5.33
4	2	2.17	658.76	0.50	5063.33	0.32	6.50
27	19	2.64	926.03	0.64	6550.70	0.34	7.84
12	11	1.47	683.81	0.52	8712.52	0.31	10.59
236	134	2.45	1113.25	0.42	7593.22	0.32	9.75
1753	1101	2.61	923.77	0.55	6828.96	0.34	8.42

(continued)

Table 11.2

Panel B. Corporate Venture

Forms of Finance	(1) Total # Investments	(2) # Inv. Start-up	(3) # Inv. Expansion	(4) # Inv. Buyout	(5) # Inv. Turnaround	(6) # Inv. High-tech
Common	226	115	91	13	3	167
Preferred	118	71	36	8	3	94
Convertible Preferred	138	75	50	9	3	118
Preferred and Warrants	4	2	1	1	0	4
Convertible Debt	153	68	67	6	9	116
Straight Debt and Warrants	0	0	0	0	0	0
Straight Debt	211	60	95	39	10	108
Warrants	3	2	1	0	0	1
Common and Straight Debt	61	14	26	16	4	23
Common and Preferred and Debt	3	1	2	0	0	0
Preferred and Debt	6	2	2	0	2	3
Preferred and Common	14	3	9	2	0	8
Common and Warrants	3	3	0	0	0	3
Other Combinations	238	139	87	7	1	170
Total	1178	555	467	101	35	815

equity has been the most frequently used security (in 28.66% of all transactions, or 28.61% of the total transaction value), followed by straight debt (15.34% of transactions, or 10.54% of the value), convertible debt (14.63% of transactions, 9.64% of the value), convertible preferred equity (10.77% of the transactions, 11.77% of the value), straight (nonconvertible) preferred equity (9.25% of the transactions, 11.56% of the value), mixes of common equity and straight debt (4.90% of the transactions, 3.94% of the value), and mixes of straight preferred equity and common (1.82% of the transactions, 1.34% of the value); other combinations make up 14.64% of all transactions (22.54% of the value). The data indicate that the use of forms of finance other than convertible preferred equity in Canada holds in every single subsample of the data as indicated in Tables 11.2a–f (by type of VC

(*continued*)

Capitalists

(7) # Inv. Syndication	(8) # Inv. New	(9) Average Round #	(10) Average $Can Invested Real 1992 ('000)	(11) Average $ Invested/ $ Deal Size	(12) Average TSX Index	(13) Average Capital Gains Tax	(14) Average Year Number Trend (1991 = 1)
161	93	2.40	1256.67	0.48	7120.91	0.33	8.92
98	32	2.68	1446.84	0.37	7309.08	0.28	10.25
115	50	2.62	1302.65	0.39	7572.82	0.31	9.83
4	0	4.50	559.96	0.06	7852.96	0.27	11.25
110	50	3.22	864.05	0.49	7490.06	0.33	9.56
0	0	0.00	0.00	0.00	0.00	0.00	0.00
101	115	2.06	1301.70	0.72	7236.76	0.35	8.94
1	0	2.67	106.61	0.60	7268.03	0.23	11.67
32	38	1.64	1341.42	0.68	6933.61	0.37	8.13
1	2	1.67	228.20	0.83	6914.13	0.32	7.67
3	4	1.50	648.65	0.68	6407.57	0.33	8.17
11	5	2.43	915.05	0.47	6759.44	0.36	7.86
2	1	1.67	1116.44	0.53	7893.37	0.28	11.33
176	85	2.45	976.62	0.38	7465.16	0.28	11.36
815	475	2.47	1170.56	0.49	7317.62	0.32	9.70

fund and by type of entrepreneurial firm, for all deal sizes, for new/staged investments, technology investments, and otherwise, etc.). Therefore, the use of different forms of finance in Canada is not a result of the definition of venture capital. The data indicate that a variety of forms of finance are used across all types of entrepreneurial firms: Subsamples of start-up or expansion investments, the subsample of high-tech investments, and so forth, contain contracts in which convertible preferred equity is not used most frequently. The univariate rankings on the frequency of use of different securities are invariant to total deal size, amounts invested, and amounts invested relative to deal size. The summary statistics also indicate the average values for the financing round, amounts invested, amounts invested relative to the total deal sizes, the average TSX index, as well as the value of a time

Table 11.2

Panel C. Labour Sponsored

Forms of Finance	(1) Total # Investments	(2) # Inv. Start-up	(3) # Inv. Expansion	(4) # Inv. Buyout	(5) # Inv. Turnaround	(6) # Inv. High-tech
Common	825	371	298	38	98	421
Preferred	247	144	79	4	18	184
Convertible Preferred	259	156	96	4	1	222
Preferred and Warrants	6	4	2	0	0	6
Convertible Debt	408	214	149	11	31	285
Straight Debt and Warrants	11	3	6	0	0	7
Straight Debt	633	230	215	27	136	286
Warrants	11	8	1	1	1	9
Common and Straight Debt	249	80	79	18	62	76
Common and Preferred and Debt	16	3	5	3	5	4
Preferred and Debt	19	6	6	2	4	11
Preferred and Common	87	31	32	8	14	29
Common and Warrants	8	4	4	0	0	4
Other Combinations	409	221	140	14	23	260
Total	3188	1475	1112	130	393	1804

trend (1991 = 1, 1992 = 2, etc.) for each security and each investor. There are trends in some of these relations, and these trends are analyzed at length in a multivariate setting the ensuing empirical analyses in the next section.

11.4 Empirical Tests

11.4.1 Methodology

The empirical analysis following considers the standard financial instruments: debt, convertible debt, preferred equity, convertible preferred equity, common equity, warrants, and combinations of debt and common equity. A broader

(*continued*)

Venture Capitalists

(7)	(8)	(9)	(10)	(11)	(12)	(13)	(14)
# Inv. Syndication	**# Inv. New**	**Average Round #**	**Average $Can Invested Real 1992 ('000)**	**Average $ Invested/ $ Deal Size**	**Average TSX Index**	**Average Capital Gains Tax**	**Average Year Number Trend (1991 = 1)**
363	362	2.45	1165.33	0.69	6917.75	0.35	8.60
165	73	3.08	1482.24	0.52	7353.41	0.31	9.81
202	85	2.76	1246.19	0.43	7357.85	0.30	10.03
6	1	3.50	1757.78	0.41	7367.19	0.23	11.83
222	135	2.74	907.60	0.57	7235.97	0.33	9.52
3	1	3.00	1145.58	0.79	7284.13	0.26	11.27
182	192	3.27	991.56	0.74	7122.48	0.32	9.45
2	4	2.55	747.12	0.80	7575.80	0.31	9.82
73	139	1.88	1120.90	0.83	6664.50	0.37	7.92
6	8	1.94	701.46	0.86	6626.72	0.35	8.06
7	6	3.11	934.68	0.73	7682.42	0.33	9.37
35	44	2.10	703.32	0.75	6865.81	0.36	8.36
5	4	3.00	364.72	0.45	7969.09	0.28	11.88
224	148	2.95	956.79	0.55	7353.49	0.32	9.88
1495	1202	2.74	1080.02	0.64	7113.46	0.33	9.23

contract space does exist in practice (see Table 11.2, Panels a–f), although it is not considered herein for a number of reasons. Works that do consider a broader contract space yield optimal contracts that resemble the standard financial instruments (see, e.g., Aghion and Bolton, 1992). The fact that the standard instruments in corporate finance are used most frequently suggests that considerable gains arise from standardization and greater transaction costs arise from designing contracts to mimic the standard forms of finance (Berglöf, 1994). Regardless, the data used to test the hypotheses developed herein have been recorded in such a way that if a contract were designed to mimic one of the standard forms of finance, then the standard form was recorded. The data make all possible distinctions between, for example, convertible debt and mixes of straight debt with warrants (mixes were much less frequent). However, such contracts were

Table 11.2

Panel D. Government

Forms of Finance	(1) Total # Investments	(2) # Inv. Start-up	(3) # Inv. Expansion	(4) # Inv. Buyout	(5) # Inv. Turnaround	(6) # Inv. High-tech
Common	578	415	136	8	16	400
Preferred	162	111	46	3	2	153
Convertible Preferred	194	123	60	8	3	177
Preferred and Warrants	9	7	0	2	0	9
Convertible Debt	308	196	91	5	15	244
Straight Debt and Warrants	3	1	1	1	0	2
Straight Debt	174	99	52	10	10	107
Warrants	7	5	2	0	0	7
Common and Straight Debt	55	26	21	2	5	30
Common and Preferred and Debt	2	0	1	0	0	0
Preferred and Debt	3	1	1	0	0	1
Preferred and Common	24	10	10	0	3	18
Common and Warrants	2	2	0	0	0	2
Other Combinations	247	175	53	5	11	192
Total	1768	1171	474	44	65	1342

grouped together in the empirical analysis where the theoretical predictions were similar. More coarse groupings of securities were also considered.[14]

Empirical tests of the hypotheses were conducted using a multinomial logit model (Theil, 1969). The left-hand-side choice variables include the forms of venture capital finance. The right-hand-side factors include the following data

[14]For example, we also considered the analysis with common equity and warrants aggregated together, straight preferred equity and straight debt aggregated together, and the remainder of the securities aggregated together. The inferences drawn are available upon request; however, because the more distinct categories presented in the tables suggested functional differences between these securities, we do not use more coarse distinctions than the ones presented.

(*continued*)

Venture Capitalists

(7)	(8)	(9)	(10)	(11)	(12)	(13)	(14)
# Inv. Syndication	# Inv. New	Average Round #	Average $Can Invested Real 1992 ('000)	Average $ Invested/ $ Deal Size	Average TSX Index	Average Capital Gains Tax	Average Year Number Trend (1991 = 1)
309	291	2.10	677.23	0.64	6131.48	0.34	7.07
136	44	3.06	924.05	0.36	7245.46	0.28	10.38
171	48	3.19	914.16	0.31	7317.02	0.29	10.59
8	2	3.33	1062.13	0.30	7833.90	0.26	11.33
227	98	3.03	474.79	0.46	7157.08	0.31	9.64
3	1	3.33	14149.48	0.26	7268.03	0.23	11.67
120	71	2.52	517.71	0.49	6538.93	0.31	9.16
7	0	4.71	573.45	0.26	8436.37	0.29	10.71
32	27	2.20	480.87	0.58	5996.55	0.35	7.40
0	1	2.00	112.80	1.00	5330.75	0.38	5.50
1	2	1.33	169.15	0.90	7083.01	0.33	9.00
12	8	2.38	530.34	0.64	5786.24	0.36	6.67
0	1	1.50	461.77	0.75	7731.72	0.23	11.00
175	93	2.44	646.62	0.39	6851.07	0.29	10.05
1201	687	2.58	685.16	0.49	6696.29	0.31	8.88

on entrepreneurial firm characteristics for each investment transaction: the stage of development (start-up, expansion, buyout, turnaround), industry type, the amount invested (and amounts relative to the total deal size), whether the firm was a new investee, and whether the transaction contemporaneously involved more than one venture capital fund. In addition, the type of venture capital fund (LSVCC or otherwise) is recorded in the data. *Akaike* and *Schwartz information criteria* were used to confirm the appropriateness of the included variables. Table 11.3 presents the correlations across the explanatory variables.

The base model regressions with a rather complete specification of right-hand-side variables are presented in Table 11.4, Panel A ("the base model estimates"). Robustness checks for different right-hand-side variables are

Table 11.2

Panel E. U.S. Venture Capitalists (Financing

Forms of Finance	(1) Total # Investments	(2) # Inv. Start-up	(3) # Inv. Expansion	(4) # Inv. Buyout	(5) # Inv. Turnaround	(6) # Inv. High-tech
Common	195	104	84	4	0	185
Preferred	116	83	32	0	1	109
Convertible Preferred	115	60	53	1	0	107
Preferred and Warrants	1	1	0	0	0	1
Convertible Debt	41	25	15	0	0	40
Straight Debt and Warrants	2	0	2	0	0	2
Straight Debt	24	7	10	5	1	15
Warrants	3	3	0	0	0	3
Common and Straight Debt	5	3	1	1	0	3
Common and Preferred and Debt	1	0	1	0	0	1
Preferred and Debt	0	0	0	0	0	0
Preferred and Common	4	0	4	0	0	3
Common and Warrants	2	1	1	0	0	2
Other Combinations	246	138	105	2	0	241
Total	755	425	308	13	2	712

presented in Panels B–E (certain variables are not simultaneously included where they are highly collinear, as indicated in Table 11.3). Panel F presents the results with instrumental variables.[15] The different specifications are provided

[15]Because adverse selection implies different forms of finance may attract different types of entrepreneurial firms, the effects of endogeneity were tested. The geographic locations (Canadian provinces) of the entrepreneurial firms were used as instrumental variables. Choice of these instruments was natural—for example, the number of expansion firms and technology firms may vary by region; however, the region will not be directly related to the forms of financing. Diagnostic tests confirmed the suitability of these instruments (securities used were not materially different in different provinces, and including provincial dummy variables in the reported regressions did not materially change any of the reported results; those results are available upon request). We present the results in Table 10.4 with and without the use of instruments to show robustness.

(*continued*)

Canadian Entrepreneurial Firms)

(7) # Inv. Syndication	(8) # Inv. New	(9) Average Round #	(10) Average $Can Invested Real 1992 ('000)	(11) Average $ Invested/ $ Deal Size	(12) Average TSX Index	(13) Average Capital Gains Tax	(14) Average Year Number Trend (1991 = 1)
172	52	2.85	4639.64	0.30	7392.33	0.30	10.03
107	17	2.91	4199.92	0.28	7745.56	0.28	10.68
112	14	3.73	3419.40	0.23	7550.11	0.30	10.28
1	1	1.00	193.30	0.09	7731.70	0.23	11.00
39	9	3.46	2779.04	0.34	7305.34	0.32	9.63
2	0	4.00	3543.81	0.28	7731.72	0.23	11.00
23	11	2.67	1028.47	0.37	6885.07	0.36	8.25
3	0	4.00	51.55	0.05	7731.72	0.23	11.00
4	3	3.40	2313.14	0.49	6683.24	0.39	7.20
1	0	2.00	17244.00	0.32	9607.70	0.37	10.00
0	0	0.00	0.00	0.00	0.00	0.00	0.00
4	3	1.25	625.14	0.24	6850.94	0.36	6.75
1	2	1.00	3340.14	0.53	7383.95	0.23	11.50
227	83	2.65	5575.36	0.24	8302.35	0.30	10.79
696	195	2.95	4424.82	0.27	7744.34	0.30	10.31

to show robustness to potential problems among collinearity and endogeneity. We explicitly show that the results are quite robust. The results are also robust to alternative specifications not presented (but are available upon request). For example, we ran the regressions on the subset of limited partnership funds that only invested in earlier-stage firms (as presented in Figure 11.2) and found very consistent results to those explicitly reported in Table 11.4 (see also the similarity between Figures 11.1 and 11.2). In each of the panels in Table 11.4, notice that we present the marginal effects and not the multinomial logit coefficients themselves to explicitly indicate economic as well as statistical significance. That is, the numbers directly indicate the probability that a security will be selected based on the specific explanatory variable.

Table 11.2

Panel F. Institutional

Forms of Finance	(1) Total # Investments	(2) # Inv. Start-up	(3) # Inv. Expansion	(4) # Inv. Buyout	(5) # Inv. Turnaround	(6) # Inv. High-tech
Common	670	344	262	21	30	445
Preferred	198	108	83	3	4	163
Convertible Preferred	215	119	79	11	4	172
Preferred and Warrants	5	5	0	0	0	5
Convertible Debt	381	162	200	8	11	271
Straight Debt and Warrants	1	1	0	0	0	1
Straight Debt	504	213	262	7	10	249
Warrants	5	3	2	0	0	5
Common and Straight Debt	125	49	63	7	5	55
Common and Preferred and Debt	3	1	2	0	0	2
Preferred and Debt	13	3	10	0	0	6
Preferred and Common	40	22	15	1	2	27
Common and Warrants	8	8	0	0	0	8
Other Combinations	342	196	127	7	10	245
Total	2510	1234	1105	65	76	1654

11.4.2 Empirical Results

There is fairly strong support for Hypothesis 11.1 that buyouts are more likely to be financed with debt. Panel A indicates buyouts are 2.7% more likely to be financed with straight debt. The economic significance of this effect is greater in the specifications indicated in Panels B, D, E, and F (as high as 8.4% in Panel F), but this effect is statistically insignificant in Panel C (the p-value is equal to 0.11). There is further evidence that buyouts are 5.4% (Panel A) less likely to be financed with convertible debt (the evidence in Panels B, C, D, and F are very similar, but this effect is marginally insignificant in Panel E). This indicates that option contracts have much less value to the venture capital fund in the case of buyouts and is therefore consistent with the proposition

(*continued*)

Investors							
(7)	(8)	(9)	(10)	(11)	(12)	(13)	(14)
# Inv. Syndication	# Inv. New	Average Round #	Average $Can Invested Real 1992 ('000)	Average $ Invested/ $ Deal Size	Average TSX Index	Average Capital Gains Tax	Average Year Number Trend (1991 = 1)
472	296	2.26	1696.17	0.57	7242.23	0.34	8.93
153	56	3.01	1548.05	0.45	7541.30	0.30	10.26
199	78	2.77	1699.22	0.36	7372.62	0.32	9.68
5	1	2.40	2399.00	0.15	7592.61	0.23	11.20
257	127	3.17	963.52	0.57	7404.16	0.32	9.61
1	0	2.00	56.70	0.02	7731.70	0.23	11.00
215	205	2.61	868.01	0.73	7343.35	0.32	9.73
5	0	7.60	3244.43	0.53	8482.13	0.29	10.60
63	73	1.99	1099.53	0.72	7150.85	0.35	8.71
2	1	1.67	2487.02	0.48	7901.01	0.32	10.33
8	4	3.46	1616.44	0.66	7465.28	0.30	9.69
30	20	1.90	1979.21	0.57	7440.54	0.36	8.65
7	5	1.50	3002.97	0.41	8817.29	0.32	10.50
265	150	2.39	3089.33	0.47	7619.50	0.31	10.29
1682	1016	2.58	1580.39	0.57	7382.21	0.32	9.55

(see Hypothesis 11.1 and accompanying text) that moral hazard costs with the venture capital fund qua agent are not pronounced. Nevertheless, there is evidence that venture capital funds are sometimes more likely (approximately 1 to 3% more likely, depending on the specification) to receive common equity when mixed with straight debt or straight preferred equity (see Panels A to F). This latter result likely reflects a certain degree of risk-taking on behalf of venture capital funds in financing buyouts.

In Hypothesis 11.2, we conjectured a pronounced incentive to use convertible preferred equity for the financing of turnarounds. The evidence does not support this proposition. Turnarounds are 5.8% more likely to receive straight debt, 1.9% more likely to receive mixes of straight debt and common equity,

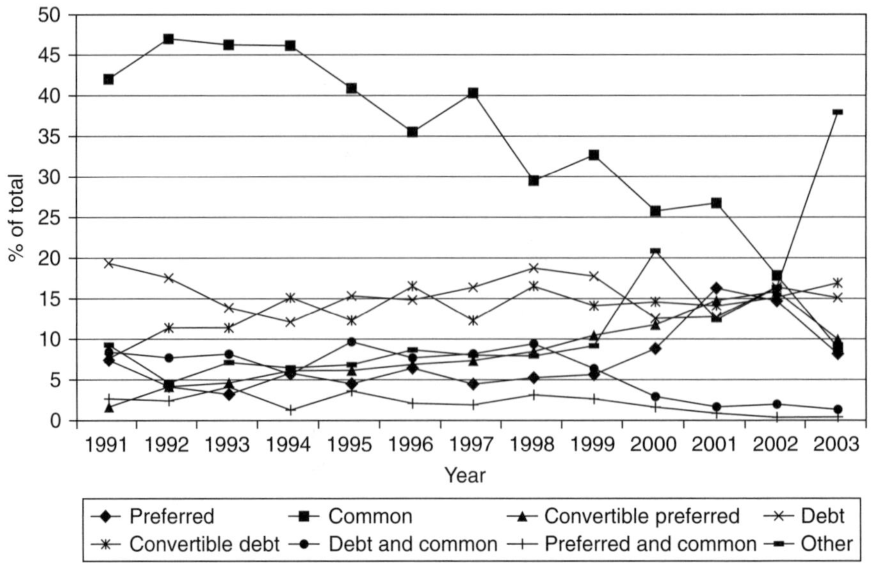

Figure 11.1 Canadian Venture Capital Securities, All Types of Venture Capital Funds and Entrepreneurial Firms, 1991 (Q1) to 2003 (Q3)

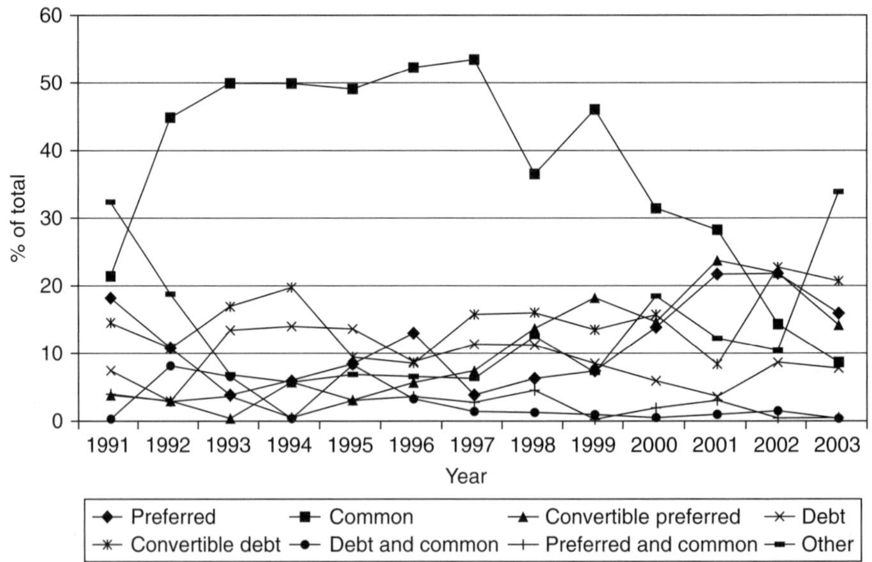

Figure 11.2 Canadian Venture Capital Securities, Private Independent Limited Partner Venture Capitalists and Start-up Entrepreneurial Firms Only, 1991 (Q1) to 2003 (Q3)

and 6.4% less likely to receive convertible preferred equity (Panel A; the evidence in the other panels is similar). We may infer from this evidence that turnarounds are structured in ways that are very similar to buyouts. Because turnarounds and buyouts are in fact often jointly considered to be more a form of "private equity" than pure "venture capital," it is perhaps not surprising that those transactions are more often structured in similar ways.[16]

Hypotheses 11.3 and 11.4 considered start-ups and expansion investments. We do not report those variables jointly because they are collinear in the data (see Table 11.3). Panels A to D and F consider the start-up marginal effects, and Panel E reports the expansion marginal effects. The evidence indicates start-ups are 2.4% (Panel A) more likely to be financed with straight preferred equity, which is in support of Hypothesis 11.4 (the effects are similarly significant in Panels B, C, D, and F). The data also indicate that start-ups are 4.0% more likely to be financed with common equity and/or warrants (Panel A; Panels C and F are similar; however, this result is marginally insignificant in Panel D and negative and significant in Panel B). Although this evidence is not completely robust, it is suggestive that investors do not always value downside protection for start-up investments. This is intuitive because start-ups have little or no assets, and this downside protection has little meaning to venture capital funds. Gilson and Schizer (2003) discuss this point at great length, and make note of the fact that it is extremely rare for a venture capital fund to fight over the assets of a failed start-up in bankruptcy proceedings. In contrast, expansion investments (which by definition have assets and a greater ability to service debt payments) are 1 to 3% more likely to be financed with some form of debt (Panel E).

The data further indicate that start-ups do not have cash flows to pay interest on debt: Securities that involve at least some debt finance are approximately 1 to 3% less likely to be employed (see Panels A–D and F). Finally, Panels D and F do indicate that start-ups are 1.3% (2.6% in Panel F) more likely to be financed with convertible preferred equity. Although this effect is not as robust, it does provide some evidence in support of the view that convertible preferred equity is an efficient form of venture capital finance.

The evidence in support of the use of convertibles is stronger in regards to the marginal effects for high-tech entrepreneurial firms. Convertible preferred equity and convertible debt are 6.1% and 2.5%, respectively, more likely for high-tech firms (Panel A; the marginal effects are similar in the other panels). This provides very strong support for Hypothesis 11.7 and indicates that the large body of literature on the optimality regarding the use of convertible securities is most applicable to the financing of high-tech firms. However, notice

[16]The inclusion of the "private equity" deals with the "venture capital" deals does not materially impact the analysis. It is helpful to consider these transactions jointly, largely because most venture capital funds in Canada are not restricted from carrying out private equity deals (that is, in the data, any given fund will invest in an array of both private equity and venture capital deals).

Table 11.3 Correlati

This table presents correlation coefficients across various dependent and explanatory variables. The securities are presen
equity and warrants, and so on. 12,363 observations. Correlations greater than 0.02 in absolute value are statistically significa

		(1)	(2)	(3)	(4)	(5)	(6)	(7)	(8)	(9)	(10)	(11)	(12)
(1)	Preferred Equity	1.00											
(2)	Common Equity	−0.20	1.00										
(3)	Convertible Preferred Equity	−0.11	−0.22	1.00									
(4)	Debt	−0.14	−0.27	−0.15	1.00								
(5)	Convertible Debt	−0.13	−0.26	−0.14	−0.18	1.00							
(6)	Debt and Common	−0.07	−0.14	−0.08	−0.10	−0.09	1.00						
(7)	Preferred and Common	−0.04	−0.09	−0.05	−0.06	−0.06	−0.03	1.00					
(8)	Other Securities	−0.13	−0.26	−0.14	−0.18	−0.17	−0.09	−0.06	1.00				
(9)	Start-up	0.07	0.04	0.05	−0.12	−0.02	−0.09	−0.03	0.05	1.00			
(10)	Expansion	−0.04	−0.03	−0.01	0.04	0.05	0.02	0.01	−0.02	−0.80	1.00		
(11)	Buyout	−0.03	0.00	−0.01	0.04	−0.03	0.07	0.03	−0.03	−0.21	−0.15	1.00	
(12)	Turnaround	−0.04	−0.01	−0.06	0.09	−0.02	0.09	0.02	−0.04	−0.25	−0.17	−0.05	1.00

Matrix

for groups which are functionally very similar; for example, convertible preferred equity includes mixes of preferred at the 5% level.

(13)	(14)	(15)	(16)	(17)	(18)	(19)	(20)	(21)	(22)	(23)	(24)	(25)

(*continued*)

Table 11

		(1)	(2)	(3)	(4)	(5)	(6)	(7)	(8)	(9)	(10)	(11)	(12)
(13)	High-tech	0.11	−0.02	0.13	−0.17	0.05	−0.16	−0.04	0.06	0.24	−0.07	−0.16	−0.18
(14)	First Round	−0.07	0.07	−0.06	0.00	−0.04	0.08	0.02	0.00	0.08	−0.10	0.10	−0.04
(15)	Round Number	0.04	−0.07	0.04	0.03	0.06	−0.08	−0.03	−0.01	−0.16	0.17	−0.06	0.05
(16)	$ Invested	0.03	0.00	0.01	−0.05	−0.05	−0.01	−0.01	0.08	−0.05	0.06	0.04	−0.04
(17)	$ Invested/$ Deal Size	−0.11	0.08	−0.16	0.17	0.00	0.12	0.04	−0.13	−0.16	0.05	0.07	0.12
(18)	Syndication	0.11	−0.06	0.16	−0.18	0.01	−0.10	−0.03	0.09	0.13	−0.04	−0.05	−0.11
(19)	Government VC	0.00	0.04	0.01	−0.06	0.03	−0.03	−0.01	−0.01	0.10	−0.07	−0.03	−0.03
(20)	LSVCC	−0.03	−0.03	−0.05	0.08	−0.02	0.09	0.04	−0.03	−0.09	−0.01	0.01	0.19
(21)	Limited Partner VC	0.02	0.06	0.04	−0.08	0.04	−0.05	0.00	−0.06	0.08	−0.05	0.00	−0.07
(22)	Corporate VC	0.01	−0.06	0.01	0.03	−0.02	0.01	−0.01	0.05	−0.04	0.03	0.08	−0.03
(23)	U.S. VC	0.05	−0.01	0.04	−0.09	−0.06	−0.05	−0.02	0.13	0.01	0.03	−0.03	−0.06
(24)	TSX Index	0.06	−0.11	0.07	−0.03	0.01	−0.08	−0.03	0.11	0.08	0.00	−0.07	−0.07
(25)	Capital Gains Tax	−0.13	0.15	−0.09	0.02	−0.01	0.12	0.06	−0.12	−0.12	0.06	0.05	0.08
(26)	Trend	0.10	−0.19	0.10	−0.02	0.03	−0.12	−0.06	0.16	0.12	−0.02	−0.08	−0.09

(continued)

(13)	(14)	(15)	(16)	(17)	(18)	(19)	(20)	(21)	(22)	(23)	(24)	(25)
1.00												
−0.21	1.00											
0.21	−0.63	1.00										
0.05	0.01	−0.02	1.00									
−0.36	0.20	−0.18	0.08	1.00								
0.33	−0.15	0.14	0.06	−0.81	1.00							
0.05	0.01	−0.01	−0.07	−0.06	0.05	1.00						
−0.17	0.00	0.03	−0.04	0.15	−0.18	−0.24	1.00					
0.10	−0.01	−0.01	−0.06	0.00	−0.03	−0.23	−0.33	1.00				
0.00	0.02	−0.03	−0.01	−0.05	0.05	−0.13	−0.19	−0.18	1.00			
0.14	−0.06	0.04	0.23	−0.18	0.16	−0.10	−0.15	−0.14	−0.08	1.00		
0.26	−0.15	0.16	0.10	−0.23	0.22	−0.10	0.01	−0.10	0.05	0.10	1.00	
−0.19	0.17	−0.18	0.00	0.32	−0.19	−0.06	0.04	0.10	−0.03	−0.09	−0.15	1.00
0.28	−0.21	0.21	0.03	−0.37	0.27	−0.04	0.01	−0.15	0.06	0.10	0.68	−0.72

Table 11.4 Multinomial Logit Analyses

Panel A. Base Model

This table presents a multinomial logit regression of the determinants of security choice among Canadian venture explanatory variables are as indicated in the table, including entrepreneurial firm characteristics, other deal characteristics, values reported are the marginal effects, not the multinomial logit coefficients themselves, for reasons of conciseness, the 10%, 5%, and 1% levels, respectively. Log Likelihood = −21667.45. Likelihood Ratio Chi-squared = 3362.665***.

	Explanatory Variables	**From Table 11.1: (Hypothesis #): Dominant Predicted Security**	**Straight Preferred Equity**	**Common Equity and/or Warrants**
	Constant		0.153***	0.387***
Entrepreneurial Firm Characteristics	Start-up	(11.3, 11.4): Convertible preferred; straight preferred	0.024***	0.040***
	Buyout	(11.1): Debt	−0.020	0.020
	Turnaround	(11.2): Convertible preferred equity	−0.004	0.023
	High-tech	(11.7): Convertible preferred equity	0.037***	0.0004
Deal Characteristics	Round Number	(11.6): Convertible preferred equity for earlier rounds	0.002	−0.007***
	$ Invested/$ Deal Size	(11.5): Less debt for higher values	−0.044***	0.038***
VC Characteristics	Government VC	(11.8): Less ownership equity	0.002	0.039**
	LSVCC	(11.9): At least some debt	0.011	−0.005
	Limited Partnership VC	(11.8): Convertible preferred equity	0.023***	0.029**
	Corporate VC	(11.8): Convertible preferred equity	0.023**	−0.084***
	U.S. VC	(11.11): Convertible preferred equity	0.055***	0.101***
Institutional and Market Factors	TSX Index	(11.12): Lower index, more debt and preferred equity	0.00001***	0.00001**
	Capital Gains Tax Rate	(11.10): Lower rate, more convertible preferred	−0.684***	0.081
	Trend	(11.11): Higher numbers (later years) more convertible preferred equity	−0.012***	−0.036***

of Security Choices

Regression Estimates

capitalists over the period 1991 (Q1) to 2003 (Q3). The dependent variable is the security selected. The
VC characteristics as well as institutional and market variables. The number of observations = 12,343. The
and to explicitly indicate the economic significance alongside the statistical significance. *, **, *** Significant at

Convertible Preferred Equity and/or Preferred and Warrants	Straight Debt	Convertible Debt and/or Debt and Warrants	Mixes of Debt and Common	Mixes of Preferred and Common	Other Combinations
−0.001	0.003	−0.092**	−0.079***	−0.051***	−0.321***
0.002	−0.033***	−0.029***	−0.013***	−0.003	0.011
0.023	0.027*	−0.054**	0.016***	0.011**	−0.023
−0.064***	0.058***	−0.018	0.019***	0.005	−0.018
0.061***	−0.079***	0.025***	−0.024***	−0.005*	−0.015*
0.00003	0.011***	0.009***	−0.004***	−0.001	−0.009***
−0.099***	0.131***	0.021**	0.020***	0.002	−0.068***
0.017*	−0.082***	0.030***	−0.011**	−0.001	0.007
0.011	−0.023***	−0.017	0.008**	0.008**	0.007
0.037***	−0.083***	0.023**	−0.020***	0.002	−0.011
0.028***	−0.003	−0.015	0.001	−0.005	0.056***
0.043***	−0.176***	−0.122***	−0.032**	−0.009	0.141***
0.000005*	−0.00001***	−0.000009**	−0.000006***	0.0000002	−0.000002
−0.209***	0.040	0.143	0.239***	0.075**	0.315***
−0.0021	0.010***	0.009***	0.002*	−0.001	0.030***

(*continued*)

Table 11.4

Panel B. Robustness Check #1: Weighted

This table presents a multinomial logit regression of the determinants of security choice among Canadian venture explanatory variables are as indicated in the table, including entrepreneurial firm characteristics, other deal characteristics, invested. The number of observations = 12,343. The values reported are the marginal effects, not the multinomial alongside the statistical significance. *, **, *** Significant at the 10%, 5%, and 1% levels, respectively. Log Likelihood =

	Explanatory Variables	From Table 11.1: (Hypothesis #): Dominant Predicted Security	Straight Preferred Equity	Common Equity and/or Warrants
	Constant		0.313***	0.582***
Entrepreneurial Firm Characteristics	Start-up	(11.3, 11.4): Convertible preferred; straight preferred	0.055***	−0.025**
	Buyout	(11.1): Debt	−0.062***	0.130***
	Turnaround	(11.2): Convertible preferred equity	−0.002	0.029
	High-tech	(11.7): Convertible preferred equity	0.047***	−0.0177
Deal Characteristics	Round Number	(11.6): Convertible preferred equity for earlier rounds	0.006***	−0.003
	$ Invested/ $ Deal Size	(11.5): Less debt for higher values	−0.106***	0.009
VC Characteristics	Government VC	(11.8): Less ownership equity	0.008	0.010
	LSVCC	(11.9): At least some debt	0.037***	−0.014
	Limited Partnership VC	(11.8): Convertible preferred equity	0.031***	0.001
	Corporate VC	(11.8): Convertible preferred equity	0.040***	−0.109***
	U.S. VC	(11.11): Convertible preferred equity	0.048***	0.069***
Institutional and Market Factors	TSX Index	(11.12): Lower index, more debt and preferred equity	0.00002***	−0.00004***
	Capital Gains Tax Rate	(11.10): Lower rate, more convertible preferred	−0.969***	0.264**
	Trend	(11.11): Higher numbers (later years) more convertible preferred equity	−0.024***	−0.007

(*continued*)

Observations by Amounts Invested

capitalists over the period 1991 (Q1) to 2003 (Q3). The dependent variable is the security selected. The VC characteristics as well as institutional and market variables. The regression is weighted by the amounts logit coefficients themselves, for reasons of conciseness, and to explicitly indicate the economic significance −20336.76 Likelihood Ratio Chi-squared = 4910.400***.

Convertible Preferred Equity and/or Preferred and Warrants	Straight Debt	Convertible Debt and/or Debt and Warrants	Mixes of Debt and Common	Mixes of Preferred and Common	Other Combinations
−0.077	−0.176***	−0.121***	−0.072***	−0.033***	−0.416***
−0.003	−0.006	−0.024***	−0.013***	0.000	0.015*
0.028	0.046***	−0.035**	0.030***	0.006**	−0.144***
−0.041	0.034***	−0.004	0.014***	−0.002	−0.028
0.079***	−0.050***	0.002	−0.031***	−0.004***	−0.025**
−0.00091	0.008***	0.008***	−0.001*	0.000	−0.017***
−0.135***	0.078***	0.023**	0.010**	0.001	0.120***
0.038***	−0.016*	0.054***	−0.007	−0.004	−0.084***
0.021**	0.027***	0.028***	0.018***	0.0001	−0.117***
0.040***	−0.021***	0.040***	−0.005	0.000	−0.087***
0.031**	0.044***	0.016	0.010**	−0.006*	−0.027
0.014	−0.150***	−0.076***	−0.014**	−0.026***	0.134***
0.000009**	−0.00002***	−0.00002***	−0.000003*	0.0000003	0.00006***
−0.039	0.432***	0.316***	0.171***	0.050**	−0.225*
−0.0016	0.009***	0.012***	0.001	0.000	0.011**

(*continued*)

Table 11.4

Panel C. Robustness Check #2:

This table presents a multinomial logit regression of the determinants of security choice among Canadian venture explanatory variables are as indicated in the table, including entrepreneurial firm characteristics, other deal characteristics, values reported are the marginal effects, not the multinomial logit coefficients themselves, for reasons of conciseness, the 10%, 5%, and 1% levels, respectively. Log Likelihood = −22018.06 Likelihood Ratio Chi-squared = 2661.440***.

	Explanatory Variables	From Table 11.1: (Hypothesis #): Dominant Predicted Security	Straight Preferred Equity	Common Equity and/or Warrants
	Constant		0.051***	−0.142***
Entrepreneurial Firm Characteristics	Start-up	(11.3, 11.4): Convertible preferred; straight preferred	0.025***	0.042***
	Buyout	(11.1): Debt	−0.014	0.021
	Turnaround	(11.2): Convertible preferred equity	−0.004	0.031
	High-tech	(11.7): Convertible preferred equity	0.041***	−0.015
Deal Characteristics	Round Number	(11.6): Convertible preferred equity for earlier rounds	0.002	−0.008***
	$ Invested/ $ Deal Size	(11.5): Less debt for higher values	−0.043	0.064***
VC Characteristics	Government VC	(11.8): Less ownership equity	−0.016**	0.056***
	LSVCC	(11.9): At least some debt	−0.007	−0.016
Tax	Capital Gains Tax Rate	(11.10): Lower rate, more convertible preferred	−0.374***	0.960***

that this result is completely robust to different definitions of "high-tech"; for example, the use of convertible securities is less likely for the subset of life science firms (see the specification in Panel D).

Hypothesis 11.5 considered the relation between syndication and capital structure. Panels A to D report the amounts invested relative to the total deal size, whereas Panels E and F report a dummy variable equal to 1 for contemporaneous syndication (these variables are not reported in simultaneous specifications due to collinearity; as indicated in Table 11.3). Panel A indicates that

(*continued*)

Alternative Explanatory Variables

capitalists over the period 1991 (Q1) to 2003 (Q3). The dependent variable is the security selected. The VC characteristics as well as institutional and market variables. The number of observations = 12,343. The and to explicitly indicate the economic significance alongside the statistical significance. *, **, *** Significant at

Convertible Preferred Equity and/or Preferred and Warrants	Straight Debt	Convertible Debt and/or Debt and Warrants	Mixes of Debt and Common	Mixes of Preferred and Common	Other Combinations
0.011	0.042**	−0.026	−0.096***	−0.066***	0.226***
0.005	−0.037***	−0.024***	−0.015***	−0.002	0.007
0.025	0.025	−0.053**	0.016***	0.010**	−0.031
−0.063***	0.058***	−0.017	0.019***	0.005	−0.029
0.065***	−0.087***	0.026***	−0.027***	−0.005**	0.002
0.00043	0.010***	0.009***	−0.005***	−0.001	−0.008***
−0.099***	0.135***	0.025**	0.020***	0.003	−0.106***
−0.006	−0.043***	0.034***	−0.001	−0.0001	−0.025**
−0.009	0.021***	−0.009	0.018***	0.008***	−0.007
−0.145***	−0.233***	−0.048	0.205***	0.099***	−0.464***

large amounts invested related to deal size are associated with a greater probability of use of common equity (an increase in the amount invested/deal size by 0.1 increases the probability of use of common equity by 0.38%), a greater probability of use securities with at least some debt (the marginal effect is greatest for straight debt, where an increase of 0.1 increases the probability of use of straight debt by 1.31%), and a smaller probability of use of straight preferred and convertible preferred securities (the marginal effect for convertible preferred is greater, where a 0.1 increase in amounts invested per deal size reduce

Table 11.4

Panel D. Robustness Check #3:

This table presents a multinomial logit regression of the determinants of security choice among Canadian venture explanatory variables are as indicated in the table, including entrepreneurial firm characteristics, other deal characteristics, values reported are the marginal effects, not the multinomial logit coefficients themselves, for reasons of conciseness, the 10%, 5%, and 1% levels, respectively. Log Likelihood = −22130.56. Likelihood Ratio Chi-squared = 2436.428***.

	Explanatory Variables	From Table 11.1: (Hypothesis #): Dominant Predicted Security	Straight Preferred Equity	Common Equity and/or Warrants
	Constant		−0.056***	0.145***
Entrepreneurial Firm Characteristics	Start-up	(11.3, 11.4): Convertible preferred; straight preferred	0.037***	0.014
	Buyout	(11.1): Debt	−0.024	0.031
	Turnaround	(11.2): Convertible preferred equity	−0.015	0.045**
	Life Sciences Industries	(11.7): Convertible preferred equity	0.002	0.053***
Deal Characteristics	Round Number	(11.6): Convertible preferred equity for earlier rounds	0.005***	−0.014***
	$ Invested/ $ Deal Size	(11.5): Less debt for higher values	−0.071***	0.115***
VC Characteristics	Government VC	(11.8): Less ownership equity	0.004	0.059***
	LSVCC	(11.9): At least some debt	0.006	−0.008
	Limited Partnership VC	(11.8): Convertible preferred equity	0.020**	0.062***
	Corporate VC	(11.8): Convertible preferred equity	0.023**	−0.084***
	U.S. VC	(11.11): Convertible preferred equity	0.066***	0.106***

the probability of use of convertible preferred by 0.99%); Panels B, C, and D indicate very similar effects. The marginal effects for syndication (Panels E and F) are a mirror image to these results, which is expected given the high negative correlation between syndication and amounts invested/deal size (Table 11.2). Syndicated investments more often involve straight preferred equity and convertible preferred equity. The evidence in regards to straight preferred equity

(continued)

Alternative Explanatory Variables

capitalists over the period 1991 (Q1) to 2003 (Q3). The dependent variable is the security selected. The
VC characteristics as well as institutional and market variables. The number of observations = 12,343. The
and to explicitly indicate the economic significance alongside the statistical significance. *, **, *** Significant at

Convertible Preferred Equity and/or Preferred and Warrants	Straight Debt	Convertible Debt and/or Debt and Warrants	Mixes of Debt and Common	Mixes of Preferred and Common	Other Combinations
−0.008	−0.043***	−0.013	−0.038***	−0.037***	0.051***
0.013**	−0.039***	−0.023***	−0.021***	−0.004	0.023***
0.010	0.041***	−0.060***	0.024***	0.012***	−0.034
−0.078***	0.067***	−0.023	0.027***	0.007	−0.030
0.002	−0.025***	0.007	−0.003	−0.009**	−0.026***
0.003**	0.009***	0.011***	−0.008***	−0.002**	−0.005**
−0.124***	0.139***	0.006	0.038***	0.007**	−0.111***
0.017*	−0.087***	0.025**	−0.012**	−0.001	−0.005
0.008	−0.016**	−0.018*	0.012***	0.009***	0.007
0.037**	−0.092***	0.019**	−0.019***	0.004	−0.031***
0.028***	−0.006	−0.014	0.000	−0.005	0.058***
0.052***	−0.190***	−0.117***	−0.043***	−0.011	0.138***

is analogous to the results discussed previously pertaining to start-ups; straight preferred equity mitigate agency problems among syndicated investors (see Hypothesis 11.4 and accompanying text). Overall, these results suggest there is both a screening and value-added role for syndication (there is no evidence that uniquely supports one view over the other) and that the security design depends on the particular transaction (see Hypothesis 11.5 and accompanying text).

Table 11.4

Panel E. Robustness Check #4:

This table presents a multinomial logit regression of the determinants of security choice among Canadian venture explanatory variables are as indicated in the table, including entrepreneurial firm characteristics, other deal characteristics, values reported are the marginal effects, not the multinomial logit coefficients themselves, for reasons of conciseness, the 10%, 5%, and 1% levels, respectively. Log Likelihood = −21994.65. Likelihood Ratio Chi-squared = 2708.258***.

	Explanatory Variables	From Table 11.1: (Hypothesis #): Dominant Predicted Security	Straight Preferred Equity	Common Equity and/or Warrants
	Constant		0.023	0.101***
Entrepreneurial Firm Characteristics	Expansion	(11.3, 11.4): Convertible preferred equity	−0.022***	−0.045***
	Buyout	(11.1): Debt	−0.035*	−0.027
	Turnaround	(11.2): Convertible preferred equity	−0.029*	−0.018
	High-tech	(11.7): Convertible preferred equity	0.035***	0.0009
Deal Characteristics	First Round	(11.6): Convertible preferred equity for earlier rounds	−0.021***	0.026***
	Syndication	(11.3, 11.4, 11.5): Straight preferred	0.039***	−0.034***
VC Characteristics	Government VC	(11.8): Less ownership equity	−0.013*	0.044***
	LSVCC	(11.9): At least some debt	−0.005	−0.014
Institutional and Market Factors	TSX Index	(11.12): Lower index, more debt and preferred equity	0.000003	−0.00003***
	Capital Gains Tax Rate	(11.10): Lower rate, more convertible preferred	−0.372***	0.957***

In regards to staging (Hypothesis 11.6), Panels A to D consider a staging variable that records the round number, whereas Panels E and F provide a dummy variable for first round (new) investments. Panels A to D indicate that later rounds are more likely to be financed with debt or convertible debt, which likely reflects the entrepreneurial firm's ability to service debt payments later in its life cycle, as there is a greater chance of revenues among more

(*continued*)

Alternative Explanatory Variables

capitalists over the period 1991 (Q1) to 2003 (Q3). The dependent variable is the security selected. The VC characteristics as well as institutional and market variables. The number of observations = 12,343. The and to explicitly indicate the economic significance alongside the statistical significance. *, **, *** Significant at

Convertible Preferred Equity and/or Preferred and Warrants	Straight Debt	Convertible Debt and/or Debt and Warrants	Mixes of Debt and Common	Mixes of Preferred and Common	Other Combinations
−0.090***	0.147***	0.000	−0.098***	−0.064***	−0.018
−0.004	0.032***	0.036***	0.011***	0.003	−0.010
0.020	0.063***	−0.022	0.028***	0.013***	−0.040*
−0.069***	0.098***	0.016	0.033***	0.007	−0.038*
0.060***	−0.088***	0.030***	−0.030***	−0.006**	−0.002
−0.011*	−0.019***	−0.022***	0.014***	0.001	0.031***
0.085***	−0.101***	−0.017**	−0.009***	−0.001	0.037***
−0.003	−0.046***	0.036***	−0.003	0.000	−0.014
−0.007	0.016**	−0.008	0.019***	0.008***	−0.010
0.000002	0.000002	−0.000001	−0.000003***	−0.0000010	0.00002***
−0.181***	−0.157***	−0.036	0.229***	0.104***	−0.543***

established firms. In regards to first round investments (Panels E and F), the evidence indicates one result that is robust to potential endogeneity concerns: Debt is approximately 2% less likely for new investments (consistent with the evidence in Panels A to D).

Hypotheses 11.8 and 11.9 were concerned with the effects of venture capital fund characteristics on capital structure. The evidence supports Hypothesis

Table 11.4

Panel F. Robustness Check #5:

This table presents a multinomial logit regression of the determinants of security choice among Canadian venture explanatory variables are as indicated in the table, including entrepreneurial firm characteristics, other deal characteristics, values reported are the marginal effects, not the multinomial logit coefficients themselves, for reasons of conciseness, the 10%, 5%, and 1% levels, respectively. Log Likelihood = −22223.64. Likelihood Ratio Chi-squared = 2250.286***.

	Explanatory Variables	From Table 11.1: (Hypothesis #): Dominant Predicted Security	Straight Preferred Equity	Common Equity and/or Warrants
	Constant		0.167***	0.374***
Entrepreneurial Firm Characteristics	Start-up	(11.3, 11.4): Convertible preferred; straight preferred	0.015**	0.040***
	Buyout	(11.1): Debt	−0.049***	−0.004
	Turnaround	(11.2): Convertible preferred equity	−0.031*	−0.002
	High-tech	(11.7): Convertible preferred equity	0.013	−0.0078
Deal Characteristics	First Round	(11.6): Convertible preferred equity for earlier rounds	−0.016	0.013
	Syndication	(11.3, 11.4, 11.5): Straight preferred	0.025***	−0.041***
VC Characteristics	Government VC	(11.8): Less ownership equity	−0.014*	0.034***
	LSVCC	(11.9): At least some debt	−0.002	−0.001
Institutional and Market Factors	TSX Index	(11.12): Lower index, more debt and preferred equity	0.00001***	0.00001***
	Capital Gains Tax Rate	(11.10): Lower rate, more convertible preferred	−0.650***	0.144
	Trend	(11.11): Higher numbers (later years) more convertible preferred equity	−0.013***	−0.035***

(continued)

Instrumental Variables

capitalists over the period 1991 (Q1) to 2003 (Q3). The dependent variable is the security selected. The
VC characteristics as well as institutional and market variables. The number of observations = 12,343. The
and to explicitly indicate the economic significance alongside the statistical significance. *, **, *** Significant at

Convertible Preferred Equity and/or Preferred and Warrants	Straight Debt	Convertible Debt and/or Debt and Warrants	Mixes of Debt and Common	Mixes of Preferred and Common	Other Combinations
−0.047	0.143***	−0.069	−0.086***	−0.058***	−0.425***
0.026***	−0.057***	0.009	−0.024***	0.003	−0.012
−0.005	0.084***	−0.047**	0.038***	0.014***	−0.030
−0.078***	0.110***	0.003	0.030***	0.006	−0.039**
0.020	−0.026**	0.031**	−0.012***	−0.011***	−0.007
−0.01807	0.027**	−0.001	−0.004	0.001	0.053***
0.111***	−0.061***	−0.014	−0.022***	−0.005	0.007
−0.013*	−0.036***	0.030***	0.009	−0.001	−0.009
0.009	0.006	−0.003	0.007*	0.005*	−0.020**
−0.000001	−0.00001***	−0.000009**	−0.000007***	0.0000007	0.000003
−0.124	−0.116	0.163*	0.241***	0.083***	0.260**
−0.006**	0.009***	0.007*	0.004***	0.000	0.035***

11.8 that limited partnerships are more likely to use securities with equity (e.g., 2.9% more likely to use common equity and 3.7% more likely to use convertible preferred equity; see Panel A; see also Panel D for similar evidence), and less likely to use debt (8.3% less likely in Panel A; the evidence in Panel D is similar). The evidence in regards to U.S. venture capital funds financing Canadian entrepreneurial firms is similar. Corporate venture capital funds are also 2.8% more likely to use convertible preferred equity but are not more likely to use straight common equity and not less likely to use debt, unlike limited partnerships.

Regarding the tax subsidized LSVCCs (see Hypothesis 11.9 and accompanying text), the evidence indicates some differences in security design. Panels C, E, and F report these effects without consideration of dummy variables for the other types of funds. There is consistent evidence that LSVCCs are 0.8% more likely to use debt and common equity as well as debt and preferred equity (Panel A; the marginal effects are similar in the other panels), which is partially supportive of Hypothesis 11.9. The evidence for LSVCCs using debt by itself is not robust to the specification (Panels C and E suggest more likely, but Panels A and D suggest less likely, whereas Panel F is insignificant).

For direct government investment programs, the evidence is quite consistent and indicates such programs are approximately 4 to 5% more likely to use common equity, approximately 3% more likely to use convertible debt, and approximately 8% less likely to use straight debt. This evidence might be a little surprising to some, depending on one's view of the appropriate role of a direct government program in the financing of innovative activities and whether or not they should be taking equity positions in the firms they finance. This issue is beyond the scope of this chapter. Further normative research on this topic is clearly warranted.

There is clear evidence that capital gains taxes affect security design. First, notice that, consistent with Gilson and Schizer (2003), higher capital gains taxes lower the probability that convertible preferred equity is used (consistent with Hypothesis 11.10; this effect is significant in Panels A to E, but in Panels B and F this effect is not statistically significant). For example, the decrease in capital gains taxes in 2000 in Canada from 36.6 to 23.3% gave rise to an increase in the probability of the use of convertible preferred equity by 2.8%.[17] This empirical effect is consistent with Gilson and Schizer (2003) because if entrepreneurial firms use stock options, then it is to the benefit of both venture capital funds and entrepreneurs to use convertible preferred equity for tax reasons. There is also evidence of an effect on the use of other securities, but the predictions and effects are a little more ambiguous in that a lowering of capital gains taxes increases the value of common equity participation to both the venture capital fund and the entrepreneur, and the sharing of this benefit depends on the bargaining power between the parties. There is evidence that straight

[17]The calculation is (0.232 – 0.366) * (−0.209), using the estimates in Panel A of Table 10.4.

preferred equity is less likely, and mixes of common equity with debt and preferred equity are more likely. There is also evidence that common equity alone is more likely (but this evidence is not significant in Panel A and E).

Hypothesis 11.11 postulated that Canadian venture capital funds would become more sophisticated over time, in the sense that they would be more likely to use convertible preferred securities. The evidence does not support this prediction. The evidence (Panels A and F) indicates a trend toward the use of securities with at least some debt (straight debt, convertible debt, and mixes of debt and common equity; where there is an increase in probability of use by 0.2 to up to 1% each year, depending on the specification and security; see Panels A and F).

Hypothesis 11.12 postulated a relation between the TSX index[18] and the selected security. Higher index values are associated with securities that provide upside potential to the venture capital fund (e.g., common equity, convertible preferred equity) and not securities with debt. For example, a 1,000-point increase in the TSX index increases the probability of use of common equity by 1% and convertible preferred equity by 0.5% (Panel A), and reduces the probability of the use of debt by 1%. This indicates venture capital funds bargain harder for upside potential in times of better economic conditions, and entrepreneurs are willing to give up equity to venture capital funds in order to obtain financing.

11.5 Limitations, Alternative Explanations, and Future Research

In this section, we briefly address a few issues that could be pertinent to the selection of different securities in the data but were not considered in the preceding empirical tests. We also suggest related research issues that could be addressed in future work.

11.5.1 Securities Regulation

Securities regulation in Canada has curtailed the formation of a secondary (resale) market for the equity of firms in their earlier stages of development in at least three important respects. First, escrow requirements (so that the entrepreneur and venture capital fund do not desert the project after a public offering) tend to be overly onerous in Canada (MacIntosh, 1994, at 114–115, 148–149), thereby limiting the incentive of entrepreneurs and venture capital funds to initiate an initial public offering (IPO). Because IPOs are typically the most attractive

[18]We do not use a variable for the returns to the TSX index because that variable is too collinear with the capital gains tax variable; as such, we use a variable that indicates the TSX level for the year in which investment took place.

form of venture capital exit in an unregulated market, escrow requirements reduce the value of the equity of firms in their earlier stages of development.

Second, the required disclosure in primary and secondary markets is cost-ineffective for smaller issuers in Canada (MacIntosh, 1994, at 115–124). For small investments (less than Can$150,000 in Ontario), a prospectus must be filed (see O.Regs. s.19(e)(1); see also Anand et al., 1999). Preparing and filing a prospectus, however, is often costly. At this level of investment, most investors require a substantial fraction of equity share in the firm; however, the reluctance of entrepreneurs to forgo equity interests is one of the most common reasons for the breakdown of contractual negotiations between small-scale investors and entrepreneurs. As a result, the onerous prospectus requirement in Canada prevents some small-scale investments from being carried out (MacIntosh, 1994, at 101–104).

Third, legislation imposing resale restrictions is particularly onerous in Canada. For example, securities purchased pursuant to a prospectus exemption prior to the firm's IPO are subject to a hold period of 12 months even where all the securities are of the same class. Hold periods are also different for different types of securities. As Canadian regulators view bonds and preferred equity to be inherently safer than common equity (this is surprising in light of adverse selection theory), hold periods for bonds and preferred equity are notably shorter (MacIntosh, 1994, at 107). Securities regulation may therefore impact the eventual exit vehicle selected; IPOs are a relatively more costly form of venture capital fund exit in Canada than in the United States (Cumming and MacIntosh, 2003). Importantly, although hold periods make preferred equity and convertible preferred equity relatively more attractive than common equity, common equity has still been the most frequently used form of finance in Canada (Tables 11.2a–f). Securities regulation cannot account for the data.

In sum, Canadian securities legislation has impeded the development of a secondary resale market for equity securities of small and medium-sized firms in Canada. A viable secondary market is needed to ensure suitable exit. Therefore, equity-type securities, and especially pure common equity securities, are less likely to be issued in financing private equity investments than that which might otherwise be the case. This will impact the overall level of observed forms of finance over the years covered by the data. Nevertheless, straight common equity has been the most frequently used form of venture capital finance in Canada in most of the years in spite of the negative liquidity effects of Canadian securities legislation (see Tables 11.2a–f and Figures 11.1 and 11.2).

11.5.2 Other Control Rights

This chapter considered a large volume of data on security design. There are other aspects of venture capital contracts that are not part of the Canadian data, including specific control and veto rights. Further work could assess the use of these other control rights in relation to different securities, as well as in relation to trust and behavioral finance considerations. Future research could also consider whether these specific contractual features differ across other countries. Evidence on topic is presented in Chapter 14.

11.5.3 Behavioral Finance Factors

Trust within the venture capital fund manager entrepreneur relationship can have an impact on venture capital contracting (Manigart et al., 2002b). It is possible that there are differences in the level of trust between parties across countries, as well as within a country. The high proportion of straight common equity contracts in Canada is suggestive that relatively more trust exists within Canadian venture capital markets when compared to the United States. That is, common equity places the entrepreneur and the venture capital fund "on the same team," as neither party has priority in bankruptcy. These Canada data, however, do not enable a direct test of the precise impact of trust and other behavioral finance variables on the contractual structure. Further research is warranted.

11.6 Conclusions

The empirical evidence indicates forms of finance other than convertible preferred equity are used by Canadian venture capital funds (Tables 11.2a–f) and there are changes in the intensity of use of different forms of finance over time (Figures 11.1 and 11.2). This is probably not due to the definition of venture capital, as the results hold in every single subsample in the data (Tables 11.2a–f). The fact that Canadian venture capital funds use securities unlike their United States counterparts, together with the fact that there is a significant tax bias in favor of the use of convertibles in the United States (Gilson and Schizer, 2003) and not in Canada (Sandler, 2001), renders the empirical analysis of venture financing structures in Canada to be both necessary and interesting.

We identified four categories of factors that impact the selected security: (1) agency costs, (2) tax, (3) sophistication and learning, and (4) market conditions. Figures 11.1 and 11.2 (as well as the empirical tests in Table 11.4) show that market conditions in the aftermath of the Internet bubble have drastically reduced the use of common equity and increased the use of securities that involve priority in bankruptcy for the investor. But the data up to 2003 do not support the view that venture capital financial contracting in Canada is evolving to more closely resemble the U.S. market (for any definition of the term *venture capital*) in terms of a convergence to only using convertible preferred equity. Likewise, U.S. venture capital funds financing Canadian entrepreneurs do not use convertible preferred equity most frequently (Table 11.2, Panel E). Hence, there is strong support for (4) market conditions but little support for (3) sophistication and learning. The data are consistent with the importance of (2) tax conditions identified by Gilson and Schizer (2003), but tax does not fully explain the heterogeneous mix of forms of finance by U.S. and Canadian venture capital funds financing Canadian entrepreneurial firms. Perhaps the most compelling explanation for the data is thus (1) agency costs. The theory and evidence are very supportive of the propositions that stage of development, asset intangibility (high-tech firms), and other nonmutually exclusive characteristics of the transacting parties affect the selected form of venture capital finance. Expected agency problems are more pronounced depending on the characteristics of the entrepreneur and the investor, and the data are consistent with the view that the securities selected systematically vary depending on venture capital fund and entrepreneur characteristics in order to mitigate such expected agency problems.

Appendix

This Appendix revisits the conditions under which fixed-fraction contracts are optimal and extends the discussion of security design for start-ups and expansion investments. For illustrative purposes, suppose an entrepreneurial venture requires \$100 of initial capital. The entrepreneur and "inside" venture capital fund (VC_1) each agree to provide \$50. Second-round financing is also required. In the second round, VC_1 and the "outside" venture capital fund (VC_2) each provide \$50. The amounts invested by the three parties in the two financing rounds are summarized in the first part of Table 11.A1. Within this context, three different contracts held by the three parties are now considered for illustrative purposes. In Case A we consider a fixed-fraction contract. Effort-related moral hazard costs are ignored in Case A. Effort-related moral hazard is introduced in Cases B and C. Case B considers the fixed-fraction contract with equal priority and moral hazard. A new contract is then proposed in Case C. Within Cases A, B, and C, we consider two cases of bankruptcy: (1) the value of the firm is \$10 without second-round investment, and (2) the value of the firm is \$140 with second-round investment (with slight modification in Cases B and C). In all cases we assume that VC_1 has inside knowledge of the future value of the firm after each financing round, but VC_2 does not have such knowledge.[19] VC_2 relies upon the information provided by VC_1 in deciding whether to invest and on what terms.

Case A Fixed-fraction contract without effort-related moral hazard

Suppose that second-round investment yields a salvage value of the firm's assets equal to \$140; this information is known to VC_1 but not to VC_2 prior to the second-round investment. Investment in the second round is efficient (a \$100 investment yields a gain of \$140 − \$10 = \$130). The fact that second-round investment yields a salvage value of the firm's assets equal to \$140 is known to VC_1 but not to VC_2 prior to the second-round investment. If the

[19]A more realistic assumption would be that the inside venture capital fund has superior knowledge than the outside venture capital fund(s); regardless, the implications and lessons from the example are the same.

Table 11.A1 Syndication Example

This table presents a syndication example to highlight the nonrobustness of the optimal contract derived by Admati and Pfleiderer (1994). Suppose there are two financing rounds. The first part of the table provides the amounts invested. The second part of the table outlines three cases (A–C). For each case, the inside VC_1 knows the salvage value of the firm if there is second-round financing. The outside VC_2 relies on the information provided by VC_1. If second-round investment does not happen then the salvage value of the firm is equal to $10.

	First-round Financing		Second-round Financing		Total Amount Invested	
Amounts invested by the three parties for Cases A, B and C	VC_1	$50	VC_1	$50	VC_1	$100
	Entrepreneur	$50	Entrepreneur	$0	Entrepreneur	$50
	VC_2	$0	VC_2	$50	VC_2	$50
	Total	$100	Total	$100	Total	$200
	Salvage Value		**Net Payoffs**		**Second-round Financing**	
Case		**VC_1**	**VC_2**	**Entrepreneur**	**Should happen?**	**Will happen?**
A. Fixed-fraction contract with equal priority and no effort-related moral hazard costs	$140	($30)	$0+[1]	($30)–[1]	Yes	Yes
B. Fixed-fraction contract with equal priority and effort-related moral hazard costs	$120 + 40ß[2]	−$100 + 0.5 (120 + 40ß)	−$50 + (0.5 − ß) (120 + 40ß)	−$50 + ß (120 + 40ß)	Yes	No[3]
C. Proposed contract with moral hazard						
VC_1: Straight preferred equity	$120 + 40ß[4]	($30)	0	($50)	Yes	Yes
VC_2: Convertible debt						
Entrepreneur: Common equity						

Notes:

[1]The price of second-stage securities must be low enough to provide (a risk neutral) VC_2 with at least 35.7% (50/140) of the firm's equity.
[2]Value of the firm itself depends on the entrepreneur's residual claim (ß) and therefore also depends on the price of securities issued at the second stage.
[3]VC_1 overstates the value of second-stage securities to minimize moral hazard (and VC_2's share, 1 – ß) and maximize the value of the firm. VC_2 will not participate.
[4]Moral hazard costs could be normalized to 0 without loss of generality with respect to optimal continuation in case C. The entrepreneur's equity share does not affect VC_1's payoff in nonbankruptcy states. In bankruptcy states, trilateral bargaining dissuades VC_1 from seeking outside VC_2 participation.

price of securities issued at the second round of investment is the same as the price of securities issued at the first stage, then the net payoffs would be as follows: VC_1 receives \$−30, VC_2 receives \$−15, and the entrepreneur receives \$−15. VC_1 would like to entice VC_2 to invest at the second round because \$140/2 – \$100 = \$−30 (>\$−45, VC_1's net payoff if there was no second-round investment). Investment in the second round is efficient (a \$100 investment yields a gain of \$140 – \$10 = \$130). However, second-round investment will not happen where VC_2 is a rational investor (because the parties are of the same priority, the entrepreneur and VC_2 each receive net payoffs equal to \$140/4 – \$50 = \$−15).

Admati and Pfleiderer (1994) argued that the preceding continuation problem may be resolved by lowering the price for the securities in the second round. If VC_2 expected the salvage value to equal \$140, then the price of the securities issued in the second round could be lowered such that VC_2 received at least (subject to risk preferences) 50/140 = 35.7% of the firm's equity (see Table 11.A1). (The entrepreneur therefore has 14.3%, and VC_1 always has 50%.) As such, VC_2's expected payoff would be slightly positive and he would invest (assuming risk neutrality; with risk aversion a greater expected payoff would be required). Changing the price of securities issued at the second stage affects the division of surplus between the entrepreneur and VC_2 but does not affect the fixed fraction received by VC_1.

Because the fraction received by VC_1 is unchanged, Admati and Pfleiderer (1994: 387) argue that "with fixed-fraction contracts, the VC's payoff is independent of the pricing of any securities issued at the second stage." Unfortunately, there is a crucial assumption driving this argument: Either there is no moral hazard or the entrepreneur's and outside VC_2's effort must be equally important to the success of the venture and the moral hazard effect of changing these parties' residual claim to the firm's assets must be identical. However, if the entrepreneur's effort is more dependent on her residual claim and has a greater impact on the success of the venture, then the inside VC_1 has an incentive to overprice securities issued at the second stage to maximize the entrepreneur's effort and the value of the firm (which in turn maximizes VC_1's payoff). In the context of a model with moral hazard, if the effect of the entrepreneur's effort on the value of the firm differs (even just infinitesimally) from that of the outside VC_2, then the inside VC_1 will always misrepresent the value of securities issued to the outside VC_2, as illustrated in Case B.

Case B Fixed-fraction contract with effort-related moral hazard

The inside VC_1 also has no role in facilitating optimal continuation and mitigating informational asymmetries between the entrepreneur and outside VC_2 under a fixed-fraction contract when residual claim affects effort and the effect of the entrepreneur's effort on the firm's payoff is different from that of the outside VC_2. For example, suppose that a reduction in the entrepreneur's equity share (denoted by ß in Table 11.A1) caused the entrepreneur to work less (even if this effect is infinitesimal), thereby reducing the expected salvage value of the firm. The fixed-fraction contract would not be robust with respect to optimal continuation: The inside VC_1 would have an incentive to overstate the value of the firm (i.e., overprice securities issued in the second round to minimize entrepreneurial moral hazard costs). A rational outside VC_2 anticipating this perverse incentive will not participate.[20] In the example in Table 11.A1, the value of the firm (equal to \$120 + 40ß) increases as the entrepreneur's equity share (ß) increases. Therefore, the inside VC_1's payoff increases as ß increases. The inside VC_1's payoff is maximized by maximizing the price of securities issued at the second stage (which is due to the fact that the example only involves entrepreneurial moral hazard and not a more complicated bilateral agency relationship in which the venture capital funds' effort also affects firm value). VC_2 will not participate because his/her payoff is less than 0 whenever $ß > 0.096$, and VC_1 has an incentive to misrepresent information to inflate the price of second-stage securities such that $ß \cong 0.5$.

After their derivation of the optimality of fixed-fraction contracts, Admati and Pfleiderer (1994: section V) introduce effort-related moral hazard in the context of an example in which it is always optimal to continue financing the project. Their example shows that an entrepreneur will have a greater incentive to put forth effort, as the entrepreneur's payoff (which depends on the prices of securities issued in the second stage) is greater when effort is expended. However, Admati and Pfleiderer (1994: 391) also assume that the inside VC_1 will not misrepresent information to outside investors because the inside VC_1 employs a fixed-fraction contract. This begs the question. By overpricing securities in the second stage, the value of the firm increases (as a result of the increase in the entrepreneur's effort), and therefore the value of the inside VC_1's fixed-fraction contract increases because the size of the pie to be divided between the parties increases. To use Admati and Pfleiderer's (1994: 374) phraseology, the inside VC_1's incentive to overprice new securities as an "old shareholder" (and thereby take away value from outside investors) is greater than his incentive as a "new shareholder" to underprice new securities (and thereby take value away from the entrepreneur). The only time that these incentives offset one another is when the value of the firm is independent of effort incentives, or when each party's effort and contribution to the value of the firm are perfect substitutes for one another.

In sum, in the general case where effort depends on residual claim and each party's effort has a unique effect on the value of the entrepreneurial firm, fixed-fraction contracts will not reduce informational asymmetries between the entrepreneur and outside investors. Where the entrepreneur's effort is more important than the outside VC_2's effort for the success of the venture, fixed-fraction contracts will exacerbate informational asymmetries because the

[20] VC_2 will participate only if VC_1 is able to convince VC_2 that the value of the securities is greater than their true value.

inside VC_1 has a financial stake in overpricing securities issued at the second stage. In view of this perverse incentive, fixed-fraction contracts do not ensure optimal continuation with outside VC_2 participation. Fixed-fraction contracts cannot achieve a first-best solution to mitigating informational asymmetry, and a superior contractual arrangement can be identified.

Case C The proposed contractual arrangement

Now consider the following contractual arrangement: VC_1 uses straight preferred equity; VC_2 uses convertible debt;[21] the entrepreneur holds common equity. As in Case B, suppose that the value of the firm is \$120 + 40ß (where ß is the entrepreneur's equity share) after second-round investment. The net payoffs to the three parties are provided in Table 11.A1. VC_1 will entice VC_2 to invest at the second round because \$120 − \$50 − \$100 = \$−30 (>\$−40, VC_1's net payoff if there is no second-round investment). VC_2 will invest whenever VC_1 encourages investment because VC_1's incentives are not distorted by the participation of VC_2. Investment in the second round is Kaldor-Hicks efficient (a \$100 investment leads to a gain of at least \$110). Second-round investment is also Pareto efficient with the proposed priority structure because no party was made worse off by investing in the second round given the initial investment. In fact, it is easy to verify that only efficient projects will be financed in the second round where the salvage value of the firm's assets is greater than or equal to \$110 when VC_1 holds straight preferred equity, VC_2 holds (convertible) debt, and the entrepreneur holds common equity.

Notice that when VC_1 (a straight preferred equity holder) and VC_2 (a convertible debt holder) are never among the same priority class, VC_1 has no incentive to misprice securities and misstate capital requirements; therefore, moral hazard costs are normalized to zero in Table 11.A1. VC_1 does not hold convertible preferred equity because perverse incentives will arise if VC_1 and VC_2 both convert to common equity and thereafter receive interdependent payoffs. Because VC_1 is never a residual claimant as a straight preferred equity holder, *there is no relation between the payoff to VC_1 and the entrepreneur's and VC_2's residual claim/effort* (see also Figure 11.A1).[22] Therefore, even if the entrepreneur's effort has a greater impact on the value of the firm than that of VC_2, VC_1 has no incentive to overstate the price of securities issued to VC_2 at second-round financing. Informational asymmetry between VC_2 and the entrepreneur is resolved by VC_1 where VC_1 is a preferred equity-holder for any possible differences in the specification of the relation between residual claim, effort, and firm value for VC_2 and the entrepreneur. In contrast, under a fixed-fraction contract, resolution of information asymmetry only occurs where

[21]The outside investor may simply hold straight debt for the purposes of this example. See also Propositions 1–3 (p. 356) and accompanying text.

[22]Bankruptcy states are an exception to this statement.

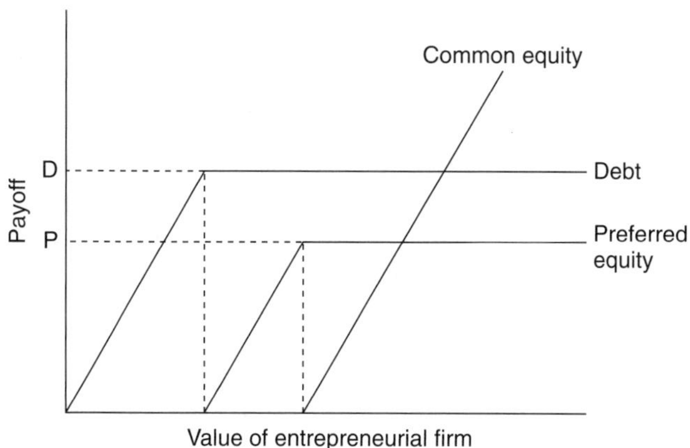

Figure 11.A1 Payoffs to Debt, Preferred Equity, and Common Equity

the efforts of VC_2 and the entrepreneur have the same relation to their equity share and the same effect on the value of the firm. In the typical case where the entrepreneur's effort is more directly related to his/her residual claim and has a greater effect on the value of the firm than that of VC_2, fixed-fraction contracts held by VC_1 do not resolve informational asymmetry and do not facilitate optimal continuation.

In bankruptcy states, there is a positive relation between entrepreneurial effort and the payoff to straight preferred equity holders. However, the inside VC_1 will never have an incentive to encourage outside VC_2 participation in anticipation of bankruptcy for two reasons. First, trilateral bargaining (Aghion and Bolton, 1992) is exacerbated when the outside VC_2 has priority and the entrepreneurial firm is anticipating bankruptcy. When an entrepreneurial firm is not earning its cost of capital, the entrepreneur has an incentive to contract with the third party to give up control over the firm to acquire additional financing at a lower cost. The inside VC_1 is worse off upon the arrival of a third-party investor who gains priority (Berglöf, 1994). The situation of the inside VC_1 is worsened when the third party acquires control over the firm and strips the assets of the firm (which are difficult to value in court; Berglöf, 1994). In contrast, the situation of the new third-party investor is improved because the investor acquires control over the firm. The situation of the entrepreneur is also improved even though the entrepreneur forgoes control over the firm because bankruptcy is avoided as a result of the lower cost financing provided by the third party. The inside VC_1 therefore does not have an incentive to search for and give up control to outside third-party investors when the entrepreneurial firm is doing poorly as the potential for trilateral bargaining is exacerbated.

In addition to trilateral bargaining problems, there is a second reason why the inside VC_1 will not be interested in encouraging outside VC_2 participation in anticipation of bankruptcy. The inside VC_1 will not have an incentive to induce outside second-round investment in anticipation of bankruptcy when the outside

VC_2 priority and VC_1 must contribute additional capital in the second round. This second reason is apparent from the part C of the syndication example.

The central ideas in the syndication example can be stated more formally. Let E_1^2 and E_2^2 represent the inside VC_1's and outside VC_2's investment in the second round, respectively (subscripts denote the agent; superscripts denote the time). For the purpose of this illustrative example, it is not important to specify the relative magnitudes of E_1^2 and E_2^2. Let X^1 and X^2 represent the salvage value of the entrepreneurial firm assets after the first- and second-round investment, respectively. Let the "proposed contract" refer to any arrangement in which the outside VC_2's security has priority over the inside VC_1's security.

Proposition 1: If $[X^2 - E_2^2 - E_1^2 < X^1]$, then the inside VC_1 will not invest E_1^2 under the proposed contract. If $[X^2 - E_2^2 - E_1^2 > X^1]$, then the inside VC_1 will invest E_1^2 under the proposed contract.

Proof: The payoff to inside VC_1 is $X^2 - E_2^2 - E_1^2$ if the inside VC_1 does invest. The payoff to the inside VC_1 is X^1 if the inside VC_1 does not invest. *Q.E.D.*

Proposition 2: Second-round investments will always be Kaldor-Hicks efficient under the proposed contract.

Proof: The Kaldor-Hicks efficiency condition is as follows: $X^2 - X^1 > E_1^2 + E_2^2$ (i.e., second-round investment adds value). This condition is satisfied only where the inside VC_1 wants to invest E_1^2: $X^2 - E_2^2 - E_1^2 > X^1$ (Proposition 1). *Q.E.D.*

Proposition 3: Second-round investments will always be Pareto efficient under the proposed contract.

Proof: The second-round investment will be made if and only if $X^2 - E_2^2 - E_1^2 > X^1$ (Proposition 1). This implies $X^2 - X^1 > E_2^2 + E_1^2$ (i.e., the increase in the salvage value of the assets more than offsets the extra amount invested in the second round); therefore, the outside VC_2 is as well off as before the investment was made (given she has first priority) and the inside VC_1 is at least as well off (given she has second priority). The entrepreneur's welfare is unchanged as a result of the second-round investment in bankruptcy states and improved in non-bankruptcy states. *Q.E.D.*

The intuition underlying Propositions 1, 2, and 3 is as follows. The inside VC_1 has no incentive to induce outside VC_2 participation when the entrepreneurial firm is facing bankruptcy and VC_2 has priority. The inside VC_1 with an informational advantage will only want to finance projects that are Kaldor-Hicks efficient when the inside VC_1 is of a lower priority class. Second-round Kaldor-Hicks inefficient investments result in a loss to the inside VC_1 when the outside VC_2 has priority in bankruptcy. Kaldor-Hicks efficient investments are also Pareto efficient as the priority rules ensure that any investment that benefits the inside VC_1 will also make the outside VC_2 better off. The entrepreneur is at least as well off because s/he does not contribute additional capital in the second round.

Corollary 1: In the presence of an information problem between VC_1 and VC_2, a priority allocation to VC_2 over VC_1 satisfies the revelation principle as mechanisms to induce VC_1 truthfully reveal information about the quality of the firm to VC_2.

Proof: This follows directly from Proposition 3 and indirectly from Propositions 1 and 2. *Q.E.D.*

The intuition underlying Corollary 1 is as follows. As mentioned, the outside VC_2 relies on information about the entrepreneurial firm provided by VC_1 in deciding whether to invest in the entrepreneurial firm as a syndicated partner with VC_1. VC_1 knows whether or not the entrepreneur is facing bankruptcy. The proposed contract specifies the payment to each party for each state of nature. If and only if priority is allocated to VC_2 over VC_1 will VC_1 truthfully reveal the quality of the entrepreneur to VC_2 for any given quality of the entrepreneur (bankruptcy or otherwise). Hence, the proposed contract satisfies the *revelation principle* (see, e.g., Mas-Colell et al., 1995, p. 493).

The framework requires VC_2 to have priority over VC_1, and alternative arrangements that satisfy this condition are suboptimal for the following reasons. Preferred is more appropriate than debt for VC_1 for start-ups that have uncertain cash flows to pay interest on debt. There are various reasons why VC_2 may use convertible debt, as opposed to straight debt or a senior preferred equity claim with or without a conversion option. Debt financing provides VC_2 with priority over VC_1 and payoffs independent of VC_1's payoffs. VC_2 may employ (convertible) debt and not a superior class of (convertible) preferred equity over VC_1 because debt reduces entrepreneurial slack (increases entrepreneurial effort) and increases the expected returns. Straight debt financing would leave the entrepreneur with incentives to risk shift thereby transferring expected wealth from the VCs to the entrepreneur; the entrepreneur maximizes his or her expected return and diminishes VC_2's expected return. Convertible debt mitigates risk shifting because the entrepreneur shares the upside potential gains from risk shifting. Notice that VC_2's convertibility option is desirable not only with risk shifting (Green, 1984) but also in light of an expansion stage firm's real growth options (Mayers, 1998). It is also noteworthy that the convertibility option mitigates entrepreneurial window-dressing in staged financing. That is, entrepreneurs have an incentive to make the firm look better than it really is at the time of performance review in staged financing. Convertibility options mitigate this problem through the threat that conversion will actually take place and diminish the entrepreneur's equity share (Cornelli and Yosha, 2003).

Key Terms

Fixed-fraction contract
Debt
Convertible debt
Preferred equity
Convertible preferred equity
Common equity
Warrants
Fixed claimant
Residual claimant
Capital structure

Security design
Staging
Syndication
Monitoring
Agency cost
Information asymmetry
Moral hazard
Bilateral moral hazard
Multitask moral hazard
Adverse selection
Free riding
Hold up
Trilateral bargaining
Window-dressing
Underinvestment
Asset stripping
Risk shifting

Discussion Questions

11.1. True/False/Uncertain and explain why: "Convertible preferred equity is the optimal form of venture capital finance."

11.2. Which of the following best explains security design in venture capital and private equity investments: (1) economic agency costs explanations, (2) tax explanations, (3) institutional, sophistication, and learning explanations, or (4) market conditions?

11.3. True/False/Uncertain and explain why: "Fixed-fraction contracts eliminate agency costs among syndicated venture capital investors."

11.4. What type of security would you normally associate with each of the following: (1) seed stage, (2) expansion stage, (3) turnaround stage, (4) buyout stage, and (5) high-tech companies? Explain which agency costs are more pronounced for these different stages and why the security you selected mitigates these agency costs.

11.5. Are government funds more likely to use convertible securities than limited partnerships? Why?

11.6. How is the capital gains tax rate related to the use of convertible preferred equity?

11.7. In what countries around the world is convertible preferred equity the most frequently used security among venture capitalists?

11.8. Do U.S. venture capitalists that finance Canadian entrepreneurial firms use convertible preferred equity more often than other securities? Why? Do U.S. venture capitalists that finance Canadian entrepreneurial firms use convertible preferred equity more often than U.S. venture capitalists that finance U.S. entrepreneurial firms? Why?

11.9. Explain whether convertible preferred equity mitigates or exacerbates each of the following agency problems: moral hazard, bilateral moral hazard, multitask moral hazard, adverse selection, free riding, hold-up, trilateral bargaining, window-dressing, underinvestment, asset stripping, and risk shifting.

12 Security Design and Adverse Selection

12.1 Introduction and Learning Objectives

This chapter considers the screening of venture capital investments. In particular, it investigates the issue of whether the use of different financial instruments (including debt, common equity, preferred equity, and convertible securities) "attract" different types of entrepreneurial firms, in terms of the adverse selection risks associated with financing low-quality firms in relation to the financial security used. A central contribution of this chapter is in the assessment of whether syndication mitigates such adverse selection risks.

As we examined in Chapter 11, firm-specific characteristics affect the choice of financial security (see also, e.g., Jensen and Meckling, 1976; Noe and Rebello, 1996; Rajan and Zingales, 1995). At the same time, however, offers of different forms of finance may attract different types of entrepreneurial firms. Seminal research on selection effects and capital structure focused on debt and common equity (DeMeza and Webb, 1987, 1992; Stiglitz and Weiss, 1981). Consistent with the seminal work of Akerlof (1970; as well as the related work of Stiglitz and Spence for the joint 2001 Nobel Memorial Prize in economic sciences), the theoretical literature shows that the offer of equity attracts firms with low expected returns (consistent with the language adopted in the literature, we hereafter refer to firms with low expected mean returns as "lemons"), whereas the offer of debt finance attracts firms with high variability in returns (hereafter referred to as "nuts"). Related research on adverse selection and capital structure has considered convertible securities; for example, Brennan and Kraus (1987) show that firms with low variability in expected returns are attracted to convertible securities. The intuition linking these different securities to different types of adverse selection risks is explained in this chapter.

The venture capital market offers an interesting forum for empirically examining the relation between adverse selection and forms of finance. Risk management is particularly important for venture capital funds. Venture capital fund managers have enhanced screening and monitoring abilities and are active value-added investors.[1] Because they finance early-stage firms for which there

[1]See, e.g., Berger and Udell (1998), Bergmann and Hege (1998), Casamatta (2003), Casamatta and Haritchabalet (2007), De Clercq and Sapienza (2001), Gompers and Lerner (1999), Kanniainen and Keuschnigg (2003, 2004), Keuschnigg (2003), Manigart et al. (2000, 2002a,b), Sapienza (1992), Trester (1998), Wright and Lockett (2003), Mayer et al. (2005).

is a comparative dearth of information, venture capital fund managers take significant steps to try to avoid financing low-quality firms. Research in venture capital is consistent with the proposition that venture capital fund managers are among the most sophisticated financial intermediaries with abilities to mitigate agency problems.[2] Therefore, in considering the venture capital market, we study not only pronounced problems of adverse selection but also specialized investors that take active steps to mitigate such problems.

In this chapter we will do the following:

- Consider which types of venture capital funds (corporate, limited partnership, etc.) are more likely to finance different types of entrepreneurial firms (start-up, expansion, high-tech, etc.)
- Consider which types of venture capital funds are more likely to syndicate their investments
- Assess the extent to which adverse selection is more problematic for different types of entrepreneurial firms and different forms of finance (debt, convertible debt, preferred equity, convertible preferred equity, common equity)
- Consider the extent to which syndication mitigates problems of adverse selection
- Draw lessons as to where venture capital fund managers can focus their due diligence efforts for different types of entrepreneurial firms

We will first develop hypotheses pertaining to adverse selection in entrepreneurial finance and then describe the Canadian Venture Capital Association data.

12.2 Adverse Selection, Capital Structure, Firm Characteristics, and Syndication

In this section we build on our discussion from Chapter 2 by developing hypotheses relating problems of adverse selection among alternative forms of finance to entrepreneurial firms at different stages of development and in different industries. We also consider the effect of syndication on adverse selection. Our theoretical discussion in this section and empirical tests in the subsequent sections are focused on first-round venture capital investments only and not follow-on staged financing rounds.

12.2.1 Theoretical Principles on Adverse Selection and Capital Structure

To understand the link between adverse selection and capital structure, it is helpful to review the properties of the different types of securities. Common equity is analogous to a call option. Common equity holders have a claim to all of a firm's cash flows but only after all other claimants have been satisfied. If the firm goes bankrupt, then equity holders are the last to be paid (debt holders have priority over preferred equity holders, who in turn have priority over

[2]See, e.g., references listed supra, note 1.

common equity holders); however, common equity holders cannot lose more than their investment in the firm by virtue of the firm's limited liability. Common equity is therefore analogous to a call option on the firm, whereby exercising the option requires that the firm be liquidated and the face value of the debt (the option price) paid off. The payoff function to common equity is bounded below by the cost of the common equity investment and unlimited potential on the upside. The payoff to straight (nonconvertible) debt, by contrast, is limited to the present discounted value of all interest payments and the principal on debt (similarly, the payoff to nonconvertible preferred equity is limited to the present discounted value of all prespecified preferred dividends). In the event of an entrepreneurial firm's failure to pay interest on debt, an investor can force a firm into bankruptcy. In the event of an entrepreneurial firm's failure to pay a prespecified preferred dividend, an investor cannot force a firm into bankruptcy, but all preferred dividends must be paid before any common dividends can be paid.

The well-known "lemons principle" (Akerlof, 1970) in the context of capital structure theory is based on the idea that the form of finance offered by an investor attracts the worst possible type of firm for that form of finance. Theoretical research has well established the propositions that common equity attracts firms with low expected returns (i.e., lemons; *adverse selection costs of common equity*; DeMeza and Webb, 1987, 1992); straight debt and straight preferred equity attract firms with high variability in returns (i.e., nuts; *adverse selection costs of straight debt and straight preferred equity*; Stiglitz and Weiss, 1981); and convertible securities attract firms with low variability of returns (*adverse selection costs of convertible securities*; Brennan and Kraus, 1987). Investors anticipate these problems and structure contracts accordingly (see, e.g., Brennan and Kraus, 1987). We review the intuition underlying these results in this subsection.

The intuition underlying the theoretical work of DeMeza and Webb (1987, 1992) linking common equity and lemons is as follows (see also Chapter 2, section 2.3.4, and Figure 2.5). A venture capital fund that finances an entrepreneurial firm with common equity receives significant upside potential in terms of obtaining an ownership interest in the entrepreneurial firm but does not obtain downside protection in terms of priority in bankruptcy. Entrepreneurial firms with lower expected mean returns have lower opportunity costs associated with giving up larger ownership interests to venture capital funds via common equity contracts, relative to entrepreneurial firms with high expected returns. Entrepreneurial firms with lower expected returns also have higher opportunity costs associated with giving up downside protection (in bankruptcy) to their venture capital fund investors. As such, venture capital funds that offer common equity contracts to their entrepreneurial investee firms face a more pronounced adverse selection problem in terms of attracting entrepreneurial firms with lower expected average returns.

The intuition underlying the theoretical work of Stiglitz and Weiss (1981) linking nonconvertible debt (and similarly nonconvertible preferred equity) and nuts is as follows (see also Chapter 2, section 2.3.4, and Figure 2.4). A venture capital fund that uses debt to finance an entrepreneurial firm does not receive any ownership interest and therefore does not derive the benefit of capturing the upside potential associated with an improvement in the quality of the firm (that is, above and beyond an increase in the probability in being paid back the interest and principal on the debt contract). Entrepreneurial firms with high expected variability (standard deviation) of returns have higher opportunity costs associated with giving up larger ownership interests to venture capital funds via equity contracts. If a risky venture happens to be successful, then the entrepreneur financed with debt captures 100% of the upside potential success. In the literature this is sometimes referred to a situation in which the entrepreneur thinks "Heads, I win" in that the firm happens to do well, and the entrepreneur captured all of the benefits associated with winning the lottery. By contrast, if a risky venture happens to fail, then the entrepreneur financed with debt has not lost to the same degree as the investor that has not been repaid. In the literature this is sometimes referred to a situation in which the entrepreneur thinks "Tails, you lose" in that the firm happens to fail, but the loss in capital provided to finance the firm is more heavily borne by the investor that provided such capital. In short, venture capital funds that offer debt contracts to their entrepreneurial investee firms face a more pronounced adverse selection problem in terms of attracting entrepreneurial firms with higher expected variability in returns.

12.2.2 Adverse Selection Risks in Venture Capital Finance

Adverse selection risks exist because of the information asymmetry in that entrepreneurs have information that venture capital funds do not have. To understand the extent to which entrepreneurs may have information that venture capital funds do not, it is necessary to identify and distinguish the entrepreneurial firm characteristics that are in fact known to venture capital funds, such as the stage of development of the entrepreneur and the industry in which the entrepreneur operates. But not all entrepreneurial characteristics can be completely known by the venture capital fund managers (such as the entrepreneur's intelligence, managerial abilities, planned work effort, scientific skills for developing patents, and technical processes for the firm, etc.). Hence, adverse selection risks will exist and will exist to different degrees, depending on the entrepreneurial firm characteristics that the venture capital fund managers can identify.

Based on prior research, we may conjecture that for entrepreneurial start-up stage firms (start-ups) without a track record (or a significant track record) and for firms in high-tech industries, venture capital fund managers are better able to screen the risks associated with financing a lemon relative to the risks associated with financing a nut. In other words, a "bad" firm is easier for a venture capital fund manager to screen than a "risky" one. The intuition is clear for four interrelated reasons. First, theoretical work (e.g., Hopenhayn and Vereshchagina, 2004; Landier and Thesmar, 2003) and empirical evidence (e.g., Moskowitz and Vissing-Jorgensen, 2002) consistently shows that entrepreneurs bear substantial risk but do not earn a return that compensates for such risks. Most all work in entrepreneurial finance is consistent with the view that entrepreneurs have significant risk tolerance and overoptimism. This means that entrepreneurs downplay the risk of variance of potential outcomes associated with their start-up firms. Second, entrepreneurs are not inclined to start a firm that they believe is a lemon due a stigma of failure and the opportunity costs of not working elsewhere. Third, venture capital fund managers can screen lemons through due diligence reviews based on the entrepreneur's track record (curriculum vitae) in terms of leisure preference,[3] as well as managerial and technical competence that had been established prior to starting the particular firm seeking venture capital finance.[4] Fourth, while a venture capital fund manager can use past performance to mitigate the risk of financing a lemon, it would be much more difficult for a venture capital fund manager to ascertain whether an entrepreneur's latest idea is best characterized as nuts based on the entrepreneur's past performance (i.e., it is easier to forecast the mean of the expected value than the variance of expected value). Taken together, these four reasons suggest the following conjecture, which is tested in the subsequent sections of this chapter.

Hypothesis 12.1: *The adverse selection risks associated with capital structure for financing risky nuts are more pronounced and difficult to mitigate through screening, relative to the adverse selection risks of financing low-quality lemons, for first-round venture capital financings of start-ups and high-tech entrepreneurial firms.*

We further hypothesize that syndication reduces informational asymmetries and adverse selection costs through information sharing and improved screening. The intuition is based on the idea that due diligence is enhanced by bringing together complementary skills and stage and/or industry expertise from venture capital fund managers employed in different venture capital funds. The prediction that syndication mitigates adverse selection risks is consistent with analyses of syndication in different contexts (in the context of venture capital finance, see Dimov and De Clercq, 2004; Jääskeläinen et al., 2006; Lerner, 1994; Lockett and Wright, 1999, 2001; Manigart et al., 2002a; Wright and Lockett, 2003; for earlier work in a general context of syndication, see Leland and Pyle, 1977). We complement and build on this prior work by analyzing for the first time the effect of syndication on problems of adverse selection associated with different securities used in venture capital finance. Based on this literature that syndication facilitates due diligence and screening, we conjecture Hypothesis 12.2.

Hypothesis 12.2: *Venture capital fund syndication in the first round of investment mitigates the adverse selection risks associated with capital structure decisions for financing start-ups and high-tech firms.*

Further to Hypothesis 12.2, note that in Canada there are a variety of different types of venture capital fund investors, including private independent limited

[3]For example, at an MBA lecture at the University of Alberta in 2003 a practicing venture capital fund manager described the due diligence process as including, but not limited to, meetings and barbeques with the entrepreneurs' family and spouse.

[4]Technical competence can be assessed from academic transcripts and peer reviews from practitioners, for example.

partnerships, corporate venture capital funds, government venture capital fund funds, labor sponsored venture capital corporations (LSVCCs), institutional investors, and as foreign (U.S.) venture capital funds. In the empirical analyses in the next sections we consider differences in the quality of the syndication among these different fund types. We expect that foreign venture capital funds face greater hurdles in screening investments due to the geographic distance. LSVCCs may also face greater difficulties in screening investments as a fund with statutory constraints that impose a time limit (from one to two years, depending on the jurisdiction in which they are incorporated) for reinvestment of capital that has been contributed by investors (see, e.g., Cumming and MacIntosh, 2006, 2007; Halpern, 1997; and Osborne and Sandler, 1998, for the statutory details).

The data used to test these hypotheses and empirical tests of the hypotheses developed herein follow. We control for the different types of venture capital funds and use artificial regressions to explore problems of adverse selection for the complete class of forms of finance among different types of entrepreneurial firms. Limitations, alternative explanations, and future research are also discussed following.

12.3 Data

To investigate problems of adverse selection in capital structure decisions, it is both necessary and interesting to consider a country in which venture capital funds finance a wide variety of different types of entrepreneurial firms and to use a heterogeneous mix of forms of finance. Research on the U.S. venture capital industry is consistent with the proposition that venture capital funds rarely use forms of finance other than convertible preferred equity (Gompers, 1998; Kaplan and Strömberg, 2003; Sahlman, 1990); therefore, the U.S. venture capital market does not offer a useful forum to address problems of adverse selection in capital structure. Nevertheless, there are reasons why venture capital funds use forms of finance other than convertible preferred equity, and data indicate a variety of forms of finance are employed by venture capital funds in all countries around the world other than the United States (see, e.g., Cumming, 2005a,b; Hege et al., 2004; Lerner and Schoar, 2004).

The data used in this chapter come from 4,114 first-round Canadian venture capital financing transactions from 1991 (Q1) to 2003 (Q3). Venture capital fund investors in Canada finance a wide variety of entrepreneurial firms and use a wide variety of financial instruments (see Table 12.1, Panels A to G). The tables show that the use of a variety of forms of finance by venture capital funds in Canada is not due to the definition of *venture capital* in Canada (e.g., early stage only, or early and expansion stage).[5] Given the heterogeneity

[5]Following the CVCA definitions, a start-up stage firm is based on a concept without a product or any marketing, or it may have a product being developed, but not yet sold commercially. An expansion stage firm requires significant capital for plant expansion and marketing to initiate full commercial production and sales.

Table 12.1 Summary of Canadian VC Investment Data by Type of Security, Type of VC Fund, and Type of Entrepreneurial Firm

This table presents the number of first-round investments by type of VC fund, type of entrepreneurial firm, and type of security. Different securities over different years and by (non-) syndication are presented. The proportions of start-up and expansion sum to 1.0. The proportion of non-high-tech is equal to 1 minus the proportion of high-tech. The proportion of nonsyndication is equal to 1 minus the proportion of syndication. The average amounts invested are in real 2000 Canadian dollars. The different types of VC funds are indicated in each Panel (A–G) separately.

Panel A. Private Independent Limited Partnership Venture Capital Funds

Type of Security	Total Number of 1st-round Investments	Proportion of Start-up	Proportion of Expansion	Proportion of High-tech	Average Amount Invested ('000)	Proportion of Syndication	Proportion in Years 1991–1998	Proportion in 1999–2000	Proportion in 2001–2003
Preferred Equity	91	0.769	0.231	0.857	1437.808	0.648	0.341	0.319	0.341
Common Equity and/ or Warrants	367	0.796	0.204	0.766	870.575	0.477	0.529	0.302	0.169
Convertible Preferred Equity	109	0.826	0.174	0.826	888.457	0.578	0.404	0.330	0.266
Debt	91	0.703	0.297	0.659	647.483	0.308	0.692	0.176	0.132
Convertible Debt	164	0.732	0.268	0.774	753.058	0.390	0.537	0.268	0.195
Debt and Common Equity	31	0.419	0.581	0.452	638.415	0.516	0.871	0.032	0.097
Preferred and Common Equity	18	0.722	0.278	0.667	591.940	0.500	0.667	0.056	0.278
Mixes of Other Securities	124	0.798	0.202	0.855	757.091	0.605	0.339	0.387	0.274

(continued)

Table 12.1 *(continued)*

Panel B. Corporate Venture Capital Funds									
Type of Security	Total Number of 1st-round Investments	Proportion of Start-up	Proportion of Expansion	Proportion of High-tech	Average Amount Invested ('000)	Proportion of Syndication	Proportion in Years 1991–1998	Proportion in 1999–2000	Proportion in 2001–2003
Preferred Equity	27	0.593	0.407	0.704	1638.536	0.778	0.333	0.296	0.370
Common Equity and/ or Warrants	82	0.622	0.378	0.671	1411.269	0.646	0.390	0.280	0.329
Convertible Preferred Equity	47	0.553	0.447	0.809	1715.965	0.766	0.234	0.447	0.319
Debt	80	0.313	0.688	0.438	1194.438	0.450	0.325	0.538	0.138
Convertible Debt	43	0.628	0.372	0.651	976.280	0.698	0.302	0.372	0.326
Debt and Common Equity	26	0.346	0.654	0.346	1081.462	0.577	0.577	0.269	0.154
Preferred and Common Equity	4	0.250	0.750	0.750	739.335	0.750	0.500	0.500	0.000
Mixes of Other Securities	77	0.662	0.338	0.584	793.493	0.623	0.065	0.234	0.701

Panel C. Government Venture Capital Funds

Preferred Equity	44	0.773	0.227	0.909	780.352	0.795	0.318	0.227	0.455
Common Equity and/or Warrants	284	0.824	0.176	0.574	575.024	0.342	0.718	0.120	0.162
Convertible Preferred Equity	49	0.796	0.204	0.837	998.616	0.816	0.265	0.163	0.571
Debt	65	0.692	0.308	0.523	537.813	0.492	0.477	0.169	0.354
Convertible Debt	96	0.771	0.229	0.615	505.848	0.615	0.448	0.177	0.375
Debt and Common Equity	28	0.643	0.357	0.607	606.096	0.536	0.536	0.107	0.357
Preferred and Common Equity	8	0.750	0.250	0.625	770.450	0.875	0.750	0.000	0.250
Mixes of Other Securities	86	0.849	0.151	0.651	579.790	0.547	0.384	0.151	0.465

in the types of firms and the use of different forms of finance, the Canadian venture capital market offers an excellent forum in which to study risks of adverse selection in capital structure. In fact, Canada is the only country in the world with industry-wide venture capital finance data to empirically study adverse selection and capital structure. For the purpose of analyzing adverse selection in venture capital finance, we control for changes in market conditions over the period considered. Our focus is on first-round investments in the start-ups and expansion stage firms only to focus on the screening of new pure venture capital fund investments (and not later-stage private equity investments). The data are summarized in Table 12.1.

There are seven types of venture capital fund investors in Canada (Chapter 11, see also Cumming, 2005b; Cumming and MacIntosh, 2003): private independent funds, corporate, government, institutional, labor-sponsored venture capital corporations (LSVCCs), foreign (United States), and other. Private independent funds (Table 12.1, Panel A) are similar to U.S. venture capital limited partnerships, but Canadian private independent venture capital funds generally have fewer and less restrictive covenants placed on the venture capital fund managers (Cumming and MacIntosh, 2003). Canadian corporate venture capital funds (Table 12.1, Panel B) are analogous to U.S. corporate venture capital funds (Gompers and Lerner, 1999) but tend to finance a somewhat more heterogeneous group of entrepreneurial firms (Table 12.2). Government venture capital funds in Canada (Table 12.1, Panel C) are managed by independent professional venture capital fund managers and finance a wide variety of different entrepreneurial firms. Institutional investors (Table 12.1, Panel D) are larger institutions that make direct venture capital fund investments. LSVCCs (Table 12.1, Panel E) are significantly different from the other Canadian venture capital funds. These differences arise through statutory restrictive covenants placed upon LSVCC managers (Cumming and MacIntosh, 2003; Osborne and Sandler, 1998). The tests that follow control for the fact that the constraints in which LSVCCs operate may influence not only their choice of types of firms in which they invest but also the types of securities they employ irrespective of the characteristics of their investee firms. Foreign investors (Table 12.1, Panel F) are U.S. limited partnership venture capital funds that invest in Canadian entrepreneurial firms. The category of "other" (including "unknown") investors (Table 12.1, Panel G) encompasses all other types of venture capital funds that less regularly appear in the CVCA data.

Table 12.1, Panels A to G, clearly shows that convertible preferred equity has not been the most commonly used form of finance by Canadian venture capital funds. This result is not due to the type of venture capital fund or the type of firms being financed, as documented in Table 12.1, Panels A to G. It is also not due to the definition of *venture capital fund*, as the results in Canada hold for the funds most similar to U.S. limited partnerships (the transactions for Canadian private independent venture capital funds are presented in Table 12.1, Panel A). The 4,114 transactions in Table 12.1, Panels A to G, will be used in the following section to test the hypotheses developed earlier in this chapter. Because the evidence in Table 12.1, Panels A to G, drastically differs from U.S. evidence on venture capital finance on the use of convertible securities (e.g., Gompers, 1998; Kaplan and Strömberg, 2003; Sahlman, 1990), we exhaustively present the data by type of venture capital fund and entrepreneurial firm. The differences between the Canadian and U.S. evidence are consistent with a tax bias in favor of convertibles in the United States (Gilson and Schizer, 2003), and this tax bias is absent in Canada (Sandler, 2001; see also Cumming, 2005b, for further details on tax aspects and security choice in Canada and the United States).

The CVCA data consider *syndication* as more than one venture capital fund managed by different venture capital fund managers and may simultaneously fund the entrepreneurial firm in the first round of the investment. Consistent with Gompers and Lerner (1999), we do not consider "co-investment" (different venture capital funds that are managed by the same venture capital fund manager) to be a syndicated investment.

The empirical analysis in this chapter considers the standard financial instruments: debt, convertible debt, preferred equity, convertible preferred equity, common equity, and combinations of debt and common equity. A broader contract space does exist in practice. For example, convertible debt is a hybrid bond that allows its bearer to exchange it for a given number of shares of common equity any time up to and including the maturity date of the bond. A broader contract space, however, is not considered herein for a number of reasons. Papers that do consider a broader contract space (e.g., Aghion and Bolton, 1992) yield optimal contracts that resemble the standard financial instruments. The fact that the standard instruments in corporate finance are used most frequently suggests that considerable gains arise from standardization, and greater transaction costs arise from designing contracts to mimic the standard forms of finance (Berglöf, 1994; Macdonald, 1992). Regardless, the data used to test the hypotheses developed herein have been recorded such that if a contract was designed to mimic one of the standard forms of finance, then the standard form was recorded.[6]

The econometric analyses in the next section consider the entire sample of 4,114 first-round investments without segmenting the sample by type of venture capital fund. Different venture capital funds syndicate more than 50% of their investments (see Table 12.1, Panels A to G, and Table 12.2). Separating the data by sectors would fail to account for venture capital fund syndicates across different venture capital fund types (Table 12.2) and therefore would significantly bias the results. Table 12.2 in fact shows a massive degree of integration across different types of venture capital funds in Canada insofar as different types of venture capital funds syndicate with one another. The use of the full dataset enables the richest array of results by accounting for interactions

[6]The inclusion/exclusion of less commonly used forms of finance was immaterial to the analyses and results.

Table 12.2 Syndication and Integration among

This table presents the total number of first-round fund investments (Column 1), the total number investments (Column 3, which is Column 2 divided by Column 1). In addition, to illustrate the extent companies for all investment rounds the following information: the total number of different companies companies in which the fund type has been involved as a syndicated investor (Column 5), the proportion which is Column 5 divided by Column 4), and the number of companies in which the fund type has totals indicates the column does not add up to the total because multiple syndications (i.e., syndications

	(1) Total Number of First-round Fund Investments	(2) Number of First-round Syndicated Fund Investments	(3) Proportion of First-round Syndicated Fund Investments	(4) Total Number of Different Companies in Which Fund Type Has Been Invested (All Rounds)	(5) Total Number of Different Companies in Which Fund Type Has Been Invested as a Syndicated Investor (All Rounds)	(6) Proportion of Different Companies in Which the Fund Type Has Invested as a Syndicated Investor (All Rounds)
Private Independent (Limited Partnership) VCs	995	489	0.491	1322	736	0.557
Corporate VCs	386	242	0.627	692	433	0.626
Government VCs	660	332	0.503	913	563	0.617
Institutional VCs	468	188	0.402	668	365	0.546
LSVCCs	959	410	0.428	1516	710	0.468
Foreign VCs	182	155	0.852	279	257	0.921
Other Types of VCs	464	405	0.873	840	770	0.917
Totals	4114	2221	0.540	3696*	1440*	0.390

among different venture capital funds in Canada, while recognizing that the Canadian venture capital market is not segmented by sectors.

12.4 Empirical Evidence

In this section, we describe econometrics methods for the determinants of forms of finance used in prior work. Then we consider the first step of a Durbin-Wu-Hausman test for the purpose of setting up the test of adverse selection, which appears in this section.

Different Types of VC Funds in Canada

of syndicated first-round fund investments (Column 2), and the proportion of first-round syndicated
of integration among different fund types in Canada, this table presents by the number of investee
in which the fund type has been involved as a syndicated investor (Column 4), the number of different
of different companies in which the fund type has been involved as a syndicated investor (Column 6,
syndicated with different types of other VCs (Columns 7–13). Notice that the * next to some of the
with more than 2 investors) across different fund types gives rise to double-counting of companies.

(7) Different Companies Syndicated with Private Limited Partnership VCs (All Rounds)	(8) Different Companies Syndicated with Corporate VCs	(9) Different Companies Syndicated with Government VCs	(10) Different Companies Syndicated with Institutional VCs	(11) Different Companies Syndicated with LSVCCs	(12) Different Companies Syndicated with Foreign VCs	(13) Different Companies Syndicated with Other Types of VCs
39						
197	25					
263	151	12				
165	121	163	16			
328	175	247	158	34		
178	109	100	68	116	7	
392	214	321	155	379	134	8
736*	433*	563*	365*	710*	257*	770*

12.4.1 *The Determinants of Forms of Venture Capital Finance*

In the Canadian context (with the absence of the U.S. tax bias; Sandler, 2001; Gilson and Schizer, 2003), Cumming (2005b) considered the determinants of the selected form of finance by estimating multinomial logit regressions of the following form (see Chapter 11):

$$\begin{aligned}\text{Probability (Security selected)} = {} & \alpha + \beta_1 \text{ Start-up} + \beta_2 \text{ High-tech} + \beta_3 \text{ Deal Size} \\ & + \beta_4 \text{ LSVCC} + \beta_5 \text{ Capital Gains Tax} \\ & + \beta_6 \text{ TSX} + \beta_7 \text{ Trend} + \varepsilon \end{aligned} \quad (12.1)$$

The right-hand-side variables in equation 12.1 include a dummy variable for start-ups (a dummy for expansion-stage firms is suppressed for reasons of perfect collinearity; other later-stage firms are excluded from the data herein), a dummy for high-tech firms, the capital required by the entrepreneurial firm (in real 2000 Canadian dollars, and in logs), a dummy variable for LSVCCs, a variable for the capital gains tax changes,[7] a dummy variable for the TSX index,[8] and a trend term to account for changes over time. These variables are also used herein in the subsequent sections, particularly in regards to assessing the potential effect of potential endogeneity of the first three variables in equation 12.1.

In the following subsections we consider in more detail the nature of this adverse selection problem associated with different forms of finance and the presence of certain types of entrepreneurial firms in the market for VC finance. Adverse selection would exist in respect of Hypothesis 12.1 where the variables Start-up and High-tech are endogenous in equation 12.1. To consider this possibility, we proceed in two steps. In the first step, we consider instrumental variables that impact the types of firms that may exist in the market for venture capital. In the second step, we use the residuals from the first-step regressions to test the effect of endogeneity on the estimated coefficients in equation 12.1. This artificial regression in the second step, a version of the Durbin-Wu-Hausman (DWH) test,[9] is not a direct test for exogeneity, but it does indicate the effect of endogeneity on the coefficient estimates in equation 12.1 and therefore provides insight into the nature of adverse selection associated with different forms of finance and different types of entrepreneurial firms.

12.4.2 Do Different Types of Investors Select Different Types of Entrepreneurial Firms?

Venture capital funds typically receive around 1,000 requests for financing each year (Sahlman, 1990). This may create noise in the matching of

[7]In 1990 the effective capital gains rate in Canada was 36%. Because marginal income tax rates rose through the 1990s, the effective capital gains rate rose as high as 39.8% (in 1995) before falling back to 36.6% in 1999. In March of 2000, the effective capital gains rate was reduced to 23.2%. The different capital gains tax rates can influence security choice in Canada as they directly affect the attractiveness of equity (capital gains) to investors. See Cumming (2005b).

[8]Different market conditions can influence security design, as investors and entrepreneurs change with changing market conditions. See Cumming (2005b).

[9]Davidson and MacKinnon (1993) discuss DWH tests for continuous variables. These specification tests have also been referred to as simply "Hausman specification tests" in various texts. Angrist (2001), Rivers and Vuong (1988), Wooldridge (2000, 2002), and others consider various ways to deal with endogeneity in limited dependent variable models. The problem of causal inference is not fundamentally different (see, e.g., Angrist, 2001, section 12.4), but limited dependent variables do present additional challenges in certain contexts, particularly for censored regression models. The DWH artificial regressions with (potentially endogenous) standard binary dummy variables in the context of this chapter are quite robust to alternative methods and specifications. The tests are also quite robust to various possible adjustments for multiple potential endogenous variables as described in, for example, Maddala (2001, chapter 12).

entrepreneurial firms to venture capital funds. But venture capital funds tend to have a preference for financing certain types of entrepreneurial firms according to their stage of development, required capital, and/or type of technology, among other things (Gompers and Lerner, 1999; Mayer et al., 2005).[10] Herein, we relate the presence of different types of firms in the venture capital market to geographic location of entrepreneurial firms[11] and to the type of venture capital fund. We estimate the binary logit regression equations 12.2 and 12.3 and OLS regression equation 12.4 of the following form:

$$\begin{aligned}\text{Probability (Start-up)} = {} & [\text{Year Fixed Effects}] + ß1\ \text{Corporate} + ß2\ \text{Government} \\ & + ß3\ \text{Institutional} + ß4\ \text{LSVCC} + ß5\ \text{LSVCC} \\ & + ß6\ \text{Foreign Investor} + ß7\ \text{Other Type of VC} \\ & + ß8\ \text{British Columbia} + ß8\ \text{Alberta} + ß9\ \text{Saskatchewan} \\ & + ß10\ \text{Manitoba} + ß11\ \text{Ontario} + ß12\ \text{Quebec} \\ & + \varepsilon_{\text{Start-up}} \end{aligned} \tag{12.2}$$

$$\begin{aligned}\text{Probability (High-tech)} = {} & [\text{Year Fixed Effects}] + ß1\ \text{Corporate} + ß2\ \text{Government} \\ & + ß3\ \text{Institutional} + ß4\ \text{LSVCC} + ß5\ \text{LSVCC} \\ & + ß6\ \text{Foreign Investor} + ß7\ \text{Other Type of VC} \\ & + ß8\ \text{British Columbia} + ß8\ \text{Alberta} + ß9\ \text{Saskatchewan} \\ & + ß10\ \text{Manitoba} + ß11\ \text{Ontario} + ß12\ \text{Quebec} \\ & + \varepsilon_{\text{High-tech}} \end{aligned} \tag{12.3}$$

$$\begin{aligned}\text{Probability (Syndication)} = {} & [\text{Year Fixed Effects}] + ß1\ \text{Start-up} + ß2\ \text{High-tech} \\ & + ß3\ \text{Log (Deal Size)} + ß4\ \text{Corporate} + ß5\ \text{Government} \\ & + ß6\ \text{Institutional} + ß7\ \text{LSVCC} + ß8\ \text{LSVCC} \\ & + ß9\ \text{Foreign Investor} + ß10\ \text{Other Type of VC} \\ & + ß11\ \text{British Columbia} + ß12\ \text{Alberta} \\ & + ß13\ \text{Saskatchewan} + ß14\ \text{Manitoba} \\ & + ß15\ \text{Ontario} + ß16\ \text{Quebec} + \varepsilon_{\text{Syndication}} \end{aligned} \tag{12.4}$$

In equations 12.2–12.4, a dummy variable for private independent limited partnerships is suppressed to avoid perfect collinearity problems; as such, the other coefficients are relative to the private independent funds. A dummy

[10]See also mission statements from venture capital firms; links are available from www.vfinance.com and www.cvca.ca.

[11]The location variables are included to account for the fact that different types of entrepreneurial firms may be more prevalent in different provinces in Canada, due to regional economic differences.

variable for the Maritime Provinces is suppressed to avoid perfect collinearity as well. Year fixed effects are used to account for the possibility of different types of firms (by stage of development, industry type, and capital requirements) present in the market for venture capital in different years due to market conditions. $\varepsilon_{\text{Start-up}}$, $\varepsilon_{\text{High-tech}}$, and $\varepsilon_{\text{Syndication}}$ are vectors of residuals for equations 12.2 to 12.4, respectively, and are used in the endogeneity tests that follow. Diagnostic tests suggested in the main that the right-hand-side variables for equations 12.2–12.4 were orthogonal to the different forms of finance (see Table 12.3) and are therefore suitable instruments for the DWH tests of endogeneity described following.[12] The main results are not sensitive to the choice of instruments (alternative regressions are on file with the author, as well as an earlier version of the chapter yielding similar results).

The estimates for equations 12.2–12.4 are presented in Table 12.4. As well, analogous to regression 3, Table 12.4 also presents regressions 4, 5, and 6 for syndications with LSVCCs only (regression 4), foreign venture capital funds only (regression 5), and syndications for all other types of investors excluding foreign venture capital funds and LSVCCs (regression 6).

There are two main results in Table 12.4. First, investments in certain types of entrepreneurial firms are related to overall investment activity in different geographic regions in Canada. In particular, venture capital–backed start-ups are less prevalent in Alberta and Saskatchewan, and high-tech venture capital–backed firms are more prevalent in British Columbia, and less prevalent in Alberta, Saskatchewan, Manitoba, and Quebec. Second, there is support for the proposition that different types of venture capital funds more often finance different types of entrepreneurial firms in Canada, as well as differences in the propensity to syndicate investments. We now elaborate on this second result, as it is more generalizable to contexts in other countries where comparative work could be considered.

Table 12.4 indicates that corporate venture capital funds are 29.8% less likely to invest in start-ups and 30.0% less likely to invest in high-tech firms relative to private limited partnerships. Institutional investors are 34.3% less likely to invest in start-ups and 32.8% less likely to invest in high-tech firms relative to limited partnerships. LSVCCs are 19.2% less likely to invest in start-ups and 34.6% less likely to invest in high-tech firms relative to limited partnerships. By contrast, government venture capital funds are 5.7% more likely to invest in start-ups and 77% less likely to invest in high-tech firms relative to limited partnerships. Foreign venture capital funds are 20.3% less

[12]Different types of venture capital funds in Canada are not restricted from using different forms of finance. Different types of funds may prefer to finance certain types of entrepreneurial firms, and different forms of finance may be more appropriate for different types of entrepreneurial firms, but there is generally no direct incentive for different types of funds to use different forms of finance. A possible exception is the case of LSVCCs (see Chapter 11); therefore, we include the LSVCC variable in the endogeneity tests.

Table 12.3 Correlations between Securities and Type of VC Fund and Location

This table presents correlation coefficients across securities and type of VC fund and location of entrepreneurial firm. Correlations greater than 0.04 are statistically significant at the 5% level of significance. Correlations are presented for first-round investments only (4,114 observations).

	Preferred Equity	Common Equity and/ or Warrants	Convertible Preferred Equity	Debt	Convertible Debt	Debt and Common Equity	Preferred and Common Equity	Mixes of Other Securities
Private Limited VC	0.04	0.05	0.04	−0.08	0.05	−0.07	−0.01	−0.05
Corporate VC	0.00	−0.08	0.03	0.06	−0.02	0.01	−0.02	0.04
Government VC	−0.01	0.10	−0.03	−0.06	0.02	−0.03	−0.02	−0.03
Institutional VC	−0.01	−0.06	−0.07	0.17	−0.01	0.06	−0.02	−0.04
LSVCC	−0.01	−0.03	−0.01	0.02	−0.02	0.09	0.05	−0.03
Foreign (U.S.) VC	0.02	−0.03	−0.01	−0.06	−0.05	−0.04	0.00	0.17
Other Type of VC	−0.03	0.01	0.03	−0.04	0.00	−0.03	0.02	0.03
British Columbia	0.02	−0.03	0.12	−0.05	−0.01	−0.05	−0.02	0.03
Alberta	0.01	0.04	0.02	−0.02	−0.03	−0.03	0.00	−0.01
Saskatchewan	−0.03	0.01	−0.03	0.07	−0.02	0.00	–0.02	−0.01
Manitoba	−0.01	0.04	0.00	0.00	−0.02	0.00	0.05	−0.03
Ontario	0.06	0.01	0.04	−0.10	−0.01	−0.07	−0.04	0.07
Quebec	−0.05	−0.02	−0.11	0.11	0.04	0.10	0.04	−0.08

Table 12.4 Logit Regressions for Start-up, High-tech, and Syndication: First-stage DWH Regressions

This table presents logit regression estimates of the determinants of start-up stage (equation 12.1) and high-tech (equation 12.2) investments, and the determinants of syndicated investments (equation 12.3). As well, equations 12.4, and 12.5, 12.6, respectively, present regressions for syndications with LSVCCs only, foreign VCs only, and other types of investors excluding foreign VCs and LSVCCs. Year fixed effects for 1991–2003 are used. Dummy variables for private limited partnerships and for the Maritime Provinces are suppressed to avoid perfect collinearity. The marginal effects are presented to explicitly show economic significance for the logit regressions. Only first-round investments are considered for a total of 4,114 observations. "—" Variable excluded for reasons of collinearity in the syndication regressions, and because they were not applicable in the start-up and high-tech regressions. *, **, *** Significant at the 10%, 5%, and 1% levels, respectively.

	(1) **Start-up**	(2) **High-tech**	(3) **Syndication: All Types of VCs**	(4) **Syndication: LSVCCs Only**	(5) **Syndication: Foreign (U.S.) VCs Only**	(6) **Syndication: Non-LSVCCs and Non-U.S. VCs Only**
Year Fixed Effects?	Yes	Yes	Yes	Yes	Yes	Yes
Start-up	—	—	**0.169*** **	0.003	**−0.025*** **	**0.155*** **
High-tech	—	—	**0.165*** **	0.009	**0.015*** **	**0.116*** **
Log (Deal Size)	—	—	**0.224*** **	**0.026*** **	**0.004*** **	**0.106*** **

Corporate	**−0.298*****	**−0.300*****	**0.120*****	—	—	—
Government	**0.057****	**−0.772*****	**0.102*****	—	—	—
Institutional	**−0.343*****	**−0.328*****	**−0.128*****	—	—	—
LSVCC	**−0.192*****	**−0.346*****	**−0.869*****	—	—	—
Foreign Investor	**−0.203*****	**0.120****	**0.122****	—	—	—
Other Type of VC	−0.037	**−0.202*****	**0.390*****	—	—	—
British Columbia	0.002	**0.165*****	**0.132****	0.042	**−0.008****	0.223
Alberta	**−0.130***	**−0.167****	−0.955	−0.003	**−0.017*****	−0.259
Saskatchewan	**−0.268*****	**−0.499*****	0.106	0.028	—	**0.161****
Manitoba	−0.057	**−0.333*****	**0.136***	**0.139***	—	−0.564
Ontario	−0.073	0.810	−0.548	0.026	**−0.020*****	**−0.119****
Quebec	−0.084	**−0.128****	**0.150****	−0.008	**−0.046*****	**0.942***
Chi-squared	403.240***	897.314***	1794.612***	206.219***	159.099***	649.963***
LogLikelihood	−2414.683	−2270.576	−1941.212	−1231.203	−580.696	−2447.950
Pseudo R^2	0.077	0.165	0.316	0.077	0.120	0.117

likely to invest in start-ups but 12.0% more likely to invest in high-tech firms relative to private independent funds.

Table 12.4 regression 3 indicates differences in the propensity of different types of venture capital funds to syndicate their investments. Relative to private independent funds, corporate venture capital funds are 12.0% more likely to syndicate, government venture capital funds are 12% more likely to syndicate, institutional investors are 12.8% less likely to syndicate, LSVCCs are 90% less likely to syndicate, and foreign venture capital funds are 12.2% more likely to syndicate. For all types of venture capital funds considered together (regression 3), we observe syndication 16.9% more frequently for start-ups and 16.5% more frequently for high-tech firms.

Syndication is also more proportionately likely the greater the total value of the deal. In regards to the economic significance of that effect, an increase in deal size from Can$1,000,000 to Can$2,000,000 increases the probability of syndication by 6.7%, whereas an increase in deal size from Can$11,000,000 to Can$12,000,000 increases the probability of syndication by 0.8%.[13]

Table 12.4 regressions 4–6 consider the determinants of the propensity of LSVCCs to syndicate (regression 4), foreign venture capital funds to syndicate with Canadian venture capital funds (regression 5), and all other types of venture capital funds taken together (that is, all excluding LSVCCs and foreign venture capital funds; regression 6). LSVCCs are considered separately (see also Osborne and Sandler, 1998). Foreign venture capital funds are considered separately because they are distinct geographically, if not in other ways as well.

Regressions 4 and 5 in Table 12.4 do in fact indicate significant differences exhibited by LSVCCs and foreign venture capital funds. The propensity of LSVCCs to syndicate is invariant for start-ups and high-tech firms, unlike other venture capital funds (compare regression 4 with regressions 3, 5, and 6). Foreign venture capital funds, by contrast, are 2.5% less likely to syndicate with Canadian venture capital funds for start-ups and 1.5% more likely to syndicate with Canadian venture capital funds for high-tech investments.

In subsection 12.4.3 below, we make use of the vectors of residuals in regressions 1 to 6 in Table 12.4 to construct artificial regressions and test for the effect of endogeneity associated with estimating equation 12.1 (the DWH test). That is, while the choice of form(s) of finance depends on the type of firm and the particular agency problems associated with the investment, are different types of firms more attracted to different

[13]The calculations are (log(12,000,000) − log(11,000,000)) * 0.224 = 0.008, and (log(2,000,000) − log(1,000,000)) * 0.224 = 0.067. Logs were used to account for a diminishing effect of deal size on the probability of syndication. Linear specifications did not materially change the results reported. Alternative specifications are available upon request.

forms of finance, and does syndication mitigate such adverse selection problems?

12.4.3 *Adverse Selection, Forms of Finance, and Firm Characteristics: Empirical Evidence*

In this subsection we test for the effect of adverse selection associated with the choice of form(s) of finance by estimating a system of artificial regressions of the following form:

$$\begin{aligned}\text{Probability (Security selected)} = {} & \varepsilon + ß1\ \text{Start-up} + ß2\ \text{High-tech} \\ & + ß3\ \text{Log (Deal Size)} + ß4\ \text{LSVCC} \\ & + ß5\ \text{Capital Gains Tax} + ß6\ \text{TSX} \\ & + ß7\ \text{Trend} + ß8\ \varepsilon_{\text{Start-up}} \\ & + ß9\ \varepsilon_{\text{High-tech}} + ß10\ \varepsilon_{\text{Syndication}} + \varepsilon \qquad (12.5)\end{aligned}$$

Recall that we said before that different forms of finance may be more appropriate for different entrepreneurial firms (equation 12.1), but the causal relation between type of firm and form of finance is not unidirectional. The key empirical insight is that where the residual vectors (ε) are not orthogonal in equation 12.5, different types of firms are attracted to different forms of finance. Statistically significant estimates indicate the residuals $\varepsilon_{\text{Start-up}}$, $\varepsilon_{\text{High-tech}}$, and $\varepsilon_{\text{Syndication}}$ are each not orthogonal to the selected security; that is, they are endogenous, such that start-ups, high-tech, and syndicated investments are each observed in the data because of presence of the particular security that is part of the venture capital financing transaction. A positive coefficient is evidence of selection toward that security, and vice versa for a negative coefficient.

Instead of providing the extended version of all of the multinomial logit regression coefficients of equation 12.5, we present only the marginal effects of such estimates. Only the marginal effects and statistical significance for $ß_8$–$ß_{10}$ are reported in Table 12.5, as these coefficients are pertinent to the issue of adverse selection by virtue of the effect of endogeneity on the coefficient estimates of equation 12.1. This has the benefit of conciseness and shows economic significance as well as statistical significance.

Table 12.5 provides evidence relating selection effects to forms of finance for the different types of firms financed by Canadian venture capital funds. Panel A of Table 12.5 considers all of the different types of venture capital funds that syndicate together. Panel B of Table 12.5 distinguishes syndication among LSVCCs only and foreign venture capital funds only from the rest of the types of venture capital funds (indicated in Table 12.1 and accompanying text).

Three primary results are apparent from Panels A and B in Table 12.5. The first primary result is that start-ups manifest adverse selection problems vis-à-vis debt finance. That is, start-ups are more likely to be attracted by offers of debt finance (Table 12.5, Panel A). This result is statistically significant at the

Table 12.5 DWH Tests of the Effect of Endogeneity vis-à-vis Firm Characteristics and Forms of Finance

This table presents DWH tests of the effect of endogeneity vis-à-vis forms of finance and firm characteristics (stage of development, industry). The regressions are multinomial logit models of equation 12.7 described in the text of the chapter. The multinomial logit regression coefficients are not presented; rather, the marginal effects are presented to explicitly show economic significance. The reported right-hand-side variables are the residuals from the regressions reported in Table 12.4. Other independent right-hand-side variables are not reported for conciseness. Only first-round investments are considered. Panel A considers all syndications among all types of VCs together. Panel B considers separately syndications that involved LSVCCs, foreign VCs, and all other types of VCs. The full sample of 4,114 first-round investments is used. *, **, *** Significant at the 10%, 5%, and 1% levels, respectively.

Panel A. All Types of Syndicated Investments Considered Together

	Preferred	Common	Convertible Preferred	Debt	Convertible Debt	Debt and Common	Preferred and Common	Other Combinations of Securities
Start-up	−0.005	**−0.053****	0.022	**0.043*****	0.016	**0.017***	−0.011	−0.029
High-tech	−0.013	0.013	**−0.092*****	**0.053*****	**−0.041****	**0.030*****	**0.017*****	**0.033****
Syndication (All Types of VCs)	0.000	**−0.058****	**−0.040*****	0.026	0.024	−0.007	−0.003	**0.057*****

Chi-square = 948.8370***; Log Likelihood = −7,162.593; Pseudo R^2 = 0.062.

Panel B. LSVCC, Foreign, and Other Syndications Considered Separately

	Preferred	Common	Convertible Preferred	Debt	Convertible Debt	Debt and Common	Preferred and Common	Other Combinations of Securities
Start-up	−0.006	**−0.061****	0.016	**0.046*****	0.014	**0.017****	−0.010	−0.015
High-tech	−0.016	0.016	**−0.088*****	**0.048*****	**−0.040****	**0.029*****	**0.017*****	**0.033****
Syndication among LSVCCs	**−0.040***	−0.027	0.026	−0.031	0.043	−0.018	−0.005	**0.052***
Syndication among Foreign VCs	−0.014	0.012	−0.014	−0.058	**−0.085****	−0.037	0.016	**0.179*****
Syndication among Other VCs	−0.011	−0.021	**0.020***	−0.012	0.009	−0.001	0.004	0.013

Chi-square = 989.935***; Log Likelihood = −7,142.044; Pseudo R^2 = 0.065.

1% level of significance, and the estimated economic significance is such that adverse selection problems are 4.3% more pronounced for start-ups (relative to expansion stage) in debt financed transactions. Similarly, the data indicate adverse selection problems for start-ups are 5.3% less pronounced for common equity finance and 1.7% more pronounced for mixes of debt and common equity finance (Panel A). This evidence is consistent with the view that start-up entrepreneurs do not like to give up common equity to their investors and would prefer to be financed by debt. Consistent with our prediction earlier in the chapter (Hypothesis 12.1), the data therefore indicate that start-ups manifest greater uncertainty as nuts as opposed to lemons. The economic and statistical significance of each of these effects are similar in Panel B in Table 12.5, illustrating the robustness of the results.

The second primary result in Table 12.5 is that adverse selection problems are much more pronounced for firms in high-tech industries, as evidenced by the greater number of statistically and economically significant coefficients for high-tech firms. The data indicate that high-tech firms are attracted toward debt. In particular, adverse selection effects for high-tech firms are 5.3% more pronounced (relative to nontech firms) for debt finance (and similarly, they are more likely to select toward mixes of debt and common, and preferred and common). The economic and statistical significance is similar for Panel B in Table 12.5 for high-tech investments. There is further evidence in both Panels A and B that high-tech entrepreneurs are more inclined to select away from securities in which they would be required to give up equity ownership to their investors; for example, in support of theoretical research on adverse selection and convertible securities (Brennan and Kraus, 1987), the evidence indicates that high-tech firms are 9.2% more likely to select away from convertible preferred equity and 4.1% more likely to select away from convertible debt. Overall, as with the evidence for start-ups just discussed, this evidence for high-tech entrepreneurial firms is consistent with the conjecture in Hypothesis 12.1 that the uncertainty associated with investment in high-tech firms is better characterized as uncertainty in the variability of returns (nuts) as opposed to uncertainty in average expected returns (lemons).

The third primary result in Table 12.5 is that, in support of Hypothesis 12.2, adverse selection is more problematic for high-tech investments than syndicated investments. That is, there are fewer statistically significant coefficients for syndication than high-tech in Table 12.5, Panel A. (Notice that the number of significant coefficients for early-stage and syndicated investments is similar in Table 12.5, but the evidence following explores differences from a companion perspective in more detail.) Further, note in Panel B of Table 12.5 that there are two statistically significant coefficients for syndication among LSVCCs, two for foreign venture capital funds, and one for syndication among the other venture capital fund types. Overall, therefore, adverse selection appears to be slightly more problematic for LSVCCs and foreign venture capital funds investing in Canada. As we said before, these latter results are expected, since foreign venture capital funds face distance hurdles in carrying out due diligence and the screening

Canadian investees. Likewise, LSVCCs face statutory covenants that require they invest capital within one to two years of receipt from the investor (or risk paying a fine to the government, or even revocation of the opportunity to operate as a LSVCC; Osborne and Sandler, 1998); this statutory covenant on LSVCCs compromises the time that LSVCC managers have for carrying out their due diligence, and hence exacerbates adverse selection problems for LSVCCs.

12.4.4 Robustness Checks on the Adverse Selection Tests

In this subsection we carry out two robustness checks on the adverse selection tests. Robust check #1 (Table 12.6) presents estimates similar to that in Table 12.5, but with syndicated and nonsyndicated investments treated separately as two different subsamples (we do not treat different types of investors in different subsamples for reasons indicated previously). The second robustness check (Table 12.7) again presents similar tests but with the difference that the $ value of the deal size is treated as a potentially endogenous variable as well. Overall, the tests we discussed in the preceding section yield quite similar results to these two alternative specifications, as explicitly shown in Tables 12.6 and 12.7 and described following.

In Table 12.6, Panel A, the tests for the subsample of nonsyndicated investments show four statistically significant coefficients for start-ups; by contrast, Table 12.6, Panel B, for the subsample of syndicated investments shows only one statistically significant coefficient for start-ups. This reinforces the view that syndication facilitates screening such that the security does not "cause" the presence of the particular entrepreneurial characteristics; that is, syndication mitigates adverse selection problems associated with start-ups. Similarly, in Table 12.6, Panel A, there are five significant coefficients for high-tech firms but only four significant coefficients for high-tech firms in Panel B. This latter difference in the number of significant coefficients for the syndication versus nonsyndication subsamples is less pronounced for high-tech firms but again still illustrates a benefit to syndication with respect to mitigating adverse selection problems. As discussed, this evidence is consistent with prior work on the rationales underlying syndication (Hypothesis 12.2; see also Lerner, 1994; Lockett and Wright, 1999, 2001; Manigart et al., 2002a; Wright and Lockett, 2003). Furthermore, notice in Table 12.6 that the coefficients are significant in a way that is very similar to those in Table 12.5; as we noted before, this supports the view that start-ups and high-tech firms are better characterized as nuts and not lemons (Hypothesis 12.1).

Table 12.7 carries out very similar tests as Table 12.6. The difference in Table 12.7 relative to Table 12.6 is that for equation 12.1 we also consider the possibility that Log (Deal Size) is endogenous as well. In Tables 12.6 and 12.7, we did not consider that variable as endogenous, since capital requirements to start a project are typically taken as exogenous in theoretical (e.g., Kanniainen and Keuschnigg, 2003, 2004; Keuschnigg, 2003) and empirical work (e.g., Manigart et al., 2002a). The estimates in Table 12.7 are presented separately

Table 12.6 DWH Tests: Robustness Check #1

This table presents DWH tests of the effect of endogeneity vis-à-vis forms of finance and firm characteristics (stage of development, capital requirements, and industry). The regressions are multinomial logit models of equation 12.7 described in the text of the chapter. The multinomial logit regression coefficients are not presented; rather, the marginal effects are presented to explicitly show economic significance. The reported independent variables are the residuals from regressions analogous to those reported in Table 12.4 (for the respective subsamples for syndicated and nonsyndicated investments). Other independent variables are not reported for conciseness. Only first-round investments are considered. Panel A considers 1,893 investments that were not syndicated. Panel B considers 2,221 investments that were syndicated. *, **, *** Significant at the 10%, 5%, and 1% levels, respectively.

	Preferred	Common	Convertible Preferred	Debt	Convertible Debt	Debt and Common	Preferred and Common	Other Combinations of Securities
Panel A. Nonsyndicated First-round Investments								
Start-up	0.014	**−0.082****	0.016	**0.055****	−0.031	0.002	**−0.019*****	**0.045*****
High-tech	−0.021	−0.007	**−0.048*****	**0.089*****	−0.013	**0.052*****	**0.018*****	**−0.069*****
Chi-square = 459.326***; Log Likelihood = −3,147.875; Pseudo R^2 = 0.068.								
Panel B. Syndicated First-round Investments								
Start-up	0.003	−0.080	0.050	0.022	0.021	**−0.059****	0.000	0.042
High-tech	**−0.071****	0.061	**−0.092****	**0.079*****	−0.001	**0.021***	−0.015	0.018
Chi-square = 482.706***; Log Likelihood = −3,932.897; Pseudo R^2 = 0.058.								

Table 12.7 DWH Tests: Robustness Check #2

This table presents DWH tests of the effect of endogeneity vis-à-vis forms of finance and firm characteristics (stage of development, capital requirements, and industry). The regressions are multinomial logit models of equation 12.7 described in the text of the chapter. The multinomial logit regression coefficients are not presented; rather, the marginal effects are presented to explicitly show economic significance. The reported independent variables are the residuals from regressions analogous to those reported in Table 12.4 (for the respective subsamples for syndicated and nonsyndicated investments), and the residuals from an analogous regression explaining the log of deal sizes. Other independent variables are not reported for conciseness. Only first-round investments are considered. Panel A considers 1,893 investments that were not syndicated. Panel B considers 2,221 investments that were syndicated. *, **, *** Significant at the 10%, 5%, and 1% levels, respectively.

Panel A. Nonsyndicated First-round Investments

	Preferred	Common	Convertible Preferred	Debt	Convertible Debt	Debt and Common	Preferred and Common	Other Combinations of Securities
Start-up	0.007	**−0.064***	0.012	**0.044***	−0.036	0.011	**−0.019****	0.044*
High-tech	−0.017	−0.015	**−0.046*****	**0.093*****	−0.011	**0.047*****	**0.018*****	**−0.069*****
Log ($ Deal Size ('000))	−0.017	0.045	−0.010	−0.026	−0.012	0.023	0.000	−0.003

Chi-square = 466.027***; Log Likelihood = −3,144.524; Pseudo R^2 = 0.069.

Panel B. Syndicated First-round Investments

	Preferred	Common	Convertible Preferred	Debt	Convertible Debt	Debt and Common	Preferred and Common	Other Combinations of Securities
Start-up	0.001	−0.075	0.047	0.026	0.028	**−0.056****	0.000	0.028
High-tech	**−0.069****	0.058	**−0.091****	**0.076*****	−0.006	0.018	−0.015	0.029
Log ($ Deal Size ('000))	−0.004	0.017	−0.002	0.012	0.025	**0.017***	−0.001	**−0.064*****

Chi-square = 504.376***; Log Likelihood = −3,922.062; Pseudo R^2 = 0.060.

for the first-round transactions that were not syndicated (Table 12.7, Panel A) and those that were syndicated (Table 12.7, Panel B), as in Table 12.6. The results in Table 12.7 are quite consistent with Table 12.6 in that for start-up and high-tech firms, adverse selection problems are mitigated by syndication. Therefore, the results pertaining to Hypotheses 12.1 and 12.2 are not affected by the treatment of the deal size variable as either exogenous or endogenous.

As an aside, notice that Table 12.7 indicates selection effects associated with a firm's capital requirements are not mitigated by virtue of syndication. Panel A (for nonsyndicated investments) indicates no statistically significant coefficients (even at the 10% level of significance) for capital requirements, while Panel B (for syndicated investments) indicates two statistically significant coefficients (one at the 1% level and one at the 10% of significance). First-round syndicated investments naturally do tend to involve larger deal sizes (average deal size for first-round syndicated investments was Can$1,501,126), whereas average deal size for first-round nonsyndicated investments was Can$1,078,892). It is therefore not surprising that adverse selection problems vis-à-vis capital requirements are not smaller by virtue of syndication (unlike the role of adverse selection problems vis-à-vis start-ups and high-tech firms), since syndication most often involves larger deals.

Finally, it is important to stress that we have consistently demonstrated in Tables 12.5 to 12.7 that syndication mitigates adverse selection problems for start-ups and high-tech firms. We have never claimed (and the data do not show) that syndication completely eliminates adverse selection. The view that agency problems can be mitigated but not eliminated has been well documented (see, e.g., Farmer and Winter, 1986).

12.4.5 Limitations and Future Research

This chapter provides new tests of the empirical tractability in adverse selection in a nonsegmented market in which financial intermediaries use any number of different forms of finance and finance a variety of types of entrepreneurial firms. We control for changes in the economic environment over the 1991 to 2003 period both in regards to types of firms in the market for venture capital finance and in regards to selected securities. As we are unaware of prior work that has carried out similar tests, we provide a few remarks about the robustness of our results and extensions to other contexts.

The approach taken in this chapter may have limitations for other contexts for a few reasons. First, we employed artificial regressions to test for the effect of endogeneity on the coefficient estimates in equation 12.1. To the extent that equation 12.1 is not appropriate for other contexts, the implied adverse selection evidence may not be generally applicable.

Second, we do not consider transaction-specific relative price changes across different securities, among certain other factors; this may limit the extent to which the results are generalizable. Increasing the price of one security relative to another may lead some entrepreneurs to switch to an alternative source of finance (e.g., from the type of financial intermediary providing debt to the type of financial intermediary providing equity); see, for example, Stiglitz and Weiss (1981) and DeMeza and Webb (1987, 1992). Given the limitation that our data do not indicate relative security prices for forms of finance in Canadian venture capital, we hold constant relative security prices and focus on adverse selection associated with the use of alternative forms of finance.[14] Similarly, our data do not indicate information pertaining to specific control rights (Gompers, 1998; Kaplan and Strömberg, 2003; Sahlman, 1990). To the extent that selection effects are associated with the allocation of specific control rights, there may be "noise" in our empirical evidence. Nevertheless, following Stiglitz and Weiss (1981), Myers and Majluf (1984), DeMeza and Webb (1987, 1992), Rebello (1995), Noe and Rebello (1992, 1996), among others, we suspect that selection effects are more broadly associated with form(s) of finance at the outset and not the particular underlying terms of the financial contract determined pursuant to contractual negotiations and fine-tuning.

Third, it is possible that pronounced differences may exist among financial intermediaries other than venture capital funds, as well as across countries, for institutional and legal reasons (see, e.g., Manigart et al., 1996, 2002a,b; Mayer et al., 2004; and Bruining et al., 2005, for differences in governance, syndication, and returns across countries).

An important finding in this chapter is that problems of adverse selection are in fact context dependent and vary depending on firm characteristics and the presence of venture capital fund syndicates. The context-dependent nature of our results suggests a number of avenues for future research. Further theoretical research could also incorporate different and/or broader contract spaces for alternative forms of finance, different types of entrepreneurial firms, and different financial intermediaries. Analyses of adverse selection in the context of work on team formation (in the spirit of Ruef et al., 2003, and Forbes et al., 2004, for example) could be carried out with more detailed hand collected data. Empirical work in different countries and/or among different financial intermediaries could also be fruitful in providing an improved understanding of adverse selection and capital structure among entrepreneurial firms.

12.5 Conclusions

This chapter provided empirical evidence from Canadian venture capital financing data that indicated the following generalizable results for other contexts.

[14]But this may not be a significant limitation for two reasons. Since all types of venture capital funds in Canada employ all forms of finance (see Table 12.1), relative security prices for entrepreneurs seeking venture financing in Canada are likely quite stable, especially compared to situations in which different forms of finance are only available from different types of financial intermediaries. Moreover, start-ups are hard to value and investors and entrepreneurs therefore delay valuation to the second round, when more information is available. We owe thanks to an anonymous referee for this latter helpful comment.

Notice that these findings pertain to the first-round investments in newly originated deals and not follow-on investments in staged investment rounds.

Investment focus of different fund types:

- Private independent venture capital funds are more likely to invest in start-ups and high-tech firms relative to corporate venture capital funds, institutional investors, and LSVCCs.
- Government venture capital funds are more likely to invest in start-ups but less likely to invest in high-tech firms relative to limited partnerships.
- Foreign (U.S.) venture capital funds investing in Canada are less likely to invest in start-ups but more likely to invest in high-tech firms relative to private independent venture capital funds.

Propensity to syndicate:

- Private independent venture capital funds are less likely to syndicate new investments than corporate venture capital funds, government venture capital funds, and foreign (U.S.) venture capital funds investing in Canada.
- Private independent venture capital funds are more likely to syndicate new investments than institutional investors and LSVCCs.
- Syndication is more common for start-ups and high-tech investments and for firms with greater capital requirements.

Adverse selection risks, given this context of stage focus, industry focus, and propensity to syndicate:

- Adverse selection risks are most pronounced for firms in start-ups. Start-ups select away from common equity and toward debt. All else being equal, early-stage entrepreneurs do not like to give up ownership to their investors if it can be avoided. This indicates the risk of financing start-ups is better characterized as a risk of financing a nut and not a lemon.
- High-tech firms are more likely to select toward debt, and are less likely to select toward convertible securities that provide the venture capital fund with upside potential and downside protection. This is consistent with the widely accepted view that high-tech firms are riskier than their non-tech counterparts and shows the risk is best characterized as the risk of financing a nut and not a lemon.
- Syndication significantly mitigates problems of adverse selection. Syndicated venture capital funds facilitate an important role in the screening potential entrepreneurial firms and mitigate the risk of financing low-quality firms associated with different capital structure decisions.

Key Terms

Adverse selection
Lemon
Nut
Debt
Convertible debt
Preferred equity
Convertible preferred equity
Common equity
Syndication
Due diligence

Discussion Questions

12.1. True/False/Uncertain and explain why: "Adverse selection costs are the risk that venture capital fund investors face with offering debt to their potential entrepreneurial firm investments."

12.2. What might explain differences in the propensity to syndicate across different types of venture capital funds? For example, why are LSVCCs less likely to syndicate than private independent venture capital funds in Canada, but foreign (U.S.) venture capital funds more likely to syndicate investments in Canada than Canadian private independent venture capital funds investing in Canada? In your response consider not only issues involving adverse selection but also fund design, fund structure and constraints, and the various motives for syndication discussed in Chapters 10 and 11.

12.3. Why might adverse selection costs in the data reviewed in this chapter for earlier stage and high-tech firms more closely resemble the risk of financing a "nut" than a "lemon"? What types of things would you consider as a venture capital fund manager in your due diligence review to mitigate these adverse selection risks? How would you structure your contracts to mitigate these risks (recall the discussion of security design and other contractual items reviewed in Chapters 10 and 11)?

12.4. Is adverse selection most pronounced in the initial investment round or in follow-on investment rounds? What agency problem(s) identified in Chapter 2 might exacerbate adverse selection risks in subsequent follow-on rounds?

12.5. Why would entrepreneurs with low expected variability in their returns be attracted to offers of finance in the form of convertible securities?

12.6. Why would entrepreneurs with high expected variability in their returns be attracted to offers of finance in the form of nonconvertible debt or nonconvertible preferred equity?

13 Corporate Venture Capital Fund Contracts

13.1 Introduction and Learning Objectives

Financial contracts between entrepreneurs and venture capital funds have been characterized as one of the most important and distinguishing features of venture capital investment (see Chapters 1, 2, and 10–12; see also Gilson and Schizer, 2003; Megginson, 2004; Sahlman, 1990). Financial contracts are vitally important to the venture capital investment process because contracts minimize information asymmetries and agency problems and appropriately provide incentives for both the entrepreneur and value-added venture capital fund manager to add value to the enterprise. Financial contracts also facilitate the exit of venture capital fund investments in entrepreneurial firms (see Chapters 14, 19–22). Given the high risk and uncertainty facing venture capital investments, financial contracts have emerged as highly sophisticated instruments that are a vital part of the venture capital cycle.

Corporate venture capital funds are widely regarded as having performance results that are inferior to limited partnership venture capital funds (Gompers, 2002; Gompers and Lerner, 1999). As such, it is worthwhile to consider whether corporate venture capital funds use financial contracts that are distinct from contracts used by limited partnership. To this end, in this chapter we build on our analysis of security design introduced in Chapters 11 and 12 by highlighting differences with corporate venture capital funds.

In this chapter we will do the following:

- Review explanations in the prior literature for corporate venture capital fund underperformance relative to limited partnership venture capital funds, including the following:
  - The comparatively autonomous structure of limited partnership venture capital funds relative to corporate venture capital funds
  - The greater pay-for-performance sensitivity among limited partnership venture capital fund managers relative to corporate venture capital fund managers
  - The strategic rationales associated with corporate investing versus the purely financial incentives of limited partnership venture capital funds
- Offer a new fourth explanation for the inferior performance of corporate venture capital funds relative to limited partnership venture capital funds: financial contracting

The central theme of this chapter is that if financial contracts do in fact influence investment performance through the appropriate allocation of cash flow and control rights, and if limited partnership venture capital funds write contracts that are superior to corporate venture capital fund contracts, then we may infer that corporate venture capital fund performance will be inferior to limited partnership venture capital fund performance.

We will first review the literature on venture capital financial contracting and then introduce data on U.S. and Canadian corporate and limited partnership venture capital funds. We discuss European evidence on corporate venture capital contracts and the link between financial contracts and investment performance. Finally, we consider lessons for setting up corporate VC funds based on the evidence in this chapter.

13.2 Financial Contracting in Venture Capital

13.2.1 A Brief Review of the Issues in Venture Capital Financial Contracting

Venture capital financial contracts allocate cash flow and control rights among the investor(s) and the entrepreneurial firm's managers and employees (Chapters 10 to 12; see also Bascha and Walz, 2001; Gompers, 1998; Kaplan and Strömberg, 2003; Sahlman, 1990). Cash flow rights refer to who gets paid what fraction of the profits of the venture and at what time. Cash flow rights may be contingent in that the division of profits depends on states of nature (bull versus bear economic conditions) and actions taken by different parties (both the entrepreneurs and the investors) that affect the value of the venture. Examples of contingencies upon which cash flow rights are allocated include, but are not limited to, measures of financial performance (e.g., meeting sales or profit figures), measures of nonfinancial performance (e.g., obtaining a patent or FDA approval), issuance of equity (e.g., failure to achieve an IPO in five years provides the venture capital fund with the right to redeem preferred shares at a certain value), and taking certain actions (e.g., founding entrepreneur must stay with firm for a certain number of years or until a key employee is hired).

Control rights refer to the allocation of rights to make decisions in respect to the firm. Control rights may be active decision rights or passive veto rights and are allocated in a contingent manner as with cash flow rights. Examples of active control flow rights include, but are not limited to, the right to replace the CEO, automatic conversion from preferred equity to common equity at exit, drag-along rights, right of first refusal at potential sale, cosale agreements, antidilution protection, protection rights against new issues, redemption rights, information rights, IPO demand registration rights, and piggyback registration rights. Passive veto rights may include rights to prevent asset sales, asset purchases, changes in control, issuance of equity, and various other rights to prevent the firm from carrying out a management decision against the interests of the rights holder. These different rights are studied in detail in Chapter 14.

Security design involves the allocation of both control and cash flow rights (see Chapters 2 and 10–12; see also Hart, 2001). Common equity holders are residual claimants whose payoff increases in proportion to the value of the firm. Equity holders also have voting rights to vote in members of the board of directors, which in turn has the right to make specific firm-related decisions. Debt holders, by contrast, are fixed claimants whose payoff does not depend on the value of the firm as long as the firm is able to repay the principal and interest payments on the debt. If the firm is unable to repay its debt, then debt holders can force the firm into bankruptcy and acquire the rights normally held by equity holders in regards to decision rights. Debt contracts can be written with convertibility clauses that enable the debt holder to convert the debt contract into common equity at prespecified rates and terms of conversion (that is, specified at the time of initial contract).

Preferred equity holders are also fixed claimants in that the value of preferred equity depends on the present discounted value of preferred dividends associated with preferred equity. Preferred equity does not by itself provide voting rights, and a firm is not obligated to pay preferred equity dividends in the same way as the obligations associated with interest payments on debt. A firm that does not pay its prespecified preferred equity dividends on a timely basis cannot be forced into bankruptcy, unlike interest payments on debt. Preferred equity holders have priority over common equity holders in bankruptcy, but preferred equity holders rank behind debt holders in bankruptcy. Preferred equity contracts can have convertibility options that enable the contract to be converted into common equity at prespecified rates and terms of conversion.

Generally speaking, prior work has established that debt is suited toward high-cash-flow businesses that can meet the ongoing interest payment obligations on debt, whereas equity is suited toward high-growth businesses (Barclay and Holderness, 1999). In the context of venture capital fund contracts, seminal papers examined the U.S. market that indicated that U.S. venture capital funds finance their entrepreneurial investee firms with convertible preferred equity. This work also made clear the fact that venture capital contracts separate cash flow and control rights to appropriately allocate incentives that best maximize the expected value of the venture. Based on the observation that convertible preferred equity is most often used in the United States, a number of theories have emerged to explain why convertible preferred equity is the apparent “optimal” form of venture capital finance (Chapter 11). Some of the reasons for the optimality of convertible preferred shares in venture capital finance are as follows. Convertible preferred equity provides the venture capital fund with a stronger claim on the liquidation value of the firm in the event of bankruptcy, thereby shifting the risk from the venture capital fund(s) to the entrepreneur. Relative to straight common equity, convertible preferred equity reduces the entrepreneur’s dilution of ownership. Convertible preferred shares also enable a greater amount of funds to be raised relative to straight debt, as the venture capital fund has some equity participation. In the context of staged financing, convertible preferred equity mitigates window-dressing problems and ensures that most positive expected NPV projects continue to receive financing. Convertible preferred shares also facilitate the conversion of illiquid holdings into cash and mitigate problems associated with selling the firm, particularly when the incentive effects of trilateral bargaining are considered.

13.2.2 Why Might Corporate Venture Capital Fund Contracts Differ from Limited Partnership Venture Capital Fund Contracts?

Corporate venture capital funds are distinct from limited partnership venture capital funds in at least three main respects, which could in turn impact the nature of the contracts written between corporate venture capital funds and their investee entrepreneurial firms (Dushnitsky and Lenox, 2006; Gompers, 2002; Maula and Murray, 2001). First, limited partnership venture capital funds are autonomous investment vehicles whereby the institutional investor limited partners cannot interfere with the day-to-day operations of the general partner venture capital fund manager. Limited partnership venture capital funds and similar forms of organization involve an assignment of rights and responsibilities in the form of a very long-term contract over a period of 10 to 13 years. The purpose of this contract is to mitigate the potential for agency problems associated with the venture capital fund managers' investing institutional investor capital in private entrepreneurial firms. The massive potential for agency problems in the reinvestment of capital, and the very long-term nature of the limited partnership contract, make extremely important the assignment of rights and obligations in the contract in the form of restrictive covenants. Corporate venture capital funds, by contrast, are much more unstable organizations whereby the existence of the corporate venture capital fund entity within the firm depends on the willingness of head office to which the corporate venture capital fund belongs. Hence, even apparently successful corporate venture capital funds, such as that within Dell, often are abandoned earlier than that which would otherwise be optimal (Gompers and Lerner, 1999). The lack of autonomy and shorter venture capital fund duration may inhibit the ability of corporate venture capital fund managers to learn by doing. For example, Kaplan et al. (2007) show that limited partnership venture capital funds in Sweden used mixes of straight debt and common equity in the 1990s but have since switched to convertible preferred equity (although see following for the evolution of venture capital contracts over time from Canadian and U.S. venture capital funds, and see Chapter 14 for European funds).

Second, corporate venture capital funds do not enjoy the same incentive compensation arrangements as those offered to limited partnership venture capital funds. Limited partnership venture capital fund managers typically receive 1 to 2% fixed fees based on the size of the fund and 20% of the profits of the fund (carried interest), which can result in enormous salaries or bonuses if the fund successfully exits investments in IPOs or acquisitions. Corporate venture capital funds, by contrast, typically do not enjoy such performance fees to maintain a level fee structure across different units of the overall corporate enterprise. Successful corporate venture capital fund managers are often recruited to work at the higher-paying limited partnership organizations. This could further limit the role of experience in writing optimal contracts among corporate venture capital funds. Corporate venture capital fund managers may also be more focused on downside protection as opposed to upside potential in writing contracts with entrepreneurs if corporate venture capital fund managers' compensation packages give rise to incentives to minimize risk as opposed to maximizing returns.

Third, corporate venture capital funds invest in a narrower range of firms that have technological promise in the industry in which the parent firm operates. To this end, a corporate venture capital fund's choice set is more limited, their investments are less diversified, and their strategic investing incentives are separate from purely financial incentives. If so, corporate venture capital funds might use stronger control rights (such as drag-along and redemption rights) that enable the corporate venture capital fund to force an acquisition exit when entrepreneurs might otherwise prefer to exit by an IPO.

In this chapter we introduce a dataset that compares some of the contractual terms used by corporate venture capital funds and limited partnership venture capital funds, as well as the evolution of contractual forms over time. But first we consider the preliminary issue as to whether convertible preferred equity is really the most efficient security choice for all venture capital transactions.

13.2.3 Is Convertible Preferred Equity Optimal in Venture Capital Finance?

The issue of whether or not convertible preferred equity is in fact the optimal form of venture capital finance has come into question by virtue of non-U.S. evidence of venture capital contracts, alongside institutional work on tax biases in favor of convertible preferred equity in the United States. Evidence from Canada (Cumming, 2005a,b), Europe (Bascha and Walz, 2007; Cumming, 2008; Hege et al., 2003; Schwienbacher, 2003), Taiwan (Songtao, 2001), and developing countries (Lerner and Schoar, 2005) clearly shows that venture capital funds use a variety of forms of finance and that convertible preferred equity is not the most frequently used security by venture capital funds in any country in the world (that is, where data have been collected) other than the United States.

There are five possible explanations for the more heterogeneous use of different securities among non-U.S. venture capital contracts. First, non-U.S. countries may have a greater presence of government investors that skew the incentives of private investors to use the most efficient security. For instance, in Canada, government-sponsored venture capital funds comprised approximately 50% of the market as of 2005, and as government funds compete for deals with private funds, they may also compete on the basis of the type of security offered to the potential investee firm (Cumming and MacIntosh, 2006). The trouble with this explanation, however, is that countries with a less significant extent of government venture capital funds are just as likely to use securities that resemble that which is observed among venture capital deals in Canada, and not the United States. For example, in the Netherlands, common equity was used twice as often as convertible securities from 1995 to 2002, and the Netherlands venture capital market has less than 10% government venture capital investments (Armour and Cumming, 2006). More generally, as just indicated, all non-U.S. countries from which venture capital contract data are available use a variety of forms of finance, unlike U.S. venture capital funds.

Second, venture capital funds outside the United States may not be as sophisticated or experienced as venture capital funds in the United States and thus may not know the best way to write contracts. There is evidence from some countries, such as Sweden, that venture capital funds are more likely to write contracts that resemble the U.S. contracts when they have had U.S. experience and that those venture capital funds that use U.S.-style contracts are more likely to survive and more likely to adopt U.S.-style contracts over time (Kaplan et al., 2007). That evidence, however, is not universally supported by evidence from other European countries (Bascha and Walz, 2007; Cumming, 2008) and from Canada (Cumming, 2005a,b).

Third, different securities could be functionally equivalent (Merton, 1995), such as common equity and warrants, straight debt and straight preferred equity, and all other securities that resemble convertible preferred equity (with both downside protection and upside potential). If so, we would expect similar securities to be used with roughly the same intensity for different financing contexts; however, empirical evidence clearly shows otherwise, and therefore there is little empirical support for the functional equivalence hypothesis (Cumming, 2005a,b).

Fourth, legal structures may be different in different countries (such as securities regulation and taxation), which could influence the extent to which venture capital funds use different securities. Lerner and Schoar (2005), for example, find evidence that law quality in regards to securities regulation and rule of law gives rise to security choices that substitute for the lack of law quality among developing countries (see also Chapter 14; Kaplan et al., 2007; and Cumming et al., 2008). The focus on securities regulation and general rule of law quality, however, is incomplete because venture capital funds in countries with similar securities regulatory structures and rule of law quality, such as Canada and the United States, use vastly different securities (as discussed following). A much more compelling explanation is provided by Gilson and Schizer (2003). In their influential paper, Gilson and Schizer show that U.S. tax law biases venture capital fund's and entrepreneur's incentives to use convertible preferred shares (see Chapters 10 and 11). This tax bias has been shown to be absent in Canada (Sandler, 2001). Unfortunately, most academic venture capital contracting studies do not acknowledge the possibility of a tax bias in favor of convertible preferred securities for venture capital funds and entrepreneurs in the United States (see, e.g., Kaplan and Strömberg, 2003; Kaplan et al., 2007; Lerner and Schoar, 2005).

A fifth explanation that could explain the use of a variety of securities other than convertible preferred equity in non-U.S. venture capital transactions is that different types of entrepreneurs are in fact different in ways that give rise to different sets of agency problems (Chapter 11). Because investments in different entrepreneurial firms are staged with different frequency based on expected agency problems, syndicated with different frequency depending on expected agency problems, and monitored with different intensity via seats on boards of directors depending on expected agency problems (Gompers and Lerner, 1999), it would be rather surprising to expect the same security choice for all entrepreneurial firms regardless of expected agency problems. The venture capital finance literature is in fact a complete outlier in the broader scope of literature on capital structure generally. Since the seminal work of Jensen and Meckling (1976), all work on capital structure (outside the realm of the narrowly focused venture capital finance literature) is consistent with the view that capital structure choices adjust to changes in expected agency problems. It is surprising that the application of this idea to the context of venture capital finance is as novel as it appears next to all prior work on the topic, particularly in view of the fact that agency problems are both very heterogeneous and very pronounced in venture capital finance.

In sum, prior evidence indicates that convertible preferred equity is the most frequently selected security for U.S. venture capital funds investing in U.S. entrepreneurial firms. International evidence from all countries around the world in which venture capital data have been collected, by contrast, indicates that a variety of forms of finance are used by venture capital funds and convertible preferred equity is not the most frequently selected security. The use of a variety of securities does not depend on the definition of *venture capital* by stage of entrepreneurial firm development, and so on. However, there is scant evidence on corporate venture capital fund contracts in prior academic research. The next section offers some new data that shed light on corporate venture capital fund contracts in an international setting with U.S. venture capital funds.

13.3 U.S. and Canadian Corporate and Limited Partnership Venture Capital Fund Investments in Canadian Entrepreneurial Firms

The data introduced in this section come from 4,820 investments in Canadian seed, early-, and expansion-stage entrepreneurial firms from 1991 to 2004. The venture capital fund investors specifically include Canadian limited partnership venture capital funds for 2,815 investments, Canadian corporate venture capital funds for 1,245 investments, U.S. limited partnership venture capital funds for 342 investments, and U.S. corporate venture capital funds for 418 venture capital investments. The U.S investments are cross-border venture capital investments in Canadian entrepreneurial firms.

The data are summarized in Table 13.1 and Figures 13.1 and 13.2, which clearly indicate that convertible preferred equity is not the most frequently

Table 13.1 Securities Used by Canadian and U.S. Venture

This table presents summary statistics of the number of investments (and the percentage partnership venture capitalists and corporate venture capitalists for investments in entrepreneurial firms are those that were in the seed, early, or expansion stage of tests for each of the four categories. *, **, *** Significant at the 10%, 5%, and 1% levels,

	Number of Investments			
	(1) Canada Limited Partnership Venture Capitalists	**(2) Canada Corporate Venture Capitalists**	**(3) U.S. Limited Partnership Venture Capitalists**	**(4) U.S. Corporate Venture Capitalists**
Common Shares	772 (27.42%)	191 (15.34%)	73 (21.35%)	76 (18.18%)
Convertible Preferred Shares	274 (9.73%)	108 (8.67%)	32 (9.36%)	37 (8.85%)
Convertible Debt	354 (12.58%)	109 (8.76%)	44 (12.87%)	36 (8.61%)
Preferred Shares	251 (8.92%)	101 (8.11%)	52 (15.20%)	35 (8.37%)
Debt	223 (7.92%)	153 (12.29%)	22 (6.43%)	82 (19.62%)
Warrants	7 (0.25%)	3 (0.24%)	2 (0.58%)	0 (0.00%)
Preferred and Common Shares	55 (1.95%)	16 (1.29%)	8 (2.34%)	1 (19.62%)
Preferred and Convertible Preferred Shares	4 (0.14%)	2 (0.16%)	1 (0.29%)	1 (0.24%)
Preferred Shares and Debt	2 (0.07%)	3 (0.24%)	2 (0.58%)	0 (0.00%)
Preferred Shares and Convertible Debt	2 (0.07%)	3 (0.24%)	2 (0.58%)	0 (0.00%)
Preferred Shares and Warrants	13 (0.46%)	3 (0.24%)	0 (0.00%)	0 (0.00%)
Common and Convertible Preferred Shares	12 (0.43%)	5 (0.40%)	0 (0.00%)	2 (0.48%)
Common Shares and Debt	44 (1.56%)	35 (2.81%)	6 (1.75%)	15 (3.59%)
Common Shares and Convertible Debt	39 (1.39%)	20 (1.61%)	1 (0.29%)	2 (0.48%)
Common Shares and Warrants	16 (0.57%)	3 (0.24%)	0 (0.00%)	1 (0.24%)

Capitalists Financing Canadian Entrepreneurial Firms

of total investments in parentheses) used by Canadian and U.S. limited entrepreneurial firms resident in Canada for the period 1991–2004. The development at the time of first investment. Comparison of proportions respectively.

Comparison of Proportions Tests					
(1) vs. (2)	(1) vs. (3)	(1) vs. (4)	(2) vs. (3)	(2) vs. (4)	(3) vs. (4)
8.35***	2.40**	4.01***	−2.64***	−1.37	1.09
1.07	0.22	0.57	−0.39	−0.11	0.24
3.53***	−0.15	2.32**	−2.28***	0.09	1.90*
0.84	−3.73***	0.37	−3.94***	−0.17	2.94***
−4.43***	0.97	−7.63***	3.06***	−3.72***	−5.26***
0.05	−1.10	1.02	−1.00	1.00	1.57
1.50	−0.48	2.51**	−1.41	1.84*	2.66***
−0.14	−0.66	−0.47	−0.50	−0.33	0.14
−1.42	−2.52**	0.55	−1.00	1.00	1.57
−1.42	−2.52**	0.55	−1.00	1.00	1.57
1.04	1.26	1.39	0.91	1.00	N/A
0.11	1.21	−0.15	1.17	−0.21	−1.28
−2.65***	−0.27	−2.89***	1.09	−0.81	−1.53
−0.54	1.71*	1.55	1.88*	1.75*	−0.41
1.41	1.40	0.87	0.91	0.01	−0.91

(*continued*)

Table 13.1

	Number of Investments			
	(1) Canada Limited Partnership Venture Capitalists	(2) Canada Corporate Venture Capitalists	(3) U.S. Limited Partnership Venture Capitalists	(4) U.S. Corporate Venture Capitalists
Convertible Preferred Shares and Debt	0 (0.00%)	1 (0.08%)	1 (0.29%)	0 (0.00%)
Convertible Preferred Shares and Convertible Debt	1 (0.04%)	1 (0.08%)	0 (0.00%)	0 (0.00%)
Convertible Preferred Shares and Warrants	15 (0.53%)	3 (0.24%)	0 (0.00%)	0 (0.00%)
Debt and Convertible Debt	1 (0.04%)	1 (0.08%)	1 (0.29%)	0 (0.00%)
Debt and Warrants	28 (0.99%)	0 (0.00%)	1 (0.29%)	0 (0.00%)
Convertible Debt and Warrants	8 (0.28%)	6 (0.48%)	0 (0.00%)	4 (0.96%)
Other Combinations of Securities or Unknown	694 (24.65%)	478 (38.39%)	94 (27.49%)	126 (20.14%)
Total	2815	1245	342	418

selected security. Table 13.1 indicates that common equity is the most frequently selected security (aside from the other/unknown category) for Canadian and U.S. limited partnership and corporate venture capital funds financing Canadian entrepreneurial firms, and a variety of other securities are used. This evidence is highly consistent with other evidence on venture capital contracts from Europe, Taiwan, and developing countries, as just discussed.

It is very striking to note that while U.S. venture capital funds finance U.S. entrepreneurs with convertible preferred equity, U.S. venture capital funds finance Canadian entrepreneurial firms with a variety of forms of finance (Table 13.1, Figures 13.2a,b). In Chapter 11, we showed that the use of a variety of forms of finance by U.S. venture capital funds for Canadian entrepreneurial firms is not attributable to the definition of *venture capital* by the stage of entrepreneurial firm development, type of industry, staging, and so forth. Likewise, U.S. venture capital funds use a variety of forms of finance and the

(continued)

Comparison of Proportions Tests					
(1) vs. (2)	(1) vs. (3)	(1) vs. (4)	(2) vs. (3)	(2) vs. (4)	(3) vs. (4)
−1.50	−2.87***	N/A	−0.98	0.58	1.11
−0.59	0.35	0.39	0.52	0.58	N/A
1.29	1.35	1.50	0.91	1.00	N/A
−0.59	−1.78*	0.39	−0.98	0.58	1.11
3.53***	1.29	2.05**	−1.91*	N/A	1.11
−0.99	0.99	−2.11**	1.29	−1.09	−1.81*
−8.15***	−1.03	−1.94*	3.40***	3.02***	−0.56

same pattern of securities as reported in Table 13.1 and Figures 13.2a,b, for investments that are not syndicated with Canadian venture capital funds.

The data in Table 13.1 and Figures 13.1 and 13.2 indicate that Canadian limited partnership venture capital funds are more likely to use common equity and convertible securities than Canadian corporate venture capital funds, whereas Canadian corporate venture capital funds are more likely to use nonconvertible debt than Canadian limited partnership venture capital funds. Similar patterns in security design are observed for cross-border U.S. limited partnership and corporate venture capital fund investments in Canadian entrepreneurial firms.

Figures 1a,b, and 2a,b, provide time series changes in the pattern of security design for the 1991 to 2004 period. Prior work explores these patterns over time and finds econometric evidence that security selection depends on four main factors (Chapter 11). First, the characteristics of the transacting parties (both the entrepreneur and the venture capital fund) affect security design.

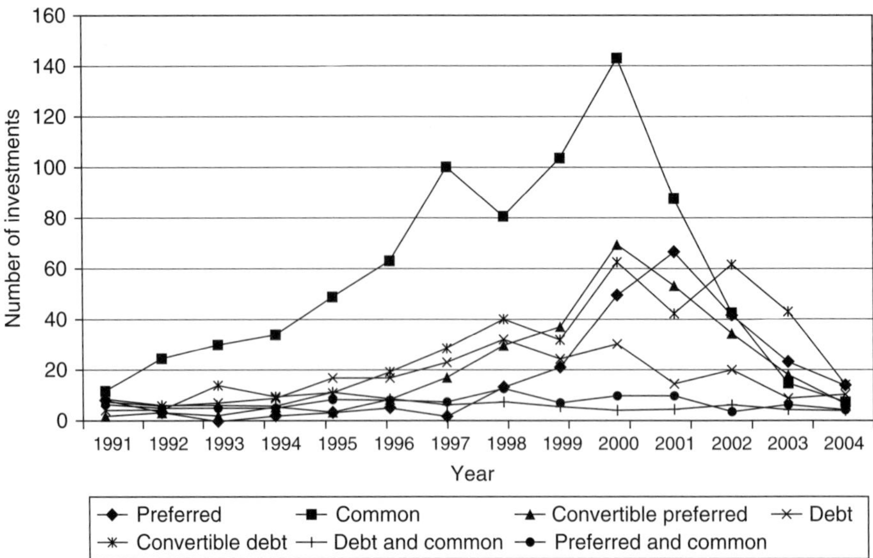

Figure 13.1a Securities Used by Canadian Limited Partnership Venture Capital Funds for Seed, Early, and Expansion Canadian Entrepreneurial Firms

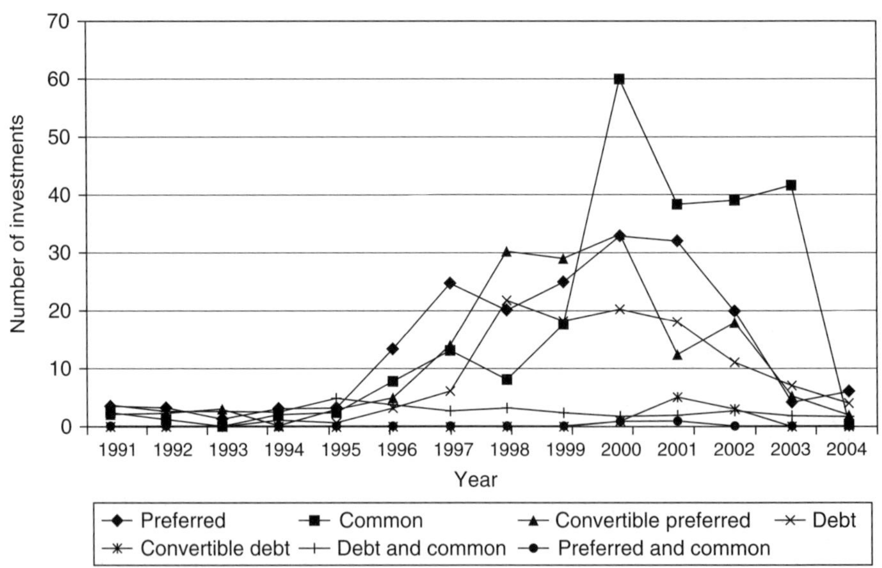

Figure 13.1b Securities Used by Canadian Corporate Venture Capital Funds for Seed, Early, and Expansion Canadian Entrepreneurial Firms

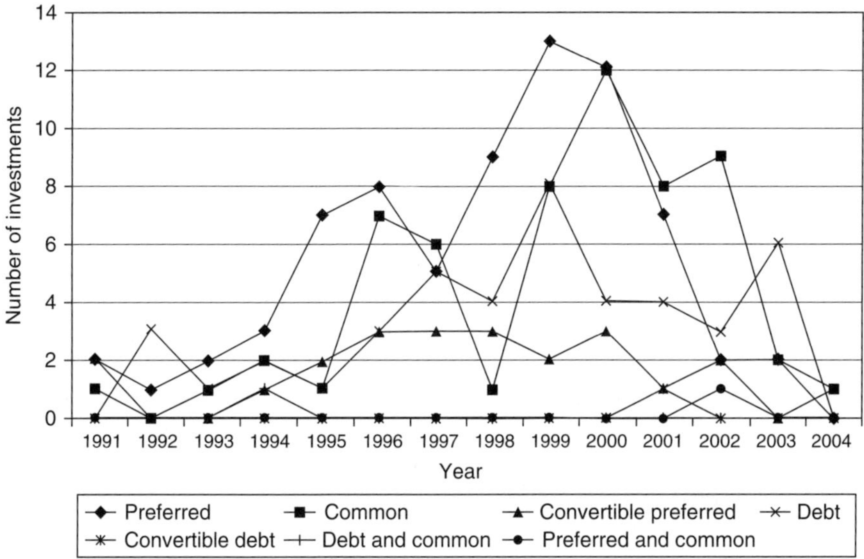

Figure 13.2a Securities Used by U.S. Limited Partnership Venture Capital Funds for Seed, Early, and Expansion Canadian Entrepreneurial Firms

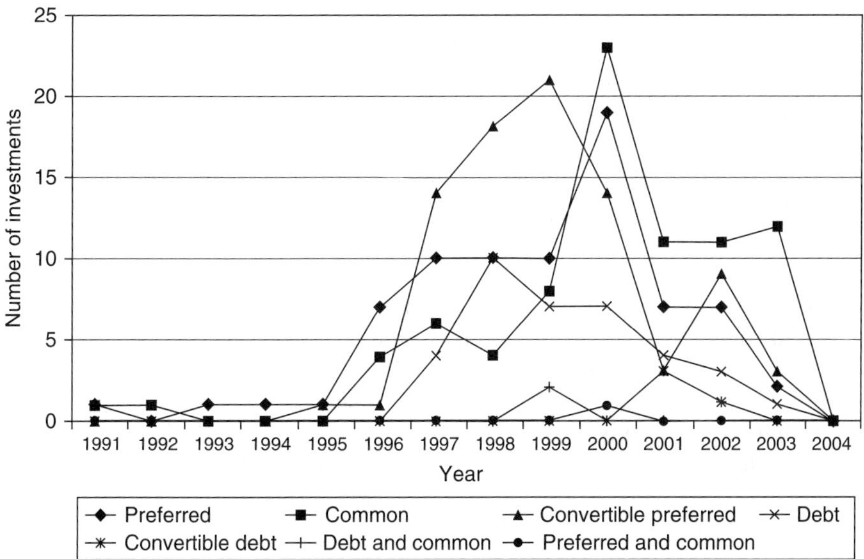

Figure 13.2b Securities Used by U.S. Corporate Venture Capital Funds for Seed, Early, and Expansion Canadian Entrepreneurial Firms

Earlier-stage high-tech firms are less likely to use securities that mandate periodic payments back to the investor prior to exit. This is intuitive, as debt-like securities are inappropriate for firms with foreseeable negative cash flows in the initial stages of development. Seed stage firms are more likely to be financed with either common equity or straight preferred equity and less likely to be financed with straight debt, convertible debt, or mixes of debt and common equity. Life science and other types of high-tech firms are more likely to be financed with convertible preferred equity. Corporate venture capital funds are less likely to use securities with upside potential, consistent with the evidence from corporate venture capital funds presented in Table 13.1 and Figures 13.1 and 13.2. Second, market conditions affect contracts. Common equity securities without downside protection are less likely to be used after the crash of the bubble, consistent with Figures 13.1 and 13.2. Third, capital gains taxation affects contracts (and in a way consistent with the work of Gilson and Schizer, just cited). Fourth, there is some evidence of learning in that time trends point to changes in the intensity of different contracts over time, but this trend is not toward the use of convertible preferred equity (at least as at 2004).

The evidence in Table 13.1 indicates that both U.S. and Canadian corporate venture capital funds are more likely to employ securities without ownership interest (that is, straight debt and/or straight preferred shares) (and see also the regression evidence in Chapter 11). The one exception to this statement is that Table 13.1 indicates U.S. limited partnership venture capital funds are more likely to use straight preferred equity than U.S. corporate venture capital funds for financing Canadian entrepreneurial firms. The most plausible explanation is that these investee firms are in different industries and financed at different points in time, consistent with prior work discussed immediately above. On a broad level, therefore, we may generally infer that corporate venture capital funds on average select investments with less upside potential, which in turn limits returns.

As just mentioned, it is important to note that Canada's venture capital market has a significant presence of government venture capital funds (Chapter 9). One may therefore worry that the securities used are at least in part attributable to the unique structure of the Canadian market. This concern, however, is mitigated by the fact that all markets around the world where venture capital fund contract data have been collected consist of securities that closely resemble the Canadian market (including Europe, Asia-Pacific, and developing countries). The outlier country in regards to venture capital security design is the United States, as it is the only country in the world whereby the market has converged on one security: convertible preferred equity.

13.4 European Corporate Venture Capital Fund Investments

Prior evidence on corporate venture capital fund contracts in Europe is limited. Schwienbacher (2003), Bascha and Walz (2007), and Kaplan et al. (2007) have data from limited partnership venture capital funds in Europe but not on corporate venture capital funds. In Chapter 14 we present data on 78 corporate and 145 noncorporate venture capital–backed firms from continental Europe. We find that 46% [44%] of corporate [noncorporate] investments are made with common equity securities, 35% [31%] of corporate [noncorporate] investments are made with convertible securities, 10% [25%] of corporate [noncorporate] investments are made with mixes of debt and preferred and common equity securities, and 9% [0%] of corporate [noncorporate] investments are made with nonconvertible preferred equity and debt securities. In regards to veto rights over asset purchases, asset sales, changes in control, and issuances of equity, corporate venture capital funds on average have one more veto right than noncorporate venture capital funds. However, only 29% of corporate venture capital fund investments allocate the right to replace the founding entrepreneur as CEO to the venture capital fund, while 46% of noncorporate venture capital fund investments allocate the right to replace the founding entrepreneur as CEO to the venture capital fund.

In brief, we show in Chapter 14 that European corporate venture capital funds are more likely to use nonconvertible preferred and debt securities than noncorporate venture capital funds. European corporate venture capital funds are also more likely to have passive veto rights. European noncorporate venture capital funds, by contrast, are more likely to have active rights such as the right to replace the founding entrepreneur as the CEO. The European corporate venture capital data are therefore consistent, within a broad level of generality, with the Canadian and U.S. corporate venture capital data introduced previously.

13.5 Venture Capital Fund Contracts, Exits, and Returns Performance

We just considered evidence indicating that corporate venture capital fund contracts are systematically different from limited partnership venture capital fund contracts. Contracts may affect performance in one of three primary ways: (1) contracts specify the division of cash flows that directly ties to venture capital fund profits, (2) contracts directly influence the actions taken by the venture capital fund(s) and the entrepreneur and thereby influence the success of the venture, and (3) contracts facilitate the exit process, which in turn relates to profits. These issues are reviewed in this section.

Prior U.S. and international evidence is highly consistent with the view that venture capital fund contracts directly influence the actions taken by venture capital fund investors. Kaplan and Strömberg (2003) argue that venture capital funds are more likely to replace CEOs when they have stronger contractual control rights. In Chapter 16 we introduce somewhat different but consistent data that measure the hours per week that venture capital fund managers spend with their entrepreneurial firms. Venture capital funds with stronger cash flow and control rights spend significantly more time with their investee companies. Similarly, countries with superior legal structures are more likely to have fewer conflicts between venture capital funds and the entrepreneurial firms due to the certainty provided by the legal system.

Theoretical research is consistent with the view that contract structures are interrelated with exit outcomes (Aghion and Bolton, 1992; Bascha and Walz, 2001; Berglöf, 1994; Hellmann, 2006). The allocation of control rights is a vital part of venture capital fund contracts, as it influences the exit outcome that may result. There are five main types of venture capital fund exit: initial public offerings (IPOs), acquisitions (in which the venture capital fund and entrepreneur both exit) to a third-party firm, secondary sales (in which the venture capital exits but the entrepreneur does not), buybacks (in which the entrepreneur repurchases the venture capital fund's shares), and liquidations (write-offs). The exit outcomes for more successful entrepreneurial firms are IPOs and acquisitions.

In the venture capital context, contracts can influence the choice between an IPO and an acquisition. The interesting issue is that the venture capital fund invariably wants the exit that gives rise to the highest financial gain, while the entrepreneur may want to go public for nonpecuniary reasons even when the financial gain from an acquisition is superior. Empirical evidence from European venture capital fund contracts is highly consistent with the view that acquisition exits are more likely to result when venture capital funds have stronger control rights, whereas IPOs are more likely when venture capital funds have weaker control rights (Chapters 20 and 21). Similarly, the data in Chapter 14 indicate that corporate venture capital funds are more likely to use a greater number of veto rights (over asset sales, asset purchases, changes in control, and issuances of equity) and more likely to use debt securities than limited partnership venture capital funds (consistent with the Canadian and U.S. data discussed in this chapter).

There is some international evidence that relates contracts to venture capital fund returns. Cumming and Walz (2004) present evidence from 3,848 venture capital funds investments in 39 developed and developing countries and show that convertible preferred equity or convertible debt contracts yield higher returns (discussed further in Chapter 22). Kaplan et al. (2007) provide consistent evidence on the survival of venture capital funds based on 145 venture capital fund investments from 23 developed countries but do not have data on returns; rather, that paper argues that venture capital fund survival is more likely where venture capital funds use convertible preferred equity. The 3,848 observations in the Cumming and Walz (2004) dataset indicate that convertible securities are correlated with greater returns. Notice that Cumming and Walz use a functional definition of convertible securities: those that actually allow for periodic cash flows back to the venture capital fund prior to venture capital fund exit and for the possibility of upside potential. The data are summarized in Figure 13.3. The average [median] return for convertible security investments (convertible preferred equity and convertible debt) is 61.89% [15.68%] (net of the MSCI index over the contemporaneous investment

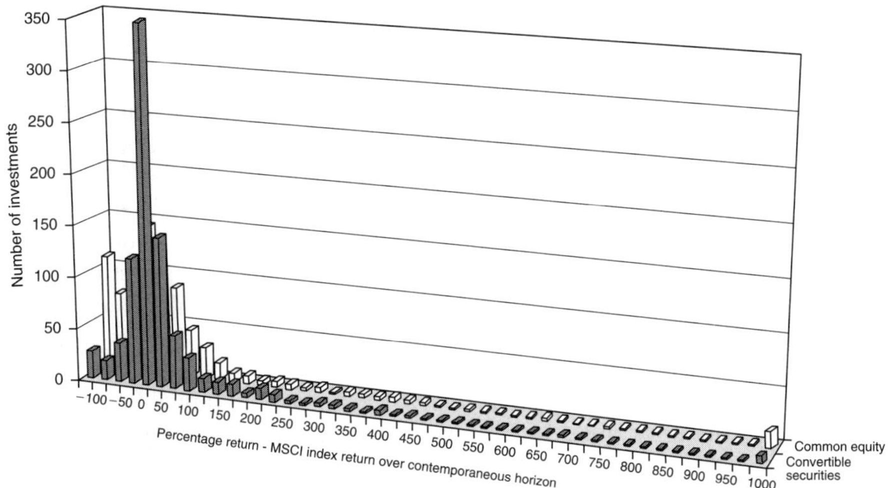

Figure 13.3 Histogram of Returns by Type of Security from 39 Countries, 1971–2003, for Start-up, Early-, and Expansion Stage Venture Capital Investments

horizon), while the average [median] return for common equity investments is 50.11% [−24.37%]. The evidence is thus consistent with theoretical work that convertible securities are comparatively more efficient for venture capital fund investments in terms of facilitating higher returns. This issue is considered in further detail in Part V.

Overall, therefore, prior evidence is highly consistent that contracts are interconnected with returns (Chapters 14, 19–22). Corporate venture capital funds are more likely to use contracts that do not involve upside potential and are more likely to use veto rights than limited partnership venture capital funds. As contracts influence the division of cash flow and control rights, influence incentives, and affect the exit process, it is natural to expect contracts to be related to returns. While there is no direct evidence on point, we may expect that based on prior work and the data introduced in this chapter that part of the reason that corporate venture capital returns lag behind those of limited partnership venture capital funds is in fact related to the differences in the contracts that these different fund types employ.

13.6 Lessons for Corporations Setting Up Venture Capital Funds

Prior evidence has shown that corporate venture capital funds are much more unstable organizations whereby the existence of the corporate venture capital entity within the firm depends on the willingness of head office to which the corporate venture capital fund belongs. Hence, even apparently successful corporate venture capital funds, such as that within Dell, often are abandoned earlier than that which would otherwise be optimal (Gompers and Lerner, 1999). Corporate venture capital fund managers do not enjoy the same incentive compensation arrangements as those offered to limited partnership venture capital funds. Limited partnership venture capital fund managers typically receive 1 to 2% fixed fees based on the size of the fund and 20% of the profits of the fund, which can result in enormous salaries and bonuses if the fund successfully exits investments via IPOs or acquisitions. Corporate venture capital funds, by contrast, typically do not enjoy such performance fees to maintain a level fee structure across different units of the overall corporate enterprise. The U.S. and Canadian corporate venture capital data just discussed indicated that corporate venture capital fund managers write contracts that more often focus on downside protection than upside potential, relative to limited partnership venture capital funds.

Corporate venture capital funds invest in a narrower range of firms that have technological promise in the industry in which the parent firm operates. To this end, a corporate venture capital fund's choice set is more limited, their investments are less diversified, and their strategic investing incentives could lead to financial contracting practices (such as veto rights, etc.) that uniquely focus on maintaining technology transfer to the corporation associated with the corporate venture capital fund.

Corporations considering setting up corporate venture capital funds should consider providing as much autonomy as possible to their corporate venture capital fund managers, as long as the corporate venture capital fund maintains its strategic direction established at the outset of the fund. The instability of corporate venture capital funds may inhibit the ability of corporate venture capital fund managers to learn which contracts do and do not work best for the types of firms that they finance. Further, corporate venture capital funds that are viewed as mere employees of the larger corporation may lack the incentives to write incentive contracts and allocate control rights for the corporate venture capital fund and their investee entrepreneurial firms in ways that are in the best interest of the corporate investor. Corporate venture capital funds should provide fund managers with incentives to write the most efficient contracts to achieve the financial and strategic directions of the fund.

13.7 Concluding Remarks and Future Research

The returns to limited partnership venture capital fund investments are widely regarded as being on average greater than the returns to corporate venture capital fund investments. Prior research is consistent with the view that the returns to corporate venture capital fund investments are lower than the returns to limited partnership venture capital fund investments due to (1) the comparatively autonomous structure of limited partnership venture capital funds relative to corporate venture capital funds, (2) the pay structures of limited partnership venture capital funds relative to corporate venture capital funds, and (3) the strategic rationales associated with corporate investing. In this chapter we explored the possibility of a fourth factor: Corporate venture capital funds are less adept at writing efficient contracts with their investee entrepreneurial firms, thereby giving rise to lower returns.

In this chapter, we examined the full range of literature on venture capital fund contracts from around the world. The literature showed that venture capital funds in the United States often use convertible preferred equity, while venture capital funds in other countries sometimes use convertible preferred equity but that is not the most commonly selected form of finance; rather, common equity is the most frequently selected form of venture capital finance in all countries around the world outside the United States. In the United States, there is a tax bias in favor of the use of convertible preferred equity.

We provided new data in this chapter from U.S. and corporate and limited venture capital cross-border investments in Canadian entrepreneurial firms, as well as Canadian corporate and limited partnership venture capital investments in Canadian entrepreneurial firms. The data indicate that convertible preferred equity investments are not the most frequently selected security by U.S. corporate or limited partnership venture capital funds investing in Canadian entrepreneurs, and likewise not by Canadian corporate and limited partnership venture capital funds investing domestically in Canada. A variety of forms of finance are used. We noted, however, that U.S. and Canadian corporate venture capital funds have a greater propensity to use nonconvertible debt, while U.S. and Canadian limited partnership venture capital funds are more likely to use common equity and convertible securities.

Companion evidence presented in this chapter from limited partnership venture capital funds indicated investments with convertible securities yield higher average returns than straight common equity. We also discussed related evidence from European venture capital fund contracts that indicate corporate venture capital fund contracts involve greater control rights and less upside potential. This European evidence also indicates corporate venture capital funds are more likely to have acquisition exits and lower returns.

At this stage, the extent to which lower corporate venture capital returns are attributable to their financial contracts with their entrepreneurial firms, or whether this is due to organizational structure or pay for performance sensitivities, is unknown. It is also possible, if not probable, that corporate venture capital funds select their contracts as a result of their organizational structure and their mix of strategic and financial incentives. Future research could more directly examine the returns of corporate venture capital funds in relation to their organizational structure in direct comparison to their financial contracts. Further research could also examine in greater detail the issue of whether contracts affect returns, or if there is a reverse causality insofar as different contracts are used for different expected returns. To date, comparatively little evidence exists from U.S. corporate venture capital fund contracts, and future research could fill this gap and examine how patterns of corporate venture capital fund contracts evolve over time.

Key Terms

Corporate venture capital
Limited partnership venture capital
Financial contracts
Debt
Convertible debt
Preferred equity
Convertible preferred equity
Common equity
Warrants

Discussion Questions

13.1. True/False/Uncertain and explain why: "Corporate venture capital underperformance relative to limited partnerships is attributable to the comparative lack of autonomy of corporate venture capital funds."

13.2. True/False/Uncertain and explain why: "U.S. corporate venture capital funds are more likely to use convertible preferred equity than Canadian corporate venture capital funds."

13.3. True/False/Uncertain and explain why: "Corporate venture capital funds are more likely to use nonconvertible preferred equity and/or nonconvertible debt than limited partnership venture capital funds, which suggests they are less sophisticated and will have worse performance."

13.4. List and explain four reasons why limited partnership venture capital fund performance may differ from corporate venture capital fund performance. Describe how a corporation setting up a venture capital division may efficiently structure the fund to maximize returns.

13.5. As an entrepreneur, would you prefer funding from a limited partnership venture capital fund or a corporate venture capital fund? Why?

14 Preplanned Exits and Contract Design

14.1 Introduction and Learning Objectives

Venture capital contracts govern long-term relations between entrepreneurs and their investors in a way that establishes cash flow and control rights. The long-term nature of venture capitalist-entrepreneur relationships leaves entrepreneurs open to exploitation by venture capitalists (Atanasov et al., 2006; Fried and Ganor, 2006) and venture capitalists open to expropriation by entrepreneurs (Casamatta, 2003; Kaplan and Strömberg, 2003; Schmidt, 2003). It is therefore natural for contracts to depend on the bargaining power of venture capitalists and the entrepreneurs, as well as the legal environment that governs the relationships between the parties. Further, as high-tech start-up entrepreneurial firms do not have cash flows to pay interest on debt or dividends on equity, contracts are established in a way that control rights are allocated over exit decisions (Black and Gilson, 1998; Sahlman, 1990; for related theoretical work, see Aghion and Bolton, 1992; Bascha and Walz, 2001; Berglöf, 1994; Neus and Walz, 2005; Schwienbacher, 2002). A successful exit may involve an initial public offering (IPO), or an acquisition (i.e., trade sale). While previous research in venture capital has identified international differences in both financial contracts and exit strategies, the precise interaction between contracts and exits has not been directly studied in empirical work. Further, empirical analyses of venture capital contracts have not fully considered international differences in venture capital contracts in relation to venture capitalist-entrepreneur bargaining power, preplanned exit strategies, and law quality. It is particularly important to consider non-U.S. evidence, as legal scholarship is consistent with the view that tax law biases U.S. venture capital contracts toward the use of convertible preferred shares (Gilson and Schizer, 2003).

In this chapter we will do the following:

- In a multicountry setting, empirically consider specific contractual terms used by venture capitalists, including security design (common equity, preferred equity, debt, convertible preferred equity, convertible debt), veto rights over asset sales, veto rights over asset purchases, veto rights over changes in control, veto rights over issuances of equity, the right to replace the CEO, rights of first refusal at sale, cosale agreement, drag-along rights, antidilution protection, protection rights against new issues, redemption rights, information rights, IPO registration rights, and contingencies in contracts (financial performance, nonfinancial performance, certain actions, default on dividend or redemption payment, future securities offerings, and founder remaining with firm)

- Consider how preplanned exit strategies influence contract design
- Consider how bargaining power influences contract design
- Consider how legal conditions influence contract design

In particular, this chapter develops three primary themes that facilitate our theoretical and empirical understanding of how entrepreneurial firms and venture capital investors write financial contracts. First, we empirically investigate the role of "preplanned" exit strategies at the time of contracting in the formation of ownership and control rights in venture capital contracts. A preplanned exit strategy is a reasonable expectation that the investor will want to dispose of the entrepreneurial investment either by IPO or acquisition (trade sale) and this expectation is formed prior to contracting with the entrepreneur. This expectation need not be revealed to the entrepreneur, and if it is revealed, it need not be fully revealed. Notice that the preplanned exit strategy is not part of the contract; rather, it is a strategy that affects the contract design. Second, we empirically examine the role of legal conditions in driving contract choices across a sample of 11 continental European countries, with a focus on antidirector rights and creditor rights. Third, we empirically study the influence of bargaining power of both the entrepreneur and the investor in the allocation of cash flow and control rights. The three themes developed and empirically studied in this chapter are not only complementary but also essential to reconciling a growing divergence in understanding financial contracting in venture capital in the academic literature. That is, the vast majority of theoretical work in venture capital contracting is based on empirical data from the United States, and U.S. tax laws significantly bias the choice of contract structure toward convertible preferred equity (Gilson and Schizer, 2003). Further, no prior study (based on U.S. data and/or international data) has considered the role of preplanned exit strategies and the bargaining power of *both* the venture capitalist and the entrepreneur in contract formation.

This chapter analyzes a hand-collected dataset involving 223 entrepreneurial firms from 35 European venture capital funds from 11 continental European countries over the period 1995–2002. Our data enable a first consideration (from any country) of how contract structure and preplanned exits are interrelated. The data indicate exit is often preplanned as either an IPO or an acquisition at the time of contracting. Venture capitalists preplanned either an IPO or an acquisition exit in 70 of 223 entrepreneurial firms (31%) in which they invested. There are 25 preplanned IPOs and 45 preplanned acquisitions; for the remainder of the investments, the venture capitalists did not have a reasonable expectation as to whether exit would be either as an IPO or an acquisition at the time of initial contract. We stress in this chapter the difference between *preplanned* exits (at the time of contract) versus *actual* exits (eventual performance in later years). Only 19% (6/32) of the actual IPOs were preplanned IPOs, and only 36% (27/74) of the actual acquisitions were preplanned acquisitions. In this chapter we do not study the factors that affect actual exit and returns performance in this chapter; that issue is considered in Chapters 20 and 21. In this chapter we focus on the relation between preplanned exits and contract formation by making use of data which comprises unique details on the investors' preplanned exit strategy prior to the time of contracting.

This chapter begins with a brief descriptive theory that outlines testable hypotheses. Data are introduced, and summary statistics and comparison tests are presented. We provide estimates from ordered logit models of the determinants of security design, veto, and control rights and discuss limitations and future research.

14.2 Hypotheses

Prior work has identified a number of potential factors that could affect the allocation of ownership and control rights in private investment contracts. For example, theoretical work has identified the role of bilateral moral hazard and adverse selection (Casamatta, 2003; Kirilenko, 2001; Schmidt, 2003), exit strategies (Aghion and Bolton, 1992; Bascha and Walz, 2001a; Berglöf, 1994; Black and Gilson, 1998), and the inalienability of human capital (Hart and More, 1994). Empirical studies have considered tests of these theoretical models (Gompers, 1998; Kaplan and Strömberg, 2003), as well as the role of legality in affecting private investment contracts (Kaplan et al., 2007; Lerner and Schoar, 2005). More important, however, empirical work has not directly tested the role of preplanned exits in venture capital contract formation. Therefore, we focus the development of testable hypotheses around the ways in which preplanned exits could play a role in shaping venture capital contract formation. Thereafter we discuss the role of law quality and bargaining power in influencing contract formation, as well as other control variables. The data and empirical tests follow in the subsequent sections.

14.2.1 Preplanned Exits and Venture Capital Contracts

Venture capitalists typically invest in entrepreneurial firms for two to seven years prior to an exit event. The two fundamental exit routes for successful entrepreneurial firms backed by venture capitalists are IPOs and acquisitions (Gompers and Lerner, 1999; Sahlman, 1990). There exists other exit routes, including buybacks (in which the entrepreneur repurchases the venture capitalist's shares) and secondary sales (in which the venture capitalist sells to another investor but the entrepreneur does not sell), as well as write-offs (also referred to as liquidations). These other exit routes, however, facilitate much lower profits upon exit (Gompers and Lerner, 1999, 2001); therefore, venture capitalists preplan their exit outcomes only as IPOs or acquisitions.

In our empirical analyses in this chapter we identify cases in which the venture capitalist has developed a clear strategy as either a preplanned IPO or a preplanned acquisition. (Notice that venture capitalists that did not specifically preplan either an IPO or an acquisition at the time of investment still always hoped for one of these outcomes.) This preplanned exit strategy is formed at the time of investment and before contract formation. The venture capitalist's preplanned exit strategy need not be revealed to the entrepreneur at the time of investment, although it could be revealed to show the good intention of the venture capitalist to develop the firm to its full potential. The preplanned exit strategy is not part of the contract. A central interest in this chapter is the study of the relation between contract formation and preplanned IPOs versus preplanned acquisitions.

A primary reason why the venture capitalist's preplanned exit strategy affects contracts is that, at the time of actual exit, venture capitalists are financial intermediaries between the entrepreneurial firm and the new owners (public shareholders in the event of an IPO, and the acquiring firm in the event of an acquisition). Venture capitalists facilitate two roles: (1) add value through active assistance provided to the entrepreneurial firm, including strategic, financial and marketing advice, as well as facilitate a network of contacts with legal and accounting advisors, investment banks, and suppliers (see Gompers and Lerner, 1999; Lockett and Wright, 2001; Manigart et al., 1996; Sahlman, 1990); and (2) certify the quality of the entrepreneurial firm to the new owners (Barry et al., 1990; Gompers and Lerner, 1999; Lerner, 1994; Megginson and Weiss, 1991; Neus and Walz, 2005). Through both roles, the sale price of the entrepreneurial firm is higher by virtue of the presence of the venture capitalist.

In theory, it is natural to expect the allocation of control and decision rights between an investor and entrepreneur to depend on a preplanned IPO versus a preplanned acquisition (Aghion and Bolton, 1992; Bascha and Walz, 2001; Berglöf, 1994; Hellmann, 2006; Neus and Walz, 2005; Zingales, 1995). Contractual governance between a private investor and an entrepreneur exists on a variety of dimensions, including security design, veto and control rights (such as the right to replace the founding entrepreneur as CEO, drag-along rights, cosale agreements, and veto rights over asset sales/purchases, changes in control and issuances of equity). Our hand-collected dataset contains information on all of these details and more.

In practice, there are two possible avenues through which preplanned exit strategies may influence contract formation. First, consider a situation in which the venture capitalist forms a preplanned exit strategy but does not reveal this strategy (or at least does not fully reveal this information) to the entrepreneur at the time of contract negotiation. The incentive for a venture capitalist to not reveal the information to the entrepreneur might be associated with preplanned acquisition exits for the following reasons. The acquisition exit is generally deemed to be the second best form of exit, with the IPO being the most preferred in terms of upside potential. More significantly, in an acquisition exit, the entrepreneur is effectively ousted from the firm as the CEO (Black and Gilson, 1998). Entrepreneurs most often find this permanent ousting out of the firm they founded to be a terribly emotional event (even described as some entrepreneurs as equivalent to the breakdown of a marriage; see Petty et al.,

1999). Many entrepreneurs are therefore reluctant to agree to an acquisition exit. As such, we conjecture that venture capitalists preplanning acquisition exits negotiate for stronger control rights in anticipation of a need to force the entrepreneur to acquiesce to an acquisition. A venture capitalist may not inform the entrepreneur about a preplanned acquisition if there is concern that the entrepreneur is reluctant to agree with the acquisition. Rather, the venture capitalist might indicate to the entrepreneur that the control rights are required by the venture capitalist for other reasons unrelated to exits, such as the risk of investing in a high-tech industry, and/or the comparative dearth of entrepreneur managerial track experience relative to that of the venture capitalist.

There are also cases where the venture capitalist preplans an exit route and does inform the entrepreneur about this strategy. An entrepreneur may rationally agree to acquiesce control rights to the venture capitalist to facilitate the acquisition exit, such that the control rights in the hands of the venture capitalist enhance the sale price of the entrepreneurial firm upon exit. The intuition is as follows. Entrepreneurs make decisions during the early life of the enterprise that have effects that are not manifest until much later in the life of the enterprise—after much of the residual claim has been sold by the entrepreneur. The implications of the decisions for future cash flows will not be observable at the time of exit. The entrepreneur's own interest in some of these decisions does not coincide with the long-term interest of the eventual owners of the firm. That is, there is an agency, or hidden action, problem in managerial decisions. A rational capital market, even where it cannot *directly* observe the future cash flow implications of past entrepreneurial decisions at the time of purchase of the residual claim, will infer that the entrepreneur's decisions were in her self-interest. The market will discount the value of the residual claim accordingly to the extent that past decisions were under control of the entrepreneur. In an acquisition exit (where the entrepreneur is effectively ousted from the firm, as discussed), the degree to which the entrepreneur's decisions early in the life of a firm are in conflict with the long-term eventual new owners of the firm will be more pronounced than in the case of an IPO exit (where the entrepreneur regains control over the enterprise). The venture capitalist and entrepreneur therefore rationally agree to allocate control rights to the venture capitalist in the initial agreement to maximize the expected value of the firm at the time of actual exit. If the entrepreneur does not want to give up control rights to the venture capitalist due to the loss of entrepreneur private benefits, it is much less likely that the firm will get financed. Firms will get financed where the venture capitalist can compensate the entrepreneur for the loss of private benefits in situations where the venture capitalist reveals the preplanned acquisition strategy to the entrepreneur.

If enhanced credibility in the "foundational value" of the enterprise at exit were the only effect of venture capital control rights, then the venture capitalist would simply be assigned all rights within the venture capitalist-entrepreneur contract. But of course there are offsetting advantages to the assignment of rights to the entrepreneur. These advantages reside in the entrepreneur's informational advantage over the venture capitalist in the day-to-day operations of the enterprise. An efficiency cost is incurred whenever rights are assigned within an organization to agents not in position of best information. The allocation of rights as between the entrepreneur and the venture capitalist is based on a trade-off between the enhanced credibility of foundational value in assigning the rights to the venture capitalist (which we term the credibility value of venture capitalist control rights) and the use of the entrepreneur's superior information in decisions for which rights are assigned to her. We therefore include control variables in our empirical tests (described following).

More important, notice that our data identify the preplanned exit at the time of contract formation. We do not test the relation between the actual exit outcome and the contract in our empirical tests (although we do provide some statistics comparing preplanned to actual exits in the subsequent sections of the chapter). The relation between contracts and actual exits is studied in Chapters 20 and 21.

14.2.2 Law Quality and Bargaining Power in Contract Formation

As indicated in Lerner and Schoar (2005; see also Kaplan et al., 2007; McCahery and Vermeulen, 2004), contracts are expected to vary by the quality of the laws in the country of investment. On the one hand, contracts can substitute for poor legal protections offered in a country so more detailed contracts may be found in countries with lower quality laws (as found in Lerner and Schoar, 2005). On the other hand, law quality can facilitate contract enforcement and give rise to more detailed contracts (as found in Bottazzi et al., 2005). We add to the body of empirical evidence in this chapter by providing additional data from a sample of continental European countries.

Investor and investee sophistication may play an equally important role in influencing contract formation given the correspondence between sophistication to bargaining power, and our data offer a unique assessment of sophistication. Consistent with theoretical work on the importance of bilateral moral hazard in shaping venture capital contracts (Casamatta, 2003; Cornelli and Yosha, 2003; Schmidt, 2003; see also Hsu, 2004, for somewhat related empirical evidence showing more sophisticated investors obtain better deal prices), we expect more sophisticated investors to have more control and veto rights and to use convertible securities for reasons of providing advice and monitoring to the investee. Conversely, and for similar reasons, we expect more sophisticated entrepreneurs to be financed with common equity and be faced with fewer veto and control rights imposed by their investors.

A number of different venture capitalist and entrepreneurial firm characteristics can affect contractual allocation of control and ownership rights, such as the type of investor (captive or limited partnership), the industry and stage of development of the entrepreneur, the entrepreneur's capital requirements, and economic conditions (both across countries and across time). The new dataset introduced following enables controls for each of these categories of variables.

14.3 Data

The data come from 223 entrepreneurial firms financed by 35 venture capital funds over the period 1995–2002 in 11 continental European countries: Austria (10 firms), Belgium (12 firms), Czech (5 firms), Denmark (11 firms), France (6 firms), Germany (50 firms), Italy (23 firms), the Netherlands (73 firms), Poland (12 firms), Portugal (6 firms), and Switzerland (15 firms). As discussed in this section, the important and unique new element in the data considered herein is in illustrating the role of preplanned exit strategies in affecting contracts, which has not been considered in any prior empirical paper on venture capital and private equity contracts.[1]

The data were obtained primarily by surveys and interviews with venture capital fund managers. In some cases, we obtained actual contracts. However, language was a significant barrier with the use of actual contracts from a diverse sample of European countries. In most cases the contracts were not written in English. As such, to properly read and understand the components of the contracts, survey and interview techniques were used. Moreover, as we incorporate information that is not part of the contract in studying the formation of contracts (including measures of entrepreneurial sophistication, and preplanned exit strategies), it was absolutely necessary to use survey and interview techniques to gather the details in the data considered herein.

The information collected from the 35 funds in our dataset is strictly confidential and not publicly available. Data were disclosed on a completely voluntary basis. Given the type of confidential information collected, naturally we cannot refer to an aggregate industry database for comparison. We can point out that our sample is similar to prior international datasets on the frequency of use of different securities (see, e.g., Hege et al., 2003; Kaplan et al., 2007; Lerner and Schoar, 2005; Schwienbacher, 2003). The scope of these other hand-collected venture capital datasets (Hege et al., 2003; Kaplan and Strömberg, 2003; Kaplan et al., 2007; Lerner and Schoar, 2005; Schwienbacher, 2003) is also very similar to our own, in terms of details and number of observations, and the frequency of use of particular contracts is similar to that reported in this study, accounting for institutional differences between the United States and Europe. The most notable institutional difference between Europe and the United States, in terms of private investor contractual governance, is in the use of convertible securities in the United States (Bergemann and Hege, 1998; Gompers, 1998; Kaplan and Strömberg, 2003; Sahlman, 1990). Tax considerations are one explanation for the dominant use

[1]Bascha and Walz (2007) and Kaplan et al. (2007) empirically study the relation between contracts and actual exits but do not have details in respect of preplanned exits. Schwienbacher (2003) and Hege et al. (2003) have some details on contracts, but these details are averaged at the fund level for all portfolio firms, and they do not have details on preplanned exits. This work is the first to have considered empirical details on the preplanned exit strategy at the time of contracting.

of convertibles in the United States (Gilson and Schizer, 2003). That there is much heterogeneity in contract choices within each fund and across funds in this dataset renders the analysis herein relevant and interesting; in fact, to test the propositions herein it is necessary to omit U.S. data.

The variables used in the empirical tests are defined and summarized in Table 14.1, Panel A. Table 14.1, Panel B, provides definitions of terms commonly found in venture capital contracts, which independently allocate cash flow and control rights (Gompers, 1998; Kaplan and Strömberg, 2003). Veto rights are passive rights that can be used to prevent certain actions taken by the board of directors and put to the shareholders for a vote. Veto rights typically cover issues relating to asset sales, asset purchases, changes in control, and issuances of equity. Veto rights may be used as threat points in negotiation and hence could influence the exit outcome; venture capitalists that preplan acquisition exits and anticipate a potential conflict of interest with the entrepreneur may therefore seek additional veto rights. Control rights, by contrast, are proactive rights that enable the holder to bring about a change in the direction of the firm because they give the investors the right to take a particular action as a residual right of control. As such, it is likely that a venture capitalist that preplans an acquisition exit will seek stronger control rights in anticipation of a potential conflict of interests with the entrepreneur at the time of sale. To this end, perhaps the most effective control right in incomplete contracting theories, like Aghion and Bolton (1992), is the right to replace the CEO. Venture capitalists typically have the right to replace the founding entrepreneur as CEO, where they have a majority of the board or a majority of the voting rights.[2] Investors may also be able to force an acquisition through other measures of residual rights of control, and, generally speaking, not all control rights are equally effective. Drag-along rights, by definition, can be particularly effective in bringing about the exit desired by the venture capitalist. Also, redemption rights can be effective in forcing an acquisition, particularly where entrepreneurs are not in a financial position to redeem the venture capitalist's shares. Antidilution rights give venture capitalists more bargaining power over sequential financing rounds, lead to a larger dilution of entrepreneurial control, and thus are useful for the venture capitalist to retain control and bring about a preplanned exit outcome. Analogous to veto rights for changes in control, a cosale right and a right of first refusal give investors protection if the *entrepreneur* tries to sell the firm in part or whole to a new owner and thus can be used as threat points in negotiation. Also, an IPO registration right can be used as a threat point in negotiation where the

[2]For this reason we do not independently report statistics for majority board seats and majority voting rights; the results were not materially different than that reported for the right to replace the founding entrepreneur as the CEO. Automatic conversion rights from preferred equity to common equity are not separately considered in the list of control rights because this right is not used to force a particular exit strategy but rather it is a precommitment by the venture capitalist to give up control rights upon a sufficiently valuable exit.

Table 14.1 Panel A Variable Definitions

This table defines each of the variables used in the text and subsequent tables in the chapter. The data are from Germany, the Czech Republic, the Netherlands, Switzerland, Italy, Denmark, France, Belgium, Poland, Austria, and Portugal. The contract terms were primarily gathered by surveys and interviews with the investors. The contracts (for the majority of the investments) were not written in English, and therefore they could not be interpreted by the authors without the use of surveys and interviews.

Variable	Definition
Preplanned Exit Strategy	
Preplanned IPO	A dummy variable equal to one if, at the time of investment and writing the contract, the investor had a reasonable expectation that the investment would be exited via an IPO. The investor may or may not have informed the investee that the anticipated exit strategy was an IPO. If the investor preplanned an acquisition exit, or did not have a preplanned exit strategy (either a preplanned IPO or preplanned acquisition), then this variable takes the value zero. Preplanned IPOs are distinct from actual IPOs (i.e., preplanned IPOs are distinct from how the investment turned out). The preplanned exit is a strategy, and not part of the contract.
Preplanned Acquisition	A dummy variable equal to one if, at the time of investment and writing the contract, the investor had a reasonable expectation that the investment would be exited via an acquisition (sometimes referred to as a "trade sale" in practice). The investor may or may not have informed the investee that the anticipated exit strategy was an acquisition. If the investor preplanned an IPO exit, or did not have a preplanned exit strategy (either a preplanned IPO or preplanned acquisition), then this variable takes the value zero. Preplanned acquisitions are distinct from actual IPOs (i.e., preplanned acquisitions are distinct from how the investment turned out). The preplanned exit is a strategy, and not part of the contract.
Market Conditions and Institutional Variables	
Legality Index	Weighted average of following legal factors of the country in which the entrepreneur is based (based on Berkowitz et al., 2003, and La Porta et al., 1998): efficiency of judicial system, rule of law, corruption, risk of expropriation, risk of contract repudiation, shareholder rights. Higher numbers indicate "better" legal systems. See Table 3.1.

(*continued*)

Table 14.1 (*continued*)

Variable	Definition
Anti-director Rights	An index aggregating the shareholder rights from La Porta et al. (1998). The index is formed by adding 1 when (1) the country allows shareholders to mail their proxy vote to the firm, (2) shareholders are not required to deposit their shares prior to the general shareholders' meeting, (3) cumulative voting or proportional representation of minorities in the board of directors is allowed, (4) an oppressed minorities mechanism is in place, (5) the minimum percentage of share capital that entitles a shareholder to call for an extraordinary shareholders' meeting is less than or equal to 10% (the sample median), or (6) shareholders have pre-emptive rights that can be waived only by a shareholders' vote.
Creditor Rights	An index aggregating different creditor rights from La Porta et al. (1998). The index is formed by adding 1 when (1) the country imposes restrictions, such as creditors' consent or minimum dividends to file for reorganization; (2) secured creditors are able to gain possession of their security once the reorganization petition has been approved (no automatic stay); (3) secured creditors are ranked first in the distribution of the proceeds that result from the disposition of the assets of a bankrupt firm; and (4) the debtor does not retain the administration of its property pending the resolution of the reorganization.
GNP per Capita	The GNP per capita of the country in which the entrepreneur is based.
Legal Origin Variables	Dummy variables equal to one for legal origin from La Porta et al. (1998), including German, Socialist, and Scandinavian (a dummy variable equal to one for French legal origin is suppressed to avoid collinearity; there are no countries of English legal origin in the data).
Investor and Investee Characteristics	
Captive Fund	A dummy variable equal to one if the fund is a captive fund. A captive fund is one that is affiliated with a bank or corporation.
Capital Managed/ Manager	The total amount of capital (in 2003 euros) for the specific fund within the investor's organization that provided data for this study, and divided by the number of venture capital fund managers employed by the fund.
Industry Market/Book	The industry market/book ratio for the industry in which the entrepreneurial firm operates.
Book Value	The value of the investors' investments in the entrepreneurial firm (in 2003 euros).

(*continued*)

Table 14.1 (*continued*)

Variable	Definition
Early-stage Investee	A dummy variable equal to zero if the entrepreneurial firm was a late-stage or buyout transaction, and one if the firm was an early- or expansion stage firm. More specific categories are not used since there are differences in definitions of investment stages across countries.
Entrepreneur Experience Rank	A subjective ranking provided by the investor about the entrepreneur's ability and experience. The ranking was provided at the time of data collection, not at the time of actual investment, but was asked as the ranking from the perspective at the time of investment. The ranking was done on a scale of 1 to 10.
Transaction Characteristics	
Sum of Veto Rights	Sum of the following veto rights used in the contract with the entrepreneur: asset sales, asset purchases, changes in control, issuance of equity, any other decisions (see Table 14.1, Panel B).
Sum of Control Rights	Sum of the following control rights used in the contract with the entrepreneur: right to replace CEO, right for first refusal at sale, co-sale agreement, drag-along rights, antidilution protection, protection rights against new issues, redemption rights, information rights, and IPO registration rights (see Table 14.1, Panel B).
Common Equity	A dummy variable equal to one where the venture capitalist uses common equity to finance the entrepreneurial firm.
Convertible Preferred Equity	A dummy variable equal to one where the venture capitalist uses convertible preferred equity (and functional equivalents, such as convertible debt) to finance the entrepreneurial firm.
Mix of Common and Preferred Equity	A dummy variable equal to one where the venture capitalist uses common equity with preferred equity and/or debt to finance the entrepreneurial firm.
Debt	A dummy variable equal to one where the venture capitalist uses nonconvertible debt and/or nonconvertible preferred equity to finance the entrepreneurial firm.
Prior Round	A dummy variable equal to one if there was at least one round of venture capitalist investment prior to observing the venture capitalist proving the data in this dataset.

(*continued*)

Table 14.1 *(continued)*

Panel B. Definitions of Specific Terms Used in Venture Capital Contracts

This table describes specific terms used in typical venture capital contracts. Contract terms are categorized into three areas: security design, veto rights, and control rights. Contract terms are independently negotiated and may or may not be used in conjunction with others.

Variable	Definition
Security	
Common Equity	Securities representing equity ownership in a corporation, providing voting rights, entitling the holder to a share of the company's success through dividends and/or capital appreciation. In the event of liquidation, common stockholders have rights to a company's assets only after debt holders and preferred stockholders have been satisfied.
Preferred Equity	Capital stock that takes precedence over common equity in the event of bankruptcy, and provides that prespecified dividends are paid before any dividends are paid to common equity. Preferred dividends are fixed and do not fluctuate. Preferred equity holders cannot force the company into bankruptcy in the event of nonpayment of dividends, but must pay all preferred dividends in arrears prior to paying dividends to common equity holders.
Debt	An amount owed to a person or organization for funds borrowed. Companies that fail to pay interest on debt can be forced into bankruptcy by debt holders.
Convertible Preferred Equity	Preferred equity that can be converted into a specified amount of common equity at the holder's option.
Convertible Debt	Debt that can be converted into a specified amount of common stock at the holder's option.
Veto Rights	
Asset Sales	The holder can prevent the board from raising the issue or resolution of asset sales at the shareholder level.
Asset Purchases	The holder can prevent the board from raising the issue or resolution of asset purchases at the shareholder level.
Changes in Control	The holder can prevent the board from raising the issue or resolution of changes in control of the company at the shareholder level.
Issuances of Equity	The holder can prevent the board from raising the issue or resolution of issuing new equity at the shareholder level.

(continued)

Table 14.1 (*continued*)

Variable	Definition
Other Decisions	The holder can prevent the board from raising any particular issue or resolution at the shareholder level. For example, these issues include, but are not limited to, hiring key personnel, external consultants, legal and accounting advisors, releasing information to the public, or other decisions.
Control Rights	
Right to Replace CEO	The holder has the right to replace the founding entrepreneur as the CEO of the company. This right is either explicit or implicit by virtue of a combination of other rights (such as through a majority of board seats or holding other rights enumerated below).
Right of First Refusal at Sale	Before the firm can be sold, the holder of the right of first refusal at sale must be offered the same terms for sale of his or her own shares. The firm cannot be sold to another party unless the holder turns down the terms that are offered.
Co-sale Agreement	Any stakeholder that wishes to sell the firm must also offer to the holder of a co-sale agreement the option to sell his or her shares at the same terms.
Drag-along Rights	The holder can force the other stakeholders to sell their shares at the same terms as that which is being sold by the holder.
Antidilution Protection	The holder is entitled to proportional equity allocations that maintain a constant equity ownership percentage in the company.
Protection Rights against New Issues	The holder has the right to vote on this issue at the stakeholder level. The votes per share may be disproportionately allocated towards certain stakeholders such as the venture capitalist.
Redemption Rights	The holder of redemption shares has the right to make the entrepreneurial firm redeem the shares as per the terms of the agreement. Typically, the terms specify the redemption price per share and the date at which the holder may seek redemption.
Information Rights	The holder has the right to obtain information above and beyond that usually provided to other stakeholders, if requested.
IPO Registration Rights	The holder can compel the company to register shares held by the investor on a stock exchange. Often the holder of IPO registration rights also has piggyback registration rights, which enables the holder to compel the company that is already in the process of filing a registration statement to extend the registration statement to cover the holder's class of shares. The sum of control rights variable in Table 14.1, Panel A, does not double count IPO registration rights and piggyback registration rights but does consider IPO registration rights.

entrepreneurial firm is not yet in a position to be a publicly listed firm. Finally, information rights typically call for the firm to supply timely financial statements and other items not generally available to other stakeholders and so may be more relevant for firms preplanning exit strategies. Overall, however, the stronger control rights in relation to preplanned exit strategies are typically the right to replace the CEO, drag-along, redemption, and antidilution rights. The other rights are also potentially relevant. In the multivariate empirical analysis following we consider the sum of these rights as well as independently analyze the rights separately.

As discussed in Chapter 10, there are examples of a term sheet, shareholders, agreement, and subscription agreement in Appendices 2, 3, and 4, respectively. These examples provide illustrative clauses for the ways in which various cash flow, control, and veto rights terms are written in practice. These examples are taken from actual transactions, but the names of the parties have been removed in the agreements for reasons of confidentiality.

Table 14.2 provides summary statistics for each of the variables in the dataset. Among the 35 funds in the data, no fund provided data on fewer than 2 entrepreneurial firms, and no fund provided data on more than 20 entrepreneurial firms. Data cannot be disclosed on a fund-by-fund basis due to confidentiality (some funds were worried their identity might be "reverse engineered" from reporting fund-specific data). Seventy-eight entrepreneurial firms in the data were financed by captive funds that were affiliated (wholly owned) by a bank or a corporation (the remainder were limited partnership venture capitalists), and 11 funds were captive funds. The typical fund manager in the data manages €30,000,000 and typically invests less than €5,000,000 (in 2003 euros) in the entrepreneurial firms. Most (67%) of the entrepreneurs in the data were in the early stage of development at the time of first investment (extra details are in Table 14.2).

Table 14.2 shows that the venture capitalists in the sample typically used all of the 5 types of veto rights as well as 5 of the 9 different control rights identified in Table 14.1, Panels A and B. Table 14.2 also shows common equity was used for 45% of the entrepreneurs; convertible preferred equity was used for 32% of entrepreneurs; debt and common was used for 19%; and straight debt was used for 4% of entrepreneurs in the data. This evidence is quite consistent with all other non-U.S. samples (Chapters 10–13; see also Bascha and Walz, 2001; Cumming, 2005a; Hege et al., 2003; Kaplan et al., 2007; Lerner and Schoar, 2005; Schwienbacher, 2003), but in the United States, venture capitalists typically use convertible preferred equity, and there is a tax incentive associated with that security in the United States (Gilson and Schizer, 2003). The securities used by year of investment are presented in Figure 14.1, and the preplanned IPOs and acquisitions by year of investment are indicated in Figure 14.2.

Table 14.2 shows that venture capitalists preplanned either an IPO or an acquisition exit in 70 of 223 entrepreneurial firms (31%) in which they invested. There are 25 preplanned IPOs and 45 preplanned acquisitions; for

Table 14.2 Summary Statistics

This table presents summary statistics of each of the variables defined in Table 1, Panel A.

Variable	Mean	Median	Standard Deviation	Minimum	Maximum	Number of Times Dummy Variable Equal to One	Number of Observations
Preplanned Exit Strategy							
Preplanned IPO	0.112	0	0.316	0	1	25	223
Preplanned Acquisition	0.202	0	0.402	0	1	45	223
Market Conditions and Institutional Variables							
Legality Index	20.090	20.76	2.045	15	21.91		223
Anti-director Rights							
Creditor Rights							
GNP per Capita	21362.511	20950	6371.435	5270	35760		223
German Legal Origin	0.336	0	0.474	0	1	75	223
Socialist Legal Origin	0.076	0	0.266	0	1	17	223
Scandinavian Legal Origin	0.049	0	0.217	0	1	11	223
Investor and Investee Characteristics							
Captive Fund	0.350	0	0.478	0	1	78	223
Capital Managed/ Manager	€46,564,302	€30,000,000	€106,359,229	€1,342,857	€666,666,667		223

(*continued*)

Table 14.2 *(continued)*

Variable	Mean	Median	Standard Deviation	Minimum	Maximum	Number of Times Dummy Variable Equal to One	Number of Observations
Industry Market/Book	3.620	4.1067	1.303	2.277	5.2		223
Book Value	€7,172,996	€3,607,000	€11,360,543	€50,000	€108,000,000		223
Early-stage Investee	0.677	1	0.469	0	1	151	223
Entrepreneur Experience Rank	6.381	6	1.675	1	10		223
Transaction Characteristics							
Sum of Veto Rights	3.570	5	2.019	0	5		223
Sum of Control Rights	4.511	5	2.541	0	9		223
Common Equity	0.448	0	0.498	0	1	100	223
Convertible Preferred Equity	0.323	0	0.469	0	1	72	223
Debt and Common	0.193	0	0.395	0	1	43	223
Debt	0.036	0	0.186	0	1	8	223
Prior Round	0.112	0	0.216	0	1	25	223

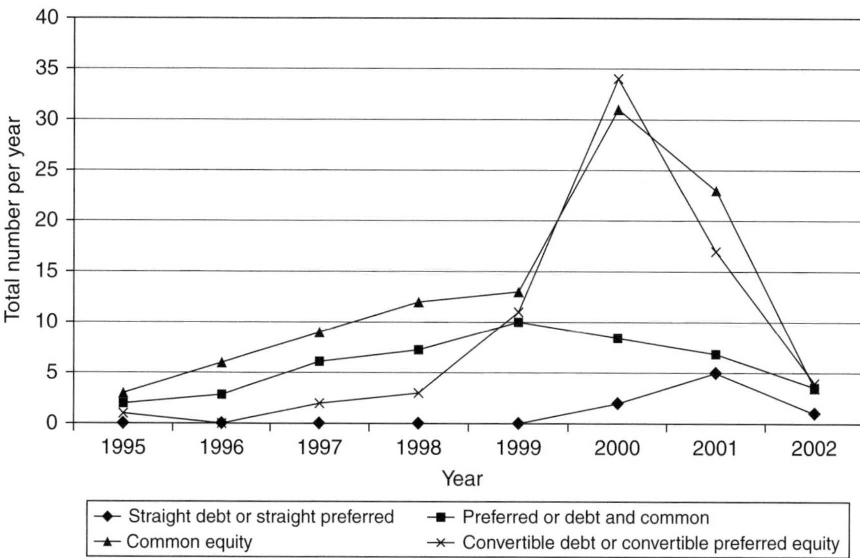

Figure 14.1 Securities Used by Year of Investment

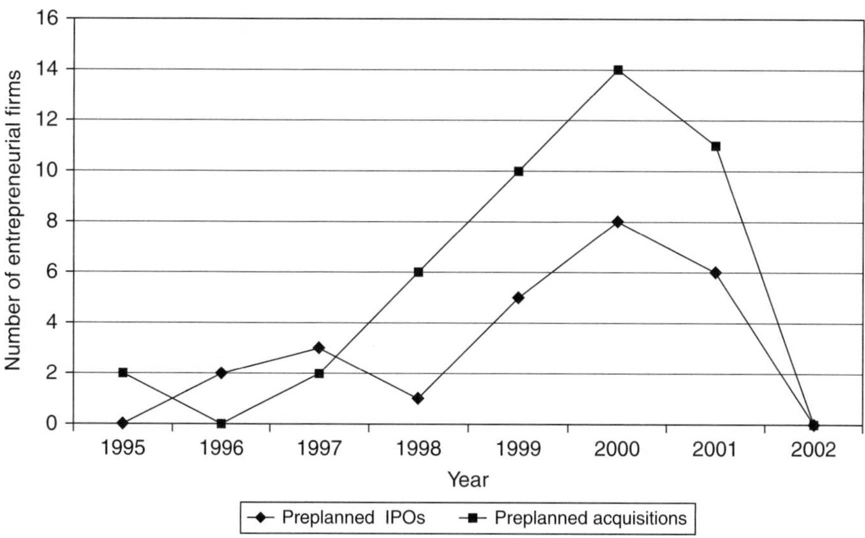

Figure 14.2 Preplanned IPOs and Acquisitions by Year of Investment

the remainder of the investments, the venture capitalists did not have a reasonable expectation as to whether exit would be either as an IPO or an acquisition at the time of initial contract. We stress in this chapter the difference between *preplanned* exits (at the time of contract) and *actual* exits (eventual performance in later years). Table 14.3 indicates that there are 187 actual exits

Table 14.3 Relationships between Preplanned Exits and Actual Exits

This table presents the relationship between preplanned exits at the time of first investment (including investments for which there was no clearly defined exit strategy in terms of seeking an IPO or acquisition at the time of first investment), and the actual exit as at 2005.

		Preplanned Exits			
		Preplanned IPO	**Preplanned Acquisition**	**No Preplanned Exit at Time of First Investment**	**Total**
Actual Exits	IPO	6	1	25	32
	Acquisition	5	27	42	74
	Buyback	0	2	15	17
	Write-off	5	9	50	64
	No Exit	9	6	21	36
	Total	25	45	153	223

as of 2005 (of the 223 entrepreneurial firms) in the data (32 actual IPOs, 74 actual acquisitions, 17 actual buybacks, and 64 actual write-offs), and among these 187 actual exits, 132 were not preplanned (71%). As well, 15 of 70 preplanned exits (21%) have not been actually exited in the data. Only 19% (6/32) of the actual IPOs were preplanned IPOs, and only 36% (27/74) of the actual acquisitions were preplanned acquisitions. We do not study the factors that affect actual exit and returns performance in this chapter; that issue is addressed in Chapters 20 and 21. In this chapter we focus on the relation between preplanned exits and contract formation by making use of data which comprise unique details on the investors' preplanned exit strategy prior to the time of contracting. Actual exits that are not preplanned do not affect contract design, since the actual exit event happens typically three to four years after first investment. By contrast, exits that are preplanned happen prior to contract formation, and therefore may affect contract design, as considered herein.

Table 14.4 provides a correlation matrix for each of the variables defined in Table 14.1, Panel A. It is noteworthy, first, that contract terms are complementary. That is, common equity is more often associated with fewer investor control and veto rights, while convertible preferred equity is more often associated with stronger investor control and veto rights, which supports recent theoretical research (Cestone, 2000).[3] Second, notice that stronger investor

[3]In Cestone's model, the intuition is based on the idea that formal control with common equity would turn into excessive real control (over interference) because venture capitalists have greater incentives to intervene with riskier claims (Cestone, 2000, p. 15). Kaplan and Strömberg (2003) similarly find that different control rights are complementary, not substitutes, in the United States, where convertible preferred equity is typically the selected security.

control and veto rights are positively correlated with preplanned acquisition exits, whereas preplanned IPOs are positively correlated with common equity contracts. Third, the data indicate legal and market conditions are related to different contract terms, as in Lerner and Schoar (2005), Kaplan et al. (2007), and Cumming et al. (2008).[4] Finally, the correlations in Table 14.4 indicate that investee and investor characteristics are related to contracts; for instance, captive funds are more likely to take veto rights, and more experienced entrepreneurs (as ranked by the venture capitalist; see Table 14.1, Panel A, for the variable definition)[5] are more likely to be financed with common equity.

Table 14.5 presents additional summary statistics and comparison of proportions, means, and medians for preplanned IPOs versus preplanned acquisitions. The data indicate that preplanned IPOs have a statistically significant greater proportion of common equity investments, while preplanned acquisitions have a statistically significant greater mean and median number of veto and control rights. These results are consistent with our theoretical predictions earlier in the chapter. In Table 14.5, the only statistically insignificant difference is in the proportion of convertible preferred equity investments between preplanned IPOs and preplanned acquisitions (but nevertheless that difference is consistent with the relations hypothesized). Overall, therefore, the univariate comparison tests in Table 14.5 (alongside the correlation matrix in Table 14.4) are quite supportive of our hypotheses. The next section investigates the univariate statistics more fully by considering multivariate tests. We then discuss limitations (such as possibly relevant details not comprised in the data, among other things) and future research.

14.4 Multivariate Tests

This section presents the regression analyses of the total number of veto and control rights used in the contracts and similarly carries out logit analyses of the determinants of the security choice. We use four alternative models with a different set of right-hand-side variables to check robustness. The same four models are used for each dependent variable analyzed.

14.4.1 Veto and Control Rights

The regression results in Table 14.6 strongly and consistently indicate that preplanned acquisitions are associated with stronger investor veto and control

[4]The relation between the legal system and contracts in our data is in some dimensions different than that reported in Lerner and Schoar (2005). For example, Lerner and Schoar find strong control rights are used in weaker legal systems; however, their sample is derived from developing countries, whereas our sample is primarily from well-developed continental European countries.

[5]This ranking was taken at the time of recording the data and in follow-up meetings and calls to the investors. The respondent was told that the ranking is intended for the time of investment, so this variable is at best an imperfect proxy. It is nevertheless a useful control variable to account for the role of entrepreneurial ability in contract formation.

Table 14.4

This table presents correlation coefficients across each of the variables defined in Table 14.1, Panel A.

	Variable	(1)	(2)	(3)	(4)	(5)	(6)	(7)	(8)	(9)
	Transaction Characteristics									
(1)	Sum of Veto Rights	1.00								
(2)	Sum of Control Rights	0.54	1.00							
(3)	Common Equity	−0.27	−0.41	1.00						
(4)	Convertible Preferred Equity	0.08	0.18	−0.62	1.00					
(5)	Debt and Common	0.21	0.21	−0.44	−0.34	1.00				
(6)	Debt	0.08	0.18	−0.17	−0.13	−0.09	1.00			
(7)	Prior Round	−0.19	−0.16	0.05	0.06	−0.10	−0.07	1.00		
	Preplanned Exit Strategy									
(8)	Preplanned Acquisition	0.18	0.29	−0.18	0.11	0.04	0.14	−0.04	1.00	
(9)	Preplanned IPO	−0.05	−0.11	0.17	−0.03	−0.17	0.01	0.10	−0.18	1.00
	Market Conditions and Institutional Variables									
(10)	Log of Legality Index	0.21	0.26	−0.04	−0.21	0.27	0.07	−0.01	0.18	0.07
(11)	Anti-director Rights	−0.28	−0.22	0.05	0.01	−0.13	0.12	−0.14	0.26	0.16
(12)	Creditor Rights	0.41	0.11	0.04	−0.18	0.23	−0.12	0.05	−0.04	0.01
(13)	Log of GNP per Capita	0.09	0.10	0.13	−0.24	0.09	0.06	0.13	0.18	0.14
(14)	German Legal Origin Dummy	−0.02	−0.04	0.12	0.02	−0.23	0.12	−0.01	0.30	0.35
	Socialist Legal Origin Dummy	−0.11	−0.10	−0.16	0.31	−0.14	−0.06	−0.10	−0.10	−0.10
(15)	Scandinavian Legal Origin Dummy	−0.12	0.03	0.00	0.11	−0.11	−0.04	0.05	0.04	−0.02
(16)	Investor and Investee Characteristics									
(17)	Captive Fund	0.24	−0.06	0.02	0.04	−0.17	0.21	−0.05	0.10	0.13
(18)	Log of Capital Managed/ Manager	0.24	0.04	−0.11	−0.07	0.18	0.07	0.19	−0.04	−0.04

Correlation Matrix

Correlations significant at the 5% level of significance are highlighted in underline font.

(10)	(11)	(12)	(13)	(14)	(15)	(16)	(17)	(18)	(19)	(20)	(21)
1.00											
0.23	1.00										
0.28	−0.41	1.00									
0.81	0.26	0.12	1.00								
0.27	0.43	−0.22	0.42	1.00							
−0.75	−0.21	−0.23	−0.86	−0.20	1.00						
0.15	0.26	0.15	0.16	−0.16	−0.07	1.00					
0.22	0.25	0.29	0.07	0.09	−0.21	0.09	1.00				
0.38	−0.24	0.36	0.49	−0.09	−0.46	0.03	0.17	1.00			

(*continued*)

Table 14.4

	Variable	(1)	(2)	(3)	(4)	(5)	(6)	(7)	(8)	(9)
(19)	Log of Industry Market/Book	−0.13	−0.11	0.08	0.01	−0.17	0.14	0.15	0.02	0.03
(20)	Log of Book Value	0.01	−0.07	0.13	−0.14	0.16	−0.35	0.10	0.00	0.08
(21)	Early-stage Investee	−0.20	−0.17	0.10	0.19	−0.42	0.13	0.09	−0.01	0.03
(22)	Entrepreneur Experience Rank	−0.05	−0.13	0.30	−0.14	−0.18	−0.06	0.06	−0.11	0.17

rights. Preplanned acquisitions increase the probability of use of five different veto rights (over asset sales, asset purchases, changes in control, issuance of equity, and other decisions) by approximately 10%.[6] Similarly, preplanned acquisitions increase the probability of use of the different control rights (over the right to replace CEO, automatic conversion at exit, right for first refusal at sale, co-sale agreement, drag-along rights, antidilution protection, protection rights against new issues, redemption rights, information rights, IPO registration rights, and piggyback registration) by approximately 5%. These results provide a unique test and strong supporting evidence of theories linking exit to contract formation (Aghion and Bolton, 1992; Bascha and Walz, 2001; Berglöf, 1994; Black and Gilson, 1998; Hellmann, 2006).

It is noteworthy that investors take fewer control rights in countries of German legal origin, relative to Socialist, Scandinavian, and French legal origin (Models 7–9; the dummy variable for French legal origin is suppressed to avoid collinearity problems). In terms of the economic significance, the probability of no control rights used in a contract with an entrepreneur resident in a German legal origin country is 11% higher than that for an entrepreneur resident in a French legal origin country, and the probability that the contract contains all the control rights enumerated in Table 14.1 is 27% lower in German legal origin countries than French legal origin countries. One possible explanation for this result is in relation to institutional factors particular to Germany, such as the bank-dominated financial system, and the incentives for private equity funds in Germany to compete with banks by offering contracts with fewer control rights (this interpretation is consistent with the German venture capital market in Becker and Hellmann, 2005). Model 2 also indicates there are fewer veto rights in Germany relative to that in France, although this difference is not statistically significant in Models 3–5, which indicate more veto rights in Socialist legal origin countries (the probability of no veto rights in these countries is 19% lower than that for French legal origin countries), while

[6]The marginal effects for the logit models were calculated using Limdep Econometric Software.

(continued)

(10)	(11)	(12)	(13)	(14)	(15)	(16)	(17)	(18)	(19)	(20)	(21)
−0.06	0.11	−0.28	0.08	0.35	−0.06	−0.17	0.18	−0.04	1.00		
0.04	−0.19	0.24	0.06	−0.14	0.00	0.15	−0.24	0.11	−0.26	1.00	
−0.14	0.11	−0.25	−0.08	0.23	0.13	0.02	0.35	−0.18	0.47	−0.42	1.00
−0.07	0.05	−0.03	−0.03	−0.06	−0.01	0.17	0.07	−0.14	−0.12	0.06	0.08

Models 2–4 indicate fewer veto rights in Scandinavian legal origin countries (the probability of no veto rights is 39% higher than that for French legal origin countries).

Notice that when we use the Legality index alone in Models 1 and 6 (separated from the legal origin and GNP per capita, due to collinearity), we find more control rights are used in countries with stronger legal protections. The economic significance is such that an increase in Legality from 19 to 20 (for example, for a move that is approximately equivalent to a move from France to the Netherlands) increases the use of an extra veto right by 2% and an extra control right by 1%. It is possible this latter result is due to more efficient contract enforcement (cost-effective, and with reasonable certainty) in countries with better legal systems, so it is worthwhile to write such contracts.[7] This evidence is consistent with an independent sample of European venture capital investments that shows that in better legal systems investors demand more contractual downside protection, using securities such as debt, convertible debt, or preferred equity (Bottazzi et al., 2005).

There is some evidence in Table 14.6 that the quality of the entrepreneur influences the extent of control rights assigned to the venture capitalist. Venture capitalists are 16% more likely to have no control rights when the quality of the entrepreneur ranking increases by 1, and 1% more likely to have all the control rights enumerated in Table 14.1 when the quality of the entrepreneur ranking increases by 1 (and these results are statistically significant at the 5% and 10% levels in Models 8 and 9, respectively). It is intuitive that venture capitalists would demand less control over entrepreneurs for which the view is being of higher quality. Table 14.6 further indicates that captive

[7]Lerner and Schoar (2005) find a somewhat different result and therefore argue that contracts substitute for poor legal protection. The difference between these results across papers is most likely attributable to the different countries considered. Lerner and Schoar study a more heterogeneous sample of developing economies from different continents, whereas our data are restricted to continental Europe.

Table 14.5 Summary Statistics and Difference Tests

This table presents difference of proportions tests for the proportion of common equity and convertible preferred equity contracts used for preplanned IPO investments and preplanned acquisition exits, as well as a variety of specific veto and control rights. This table further presents difference of means and medians tests for the number of veto and control rights (for the different rights enumerated in Table 14.1) for preplanned IPOs and preplanned acquisitions. *, **, *** Statistically significant at the 10%, 5%, and 1% levels, respectively.

Variable	Preplanned IPOs				Preplanned Acquisitions				Difference of Proportions Test	Difference of Means Test	Difference of Medians Test
	Number of Preplanned IPOs	Proportion	Mean	Median	Number of Preplanned Acquisitions	Proportion	Mean	Median			
Common Equity	25	0.68	—	—	45	0.27	—	—	3.36***	—	—
Convertible Preferred Equity	25	0.28	—	—	45	0.42	—	—	−1.18	—	—
Number of Veto Rights	25	—	3.28	5	45		4.29	5	—	−2.05**	$p \leq 0.052$*
Number of Control Rights	25	—	3.92	4	45		6.24	6	—	−4.27***	$p \leq 0.001$***
First Refusal in Sale	25	0.68	—	—	45	0.67	—	—	0.11	—	—

Co-sale Rights	25	0.76	—	—	45	0.89	—	—	−1.42	—	—
Anti-dilution Rights	25	0.36	—	—	45	0.89	—	—	−4.63***	—	—
Drag-along Rights	25	0.08	—	—	45	0.36	—	—	−2.53**	—	—
Redemption Rights	25	0.24	—	—	45	0.58	—	—	−2.74***	—	—
Protection Rights against New Issues	25	0.48	—	—	45	0.82	—	—	−2.97***	—	—
Veto Asset Sales	25	0.68	—	—	45	0.89	—	—	−2.15**	—	—
Veto Asset Purchases	25	0.68	—	—	45	0.84	—	—	−1.61	—	—
Veto Changes in Control	25	0.64	—	—	45	0.84	—	—	−1.95*	—	—
Veto Issue Equity	25	0.68	—	—	45	0.84	—	—	−1.61	—	—

Table 14.6 Regression Analyses of

This table presents ordered logit estimates of the number of veto and control rights. The logit coefficients are presented; marginal effects are discussed in the text of the chapter 5, 9, and 10 use dummy variables for all years 1995–2001; a dummy variable for 2002 late-stage investments from the sample. *, **, *** Significant at the 10%, 5%, and

	LHS Variable = Sum of Veto Rights				
	Model 1	**Model 2**	**Model 3**	**Model 4**	**Model 5**
Constant	−7.578***	−7.530*	−10.018**	−9.148*	−12.600**
Year of Investment Dummy Variables?	No	No	No	Yes	Yes
Preplanned Exit Strategy					
Preplanned Acquisition	0.522**	0.681***	0.555**	0.689***	0.974***
Preplanned IPO			−0.219	−0.208	−0.451
Legal and Economic Environment					
Log (Legality)	2.787***				
Log (GNP per Capita)		0.850**	1.147**	1.055*	1.294**
German Legal Origin		−0.393*	−0.040	−0.074	0.246
Socialist Legal Origin		0.287	1.481**	1.556**	2.788***
Scandinavian Legal Origin		−0.989**	−1.141**	−1.252***	−0.622
Investor and Investee Variables					
Captive Investor			0.892***	0.965***	1.414***
Log (Capital Managed ['000]/Manager)			0.128	0.148	0.156
Log (Industry Market/ Book)			−0.469*	−0.464*	−0.179
Log (Book Value)			−0.129*	−0.136*	−0.152
Early-stage Investee			−0.857***	−0.830***	
Entrepreneur Experience			0.018	0.030	0.034
Ordered Logit Cut-off Parameters					
m_1	0.077**	0.078**	0.092**	0.094**	0.108**
m_2	0.107***	0.108***	0.127***	0.129***	0.134**
m_3	0.312***	0.315***	0.359***	0.366***	0.433***
m_4	0.674***	0.675***	0.760***	0.777***	0.935***

Sum of Veto and Control Rights

variables are as defined in Table 14.1. For conciseness, the standard (the marginal effects differ for each outcome 0, 1, 2, 3, etc.). Models 4, is excluded to avoid perfect collinearity. Models 5 and 10 exclude 1% levels, respectively.

LHS Variable = Sum of Control Rights				
Model 6	**Model 7**	**Model 8**	**Model 9**	**Model 10**
−5.703***	−2.574	0.549	2.073	4.365
No	No	No	Yes	Yes
0.662***	0.877***	0.884***	1.083***	1.282***
		0.135	0.210	0.053
2.265***				
	0.381	0.365	0.211	−0.098
	−0.501***	−0.503**	−0.566**	−0.112
	−0.016	−0.146	−0.160	0.229
	−0.138	0.192	0.068	0.836*
		−0.221	−0.219	−0.257
		−0.052	−0.033	0.037
		−0.056	−0.045	0.084
		−0.182***	−0.189***	−0.289***
		−0.328*	−0.319	
		−0.088**	−0.074*	−0.022
0.109**	0.106**	0.110**	0.115**	0.059
0.351***	0.343***	0.353***	0.369***	0.277***
0.611***	0.602***	0.616***	0.640***	0.579***
0.923***	0.913***	0.931***	0.969***	0.871***

(*continued*)

Table 14.6

	LHS Variable = Sum of Veto Rights				
	Model 1	Model 2	Model 3	Model 4	Model 5
m_5					
m_6					
m_7					
m_8					
m_9					
Model Diagnostics					
Number of Observations	223	223	223	223	151
LogLikelihood	−258.887	−259.779	−240.659	−237.046	−167.852
Pseudo R^2	0.049	0.045	0.116	0.129	0.163
Chi-squared Statistic	26.456***	24.672***	62.911***	70.138***	65.206***

investors are approximately 20% more likely to take a greater number of veto rights. This result is consistent with Gompers and Lerner (1999) and Riyanto and Schwienbacher (2006), who indicate strategic reasons (alongside financial goals) for corporate venture finance increase the probability of control among the investors so the venture capitalist can appropriate the innovation in ways consistent with the venture capitalist's companion corporate operations.

The control variables include various other venture capital fund characteristics and entrepreneurial firm characteristics, international differences across the countries considered, as well as differences over time (the sample spans the years 1995–2002, and dummy variables for each year except 2002 are used in Models 4 and 8 to check for robustness). It is noteworthy that perhaps somewhat unexpectedly, we observe fewer veto rights for earlier-stage investees. We may have expected a greater number of investor veto rights for early-stage investees due to the increased risk. One possible explanation is related to the time period considered around the Internet bubble and the phenomenon of money chasing deals with few control rights for high-tech start-ups (Gompers and Lerner, 2000), which is consistent with more favorable deal terms for early-stage investees.

As a further robustness check, Table 14.7 provides logit analyses of specific control and veto rights (instead of the sum of the control rights and the sum of the veto rights as in Table 14.6). The results are generally consistent with Table 14.6 but indicate more precisely which control and veto rights are directly influenced by each explanatory variable. Preplanned acquisitions are statistically associated with a greater probability of use of the right to replace the founding entrepreneur as CEO (the economic significance is a 28.2% higher

(*continued*)

LHS Variable = Sum of Control Rights				
Model 6	Model 7	Model 8	Model 9	Model 10
1.347***	1.330***	1.356***	1.410***	1.459***
1.819***	1.800***	1.852***	1.919***	2.199***
2.405***	2.391***	2.488***	2.572***	2.552***
3.036***	3.028***	3.155***	3.256***	3.015***
3.749***	3.744***	3.901***	4.012***	3.877***
223	223	223	223	151
−475.368	−476.820	−468.668	−461.635	−296.787
0.032	0.029	0.046	0.060	0.084
31.348***	28.444***	44.748***	58.814***	54.578***

probability in Model 11), first refusal in sale (19.9% higher probability in Model 12), co-sale rights (44.7% higher probability in Model 13), antidilution (48.5% higher probability in Model 14), redemption rights (13.9% higher probability in Model 16), protection rights against new issues (26.2% higher probability in Model 17), veto rights over asset sales (22.6% higher probability in Model 18), veto rights over asset purchases (20.3% higher probability in Model 19), and veto rights over changes in control (14.8% higher probability in Model 20). Preplanned IPOs are associated with a 14.9% lower probability of drag-along rights, and preplanned acquisitions are associated with a 5.7% greater probability of drag-along rights.[8] All of these results are consistent with prior theory that venture capitalist control is more important when venture capitalists preplan acquisition exits and less important when venture capitalists preplan IPO exits, since venture capitalists are more likely to have to use their control rights to force an acquisition on an unwilling entrepreneur.

Table 14.7 shows that German legal origin countries are 11.3% less likely to use antidilution rights (Model 14), 6.8% less likely to use redemption rights (Model 16), and 30.6% less likely to use protection rights against new issues (Model 17) than French legal origin countries. Socialist legal origin countries are 29.1% more likely to have contracts with protection rights against new issues (Model 17) and veto rights of issuing equity (Model 21) than French legal origin countries. Scandinavian legal origin countries are 44.4% less

[8]With a more parsimonious specification, drag-along rights are 14.7% more likely to be observed when the venture capitalist preplans an acquisition exit.

Table 14.7 Regression Analyses of

This table presents binary logit estimates of specific veto and control rights. The variables highlight economic significance alongside statistical significance. Dummy variables for avoid perfect collinearity. Various legal origin variables were excluded in Models 11 and levels, respectively.

	Model 11: Replace CEO	**Model 12: First Refusal**	**Model 13: Co-sale**	**Model 14: Anti-dilution**	**Model 15: Drag-along**
Constant	−6.777***	−2.820	−4.068	−0.709	−1.028
Year of Investment Dummy Variables?	Yes	Yes	Yes	Yes	Yes
Preplanned Exit Strategy					
Preplanned Acquisition	0.282**	0.199**	0.447***	0.485***	0.057*
Preplanned IPO	−0.034	0.174	0.223	−0.015	−0.149**
Legal and Economic Environment					
Log (GNP per Capita)	0.682***	0.234	0.541*	0.115	0.136
German Legal Origin	−0.123		−0.247	−0.113**	0.080
Socialist Legal Origin		0.402***	−0.949	−0.638	0.411
Scandinavian Legal Origin	−0.163		0.701	−0.088	0.029
Investor and Investee Variables					
Captive Investor	−0.106	0.005	0.269**	−0.036	0.017
Log (Capital Managed ['000]/Manager)	0.106**	0.025	0.812	−0.026	−0.003
Log (Industry Market/ Book)	−0.182	0.051	−0.237	0.123*	−0.0002
Log (Book Value)	−0.062*	−0.022	−0.177***	−0.007	−0.016
Early-stage Investee	−0.323***	0.210**	−0.423***	−0.080	−0.152*
Entrepreneur Experience	−0.029	0.031	0.446	−0.020	−0.053***
Model Diagnostics					
Number of Observations	223	223	223	223	223
LogLikelihood	−110.177	−139.401	−74.510	−115.044	−109.634
Pseudo R^2	0.267	0.090	0.443	0.247	0.103
Chi-squared Statistic	80.445***	27.533***	118.330***	75.273***	25.309**

Specific Veto and Control Rights

are as defined in Table 14.1. The marginal effects are presented to explicitly
1999 and 2000 are used; dummy variables for other years are excluded to
12 for reasons of collinearity. *, **, *** Significant at the 10%, 5%, and 1%

Model 16: Redemption	Model 17: Protection Rights against New Issues	Model 18: Veto Asset Sale	Model 19: Veto Asset Purchases	Model 20: Veto Change Control	Model 21: Veto Issue Equity
−0.601	−2.403	0.426	0.633	0.741	−3.452**
Yes	Yes	Yes	Yes	Yes	Yes
0.139***	0.262***	0.226***	0.203***	0.148**	0.077
0.015	−0.003	0.005	0.021	−0.064	−0.193
0.061	0.379*	−0.007	−0.057	−0.154	0.335*
−0.068***	−0.306**	0.035	0.031	0.048	−0.132
−0.355	0.291***	0.171	0.147	0.122	0.196***
−0.001	−0.319*	−0.444**	−0.414**	−0.209	−0.699***
−0.005	0.086	0.191***	0.181**	0.172**	0.405***
0.002	−0.088**	0.034	0.049	0.133***	0.013
0.048*	0.096	−0.147	−0.178*	−0.025	−0.037
−0.002	−0.019	−0.033	−0.013	−0.042	0.023
−0.045*	−0.172**	−0.253***	−0.198***	−0.163**	−0.147***
−0.006	−0.016	0.010	0.009	0.011	0.012
223	223	223	223	223	223
−120.720	−128.542	−108.042	−114.767	−106.224	−90.045
0.180	0.106	0.186	0.153	0.169	0.284
52.972***	30.356***	49.423***	41.368***	43.177***	71.260***

Table 14.8 Regression Analyses

This table presents binary logit estimates of the use of common equity and convertible preferred are presented to explicitly highlight economic significance alongside statistical significance. Models dummy variable for 2002 is excluded to avoid perfect collinearity. Models 26 and 31 exclude late-5%, and 1% levels, respectively.

	LHS Variable = Common Equity				
	Model 22	Model 23	Model 24	Model 25	Model 26
Constant	0.111	4.406	−1.023	−0.259	5.221
Year of Investment Dummy Variables?	No	No	No	Yes	Yes
Preplanned Exit Strategy					
Preplanned Acquisition	−0.226***	−0.315***	−0.328***	−0.336***	−0.353***
Preplanned IPO			−0.036	−0.077	−0.087
Legal and Economic Environment					
Log (Legality)	−0.039				
Log (GNP per Capita)		−0.438	0.043	−0.041	−0.437
German Legal Origin		0.196*	0.152	0.176	0.104
Socialist Legal Origin		−0.581***	−0.417***	−0.457***	−0.659***
Scandinavian Legal Origin		−0.113	−0.166	−0.126	−0.343**
Investor and Investee Variables					
Captive Investor			0.005	0.024	0.001
Log (Capital Managed ['000]/Manager)			−0.123**	−0.143***	−0.255***
Log (Industry Market/Book)			0.040	0.031	−0.120
Log (Book Value)			0.131***	0.126***	0.241***
Early-stage Investee			0.188*	0.223**	
Entrepreneur Experience			0.092***	0.099***	0.051
Model Diagnostics					
Number of Observations	223	223	223	223	151
LogLikelihood	−149.454	−142.179	−123.222	−118.015	−67.857
Pseudo R^2	0.026	0.073	0.197	0.231	0.351
Chi-squared Statistic	7.858**	22.410***	60.324***	70.737***	73.450***

of Security Design

equity. The variables are as defined in Table 14.1. The marginal effects
25, 26, 30, and 31 use dummy variables for all years 1995–2001; a
stage investments from the sample. *, **, *** Significant at the 10%,

LHS Variable = Convertible Preferred Equity				
Model 27	**Model 28**	**Model 29**	**Model 30**	**Model 31**
2.757***	1.069	2.650	0.833	1.322
No	No	No	Yes	Yes
0.188**	0.143*	0.184*	0.136**	0.301*
		0.098	0.113	0.220
−0.989***				
	−0.137	−0.314	−0.105	−0.256
	0.118	0.140	0.050	0.002
	0.467**	0.387	0.554*	0.692***
	0.362**	0.495***	0.348**	0.579***
		−0.067	−0.046	−0.152
		0.090**	0.056**	0.163**
		−0.113	−0.060	0.029
		−0.054	−0.025	−0.072
		0.185**	7.09E–02	
		−0.046**	−0.029**	−0.065**
223	223	223	223	151
−133.011	−125.595	−116.109	−106.723	−69.982
0.052	0.105	0.172	0.239	0.304
14.519***	29.350***	48.322***	67.093***	61.180***

likely to have contracts with veto rights over asset sales (Model 18), 41.4% less likely to have veto rights over asset purchases (Model 19), and 69.9% less likely to have veto rights over issuing new equity (Model 21) than French legal origin countries.

Table 14.7 also indicates that the quality of the venture capitalist and the entrepreneur matter for the allocation of control and veto rights. More experienced investors (proxied by capital managed per manager) are more likely to have the right to replace the CEO and veto rights over changes in control (an increase from €30,000,000 to €40,000,000 in capital managed increases the probability of the right to replace the CEO by 3% [Model 11] and veto rights over changes in control by 4% [Model 20]), which is consistent with the view that more experienced investors can demand greater control rights.[9] Similarly, more experienced entrepreneurs are less likely to have contracts that give up drag-along control rights to venture capitalists: An increase in the entrepreneur experience rank by 1 reduces the probability of drag-along rights by 5.3% (Model 15).

The other control variables in Table 14.7 are generally consistent with those discussed pertaining to Table 14.6. At a broad level, regardless of the specification, the general lessons from Tables 14.6 and 14.7 are that venture capitalists use stronger control and veto rights when they preplan acquisition exits, and weaker control rights in countries of German and Scandinavian legal origin, and weaker control rights when the entrepreneur has stronger bargaining power and the venture capitalist has weaker bargaining power. The next subsection considers complementary evidence for security design in terms of the use of straight common equity versus convertible preferred equity.

14.4.2 Security Design

Consistent with the regressions in Tables 14.6 and 14.7, the regression results in Table 14.8 indicate that preplanned acquisition exits increase the probability that convertible securities will be used by approximately 18% (Models 27–31; the coefficients are significant at 10% or higher in all models, and the economic significance ranges from 13.6 to 30.1%), and lower the probability that common equity will be used by approximately 33% (Models 22–26; the coefficients are significant at the 1% level in all models, but the economic significance ranges from 22.6 to 35.3%). As before, these results provide a unique test of theories linking exit to contract formation (Aghion and Bolton, 1992; Bascha and Walz, 2001; Berglöf, 1994; Black and Gilson, 1998; Hellmann, 2006; Neus and Walz, 2005;). The results are consistent with the view that venture capitalists take stronger control rights to force acquisition exits on potentially unwilling entrepreneurs that might prefer to otherwise become the

[9]However, more experienced investors are also less likely to have protection rights against new issues (Model 17), and there does not appear to be a good explanation for that coefficient (except that more parsimonious models gave rise to statistical significance of this one result in Model 17).

CEO of a publicly traded firm (see Black and Gilson, 1998, for a supportive theory, and Petty et al., 1999, for supportive case studies).

The results in Table 14.7 also indicate that investors are more likely to use common equity in countries of German legal origin (Model 23 indicates 19.6% more likely; however, this result is significant only at the 10% level and insignificant in the other models), relative to French legal origin. These results highlight a role for legal and institutional differences across countries in affecting private investment contracts (as in Lerner and Schoar, 2005; Kaplan et al., 2007). The results regarding German legal origin and common equity in Table 14.8 are consistent with Table 14.6 (showing German legal origin is associated with weak control and veto rights) in that common equity similarly involves weaker investor protection than preferred equity in bankruptcy states. Perhaps somewhat surprisingly, Social and Scandinavian legal origin countries are much less likely to be associated with common equity and more likely to be associated with convertible preferred equity than French legal origin countries. These latter results are generally statistically significant at the 1% level in Models 23–26 and Models 28–31, and economically large (the economic significance generally ranges from 30 to 69% in the various models). Our discussions with venture capitalists in these countries indicated tax reasons for adopting these securities (in a way consistent with Gilson and Schizer, 2003), and the large tax rates made this a primary concern. We were generally informed that specific details depended on the entrepreneurial firm's situation and the country in which the firm was resident, but we were not privy to obtaining any specific details. The specific nature of the tax codes and tax benefits with different securities in different countries is beyond the scope of our analysis; further research is warranted.

Finally, note that the results in Table 14.8 indicate more experienced entrepreneurs are more likely to be financed with common equity (Models 24–26) and less likely to be financed with convertible preferred equity (Models 29–31). The economic significance is such that an increase in the entrepreneur's experience ranking by 1 increases the probability of use of common equity by 9 to 10% (Models 24 and 25; however, this effect is not statistically significant in Model 26 for the subsample of earlier-stage investments) and decreases the probability of use of convertible preferred equity by 2.9 (Model 30) to 6.5% (Model 31, for the subsample of earlier-stage investments). Similarly, more experienced investors (proxied by the amount of capital raised per manager) are more likely to use convertible preferred equity and less likely to use common equity, and this effect is statistically significant at at least the 5% level in each of Models 24–26 and Models 29–31. The economic significance indicates that an increase in capital per manager from €30,000,000 to €40,000,000 reduces the probability of use of common equity by approximately 4 (Model 24) to 7% (Model 26 for the subsample of earlier-stage investments) and increases the probability of use of convertible preferred equity by approximately 2 (Model 30) to 5% (Model 31 for the subsample of earlier-stage investments). These results are very supportive of bilateral moral theories (e.g., Casamatta, 2003; Schmidt, 2003). These results are also consistent with U.S.

evidence provided by Hsu (2004) that shows more sophisticated investors tend to obtain more favorable deal terms for themselves, and entrepreneurs are happy to pay for affiliation with more sophisticated investors in terms of signing contracts that are more favorable to the investor.

In sum, the data indicate in Table 14.8 strong robustness of the results that security design is a significant function of preplanned exits, legal origin, and the bargaining power of the venture capitalist and entrepreneur, consistent with the allocation of control rights (Tables 14.6 and 14.7). Common equity is more often used in countries of German legal origin and among higher-quality entrepreneurs, while convertible preferred equity is more often used for preplanned acquisition exits, in countries of Socialist and Scandinavian legal origin, and for venture capitalists of higher quality in terms of their capital managed per manager.

14.5 Limitations and Future Research

We have presented many robustness checks with a wide variety of explanatory variables and dependent variables. Numerous alternative specifications were considered. We controlled for a very large number of different firm-specific and private investor–specific characteristics, market conditions, and institutional factors. The information considered was hand-collected, and highly confidential. We have no reason to believe that the variables considered in this chapter are incomplete, although more detailed data and/or a greater volume of data could shed further light on the issues raised. It is possible that other confidential data are relevant, but inclusion/exclusion of our control variables did not point to any pronounced concerns about robustness of the tests of the central hypotheses considered. We nevertheless outline a number of suggestions for future work.

First, the ways in which contracts between investors are negotiated in respect of preplanned exit behavior might be a fruitful avenue of further theoretical and empirical work. For instance, one might build into the analyses behavioral factors related to trust and/or overoptimism in the spirit of Landier and Thesmar (2007) and Manigart et al. (2002). Ideally, such data would enable controls for the expected performance and perceived quality of the venture. Our dataset provided some new control variables for entrepreneurial firm quality and venture capital fund quality; future work might consider more refined control variables with more detailed data. Further empirical research along these lines could also consider investor valuations practices and due diligence reviews, as well as the interplay among contractual governance, innovation, and performance (in the spirit of Kortum and Lerner, 2000; Baker and Gompers, 2003). Further empirical work in this regard might also consider sources of funds in the spirit of Mayer et al. (2005); our data only enabled a control variable for captive investors versus non-captives.

Second, recall that our intuition linking preplanned exits to contracts involved two themes: One involved the venture capitalist disclosing to the entrepreneur the exit strategy, and the other did not. We argued that both themes yielded similar predictions that were supported in the data. However, there may theoretically be cases in which the entrepreneur faces a trade-off when he knows the venture capitalists preplanned exit strategy is an acquisition. If he gives the venture capitalist more control, the firm is going to have a higher exit value, but at the same time he loses his private benefits. If he gives the venture capitalist less control, the firm is going to have a lower exit value, but the entrepreneur is able to retain his private benefits. We may also expect, however, that firms will not get financed in the latter case where the venture capitalist's preplanned exit strategy is toward an acquisition and an entrepreneur does not want to give up control rights. Regardless, as discussed we were unable to empirically distinguish between these two themes due to an inability to obtain details from the investors as to when the preplanned exit strategy was revealed to the entrepreneur (the vast majority of the venture capitalists did not want to disclose this information). Further empirical work might shed more light on this issue if and where new data can be obtained.

Third, other variables considered but not explicitly reported included portfolio size per manager and tax differences across countries (in the spirit of Kanniainen and Keuschnigg, 2003, 2004; Keuschnigg, 2004; Keuschnigg and Nielsen, 2001, 2003a,b, 2004a,b). These factors did not materially impact the analysis of the variables already considered. It is most likely that preplanned exits influence portfolio size per manager, which could be the subject of a new and different paper; but our data come from 35 venture capital funds, and it is therefore not possible to fully consider this issue.

Fourth, the unit of analysis is the entrepreneurial firm and not an investment round or syndicated investor. Syndicated investors almost invariably used the same securities as those used by the investors that provided these data. Only in 6 of 223 cases were differences observed (where the syndicated investor used common equity or warrants when the respondent investor used a security involving debt and/or preferred equity). It is also noteworthy that the private investors did not indicate significant alterations to their contract structures across financing rounds (since they felt that the negotiation and transactions costs would outweigh any benefits). Further theoretical work in the spirit of Casamatta and Haritchabalet (2003) and empirical work in the spirit of Lerner (1994), Lockett and Wright (2001), and Gompers (1995) could consider staging and syndication vis-à-vis preplanned exits; those topics are beyond the scope of this chapter.

Finally, notice that our empirical analysis is specific to the venture capital context in which investment is *invariably* made with a view toward exit in the form of an IPO or acquisition. Other theories about going public (e.g., Boot and Thakor, 2006; Chemmanur and Fulghieri, 1999) more generally consider companies that are not necessarily financed by venture capitalists that invest with a view toward an IPO or acquisition. As our tests carried out in this chapter are in a somewhat more restricted context, future research could explore more direct tests of those models (in the spirit of Pagano et al., 1998; Pagano and Roell, 1998; and Roell 1996).

14.6 Conclusions

This chapter introduced an empirical analysis of the relation between preplanned IPO and acquisition exits and contractual ownership and control rights. We provide a unique test and supporting evidence of theories linking exit to contract formation (Aghion and Bolton, 1992; Bascha and Walz, 2001; Berglöf, 1994; Black and Gilson, 1998; Neus and Walz, 2005). We considered a new data sample of 223 investments from 35 venture capital funds in 11 continental European countries. The data uniquely enabled consideration of the role of preplanned exits in contract formation in venture finance. A preplanned exit strategy is a reasonable expectation that the investor will want to dispose of the entrepreneurial investment either by IPO or acquisition, and this expectation is formed prior to contracting with the entrepreneur.

The data indicated that preplanned acquisitions are associated with stronger investor veto and control rights, a greater probability that convertible securities will be used, and a lower probability that common equity will be used. An acquisition exit typically involves the ousting of the entrepreneur from the firm or at least a reduced scope of authority from the original position as CEO of the firm he or she founded; either way, the permanent loss of control is typically distasteful to the entrepreneur (see Petty et al., 1999, for supportive case studies; see also Black and Gilson, 1998, for a supportive qualitative theory). As such, it was expected that venture capitalists preplanning acquisition exits would negotiate for stronger control rights in case it became necessary to force an entrepreneur to acquiesce to an acquisition. We also hypothesized that it would be in the interest of both the venture capitalist and entrepreneur to allocate stronger control rights to the venture capitalist to maximize the value of the firm upon an acquisition exit.

In testing the theories pertaining to preplanned exit and contracts with the use of a variety of control variables, it is noteworthy that we found that investors take fewer control and veto rights and use common equity in countries of German legal origin, relative to Socialist, Scandinavian, and French legal origin. The data also indicated that more experienced entrepreneurs are more likely to get financed with common equity and less likely to get financed with convertible preferred equity, while more experienced investors are more likely to use convertible preferred equity and less likely to use common equity. These results strongly support recent theoretical work on bilateral moral hazard and contracting in venture capital finance (Casamatta, 2003; Schmidt, 2003).

Key Terms

Common equity
Preferred equity
Debt
Convertible preferred equity
Convertible debt
Veto rights over asset sales
Veto rights over asset purchases
Veto rights over changes in control
Veto rights over issuances of equity
The right to replace the CEO
Rights of first refusal at sale
Co-sale agreement
Drag-along rights
Antidilution protection
Protection rights against new issues
Redemption rights
Information rights
IPO registration rights
Contingencies in contracts
Financial performance
Nonfinancial performance
Certain actions
Default on dividend or redemption payment
Future securities offerings
Founder remaining with firm

Discussion Questions

14.1. List five different types of control rights that are allocated in venture capital contracts. What is the significance associated with each control right?

14.2. List four different types of contractual contingencies commonly found in venture capital contracts. Provide an example of each type of contingency. What is the rationale for including each contingency?

14.3. What is a preplanned exit? How do preplanned exits affect the structure of venture capital contracts?

14.4. In what ways do venture capitalist and entrepreneur bargaining power influence financial contracts?

14.5. True/False/Uncertain: Stronger legal environments are associated with a greater likelihood that venture capitalist-entrepreneur contracts will involve convertible shares and more investor veto and control rights.

14.6. Which clauses from Table 14.1, Panel B, can you find in example agreements in Appendices 2, 3, and 4?

14.7. As an entrepreneur, would you agree to the *Special Rights* listed in the term sheet in Appendix 2? Why or why not? If not, what rewording of that clause would you propose?

Part Four

Investor Effort

15 Investor Value-added

15.1 Introduction and Learning Objectives

Part IV consists of Chapters 15 to 18, and it considers the efficiency of venture capital investment in terms of investor value-added. Investor value-added may be viewed as involving the following issues:

1. The relation between venture capital and private equity and innovative activity
2. Contract terms and investor value-added
3. Location of investee firms (e.g., intra- versus interprovincial)
4. Optimal portfolio size/manager
5. Investment duration

This chapter provides a brief overview of the issues pertaining to each of the preceding items. Further, in this chapter we provide a road map of items considered in more detail in Chapters 16 to 18.

15.2 Innovation and Efficiency

At the outset, it is important to highlight the fact that empirical evidence shows that both venture capital and private equity investment enhance entrepreneurship, innovative activity, and operating efficiency of investee companies. In the context of early-stage venture capital investment, Kortum and Lerner (2000) show that venture capital has a significant impact on innovation and productivity. They report that venture capital averaged less than 3% of corporate R&D from 1983 to 1992, but venture capital's share of U.S. industrial innovations was 8%, and by 1998 venture capital funding accounted for 14% of U.S. innovative activity. Based on a sample of patents issued to 20 manufacturing industries between 1965 and 1992, Kortum and Lerner show that US$1 of venture capital gives rise to an increase in patenting by three times. They argue, and find evidence in support of their view, that venture capital causes R&D spending and patent activity (and not the reverse causality).[1] Also, Kortum and

[1]Ueda and Hirukawa (2003) find stronger evidence of the reverse causality—that is, evidence that innovation causes venture capital.

Lerner (2000) and Lerner (2002) provide evidence that venture capitalists add less value and contribute less to innovation among their entrepreneurial investee firms in boom periods relative to more normal times.

A long history of academic work has shown that private equity and buyout transactions enhance productivity. Lichtenberg and Siegel (1990) and Harris et al. (2005) find evidence from the U.S. and U.K. buyouts, respectively, that management buyouts significantly improve productivity. Lichtenberg and Siegel used U.S. Census Bureau's Longitudinal Research Database, which contained data on more than 19,000 mostly large U.S. manufacturing plants for the years 1972 to 1988. They found that management buyout (MBO)[2] plants had enhanced total factor productivity[3] relative to representative establishments in the same industry after the MBO. This enhancement in economic performance could not be attributed to reductions in R&D, wages, capital investment, or layoffs of blue-collar personnel. Harris et al. studied longitudinal data for approximately 36,000 U.K. manufacturing establishments and found that MBO plants experienced a substantial increase in productivity after a buyout (+70.5% and +90.3% more efficient in the short and long run, respectively). Overall, the evidence is consistent with the view that MBOs are a useful mechanism for reducing agency costs and enhancing economic efficiency. Similarly, Chemmanur et al. (2007) show that venture capital enhances total factor productivity among a sample of venture capital– versus nonventure capital–backed firms in the United States.

The media in 2007, however, focused on the effect of buyouts on jobs. In a famous speech in 2004, social Democrat politician Franz Müntefering from Germany argued that private equity firms were value destroyers that killed jobs:

> We support those companies, who act in interest of their future and in interest of their employees against irresponsible locust swarms, who measure success in quarterly intervals, suck off substance, and let companies die once they have eaten them away.[4]

Recent European evidence has studied the question as to whether private equity buyouts kill jobs. Bruining et al. (2005) report that MBOs in the United Kingdom result in higher levels of employment, employee empowerment, and wages. These effects were found to be stronger in the United Kingdom than in Holland and emphasize the importance of understanding different institutional contexts even within Europe. Amess and Wright (2007) consider a panel of 1,350 U.K. LBOs observed over the period 1999 to 2004. Their data indicate that when LBOs are disaggregated, employment growth is 0.51% higher

[2]See Chapter 1 for definitions.

[3]Total factor productivity refers to growth in output not caused by a growth in inputs (Hornstein and Kruseel, 1996; see also http://en.wikipedia.org/wiki/Total_factor_productivity).

[4]See http://en.wikipedia.org/wiki/Locust_(private_equity).

for MBOs after the change in ownership and 0.81% lower for management buyins (MBIs). These findings indicate that MBOs create economic efficiencies and therefore enhance employment, while MBIs typically require considerable restructuring. Preliminary evidence from the United States is consistent with the view that buyouts do not lead to employment reductions. Overall, therefore, the vast majority of empirical evidence is inconsistent with the view that private equity funds are "locusts" that kill jobs.[5]

Despite the evidence on the efficiency of private equity transactions, including buyouts, some countries have imposed significant regulation on private equity. For instance, prior to 2004, in Italy leveraged buyouts were deemed illegal by the Italian Supreme Court. Cumming and Zambelli (2007) show that this prohibition did not eliminate buyouts but did lower the frequency of buyouts. As well, during the period of prohibition, transactions were structured in ways that allocated fewer cash flow and control rights to private equity investors. Further, during the period of prohibition, due diligence was focused on the agreeableness of the target firm management and not substantive issues associated with the quality of the investment. The empirical evidence in Cumming and Zambelli shows that removal of the prohibition on leveraged buyouts by the Italian legislature was appropriate, as it enabled enhanced due diligence and improved transaction structures.

In Chapter 4 (e.g., Figure 4.25), we saw significant discrepancies in the performance of different fund managers and documented persistence in performance. It is therefore worth considering why investor value-added might be different across different funds. Following, we highlight the role of contracts, location, and portfolio size.

15.3 Do Contract Terms Facilitate Investor Effort?

Chapter 16 considers directly the issue of whether contracts have an impact on agency problems. Specifically, we consider whether contractual terms used by venture capitalists impact their advice and monitoring provided to their investee firms. As well, we consider the possibility that contracts influence the extent of disagreement between the investor and investee. These issues are considered by empirically examining an international dataset from continental Europe that matches actual contract terms with the activities of the investor for each investee firm.

We note, however, that contracts are incomplete. That is, it is not possible to write contracts on all eventualities that may arise in a long-term financing arrangement. As such, other factors, such as distance and portfolio size, may indirectly play a significant role above and beyond contracts.

[5]There is evidence, however, that buyouts reduce employment in one study with a sample of 48 U.K. buyouts (Cressy et al., 2007).

15.4 Location

In practice, fund managers are significantly concerned about the locations or proximity of investee firms:

> Venture capital is not about the people you know but rather where you are: FIBRE networks cross the world. Data bits move at light speed. The globe has been flattened, and national boundaries obliterated. Yet . . . physical distance is very much on the minds of the investors who provide venture capital.[6]

Many fund managers consider only companies that are within a 20-minute drive of the venture firm's offices.[7] This is due to the amount of work required by the fund manager in assisting the venture to successful outcome and the limited time the fund manager has to offer his investee firms. If the fund manager's time cost is measured, then even that 20-minute drive over the number of years of the investment in the investee firm may add up to tens of thousands of dollars. Of course, there are many fund managers who do take on investee firms not within close proximity, but it is not something they prefer to do.

Cumming and Dai (2007) consider local bias of venture capital investments in the United States over the period between 1980 and 2000 (for related evidence, see Tian, 2007). They find that venture capitalists in 22 states finance a majority of ventures in their home states (see Table 15.1). For the remainder of the states, venture capitalists have the strongest preference for California. In California, and especially Silicon Valley, there is a cluster of computer-related ventures, while near Boston, Massachusetts (Route 128), there is a cluster of biotechnology-related companies. Cumming and Dai show that about 65% of the new ventures are located in California, Massachusetts, New York, and Texas. About 62% of venture capital firm headquarters are located in these four states. The same four states are most popular in terms of establishing branch offices for venture capital firms.

Cumming and Dai (2007) find that larger venture capital firms, older venture capitalists, and venture capitalists with more previous investment experience exhibit stronger local bias. They explain this finding by the two-sided selection process in venture capital markets (entrepreneurs chose their investor, and investors chose their entrepreneurs). Cumming and Dai further show that distance matters for the eventual performance of venture capital investments in that local investments tend to perform better.

Chapter 17 considers local bias across Canadian provinces. Chapter 20 presents evidence relating local bias to the exit performance of investments.

[6]Stross, Randall, "It's not the people you know. It's where you are." *The New York Times*, October 22, 2006.
[7]Ibid.

Table 15.1 Home Bias in the U.S. Venture Capital Industry

This table summarizes the percentage of same state investments by venture capitalists in the United States over the period 1980–2000.

U.S. State	Percentage of Investments in the Same State	U.S. State	Percentage of Investments in the Same State	U.S. State	Percentage of Investments in the Same State
Idaho	87.70%	Tennessee	53.05%	New Mexico	35.75%
Vermont	86.61%	Kentucky	50.75%	Delaware	33.91%
South Carolina	71.81%	Colorado	50.47%	Maryland	32.34%
Maine	70.54%	Georgia	50.21%	New Jersey	30.11%
North Carolina	65.46%	Nebraska	50.08%	New York	28.86%
California	64.50%	Montana	47.21%	Illinois	28.19%
Hawaii	64.30%	Pennsylvania	46.35%	Alabama	26.98%
Rhode Island	61.57%	Virginia	45.78%	Kansas	26.87%
Massachusetts	60.13%	Texas	45.69%	Michigan	25.42%
Washington	58.86%	Ohio	43.82%	Iowa	25.30%
Arizona	56.77%	Connecticut	42.89%	Arkansas	24.09%
Minnesota	56.34%	Louisiana	40.72%	Montana	23.90%
Oregon	56.18%	Washington, D.C.	39.58%	West Virginia	10.33%
Utah	55.97%	South Dakota	38.70%	Wyoming	3.60%
New Hampshire	54.86%	Indiana	38.03%	Nevada	−3.32%
Wisconsin	54.81%	Florida	35.96%	Mississippi	−19.27%
Oklahoma	54.68%				

Source: Cumming and Dai (2007).

Consistent with Cumming and Dai (2007), there is some evidence that local investments perform better.

15.5 Portfolio Size

Kanniainen and Keuschnigg (2003, 2004), Keuschnigg (2004), and Bernile et al. (2007) have developed theoretical work pertaining to the optimal size of a venture capitalist's portfolio in terms of the number of investees per fund manager. Increasing the size of the portfolio offers potential benefits of diversification and synergies across investee firms, but it comes at the expense of less effort provided to each investee. The optimal portfolio size for each fund will differ as skill sets, intensity of monitoring, and characteristics of specific firms within a portfolio differ across funds. These trade-offs are empirically examined in Chapter 18. Chapters 19 and 22 discuss evidence from Cumming and Walz (2004) on how venture capital funds with very large portfolios per fund manager tend to have significantly lower returns.

15.6 Investment Duration

Venture capital fund managers primarily invest for capital gains upon an exit or sale transaction, particularly since investee firms often do not have cash flows to pay interest on debt or dividends on equity. As such, an important aspect of the investment process is deciding when to exit an investment—that is, how long to invest. Following earlier work (Cumming and MacIntosh, 2001), Cumming and Johan (2007d) conjecture that venture capitalists will continue to invest in a firm as long as the marginal value-added that they provide exceeds the marginal cost of maintaining the investment. Hence, their central theoretical prediction is that the duration of venture capital investment will vary depending on the expected strategic advantage that the venture capitalist brings to the entrepreneurial firm. Where the value-added provided by the venture capitalist is greater, all else being equal, investment duration will be longer. This issue is addressed in further detail in Chapter 19 and Part V.

15.7 Summary

This chapter summarized evidence in venture capital and private equity related to location, portfolio size, and the effect on innovative activity. We will now examine in more detail the impact of contracting on the advice and monitoring provided by the investor (Chapter 16), local bias in venture capital investments (Chapter 17), and portfolio size (Chapter 18). Thereafter, Part V addresses issues involving exits and returns.

Key Terms

Home bias
Portfolio size
Total factor productivity
Private equity locusts

Discussion Questions

15.1. To what degree do venture capital and private equity fund managers exhibit home bias? Is home bias related to subsequent investment performance?
15.2. How does venture capital impact innovative activity?
15.3. What is the mechanism by which venture capital enhances total factor productivity? Is this mechanism the same for private equity buyouts?
15.4. How does private equity impact the efficiency of its investee companies?
15.5. True/False/Uncertain (and explain why): "Private equity funds are locusts that kill jobs."

16 Contracts and Effort

16.1 Introduction and Learning Objectives

A common theme across the literature in economics, finance, law, and management is the role of formal mechanisms (e.g., actual contracts that specify ownership and control, and the law that governs the enforcement of such contracts) versus informal mechanisms (e.g., trust, reputation, and management structures) in governing relationships. Contracts are by definition incomplete, as not all eventualities can be anticipated at the time of writing a contract (see, e.g., Hart and Moore, 1999). We may therefore expect informal governance mechanisms to play a strong role in relationships that are formed by contract. For example, Kanniainen and Keuschnigg (2003, 2004) and Keuschnigg (2004) show an important role for formal and informal governance mechanisms in the context of portfolio size per venture capital fund manager, which actively seek to add value to privately held entrepreneurial firms.[1]

At issue in this chapter is the comparative importance of the more formal contracts and legal settings versus other informal noncontractual governance mechanisms for governing relationships.

In this chapter we will do the following:

- Compare the role of contracts to other governance mechanisms in facilitating venture capital fund manager advice and monitoring to entrepreneurs versus mitigating venture capital fund manager-entrepreneur conflicts[2]

[1]See also Keuschnigg (2003) and Keuschnigg and Nielsen (2001, 2003a,b, 2004a,b,c) for related analyses of taxation, agency costs, and entrepreneurship.

[2]In this chapter, we use the term *venture capital* in the broad (European) definition of the term. In Europe, the venture capital is defined more broadly than it is in the United States. All of the funds in our sample do invest in earlier stages of development, but some funds also finance later-stage investments (which is referred to as *private equity* in the United States). Hence, we do not exclude investments from the sample data on the basis of the stage of development because the same venture capital managers in our sample have contemporaneously invested in both early-stage projects and buyouts. That venture capital managers finance different types of entrepreneurs in different stages is not unheard of in the United States. Many venture capital funds in the U.S. Venture Economics database, for example, indicate a range of investments from seed to buyout, although other U.S. venture capital funds are prohibited from financing buyouts (see Gompers and Lerner, 1999a, 2001a), as are non-U.S. funds (Chapter 5).

- Assess the role of legal systems in mitigating venture capital fund manager-entrepreneur conflicts
- Match detailed venture capital fund contracts to actions taken by venture capital fund managers in an international context

The venture capital setting is an interesting one in which to analyze the role of laws and contracts versus noncontractual mechanisms in business relationships. It is widely recognized that entrepreneurship is characterized by problems of information asymmetry, illiquidity, and nondiversification, and is therefore high risk in terms of both idiosyncratic and market risk. An overriding issue is thus the role of the "expert" investor in facilitating the entrepreneurial venture. In fact, one of the primary explanations for the existence of venture capital funds is the presence of pronounced problems of adverse selection and moral hazard in financing entrepreneurial firms (Amit et al., 1998; Kanniainen and Keuschnigg, 2003, 2004; Mayer et al., 2005; Sapienza, 1992; Zacharakis and Shepherd, 2001, 2005). Inherent in the venture capital fund managers' ability to use their expertise to provide valuable advice to the entrepreneurial firm is their ability to interfere in business or operational decision making of the entrepreneurial firm. For example, venture capital fund managers often take board seats to ensure participation in management decisions and are even able to replace the founder entrepreneur with a professional manager when they feel that the firm is best served, or their objectives are best served, by a manager with different skill sets to further develop the firm, regardless of the sweat equity put in by the founding entrepreneur. The venture capital setting is thus an interesting and important context in which to explore the management of investor-investee relations (or in this case, venture capital fund manager-entrepreneur/entrepreneurial firm relations), since the advice may be as important as the contributed capital, and conflict as detrimental as the absence of the contributed capital (Manigart et al., 2000, 2002a,b,c). Further, it is useful to assess legal systems in conjunction with contracts, as the law provides enforcement mechanisms for contracts, as well as provides a basis for the interpretation of incomplete contracts (i.e., the law provides a set of default rules).

In the investigation of the venture capital fund manager-entrepreneur relationship in this chapter, we consider "effort" put in by the venture capital fund manager, or the total number of hours per month spent with the entrepreneurial firm by venture capital fund managers. We then differentiate this venture capital fund manager commitment to the entrepreneurial firm along two effort dimensions, which we will further refer to as the provision of "advice" and addressing "conflict." We directly measure effort exertion on advice and conflict based on the premise that providing advice is congruent, whereas conflict is dissonant with respect to entrepreneurial interests. In particular, advice is the average of the venture capital fund managers' rankings, on a scale 1 (lowest) to 10 (highest), of the venture capital fund managers' contribution to the venture in the following advising fields: strategy, marketing, issues related to financing, R&D, product development, human resources, exit strategy advice, interpersonal support, help in networking, and any other. Conflict is the total number of issues for which the venture capital fund manager reported disagreement with the entrepreneur, including strategy, marketing, issues related to financing, R&D, product development, human resources, replacement of founder, and any other. Advice is equivalent to the provision of effort or expertise by the venture capital fund manager that constructively contributes to the value of the venture. On the other hand, conflict refers to a state of affairs that call for the venture capital fund manager's effort to monitor, govern, and interfere with the entrepreneur's activity. Notice that advice and number of hours per month are correlated (the correlation coefficient is 0.39) but not perfectly so as hours per month spent with the venture may also involve conflict, and venture capital fund managers may rank advice higher without spending more time advising the firm.

This chapter is distinct from prior academic works in that we develop a framework for distinguishing the role of contracts (specific details on venture capital fund cash flow and control rights) from legal settings (the law of the country in which the entrepreneurial firm resides) for providing formal governance mechanisms for venture capital fund manager-entrepreneur relationships. We further consider and compare the role of formal governance mechanisms (contracts and legal systems) versus other informal noncontractual governance mechanisms (proxied by variables such as syndication and portfolio size per fund manager) and variables for project risk and success potential, among other things. Prior studies have not provided a unifying look into the role of actual venture capital fund contracts and legal settings versus other noncontractual governance mechanisms, risk and success potential on venture capital fund manager-entrepreneur relationships in an international context.

We begin by outlining our hypotheses and then describing the methodology employed to test the hypotheses. Then the data are presented, and the core empirical results together with robustness checks are detailed. We also discuss limitations and alternatives for future research.

16.2 Hypotheses

Our hypotheses concerning the determinants of effort exertion by venture capital fund managers are based on a number of theories modeling the venture capital fund manager's involvement in the entrepreneurial firm through exerting effort. These theories focus on three specific issues: (1) whether the cash flow allocation has a role in implementing optimal incentive schemes for the entrepreneur and the venture capital fund manager, (2) whether the allocation of control rights provides implicit incentives for the venture capital fund manager to interfere in entrepreneurial decision making, and (3) the quality of the legal system of the jurisdiction in which the entrepreneurial firm is located. Following, we briefly discuss the most important theories addressing these issues and their empirical implications.

16.2.1 Allocation of Cash Flow Rights

The allocation of cash flow rights affects the effort that the venture capital fund manager and the entrepreneur will contribute to the entrepreneurial venture. Prior research has established that the efficient effort is elicited from venture capital fund managers where venture capital funds are allocated convertible securities (convertible debt or convertible preferred equity) (Casamatta, 2003; Schmidt, 2003).[3] First, consider nonconvertible debt or nonconvertible preferred equity relative to convertible securities. If the venture capital fund utilizes nonconvertible debt or nonconvertible preferred equity, the venture capital fund does not obtain any ownership interest in the entrepreneurial firm and therefore does not typically have a financial incentive to provide effort. The only case where the venture capital fund manager has an incentive to provide effort is in cases of expected liquidation (where the entrepreneurial firm is potentially experiencing liquidation, the venture capital fund manager does have an incentive to provide effort as the amount paid to the venture capital fund varies directly with the residual value of the entrepreneurial firm; see also Zimmermann, 2002). Hence, convertible securities enable stronger incentives for the venture capital fund manager to provide effort than straight debt or straight preferred equity because the venture capital fund manager has the incentive to provide effort both in times of financial distress and in good times when the firm is not expecting liquidation.

Second, if the venture capital fund utilizes common equity, the venture capital fund manager does not have the high-powered incentives to help the firm in times of financial distress (typically early in the life of the entrepreneurial firm), unlike the case where the venture capital fund holds convertible debt or preferred equity (Berglöf, 1994). As just mentioned, when a firm is in financial distress, debt or preferred equity provides stronger incentives to the venture capital fund manager to provide effort because the entire increase in the value of the firm immediately prior to liquidation goes directly to the debt or preferred equity holder. In good times (when not experiencing financial distress), the contingent claim associated with convertible securities provides stronger incentives for the venture capital fund manager to provide effort (Casamatta, 2003; Hellmann, 1998; Schmidt, 2003).

Pursuant to staged financing rounds, there is an agency problem that is sometimes colloquially referred to as "cooking the books" or "window-dressing." That is, entrepreneurs may make the firm look better than it really is to secure the next financing round from the venture capital funds. Window-dressing problems are typically considered to be more pronounced for informationally opaque firms (early-stage and high-tech firms). The entrepreneur's incentive to window-dress is mitigated when the venture capital fund holds a convertible debt or convertible preferred security (Cornelli and Yosha, 2003), because the venture capital fund may convert its preferred security too early (from the perspective of that which would otherwise be optimal for the entrepreneurial

[3]See Gorman and Sahlman (1989), Sahlman (1990), and Repullo and Suarez (2004) for theoretical work and discussions; see also evidence in Kaplan and Strömberg (2004) and Cumming (2005a,b).

firm) if the entrepreneur provides a biased signal of quality. Window-dressing may give rise to a conflict between entrepreneurs and venture capital fund managers; because convertible securities have been theoretically shown to mitigate the incentive to window-dress (Cornelli and Yosha, 2003), there is reason to believe that convertible securities may also mitigate the extent of venture capital fund manager-entrepreneur conflicts.

Hypothesis 16.1a: *Venture capital fund managers provide more effort and advice to entrepreneurial firms financed with convertible securities (instead of common equity or debt). Moreover, the effort exerted by the venture capital fund manager and advice provided are directly correlated with the venture capital fund's ownership percentage.*

Hypothesis 16.1b: *There are fewer venture capital fund manager-entrepreneur conflicts within entrepreneurial firms financed with convertible securities.*

16.2.2 Allocation of Control Rights

Theoretical work in venture capital finance has indicated that control rights also matter for venture capital fund manager effort incentives. Chan et al. (1990) claim that venture capital fund managers require substantial control rights because of the internal risk associated with the quality of the founding entrepreneur. For example, control rights provide the venture capital fund manager with incentives to engage in an executive search so he can substitute the original manager or founding entrepreneur once that manager turns out to be insufficiently skilled as the firm progresses or develops. Therefore, the more internal risk involved with the venture, the more control is allocated to the venture capital fund manager, and the more intense the venture capital fund manager's effort exertion. Where venture capital fund managers exercise control rights to replace the founding entrepreneur or existing manager with a new manager, conflicts are also more likely to arise between the entrepreneur and the venture capital fund manager. For instance, Hellmann and Puri (2002) show that venture capital fund managers are more likely to replace the founder with an outside CEO, both in situations that appear adversarial and otherwise (as well as facilitate a number of professionalization measures for the entrepreneurial firm such as adopting stock option plans [see also Ammann and Siez, 2005], human resource policies, and hiring key personnel). In addition to internal risk regarding the founding entrepreneur's skill, there is also risk regarding the quality of the project and the likelihood of market adoption. Hellmann (1998) and Kirilenko (2001) argue that a higher degree of external risk associated with project quality and market adoption requires that in equilibrium more control is allocated to the venture capital fund. If riskier projects require more effort, the provision of control to the venture capital fund should exacerbate the venture capital fund manager's contribution.[4]

[4]Several theories outside the venture capital context also suggest that investors' control rights enhance interference. The most well-known examples are Aghion and Bolton (1992) and Burkart et al. (1997).

Recent work is further consistent with the view that the provision of control rights to the venture capital fund may exacerbate the inequality in bargaining power between the entrepreneur and the venture capital fund manager, and allow the venture capital fund manager to act opportunistically vis-à-vis the entrepreneur. Fried and Ganor (2006) show that venture capital fund managers with strong control rights may have an incentive to choose lower-value, lower-risk investment and exit strategies over higher-value, higher-risk strategies. For example, venture capital fund managers may prematurely push for liquidation events, such as dissolutions or mergers that hurt entrepreneurs as ordinary common shareholders but benefit venture capital fund managers as preferred shareholders. Where entrepreneurs disagree with the control rights exercised by the venture capital fund manager, there is also greater scope for potential conflict between the venture capital fund manager and entrepreneur. These theories imply the Hypotheses 16.2a and 16.2b.

Hypothesis 16.2a: *Venture capital fund managers provide more effort and advice for entrepreneurial firms for which the venture capital fund has been allocated greater control rights.*

Hypothesis 16.2b: *Venture capital fund manager-entrepreneur conflicts are more likely among investee firms for which the venture capital fund has been allocated greater control rights.*

In testing Hypotheses 16.2a and 16.2b (discussed following), we control for the various types of risk associated with the investment (among other things) to ascertain the role of control rights.

16.2.3 Quality of Legal System

Countries differ in terms of the strength of legal protections afforded to investors and entrepreneurs alike, including the efficiency of the judicial system, the rule of law, corruption, risk of expropriation, risk of contract repudiation, and shareholder rights (in other words, the substantive content of laws pertaining to investing, the quality of their enforcement, and the likelihood that they will need to be enforced). La Porta et al. (1997, 1998) have developed indices that account for the strength of each of these legal factors across countries, and Berkowitz et al. (2003) have developed a Legality index, which is a weighted sum of these indices derived from La Porta et al. (1997, 1998) (see Chapter 3, Table 3.1).

There are at least three primary reasons to believe that Legality matters in the context of managing venture capital fund manager-entrepreneur relationships. All else being equal, a higher Legality index in a country is associated with more certain enforcement of contract terms and a clearer delineation of the rights and responsibilities of the venture capital fund manager and entrepreneur. Better legal systems mitigate information asymmetries associated with decision making pursuant to rights granted via contracts (consistent with La Porta et al., 1997, 1998; however, see also Drobetz, 2002, and Bührer et al.,

2005). Moreover, better legal systems provide a clearer interpretation of incomplete contracts. Contracts are by their nature incomplete, as not all contingencies and eventualities can be anticipated at the time of investment and incorporated into a written contract. Terms, items, and eventualities not considered and incorporated into contracts are interpreted by the legal system of the country of domicile of the entrepreneurial firm. Matters that govern relationships between firms and their investors depend on the quality of the legal system. Therefore, we expect that Legality will mitigate the scope of venture capital fund manager-entrepreneur conflicts and facilitate the provision of venture capital fund manager advice.

Hypothesis 16.3: *Countries with better legal systems mitigate the scope for venture capital fund manager-entrepreneur conflict, as better legal systems facilitate more certainty in the enforcement of contracts as well as the interpretation of incomplete contracts.*

The primary methods for studying the three central hypotheses are described in the next section. A description of the data and empirical tests follow thereafter in the subsequent sections.

16.3 Methodology

In this section we first describe the measurement of the dependent variables for measuring advice and conflict, and compare our measurements to that used in related work. Thereafter we discuss the variables for testing the central hypotheses and the set of control variables.

16.3.1 Dependent Variables: Hours per Month, Advice, and Conflict

The unit of analysis in this chapter is the entrepreneurial firm. Our empirical analyses proxy the involvement of the venture capital fund manager by the total number of hours per month spent with the entrepreneurial firm. We also asked venture capital fund managers to rank the importance of their contribution to the venture in a number of different fields of activities on a scale of 1 to 10 (lowest to highest). Although this measure is subject to the venture capital fund managers' own performance evaluation, it is indicative that in most advising activities considered, venture capital fund managers reported a significantly higher number of monthly hours for ventures for which they gave higher advice rankings. It was important to distinguish "advice" from "total hours" because certain hours spent may be attributable to addressing "conflict" and not providing the more constructive "advice."

Our measure for conflict is based on the number of different types of disagreements with the entrepreneur. We asked venture capital fund managers to report whether they had disagreements with the entrepreneurial firm concerning different matters including strategy, marketing, financial matters, R&D, human resource, and product development. Our proxy for conflict is the sum of these potential areas of disagreement; that is, it is a measure of the scope of disagreement.[5] We do not count the frequency of disagreements over the same issue, as that was not empirically tractable (venture capital fund managers could not count how many times they disagreed with, for example, human resource policies; it was either an issue of conflict or it was not).

Notice that our measure of conflict (the scope of disagreement) may be correlated with venture capital fund manager monitoring activities carried out during total hours spent on firm business; that is, more intensive monitoring increases the possibility for the venture capital fund manager to discover entrepreneurial shirking and thus gives rise to a higher number of conflicts between the two parties. However, unlike prior work that has directly examined monitoring versus advice (e.g., Kaplan and Strömberg, 2004), in our empirical analysis we focus on advice in terms of all types of value-added assistance provided by the venture capital fund manager and distinguish advice from conflict in terms of the scope of venture capital fund manager-entrepreneur disagreement, which is dissonant with respect to entrepreneurial interests. As indicated, we also provide a measure of total effort in terms of the total number of hours per month the venture capital fund manager spent with the entrepreneurial firm. We provide a new contribution to the literature by examining effort, advice, and conflict in relation to very detailed terms used in venture capital contracts, among other variables described following.

Our empirical strategy is related to a few important empirical papers focusing on investors' involvement in the development of entrepreneurial firms. Most notably, Sapienza et al. (1996) measure effort on advice in two dimensions. They consider venture capital fund managers' rankings of the importance and effectiveness of their contribution. Their measure of advice comes from multiplying the rate of importance with the rate of effectiveness.[6] Sapienza et al. (1996) further examine venture capital fund manager governance in terms of the frequency of face-to-face interactions the venture capital fund manager has with the venture CEO and the number of working hours devoted to the venture.

[5]It is of course true that not all areas of disagreement may be equal, but when we redefined the dependent variable for disagreement as a subset of different types of disagreement, the results did not materially change. (That is, if we changed the variable to a small degree by deleting one or two types of disagreement, then the results did not drastically change.) We felt it was appropriate to consider all types of disagreement mainly because we did not have a theoretical basis for doing otherwise. Additional specifications are available upon request.

[6]In Sapienza et al. (1996), the rate of importance of the venture capitalist's contribution is ranked on a scale of 1 to 5 (1 = not important at all, 5 = of great importance), while the effectiveness ranking is on a scale of 1 to 10 (1 = not effective at all, and 10 = extremely effective). The measure for advice comes from multiplying the importance and the effectiveness ranking. In related work, Gorman and Sahlman (1989) point out the role of venture capital fund managers in strategic analysis, management recruiting, and CEO replacements. Gompers (1995) finds that venture capital fund managers become more active when the risk and growth options involved in their investee firms are high. Sapienza (1992) shows that it is the highly innovative entrepreneurs that benefit most from value-added by venture capital funds. De Clercq and Sapienza (2005), De Clercq et al. (2005), and Sapienza et al. (2005) examine related issues of learning among venture capital fund managers and entrepreneurs.

In related work, Kaplan and Strömberg (2004) provide proxies for advice and monitoring with the use of binary dummy variables. As in Sapienza (1992) and Sapienza et al. (1996), our data consist of significant variation in the dependent variables (among other things).[7]

16.3.2 Explanatory Variables to Test Hypotheses 16.1 to 16.3

To test Hypotheses 16.1a and 16.1b, we use a convertible security dummy variable for investments financed by convertible debt or preferred equity. We exclude dummy variables for other types of securities due to collinearity. To consider the impact of equity holdings, we include the percentage of the venture capital fund's ownership share in the firm (in the best-case scenario) as an explanatory variable. A more detailed definition of each dependent and independent variable used in the analysis is presented in Table 16.1.

To test Hypotheses 16.2a and 16.2b, we use three different proxies to measure the extent of venture capital fund manager control. First, we use the venture capital fund veto rights, which measure the number of veto rights held, such as veto on asset sales or purchases, changes in control, issuance of equity, and other decisions. Second, we measure control rights, such as the right to replace the CEO, the right for first refusal in sale, or IPO registration rights (among other things defined in Table 16.1). The distinction between venture capital fund control and venture capital fund veto rights is important. Venture capital veto rights are passive rights, where it can be said that although the venture capital fund manager is *not* "actively managing" the firm, it is influencing the outcome of the business decision to be made, especially if the decision requires a unanimous consensus. Venture capital control rights, such as the right to replace the founding entrepreneur are active rights, as the outcome of the issue is dependent on the venture capital fund manager's resolve. Cronbach's alpha statistic confirmed the appropriateness of the grouping of the veto versus control rights for the data.[8] As well, in the empirical analysis we account for the

[7]This is unlike Kaplan and Strömberg (2004). It is noteworthy that Kaplan and Strömberg (2004) do not consider potential endogeneity of contracts to effort, unlike our analyses.

[8]Since it is not necessarily appropriate to lump together different types of veto and control rights into a single variable, we computed the Cronbach alpha statistic to check the appropriateness of the grouping of the veto versus control rights. Cronbach's alpha is equal to N * r/(1 + (N – 1) * r, where N is equal to the number of items and r is the average of the interitem correlation among the items. For the grouping of veto rights (asset sales, asset purchases, changes in control, issuances of equity, and other veto rights), the alpha was 0.9581. For the other types of control rights (nonveto rights, including right to replace CEO, automatic conversion at exit, right for first refusal at sale, co-sale agreement, antidilution protection, protection rights against new issues, redemption rights, information rights, IPO registration rights, piggyback registration; see Table 16.1), alpha is 0.7742. For the grouping of the different risk measures enumerated in Tables 16.1 and 16.2, alpha is 0.8351. For the different types of disagreement, alpha is 0.7965. For the different types of advice rankings, alpha is 0.8628. For most social science applications, a reliability coefficient of 0.80 is considered acceptable (see, e.g., http://www.ats.ucla.edu/stat/spss/faq/alpha.html; accessed January 1, 2006; and we also checked dimensionality of the data and did not find reasons to be concerned with the groupings).

Table 16.1 Definition of Variables

This table provides an exact definition for each of the most important variables considered in the chapter. This table does not list several control variables in the chapter that are easy to interpret (these variables are indicated in Table 16.2).

Dependent Variables: Venture Capital Fund Manager Effort and Conflict	
Venture Capital Fund Manager Hours	Monthly number of hours the venture capital fund manager spends with the venture.
Advice	Average of the venture capital fund manager's rankings, on a scale 1 (lowest) to 10 (highest), of the venture capital fund manager's contribution to the venture in the following advising fields: strategy, marketing, issues related to financing, R&D, product development, human resources, exit strategy advice, interpersonal support, help in networking, and any other. If no advice was provided for a field, then the value "0" was entered.
Conflict	Total number of fields for which the venture capital fund manager reported disagreement with the entrepreneur. Fields considered: strategy, marketing, issues related to financing, R&D, product development, human resources, replacement of founder, and any other.
Variables to Test Hypotheses: Venture Capital Fund Manager Contractual Terms and Legal Conditions	
Convertible Security (H16.1)	Dummy variable for investees financed either with convertible debt or convertible preferred equity.
Venture Capital Fund Manager Ownership Share (H16.1)	% Ownership of venture capital fund manager; given contingencies in contracts, the best-case scenario for the entrepreneurial firm performance is considered.
Veto Rights (H16.2)	The sum of the following veto right dummies: asset sales, asset purchases, changes in control, issuance of equity, any other decisions. "Full veto control" means that all five types of control rights were used in the investment.
Special Control Rights (H16.2)	The sum of the following control dummies (dummy takes value 1 if venture capital fund manager has the right): right to replace CEO, automatic conversion at exit, right for first refusal at sale, co-sale agreement, antidilution protection, protection rights against new issues, redemption rights, information rights, IPO registration rights, piggyback registration.
Board Rights (H16.2)	Venture capital fund manager board seats as % of total number of board seats at the company.
Legality (H16.3)	Weighted average of following factors (based on Berkowitz et al., 2003): civil versus common law systems, efficiency of judicial system, rule of law, corruption, risk of expropriation, risk of contract repudiation, shareholder rights. Higher numbers indicate "better" legal systems.

(*continued*)

Table 16.1 *(continued)*

Selected Control Variables (Others Are Listed in Table 16.2)	
Project Risk	Average of the venture capital fund manager's rankings of the following risk factors: uncertain market size, uncertainty about product, risky competitive position, uncertain customer adoption, risks in business strategy, questionable performance to date, contractual structure, high valuation, costly to monitor, exit conditions, negative influence of other investors.
Entrepreneur Experience	Venture capital fund manager's ranking of the entrepreneur's experience on a scale of 1–10.
Hours from Syndicated Partners	The average number of hours per month that the syndicated venture capital fund manager investors spent with the investee firm.
Investment Rounds	Number of staged financing rounds the venture capital fund manager financed the investment.
Book Value	Log of the book value of the investment at the time of first investment, measured in € '000.
Investment Months	Number of investment months from first investment date to exit (for exited investments) or to 12/2002 (for nonexited investments).
MSCI	The Morgan Stanley Capital International Index (www.msci.com) for the public stock market return in the investee country from the time of first venture capital fund manager investment until exit, or until 12/2002 if there has not been an exit.
Venture Capital Fund Manager Portfolio Size/# Venture Capital Fund Manager Managers	The number of entrepreneurial firms in the venture capital fund manager fund portfolio per the number of venture capital fund manager managers.

potential endogeneity of both the control and cash flow rights variables and the venture capital fund manager effort variables. We further control for the proportion of board seats held by the venture capital fund manager.

To test the quality of laws on venture capital fund manager-entrepreneur relations in Hypothesis 16.3, we use the Legality index, which accounts for the substantive content of laws pertaining to investing, the quality of their enforcement, and the likelihood that they will need to be enforced. Based on Berkowitz et al. (2003) and derived from (La Porta et al., 1997, 1998), the Legality index is a weighted sum of the following factors: the efficiency of the judicial system, the rule of law, corruption, risk of expropriation, risk of contract repudiation, and shareholder rights.[9] Higher numbers indicate "better"

[9]We do not use separate variables for each of these legal factors because they are very highly correlated.

legal systems. Because the subcomponents of the Legality index are highly collinear, we focus on the Legality index in our regressions to avoid the appearance of data mining. We did consider specific components of the Legality index but found much similarity in the qualitative results, so we focus on the overall Legality index variable.

16.3.3 Other Governance Mechanisms, Risk, and Controls for Other Factors

Sapienza et al. (1996) consider the determinants of advice and governance by examining agency risk (represented by CEO experience) and other project and environment-related uncertainty (business risk ranking, the firm's stage of development, and the innovativeness of the project). Although they find no evidence of more intense advice or governance in ventures with less CEO experience, they find that project- and environment-related uncertainty matters: Venture capital fund managers become more involved in early-stage ventures and in projects with higher risk assessment. We likewise control for various measures of risk in our empirical analyses. Similar to Sapienza et al. (1996), Kaplan and Strömberg (2004) use venture capital fund managers' investment memoranda and identify three different types of risk measures: "internal risk," which is a consequence of asymmetric information between the parties; "external risk," which refers to environment-related uncertainty; and "project complexity" risk, which arises from the difficulty and complexity of project realization. We use several risk variables that capture the different project- and environment-related uncertainty inherent in an investment. The most important are the venture capital fund managers' ranking of the "entrepreneur's experience" and "project risk" on a scale of 1 to 10. To establish an overall project risk measure, we build on Kaplan and Strömberg (2004).[10] We ask venture capital fund managers to rank their investments on a scale of 1 to 10 for a number of risk types, such as uncertainty about product/technology, risky competitive position, uncertain customer adoption, and so on. We employ an average of these risk factors[11]—excluding the entrepreneur's experience, which is considered separately—in the empirical analysis. Since early-stage investments and firms in high-tech industries usually represent greater uncertainty, a stage dummy variable and industry dummies for the biotechnology, electronics,

[10]Based on an analysis of venture capitalists' investment memoranda, Kaplan and Strömberg (2004) identify the following risk factors of start-up investments: uncertain market size, uncertainty about product/technology, risky competitive position, uncertain customer adoption, risk in business strategy, quality of entrepreneur's management and business skills, questionable performance to date, contractual structure and downside risk, high valuation, costly to monitor investment, negative influence of other investors, and uncertain financial market and exit conditions.

[11]This is in contrast to Kaplan and Strömberg (2004), who categorize the different risk factors as internal, external, and complexity risk. In our sample, these risk distinctions were not statistically or economically significant, and the risk measures were very highly correlated (generally the correlation coefficients are greater than 0.5).

and Internet investments are also considered as additional proxies for the risk involved. Moreover, since foreign investments may also be riskier for the venture capital fund manager, we include a "foreign investment" dummy variable (this issue of location is studied further in Chapter 17).

Most venture investments are syndicated transactions. In an empirical investigation of the U.S. biotechnology industry, Lerner (1994) finds that older, larger, and thus more experienced venture capital fund managers tend to syndicate with other established venture funds, which refers to complementarities concerning skills of syndicate members. Brander et al. (2002), Chemmanur and Tian (2008), and Tian (2008) argue that venture capital syndication facilitates value-added advice provided to the entrepreneur. Wright and Lockett (2003) emphasize the importance of nonlegal sanctions in mitigating opportunistic behavior by dominant equity holders, particularly through informal mechanisms and reputation concerns. The theoretical analysis in Casamatta and Haritchabalet (2003) is consistent in that it argues that effort exertion by syndicate members depend on their experience: Less experienced venture capital fund managers will exert too little, whereas more experienced venture capital fund managers will provide too much effort to increase the chance for success. These theories suggest that complementarities of effort exertion will characterize syndicated transactions: Venture capital fund managers work more when their syndicating counterparts also exert increased effort. We therefore consider the impact of the average number of monthly hours provided by syndicating partners on the three measures of venture capital fund managers' involvement. The preceding discussion suggests that effort exertion in investment syndicates will depend on the participating venture capital fund managers' skills and experience. Since venture capital fund managers that exert more effort may accumulate more experience and thus participate in more efficient syndicates, syndication may be endogenous to effort exertion by venture capital fund managers; thus, the direction of causality requires further scrutiny. The problem is addressed in the empirical analyses following.

Moreover, considering the size of the venture capital fund per number of managers, we test whether the extent of the venture capital fund manager involvement depends on portfolio size, as modeled by Kanniainen and Keuschnigg (2003, 2004) and Keuschnigg (2004; see also Cumming, 2006a, and Gygax and Griffiths, 2007). As well, notice that since venture capital fund managers exerting more effort are able to manage larger portfolios, the variable we employ in the analysis (the number of entrepreneurial firms in the portfolio per number of venture capital managers)[12] may be endogenous to our

[12]Controls for the amount of capital in the venture capital fund per the number of fund managers were too highly correlated with the variable for this measure of portfolio size per fund manager and therefore were not used. Either way, the other variables are not affected. The number of observations per fund does not enable us to use fund fixed effects. Nevertheless, we have considered a variety of different controls and robustness checks. For instance, we considered excluding one fund at a time to see if the results changed, and they did not. Other variables such as fund size, fund type, fund age, and so forth, did not effect the tests of the hypotheses and control variables.

advising and conflict measures. We address this issue in the empirical analysis. We also use variables for the characteristics of the venture capital fund, including variables that distinguish independent venture capital funds (also referred to as limited partnerships) from bank-affiliated or funds owned by large corporations.[13]

Another group of control variables consists of investment performance characteristics such as dummy variables for successful exits. Since venture capital fund managers generate most of their profits from a small number of very profitable investments (so-called high-flyers or home runs), which often yield more than five times the value of the initial investment, their projects' inherent success potential seems to be important for success. Related evidence is provided by Sahlman (1990): In a sample of 383 investments, about 35% of all projects turned out to be a total failure, 15% were highly profitable, and the remaining 50% were moderately successful. We presume that venture capital fund managers exert more effort on their inherently successful projects. We test this assumption by involving dummy variables for successful IPO or acquisition exits. Further, we assume that if venture capital fund managers exert more effort on a few successful investments, they will exert less effort on their "moderately successful" projects, which remain in their portfolio for a long time. In that case, the length of the investment period, which we proxy with the number of investment months, must be negatively related to their involvement. To the extent that successful exits occur as a consequence of intense advising by venture capital fund managers, concerns for endogeneity naturally arise for this group of variables. The issue is addressed in the subsequent empirical analysis.

Finally, we include the book value of the investment and the number of investment rounds as transaction-related control variables. The first is to test whether the involvement of venture capital fund managers varies according to investment size. The latter accounts for the fact that staging is a monitoring device: Investments in several rounds require more intense involvement by venture capital fund managers, especially in the monitoring task (Witt and Brachtendorf, 2006). To the extent that staging happens as a consequence of the venture capital fund manager's ex-ante appraisal of project risk, the number of investment rounds may be endogenous to effort exertion, especially monitoring. Thus, in the empirical analysis, we treat the number of rounds as a potential endogenous variable.

[13]In Europe, many venture capital funds are affiliated with larger financial institutions such as banks. We do not restrict our attention to limited partnerships (the more common venture capital structure in the United States) but control for the type of fund in the empirical analysis. We also considered the possibility that other venture capital fund characteristics matter for advice and conflicts, such as fund age and size, but did not find material differences for the regressions reported below. We further considered the possibility of a "halo effect" for different portfolio firms from the same investor by excluding different funds (one at a time) from the dataset and rerunning the regressions and did not find material influences due to one of the funds. Notice, however, that the sample size did not allow the use of fixed-effect dummy variables for the different funds in the data.

There are a variety of other variables that were collected to control for other potential factors that influence the venture capital fund manager-entrepreneur relationship. These are described in detail in the next sections, which report the tests of Hypotheses 16.1 to 16.3.

16.4 The Dataset

16.4.1 Data Collection

The data were obtained by a mail survey and follow-up interviews of venture capital fund members of the European Venture Capital Association (EVCA). In total, there are data on 121 investment rounds in 74 entrepreneurial firms from 14 venture capital funds in 7 continental European countries (Belgium, Denmark, Germany, Hungary, Italy, Portugal, and the Netherlands). Approximately 250 private (nongovernmental) funds were contacted in the initial data collection effort. Those funds were selected based on a random sample of private venture capital funds from the EVCA in continental Europe. Approximately 30% initially expressed interest in participating in the study; however, upon informing the funds of the extent of details requested, only 14 (5%) agreed to provide full access to contracts used by their funds. Hence, from the broad initial effort, the response rate was slightly more than 5%, which is consistent with the only prior study on topic with the detailed information on contracts used in Kaplan and Strömberg (2004; as described following, their sample is a U.S.-only sample involving 11 venture capital funds and 67 entrepreneurial firms, whereas our sample comprises 14 European venture capital funds and 74 entrepreneurial firms). Funds that had an interest in participating in the study were interviewed (directly for some funds and by phone calls for other funds for which travel was not possible) in 2003 and 2004. The details pertaining to the venture capital fund contract terms and effort exerted for their investee firms involved compiling a mix of hard contract data alongside qualitative data on effort and actions taken by the venture capital fund managers.

It is difficult to quantitatively comment on the representativeness of the data. Normally, we would compare the publicly available information of the respondents versus the nonrespondents on a fund level. However, in our case we have details from 14 funds, which makes it difficult to carry out meaningful comparison of means and medians tests. To ensure the integrity of the data collected, the respondents were provided assurances that the information collected would remain strictly confidential (particularly the actual contract terms) and not be made publicly available. Data were disclosed on a completely voluntary basis. Given the type of confidential information collected (particularly for actual contract terms), naturally we cannot refer to an aggregate industry database for comparison.

We can point out that our sample is similar to prior datasets on private equity exits in terms of the frequency of use of different securities and specific contract terms (e.g., Kaplan et al., 2005; Lerner and Schoar, 2005). The scope of prior datasets on venture capital fund manager activities (see, e.g., Sapienza, 1992; Sapienza et al., 1996) is also similar to that reported herein. The scope of other venture capital datasets with detailed venture capital contract terms (Bascha and Walz, 2007; Kaplan et al., 2007; Lerner and Schoar, 2005; Schwienbacher, 2008) is also very similar to our own in terms of details and number of observations, and the frequency of use of particular contracts is similar to that reported in this study. For example, the only other study that matches venture capital fund contract terms (with the level of detail used in this study) to venture capital fund manager effort (Kaplan and Strömberg, 2004) consists of 67 entrepreneurial firms from 11 venture capital funds in the United States, and that study only has binary measures of effort. Our study is unique in that we provide international evidence from continental Europe and have more variation in venture capital fund manager effort in terms of details on hours spent, and so forth (not merely binary measures of effort).

It is important to point out that the unit of analysis is the entrepreneurial firm, so our regression analyses consist of 74 observations. In the dataset, no fund provided data on more than 7 investments, and one provided data on just 2 firms. The number of deals provided by the fund depended on the number of deals in which the managing partner of the venture capital fund that provided the data had direct familiarity with (crucial in terms of her effort measurement and in terms of the hard contract data); not all fund managers within each of the 14 funds were involved in the study, as venture capital fund managers are not directly involved in every investee firm in which their fund invests.[14] Thus, the results that follow are not uniquely attributable to any given fund in the data (see also footnote 9 and accompanying text). While we do not have all investee firms for all venture capital funds, we do have all investee funds for all venture capital fund managers that participated in the study.

16.4.2 Data Summary

Table 16.1 defines many of the variables in the dataset (and excludes a number of variables that are self-explanatory). Table 16.2 provides summary statistics for most all of the variables in the dataset. The typical venture capital fund manager in the data provides approximately 15 hours of work per month to an entrepreneurial firm. This is similar to seminal work of Gorman and Sahlman (1989), who report lead venture capital fund managers in the United States spending 4 to 5 hours in direct contact with entrepreneurs (non-lead venture capital fund managers report spending 2 to 3 hours in their visits on average) and extra time helping venture capital fund managers when not in direct contact with entrepreneurs. The average fund in our data finances on average 2.1 entrepreneurial firms per venture capital fund manager, which is

[14]The small number of the entrepreneurial firms in our sample is attributable to the fact that we requested a significant amount of confidential data on each financing transaction.

Table 16.2 Descriptive Statistics

This table provides the mean, median, standard deviation, and minimum and maximum values for most of the variables in the data. The number of observations for each variable is 74 (74 investee companies). The unit of analysis is the entrepreneurial investee firm.

	Average	Median	Standard Deviation	Minimum	Maximum
Dependent Variables: Venture Capital Fund Manager Effort and Conflict					
Hours per Month	15.48	10	15.59	0	60
Advice	2.39	1.83	1.79	0	6.78
Conflict	0.89	0	1.42	0	7
Contractual Terms and Legal Conditions					
Convertible Preferred Equity Dummy Variable	0.38	0	0.49	0	1
Venture Capital Fund Manager Ownership Percentage	0.29	0.25	0.16	0	0.87
Venture Capital Fund Manager Veto Rights	3.80	5	1.98	0	1
Venture Capital Fund Manager Control Rights	5.97	6	2.56	0	1
Venture Capital Fund Manager Board Seats	0.25	0.20	0.22	0	1
Legality Index of Investee Country	19.53	20.44	2.72	12.80	21.78
Control Variables: Entrepreneurial Firm Characteristics					
Early-stage Investee Company at Time of First Investment	0.72	1	0.45	0	1
Late-stage Investee Company	0.28	0	0.45	0	1
Medical Dummy Variable	0.07	0	0.25	0	1
Computer Dummy Variable	0.27	0	0.45	0	1
Internet Dummy Variable	0.18	0	0.38	0	1
Foreign Investment Dummy Variable	0.19	0	0.39	0	1
Project Risk	3.30	2.77	2.21	1	8.30
Entrepreneur Experience	6.57	7	2.25	1	10

(continued)

Table 16.2 (*continued*)

	Average	Median	Standard Deviation	Minimum	Maximum
Venture Capital Fund Manager Fund Characteristics					
Limited Partner Venture Capital Fund Manager Dummy Variable	0.51	1	0.50	0	1
Capital under Management ('000 Euro)	389069	150000	604698	70000	2500000
Capital under Management ('000 Euro)/ Venture Capital Fund Manager	21605	16714	11594	7143	38462
Number of Investee Firms/ Venture Capital Fund Manager	2.15	1.59	1.68	0.190	6.00
Investment Characteristics and Performance					
Lead Investor Dummy Variable	0.66	1	0.48	0	1
Number of Syndicated Venture Capital Fund Managers	1.28	1	1.24	0	5
Hours per Month of Syndicated Venture Capital Fund Managers	10.41	6	16.83	0	70
Book Value of Investment at Time of First Investment ('000 Euro)	5570.10	2257.30	9253.36	150.00	52000
Number of Financing Rounds	1.64	1	0.85	1	5
Investment Months	30.73	31	15.99	3	84
MSCI Market Return over Investment Period	−0.08	−0.08	0.14	−0.33	0.36
IPO Exit Dummy Variable	0.16	0	0.37	0	1
Trade Sale Exit Dummy Variable	0.45	0	0.50	0	1
Write-off Exit Dummy Variable	0.07	0	0.25	0	1

identical to prior work on venture capital portfolio size per manager reported in a Canadian dataset by Cumming (2006a). In our sample, 37.8% of transactions use convertible preferred stock, which is less than the 53.8% reported by Kaplan et al. (2007) for an international sample of venture capital fund managers (although Schwienbacher, 2008, reports that venture capital fund managers in Europe use convertibles for approximately 20% of transactions, which is significantly less than that reported by Kaplan et al.'s, 2007, international sample). In our sample, 66% of the entrepreneurial firms financed (49 of 74) involved syndicated deals, which is about twice as great as that reported for Europe (see the EVCA yearbook). The difference is likely due to the high proportion of early-stage investments in our sample (72%). Schwienbacher (2008) reports that European venture capital funds syndicate 54% of their deals, which is consistent with our dataset. Wright and Lockett (2003) report a greater number of syndicated partners for early-stage deals, which is also consistent with our data. The average number of syndicated venture capital fund managers in our data is 1.284, which is also consistent with Wright and Lockett (2003) and Schwienbacher (2008). A majority of the exited investments were by way of trade sales, consistent with Schwienbacher's European sample of exits; although notice that 32.4% of the investments had not yet been exited at the time of collection of our sample. The average fund size and the investment amounts per investee are quite consistent with figures reported by Wright and Lockett (2003) for the United Kingdom, Bascha and Walz (2007) for Germany, and Schwienbacher (2008) for Europe.

Table 16.3 (Panels A and B) depicts the data by different numbers of hours worked by the venture capital fund manager. The data are presented by entrepreneurial firm, mainly because we do not observe significant variation across different financing rounds. The first column in Table 16.3 presents the data for all the entrepreneurial firms in the sample. The next columns break down the information by the number of hours of support received by the entrepreneurial firms from their venture capital fund managers, including the managing partners and their associates.[15]

The first group of numbers in Table 16.3, Panel A, describe the most important contracting features employed in the investments in our sample. Most of the transactions were financed by convertible securities or straight equity, but we observe a small number of debt investments as well.[16] The use of convertible securities does not seem to enhance the number of hours venture capital fund managers spend with entrepreneurs. Board representation and the allocation of veto rights reflect, however, that investors are more involved in firms

[15]We do not report the entrepreneurs' average hours worked simply because entrepreneurs generally work full time and it was not feasible to track any variation in entrepreneur hours (see further the discussion in the section on limitations and future research).

[16]The pattern of financial contracts observed in this dataset is similar to that reported by Bascha and Walz (2007) and Schwienbacher (2008) for venture capital fund managers in Europe; similar evidence is also found in Canada (Cumming, 2005a,b).

Table 16.3 Summary of the Data by Monthly Hours Spent with the Entrepreneurial Firm

This table presents a summary of the data in terms of the average number of hours per month spent with the entrepreneurial firm by the respondent venture capital fund manager. Panel A presents the characteristics of the respondent venture capital fund managers (type of venture capital fund manager, capital under management), entrepreneurial firm characteristics (Legality index of the country of location, foreign versus domestic investments, stage of development, industry), transaction specific (number of hours for syndicated partners, type of securities used, board composition, allocation of veto and ownership rights, number of rounds, and book value) and performance characteristics (investment duration, and the actual and expected IPOs and acquisitions). Panel B shows the average advice ranking for 9 different advising fields, the number of disagreements in 8 possible matters including appointing a new CEO, the number of conflicts related to exit with founder and other parties, the average risk ranking of investments for 13 different risk factors, and the average rank of the entrepreneurs' experience. Some important variables are typed bold.

	Panel A				
	Total	**Hours $<$ 10**	**10 $\leq$ Hours $<$ 20**	**20 $\leq$ Hours $<$ 30**	**30 $\leq$ Hours**
Respondent Venture Capital Fund Manager Hours	74	31	17	9	17
Contractual Terms and Legal Conditions					
Number of Common Equity and/or Warrant Investments	38	18	9	3	8
Number of Convertible Pref. Equity and/or Conv. Debt Inv.	28	12	6	2	8
Number of Debt and/or Preferred Equity Investments	8	1	2	4	1
Average Venture Capital Fund Manager Ownership	0.29	0.31	0.26	0.22	0.32
Average Venture Capital Fund Manager Board Seats/ Total Board Seats	0.25	0.23	0.22	0.30	0.31

Number of Investments with Partial or No Veto Control	27	13	11	2	1
Number of Investments with Full Veto Control	47	18	6	7	16
Average Legality Index in Entrepreneur's Country	19.53	20.06	19.29	17.89	17.68
Project and Environment Related Risk					
Average Overall Risk Ranking	4.46	4.42	4.03	3.69	4.37
Average ENT Experience Ranked on Scale 1–10	6.57	6.65	6.35	6.58	6.76
Number of Early (Seed Start-up/Expansion) Stage Inv.	53	21	11	7	13
Number of Late (Late/Buyout/Turnaround) Stage Inv.	21	10	6	1	4
Number of Investments in High-tech Industry	38	14	9	9	6
Number of Investments in Nontech Industry	36	17	8	0	11
Number of Foreign Venture Capital Fund Manager Investments	14	8	1	0	5
Number of Domestic Venture Capital Fund Manager Investments	60	23	16	9	12
Investment Characteristics and Performance					
Average Number of Financing Rounds	1.64	1.35	1.76	1.56	2.06
Syndicated Venture Capital Fund Manager Hours	74	46	12	4	12
Average Book Value ('000)	5,570	3,255	11,939	2,616	4,987
Average Investment Duration (Months)	30.73	33.93	33.88	25.11	24.70
Number of Actual IPOs	5	1	0	2	2

(*continued*)

Table 16.3 (*continued*)

	Panel A				
	Total	Hours < 10	10 ≤ Hours < 20	20 ≤ Hours < 30	30 ≤ Hours
Number of Expected IPOs	7	4	2	0	1
Number of Actual Acquisitions	11	2	6	0	3
Number of Expected Acquisitions	22	4	7	6	5
Venture Capital Fund Manager Characteristics					
Number of Limited Partnership Venture Capital Fund Managers	38	16	10	4	8
Number of Bank-affiliated Venture Capital Fund Managers	36	15	7	5	9
Average Capital under Management ('000) per Venture Capital Fund Managers	17,888	21,922	18,290	24,422	23,217
Venture Capital Fund Manager Portfolio Size per # Venture Capital Fund Managers	2.15	2.97	1.06	1.72	2.00
	Panel B				
Average Venture Capital Fund Manager Advice Ranked on Scale 1–10					
Strategic Advice	3.99	3.10	3.94	5.22	5.00
Marketing Advice	1.91	1.29	1.65	4.00	2.18

Financial Advice	4.64	4.65	3.35	6.11	5.12
R&D Advice	0.80	0.84	0.18	1.11	1.18
Product Development Advice	0.88	0.84	0.41	0.56	1.59
Human Resource Advice	1.91	1.29	1.53	2.78	2.94
Exit Strategy Advice	3.04	2.74	3.53	1.56	3.88
Interpersonal Support	1.66	0.94	1.76	1.67	2.88
Help in Networking	2.73	1.94	1.76	3.89	4.53
Average Overall Advice Ranking	2.39	1.96	2.01	2.99	3.25
Number of Disagreements with Management Team					
Strategy	21	4	6	2	9
Marketing	8	1	1	3	3
Financial	11	3	1	0	7
R&D	3	1	0	1	1
Product Development	8	1	1	1	5
Human Resources	7	1	1	1	4
Other	1	1	0	0	0
Venture Capital Fund Manager Has Replaced Founder as CEO	7	1	0	0	6
Total Number of Disagreements	66	13	10	8	35

in which they have more extensive control. In particular, venture capital fund managers with more extensive board representation tend to provide a greater number of hours. Moreover, the average number of hours spent is proportionately less when the venture capital fund managers have partial or no veto control as opposed to full veto control. These observations indicate univariate support for the hypothesis that control rights increase the involvement of venture capital fund managers in their entrepreneurial firms (Hypothesis 16.2b).

Our data include a number of project risk characteristics. Noteworthy is that contrary to our expectations, venture capital fund managers spend the highest number of hours with entrepreneurs with the highest experience rankings. Further, there seems to be a strong positive correlation between the number of hours and the stage of development.[17] We observe more hours of support for early-stage investments. About half of the firms in the sample were in high-tech industries (biotech, electronics, or Internet). There do not appear to be any differences in the involvement of venture capital fund managers by industry type. However, venture capital fund managers report a greater number of hours for investments in countries with lower Legality indices. These observations indicate univariate support for the hypothesis that venture capital fund managers exert more effort on riskier investments (Hypothesis 16.2a).

Concerning the performance of investments, the data suggest that there is generally a negative relation between the average hours of support and total investment duration.[18] This refers to a number of investments in the venture capital fund managers' portfolio that are neither profitable enough to be exited nor represent failures, but at the same time they are not worth the venture capital fund manager's extensive involvement. Moreover, the information on exit outcomes reflects that most of the IPOs (the most successful exits) to date have received an average of more than 20 hours per month of support.

The last group of numbers in Table 16.3, Panel A, reflect the characteristics of the respondent venture capital fund managers. Thirty-eight of the entrepreneurial firms were financed by limited partnership venture capital funds, and 36 by bank-affiliated venture capital funds. We do not observe significant differences in the distribution of hours, depending on venture capital fund manager type. Portfolio size per manager, however, is notably larger among the entrepreneurs that receive fewer than 10 hours per month of support from

[17]The venture capital funds classified the investments as being in one of the following categories: seed, early, expansion, buyout, late, and turnaround stage. This classification corresponds to the definition of stages by the EVCA. We use a simplified classification: We consider the investments as of early (i.e., seed, early, or expansion phase) or late (late, buyout, or turnaround phase) stage. The main reason for this classification is that the definitions of early-stage investments are somewhat blurred across funds and across countries, and our data comprise very few (5) buyout and turnaround investments, which did not warrant separate variables.

[18]Another factor influencing the relation between number of investment months and average hours per month is the escalation of commitment. Because venture capital fund managers may want to avoid being associated with failures, they may be spending more time with their firms in an effort to make them more successful. For work on this topic, see, for example, Birmingham et al. (2003).

the venture capital fund manager, consistent with Kanniainen and Keuschnigg (2003, 2004) and Keuschnigg (2004b).

Table 16.3, Panel B, provides information pertaining to our advice and conflict measures. A number of rankings of the importance of venture capital fund manager advice are provided in the first group of numbers, including strategic, marketing, financial, R&D, product development, human resource, exit strategy, interpersonal support, and help in networking. The table indicates that for most support activities, venture capital fund managers report higher advice rankings if they spend a higher number of hours with the firm. This observation holds also for the average advice ranking, which we employ in the multivariate empirical analysis.

The second group of numbers in Table 16.3, Panel B, report various types of disagreement between the venture capital fund manager and entrepreneur (including situations in which the venture capital fund manager has replaced the founder with another professional manager as CEO).[19] The most disagreements were with entrepreneurial firms for which venture capital fund managers spent at least 30 hours per month. The positive relationship between disagreements and the time spent with the venture is suggestive that conflicts proxy the venture capital fund manager's monitoring effort.

A correlation matrix is provided in an extended version of the chapter, which is available upon request. The correlations provide some support for Hypotheses 16.1 to 16.3, in that veto rights are significantly positively correlated with monthly hours (the correlation statistic is 0.35) and advice (0.53), and Legality is significantly negatively correlated with disagreement (−0.23). It is also noteworthy that the hours from syndicated partners are very highly correlated with the respondent venture capital fund manager hours (0.48), consistent with Wright and Lockett (2003). Portfolio size per fund manager is highly negatively correlated with disagreement (−0.24). Overall, therefore, the univariate correlations provide suggestive evidence that is consistent with the theory discussed previously in conjunction with the hypotheses and control variables. Multivariate tests provided in the next section supply more robust and conclusive evidence.

The correlation matrix also provided guidance in terms of considering issues of collinearity in the regressions in subsequent sections. We test for collinearity by excluding various variables in alternative regression specifications in the next section. The correlation coefficients between pairs of independent variables are generally lower than 0.4, suggesting that significant collinearity problems are unlikely (see, e.g., Judge et al., 1982, p. 620). Nevertheless, since collinearity may be present among a multitude of independent variables, we also computed the variance inflation factors (VIFs). For one variable, a dummy variable for limited partnership venture capital funds, we found the VIFs to be 2.4. In all other cases, the VIFs were significantly below 2, suggesting that

[19]Exit-related disagreements are excluded from the sum total of different disagreements because not all firms in the sample have gone through the exit process and because most of the exit conflicts were not with the entrepreneurial team but rather with other parties.

multicollinearity is not a severe problem for the econometric regressions presented in the next section (Kennedy, 1998, p. 190). It is perhaps not altogether surprising that the limited partnership dummy variable has a significant VIF, as the type of venture capital fund significantly affects its investments (see, e.g., Gompers and Lerner, 1999). In the case of the dummy variable for limited partnerships, we also considered excluding that variable, and the reported results were not materially different. The next section provides a number of different specifications of the variables. Additional specifications not presented are available upon request.

16.5 Econometric Analysis

This section provides OLS and 2SLS estimations of the three different proxies of the involvement of venture capital fund managers as dependent variables: the total number of hours per month spent with the entrepreneurial firm, the average advice ranking, and the total number of disagreements between the venture capital fund manager and the entrepreneur. Table 16.4 presents the results for the number of hours, Table 16.5 for the advice measure, and Table 16.6 for the disagreement variable. To account for the discrete nature of the disagreement variable, we show both least squares and ordered logit estimates in Table 16.6. Each table presents five regressions to check for the effect of specification bias and collinearity among the explanatory variables. Models 1 to 4 in each table present alternative explanatory variables to show the possible influence of collinearity. Each table also provides a 2SLS specification (Model 5) to check for the effect of potential endogeneity.

Our explanatory variables are broken down into four categories. The relevant variables to test the impact of contractual terms on effort exertion by venture capital fund managers (namely Hypotheses 16.1 to 16.3) are shown in the first group in each table. To consider how the risk involved in an investment affects the venture capital fund manager's involvement (Hypothesis 16.2), we employ a number of different proxies for project- and environment-related uncertainty, which are presented in the second group. The last two categories include controls for investment performance and venture capital fund characteristics in each table. For reasons discussed alongside the development of the preceding hypotheses, several contract-specific and investment performance variables may be endogenous to the involvement of venture capital fund managers. We control for the potential endogeneity by using two-stage least squares estimations of the following explanatory variables: the convertible security dummy, the venture capital fund manager's ownership share, veto rights, board rights, special control rights, the number of hours by syndicating partners, IPO and acquisition exit dummies, investment months, investment rounds, and venture capital portfolio size per number of venture capital managers. In the first step of the regression, we estimate these variables as functions of exogenous instruments, such as project- and environment-related risk characteristics, investment and exit year dummies, and returns to the Morgan Stanley Capital International Inc. (MSCI) index over the period of the investment.[20] The instruments might be correlated with, for example, exit potential or the experience of venture capital fund managers, but they are less likely to be correlated with the advice and conflict measures.[21] In an extended version of this chapter we present correlations across a variety of potentially endogenous variables and various instruments. In brief, the instruments used are useful (although not 100% perfect), as the correlations with the instruments and dependent variables are generally less statistically significant than the correlations between the instruments and the potentially endogenous explanatory variables.

16.5.1 Hypotheses 16.1 to 16.3: The Impact of Contracts and Laws on Venture Capital Fund Manager-Entrepreneur Relationships

In regards to Hypothesis 16.1a, there is some evidence consistent with the view that the use of convertible securities and the allocation of a substantial ownership percentage to venture capital funds enhance venture capital fund managers' effort and advice (consistent with the predictions of Casamatta, 2003; Repullo and Suarez; 2004; and Schmidt, 2003), but the results are sensitive to the econometric specification. Large ownership percentages induce venture capital fund managers to spend more hours with entrepreneurial firms: A 10% increase in the venture capital fund manager's ownership share increases the time spent with the entrepreneur by 3 hours per month on average (Models 3 to 5 in Table 16.4). When convertible securities are used, venture capital fund managers value their contribution roughly 10% more important (see Models 1, 2, and 4 in Table 16.5). Contrary to expectations, we find no significant effect of the ownership variable to the intensity of advice (Table 16.5).

[20]For identification, there must be at least as many instruments as the number of explanatory variables. We use a number of instruments that are not included among the original set of explanatory variables. We also treat some of the original variables as instruments (for which endogeneity is not potentially problematic), which is appropriate for obtaining asymptotically efficient estimates and necessary to satisfy the identification criterion with our variables.

[21]Kortum and Lerner (2000) find that venture capital fund managers contribute approximately 15% less to innovation in boom periods in the United States, which suggests that our instruments are not ideal. In this European dataset, however, the correlations are not as correlated with the dependent variables and the potentially endogenous explanatory variables (this information was presented in an extended version of this chapter and is available upon request). The interaction between effort and years is indirect, via exit conditions and contract decisions. That is, our instruments are based on the premise that investment contract decisions and exits are more closely related to market conditions and year effects, consistent with Gompers and Lerner (1999, 2001), Lerner and Schoar (2004, 2005), Bessler and Kurth (2007), Lauterbach et al. (2007), Tykvova (2006), Tykvova and Walz (2007), Witt (2006), and others. Our instruments in this context were not selected on the basis of prior work directly on topic of advice, as such papers (e.g., Kaplan and Strömberg, 2004) did not control for endogeneity. We considered alternative specifications, which generally yielded similar results. Other specifications are available upon request.

Table 16.4 Multivariate

This table presents OLS and 2SLS estimates of the number of hours per month that the variables are as defined in Table 16.1. Models 1–4 use OLS; Model 5 uses 2SLS where preferred equity dummy, the fraction of veto rights, board rights, and other "special" venture capital fund manager's ownership share, the number of hours per month from number of investment months, exit outcomes, and the capital under management per instruments: the venture capital fund manager's ranking of project risk and entrepreneur country of the investment, a dummy for entrepreneurs in foreign countries, a late-stage for the venture capital fund manager, dummy variables for the investment and exit years, HCCME is used. *, **, *** represent estimates significant at the 1%, 5%, and 10%

Independent Variables	Model 1 OLS		Model 2 OLS	
	Coefficient	t-Statistic	Coefficient	t-Statistic
Constant	**10.75**	**2.00***	1.43	0.17
Contractual Terms and Legal Conditions				
Convertible Security (H16.1)	2.25	0.51	1.88	0.50
Ownership % (H16.1)	4.55	0.30	20.83	1.50
Veto Rights (H16.2)	**13.44**	**4.98*****	**7.96**	**2.10****
Board Rights (H16.2)	−0.004	−0.48	−0.001	−0.15
Special Control Rights (H16.2)				
Country Legality (H16.3)				
Project- and Environment-Related Risk				
Project Risk Ranking	−4.67	−0.56	−9.77	−1.12
Entrepreneur Experience Ranking				
Late or Buyout Stage	**−8.35**	**−2.13****	**−10.50**	**−3.22*****
Medical/Biotechnology				
Computer/Electronics				
Communications/Internet				
Foreign Investment	0.46	0.10	−2.85	−0.63
Investment Characteristics and Performance				
Hours from Syndicated Partners			**0.49**	**5.60*****
Investment Rounds				
(Log of) Book Value			0.51	0.72
Investment Months				
IPO Exit				
Acquisition Exit				

Analyses of Hours per Month

venture capital fund manager spends with the entrepreneurial firm. Independent the following variables that are treated as potentially endogenous: the convertible control rights held by the venture capital fund manager, the percentage of the syndicated venture capital fund managers, the number of investment rounds, the venture capital fund manager fund managers. The following variables are used as experience, the log of the book value of the investment, the Legality index of the investment dummy, industry dummy variables, the limited partnership dummy variable and the log of the MSCI returns over the period of the investment. White's (1980) levels, respectively.

Model 3 OLS		Model 4 OLS		Model 5 2SLS	
Coefficient	t-Statistic	Coefficient	t-Statistic	Coefficient	t-Statistic
10.20	1.02	14.87	0.46	−3.55	−0.10
−3.23	−0.92	−2.22	−0.66	**−10.33**	**−1.87****
25.69	**2.30****	**30.67**	**2.67*****	**38.76**	**1.64***
11.36	**3.26*****	**12.15**	**3.22*****	−0.87	−0.07
0.003	0.65	0.002	0.44	−0.03	−0.91
		−1.49	−0.23		
		−0.39	−0.50		
−4.07	−0.46	2.51	0.29	−6.01	−0.37
0.21	0.40	0.24	0.43	0.36	0.26
−9.15	**−2.47****	**−7.44**	**−1.89***	−5.87	−0.66
−4.70	−0.92	−5.33	−0.93	2.77	0.31
−4.92	−1.54	−3.95	−1.13	−4.31	−0.78
−11.58	**−2.82*****	**−11.16**	**−2.48****	−9.70	−1.58
−0.79	−0.20	1.87	0.39	2.75	0.44
0.40	5.51***	0.38	5.07***	**0.67**	**2.07****
3.81	**2.59****	**4.00**	**2.55****	1.64	0.19
−0.21	−0.28	−0.96	−1.13	0.94	−0.06
−0.30	−3.35***	−0.30	−3.61***	**17.09**	**1.74****
10.76	**2.44****	**16.26**	**3.26*****	0.25	0.03
		7.74	**2.09****		

(*continued*)

Table 16.4

Independent Variables	Model 1 OLS		Model 2 OLS	
	Coefficient	t-Statistic	Coefficient	t-Statistic
Venture Capital Fund Manager Fund Characteristics				
Limited Partnership Venture Capital Fund Manager			1.74	0.42
Venture Capital Fund Manager Portfolio Size/# of Venture Capital Fund Manager Managers	**−1.98**	**−2.53****	−1.19	−1.55
Number of Observations	74		74	
Adjusted R^2	0.10		0.31	
Log Likelihood	−299.77		−287.98	
Akaike Information Criterion	8.35		8.10	
f-Statistic	1.96*		3.99***	

The results do not support Hypothesis 16.1b; that is, convertible securities do not mitigate venture capital fund manager-entrepreneur conflicts. On the contrary, there is evidence that a large venture capital fund ownership percentage is associated with a greater scope of venture capital fund manager-entrepreneur disagreements (Table 16.6, Models 2 and 4). One explanation is that venture capital fund managers have pronounced incentives to monitor the activities of the entrepreneur when venture capital funds have larger ownership stakes, which in turn leads to conflict.

The data provide much stronger support for Hypothesis 16.2a than Hypotheses 16.1a and 16.1b. In regards to Hypothesis 16.2a, the data indicate that the more control given to the venture capital fund manager in the form of veto rights, the more intense his effort exertion, especially with respect to the intensity of advising. Venture capital fund managers with full veto control with respect to the five issues considered (asset sales, asset purchases, changes in control, issuance of equity, and other veto rights; see Table 16.1) provide roughly 30% more advice than venture capital fund managers who have no veto rights in any of these decisions (Table 16.5, Models 1 to 5). This effect survives when we control for the endogeneity of the "veto rights" variable (Table 16.5, Model 5). We find that control increases the time spent with the firm, too, by roughly 10 to 12 hours per month (Table 16.4, Models 1 to 4), but this effect is not robust to potential endogeneity of the variable (see Table 16.4, Model 5). These results indicate that venture capital fund manager veto rights are an extremely important and effective mechanism for venture capital fund managers to exercise their views on how to bring the project to fruition

(*continued*)

Model 3 OLS		Model 4 OLS		Model 5 2SLS	
Coefficient	t-Statistic	Coefficient	t-Statistic	Coefficient	t-Statistic
0.96	0.29	−2.92	0.74	3.00	0.62
−2.39	**−2.67*****	**−1.69**	**−1.88***	−3.01	−1.40
74		74		74	
0.47		0.48		0.24	
−273.92		−271.29		−285.52	
7.92		7.93		8.28	
4.57***		4.16***		2.18***	

and are more effective than information rights and other specific contractual terms. As mentioned earlier, veto rights are passive rights, where it can be said that although the venture capital fund manager is not "actively managing" the firm, it is influencing the outcome of the business decision to be made, especially if the decision requires a unanimous consensus. When involving itself in a high-risk project such as a start-up entrepreneurial firm, a venture capital fund manager will risk being blamed for the failure of the firm in the more than likely event of its failure. By exercising veto rights, it can avoid having to shoulder full blame, as it is not the venture capital fund manager alone that decides various issues related to, for example, asset sales or asset purchases; it is just failure to reach a consensus by the "whole managing team" that determines which course of action is to be taken. This indirect control is also pertinent in the event there is an attempt to argue that the corporate veil was pierced (some venture capital fund managers exercise their veto rights as shareholders and not board members). The more veto rights the venture capital fund manager wields, the more secure it feels in involving itself with the firm.

In Model 3 in Table 16.6, contrary to expectations (Hypothesis 16.2b), we find support that venture capital fund manager control mitigates the number of venture capital fund manager-entrepreneur disagreements. This indicates venture capital fund managers have fewer conflicts with entrepreneurs when they have the right to interfere in entrepreneurial decision making; however, this effect is not robust to the inclusion/exclusion of the other explanatory variables and controls for endogeneity.

Table 16.5 Multivariate

This table presents OLS estimates of the venture capital fund manager's average advice are as defined in Table 16.1. Models (1)–(4) use OLS; Model (5) uses 2SLS where the equity dummy, the fraction of veto rights, board rights, and other "special" control rights manager's ownership share, the number of hours per month from syndicated venture months, exit outcomes, and the capital under management per venture capital fund capital fund manager's ranking of project risk and entrepreneur experience, the log of the dummy for entrepreneurs in foreign countries, a late stage investment dummy, industry fund manager, dummy variables for the investment and exit years, and the log of the *** represent estimates significant at the 1%, 5%, and 10% levels, respectively.

Independent Variables	Model (1) OLS		Model (2) OLS	
	Coefficient	t-Statistic	Coefficient	t-Statistic
Constant	0.44	0.85	**2.31**	**2.96****
Contractual Terms and Legal Conditions				
Convertible Security (H16.1)	**0.97**	**2.87*****	**0.83**	**2.59****
Ownership % (H16.1)	−0.52	−0.53	−0.11	−0.12
Veto Rights (H16.2)	**2.63**	**6.90*****	**2.57**	**5.63*****
Board Rights (H16.2)	**0.001**	**1.69***	0.001	1.51
Special Control Rights (H16.2)				
Country Legality (H16.3)				
Project- and Environment-Related Risk				
Project Risk Ranking	1.36	1.51	**2.15**	**2.59*****
Entrepreneur Experience Ranking				
Late or Buyout Stage	**−1.34**	**−4.46*****	**−0.98**	**−2.92*****
Medical/Biotechnology				
Computer/Electronics				
Communications/Internet				
Foreign Investment	−0.29	−0.84	−0.26	−0.74
Investment Characteristics and Performance				
Hours from Syndicated Partners			−0.003	−0.29
Investment Rounds				
(Log of) Book Value			**−0.25**	**−2.98*****
Investment Months				
IPO Exit				
Acquisition Exit				

Analysis of Advice

ranking for assistance provided to the entrepreneurial firm. Independent variables following variables are treated as potentially endogenous: the convertible preferred held by the venture capital fund manager, the percentage of the venture capital fund capital fund managers, the number of investment rounds, the number of investment manager fund managers. The following variables are used as instruments: the venture book value of the investment, the Legality index of the country of the investment, a dummy variables, the limited partnership dummy variable for the venture capital MSCI returns over the period of the investment. White's (1980) HCCME is used. *, **,

Model (3) OLS		Model (4) OLS		Model (5) 2SLS	
Coefficient	t-Statistic	Coefficient	t-Statistic	Coefficient	t-Statistic
1.64	1.64	3.31	1.19	−2.24	−0.72
0.48	1.27	**0.62**	**1.93***	−0.11	−0.19
−0.19	−0.24	−0.07	−0.09	0.09	0.04
2.63	**5.63*****	**2.45**	**5.17*****	**3.80**	**3.67*****
0.001	1.20			**−0.007**	**−2.61****
0.24	0.31				
		−0.07	−0.64		
2.46	**2.83*****	**2.30**	**2.60****	**3.10**	**2.33****
0.14	**1.98****	**0.14**	**1.85****	**0.27**	**2.07****
−0.86	**−1.88****	**−0.80**	**−1.80****	−0.48	−0.59
−0.47	−0.63	−0.46	−0.68	0.32	0.33
0.30	0.75	0.26	0.64	**0.93**	**1.73***
−1.03	−1.50	**−1.06**	**−1.68***	−0.68	−1.10
−0.28	−0.82	−0.19	−0.63	0.45	0.78
−0.008	−0.78	−0.008	−0.77	−0.01	−0.46
0.25	1.10	0.34	1.36	0.99	1.21
−0.30	**−4.13*****	**−0.30**	**−3.65*****	**−0.29**	**−1.95***
−0.008	−0.84	−0.006	−0.71	0.10	0.11
0.12	0.33	−0.05	−0.13	**0.002**	**2.11****
		−0.24	−0.61		

(*continued*)

Table 16.5

Independent Variables	Model (1) OLS		Model (2) OLS	
	Coefficient	t-Statistic	Coefficient	t-Statistic
Venture Capital Fund Manager Fund Characteristics				
Limited Partnership Venture Capital Fund Manager			−0.18	−0.43
Venture Capital Fund Manager Portfolio Size/# of Venture Capital Fund Manager Managers	−0.07	−0.78	−0.14	−1.59
Number of Observations	74		74	
Adjusted R^2	0.38		0.40	
Log Likelihood	−125.30		−122.34	
Akaike Information Criterion	3.63		3.63	
f-Statistic	6.69^{***}		5.50^{***}	

In regards to Hypothesis 16.3, considering the impact of investor protection and legal rules, we find that venture capital fund managers experience more disagreements with entrepreneurs in countries with lower Legality indices (Table 16.6). The estimates indicate that an approximately 5-point increase in Legality (which is roughly the difference in the Legality index between Portugal and the Netherlands) gives rise to on average one less dispute. Recall as well that the correlation between Legality and conflicts is −0.23 and significant at the 5% level. The estimated coefficient for Legality in Table 16.6, however, is sensitive to all possible specifications (for other specifications not explicitly reported); overall, therefore, we may infer that the evidence relating higher Legality to fewer conflicts is highly suggestive but not absolutely conclusive. One might intuitively expect better laws and legal certainty to mitigate the scope for disagreement, since better laws provide greater certainty in enforcing contracts and interpreting incomplete contracts (La Porta et al., 1997, 1998). Notice as well that while venture capital fund manager-entrepreneur conflicts are negatively related, venture capital fund manager advice is statistically unrelated to Legality.

In sum, there is some support for the hypotheses pertaining to formal control mechanisms and legal systems in facilitating venture capital fund manager advice and mitigating venture capital fund manager-entrepreneur conflicts. First, in regards to venture capital fund manager advice, the most economically significant and statistically robust effect on venture capital fund manager advice was in relation to venture capital fund manager veto rights. The use of convertible securities and venture capital fund manager ownership percentages also matter for venture capital fund manager advice, but those effects are

(*continued*)

Model (3) OLS		Model (4) OLS		Model (5) 2SLS	
Coefficient	t-Statistic	Coefficient	t-Statistic	Coefficient	t-Statistic
−0.01	−0.04	−0.16	−0.45	0.57	1.08
−0.22	−2.21**	−0.26	−2.78***	−0.37	−1.76*
74		74		74	
0.44		0.44		0.44	
−114.90		−114.98		−114.98	
3.65		3.65		3.65	
4.02***		4.01***		4.01***	

not completely robust to the econometric specification.[22] Second, in regards to venture capital fund manager-entrepreneur conflicts, conflicts are not related to contracts in a statistically significant way but are significantly mitigated by the strength of the legal system.

16.5.2 Other Governance Mechanisms, Risk, and Control Variables

The data indicate noncontractual governance mechanisms (such as syndication arrangements and portfolio size in terms of number of investees per venture capital manager), entrepreneur and venture capital fund manager characteristics, project and environment risk, and project success potential all matter for enhancing the active involvement of venture capital fund managers in the entrepreneurial firms that they finance. The results pertaining to these variables in Tables 16.4–16.6 are described next for syndication, venture capital fund

[22]We may expect that cash flow rights will not be effective in eliciting more venture capitalist support if the venture capital fund manager isn't at the same time endowed with more control rights. Without sufficient control rights, the venture capital fund manager probably cannot assure that his advice is being adhered to in the firm. Hence, financial incentives won't be effective in eliciting more advice. With powerful control rights, however, the venture capital fund manager will be very effective in pushing through any suggestions for improvement, and he will thus engage more if he has more financial incentives. In this sense, financial incentives and control rights should be complements. We considered this possibility by including interaction terms in the regressions. However, such terms were generally insignificant. Additional data collection may shed further light on this issue in future research.

Table 16.6 Multivariate

This table presents OLS and ordered logit estimates of the number of disagreements variables are as defined in Table 16.1. OLS is used in Models (1) and (2); ordered logit Model (5) with the following variables that are treated as potentially endogenous: the control rights held by the venture capital fund manager, the venture capital fund manager's fund managers, the number of investment rounds and investment months, exit outcomes, as instruments: the venture capital fund manager's ranking of project risk and entrepreneur country of the investment, a dummy for entrepreneurs in foreign countries, a late stage variables for the investment and exit years, and the log of the MSCI returns over the estimates significant at the 1%, 5%, and 10% levels, respectively.

Independent Variables	**Model (1) OLS**		**Model (2) OLS**	
	Coefficient	**t-Statistic**	**Coefficient**	**t-Statistic**
Constant	0.53	0.61	7.75	**2.72*******
Contractual Terms and Legal Conditions				
Convertible Security (H16.1)	−0.04		0.31	1.01
Ownership % (H16.1)	1.21	1.22	**1.55**	**1.67***
Veto Rights (H16.2)	0.27	0.86	−0.42	0.95
Board Rights (H16.2)	0.83	0.15		
Special Control Rights (H16.2)				
Country Legality (H16.3)			**−0.29**	**3.10*****
Project- and Environment-Related Risk				
Project Risk Ranking (H16.2)	−0.23	0.28	0.41	0.49
Entrepreneur Experience Ranking (H16.2)			**−0.16**	**1.83***
Late or Buyout Stage (H16.2)	**−0.88**	**0.83*****	−0.34	1.09
Medical/Biotechnology (H16.2)			1.15	1.43
Computer/Electronics (H16.2)			−0.33	0.90
Communications/Internet (H16.2)			**−0.78**	**1.80***
Foreign Investment	0.21	0.60	0.48	1.19
Investment Characteristics and Performance				
Hours from Syndicated Partners	**0.03**	**3.72*****	**0.03**	**4.00*****
Investment Rounds			0.16	1.14
(Log of) Book Value	0.03	0.34	0.03	0.33
Investment Months			**−0.01**	**1.787***
IPO Exit			−0.14	0.28
Acquisition Exit			−0.02	0.04

Analysis of Disagreement

between the venture capital fund manager and the entrepreneurial firm. Independent
is used in Models (3) and (4); ordered logit with instrumental variables is used in
convertible preferred equity dummy, the fraction of veto, board, and other "special"
ownership share (%), the number of hours per month from syndicated venture capital
and the capital under management per fund managers. The following variables are used
experience, the log of the book value of the investment, the Legality index of the
investment dummy, industry dummy variables, the limited partnership dummy, dummy
period of the investment. White's (1980) HCCME is used. *, **, *** represent

Model (3) Ordered Logit		Model (4) Ordered Logit		Model (5) IV Ordered Logit	
Coefficient	t-Statistic	Coefficient	t-Statistic	Coefficient	t-Statistic
3.67	1.50	**9.97**	**2.07****	7.79	**2.13****
0.03	0.40	0.36	0.48	0.20	0.15
3.14	1.14	**3.03**	**1.76***	−0.34	0.06
−0.12	0.11	−0.93		−2.57	0.81
3.27	1.15			0.002	0.48
−2.92	**1.75***			1.64	0.26
		−0.40	**2.17****		
0.73	0.20	0.34	0.14	−0.89	0.40
−0.39	**1.81***	**−0.32**	**1.84***	**−0.39**	
−2.76	**2.46****	−1.30	1.08	**−2.15**	**2.02****
1.93	1.45	1.10	0.93	−0.08	0.05
0.44	0.53	−0.06	0.09	−0.47	0.41
−1.05	−0.93	−1.29		−1.19	
0.81	0.75	0.78	0.86	−0.58	0.25
0.09	**2.24****	**0.06**	**2.40****	0.02	0.44
−0.42		0.06	0.13	**−2.57**	**2.38****
0.19	0.90	0.14	0.61	0.12	0.50
−0.04	−1.35	−0.02	−1.02	1.96	1.38
0.16	0.19	0.81	0.90	0.43	0.52
		0.53	0.73		

(continued)

Table 16.6

Independent Variables	Model (1) OLS		Model (2) OLS	
	Coefficient	t-Statistic	Coefficient	t-Statistic
Venture Capital Fund Manager Fund Characteristics				
Limited Partnership Venture Capital Fund Manager			−0.98	2.24**
Venture Capital Fund Manager Portfolio Size/# of Venture Capital Fund Manager Managers	−0.23	3.22***	−0.18	2.20**
Mu (1)				
Mu (2)				
Mu (3)				
Mu (4)				
Number of Observations	74		74	
Adjusted R^2 (Pseudo R^2 for Models (3)–(5))	0.16		0.32	
Log Likelihood	−118.31		−104.99	
Akaike Information Criterion	3.50		3.37	
f-Statistic (Chi-square for Models (3)–(5))	2.44**		2.81***	

manager fund characteristics, entrepreneur characteristics and project risk, and success potential, respectively.

Syndication

The data indicate an hour extra support from other syndicating partners increases the time spent by the venture capital fund manager with the entrepreneur by approximately 0.5 to 1 hour per month (see Table 16.4). This effect is highly statistically significant (Models 1 to 5 in Table 16.4) and very robust to consideration of potential endogeneity (Model 5 in Table 16.4). This result is consistent with empirical regularities of investment syndication in the United States (Lerner, 1994) and Europe (Wright and Lockett, 2003). The data therefore suggest that syndicated transactions can be characterized by complementarities (as opposed to free riding) in effort exertion by syndicate members. Notice, however, that the syndication variable is not significant in Table 16.5 for the venture capital fund managers' advice ranking. In Table 16.6, syndication

(continued)

Model (3) Ordered Logit		Model (4) Ordered Logit		Model (5) IV Ordered Logit	
Coefficient	**t-Statistic**	**Coefficient**	**t-Statistic**	**Coefficient**	**t-Statistic**
−0.53	0.62	−1.23	1.43	−0.61	0.82
−0.79	**1.91***	−0.74		−0.42	
0.95	3.03***	0.84	2.74***	0.66	2.96***
1.30	2.41**	1.20	3.10***	0.95	3.42***
2.59	2.52**	2.60	3.09***	2.01	3.37***
3.69	2.78***	3.77	2.74***	2.98	2.35**
74		74		74	
0.38		0.34		0.31	
−55.11		−58.29		−69.62	
Chi-squared: 67.30***		Chi-squared: 60.94***		Chi-squared: 38.28***	

appears to be positively related to the scope of conflict, but this effect is not robust to controls for endogeneity (Model 5 in Table 16.6).

Venture Capital Fund Characteristics

Concerning the impact of venture capital fund characteristics, we find that venture capital funds with large portfolios (in terms of the number of investee firms) per number of fund managers become less involved in the development of their ventures. In particular, venture capital funds with one extra entrepreneurial firm per manager in their portfolio provided on average 2 to 3 hours less support per month, 20% less advice, and had 0.2 to 0.3 fewer disagreements with entrepreneurs (Tables 16.4 to 16.6). This result is robust to the endogeneity of the portfolio size per number of fund managers variable. The evidence is suggestive that there is an upper bound to the number of ventures that fund managers can efficiently advise, which is an intuitive result and supports Kanniainen and Keuschnigg (2003, 2004), Keuschnigg (2004b), Cumming

(2006), and Jääskeläinen et al. (2006). We find no significant impact of fund type on effort exertion by venture capital fund managers: In our sample, bank-affiliated and limited partnership funds are similar in this respect. As indicated (see footnote 12), other controls for venture capital fund characteristics were not material to the results.

Entrepreneur Characteristics and Project Risk

The data indicate that venture capital fund managers spend less time with their late-stage investments. Venture capital fund managers also value their advice as less important for late-stage investments. Conflicts are also less frequent for late-stage firms (Tables 16.4 to 16.6). These effects are large and statistically significant: Late-stage ventures in our sample received on average 8 to 10 hours less time per month, 10% less advice, and had fewer disputes concerning one or two more issues with their venture capital fund managers. Early-stage investments require a much greater effort commitment for venture capital fund managers, which is consistent with earlier findings in Gompers (1995) and Sapienza et al. (1996). Evidence on the size of the investment in Table 16.5 is also robust and supportive of the view that the smaller the investment (for earlier stages of development), the greater the importance the venture capital fund manager's advice.

The data also indicate a statistically significant and large positive effect of project risk on advice. When venture capital fund managers value a project as 10% riskier, they give roughly 25 to 30% more advice (Table 16.5). The risk variable is built on the assessment of venture capital fund managers of both project- and environment-related risk, such as "uncertain market size," "uncertainty about product/technology," "risky competitive position," and so on (see Table 16.1). As a result, it accounts for both "internal" and "external" uncertainty, following the classification used by Kaplan and Strömberg (2004). The distinction between the two risk measures was not meaningful in our data, since they turned out to be very highly (positively) correlated in the sample. Therefore, we use an aggregate of all these risk factors. The result that venture capital fund managers provide more advice to entrepreneurs with riskier projects is nevertheless consistent with both Sapienza et al. (1996) and Kaplan and Strömberg (2004).

The entrepreneur variable is employed to account for the impact of uncertainty related to the entrepreneur's skills and ability. The results show a positive relation between the entrepreneur's experience and venture capital fund manager advice (Table 16.4) and a negative relation between the entrepreneur's experience and venture capital fund manager-entrepreneur disagreements (Table 16.6). Although both effects are rather small, they are statistically significant and robust to alternative specifications. The positive relation between entrepreneurial experience and advice supports the notion of complementarities of effort by the contracting parties, as assumed in several theoretical models on venture capital finance (e.g., Casamatta, 2003; Cestone, 2001; Repullo and Suarez, 2004).

An interesting result is that venture capital fund managers tend to get involved in Internet-based firms to a significantly lesser extent than in other types of firms. Venture capital fund managers spend approximately 10 to 12 hours less time each month with their ventures in the Internet or communications industries (Table 16.4). Moreover, they give 10% less advice to and have on average one less disagreement with the management of these firms (Tables 16.5 and 16.6). Although not robust to all specifications, it is noteworthy that this negative relation between the Internet dummy and venture capital fund manager effort exists for all the three dependent variables. Related evidence is consistent with the view that venture capital fund managers financed more and advised less while taking advantage of the Internet bubble (Kortum and Lerner, 2000). Evidence from the United States that many venture capital fund managers were able to successfully exit their Internet investments, even though many such firms subsequently went bankrupt, is consistent with this interpretation (that is, while our data sample does not enable direct tests of the same phenomenon, our evidence shows that European venture capital fund managers similarly tend to spend less time with Internet investees). Also noteworthy is that there were no other significant differences with respect to the venture capital fund managers' involvement in the other two high-tech industries in the data (biotechnology and electronics).

Success Potential

Our evidence with respect to the relation between the venture's success potential and venture capital fund managers' involvement is ambiguous. Similarly, the evidence on the length investment horizon is not robust. Based on motives discussed alongside the development of the preceding hypotheses, we associate the venture's success potential with the probability of successful exit and consider whether actual and planned exits can be associated with more intense involvement. In the sample, exits via IPO and acquisition do not have a robust impact on the advising activities and conflicts (Tables 16.5 and 16.6). Models 3 and 4 in Table 16.4 suggest a positive relation between effort and IPOs, but this effect is not robust to controls for endogeneity. In Model 5 in Table 16.5, the IPO dummy is statistically significant with the control for endogeneity; however, the economic significance of the estimate is close to zero. Thus, our analysis cannot provide clean evidence for the role of inherently successful ventures in spurring venture capital fund managers' involvement, but there is nevertheless suggestive evidence that venture capital fund managers spend more time with, and provide more advice to, their better-performing investee firms.

16.6 Limitations, Alternative Explanations, and Future Research

The analysis in this chapter is based on a new and fairly comprehensive dataset. However, there are limitations to the breadth and depth of the data that are important to mention. For example, our data do not include details on the investor fixed and performance fees, covenants surrounding the management of the fund, experience of the fund managers, sources of the funds (from pension funds [see also Ammann, 2003], banks, etc.), changes in effort measures over time, among other things. Albeit, to the extent that we were able to obtain these details from a subset of the funds, we did not find significant differences in some of these variables, and other variables were correlated with the variables already considered in the chapter. Hence, despite the large number of details that are available in the data, there are other elements that could add to the richness in an analysis of investor activities. Moreover, the number of observations for which we could obtain sufficient details is limited (although similar to related prior work on the topic; see Kaplan and Strömberg, 2004, for a sample of 67 entrepreneurial firms from 11 venture capital funds that are derived from a U.S.-only sample). This is primarily due to the fact that most venture capital funds are loath to disclose (some even contractually restricted from disclosing) confidential information, which limits the breadth and depth of the data that can be analyzed. Nevertheless, despite these limitations, we do not believe there are reasons to expect the preceding results to be materially biased by excluded variables or sample selection problems. Future work could seek to expand the scope of data, and the role of contracts and legal systems for managing investor-investee relationships in different countries, such as in emerging markets. Future work could also consider different types of investors, such as hedge funds (see also Eling, 2006; Kassberger and Kiesel, 2006; and Le Moigne and Savaria, 2006).

A unique and useful feature of our data is that they enable an analysis of contract and legal variables alongside information regarding the entrepreneur's and venture capital funds' characteristics, including the syndicate venture capital funds' characteristics. Our data, however, are derived primarily from the venture capital fund managers, not the entrepreneurs', and syndicate venture capital fund managers'. We were able to confirm the accuracy of the information provided in cases where the identities of the entrepreneurs and syndicate venture capital fund managers could be revealed (in a few ongoing investments this information was considered to be classified) and did not find any material discrepancies or reporting bias.

Finally, we note that the distinction between advice and conflict can be difficult to disentangle in practice. Our data were derived by meeting with the venture capital fund managers themselves and reviewing their tasks. The venture capital fund managers consistently identified the data presented herein as exemplifying advice versus conflict. In practice, however, a few venture capital fund managers did point out that the distinction can become blurred depending on the specific context. Our analysis of specific tasks (as detailed in the summary statistics) did not suggest differences depending on broad versus narrow definitions of advice versus conflict. Further, the broad picture of advice versus conflict was quite consistent with the ways in which venture capital fund managers viewed their role in facilitating the development of entrepreneurial firms.

16.7 Conclusions

This chapter considered three different proxies to effort exerted by venture capital fund managers: the hours per month spent with entrepreneurs (total effort), the investors' rankings of the importance of their contribution pertaining to different advising fields (advice), and the scope of investor-entrepreneur disagreements (conflict). Our results show that the allocation of cash flow and control rights and the different project- and environment-related risk factors affect the three effort measures in different ways. Cash flow and control rights seem to enhance advice but do not affect the likelihood of conflict. In particular, venture capital fund managers holding a convertible claim provide on average 10% more advice, large venture capital fund ownership percentages significantly increase the amount of venture capital fund manager hours spent with entrepreneurs, and venture capital fund managers with full veto control give roughly 30% more advice than venture capital fund managers who have no veto rights.

The quality of a country's legal system matters for the propensity of conflicts between entrepreneurs and their investors. In particular, the data indicate that an approximately 5-point increase in Legality (which is roughly the difference in the *Legality* index between Portugal and the Netherlands) gives rise to on average one type of venture capital fund manager-entrepreneur dispute (such as in regards to strategic decisions, human resource policies of the firm, and the like).

It is important to note that many nonlegal and noncontractual features are also vital to both venture capital fund manager advising activities as well as venture capital fund manager-entrepreneur conflicts. For instance, when venture capital fund managers consider a project to be 10% riskier, they provide on average 25% more advice. Moreover, venture capital fund managers spend on average 8 to 10 hours more with their early-stage ventures and provide them roughly 10% more advice. They also have on average 1 or 2 more different types of disagreements with entrepreneurs at their early stages of development. We also find that if syndicate members provide one hour more every month, the venture capital manager will also spend up to an hour more with the entrepreneur. A related result in this chapter is that venture capital fund managers give more advice to, and disagree less with, more experienced entrepreneurs. This implies that venture capital fund managers and entrepreneurs tend to have complementary skills or expertise, consistent with many theoretical models of venture capital financing (Casamatta, 2003; Cestone, 2001; Repullo and Suarez, 2004).

Our evidence also indicates that venture capital funds that have more investments per number of managers tend to contribute less, as expected (Cumming, 2006a; Kanniainen and Keuschnigg, 2003, 2004; Keuschnigg, 2004b). In our sample, venture capital funds with one extra entrepreneurial firm per manager in their portfolio provided on average of 2 to 3 hours less support per month, gave 20% less advice, and had 0.2 to 0.3 fewer disagreements with entrepreneurs. We also find a positive relationship between venture capital fund managers' involvement and successful exits, but the direction of causality in this context is highly ambiguous.

Overall, the data are consistent with the view that both formal contracts and legal systems are important to managing venture capital fund manager-entrepreneur relationships. But contracts and laws operate alongside other informal governance mechanisms such as syndication and portfolio size, as well as risk factors and success potential. Further work could continue to study the comparative importance of formal contracts and laws versus other governance mechanisms in managing investor-investee relationships in different financing contexts and in less developed countries.

Key Terms

Convertible securities
Common equity
Veto rights
Control rights
Advice
Monitoring
Disagreement
Legality

Discussion Questions

16.1. True/False/Uncertain and explain why: "Legal differences across countries have nothing to do with either the advice or monitoring provided by a venture capital fund manager to an investee entrepreneurial firm."

16.2. True/False/Uncertain and explain why: "Greater venture capital fund veto and control rights enhance venture capital fund manager monitoring but not venture capital fund manager effort."

16.3. True/False/Uncertain and explain why: "Convertible securities provide greater incentives to venture capital fund managers to provide effort but not monitoring to their investee entrepreneurial firms."

16.4. True/False/Uncertain and explain why: "In practice, syndicated investors tend to free ride on the effort provided by the other investors."

16.5. True/False/Uncertain and explain why: "In practice, venture capital fund managers provide more assistance to entrepreneurial firms that have a better chance of being successful and going public."

16.6. True/False/Uncertain and explain why: "The size of a venture capital fund manager's portfolio in terms of number of investee entrepreneurial firms per manager does not affect advice, monitoring, or disagreement in venture capital fund manager-entrepreneurial firm relationships."

17 Home Bias

17.1 Introduction and Learning Objectives

Private equity markets are characterized by informational asymmetries and agency problems (see Chapter 2). In fact, the very existence of fund managers has been attributed to difficulty at screening high-tech investments for which there has been scant track record and pronounced problems of information asymmetries. In view of the informational problems and institutional aspects that characterize private equity markets, it is expected that fund managers will exhibit a "local bias" to mitigate information problems. Private equity fund managers, particularly those managing venture capital funds, are widely regarded as active value-added investors that spend a significant amount of time on due diligence as well as serving on entrepreneurial firm board of directors, providing strategic, financial, marketing, and administrative advice.[1] Venture capital funds frequently retain strong veto and control rights over the firm, including the contractual right to replace the founding entrepreneur as CEO of the firm (Chapters 10–14). It is therefore natural to expect fund managers to prefer to invest in geographically proximate entrepreneurial firms.

But because contracts are incomplete—it is not possible to write contracts that cover all eventualities—it is worth considering factors that affect geographic proximity. Proximity may independently influence governance above and beyond that which is specified in a contract.

Despite the apparent importance of geographic proximity for private equity investment, there has been a comparative lack of research on this topic. So far, existing literature has focused exclusively on the U.S. venture capital market. Lerner (1995) shows venture capitalists that are geographically closer to their entrepreneurial investee firms are more likely to serve on the firm's board of directors.[2] Similarly, Sorenson and Stuart (2001) show the likelihood of a venture capitalist investing in an entrepreneurial firm increases as the greater

[1]See, for example, Barry et al. (1990a); Cressy (2002); Gompers (1995, 1996, 1998); Gompers and Lerner (1999a, 2000, 2001a); Gorman and Sahlman (1989); Hellmann and Puri (2002); Hsu (2004); Kanniainen and Keuschnigg (2003, 2004); Keuschnigg (2003, 2004a); Keuschnigg and Nielsen (2001, 2003a,b); Lerner (1994, 1995); Litvak (2004a,b); Bascha and Walz (2001); Mayer et al. (2005); and Atanasov et al. (2006).

[2]See also Gompers and Lerner (1999).

the degree of proximity between the investor and entrepreneur.[3] In short, the "home bias" preference is found in U.S. venture capitalist financings of privately held firms (see Cumming and Dai, 2007, and Tian, 2007, for recent work on topic with U.S. data). This finding of home bias in private equity is consistent with evidence from U.S. mutual fund investments which show a geographically proximate preference for investments in publicly traded firms (Coval and Moskowitz, 1999, 2001).[4]

In this chapter we will do the following:

- Explore the factors that give rise to interprovincial (for investors and entrepreneurs that reside in different provinces) versus intraprovincial (for investors and entrepreneurs that reside in the same province) investment activity
- Study both institutional and agency factors in influencing geographic proximity in private equity investment
- Study home bias in a non-U.S. setting: Canada. It is interesting and relevant to study a non-U.S. context because it enables the following:
    - A comparison of home-province preferences for Quebec (a French-speaking civil law province) and other provinces (English-speaking common law provinces)
    - An examination of differences in home bias over time for a relatively young venture capital market as it has matured over the 1991 to 2003 period
    - An examination of home bias for a diverse group of entrepreneurial firms than those studied elsewhere, which enables a more complete analysis of agency factors in geographic proximity
    - An examination of home bias for different types of private equity investors, including wholly private (corporate, limited partnerships, and institutional investors) and government-sponsored funds

The data used in this study were provided by Macdonald & Associates Limited, which has built the most comprehensive database on venture capital and private equity activity in Canada. We included 13,729 investments over the period from 1991 (first quarter) to 2003 (first quarter). Transactions comprising numerous types of investors, entrepreneurial investee firms in various stages of development and industries, and both privately held and publicly traded firms, are included in the dataset. Differences in securities used and deal types such as syndication, staging, and investment amounts are specified in the data.

The data indicate a strong tendency for intraprovincial investment within the Canadian private equity market. For all types of investors and entrepreneurial firms, in terms of the number of investments (13,729 transactions), 84.42% of investments involved an investor and entrepreneur that resided in the same province. In terms of the total value of these transactions ($20,193,896,909 in 1997

[3]The Sorenson and Stuart (2001) study is based on an artificially constructed dependent variable of feasible investments for the venture fund. We adopt a different approach without the use of artificially generated variables in this chapter, and address a different set of issues. A recent working paper with U.S. data adopts an approach that is more similar to ours (Cumming and Dai, 2007).

[4]It is noteworthy that a geographically proximate investment strategy (within a 100-kilometer radius) increases the average annual mutual fund returns by 2.67%. See, for example, Coval and Moskowitz (1999, 2001).

dollars),[5] 61.15% of the investment value was intraprovincial. We also find differences in the frequency of interprovincial investment transactions and provide evidence that certain economic and institutional factors systematically give rise to differences in the frequency of inter- versus intraprovincial investments.

In this chapter, we develop testable hypotheses with the institutional structure with reference to prior research. The data are described and univariate comparison tests are carried out on the proportion of inter- versus intraprovincial investments for different characteristics of the investments. Multivariate tests of inter- versus intraprovincial investment are carried out, and a discussion of limitations with the data and the types of tests that can be carried out in future research follows.

17.2 Institutional Structure, Prior Research, and Testable Hypotheses

In this section we describe agency cost barriers and legal and institutional impediments to interprovincial investment. These hypotheses are tested with a dataset provided.

17.2.1 Agency Impediments to Interprovincial Investment

Private equity investors invest in firms that are geographically proximate for at least three reasons (Gompers and Lerner, 1999; Sorenson and Stuart, 2001). First, it is more convenient to conduct due diligence and screening of firms that are geographically proximate. Fund managers typically receive more than 1,000 business plans per year but seriously consider fewer than 50 firms, and they carry out fewer than 30 investments (Cumming, 2006a; Sahlman, 1990).[6] Second, geographic proximity facilitates information flow and monitoring, as well as the ability to serve effectively on a board of directors and provide value-added services such as strategic, marketing, administrative, and financial advice. Third, while data are unavailable to date, one may postulate[7] that because there will be more interaction between the fund manager and entrepreneurial firm during the crucial divestment period, this can only be facilitated by proximity, so the investment is more profitable when the fund manager and entrepreneur are geographically proximate. In sum, regardless of institutional impediments, we expect to find a small number of interprovincial investments relative to intraprovincial investments. Overall, we expect intraprovincial investment, or home bias, will be more likely when information asymmetries and agency costs are more pronounced. This gives rise to Hypothesis 17.1.

[5]We use 1997 Canadian dollars as a reference point as the midpoint of the data that are from 1991 to 2003.

[6]Often there are fewer than 30 firms in a venture portfolio and fewer than 5 investee firms per fund manager; see Chapter 18.

[7]This is based on mutual fund evidence provided by Coval and Moskowitz (1999, 2001).

In the empirical tests we proxy the extent of information asymmetries and agency costs by a variety of observable factors in the data.

Hypothesis 17.1: *The more pronounced the extent of information asymmetries and agency costs, the greater the probability of intraprovincial private equity investment.*

Stage of Investee Firm Development: The earlier the firm's stage of development, the greater the required screening, due diligence, and monitoring (Gompers, 1995; Gompers and Lerner, 1999). We would therefore expect a greater proportion of earlier-stage firms to be intraprovincial investments.

Investee Capital Requirements: For reasons that are similar to *Stage of Investee Firm Development*, we expect smaller investment requirements to be associated with intraprovincial investment.

Entrepreneurial Firm Industry: High-tech firms present greater informational problems for fund managers, and therefore they require more intensive screening and monitoring (Gompers, 1995; Gompers and Lerner, 1999), and are more likely to be intraprovincial investments.

Privately Held versus Publicly Traded Investees: Publicly traded firms face a number of reporting requirements and therefore are much easier to value and monitor than privately held firms. We expect a greater proportion of publicly traded firms to have fund managers from other provinces than privately held firms.

Transaction-specific Factors: The types of security, staging, and syndication are expected to be correlated with the likelihood of interprovincial investment but not expected to be determinants of interprovincial investment (i.e., the causal connection is ambiguous). Syndicated investments are more likely to be interprovincial, as syndication facilitates due diligence, risk sharing, and monitoring (Lerner, 1994). Staging frequency is related to monitoring intensity, and more frequent staging is therefore more likely to be correlated with intraprovincial investments. Investments with debt and preferred equity securities are more likely to be correlated with the interprovincial investments, as such securities mitigate the costs associated with bankruptcy.

17.2.2 Institutional Impediments to Interprovincial Investment

Canada contains 10 provinces and 3 Northern Territories. Because the private equity database considered herein does not consist of fund managers or entrepreneurial firms from the Northern Territories, our focus is on the 10 provinces (from west to east): British Columbia, Alberta, Saskatchewan, Manitoba, Ontario, Quebec, Newfoundland, New Brunswick, Nova Scotia, and Prince Edward Island. There are at least three institutional barriers to interprovincial private equity investment in Canada: legal, language, and statutory provision applicable to government private equity funds.

Legal differences across provinces may exacerbate the extent of intraprovincial investment, as nonharmonious regulations increase the direct costs of interprovincial investment. Perhaps most importantly, the Province of Quebec in Canada is a civil law province, while all other provinces are common law.[8] Further, Quebec residents are primarily of French origin, while residents in all other provinces are primarily of English origin. Thirty-eight percent of Quebec residents can converse in both languages, compared with only 10% of the rest of Canada.[9] It is not within the scope of this chapter to discuss the extent of the differences between Quebec and the rest of the Canadian provinces, however, other cultural differences outside of the preceding institutional differences are well established by previous research.[10] Intraprovincial investment is much more likely in Quebec than other Canadian provinces. Similarly, we would expect neighbor provinces in Eastern Canada (including Ontario and the Maritime Provinces that border Quebec) to involve less frequent interprovincial investment than the neighboring English-speaking provinces in Western Canada.

It is also noteworthy that securities laws and securities commissions in Canada differ in each province. For the purpose of private equity investment, the most striking difference is the exemptions from the prospectus requirement among the provinces.[11] These differences are relevant for the smaller ranges of investment of less than approximately $100,000 to $150,000, depending on the province of course. Interprovincial differences in securities regulation present obvious impediments to interprovincial investment activity, especially in light of the requirement that not only must all legal provisions of both provinces be met but also certified as such by lawyers from both provinces.[12]

Corporate laws in Canada also differ by province, and there is a federal incorporation option in Canada. Over the period from 1975 to 1990, the provinces adopted changes to harmonize corporate laws, but there are nevertheless differences across provinces. Most firms in Canada are incorporated under either the laws of their home province or federally (Cumming and MacIntosh 2000b; Daniels, 1991). Different corporate codes also present a small institutional impediment to investment activities across the different Canadian provinces, as they necessitate dissimilar transaction structures, which increase transaction costs.

Corporate tax in Canada is calculated on the basis of where the business is conducted. Different tax rates across provinces may discourage interprovincial

[8]Similarly, prior work on law and finance is consistent with the notion that national differences may impede flows of capital across countries, among other things. For seminal work in this area of law and finance, see La Porta et al. (1997, 1998); see also Leleux and Surlemont (2003) for an application to private equity.

[9]http://www.isteve.com/2001_Canada_Bilingual.htm.

[10]For a more in-depth understanding of how culture affects commerce, please see Booth et al. (2006), and see also the five Hofstede Cultural Dimensions (http://www.geert-hofstede.com/), specifically http://www.geert-hofstede.com/hofstede_canada.shtml for Canada.

[11]See, for example, Gillen (1998); see also the various Canadian securities commissions' web pages, including http://www.osc.gov.on.ca/ for the Ontario Securities Commission.

[12]Harris (2002) discusses numerous pros and cons associated with the current provincial securities regulatory structure in Canada.

investment from provinces with higher tax rates.[13] It is noteworthy in the venture capital context that nearly all of the provinces, except Alberta, have R&D tax credit programs, which reduces the after-tax cost of R&D to between \$0.29 to \$0.58 per dollar of R&D expenditure, depending on the size of the firm and the particular province.[14]

Government bodies across Canada, with the exception of Alberta and Newfoundland, have created tax-subsidized venture capital funds known as Labour-Sponsored Venture Capital Corporations (LSVCCs). Briefly, LSVCCs are tax-subsidized mutual funds that invest in private equity. Investors in LSVCCs are limited to individuals, unlike private limited partnerships that receive the majority of their capital from institutional investors like pension funds.[15] LSVCCs have accumulated the most capital under management in recent years—approximately 50% of all private equity in Canada—which can be explained by the tax incentives for investors in LSVCCs.[16] LSVCCs may affect interprovincial investing activities in two ways. First, LSVCCs are required by statute to invest in the province in which they reside. Second, provinces without LSVCCs may have a greater demand for private equity that cannot be fulfilled by local investors.[17] We may therefore conjecture less interprovincial investment among provinces with LSVCCs and greater interprovincial private equity investment into Alberta and Newfoundland, the two provinces that do not have LSVCCs. As a related matter, there is a small presence of other types of government funds (not LSVCCs) in Canada (about 2% of the total private equity market; Cumming and MacIntosh, 2006), and these funds are highly unlikely to invest outside their own province. The government funds are directly funded from provincial tax revenues, and it would be politically unwise for them to invest in firms that reside outside the province.

Hypothesis 17.2: *The greater the costs associated with institutional differences across provinces, the greater the probability of intraprovincial private equity investment.*

In the empirical tests we proxy the extent of institutional costs with the following variables from the data, including the following.

[13]Combined federal-provincial corporate income tax rates on large nonmanufacturing corporations (excluding special exemptions for subsidized small firms in certain sectors in certain regions) are as follows: British Columbia 35.5%, Alberta 33.5%, Saskatchewan 39%, Manitoba 37%, Ontario 30%, Quebec 31%, New Brunswick 35%, Nova Scotia 38%, Prince Edward Island 38%, and Newfoundland 36% (in the United States the 2002 rate is 39%). http://www.innovationstrategy.gc.ca/cmb/innovation.nsf/ProvincialProfiles/.

[14]http://www.innovationstrategy.gc.ca/cmb/innovation.nsf/ProvincialProfiles/.

[15]Osbourne and Sandler (1998) discuss LSVCCs in much greater detail. The CVCA Annual Reports (posted at http://www.cvca.ca/statistical_review/index.html) provide details on the sources of capital by type of institutional investor.

[16]Osborne and Sandler (1998); Cumming and MacIntosh (2006).

[17]This statement assumes that there is a market failure in the provision of private equity among private venture capital funds (i.e., too few private venture capital funds) and that the LSVCCs correct such a market failure. An alternative view is that government funds and/or LSVCCs crowd out private investment. For a more detailed discussion, see Cumming and MacIntosh (2006).

Province-specific Dummy Variables: Quebec, as a French-speaking civil law province in Eastern Canada, is more likely to have intraprovincial investment, as are the provinces that border Quebec, Ontario, and the Maritime Provinces. Western Canadian provinces that are English speaking and common law based are more likely to have interprovincial investment. Alberta and Newfoundland investees (the two provinces without LSVCCs) are more likely to have investors from other provinces.

Year of Investment: Interprovincial investment activity is expected to increase over time as investors become more sophisticated and information sharing and strategic networks develop. There could be an increasing role of information technology in expanding the geographic reach of venture capital and other forms of private equity; that is, the meaning of *geographic proximity* could be changing that would lead one to expect the importance of interprovincial activity to continue to grow. Interprovincial investment may also be expected to be greater in the bubble years of 1999 and 2000, as there was a surplus of capital chasing fewer deals (Gompers and Lerner, 2000).

Type of Investor: We expect government funds and LSVCCs to invest more frequently in entrepreneurial firms located in the same province. There may exist differences among limited partnerships, corporate funds, and institutional investors, depending on the extent of sophistication and risk taking across fund managers at different fund types; however, a priori, we have no reason to expect systematic differences across these different types of Canadian funds.

The next section of the chapter introduces the dataset used to test Hypotheses 17.1 and 17.2 and summary statistics. Thereafter, we provide multivariate tests of Hypotheses 17.1 and 17.2. A discussion of the results and potential avenues for further research, as well as concluding remarks follow in the final sections of the chapter.

17.3 Data

The data used in this study are from Macdonald & Associates Limited, which has built the most comprehensive database on venture capital and private equity activity in Canada. The majority of economic activity in Canada is generated in Ontario, Quebec, British Columbia, and Alberta.[18] Likewise, a majority of private equity transactions in Canada are carried out in Quebec and Ontario (Cumming and MacIntosh, 2006). Canada's private equity funds managed in total approximately \$22.5 billion in capital in 2002 (or approximately \$20 billion in 1997 dollars).[19] Total investment activity in Canada's private equity markets amounted to approximately 0.38% of GDP in Canada over the 1998 to 2001 period, compared to 0.63% in the United States and 0.30% in the European Union.[20]

[18]http://www.innovationstrategy.gc.ca/cmb/innovation.nsf/ProvincialProfiles/.

[19]See http://www.cvca.ca.

[20]OECD http://r0.unctad.org/en/subsites/dite/pdfs/Frank_Lee.pdf.

We included 13,729 investments over the period from 1991 (first quarter) to 2003 (first quarter). Transactions are from numerous different types of investors: corporate, institutional, government, private limited partnerships, LSVCCs, and "other" types of investors with an interest in specific private equity deals but without a permanent market presence.[21] The types of entrepreneurial firms in the database are also broad in scope: various stages of development such as start-up, expansion, buyout, turnaround, and "other," which are not specifically identified, industries such as life sciences, other high-tech, and traditional non-high-tech, and entrepreneurial firms both privately held and publicly traded on a stock exchange. A wide variety of securities appear in the data, including common equity, preferred equity, convertible preferred equity, debt, convertible debt, warrants, mixes of debt and common equity, mixes of preferred equity and common equity, and other combinations. Differences in deal types such as staging, syndication, and the amounts invested, which range from less than $10,000 to more than $100,000,000, are specified in the data.

A snapshot of the complete dataset for all 13,729 transactions is provided in Table 17.1, which shows that a majority of investment activity is intraprovincial. For all types of fund managers and entrepreneurial firms, in terms of the number of investments (13,729 transactions), 84.42% of investments was intraprovincial. In terms of the total value of these transactions ($20,193,896,909 in 1997 dollars), 61.15% of the investment value was intraprovincial. The investee firms in Alberta, Newfoundland, and Prince Edward Island received capital from non-resident fund managers in a majority of the investments.

Table 17.2 provides a detailed summary of the data. The proportions of intraprovincial investments are explicitly presented for a number of different fund managers, entrepreneurial firms, and transaction-specific characteristics. Univariate comparison tests are also provided. The statistically significant test statistics indicate support for both agency costs and institutional explanations for differences between inter- and intraprovincial investment activities.

In regards to agency costs explanations for intraprovincial investment (Hypothesis 17.1), first notice that the stage of investment is important for intra- versus interprovincial investment. The data indicate 97% of turnaround investments are intraprovincial (Test #3 in Table 17.2). This suggests that the risk of financing a lemon is considerable for turnarounds, as by definition these are investments in firms that are failing, and fund managers therefore must get closely involved in these investments. The proportion of intraprovincial investments for turnarounds is significantly greater than that for seed, expansion, and buyout investments that are intraprovincial in 83%, 84%, and 85% of investments, respectively. Notice, however, that the size of investment per private equity fund and total deal size, including syndicated deals, are significantly related to the propensity to invest intraprovincially (Tests #18 to 25): Generally, smaller investments are more likely to be intraprovincial.

[21]Each of these types of funds in Canada has been described in previous research. See, for example, Macdonald (1992); MacIntosh (1994); Halpern (1997); Amit et al. (1998); Brander et al. (2002); and Cumming (2005).

Table 17.1 Are Entrepreneurs and Investors Located in the Same Province?

This table presents the number of investments by private equity investors (of all types) and by entrepreneurs (of all types at different stages of development and different industries), for each province. The location of the entrepreneurs is based on their place of business (or primary place, in a minority of cases where entrepreneurs carried on business in more than 1 province), as recorded by Macdonald and Associates, Ltd. The location of the investor is recorded as follows: If the investor has an office in the same province as the entrepreneur, then only that province is recorded; otherwise, the office in the primary other province of residence is recorded in this table. 13,729 observations. 1991 quarter 1 to 2003 quarter 1.

		Primary Location of Entrepreneurial Firm											
		BC	**AB**	**SK**	**MB**	**ON**	**QC**	**NF**	**NB**	**NS**	**PEI**	**Total**	**% Investors Financing Entrepreneurs in Same Province**
Primary Location of Investor	BC	999	8	0	2	9	3	0	0	0	0	1021	97.85%
	AB	21	156	4	6	16	3	0	0	0	1	207	75.36%
	SK	5	9	146	0	3	0	0	0	0	0	163	89.57%
	MB	11	0	2	315	13	1	0	2	1	0	345	91.30%
	ON	247	200	39	40	3530	287	14	42	56	8	4463	79.09%
	QC	55	44	0	9	222	4962	2	9	2	0	5305	93.53%
	NF	0	0	0	0	0	0	0	0	0	0	0	NA
	NB	0	0	0	0	1	1	0	18	0	0	20	90.00%
	NS	2	1	0	0	7	0	13	10	101	0	134	75.37%
	PEI	0	0	0	0	0	0	0	0	0	5	5	100.00%
	Foreign	113	19	0	1	259	62	0	3	1	0	458	NA
	Unknown	280	96	35	29	586	534	12	13	19	4	1608	NA
	Total	1733	533	226	402	4646	5853	41	97	180	18	13729	
% Entrepreneurs Financed by Investors in Same Province, Including Foreign, Excluding Unknown	68.75%	35.70%	76.44%	84.45%	86.95%	93.29%	0.00%	21.43%	62.73%	35.71%		84.42%	

Table 17.2 Comparison of Proportions Tests for Proportions of Investments Where Entrepreneurs and Investors Are in the Same Province

This table reports comparisons of proportions tests of the number of times investments occurred in which investors and entrepreneurs were in the same province as a proportion of the total number of financings for the listed characteristics of the venture capitalist, entrepreneur, and financing arrangement. A positive (negative) and significant number indicates that the top number is that a greater (smaller) proportion of investors and entrepreneurs were in the same province. *, **, *** Significant at the 10%, 5%, and 1% levels, respectively.

	#	Proportion	Proportion Equal?		#	Proportion	Proportion Equal?
1. Seed Stage versus				10. Limited Partnership			
Expansion Stage				VCs versus LSVCCs			
Seed Stage	4967	0.83	−0.65	Private Independent	2753	0.82	−12.52***
Expansion Stage	3944	0.84		Limited Partnerships			
				LSVCCs	3404	0.92	
2. Seed Stage versus				11. Investment Years			
Buyout Stage				1991–1994 versus			
Seed Stage	4967	0.83	−0.84	1995–1998			
Buyout Stage	410	0.85		1991–1994	962	0.89	1.63
				1995–1998	3243	0.87	
3. Seed Stage versus				12. Investment Years			
Turnaround Stage				1991–1994 versus			
Seed Stage	4967	0.83	−9.35***	1999–2000			
Turnaround Stage	654	0.97		1991–1994	962	0.89	3.92***
				1999–2000	3016	0.83	
4. Privately Held				13. Investment Years			
versus Publicly Traded				1991–1994 versus			
Entrepreneurs				2001–2003 (Q1)			
Privately Held	8748	0.85	1.42	1991–1994	962	0.89	3.15***
Publicly Traded	1484	0.83		2001–2003 (Q1)	339	0.82	

5. Life Sciences				14. Syndication versus			
versus Other Types of				Nonsyndication			
High-tech				Syndication	5477	0.80	−13.15***
Life Sciences	2082	0.81	−1.01	Nonsyndication	4755	0.90	
High-tech	4544	0.82					
6. Life Sciences				15. Initial Investment			
versus Traditional				Round 1 versus Staged			
(Non-high-tech)				Rounds 2–5			
Life Sciences	2082	0.81	−8.28***	Round 1	3829	0.87	6.22***
Traditional	3606	0.89		Rounds 2–5	5264	0.83	
7. Limited Partnership				16. Initial Investment			
VCs versus Corporate				Round 1 versus Staged			
Investors				Rounds 6–10			
Private Independent	2753	0.82	−1.18	Round 1	3829	0.87	4.58***
Limited Partnerships				Rounds 6–10	1036	0.82	
Corporate	1014	0.83					
8. Limited Partnership				17. Initial Investment			
VCs versus Government				Round 1 versus Staged			
Investors				Rounds 11–15			
Private Independent	2753	0.82	−14.73***	Round 1	3829	0.87	−0.17
Limited Partnerships				Rounds 11–15	103	0.88	
Government	1722	0.97					
9. Limited Partnership				18. Amounts Invested			
VCs versus Institutional				<$100,000 versus			
Investors				$100,000–$500,000			
Private Independent	2753	0.82	−4.52***	<$100,000	1119	0.82	−6.00***
Limited Partnerships				$100,000–$500,000	3782	0.89	
Institutional	1144	0.87					

(*continued*)

Table 17.2 (*continued*)

	#	Proportion	Proportion Equal?		#	Proportion	Proportion Equal?
19. Amounts Invested <$100,000 versus $500,000–$1,000,000				28. Common Equity versus Convertible Preferred Equity			
<$100,000	1119	0.82	−3.61***	Common Equity	3212	0.85	3.76***
$500,000–$1,000,000	1916	0.87		Convertible Preferred Equity	893	0.80	
20. Amounts Invested <$100,000 versus $1,000,000–$5,000,000				29. Common Equity versus Debt			
				Common Equity Debt	3212	0.85	−4.93***
<$100,000	1119	0.82	−0.10		1630	0.90	
$1,000,000–$5,000,000	2948	0.82					
21. Amounts Invested <$100,000 versus >$5,000,000				30. Common Equity versus Convertible Debt			
				Common Equity	3212	0.85	0.40
<$100,000	1119	0.82	8.09***	Convertible Debt	1209	0.84	
>$5,000,000	467	0.63					
22. Deal Size <$100,000 versus $100,000–$500,000				31. Common Equity versus Warrants			
<$100,000	610	0.93	0.61	Common Equity	3212	0.85	0.42
$100,000–$500,000	2486	0.92		Warrants	53	0.83	

23. Deal Size <$100,000 versus $500,000–$1,000,000				32. Common Equity versus Mixes of Debt and Common Equity			
<$100,000	610	0.93	2.60***	Common Equity	3212	0.85	−5.17***
$500,000–$1,000,000	1483	0.89		Debt and Common	529	0.93	
24. Deal Size <$100,000 versus $1,000,000–$5,000,000				33. Common Equity versus Mixes of Preferred and Common Equity			
<$100,000	610	0.93	4.72***	Common Equity	3212	0.85	−1.23
$1,000,000–$5,000,000	3619	0.86		Preferred and Common	187	0.88	
25. Deal Size <$100,000 versus >$5,000,000				34. Common Equity versus Other Combinations			
<$100,000	610	0.93	11.06***	Common Equity	3212	0.85	3.58***
>$5,000,000	2034	0.71		Other	1641	0.81	
26. Investor Has Offices in >1 Province versus Only 1 Province				35. ON Entrepreneurs versus BC Entrepreneurs			
				ON	3530	0.87	13.50***
Investor has offices in More Than 1 Province	2968	0.89	19.94***	BC	999	0.69	
Investor has Offices in 1 Province Only	7264	0.70				0.69	
27. Common Equity versus Preferred Equity				36. Entrepreneurs versus AB Entrepreneurs			
Common Equity	3212	0.85	3.73***	ON	3530	0.87	17.44***
Preferred Equity	878	0.80		AB	156	0.36	

(continued)

Table 17.2 *(continued)*

	#	Proportion	Proportion Equal?		#	Proportion	Proportion Equal?
37. ON Entrepreneurs versus SK Entrepreneurs				45. ON Investors versus AB Investors			
ON	3530	0.87	3.65***	ON	3530	0.79	1.12
SK	146	0.76		AB	156	0.75	
38. ON Entrepreneurs versus MB Entrepreneurs				46. ON Investors versus SK Investors			
ON	3530	0.87	1.25	ON	3530	0.79	−3.07***
MB	315	0.84		SK	146	0.90	
39. ON Entrepreneurs versus QC Entrepreneurs				47. ON Investors versus MB Investors			
ON	3530	0.87	–9.89***	ON	3530	0.79	−5.20***
QC	4962	0.93		MB	315	0.91	
40. ON Entrepreneurs versus NF Entrepreneurs				48. ON Investors versus QC Investors			
ON	3530	0.87	NA	ON	3530	0.79	−19.85***
NF	0	0.00		QC	4962	0.94	

41. ON Entrepreneurs versus NB Entrepreneurs				49. ON Investors versus NF Investors			
ON	3530	0.87	8.14***	ON	3530	0.79	NA
NB	18	0.21		NF	0	0.00	
42. ON Entrepreneurs versus NS Entrepreneurs				50. ON Investors versus NB Investors			
ON	3530	0.87	6.97***	ON	3530	0.79	−1.14
NS	101	0.63		NS	18	0.90	
43. ON Entrepreneurs versus MB Entrepreneurs				51. ON Investors versus NS Investors			
ON	3530	0.87	3.39***	ON	3530	0.79	0.90
PEI	5	0.36		NS	101	0.75	
44. ON Investors versus BC Investors				52. ON Investors versus PEI Investors			
ON	3530	0.79	−14.01***	ON	3530	0.79	−1.15
BC	999	0.98		PEI	5	1.00	

Some of the results in regards to the type of investment, however, were not expected. The proportions of intraprovincial investment for private and public firms are 85% and 83%, respectively, and therefore not materially different. The proportion of investments in life sciences and other types of high-tech industries is 81% and 82%, respectively (Table 17.2, Test #5). By contrast, traditional non-high-tech industries such as manufacturing, comprised 89% of intraprovincial investment (Test #6). As informational asymmetries and agency costs are generally viewed as more pronounced for high-tech investments, we had expected a greater proportion of intraprovincial investment in high-tech industries. A likely explanation for this result is that profit opportunities are greater for high-tech industries, and deal flow is not sufficiently large for Canadian investors to focus only on intraprovincial high-tech investment.

Other evidence in the data is consistent with the importance of agency explanations for inter- versus intraprovincial investment. We find that 80% of syndicated investments are intraprovincial, whereas 90% of nonsyndicated investments are intraprovincial (Test #14). This suggests syndication facilitates deal screening and monitoring thereby lowering potential agency problems, consistent with prior work (Brander et al., 2002; Lerner, 1994). The data also indicate that 87% of first-round investments are intraprovincial, while only 83% of follow-on investments are intraprovincial (Tests #15–17), which, as expected, indicates first-round investments require greater screening (Gompers, 1995). Notice that these variables for syndication and staging do not "cause" intra- versus interprovincial investment, so they are not explanatory variables in the next section where we carry out multivariate tests.

We find that the type of security is correlated with the extent of intraprovincial investment. The data indicate that 80% of investments with convertible preferred equity, 85% of common equity investments, and 90% of investments using pure debt are intraprovincial (see generally Tests #27 to 34). Common equity investments, which provide upside potential without downside protection in bankruptcy, are more likely to be carried out in the same province to mitigate failure. Conversely, investments with pure debt provide investors with downside protection in bankruptcy but no upside potential. This indicates that investors are only willing to make interprovincial investments if the added risk is mitigated with downside protection, and their risk taking is additionally rewarded with upside potential, which is available with the use of convertible preferred equity. As with the staging and syndication variables, notice that these variables for the type of security are also choice variables and do not cause intra- versus interprovincial investment, so they are not explanatory variables in the next section with multivariate tests. Nevertheless, these statistics are reported, as they lend support to the view that intra- versus interprovincial investment is related to agency costs as predicted (Hypothesis 17.1).

Fund manager characteristics are significantly related to the extent of intraprovincial investment (Tests #7–10 in Table 17.2). Managers of government funds (including LSVCCs) are much more likely to invest intraprovincially. One item of interest is that despite covenants restricting LSVCCs from investing interprovincially, 8% of LSVCC investments are interprovincial (Test #10). This indicates institutional features are important for intraprovincial investment, consistent with Hypothesis 17.2.

Private fund managers with offices in more than one province are more likely to invest interprovincially (Test #26): 70% of investments are intraprovincial among fund managers with offices in more than one province, while 89% of investments are intraprovincial among fund managers based in only one province. Notice that the CVCA data comprise incomplete details on fund size in terms of total capital managed by each specific fund, and therefore we cannot investigate such details in the data. Nevertheless, we may expect that fund managers with offices in more than one province are typically more established with greater capital under management, and therefore we could postulate that such fund managers will be more sophisticated and thus able to incur extra risks of interprovincial investment.

The data indicate that 93% of investment is intraprovincial in Quebec (Test #39 for Quebec entrepreneurs; see also Test #48 for Quebec-based investors), which is greater than any other province based on the province of residence of the entrepreneurs (Tests #35 to 43). This result was expected, since Quebec is a civil law French province and all other provinces are common law based with residents that primarily speak English (Hypothesis 17.2 and accompanying text). Ontario comprises the second highest proportion of intraprovincial investment, which was also expected. The data also indicate that intraprovincial investing has decreased over time, from approximately 89% in 1991 to 1994, to 87% in 1995 to 1998, to 83% in 1999 to 2000, and to 82% in 2001 to 2003, which is consistent with improvements in technology and communication networks, as well as greater fund manager experience over time.

Table 17.3 presents a matrix of correlation coefficients. The reported correlation coefficients for the first column between the proportion of intraprovincial investment and the other variables are consistent with the conclusions drawn from the comparison of proportion tests in Table 17.2. The variables in Table 17.3 are used in the next section to further explore the robustness of the univariate test statistics by analyzing the determinants of inter- versus intraprovincial investment in a multivariate context. The relatively small correlation coefficients across the variables indicate that we do not have a concern with collinearity problems among the considered explanatory variables. However, other explanatory variables are not used, as the correlations were much higher, as we will discuss in the next section.

17.4 Multivariate Logit Tests

In this section we investigate the determinants of inter- versus intraprovincial investment decisions in a multivariate setting. Table 17.4 presents binomial logit regressions of the likelihood that a fund manager and entrepreneur reside in the same province. Model 1 considers all provinces together, while

Table 17.3 Correlation Matrix

This table presents the correlation coefficients between a dummy variable for investments with entrepreneurs and investors located in the same province, and a number of investor and entrepreneur characteristics, as well as the log of the deal size, and dummy variables for the province of residence of the entrepreneur. Correlations greater than 0.02 in absolute value are statistically significant at the 5% level. These variables are used for the multivariate tests in Table 17.4.

		(1)	(2)	(3)	(4)	(5)	(6)	(7)	(8)	(9)	(10)	(11)	(12)	(13)	(14)	(15)
(1)	Dummy Variable for Investor and Entrepreneur in Same Province	1.00														
(2)	Dummy Variable for Government Investor or LSVCC	0.17	1.00													
(3)	Dummy Variable for Public Company	−0.05	0.03	1.00												
(4)	Dummy Variable for Buyout Company	0.01	0.01	0.02	1.00											
(5)	Dummy Variable for Turnaround Company	0.08	0.15	0.00	−0.05	1.00										
(6)	Dummy Variable for Tech Company (Life Science or Other High-tech)	−0.06	−0.12	0.08	−0.11	−0.17	1.00									
(7)	Log of the Total Deal Size	−0.15	−0.05	0.07	0.06	−0.15	0.25	1.00								

(8)	# Provinces in Which Investor Has Offices	0.05	0.24	0.05	0.01	−0.05	0.13	0.16	1.00							
(9)	Dummy Variable for Alberta Entrepreneur	−0.28	−0.09	0.05	0.01	–0.04	–0.05	0.02	0.03	1.00						
(10)	Dummy Variable for Saskatchewan Entrepreneur	0.00	0.10	−0.01	0.04	−0.03	−0.05	−0.02	0.06	−0.02	1.00					
(11)	Dummy Variable for Manitoba Entrepreneur	0.00	0.07	−0.02	−0.01	−0.03	−0.10	−0.06	−0.06	−0.04	−0.02	1.00				
(12)	Dummy Variable for Ontario Entrepreneur	0.06	0.01	0.07	−0.02	−0.09	0.15	0.19	0.09	−0.12	−0.08	−0.12	1.00			
(13)	Dummy Variable for Quebec Entrepreneur	0.20	0.02	−0.11	0.03	0.17	−0.13	−0.22	−0.29	−0.19	−0.13	−0.19	−0.63	1.00		
(14)	Dummy Variable for New Brunswick Entrepreneur	−0.16	−0.02	−0.02	0.00	−0.02	0.02	0.01	0.03	−0.02	−0.01	−0.02	−0.05	−0.08	1.00	
(15)	Dummy Variable for Nova Scotia Entrepreneur	−0.07	−0.02	−0.04	0.00	−0.03	0.05	−0.04	0.04	−0.02	−0.01	−0.02	−0.07	−0.11	−0.01	1.00
(16)	Dummy Variable for PEI Entrepreneur	−0.06	−0.01	0.00	0.05	−0.01	−0.01	−0.02	0.03	−0.01	0.00	−0.01	−0.02	−0.04	0.00	0.00

Table 17.4 Multivariate Logit Regressions for the Likelihood

Dependent variable: a dummy equal to one if the entrepreneur and the investor are located other explanatory variables are as defined. There are 10,450 observations in the full sample was unknown). The number of provinces in which the investor has offices was necessarily problems. The provincial dummy variables are similarly excluded for the subsamples for estimator used in all regressions. t-Statistics are in parentheses. *, **, *** Significant at

	Model 1: Full Sample		Model 2: Quebec Subsample	
	Coefficient	**Marginal Effect**	**Coefficient**	**Marginal Effect**
Constant	1.93 (6.29***)	0.13	5.16 (10.82***)	0.14
Dummy Variable for Government Investor or LSVCC	0.67 (8.46***)	0.04	0.95 (6.19***)	0.03
Dummy Variable for Public Company	−0.22 (−2.32**)	−0.01	−0.44 (−2.57**)	−0.01
Dummy Variable for Buyout Company	0.26 (1.29)	0.02	0.43 (1.24)	0.01
Dummy Variable for Turnaround Company	1.16 (3.50***)	0.08	1.25 (2.65***)	0.03
Dummy Variable for Tech Company (Life Science or Other High-tech)	−0.28 (−3.32***)	−0.02	−0.81 (−4.57***)	−0.02
Log of the Total Deal Size	−0.30 (−13.01***)	−0.02	−0.52 (−10.92***)	−0.01
# Provinces in Which the Investor Has Offices	0.45 (12.29***)	0.03	−0.17 (−2.88***)	−0.004
Dummy Variable for Alberta Entrepreneur	−1.31 (−9.31***)	−0.09		
Dummy Variable for Saskatchewan Entrepreneur	0.53 (2.05***)	0.04		
Dummy Variable for Manitoba Entrepreneur	1.06 (5.47***)	0.07		
Dummy Variable for Ontario Entrepreneur	1.80 (17.36***)	0.12		
Dummy Variable for Quebec Entrepreneur	2.13 (20.41***)	0.14		
Dummy Variable for New Brunswick Entrepreneur	−2.47 (−7.81***)	−0.16		
Dummy Variable for Nova Scotia Entrepreneur	−0.24 (−1.11***)	−0.02		
Dummy Variable for PEI Entrepreneur	−2.45 (−3.76***)	−0.16		

That the Entrepreneur and the Investor Are in the Same Province

in the same province. The deal size is measured in thousands of Canadian dollars;
(excluded: foreign investments and investments in which the location of the investor
excluded in the Ontario and British Columbia subsamples due to collinearity
the different provinces. White's (1980) heteroskedasticity consistent covariance matrix
the 10%, 5%, and 1% levels, respectively.

Model 3: Ontario Subsample		Model 4: British Columbia Subsample		Model 5: Alberta Subsample	
Coefficient	**Marginal Effect**	**Coefficient**	**Marginal Effect**	**Coefficient**	**Marginal Effect**
1.03 (1.96**)	0.05	1.52 (2.55**)	0.28	1.78 (2.09**)	0.41
2.25 (11.20***)	0.11	0.89 (6.03***)	0.16	−1.95 (−3.76***)	−0.45
−0.32 (−1.68*)	−0.02	−0.24 (−1.40)	−0.05	−0.71 (−2.00**)	−0.16
0.75 (1.53)	0.04	−0.21 (−0.44)	−0.04	1.69 (2.53**)	0.39
1.19 (1.61)	0.06	0.82 (1.024)	0.12	−0.33 (−0.19)	−0.08
0.19 (0.99)	0.01	0.28 (1.68*)	0.05	0.41 (1.35)	0.10
0.02 (0.51)	0.001	−0.19 (−3.85***)	−0.03	−0.16 (−1.78*)	−0.04
				0.58 (4.29***)	0.14

(continued)

Table 17.4

	Model 1: Full Sample		Model 2: Quebec Subsample	
	Coefficient	Marginal Effect	Coefficient	Marginal Effect
Dummy Variable for Investment in 2003	0.23 (0.73)	0.02	2.60 (4.43***)	0.07
Dummy Variable for Investment in 2002	0.45 (1.67*)	0.03	2.38 (5.67***)	0.06
Dummy Variable for Investment in 2001	0.47 (1.74*)	0.03	2.51 (5.95***)	0.07
Dummy Variable for Investment in 2000	0.36 (1.34)	0.02	2.10 (5.30***)	0.06
Dummy Variable for Investment in 1999	0.17 (0.63)	0.01	2.09 (5.10***)	0.06
Dummy Variable for Investment in 1998	0.24 (0.87)	0.02	2.12 (5.03***)	0.06
Dummy Variable for Investment in 1997	0.04 (0.13)	0.00	1.43 (3.57***)	0.04
Dummy Variable for Investment in 1996	0.09 (0.32)	0.01	1.25 (3.01***)	0.03
Dummy Variable for Investment in 1995	0.38 (1.19)	0.03	1.01 (2.40**)	0.03
Dummy Variable for Investment in 1994	0.41 (1.19)	0.03	1.71 (3.25***)	0.05
Dummy Variable for Investment in 1993	0.80 (2.16**)	0.05	2.12 (3.59***)	0.06
Dummy Variable for Investment in 1992	0.57 (1.58)	0.04	0.32 (0.65)	0.01
Model Diagnostics:				
Number of Observations	10450		5152	
Log Likelihood	−2931.38		−907.54	
Pseudo R^2	0.38		0.16	
Chi-square	1853.67***		343.16***	
	Predicted Outcomes		Predicted Outcomes	
Actual Outcomes	0	1	0	1
0	350	916	1	276
1	192	8992	3	4872

(*continued*)

Model 3: Ontario Subsample		Model 4: British Columbia Subsample		Model 5: Alberta Subsample	
Coefficient	**Marginal Effect**	**Coefficient**	**Marginal Effect**	**Coefficient**	**Marginal Effect**
−0.36 (−0.62)	−0.02	0.22 (0.35)	0.04	−2.65 (−2.63***)	−0.61
−0.02 (−0.05)	0.00	0.42 (0.82)	0.07	−2.70 (−3.74***)	−0.63
0.22 (0.45)	0.01	0.56 (1.09)	0.10	−2.20 (−3.10***)	−0.51
0.28 (0.57)	0.01	0.39 (0.77)	0.07	−2.08 (−3.15***)	−0.48
0.24 (0.48)	0.01	0.26 (0.51)	0.05	−2.76 (−3.80***)	−0.64
0.26 (0.52)	0.01	0.31 (0.59)	0.05	−2.21 (−3.17***)	−0.51
0.45 (0.88)	0.02	0.13 (0.24)	0.02	−3.10 (−4.13***)	−0.72
0.53 (0.95)	0.03	0.89 (1.50)	0.13	−1.99 (−2.40**)	−0.46
2.85 (2.57**)	0.14	0.88 (1.37)	0.13	1.76 (1.40)	0.41
0.26 (0.42)	0.01	0.95 (1.49)	0.14	0.23 (0.18)	0.05
0.91 (1.39)	0.04	1.59 (1.77*)	0.19	−0.45 (−0.49)	−0.11
2.49 (2.24**)	0.12	0.56 (0.82)	0.09	0.06 (0.07)	0.01
3005		1158		360	
−784.87		−633.71		−181.29	
0.13		0.06		0.25	
241.80***		76.08***		121.17***	
Predicted Outcomes		Predicted Outcomes		Predicted Outcomes	
0	1	0	1	0	1
0	269	9	300	177	40
0	2736	8	841	65	78

Models 2 to 5 consider the subsamples for entrepreneurs resident in Quebec, Ontario, British Columbia, and Alberta, respectively.[22] In each regression, the dependent variable is equal to one if the entrepreneur and fund manager reside in the same province. The independent variables are as follows:

- A dummy variable equal to one if the fund manager was an actual government fund or a LSVCC and zero for private limited partnerships, institutional investors, and corporate investors. Separate variables for each investor type were not used to avoid collinearity bias.
- A dummy variable equal to one if the entrepreneurial firm was a publicly traded firm and zero for privately held firms.
- A dummy variable equal to one for buyout stage firms and zero otherwise, and a dummy variable equal to one for turnaround stage firms and zero otherwise. Separate dummies for start-up and expansion stage firms were suppressed to avoid problems arising from collinearity.
- A dummy variable equal to one for high-tech firms (either life science or other high-tech) and zero for firms in traditional industries (e.g., manufacturing, etc.). Dummies for different industries were not used to avoid collinearity problems.
- The log of the total deal size, including all syndicated investment. Consistent with a large prior literature in financial economics, this variable is expressed in logs as the effect of larger sizes becomes smaller as size becomes larger. We use total deal size and not the amount invested by a particular fund manager, as entrepreneurial firm capital requirements are exogenously determined by the financial needs of the entrepreneur. As discussed following, certain other variables are not exogenous to the likelihood of interprovincial investment activity.
- Dummy variables for entrepreneurs resident in different provinces. Dummy variables for British Columbia and Newfoundland were suppressed in order to avoid perfect collinearity.
- Dummy variables for different investment years. A dummy variable for 1991 was suppressed to avoid perfect collinearity.

In an earlier stage of this research, we presented a number of models with different right-hand-side variables to illustrate the robustness of the results. We also considered many alternative specifications, which are available upon request; however, the results were not materially different. The right-hand-side variables do not include "choice" variables, such as staging, syndication, and capital structure. Such variables are not exogenous to the decision to invest in a firm resident in a different province (or not). Previously we reported comparison of proportion tests to ascertain correlations between certain choice variables and inter- versus intraprovincial investment, but such choice variables are not appropriate for the multivariate tests, which have a causal structure.

The multivariate regressions provide some support for Hypothesis 17.1. That is, agency explanations are important for geographic proximity, as the likelihood of intra- versus interprovincial investing depends on firm- and transaction-specific characteristics. As discussed previously, firm-specific characteristics proxy the degree in agency problems. Model 1 indicates intraprovincial investing

[22]Subsamples from other provinces were not considered due to a comparative dearth of data from those provinces.

is approximately 8% more likely for turnaround investments relative to both buyouts and early- and expansion-stage investments.[23] Turnaround investments are investments in firms facing potential bankruptcy because they are not currently earning their cost of capital. The data are supportive of the view that such investments require more intensive screening and monitoring than earlier-stage investments and buyouts. The summary statistics from Table 17.2 (Tests #1–3) are consistent with this view.

Industry factors in Model 1 run counter to our expectations under Hypothesis 17.1. Model 1 indicates that firms in traditional industries, as opposed to life science and other types of high-tech firms, are approximately 2% more likely to be interprovincial investments. We had expected a greater proportion of intraprovincial investments for high-tech firms, as information asymmetries and agency problems are more pronounced for high-tech firms. We may infer from the evidence that fund managers will seek greater expected returns with high-tech investments by considering more often firms that are not resident in the same province. Another explanation for this result is that fund managers that do actually finance high-tech firms have superior information networks, such as strategic alliances with other fund managers or consultants that can facilitate the investment to lower the agency costs and information asymmetries associated with investment in high-tech firms. Notice as well that the Quebec subsample is mainly driving the results for the high-tech coefficient in Model 1. In British Columbia (Model 4), high-tech investments are 4% more likely to be intraprovincial, which is consistent with expectations (Hypothesis 17.1). The high-tech coefficient is insignificant in the Ontario and Alberta subsamples. Hence, Quebec is an outlier in regards to high-tech entrepreneurs being financed by non-Quebec investors, since Model 2 for Quebec shows high-tech firms are less likely to be intraprovincial in Quebec, which is in contrast to Models 3 to 5 for Ontario, British Columbia, and Alberta.

Consistent with Hypothesis 17.1, publicly traded firms are 1% more likely to be interprovincial investments in Model 1. While this result is statistically significant, we might have expected greater economic significance. A greater amount of information is typically known about publicly traded firms. But referring back to Test #4 in Table 17.2, recall that 85% of private investments were intraprovincial and 83% of investments in publicly traded firms were intraprovincial. The comparison test was not statistically significant. In the more rigorous multivariate context that simultaneously controls for many factors, we do find a statistically significant difference between privately held and publicly traded securities, but again, the magnitude of the difference is not large.[24] The correlation between deal size (in logs) and the variable for public firms is only 0.07 (see Table 17.3). The statistical significance of the estimates does not depend on the simultaneous inclusion of the public company and

[23]The early- and expansion-stage dummy variables are excluded to avoid collinearity problems.

[24]Notice that our evidence that compares private versus publicly traded securities in this chapter is based on a relatively small number of public equity investments, since private equity funds typically do not invest in publicly listed securities.

deal size variables in the same model (see the alternative specifications in Table 17.3). The economic significance on the public company variable is about twice as large in Models 1 to 3 relative to Models 4 and 5, but the difference is due to the inclusion of the variables for the provinces and not the deal size variable (see Model 3 versus Model 4).

Model 1 indicates that entrepreneurial firms that require more capital are more likely to receive that capital from a fund manager domiciled in a different province. This effect, however, is small and diminishes with larger deal sizes: An increase in deal size from $500,000 to $1,000,000 increases the likelihood of interprovincial investment by 0.60%, while an increase in investment from $9,500,000 to $10,000,000 increases the likelihood of interprovincial investment by 0.04%.[25]

Overall, the multivariate regressions support Hypothesis 17.1 in terms of expected findings for turnaround investments, public firms, and deal sizes, but not in regards to industry factors. The summary statistics in Table 17.2 also provided additional “choice” variables pertaining to capital structure, staging, and syndication, which also supported Hypothesis 17.1. As discussed, those variables are not explanatory variables in the regressions as they are choice variables and selected when needed to mitigate the agency problems that are more pronounced among interprovincial investments.

In addition to agency explanations for inter- versus intraprovincial investment, the data also indicate that institutional explanations are important for geographic proximity. Perhaps most notably, in Model 1, intraprovincial investment is also 12% more likely for entrepreneurs resident in Ontario and 14% more likely for entrepreneurs resident in Quebec. Quebec and Ontario are neighboring provinces in Eastern Canada, but Quebec is a French civil law province, whereas Ontario is an English common law province. In Model 1 of Table 17.4, the Alberta and Maritime Provinces (Newfoundland, New Brunswick, Nova Scotia, and Prince Edward Island) variables are negative and significant, indicating interprovincial investments are more likely for entrepreneurs in those provinces relative to the others, whereas the variables for the other provinces are positive and significant, indicating intraprovincial investments are more likely for entrepreneurs in those provinces relative to the others.[26] This generally indicates that there is a comparative dearth of local fund managers in Alberta and the Maritime Provinces, as entrepreneurs in those provinces are more likely to receive capital from investors in other provinces. Note as well that all of the dummy variables that capture province-specific effects in the analysis of the complete set of data are statistically significant, which is consistent in spirit with Hypothesis 17.2.

Model 1 in Table 17.4 indicates that government funds and LSVCCs are 4% more likely to carry out intraprovincial investments relative to interprovincial investments, as expected (Hypothesis 17.2), and this result is significant at

[25]The calculation is [Log($10,000) – Log($9,500)] * (–2%). Notice that the deal size values in the data are expressed in thousands of Canadian dollars, so $10,000 in the calculation is actually $10,000,0000.

[26]The dummy variable for British Columbia is suppressed to avoid perfect collinearity.

the 1% level of significance. The same result holds in all subsamples with the exception of Alberta (Model 5), which is expected, since there are no government funds in Alberta and so government investment is interprovincial.

Model 1 also indicates that the number of provinces in which the fund manager has offices is positively related to the probability that the fund manager carries out intraprovincial investments. With each extra office, there is a 3% reduction in the probability of interprovincial investment. Some of the fund managers in the dataset had offices in as many as 6 of the 10 provinces. The need to consider entrepreneurs domiciled in other provinces naturally diminishes when geographic scope of office location is more complete. Notice, however, that in the Quebec regression (Model 2), the coefficient for number of provinces in which the fund manager has offices is negative and significant. Referring back to Table 17.3, recall that the correlation between the number of offices and the variable for Quebec was –0.29 but positive in the other provinces (except Manitoba). Therefore, the data indicate Quebec fund managers are much more regionally isolated and less likely to have offices in multiple jurisdictions, as might be expected.

The data strongly indicate that the year of investment matters for intra- versus interprovincial investment. Controlling for the previously mentioned factors, Model 1 indicates that years 2002, 2001, and 1993 show relatively more frequent intraprovincial investment. These were years of "bust" periods in private equity investment. A natural interpretation is that intraprovincial investment activity increases when economic activity is in decline, which suggests that investors are more risk averse in bust periods. Recall from the summary statistics (Table 17.2) that we observed intraprovincial investment decreased over time (from approximately 89% in 1991 to 1994, to 87% in 1995 to 1998, to 83% in 1999 to 2000, to 82% in 2001 to 2003). The coefficients in Model 1 suggest that these year changes over time are directly attributable to changes in the types of investment, such as high-tech investment, and so on. However, the year coefficients in the full sample in Model 1 are significantly influenced by the Quebec observations. In a regression excluding Quebec observations (not reported), we find that the coefficients for the year investments show a trend toward less intraprovincial investment over time. The year dummy variables in Model 2 are all positive and significant and trend upward over time, with the exception of slight drops in magnitude in 2002 and 2003, which suggests more intraprovincial investment in Quebec over time. This is consistent with an increased degree in political isolationism in Quebec, as the province has vigorously pursued separation from the rest of Canada over the years considered.

17.5 The Scope of the Data and Generalizations That Can Be Drawn from the Empirical Analysis

There are certain limitations associated with the analysis of private equity investments carried out in this chapter. First, the coverage of the data is obviously not

100% of all transactions in Canada. The CVCA covers industries traditionally targeted by private equity funds. The CVCA covers the following high-tech industries: biotechnology, medical/health related, communications, computer related, Internet related, electronics, and "other" technology. The CVCA also covers the following traditional industries: consumer related, manufacturing, and "miscellaneous."[27] Certain industries like mining and oil and gas are not covered in the database, and to our knowledge, systematic data on intra- versus interprovincial investment in these and other industries do not exist in Canada.

Second, the data are focused on private equity limited partnerships, corporate venture funds, LSVCCs, certain institutional investors that directly invest in entrepreneurial firms,[28] government venture programs, and "other" types of investors with an interest in specific private equity deals but without a permanent market presence. The data do not comprise investments from mutual funds, hedge funds, banks, and any other individual or institutional investor that does not fit within the scope of investors covered by Macdonald & Associates Limited. Based on the empirical tests carried out in this chapter, the data are consistent with the view that there is significantly less provincial bias for mutual funds, hedge funds, and other investors of publicly traded firms.

Third, we do not know the exact intraprovince location and rural versus urban investments in Canada. Ideally, we would like to know the exact location. Nevertheless, we believe the intra- versus interprovincial test is the most appropriate one, as the institutional barriers to interprovincial investment likely outweigh a measure of geography based on miles. For similar analyses in the U.S. context with data based on miles, see Cumming and Dai (2007) and Tian (2007).

Fourth, the data cover investments and not sales of investments through IPOs and acquisitions, and so forth. In Chapter 20 we consider the performance implications of intra- versus interprovincial investment.

17.6 Conclusions and Implications

This chapter presented evidence on the frequency with which investors and entrepreneurs are located in different provinces. For all types of investors and entrepreneurial firms, in terms of the number of investments (13,729 transactions), 84.42% of investments involved an investor and entrepreneur that resided in the same province. In terms of the total value of these transactions ($20,193,896,909 in 1997 dollars), 61.15% of the investment value was intraprovincial.

The data indicate agency factors are important for geographic proximity in private equity investment. In regards to agency explanations, we find the likelihood of intra- versus interprovincial investing depends on firm- and transaction-specific

[27]See http://www.cvca.ca/statistical_review/table_3x2002.html.

[28]The identity of any given investor is not specifically revealed in the raw data (whereby each transaction can be observed) from Macdonald and Associates, Ltd., for reasons of confidentiality. A list of investors that are members of the Canadian Venture Capital Association is available at http://www.cvca.ca/full_members/index.html.

characteristics. Interprovincial investing is more likely for publicly traded firms and for larger deal sizes, and intraprovincial investing is more likely for turnaround investments. The extent of intra- versus interprovincial investment is also significantly correlated with staging, syndication, and capital structure.

It is noteworthy that investors more often carried out interprovincial investments if the added risk is mitigated with downside protection, and their risk taking is additionally rewarded with upside potential, which is available with the use of convertible preferred equity. By contrast, a greater proportion of intraprovincial investment was with common equity securities.

In addition to agency explanations for inter- versus intraprovincial investment, the data also indicate institutional explanations are very important for geographic proximity, as the likelihood of intra- versus interprovincial investing increases among government-subsidized funds, increases over time, and differs across different provinces. Intraprovincial investment is more likely for entrepreneurs resident in Quebec. Quebec is a French civil law province, unlike all other Canadian provinces. The data are consistent with the view that differences in regulations across provinces exacerbate the degree of home bias.

Key Terms

Home bias
Intraprovincial investment
Interprovincial investment
Common law
Civil law

Discussion Questions

17.1. Why do information asymmetries and agency costs matter for investment location decisions?

17.2. Do investment location decisions systematically vary with the characteristics of the entrepreneurial firm (such as stage of development and industry), characteristics of the fund manager (such as private limited partnerships versus government funds), and/or structure of the investment (such as staging, syndication, and capital structure)?

17.3. True/False/Uncertain (and explain why): "A greater proportion of interprovincial investments involve the use of convertible securities."

17.4. In what ways might institutional factors influence the location of investment? Would you expect more intraprovincial investment activity in Quebec than other regions of Canada? Why?

17.5. Would you expect information asymmetries and agency costs to be more or less important than institutional factors in influencing the determinants of intraprovincial investment? Why?

18 Portfolio Size

18.1 Introduction and Learning Objectives

In Chapter 16 we provided evidence that contracts matter for investor effort and governance. But, as we have discussed, contracts are incomplete and therefore other factors matter for governance, such as location (Chapter 17). In this chapter, we focus on the role of portfolio size.

Mutual funds and private equity funds are similar in many ways. They both provide means for fund investors to pool their money, to have their capital managed by professional fund managers, and to have the professional fund managers make multiple investments, also known as the portfolio, which will eventually reap rewards for all those involved. Both investment vehicles are also used by their investors for diversification and risk mitigation purposes. This is probably where the similarities end, though, as the transaction-specific characteristics of their portfolio diverge. Mutual funds in general take diversification to a whole new level as their portfolios consist of numerous different investments in publicly listed firms and/or bonds in a variety of industries. This makes mutual fund investment extremely diversified, convenient, and liquid. Private equity funds, by contrast, invest in a small, undiversified, illiquid portfolio of privately held firms that are not yet listed on stock exchanges. Private equity fund managers are unable to hold portfolios that are too large or diversified, as they are, unlike mutual fund managers, active value-added investors who invest in nascent firms and use their unique technological, management, and financial contracting know-how to mitigate the informational asymmetries and agency costs involved in the investment in such nascent firms (e.g., Bergmann and Hege, 1998; Sahlman, 1990; Gompers, 1995, 1998; Gompers and Lerner, 1999a,b, 2000, 2001; Kirilenko, 2001; Neus and Walz, 2005; Schmidt, 2003; Trester, 1998).

Size, diversification, and risk management are particularly important for private equity funds as increases in portfolio size dilute the advice and monitoring provided to each entrepreneurial firm. The efficient size of a fund manager's portfolio therefore balances the trade-off between diversifying risks with the dilution of value-added advice, among other things (Kanniainen and Keuschnigg, 2003; Keuschnigg, 2003; and Keuschnigg and Nielsen, 2001, 2003a, 2004a,b).

In this chapter we will do the following:

- Consider four main factors that influence the determinants of portfolio size in terms of the number of entrepreneurial firms in the venture capital fund portfolio, as well as portfolio size per fund manager per year of investment:
  - The fund's characteristics, such as type of fund, fund size, and fund management firms that operate more than one fund
  - The characteristics of the entrepreneurial firms in the venture capitalist fund managers' portfolio, including entrepreneurial firm development stage, technology, and location
  - The structure and characteristics of the financing transactions, including staging, syndication, and forms of finance
  - Market conditions

In Chapter 22 we show that portfolio size is extremely important in understanding differences in realized rates of return across private equity funds. Funds that finance too many entrepreneurial firms per fund manager tend to perform much worse because of the diminished value-added provided to each entrepreneurial firm. As such, an extremely important part of the investment process is the design of an efficient portfolio size in terms of the number of entrepreneurial firms.

In this chapter we first consider the factors that may affect the size of a venture capital fund manager's portfolio. The Appendix to this chapter complements the discussion of the theory by providing an analysis of nonlinearities in the comparative statistics. We then discuss the data and present empirical estimates.

18.2 Comparative Statistics and Hypotheses

This section builds upon previous theoretical research (Kanniainen and Keuschnigg, 2003) on venture capital fund portfolio size by developing a number of proxies for the costs and benefits of having additional entrepreneurial firms in a venture capital fund's portfolio. The factors that affect venture capital fund portfolio size are analyzed at the venture capital *fund* level, with consideration to venture capital management firms that manage more than one venture capital fund. We study the total number of entrepreneurial firms in a venture capital fund's portfolio, as well as the number of entrepreneurial firms in the portfolio per venture capital fund manager. We use various proxies to account for benefits and costs associated with changing portfolio size because not all operational data are available from privately run venture capital funds, and therefore not all pecuniary costs and benefits associated with active value-added venture capital investment can be directly measured.

The testable hypotheses are based on the premise that there exists a projected marginal benefit (PMB) and a project marginal cost (PMC) function associated with the addition of an entrepreneurial firm to a venture capital fund's portfolio (analogous to Kanniainen and Keuschnigg, 2003). "Projected" refers to expected costs or benefits over the investment horizon. At the point of optimality, a venture capital fund manager will decide to invest in an entrepreneurial firm when the PMB as a result of the venture capital fund manager's efforts is greater than or equal to the PMC. The relationship between PMB and PMC is depicted in Figure 18.1. Most important, notice that the theory and empirical tests do not rely on the concavity or convexity of the PMB and PMC functions as depicted in Figure 18.1. The empirics directly test for the presence of concavity versus convexity. The nature of the PMB and PMC functions in Figure 18.1 is discussed in detail in the Appendix, along with the nonlinearities in the comparative statistics.

The factors that shift the PMB and PMC curves (see Figure 18.1) could include (1) the type of venture capital management firm and the number of venture capital funds managed, the age of the venture capital fund, the number of venture capital fund managers, venture capital fundraising; (2) the type of entrepreneurial firm (technology, stage of development, geographic location); (3) the nature of the financing arrangement (security, deal size, syndication, and staging); and (4) market conditions. As discussed following, in some cases predictions based in the comparative statistics largely depend on which effect is emphasized. The fact that the comparative statistics do not provide complete guidance renders the empirical tests in the subsequent section both necessary and interesting.

18.2.1 Venture Capital Fund Characteristics

We naturally expect that the PMB of portfolio expansion will be greater, and therefore portfolio size will be larger, among venture capital funds that have raised more capital, that have had a longer time to invest such capital, and that have a greater number of fund managers.

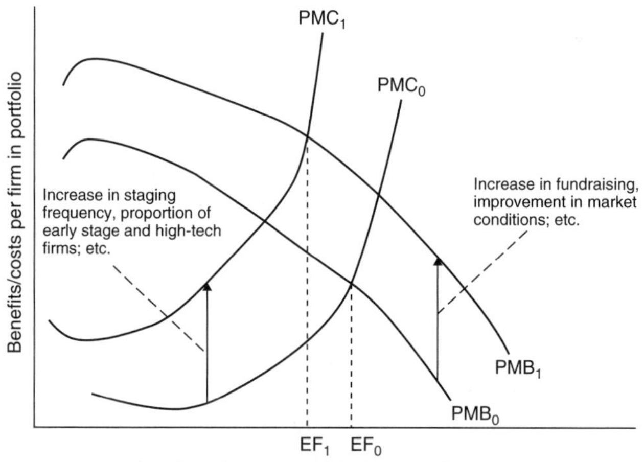

Figure 18.1 Efficient Venture Capital Portfolio Size and Comparative Statistics

Public funds typically have lower productivity due to less human capital, lower salaries and incentive pay, and political pressures to do a greater number of financings in more geographically disparate areas (the political economy literature discussed by Lerner, 1999, 2002b, suggests that these pressures are powerful). These factors tend to lead public funds to provide much less advice to their entrepreneurial firms (Lerner, 1999). If so, marginal costs of portfolio expansion in terms of providing advice are smaller for public funds (PMC for public funds is below PMC for private funds in Figure 18.1). Portfolio size is therefore expected to be greater among public funds (Keuschnigg, 2004b).

Some venture capital funds are managed by venture capital management firms that manage more than one venture capital fund. On the one hand, there are various reasons to indicate that this may have a positive effect on portfolio size. Venture capital fund managers that work for a management firm with more than one fund may share resources and effort across funds. In terms of Figure 18.1, the PMC is lower for any given number of entrepreneurial firms in the portfolio. Increasing the size of a venture capital fund's portfolio may therefore lead to less of a reduction in the venture capitalist's effort within a venture capital management firm that operates more than one venture capital fund. There may also be greater networking benefits, complementarities in effort, and benefits to the fund from co-investment (see also Gompers and Lerner, 1996) in entrepreneurial firms financed by partner funds (PMB is greater). If so, we would expect that venture capital funds that are managed by venture capital management firms that manage more than one fund will have larger portfolios. However, on the other hand, there are reasons why operating more than one fund may lead to a reduction in portfolio size. For example, venture capital fund managers may take time away from operating and actively investing the capital from the initial fund to start up a second one (hence, many limited partnership agreements have covenants to mitigate this problem; see Chapter 5). It is necessary to consider the data to see which effect dominates.

18.2.2 Entrepreneurial Firm Characteristics

The composition of the portfolio with regard to entrepreneurial firm characteristics affects the relative position of the PMB and PMC curves (see Kanniainen and Keuschnigg, 2003). We may expect earlier-stage firms and firms in high-tech industries with intangible assets to have relatively greater PMB and PMC curves (i.e., PMB shifts to the right and PMC shifts to the left). Earlier-stage firms and firms with intangible assets have more pronounced information asymmetries (Gompers, 1995) and are therefore associated with higher PMCs. PMBs may also be higher for funds with a focus on earlier-stage and high-tech firms because there could be complementarities across firms of similar technologies and stages of development. Many venture capital funds specialize in particular technologies for this very reason. The net effect of a higher proportion of earlier-stage and high-tech investments on portfolio size therefore requires empirical scrutiny.

Entrepreneurial firms that are more geographically disperse relative to the venture capital fund require extra effort to monitor (see Gompers and Lerner, 1999, 2001; Lerner, 1995, 1999; Sorenson and Stuart, 1999). This increases the marginal costs of portfolio expansion (PMC) and lowers efficient portfolio size (see Kanniainen and Keuschnigg, 2003; Keuschnigg, 2004b).

18.2.3 Nature of the Financing Arrangement

Venture capital transaction structures are multifaceted, involving security design, staging, and syndication, among other things. The use of different securities has an impact on the downside protection and upside potential of venture capital funds. This in turn affects the venture capital fund manager's interest in taking time to actively manage and monitor any particular investment (see Kanniainen and Keuschnigg, 2003). The venture capital literature is consistent with the proposition that convertible securities are the optimal form of finance (see, e.g., Bascha and Walz, 2001; Casamatta, 2003; Gompers, 1997; Kaplan and Strömberg, 2003; Sahlman, 1990; and Schmidt, 2003). Since convertible securities are a more flexible instrument to allocate incentives to venture capital funds and entrepreneurs, this might strengthen incentives for venture capital fund managers to provide advice and thereby lead them to focus attention on a smaller number of firms where they can add more value.

We would expect the size of the venture capital fund's capital contribution to an entrepreneurial firm, relative to the amount of capital provided by the other sources, to be correlated with the venture capital fund's ownership percentage and control rights.[1] This in turn could affect the costs and benefits of investment in many ways. On the one hand, the greater the venture capital fund's relative stake, the greater the benefits to increasing active value-added investing, as a greater proportion of the benefits are retained by the venture capital fund. For this reason, portfolio size would be smaller among venture capital funds that invest a greater proportion of the total capital raised by the entrepreneurial firm. On the other hand, if a venture capital fund acquires a greater proportion of control rights, this could increase the benefits (both pecuniary and nonpecuniary benefits from having control) and lower the costs (e.g., the expected costs of conflicts of interest between the venture capital fund manager and/or with the entrepreneur). Therefore, an increase in the amount invested as a proportion of the total amount of capital raised by the entrepreneurial firm could shift the PMB curve up and the PMC curve down. And it is also possible that venture capital funds that invest a greater proportion of the entrepreneurial firm's total capital will have larger portfolios. In short, theory does not provide unambiguous guidance as to the effect on portfolio size from the

[1]Gompers (1998) and Kaplan and Strömberg (2003) find that control rights and cash flow rights are independently allocated. Nevertheless, this is not inconsistent with a prediction that larger capital commitments from an investor give rise to more investor bargaining power to demand more scope for control (see, e.g., Noe and Rebello, 1996; Cumming, 2005a,b).

relative size of the venture capital fund's capital contribution. We nevertheless control for the size of capital contributions in the empirics.

Venture capital fund managers typically stage and syndicate their investments. More frequent staging is tantamount to more intensive monitoring (Gompers, 1995). Relatedly, syndication facilitates risk sharing, monitoring, and screening (Lerner, 1994). Staging involves intensive monitoring (high PMC) and dilution of venture capital effort (low PMB). However, staging also provides the venture capital fund manager with the option to wait and not precommit funds, and it provides the venture capital fund manager with the opportunity to renegotiate the terms of the agreement if milestones are not reached (Gompers, 1995, 1998; Kaplan and Strömberg, 2003). A myriad of theoretical possibilities could arise with the issue of syndication; for example, risk sharing, monitoring, and screening may suggest larger portfolios, but agency problems between syndicated investors may suggest smaller portfolios.[2] Any predictions on the net impact of these variables on portfolio size would depend on the aspect that is stressed. These limitations of theory are overcome herein by tests with the new data.

The causal relation between these variables is not unambiguous (see, e.g., Bernile et al., 2007). For any particular investment, the staging decision (and possibly the syndication decision, if syndication comes in at latter follow-on financing rounds) would be made after that of whether to invest. It is also possible that unobserved third factors independently shape these variables. However, the staging and syndication variables herein are measured as the average frequency of staging and syndication for all investees of the venture capital fund and therefore reflect the degree of monitoring that a venture capital fund has on a typical entrepreneurial firm in the portfolio. Factors that affect staging (Gompers, 1995) and syndication (Lerner, 1994) are *transaction specific*. The staging and syndication variables are averaged across all transactions in a fund in this chapter. By including staging and syndication variables as determinants of portfolio size, we are considering the impact of the typical frequency of staging and syndication on *typical* investments on the *marginal* decision to add an additional *new* entrepreneurial firm to the venture capital fund portfolio. The reverse causality would only apply to an analysis of staging and syndication on a transaction-by-transaction level (Gompers, 1995; Lerner, 1994), whereas our staging and syndication variables are defined as *fund averages* and not on a transaction-by-transaction basis. The same reasoning applies to all choice variables that are transaction specific: The average of all

[2]Jääskeläinen et al. (2002) provide some evidence of a positive relation between portfolio size and syndication using correlation coefficients and U.S. data, but they do not provide any tests of the determinants of portfolio size. Their focus is on the impact of portfolio size on exit outcomes. Manigart et al. (2006) provide some evidence of a negative relation between portfolio size and syndication using correlation coefficients and European data, but they do not any provide formal tests of the determinants of portfolio size.

transaction-specific variables is used to asses the impact on overall portfolio size and therefore endogeneity is not a significant concern (see also footnote 11).

18.2.4 Market Conditions

Lerner (2002b; see also Kortum and Lerner, 2000) finds that the impact of venture capital on innovation is approximately 15% lower during boom periods as compared with normal periods, and this difference is strongly statistically significant. Lerner's empirical work thus points to an important trade-off between portfolio size and venture capital involvement (advice) and also points to variations over the business cycle (for supportive theoretical work on topic, see Keuschnigg, 2004b; Kanniainen and Keuschnigg, 2003). We therefore control for market conditions using MSCI real returns[3] over the period from the date of the first venture capital fund investment to the date of last venture capital fund investment. We expect that, for example, portfolios formed over the 1991 to 1993 period will be smaller than portfolios formed over the period 1997 to 1999 because returns were greater in the later period.

The variables just described and used in the empirical tests that follow are summarized in Table 18.1. As mentioned, nonlinearities are important in the comparative statistics, and these nonlinearities are explained in the Appendix. Before proceeding with the empirical tests, the data are first described.

18.3 Data

18.3.1 Description of the Data

The data were obtained from a large sample of venture capital financing transactions over the years 1991 to 2000 from Macdonald & Associates, Ltd.,[4] for the Canadian Venture Capital Association (CVCA). Canadian data are used primarily because the CVCA has assembled a unique venture capital database with details that are not available from venture capital associations in the United States or other countries around the world. Not all the funds in the Macdonald & Associates database are used herein. To mitigate the possibility of missing investments, we excluded from the data funds that were tracked by Macdonald &

[3]We use industry rates of return, and not rates of return from the venture capital funds themselves, as these returns are arguably endogenous (i.e., portfolio size determines individual venture capital fund rates of return and not vice versa; see, e.g., Jääskeläinen et al., 2002). We did consider annualized versus total Morgan Stanley Capital International (MSCI) rates of return as well as other industry rates of return (e.g., U.S. venture capital fund rates of return, as reported in Lerner, 2002b), but the qualitative conclusions were not materially different. We report the MSCI rates of return because these returns are widely regarded as a measure of market sentiment, and arguably the most reliable measure of returns in the Canadian market.

[4]See www.canadavc.com.

Table 18.1 Definitions of Variables

Variable Name	Variable Description
Venture Capital Fund Characteristics	
Portfolio Size	The number of entrepreneurial firms in the venture capital fund portfolio.
Average # Portfolio Firms/# Venture Capital Fund Managers	The number of entrepreneurial firms in the venture capital fund portfolio/# venture capital fund managers.
Average # Portfolio Firms/# Venture Capital Fund Managers/# Years	The number of entrepreneurial firms in the venture capital fund portfolio/# venture capital fund managers/investment period duration period (measured in years, with accuracy to quarters). (i.e., this variable measures the investment rate/ fund manager).
Corporate Venture Capital	A dummy variable that is equal to one if the venture capital fund is a corporate fund.
Government Venture Capital	A dummy variable that is equal to one if the venture capital fund is a Canadian government fund.
LSVCC	A dummy variable that is equal to one if the venture capital fund is a Canadian Labour Sponsored Venture Capital Fund.
Private Independent Venture Capital	A dummy variable that is equal to one if the venture capital fund is a limited partnership fund.
2 or more Venture Capital Funds Managed by the Venture Capital Management Firm	A dummy variable equal to one if the venture capital fund is part of a venture capital firm that manages 2 or more venture capital funds.
Venture Capital Funds Raised (Draw Downs)	The amount of funds raised by the venture capital fund, proxied by the total draw downs by the fund.
# Years Fund Investments Tracked by CVCA	The number of years for which the venture capital fund is tracked by the Canadian Venture Capital Association (Macdonald and Associates, Ltd.) in the database. This variable is only used to exclude the funds in the data that have been tracked for fewer than 2 years.
Investment Duration Period (Quarters)	The duration of time (measured in quarters of years) over which the venture capital fund invested in entrepreneurial firms. Could be less than 2 years or even 1 year if all fund investments occurred towards the end of 1 year and the beginning of the next year.

Table 18.1 (*continued*)

Variable Name	Variable Description
# Venture Capital Fund Managers	The number of venture capital fund managers employed by the fund management firm.
Entrepreneurial Firm Characteristics	
Early Stage	The proportion of entrepreneurial firms in the start-up and expansion stage of development at the time of first venture capital investment.
Life Sciences	The proportion of entrepreneurial firms in life sciences industries.
Other High-tech	The proportion of entrepreneurial firms in technology industries other than life sciences.
Entrepreneur/Venture Capital Different Provinces	The proportion of entrepreneurial firms resident in provinces in which the venture capital fund does not have an office.
Financing Transaction Characteristics	
Staging Frequency	The proportion of staged investments.
Syndication Frequency	The proportion of syndicated investments.
Venture Capital Investments/ Ent. Capital	The amount of venture capital fund capital provided to entrepreneur/the total capital raised by the entrepreneurial firm at the time of venture capital investment.
Convertible Securities	The proportion of investments with the use of convertible debt and/or convertible preferred equity.
Market Conditions	The Morgan Stanley Capital International Index real return from the date (year and quarter) of the venture capital fund first investment to date of last investment.
MSCI Return	
Returns to Scale	
λ	The degree of curvature of the output function, based on the Box-Cox transformation.

Associates for fewer than two years.[5,6] In net, 214 funds were included: 104 private independent limited partnership venture capital funds, 18 corporate funds, 15 government funds, 29 Labour-sponsored venture capital corporations (LSVCCs), and 48 institutional funds. The results are quite robust to the inclusion/exclusion of the full set of 214 funds, but there are notable differences between the full sample of all 214 funds and the subsample of 104 limited partnerships; these differences are most likely attributable to fund structures, as explained following.

Notice that we distinguish between the duration from first to last investment and the numbers of years the fund's investments were tracked by Macdonald & Associates. The number of years the fund was tracked is used only to define the sample, as just discussed. The period of investment duration (time from quarter of the first investment to the quarter of the last investment) is used hereafter in the empirics. Of all the funds in the sample, nine had investment durations of less than one year (i.e., these nine funds were tracked for at least two full years, but made investments toward the latter part of the first year and earlier part of the second year only).

Each type of venture capital fund in Canada has been discussed elsewhere (e.g., Halpern, 1997; Macdonald, 1992; MacIntosh, 1994). Briefly, private independent limited partnerships are analogous to those in the United States (Gompers and Lerner, 1996, 1999a), as are corporate funds (Gompers and Lerner, 1999a,b; Hellmann, 2002; Riyanto and Schwienbacher, 2006). Government funds are direct investment programs financed by the government and run by professional venture capital managers. LSVCCs are mutual funds with tax incentives for individual investors to contribute capital, and this capital is reinvested in entrepreneurial firms. LSVCC governance mechanisms are based in statute, unlike limited partnership covenants (as studied in Chapter 5).

Summary statistics for the duration of the fund, fundraising, the average amounts invested, and the average total deal sizes (total capital raised by the entrepreneurial firm) are provided in Tables 18.2a–c. Corporate venture capital funds and private independent limited partnerships have smaller portfolios than LSVCCs and government venture capital funds in the sample (see Table 18.2a). Most all funds in Canada invest in earlier stages (start-up and expansion stages), and most invest in high-tech industries. In the data employed herein, the information on fundraising was incomplete. Fundraising is therefore proxied by fund draw downs (i.e., amounts invested) from capital commitments. This proxy is suitable because we also account for the number of years in which the fund has been investing capital in entrepreneurial firms, which gives an indication of the proportion of total capital raised that has been invested by the venture capital

[5]This was suggested by Macdonald and Associates, Ltd.; see www.canadaa.com. A prior version of the chapter (on file with the authors) excluded funds that invested in 1991, 1999, and 2000 (a total of 79 funds). See also footnote 17.

[6]It is noteworthy, however, that there may still exist some "unobserved" (pre-1991 and post-2000) investments in the data. To account for this problem in the econometric estimates, a heteroscedastic specification is used with duration as the weighting variable.

Table 18.2a Summary of the Data by Type of Venture Capital Fund

Variable Names	Corporate Venture Capital	Government Venture Capital	LSVCC	Private Limited Partnership	Other Institutional Venture Capital	Total
Venture Capital Fund Characteristics						
Total Number of Funds	18	15	29	104	48	214
2 or More Venture Capital Funds Managed by the Venture Capital Management Firm	0	3	3	14	12	32
Venture Capital Funds Raised (Draw Downs) ('000)	\$70,650	\$48,343	\$117,273	\$24,307	\$110,071	\$61,724
# Years Fund Investments Tracked by CVCA	4.222	5.533	4.586	4.663	4.750	4.696
Investment Duration Period (Quarters)	3.625	4.850	4.043	3.959	4.073	4.030
# Venture Capital Fund Managers	6.000	8.533	6.379	5.673	8.083	7.075
Entrepreneurial Firm Characteristics						
Average # Portfolio Firms	17.056	32.467	37.966	8.221	30.500	19.692
Average # Portfolio Firms/ # Venture Capital Managers	2.793	7.460	6.379	2.589	4.939	4.003
Average # Portfolio Firms/ # Venture Capital Managers/ # Years	0.863	1.695	1.674	0.843	1.632	1.194
Early Stage	0.819	0.900	0.897	0.857	0.776	0.844

(*continued*)

Table 18.2a (*continued*)

Variable Names	Corporate Venture Capital	Government Venture Capital	LSVCC	Private Limited Partnership	Other Institutional Venture Capital	Total
Life Sciences	0.066	0.200	0.229	0.198	0.088	0.167
Other High-tech	0.597	0.393	0.427	0.510	0.428	0.479
Entrepreneur/Venture Capital Different Provinces	0.297	0.083	0.052	0.161	0.286	0.180
Financing Transactions Characteristics						
Staging Frequency	0.560	0.471	0.497	0.544	0.489	0.521
Syndication Frequency	0.624	0.456	0.519	0.490	0.536	0.513
Venture Capital Investments/Ent. Capital	0.526	0.509	0.409	0.481	0.630	0.511
Convertible Securities	0.237	0.201	0.272	0.262	0.200	0.243
Market Conditions						
MSCI Return	0.296	0.268	0.360	0.268	0.334	0.297

Note: Data over the period 1991–2000. Venture capital funds that invested for 1 year only in the data are excluded. Canadian venture capitalists only. *Source:* Macdonald and Associates, Ltd., Toronto.

Table 18.2b Summary Statistics for All Types of Venture Capital Funds in the Data (214 Funds)

Variable Names	Mean	Standard Deviation	Skewness	Kurtosis	Minimum	Maximum
Venture Capital Firm Characteristics						
Venture Capital Funds Raised (Draw Downs) ('000)	$61,724	138,313	5.089	34.636	150	$1,219,360
# Years Fund Investments Tracked by CVCA	4.696	2.464	0.822	2.538	2	10
Investment Duration Period (Quarters)	4.030	2.376	0.760	2.538	0.5	9.25
# Venture Capital Fund Managers	7.075	7.505	2.804	13.965	1	48
Entrepreneurial Firm Characteristics						
Average # Portfolio Firms	19.692	42.220	5.698	43.403	1	408
Average # Portfolio Firms/# Venture Capital Managers	4.003	6.626	3.966	22.686	0.091	48.4
Average # Portfolio Firms/# Venture Capital Managers/# Years	1.194	1.936	5.651	47.929	0.026	20
Early Stage	0.844	0.207	−1.731	5.801	0	1
Life Sciences	0.167	0.271	2.104	6.460	0	1
Other High-tech	0.479	0.338	0.063	1.734	0	1
Entrepreneur/Venture Capital Different Provinces	0.180	0.277	1.749	5.112	0	1
Financing Transactions Characteristics						
Staging Frequency	0.521	0.211	−0.434	2.789	0	0.933
Syndication Frequency	0.513	0.313	0.028	1.827	0	1
Venture Capital Investments/Ent. Capital	0.511	0.275	0.293	1.948	0.047	1
Convertible Securities	0.243	0.194	0.828	3.500	0	1
Market Conditions						
MSCI Return	0.297	0.198	1.628	7.315	−0.067	1.192

Note: Data over the period 1991–2000. Venture capital funds that invested for 1 year only in the data are excluded. Canadian venture capitalists only. *Source:* Macdonald and Associates, Ltd., Toronto.

Table 18.2c Summary Statistics for Private Limited Partnership Funds Only (104 Funds)

Variable Names	Mean	Standard Deviation	Skewness	Kurtosis	Minimum	Maximum
Venture Capital Firm Characteristics						
Venture Capital Funds Raised (Draw Downs) ('000)	24,306.5	29,385.7	1.969	6.645	600	149,316
# Years Fund Investments Tracked by CVCA	4.663	2.400	0.808	2.489	2	10
Investment Duration Period (Quarters)	3.959	2.297	0.758	2.564	0.75	9.25
# Venture Capital Fund Managers	5.673	4.788	1.261	3.840	1	19
Entrepreneurial Firm Characteristics						
Average # Portfolio Firms	8.221	6.987	2.152	9.167	1	42
Average # Portfolio Firms/# Venture Capital Managers	2.589	3.385	3.244	16.187	0.200	23
Average # Portfolio Firms/# Venture Capital Managers/# Years	0.843	0.877	1.680	5.519	0.048	4
Early Stage	0.857	0.213	−1.843	5.948	0.071	1
Life Sciences	0.198	0.321	1.626	4.224	0	1
Other High-tech	0.510	0.364	−0.074	1.582	0	1
Entrepreneur/ Venture Capital Different Provinces	0.161	0.236	1.638	5.152	0	1
Financing Transactions Characteristics						
Staging Frequency	0.544	0.236	−0.686	2.819	0	0.933
Syndication Frequency	0.490	0.293	−0.041	1.998	0	1
Venture Capital Investments/Ent. Capital	0.481	0.283	0.485	2.032	0.047	1
Convertible Securities	0.262	0.192	0.750	3.072	0	0.875
Market Conditions						
MSCI Return	0.268	0.180	1.218	5.000	−0.067	0.944

Note: Data over the period 1991–2000. Venture capital funds that invested for 1 year only in the data are excluded. Canadian venture capitalists only. *Source:* Macdonald and Associates, Ltd., Toronto.

fund.[7] LSVCCs on average have raised the most capital (due to favorable tax treatment), whereas limited partnerships have raised significantly less capital.

Lerner (1994), Gompers (1995), and Gompers and Lerner (1999a, 2001) analyze the staging and syndication decision in terms of agency problems, monitoring, and risk sharing. In this dataset, as a percentage of all investments (first and latter financing rounds), roughly half (47% for government venture capital funds, 54% for private independent venture capital funds, and 56% for corporate venture capital funds) were staged. Corporate venture capital funds syndicated their investments more frequently (62% of their total investments), and government venture capital funds syndicated least frequently (46%). Relatedly, institutional investors on average provided the most capital as a fraction of the total entrepreneurial capital at the time of investment (63%), whereas private independent limited partners provided the smallest proportion of entrepreneurial capital (48%) among the funds in the sample. Although the details in the data do not enable an analysis of urban versus rural investments, we nevertheless control for entrepreneurial firm location relative to the investor with the use of a variable that measures the frequency of intra- versus interprovincial investment. On average, more than 80% of investments were intraprovincial (in which the venture capital fund manager and entrepreneurial firm resided in the same province).

LSVCCs used convertible securities (convertible debt and/or convertible preferred equity) most frequently (27% of investments); government and institutional venture capital funds used convertibles least frequently (20%).[8] Variables for other securities are not considered in the empirics that follow to mitigate problems associated with collinearity. As discussed before, we focus on the securities that are regarded as optimal in venture capital finance: convertible securities.

18.3.2 Comparison Tests and Correlation Matrix

Table 18.3 provides a number of comparison tests for average portfolio size, as well as the average portfolio size per number of venture capital fund managers per year, depending on the values of the explanatory variables just discussed. The cut-off points for the comparison tests were somewhat arbitrarily chosen to be close to the means of the variables (as indicated in Table 18.2); additional comparison tests are available upon request. The tests are provided for the full sample of all 214 funds and the subsample of 104 limited partnerships.

[7]It is possible that other factors could impact draw downs independent of fundraising. The data in this chapter do not enable full consideration of this issue. Further research is warranted. See also Ljungqvist and Richardson (2003) and Cumming et al. (2005b) on fundraising versus draw downs.

[8]The use of a variety of forms of finance for Canadian entrepreneurial firms is not due to the definition of venture capital (by type of venture capital fund or by type of entrepreneurial firm); Chapters 11–13. See Chapter 14, Bascha and Walz (2007), Schwienbacher (2008), and Cumming (2008) for similar evidence from independent samples derived from the population of European venture capital funds; see Lerner and Schoar (2003) for similar evidence from developing countries. In the United States, by contrast, convertible preferred equity is most common in venture capital (Gompers, 1998; Kaplan and Strömberg, 2003). One explanation for this difference across countries is that there is a unique tax bias in favor of convertible preferred equity in the United States (Gilson and Schizer, 2003).

Table 18.3 Difference Tests

This table presents difference of means tests comparison of means tests for the number of entrepreneurial firms in the venture capital fund portfolio and for the number of entrepreneurial firms per venture capital manager per years of investment, for different characteristics of the portfolio, as per variables defined in Table 18.1. *, **, *** Significant at the 10%, 5%, and 1% levels, respectively.

	All 214 Funds				104 Limited Partnerships Only			
	Average # Portfolio Firms	Difference Test	Average # Portfolio Firms/# Venture Capital Managers/ Years	Difference Test	Average # Portfolio Firms	Difference Test	Average # Portfolio Firms/# Venture Capital Managers/ Years	Difference Test
Limited Partnership Venture Capital Fund	8.221	−7.483***	0.843	−0.102	—	—	—	—
Corporate Venture Capital Fund	17.056		0.863		—		—	
Limited Partnership Venture Capital Fund	8.221	−19.515***	0.843	−2.805***	—	—	—	—
LSVCC Fund	37.966		1.674		—		—	
Limited Partnership Venture Capital Fund	8.221	−14.247***	0.843	−2.566**	—	—	—	—
Government Venture Capital Fund	32.467		1.695		—		—	
Venture Capital Mgmt. Firm with 1 Fund	17.790	−5.044***	1.214	0.242	6.956	−6.313***	1.059	−0.517
Venture Capital Mgmt. Firm with 2 or More Funds	22.311		1.166		10.611		1.166	

Venture Capital Fund with More Than $50,000,000 Draw Downs	50.155		1.428		16.400		0.574	
		36.749***		1.446		11.085***		−1.598
Venture Capital Fund with Less Than $50,000,000 Draw Downs	8.365		1.107		6.843		0.889	
Investment Duration Period >4 Years	24.730		0.985		10.333		0.623	
		14.880***		−2.780***		13.136***		−3.100***
Investment Duration Period <4 Years	10.727		1.565		4.553		1.226	
# Managers >7	35.246		0.530		12.185		0.275	
		22.060***		−5.915***		8.469***		−5.330***
# Managers <7	12.290		1.510		6.831		1.043	
Early Stage >0.75	20.067		1.211		8.265		0.895	
		1.465		0.331		0.308		1.265
Early Stage <0.75	18.429		1.136		8.048		0.638	
Life Sciences >0.5	10.045		1.318		9.250		0.858	
		−12.790***		0.485		1.413		0.061
Life Sciences <0.5	20.797		1.180		8.034		0.841	
Other High-tech >0.5	15.626		1.063		7.154		0.794	
		−8.938***		−1.268		−4.268***		−0.541
Other High-tech <0.5	23.191		1.306		9.288		0.893	
Venture Capital/ Entrepreneur Different Province >0.15	10.452		0.688		7.474		0.633	
		−19.352***		−4.701***		−2.336**		−1.956*
Venture Capital/ Entrepreneur Different Province <0.15	24.475		1.456		8.652		0.964	

(continued)

Table 18.3 *(continued)*

	All 214 Funds				104 Limited Partnerships Only			
	Average # Portfolio Firms	Difference Test	Average # Portfolio Firms/# Venture Capital Managers/ Years	Difference Test	Average # Portfolio Firms	Difference Test	Average # Portfolio Firms/# Venture Capital Managers/ Years	Difference Test
Staging Frequency >0.5	21.575	4.470***	0.862	−3.758***	9.164	4.406***	0.609	−3.046***
Staging Frequency <0.5	17.584		1.565		6.884		1.176	
Syndication Frequency >0.5	15.783	−9.065***	0.700	−5.588***	7.833	−1.406	0.588	−2.706***
Syndication Frequency <0.5	23.528		1.679		8.554		1.062	
Venture Capital Investments/ Entrepreneurial Capital >0.5	21.970	4.740***	1.514	3.127***	7.390	−2.590***	1.099	2.212**
Venture Capital Investments/ Entrepreneurial Capital <0.5	17.730		0.919		8.762		0.676	
Convertible Securities >0.5	9.333	−13.839***	1.277	0.314	8.700	0.568	1.083	0.753
Convertible Securities <0.5	20.643		1.186		8.170		0.818	
MSCI >0.25	19.775	0.216	1.335	1.795*	6.980	−4.816***	0.761	−0.879
MSCI <0.25	19.585		1.014		9.415		0.922	

The comparison tests generally indicate that larger overall portfolios are observed among the corporate, government funds, and LSVCCs (relative to limited partnerships), as well as among venture capital management firms with two or more funds under management, venture capital funds that have more than real 2,000 Can$50,000,000 capital, funds that have been investing for at least four years, funds with more than seven fund managers, funds with less than 50% of the investments in life science or other types of high-tech firms, funds that invest more frequently in entrepreneurial firms resident in the same province, and among funds that stage more but syndicate less frequently. Some differences in overall portfolio size are observed between the full sample of 214 funds and the subsample of 104 limited partnerships. Among the full sample, all types of venture capital funds other than limited partnerships that invest a greater proportion relative to the entrepreneurial firms' other sources of capital have larger portfolios. Limited partnerships have smaller portfolios. Funds that invest in life science industries and use convertible securities more frequently among the full sample of 214 funds have smaller portfolios, but these differences of means are not statistically significant among the 104 limited partnerships. Overall portfolio size seems invariant to MSCI returns over the investment period among the full sample of funds, but portfolio size is smaller among funds that invested in boom periods among the subsample of limited partnerships.

The comparisons of means tests for portfolio size per manager per year (investment rates per manager) yield similar results, with the following exceptions. First, investment rates are invariant among venture capital management firms with and without more than one venture capital fund, fundraising, and entrepreneur industry (where these factors were significant for overall portfolio size). Second, investment rates are higher when MSCI returns are higher among the full sample of all 214 funds (but not among the limited partnerships, and different results are also observed in regards to overall portfolio size in the difference of means tests). Finally, it is noteworthy that investment rates are higher among government venture capital funds and LSVCCs, but there is no difference in investment rates among corporate venture capital funds and limited partnerships (despite the finding that corporate funds have larger overall portfolios, as just mentioned).[9]

The comparison tests in Table 18.4 provide a useful starting point for analyzing the data. Additional empirical tests in a multivariate context are obviously warranted. Portfolio size is not uniquely attributable to any single variable. Moreover, the theory described in the Appendix predicts a nonlinear relation between portfolio size and the enumerated factors just discussed, and this nonlinear relation is best tested in a multivariate setting.

[9]In regards to investment duration, one may speculate that investment rates slow down over the life of a fund. For the number of managers, one could argue that investment rates slow down if it is inefficient for a greater number of venture capital fund managers to be working together. In the regression specifications in Tables 18.5, Panel B and 18.6, Panel B, notice that we do not include the number of fund managers and investment duration as right-hand-side variables. When these variables are included, they tend to be negative and significant (at around the 10% level of significance), without significantly impacting the other included right-hand-side variables. The main reason for their exclusion is that these variables would appear on both the right- and left-hand side of the regression equations, which is obviously undesirable.

18.4 Empirical Evidence

18.4.1 Empirical Methods

Two different dependent variables are considered: the total number of entrepreneurial firms in the portfolio (Panel A in Tables 18.5 and 18.6) and the total number of entrepreneurial firms/the number of fund managers/the time period of investment (Panel B in Tables 18.5 and 18.6). The first considers overall portfolio size, and the second considers that investment rate. We employ similar strategies for estimating both variables, and compare the results. The data are segregated for the subsample of private independent funds (Table 18.6), as well as pooled with all firm types together (Table 18.5). (Other subsamples are not considered, due to the comparative dearth of observations.) The advantage of segregating the data is that differences may exist across types of venture capital management firms. In the pooled sample, dummy variables for the type of venture capital management firm are employed (a dummy for "other institutional" types is suppressed to avoid collinearity).

Two different regression models are presented in the tables: a linear model and Box-Cox transformations of the right-hand-side variables with a heteroscedastic specification. The Box-Cox specification is consistent with the theory explained in the Appendix. Right-hand-side variables include all the entrepreneurial firm and transaction characteristics discussed previously. Each variable is defined as the proportion of the total venture capital fund portfolio with the particular characteristic. For example, the variable "Life Sciences" is the proportion of all investments in a venture capital fund's portfolio that were in life science (biotechnology and medical) firms. Dummy variables are included for the type of venture capital management firm in the full sample estimates. Transformations to independent variables (other than the dummy variables) are presented to capture nonlinearities in the relationship between portfolio size and the factors described previously. The variables used in the empirical analysis are summarized in Table 18.1.

Following the conventional notation, λ is used to denote the transformation variable for the right-hand-side variables. The transformation yields a convex relation when $\lambda > 1$ and a concave relation (as depicted in Figure 18.A2) when $\lambda < 1$. Maximum likelihood optimization and grid searches were used to optimize the value of the log likelihood function to ascertain the appropriate value for λ given the data. The Box-Cox grid search was sufficiently broad (-2 to $+2$) to allow for the possibility of concavity (diminishing returns to scale in the number of investees) as well as convexity (increasing returns to scale in the number of investees). The Box-Cox transformation is as follows:

$$B(x, \lambda) = \begin{cases} \dfrac{x^{\lambda} - 1}{\lambda} \text{ when } \lambda \neq 0\,; \\ \log(x) \text{ when } \lambda = 0. \end{cases}$$

where x represents the independent variables, and $\log(x)$ is the limit of $(x^{\lambda} - 1)/\lambda$ as $\lambda \rightarrow 0$. Note that the transformation is applied to variables that are *not* dummy variables (see, e.g., Greene, 1997).

The linear OLS model is presented for comparison (Model 2); Models 1 and 3–5 involve Box-Cox estimations, with consideration to heteroscedasticity. Significant correlations are observed among some of the variables, particularly the entrepreneurial firm and transaction-specific variables; as such, regressions are provided with alternative right-hand-side variables to show robustness.

The heteroscedastic specification is $\text{Var}(e) = (s^2)[w^2]^{(\lambda)}$, where w = fund duration. This heteroscedastic specification was employed for the estimates of portfolio size (only)[10] in Panel A of Tables 18.5 and 18.6 to account for the possibility of unobserved observations in the data (see footnotes 5 and 6 and accompanying text). The likelihood dominance criterion (Davidson and MacKinnon, 1993, p. 492) indicated that this heteroscedastic Box-Cox transformation outperformed other specifications (reported and otherwise). For example, the LR statistic is equal to 307.25 for Table 18.5, Panel A (comparing Models 1 and 2), which is significant at the 1% level. (The reported log likelihood values are directly comparable across transformations within each panel.) The LR statistics support the Box-Cox specifications in Panel A of Tables 18.5 and 18.6, but the tests are inconclusive for distinguishing between the models in Panel B of Tables 18.5 and 18.6. Alternative specifications (not presented but available upon request) did not perform better than the heteroscedastic Box-Cox specification (Model 1 in Tables 18.5 and 18.6).

The likelihood dominance criterion and the various information criterion statistics were supportive of the complete set of explanatory variables; therefore, the focus of the discussion herein is on the complete set of explanatory variables in the heteroscedastic Box-Cox specification (Model 1).[11] The other models are provided in the tables for comparison. The estimates are very similar across the six models in Tables 18.5 and 18.6, and differences in results

[10]The heteroscedastic specification is not relevant in the Panel B estimates in Tables 18.5 and 18.6 that explain the rate of investment because each investment per year is observed in each year in which the funds exist in the data; see also footnote 9.

[11]As discussed, some of the right-hand-side variables are choice variables, such as staging and syndication. The decision to add another entrepreneurial firm to the portfolio depends on the prior structure of the portfolio, including the proportion of investments that were staged and syndicated, and the proportion of firms that are financed with convertible securities, and so on. Portfolio size is not uniquely determined at the outset prior to knowing all investment opportunities, and each entrepreneurial firm's required capital and the needs associated with advice and/or monitoring for each firm, and so on. Financing structure, including staging, syndication, and contracting, depends on entrepreneurial firm–specific factors (Gompers, 1995, 1998; Gompers and Lerner, 1999a; Lerner, 1994). Marginal effects on the decision to expand portfolio size depend on prior investment decisions, among other things. Note we also considered specification tests (e.g., Durbin-Wu-Hausman tests; Davidson and MacKinnon, 1993) for endogeneity, and so on, which did not indicate a reason to be concerned with endogeneity, and numerous alternative specification tests suggested that these variables should be included.

Table 18.4a Correlations across

This table presents correlation coefficients across the dependent and independent lighted in underline font.

	(1)	(2)	(3)	(4)	(5)	(6)	(7)	(8)
(1) # Portfolio Firms	1.00							
(2) # Portfolio Firms/ # Venture Capital Managers	0.54	1.00						
(3) # Portfolio Firms/ # Venture Capital Managers/Year	0.34	0.61	1.00					
(4) Corporate Venture Capital	−0.02	−0.05	−0.05	1.00				
(5) Government Venture Capital	0.08	0.14	0.07	−0.08	1.00			
(6) LSVCC	0.17	0.14	0.10	−0.12	−0.11	1.00		
(7) Private Limited Partnership	−0.26	−0.21	−0.18	−0.29	−0.27	−0.38	1.00	
(8) 2 or More Venture Capital Funds in Venture Capital Mgmt. Firm	0.05	0.00	−0.01	−0.02	−0.09	−0.03	−0.15	1.00
(9) Funds Raised (Draw Downs)	0.56	0.34	0.06	0.02	−0.03	0.16	−0.26	0.14
(10) Investment Duration (Quarters)	0.31	0.35	−0.11	−0.05	0.09	0.00	−0.03	0.09
(11) # Venture Capital Fund Managers	0.40	−0.17	−0.21	−0.04	0.05	−0.04	−0.18	0.25
(12) Early Stage	0.01	0.00	0.01	−0.04	0.07	0.10	0.06	−0.02
(13) Life Sciences	−0.02	−0.03	0.01	−0.11	0.03	0.09	0.11	0.04
(14) Other High-tech	−0.09	−0.16	−0.08	0.11	−0.07	−0.06	0.09	−0.03
(15) Venture Capital/ Entrepreneur Different Province	−0.09	−0.16	−0.14	0.13	−0.10	−0.18	−0.07	0.04
(16) Staging	−0.05	−0.07	−0.27	0.06	−0.07	−0.05	0.10	0.06
(17) Syndication	−0.12	−0.21	−0.29	0.11	−0.05	0.01	−0.07	0.17
(18) Venture Capital Investments/Ent. Capital	0.07	0.09	0.23	0.02	0.00	−0.15	−0.10	−0.08
(19) Convertible Securities	−0.13	−0.13	−0.13	−0.01	−0.06	0.06	0.10	−0.04
(20) MSCI Return	−0.02	−0.06	0.28	0.00	−0.04	0.13	−0.15	0.07

Variables (Full Sample of 214 Funds)

variables (as defined in Table 18.1). Correlations significant at the 5% level are high-

(9)	(10)	(11)	(12)	(13)	(14)	(15)	(16)	(17)	(18)	(19)	(20)
1.00											
0.47	1.00										
0.22	0.21	1.00									
−0.03	0.02	−0.06	1.00								
0.01	0.08	0.03	0.30	1.00							
0.01	−0.14	−0.05	0.35	−0.38	1.00						
−0.02	−0.02	0.15	−0.02	−0.13	−0.06	1.00					
0.13	0.32	0.09	0.17	0.13	0.25	0.00	1.00				
0.04	0.01	0.09	0.20	0.17	0.26	0.01	0.35	1.00			
0.10	−0.14	−0.06	−0.32	−0.16	−0.30	0.12	−0.44	−0.67	1.00		
−0.09	−0.03	−0.06	0.21	0.15	0.17	−0.04	0.17	0.18	−0.16	1.00	
−0.04	−0.31	−0.05	0.15	0.05	0.19	−0.11	−0.24	0.01	0.07	0.00	1.00

Table 18.4b Correlations across Variables (Private

This table presents correlation coefficients across the dependent and independent lighted in underline font.

	(1)	(2)	(3)	(4)	(5)	(6)
(1) # Portfolio Firms	1.00					
(2) # Portfolio Firms/ # Venture Capital Managers	0.43	1.00				
(3) # Portfolio Firms/ # Venture Capital Managers/Year	0.09	0.64	1.00			
(4) 2 or More Venture Capital Funds in Venture Capital Mgmt. Firm	0.25	−0.23	−0.34	1.00		
(5) Funds Raised (Draw Downs)	0.51	0.12	−0.16	0.18	1.00	
(6) Investment Duration (Quarters)	0.52	0.31	−0.27	0.14	0.45	1.00
(7) # Venture Capital Fund Managers	0.31	−0.40	−0.53	0.52	0.24	0.22
(8) Early Stage	0.00	−0.04	0.05	0.14	−0.08	−0.11
(9) Life Sciences	0.10	0.10	−0.04	0.26	0.05	0.03
(10) Other High-tech	−0.14	−0.27	−0.11	−0.03	0.02	−0.19
(11) Venture Capital/ Entrepreneur Different Province	−0.02	−0.08	−0.11	−0.06	0.11	0.07
(12) Staging	0.09	−0.02	−0.36	0.22	0.31	0.39
(13) Syndication	−0.06	−0.30	−0.37	0.24	−0.03	−0.04
(14) Venture Capital Investments/Ent. Capital	−0.11	0.12	0.32	−0.26	0.01	−0.16
(15) Convertible Securities	−0.05	−0.16	−0.03	0.12	−0.11	−0.06
(16) MSCI Return	−0.12	−0.19	0.06	0.06	−0.04	−0.29

Independent Limited Partnerships Sample of 104 Funds)

variables (as defined in Table 18.1). Correlations significant at the 5% level are high-

(7)	(8)	(9)	(10)	(11)	(12)	(13)	(14)	(15)	(16)
1.00									
−0.01	1.00								
0.20	0.31	1.00							
0.02	0.40	−0.48	1.00						
−0.03	−0.15	−0.15	0.01	1.00					
0.27	0.13	0.17	0.15	−0.04	1.00				
0.30	0.27	0.22	0.15	−0.07	0.32	1.00			
−0.29	−0.39	−0.18	−0.28	0.09	−0.46	−0.78	1.00		
0.02	0.27	0.02	0.13	−0.05	0.16	0.06	−0.06	1.00	
−0.03	0.36	0.04	0.32	−0.10	−0.22	0.14	−0.13	−0.01	1.00

Table 18.5 Regressions with All Types of

This table presents OLS and Box-Cox regressions of the determinants of venture capital portfolio size. The The independent variables are as defined in Table 18.1. Box-Cox specification: $B(x,\lambda) = (x^{\lambda} - 1)/\lambda$ when λ is not log likelihood. Panel A uses a heteroscedastic specification: $Var(\varepsilon) = (\sigma^2)[w^2]^{(\lambda)}$, where w = fund duration. The did not materially affect the marginal effects, as the high R^2 values indicate relatively small residuals. f-Statistics respectively. Two-sided tests. "—" = Not applicable, or variable excluded for robustness checks and/or to avoid

Panel A. Dependent Variable: # of Entreprene

Independent Variables	**(1) Box-Cox**				**(2) Linear**	
	Coefficient	**t-Statistic**	**Slope**	**Elasticity**	**Coefficient**	**t-Statistic**
Constant	21.997	4.415***	21.997	0.579	147.656	2.365**
Venture Capital Fund Characteristics						
Corporate Venture Capital	−5.027	−2.885***	−5.027	−0.010	0.847	0.094
Government Venture Capital	1.141	0.639	1.141	0.003	0.610	0.061
LSVCC	1.910	1.196	1.910	0.007	1.887	0.224
Private Independent Venture Capital	−10.757	−8.669***	−10.757	−0.136	−9.110	−1.416
2 or More Venture Capital Funds in the Venture Capital Mgmt. Firm	−13.920	−15.435***	−13.920	−0.163	−6.379	−1.351
Venture Capital Funds Raised (Draw Downs) ('000)	0.164	4.397***	0.0002	0.4872	0.0002	7.698***
Venture Capital Fund Duration	−2.482	−3.985***	−0.870	−0.137	0.265	0.225
# Venture Capital Fund Managers	7.954	20.253***	2.210	0.515	1.818	5.748***
Entrepreneurial Firm Characteristics						
Early Stage	17.833	5.305***	12.438	0.605	15.613	1.344
Life Sciences	—	—	—	—	—	—
Other High-tech	—	—	—	—	—	—
Entrepreneur/Venture Capital Different Provinces	−23.242	−11.909***	−21.121	−0.655	−16.779	−2.000**
Financing Transactions Characteristics						
Staging Frequency	−33.607	−9.741***	−25.932	−1.062	−26.072	−2.093**
Syndication Frequency	−32.113	−11.494***	−25.159	−1.004	−30.731	−2.952***
Venture Capital Investments/ Ent. Capital	−24.588	−6.717***	−19.441	−0.764	−22.264	−1.706*
Convertible Securities	−13.253	−4.556***	−11.679	−0.382	−10.028	−0.851
Market Conditions						
MSCI Return	−10.956	−2.632***	−9.535	−0.318	−8.607	−0.697
Returns to Scale						
λ	0.413	21.405***	—	—	—	—
Adjusted R^2	0.891				0.443	
Log Likelihood	−880.144				−1033.740	
Akaike Information Criterion	8.375				9.811	
# Observations	214				214	

Venture Capital Funds in the Same Sample

dependent variable is the number of entrepreneurial firms in the venture capital fund's portfolio in Panel A. equal to 0; log(x) when $\lambda = 0$; x = independent variables. Grid searches for λ from -2 to $+2$ to maximize the marginal effects are computed ignoring the residuals. Various assumptions about the distribution of the residuals for all 6 models are significant at the 1% level. ***, **, * Significant at the 1%, 5%, and 10% levels, collinearity.

urial Firms in Venture Capital Fund Portfolio

(3) Box-Cox		(4) Box-Cox		(5) Box-Cox		(6) Box-Cox	
Coefficient	**t-Statistic**	**Coefficient**	**t-Statistic**	**Coefficient**	**t-Statistic**	**Coefficient**	**t-Statistic**
−10.119	−2.891***	−2.547	−0.588	−11.137	−2.700***	1.442	0.510
−7.521	−3.694***	−6.307	−3.087***	−7.016	−3.429***	−5.058	−2.875***
6.614	3.203***	5.547	2.659***	6.461	3.120***	5.809	3.232***
3.504	2.056**	4.760	2.707***	5.699	3.238***	7.811	5.210***
−6.489	−4.708***	−7.870	−5.593***	−5.694	−4.092***	−6.469	−5.355***
−15.670	−15.114***	−13.295	−12.637***	−15.406	−14.731***	−14.615	−15.997***
0.338	3.857***	0.346	3.697***	0.329	3.682***	0.145	4.050***
−2.633	−3.273***	0.370	0.466	−1.698	−2.037**	−2.067	−3.370***
8.297	16.847***	8.468	16.346***	8.441	16.377***	8.313	19.372***
—	—	—	—	—	—	—	—
—	—	0.431	0.176	—	—	2.271	1.089
−19.152	−9.454***	—	—	−16.129	−7.230***	—	—
−26.509	−11.432***	−27.626	−11.770***	−27.880	−11.940***	−23.206	−11.756***
—	—	−40.845	−10.002***	—	—	—	—
—	—	—	—	—	—	−25.178	−12.816***
—	—	0.502	0.164	5.165	1.783*	—	—
—	—	—	—	−14.257	−4.224***	−12.909	−4.443***
3.357	0.711	−7.190	−1.497	1.253	0.264	−5.120	−1.243
0.346	15.498***	0.340	14.543***	0.344	14.710***	0.414	19.778***
0.869		0.870		0.869		0.887	
−899.801		−899.093		−899.483		−884.238	
8.522		8.534		8.537		8.395	
214		214		214		214	

Table 18.5

This table presents OLS and Box-Cox regressions of the determinants of venture capital portfolio size. The venture capital managers/the number of investment years in Panel B. The independent variables are as defined in by the number of investment years in order to match the transformation of the dependent variable. Box-Cox for λ from −2 to +2 to maximize the log likelihood. The marginal effects are computed ignoring the residuals. for all 6 models are significant at the 1% level. ***, **, * Significant at the 1%, 5%, and 10% levels, respectively.

Panel B. Dependent Variable: # of Entrepreneurial Firms in Venture Capital						
Independent Variables	(1) Box-Cox				(2) Linear	
	Coefficient	t-Statistic	Slope	Elasticity	Coefficient	t-Statistic
Constant	2.917	2.860***	2.917	2.241	8.099	2.502**
Venture Capital Fund Characteristics						
Corporate Venture Capital	−0.471	−1.030	−0.471	−0.030	−0.376	−0.799
Government Venture Capital	0.081	0.158	0.081	0.004	0.064	0.120
LSVCC	−0.206	−0.485	−0.206	−0.021	−0.212	−0.480
Private Independent Venture Capital	−0.515	−1.590	−0.516	−0.193	−0.529	−1.563
2 or More Venture Capital Funds in the Venture Capital Mgmt. Firm	−0.160	−0.667	−0.160	−0.052	−0.194	−0.787
Venture Capital Funds Raised (Draw Downs) ('000)	0.006	0.535	0.0003	0.426	0.0002	4.628***
Entrepreneurial Firm Characteristics						
Early Stage	0.648	0.895	0.508	0.720	0.487	0.790
Life Sciences	—	—	—	—	—	—
Other High-tech	—	—	—	—	—	—
Entrepreneur/Venture Capital Different Provinces	−0.739	−1.517	−0.692	−0.627	−0.646	−1.459
Financing Transactions Characteristics						
Staging Frequency	−2.088	−2.687***	−1.769	−2.068	−1.616	−2.495**
Syndication Frequency	−2.476	−3.927***	−2.102	−2.443	−2.147	−3.956***
Venture Capital Investments/ Ent. Capital	−1.578	−1.949*	−1.340	−1.556	−1.267	−1.810*
Convertible Securities	−0.383	−0.572	−0.352	−0.336	−0.405	−0.648
Market Conditions						
MSCI Return	1.764	2.494**	1.591	1.586	1.801	2.854***
Returns to Scale						
λ	0.605	2.549**	—	—	—	—
Adjusted R^2	0.316				0.257	
Log Likelihood	−404.936				−405.990	
Akaike Information Criterion	3.915				3.925	
# Observations	214				214	

(*continued*)

dependent variable is the number of entrepreneurial firms in the venture capital fund's portfolio/the number of
Table 18.1, with one exception in Panel B: Funds raised are divided by the number of venture capital managers and
specification: B(x,λ) = (x^{λ} − 1)/λ when is λ not equal to 0; log(x) when λ = 0; x = independent variables. Grid searches
Various assumptions about the distribution of the residuals did not materially affect the marginal effects. f-Statistics
Two-sided tests. "—" = Not applicable, or variable excluded for robustness checks and/or to avoid collinearity.

Fund Portfolio/# Venture Capital Fund Managers/Investment Years

(3) Box-Cox		(4) Box-Cox		(5) Box-Cox		(6) Box-Cox	
Coefficient	**t-Statistic**	**Coefficient**	**t-Statistic**	**Coefficient**	**t-Statistic**	**Coefficient**	**t-Statistic**
0.631	1.160	1.095	1.364	0.305	0.460	1.487	2.802***
−0.513	−1.055	−0.519	−1.093	−0.455	−0.941	−0.426	−0.913
0.393	0.738	0.360	0.683	0.438	0.826	0.230	0.445
0.031	0.072	0.137	0.317	0.215	0.494	0.006	0.013
−0.266	−0.799	−0.258	−0.781	−0.187	−0.562	−0.458	−1.420
−0.357	−1.436	−0.223	−0.894	−0.278	−1.104	−0.172	−0.709
0.005	0.488	0.013	0.531	0.005	0.435	0.002	0.395
—	—	—	—	—	—	—	—
—	—	0.379	0.723	—	—	0.537	1.115
−1.060	−2.445**	—	—	−0.727	−1.574	—	—
−0.791	−1.554	−0.817	−1.565	−0.861	−1.691*	−0.741	−1.552
—	—	−2.429	−2.914***	—	—	—	—
—	—	—	—	—	—	−1.952	−4.130***
—	—	0.441	0.686	0.844	1.419	—	—
—	—	—	—	−0.765	−1.117	−0.619	−0.954
2.662	3.574***	1.643	2.191**	2.513	3.349***	2.258	3.284***
0.624	2.408**	0.499	2.037**	0.624	2.147**	0.724	2.307**
0.229		0.259		0.242		0.287	
−417.647		−413.407		−415.887		−409.382	
3.997		3.976		3.999		3.938	
214		214		214		214	

Table 18.6 Regressions with Private

This table presents OLS and Box-Cox regressions of the determinants of venture capital portfolio size. The independent variables are as defined in Table 18.1. Box-Cox specification: $B(x,\lambda) = (x^{\lambda} - 1)/\lambda$ when λ is not equal lihood. Panel A uses a heteroscedastic specification: $Var(\varepsilon) = (\sigma^2)[w^2]^{(\lambda)}$, where w = fund duration. The marginal materially affect the marginal effects, as the high R^2 values indicate relatively small residuals. f-Statistics for all 6 sided tests. "—" = Not applicable, or variable excluded for robustness checks and/or to avoid collinearity.

Panel A. Dependent Variable: # of Entrepreneurial

Independent Variables	(1) Box-Cox				(2) Linear	
	Coefficient	t-Statistic	Slope	Elasticity	Coefficient	t-Statistic
Constant	8.396	22.907***	8.396	0.824	41.031	2.976***
Venture Capital Fund Characteristics						
2 or More Venture Capital Funds in the Venture Capital Mgmt. Firm	−0.120	−1.673*	−0.120	−0.004	1.232	0.954
Venture Capital Funds Raised (Draw Downs) ('000)	0.0003	4.052***	0.0001	0.2315	0.0001	4.788***
Venture Capital Fund Duration	1.498	22.837***	1.195	0.683	1.008	3.522***
# Venture Capital Fund Managers	0.342	20.268***	0.266	0.187	0.234	1.757*
Entrepreneurial Firm Characteristics						
Early Stage	0.244	1.157	0.226	0.041	2.183	0.734
Life Sciences	—	—	—	—	—	—
Other High-tech	—	—	—	—	—	—
Entrepreneur/Venture Capital Different Provinces	−2.948	−21.244***	−2.889	−0.332	−2.374	−1.069
Financing Transactions Characteristics						
Staging Frequency	−7.530	−33.593***	−7.096	−1.107	−10.647	−3.722***
Syndication Frequency	−3.883	−20.235***	−3.692	−0.538	−6.839	−2.301**
Venture Capital Investments/ Ent. Capital	−6.514	−26.969***	−6.206	−0.890	−8.983	−2.602***
Convertible Securities	1.661	8.419***	1.613	0.199	1.263	0.437
Market Conditions						
MSCI Return	−0.014	−0.046	−0.013	−0.002	−4.907	−1.463
Returns to Scale						
λ	0.872	38.155***	—	—	—	—
Adjusted R^2	0.975				0.447	
Log Likelihood	−169.777				−312.608	
Akaike Information Criterion	3.496				6.242	
# Observations	104				104	

Independent Limited Partnerships Only

dependent variable is the number of entrepreneurial firms in the venture capital fund's portfolio in Panel A. The to 0; log(x) when $\lambda = 0$; x = independent variables. Grid searches for λ from -2 to $+2$ to maximize the log like- effects are computed ignoring the residuals. Various assumptions about the distribution of the residuals did not models are significant at the 1% level. ***, **, * Significant at the 1%, 5%, and 10% levels, respectively. Two-

Firms in Venture Capital Fund Portfolio

(3) Box-Cox		(4) Box-Cox		(5) Box-Cox		(6) Box-Cox	
Coefficient	**t-Statistic**	**Coefficient**	**t-Statistic**	**Coefficient**	**t-Statistic**	**Coefficient**	**t-Statistic**
0.426	1.864*	4.642	15.401***	0.252	1.032	0.376	1.643
−0.188	−2.439**	0.060	0.693	−0.307	−3.912***	−0.252	−3.193***
0.0003	2.910***	0.001	3.399***	0.0003	3.017***	0.0002	2.914***
1.454	17.545***	1.830	19.563***	1.408	18.204***	1.379	17.299***
0.333	14.942***	0.296	16.594***	0.336	15.518***	0.374	15.038***
—	—	—	—	—	—	—	—
—	—	1.333	8.866***	—	—	0.701	5.040***
−0.463	−3.982***	—	—	−0.600	−5.096***	—	—
−1.764	−11.605***	−3.503	−20.585***	−1.600	−10.534***	−1.094	−7.569***
—	—	−7.445	−28.408***	—	—	—	—
—	—	—	—	—	—	−1.272	−8.384***
—	—	−3.144	−16.431***	−0.235	−1.461	—	—
—	—	—	—	1.279	6.190***	0.740	3.685***
2.236	6.902***	0.229	0.658	2.449	7.516***	2.242	7.302***
0.847	26.704***	0.802	29.251***	0.856	27.986***	0.865	27.128***
0.970		0.970		0.970		0.971	
−180.586		−179.042		−179.376		−178.031	
3.627		3.635		3.642		3.616	
104		104		104		104	

Table 18.6

This table presents OLS and Box-Cox regressions of the determinants of venture capital portfolio size. The venture capital managers/the number of investment years in Panel B. The independent variables are as defined in by the number of investment years in order to match the transformation of the dependent variable. Box-Cox searches for λ from −2 to +2 to maximize the Log Likelihood. The marginal effects are computed ignoring the f-Statistics for all 6 models are significant at the 1% level. ***, **, * Significant at the 1%, 5%, and 10% levels, collinearity.

	Panel B. Dependent Variable: # of Entrepreneurial Firms in Venture Capital Fund					
Independent Variables	(1) Box-Cox				(2) Linear	
	Coefficient	t-Statistic	Slope	Elasticity	Coefficient	t-Statistic
Constant	−0.167	−0.054	−0.167	−0.183	4.810	2.527**
Venture Capital Fund Characteristics						
2 or More Venture Capital Funds in the Venture Capital Mgmt. Firm	−0.446	−2.935***	−0.446	−0.169	−0.480	−2.976***
Venture Capital Funds Raised (Draw Downs) ('000)	0.414	0.352	0.0002	0.2212	0.0002	2.552**
Entrepreneurial Firm Characteristics						
Early Stage	1.212	1.691*	0.612	1.242	0.650	1.547
Life Sciences	—	—	—	—	—	—
Other High-tech	—	—	—	—	—	—
Entrepreneur/Venture Capital Different Provinces	−0.913	−2.176**	−0.774	−0.982	−0.568	−1.791*
Financing Transactions Characteristics						
Staging Frequency	−1.671	−2.941***	−1.035	−1.745	−1.255	−3.159***
Syndication Frequency	−1.129	−1.931*	−0.727	−1.184	−0.931	−2.302**
Venture Capital Investments/ Ent. Capital	−0.306	−0.425	−0.198	−0.321	−0.413	−0.845
Convertible Securities	0.107	0.205	0.083	0.114	0.210	0.506
Market Conditions						
MSCI Return	−0.662	−1.060	−0.510	−0.706	−0.298	−0.630
Returns to Scale						
λ	−0.104	−0.226	—	—	—	—
Adjusted R^2	0.372				0.283	
LogLikelihood	−110.213				−111.347	
Akaike Information Criterion	2.312				2.334	
# Observations	104				104	

(*continued*)

dependent variable is the number of entrepreneurial firms in the venture capital fund's portfolio/the number of
Table 18.1, with one exception in Panel B: Funds raised are divided by the number of venture capital managers and
specification: B(x,λ) = $(x^{\lambda} - 1)/\lambda$ when λ is not equal to 0; log(x) when λ = 0; x = independent variables. Grid
residuals. Various assumptions about the distribution of the residuals did not materially affect the marginal effects.
respectively. Two-sided tests. "—" = Not applicable, or variable excluded for robustness checks and/or to avoid

Portfolio/# Venture Capital Fund Managers/Investment Years

(3) Box-Cox		(4) Box-Cox		(5) Box-Cox		(6) Box-Cox	
Coefficient	t-Statistic	Coefficient	t-Statistic	Coefficient	t-Statistic	Coefficient	t-Statistic
−4.044	−0.387	−2.053	−0.318	−23.888	−0.421	−38.798	−0.373
−0.637	−4.006***	−0.481	−2.995***	−0.543	−3.356***	−0.514	−3.147***
2.318	0.344	1.294	0.366	19.821	0.337	38.378	0.312
—	—	—	—	—	—	—	—
—	—	0.265	0.725	—	—	0.197	0.441
−0.644	−1.710*	—	—	−0.453	−1.066	—	—
−0.938	−1.930*	−1.045	−2.267**	−1.178	−2.215**	−1.207	−2.209**
—	—	−1.709	−2.797***	—	—	—	—
—	—	—	—	—	—	−1.908	−2.628***
—	—	0.507	0.860	1.503	1.965**	—	—
—	—	—	—	0.205	0.322	0.045	0.070
0.322	0.478	−0.428	−0.662	0.464	0.630	0.370	0.507
−0.391	−0.790	−0.286	−0.623	−0.799	−1.434	−0.945	−1.528
0.243		0.325		0.283		0.297	
−119.964		−114.011		−117.104		−115.572	
2.422		2.346		2.406		2.376	
104		104		104		104	

are explained following alongside the discussion of statistical and economic significance.[12]

18.4.2 Empirical Results

For reasons indicated immediately preceding, unless otherwise indicated we focus the discussion on Model 1 in each of the tables and panels. The other models are presented to indicate robustness. Table 18.5, Panel A, analyzes the overall portfolio sizes as measured by the total number of entrepreneurial firms. The dummy variables for private independent limited partnership venture capital funds and corporate venture capital funds indicate that these funds have smaller portfolios (the coefficients are negative and significant at the 1% level). (Recall that a dummy for other institutional investors was suppressed to avoid perfect collinearity.) This was an expected result given that corporate and private independent venture capital funds are reputed to be the most value-added active investors. The corporate and private funds have on average approximately 5 and 11, respectively, fewer entrepreneurial firms in their portfolios, other things being equal across funds. Model 1 indicates the tax-subsidized LSVCC and government venture capital funds' coefficients are positive but statistically insignificant, whereas Models 3 to 6 indicate positive and significant coefficients (these public funds have approximately 5 more entrepreneurial firms in their portfolios, other things being equal).

Table 18.5, Panel B, analyzes the rate of investment (number of entrepreneurial firms per fund manager per year). Unlike overall portfolio sizes, significant differences in rates of portfolio size expansion are not observed across the different types of funds in the full sample. Nevertheless, as discussed following, we do observe differences in the determinants of the rates of investment between the full sample (Table 18.5, Panel B) and the subsample of limited partnerships (Table 18.6, Panel B).

In the full sample estimates (Table 18.5, Panel A), venture capital funds that are managed by venture capital management firms with two or more venture capital funds under their umbrella have 14 fewer entrepreneurial firms in their portfolio. In the subsample of private independent funds (Table 18.6, Panel A), venture capital management firms with more than one fund also have smaller

[12]There is a statistical modeling issue with making exact predictions regarding economic significance with the Box-Cox model. In particular, in contrast to the linear regression Model 2, the error disturbance term does not drop out of the expectation in a Box-Cox model. Abrevaya (2002) suggests various ways to account for the error term by introducing new distributional assumptions. Greene (1997), on the other hand, advocates ignoring the error term (which of course makes the most sense when the residuals are small). Given the unusually high adjusted R^2 for the Box-Cox regressions in Tables 18.5 and 18.6 (for Model 1, equal to 0.89 and 0.98 in Tables 18.5, Panel A, and 18.6, Panel A, respectively), we adopt the approach advocated by Greene (1997) in the presentation of the marginal effects in Tables 18.5 and 18.6 for Model 1. (Regardless, the alternative approach of Abrevaya generally yields similar results for the economic significance under most distributional assumptions.)

portfolios (but the marginal effect is much smaller, at approximately 0.2 fewer entrepreneurial firms in their portfolio depending on the specification).[13] The rates of investment are not materially different for venture capital management firms with two or more funds in the full sample (Table 18.5, Panel B) but are slower among the subsample of limited partnerships (Table 18.6, Panel B), whereby there are approximately 0.5 fewer entrepreneurial firms in a portfolio per venture capital fund manager per year. There are two potential interpretations of these results. On the one hand, one may view these results as suggestive of agency problems in the allocation of venture capital effort in the establishment of the second and subsequent funds in the same venture capital management firm (see Gompers and Lerner, 1996). That is, venture capital fund managers appear to be investing less and possibly spending more time on fundraising efforts when setting up multiple funds. The benefits of venture capital managerial experience value-added, networking, complementarities, among other things (see Gompers and Lerner, 1999a, 2001; Sahlman, 1990), appear to mitigate the agency effect for the subsample of limited partnerships. The results also suggest that, consistent with Gompers and Lerner (1996), private independent limited partnerships have stronger governance mechanisms pertaining to fundraising and the establishment of new venture capital funds. On the other hand, one may view these results as indicating a greater degree of skill among venture capital fund managers in firms that manage more than one fund, and therefore these funds are better off by financing less and advising more. It would be fruitful to investigate this issue further in follow-up work to see how exactly a venture capital fund managers' time is allocated between fundraising and advising. The fact that private independent funds are widely regarded as providing more advice relative to other fund types, together with the fact that private independent funds typically have strong governance mechanisms in setting up follow-on funds, suggests the second interpretation is more plausible: Venture capital management firms with two or more funds under their umbrella have venture capital fund managers that spend more time advising than financing.

As expected, the multivariate results in Tables 18.5 and 18.6 (Panel A) also indicate that more fundraising (proxied by total draw downs) leads to larger portfolios. Raising an additional Can$10,000,000 in capital would increase portfolio size by two entrepreneurial firms for the full sample of all fund types (Table 18.5, Panel A) but only one extra entrepreneurial firm in the portfolio

[13]It is worthwhile reconciling this result with the comparison tests in Table 18.4. The comparison tests, which indicate larger portfolios for two or more venture capital funds per venture capital management firm, is attributable to a greater number of venture capital fund managers and larger values for fundraising (draw downs) among venture capital management firms with two or more venture capital funds. Portfolio size per fund manager and portfolio size per amount of fundraising (draw downs) is smaller among funds with two or more venture capital funds per venture capital management firm relative to funds with only one venture capital fund per venture capital management firm. The effects of the number of fund managers and fundraising (draw downs) are picked up in the regressions.

of a private independent limited partnership (Table 18.6, Panel A). Rates of investment are unaffected by fundraising (as indicated in the Panel B estimates, with the exception of the OLS model).[14]

In Table 18.6, Panel A, the duration coefficient is positive and significant, which was expected; other things being equal, an extra year of investing on average leads to slightly more than 1 new entrepreneurial firm in the portfolio. However, the coefficient for the duration variable is either negative and significant or insignificant in Table 18.5, depending on the specification in Models 1 to 5. It is likely that the presence of LSVCCs in the data used for Table 18.5 distorts the duration effect in Table 18.5. LSVCCs do not have a finite horizon (unlike limited partnerships) and face a large number of statutory restrictive covenants that may distort the duration variable. Similar distortions to the duration coefficient may arise from the presence of government funds in the full sample in Table 18.5 (see Chapter 9; see also Halpern, 1997; Lerner, 1999, 2002a; MacIntosh, 1994).[15]

Consistent with Kanniainen and Keuschnigg (2003), there is a positive and significant (at the 1% level) relation between the number of venture capital fund managers and the number of entrepreneurial firms in the venture capital fund's portfolio. Adding one venture capital fund manager in the full sample of funds (Table 18.5, Panel A) gives rise to approximately two additional entrepreneurial firms in the fund's portfolio, but it would take an extra eight limited partnership venture capital fund managers to increase portfolio size by two entrepreneurial firms (8 * 0.266; see Table 18.6, Panel A). The evidence thus indicates that limited partnership venture capital fund managers have a more active role in their entrepreneurial firms. More generally, the evidence provides very strong support for the proposition that the characteristics of the venture capital fund affect the size of the venture capital portfolio.

The evidence also indicates that entrepreneurial firm characteristics affect portfolio size. Venture capital funds that invest in a greater proportion of early-stage entrepreneurial firms have larger portfolios in the full sample of all types of venture capital funds (Table 18.5, Panel A; an increase of 10% in the proportion

[14]To match the definition of the dependent variable on the estimates of rates of investment in Panel B, we scaled the fundraising (draw downs) variable by dividing it by the number of fund managers and the number of years. Failure to do this would lead to estimates of very large increasing returns to scale (i.e., the econometric specification would be looking at lots of capital per fund manager to invest each year compared to very low investment rates). Alternative specifications are available upon request.

[15]The duration coefficient in Table 18.5 may also be explained by the pronounced amount of uninvested capital on behalf of funds without a finite termination date (particularly LSVCCs and government funds). We just noted that the fundraising (proxied by draw downs) and duration variables go hand-in-hand: over a longer period, a greater proportion of the fund's capital will be invested, particularly as the fund termination date looms. There is no fund termination date for LSVCCs and government funds. As well, note that collinearity was a problem with the duration variable in Table 18.5, which gave rise to either negative and significant or insignificant coefficients depending on the specification. Nevertheless, note that no specification yielded estimates of a positive relation between duration and portfolio size.

of start-ups gives rise to approximately one more entrepreneurial firm in the portfolio), but this effect is insignificant in the subsample of limited partnerships (Table 18.6, Panel A). Investment rates are not materially different for early-stage entrepreneurial firms among all types of funds (Table 18.5, Panel B) but are higher among the subsample of limited partnerships (Table 18.6, Panel B) such that an increase of 10% in the proportion of early-stage investments increases portfolio size by 0.06 firms per fund manager per year. These results are suggestive of scale economies through specialization in early development stages.

The life science, other high-tech, and early-stage variables are not reported together due to collinearity problems. For reasons of succinctness, we do not report the marginal effects in the tables for the other specifications within the tech variables, but discuss these marginal effects following. The evidence in Table 18.6, Panel A, indicates funds with a 10% greater proportion of life science (biotechnology and health) entrepreneurial firms tend to have larger portfolios by approximately 0.1 entrepreneurial firms (but this effect is insignificant for rates of investment in Table 18.6, Panel B, and insignificant in the full sample in Table 18.5, Panels A and B). Funds with other types of high-tech firms are typically associated with smaller portfolios and slower rates of investment (Tables 18.5 and 18.6, Panels A and B). Generally, the evidence indicates that increasing the proportion of other high-tech firms in the portfolio across all fund types (Table 18.5, Panel A, Models 3 and 5) by 10% would reduce the portfolio size by 1 entrepreneurial firm; whereas increasing the proportion of other high-tech firms in the subsample of private independent funds (Table 18.6, Panel A, Models 3 and 5) would reduce portfolio size by 0.05 entrepreneurial firms. There is some evidence that rates of investment are also slower among tech firms (Tables 18.5 and 18.6, Panel B, Model 3), such that a 10% increase in tech investments slows the rate of portfolio expansion by 0.09 entrepreneurial firms per year per fund manager among all types of funds, and by 0.04 entrepreneurial firms per year per fund manager among limited partnership funds. Differences between the effect of life science investments and other high-tech investments could be attributable to the time it takes to bring an investment to fruition, or the degree to which complementarities may exist among different entrepreneurial firms in the venture capital portfolio. The data suggest that life science investments take longer between the first investment date and exit date (possibly due to delays in obtaining patent approval, testing, and regulatory approval etc.), which would be associated with an increase in portfolio size as the venture capital fund's effort can be spread across a greater number of firms at different periods of time. The data are also consistent with the idea that complementarities across entrepreneurial firms are greater among funds with a focus on firms in the life science industries.

There is fairly strong evidence that geographic proximity impacts overall portfolio size as well as the rate of portfolio expansion. A 10% increase in interprovincial investment lowers portfolio size by approximately 2 entrepreneurial firms among all types of funds (Table 18.5, Panel A) and by 0.3 entrepreneurial firms among the subsample of limited partnerships (Table 18.6,

Panel A). Likewise, the rate of investment is lower among funds that invest more frequently in out-of-province entrepreneurial firms: A 10% increase in interprovincial investments decreases the rate of investment by 0.07 entrepreneurial firms per venture capital fund per year (this effect is significant in Table 18.6, Panel B, in all specifications, but only significant at the 10% level in Model 5 of Table 18.5, Panel B). The evidence thus indicates that geographic distance requires extra monitoring, which increases PMC and therefore lowers portfolio size.

The coefficients for the proportion of all investments that are staged and syndicated are negative and significant at the 1% level in each of Tables 18.5 and 18.6, Panels A and B. Specifically, increasing staging frequency by 10% across all types of funds (Table 18.5, Panel A) leads to a decrease in portfolio size by approximately 2.6 entrepreneurial firms (0.10 * −25.932); by comparison, it would require an increase in staging frequency by 30% to give rise to a decrease in portfolio size by 2 entrepreneurial firms for the private independent funds (Table 18.6, Panel A). Syndicating an additional 10% of investments leads to an average of 2.5 fewer entrepreneurial firms in the portfolios of all types of venture capital funds (Table 18.5, Panel A), but only 0.4 fewer entrepreneurial firms in a private independent limited partnership venture capital fund portfolio (Table 18.6, Panel A). Similarly, a 10% increase in staging and syndication frequency lowers the rate of portfolio expansion by approximately 0.2 entrepreneurial firms per fund manager per year among all types of funds (Table 18.5, Panel B) and by 0.1 entrepreneurial firms per fund manager per year among the limited partnerships (Table 18.6, Panel B). The staging coefficient is consistent with the proposition that more intensive monitoring by the venture capital fund managers gives rise to fewer entrepreneurial firms in the venture capital fund portfolio (see also Gompers, 1995). The syndication coefficient is somewhat surprising because syndication facilitates risk sharing, monitoring, and screening (Lerner, 1994), and therefore may enable larger portfolios (PMB shifts up; Figure 18.1). In this dataset, the syndication coefficient points to the greater importance of agency problems among syndicated investors (i.e., free-riding, misrepresentation of information between lead inside and follow-on outside venture capital funds; see Lerner, 1994), which exacerbates the costs of adding another entrepreneurial firm to a portfolio (PMC shifts up, and this effect more than offsets the move in the PMB curve; Figure 18.1). PMC is higher because each venture capital fund must monitor other syndicated venture capital investors, and not just the entrepreneurial firm.

The coefficient for amount invested per entrepreneurial firm relative to the total amount of capital raised by the entrepreneurial firm is negative and significant. A 10% increase on average gives rise to 2 fewer firms in the portfolio among all venture capital fund types (Table 18.5, Panel A), and 0.6 fewer firms in a private independent venture capital fund portfolio (Table 18.6, Panel A). Similarly, a 10% increase gives rise to 0.1 fewer firms per manager per year among the full sample of funds (Table 18.5, Panel B; but this effect is insignificant among the subsample of limited partnerships in Table 18.6, Panel B).

Overall, this evidence is generally consistent with the prediction that venture capital funds obtain a greater ownership interest in entrepreneurial firms as they provide more capital relative to the total amount of entrepreneurial capital. As such, a venture capital fund's incentive to add value to a small number of firms is high because the opportunity cost of portfolio expansion is high and the venture capital fund retains a larger proportion of the benefits.

The convertible securities coefficient is negative and significant in the full sample of all 214 funds. A 10% increase in the use of convertible securities gives rise to a smaller portfolio by 1.2 entrepreneurial firms when all funds are considered together (Table 18.5, Panel A). Because convertible securities are widely regarded as optimal in venture capital finance (Gompers, 1997; Kaplan and Strömberg, 2003; Sahlman, 1990), we had expected a significant and negative coefficient (there is an incentive to advise more and finance fewer firms). Although we do find support for this conjecture in the sample of all 214 venture capital funds in Table 18.5, the coefficient for convertible securities is positive and significant among the subsample of 104 limited partnership funds only in Table 18.6, Panel A (a 10% increase in the use of convertible securities increases portfolio size by approximately 0.2 entrepreneurial firms among private independent funds). The data thus indicate that there are benefits to the use of convertible securities among most venture capital funds (in terms of providing incentives to focus efforts on advising more and financing less), but not the limited partnership funds. Although there has been little research on venture capital structure in relation to venture capital characteristics (such as different types of limited partnership agreements and restrictive covenants, and the structure of corporate and government funds, etc.), this evidence suggests that there are important differences worthy of further study. It is further noteworthy that the use of convertible securities does not affect the rate of portfolio expansion in this dataset (Tables 18.5 and 18.6, Panel B).

Based on Lerner (2002), we had expected venture capital funds to invest more and finance less in boom economic periods. There is some evidence consistent with this prediction. The overall total size of venture capital fund portfolios among all fund types (Table 18.5, Panel A) is generally invariant to the MSCI returns over the period in which the portfolio was formed (with the exception of Model 1, but this evidence is not robust), but there is evidence of a positive effect among some of the specifications for the subsample of limited partnerships (Models 3, 5, and 6 in Table 18.6, Panel A). In particular, for limited partnerships a 10% increase in MSCI returns gives rise to greater portfolio sizes by approximately 0.2 entrepreneurial firms. There is further evidence that higher MSCI returns over the investment period increase the rate of portfolio expansion among all fund types (Table 18.5, Panel B, Models 1 to 6): A 10% increase in MSCI returns increases portfolio size per fund manager per year by approximately 0.2 entrepreneurial firms (but this effect is not significant among the Table 18.6, Panel B, results for limited partnerships). The partial nonrobustness of the results is likely attributable to the impreciseness associated with a single market returns variable to measure expectations. We considered alternative measures (e.g., small cap index returns) but did not find a better fit, and alternative measures for returns are not simultaneously included to avoid collinearity.[16] Overall, despite the fact that these results are not quite as robust as most of the other effects, we may infer from the evidence that there exists a positive connection between portfolio sizes and market returns. Consistent with Kortum and Lerner's (2000) and Lerner's (2002b) evidence that venture capital funds contribute less to innovation in boom periods (for a supportive theory, see also Kanniainen and Keuschnigg, 2003), in boom periods venture capital funds also finance more but advise less.

The results also provide the first look at empirical evidence on portfolio size and returns to scale in venture capital finance. The CVCA data indicate that returns to scale are in fact diminishing ($\lambda < 1$ in both Tables 18.5 and 18.6, as depicted in Figure 18.A2; see the Appendix) for the number of entrepreneurial firms in a venture capital fund portfolio.[17] As well, notice that Models 1 and 3–5 in Tables 18.5 and 18.6 indicate that λ is significantly different from zero; therefore, the relationship should not be approximated by a simple log specification. Table 18.6 indicates that the extent to which scale economies are diminishing ($\lambda < 1$) is much smaller for the subsample of 104 private independent limited partnership venture capital funds ($\lambda = 0.8$; Table 18.6, Panel A) relative to the full sample of all types of funds ($\lambda = 0.4$; Table 18.5, Panel A). That the private independent limited partnerships have less pronounced diminishing returns to scale indicates that increases in inputs (e.g., more funds raised, etc.), ceteris paribus (given the same coefficients and same changes in the variables, etc.),[18] would lead to a greater portfolio expansion relative to other types of venture capital funds. However, in regards to rates of portfolio expansion, scale economies diminish quicker for private funds ($\lambda = 0$, which

[16]See also footnote 3. Notice that the duration and returns variables are somewhat correlated, but the inclusion or exclusion of either of these variables does not materially affect the significance of these results. Alternative specifications are available upon request.

[17]A prior version of this chapter studied funds that had invested over the 1992 to 1998 period (see footnotes 14 and 15), whereas the current chapter studies funds that invested over the 1991 to 2000 period (as discussed, the current chapter excludes funds that had invested for only one year from the CVCA data). There were fewer funds in the prior chapter (79) and therefore fewer degrees of freedom in the econometric tests, which gave rise to less robust results in estimating the returns to scale. With the more complete sample of funds used in Table 18.5 (214 funds) and Table 18.6 (104 funds), the results are very robust to alternative specifications. It is further noteworthy that when the dependent variable is expressed as the number of investors/venture capital fund manager, it is possible for λ to be greater than 1 without redefining some of the right-hand-side variables (for reasons related to the discussion in footnote 14).

[18]Notice, however, the economic effects of the various explanatory factors on portfolio size are generally larger in Table 18.5 for all funds considered in unison, relative to the subsample of private independent limited partnerships in Table 18.6. One may infer that the main reason for the smaller coefficients among the private limited partnerships in Table 18.6 is that the private funds themselves are generally smaller (i.e., they employ fewer venture capital fund managers and have less capital under management, etc.; see Tables 18.2a, b, and c) and face more onerous restrictive covenants, which makes it relatively more difficult to change investment strategies (see Chapter 5).

is equivalent to a log specification; Table 18.6, Panel B) than for all fund types ($\lambda = 0.6$; Table 18.5, Panel B). This indicates that it is less efficient for limited partnerships to expand their portfolios quickly relative to other fund types. Overall, the evidence is consistent with the view that limited partnerships provide more advice to their investees.

18.4.3 Further Robustness Checks, Limitations, and Alternative Explanations

This chapter provides a first look at the empirical determinants of venture capital fund portfolio size. A broad array of factors was considered within four primary categories: venture capital fund characteristics, entrepreneurial firm characteristics, the structure of the financing transactions, and market conditions.

A variety of robustness checks were provided earlier in the chapter. There are additional issues of robustness not provided in the tables (for reasons of conciseness; however, these robustness checks are available upon request from the authors). Some examples are mentioned here. First, the degree of curvature in the Box-Cox transformation may be different for different variables. Second, we may exclude different funds from the complete sample in Table 18.5, such as the LSVCCs. Third, we may exclude funds from the sample based on the structure of their transactions and/or the types of entrepreneurial firms that they finance. In general, to the extent that we are able to make inferences with the data, these various alternative specifications did not materially impact the results and conclusions arising from the data just presented.

There are additional robustness checks that we would have liked to have been able to consider, but were not feasible with the data availed to us. For example, we do not have accurate data that distinguishes the number of people that work in the capacity of the fund manager, fund advisor, fund analyst, fund support staff, and fund consultants for each of the funds. We do know (based on anecdotal evidence) that at least some of the funds in Canada have staff that work in these different roles. But despite this data limitation, note that fund size based on staff working in different capacities is significantly positively correlated with the number of venture capital fund managers and capital under management (again, based on anecdotal evidence), which are both accounted for in the data and tests (among other things). As such, we do not believe that these additional details would materially affect the inferences that can be drawn from the available data.

There are further details that could be useful in the empirical analysis of venture capital fund portfolio size. For example, in this dataset we do not know the relative importance of financial, administrative, marketing, strategic, and so on, advice provided by each fund to their entrepreneurial firms, as well as the number of days per month spent with the firms. We also do not know the valuations assigned to the different entrepreneurial firms in the portfolios (which may be positively correlated with fundraising; see Gompers and Lerner, 2000). In addition, we do not know the extent to which different venture capital funds use different covenants to govern their relationship with their entrepreneurial firms. Again, these are limitations in detail that are difficult (or impossible) to overcome in the collection of confidential venture capital data. We nevertheless do stress that we considered robustness across a wide variety of types of venture capital funds (limited partnerships, corporate venture capitalists, government venture capitalists, etc.). As well, despite the limitations, this is the first dataset for which it is possible to test the determinants of venture capital fund portfolio size, and we have considered a broad array of factors for venture capital fund and entrepreneurial firm characteristics, the nature of the financing transactions, and market conditions.

18.5 Conclusions

The empirical evidence supports the theoretical proposition that there is a trade-off between venture capital assistance to entrepreneurial firms in the venture capital fund's portfolio and the size of the portfolio (Kanniainen and Keuschnigg, 2003). Consistent with recent developments in the banking literature (Hughes et al., 2001), portfolio size in venture capital is affected by risk taking, capital structure and a number of other factors related to agency costs, costs of investing and monitoring, and the potential for value maximization. The data introduced in this chapter enable a first look at the empirical determinants of venture capital fund portfolio size and whether there are diminishing returns to scale in the number of entrepreneurial firms in a venture capital fund portfolio.

The nature of value-added active venture capital investing requires the use of pecuniary measures of investment costs as well as proxies for the non-pecuniary costs and benefits associated with changes in portfolio size. The data indicate four main categories of significant factors that affect portfolio size: (1) characteristics of the venture capital fund, (2) characteristics of the entrepreneurial firms, (3) characteristics of the financing arrangements, and (4) market conditions. First, fundraising and the number of funds operated by the venture capital management firm have a significantly positive impact on venture capital fund portfolio size. Government-sponsored venture capital funds have larger portfolios, and corporate and private independent limited partnerships have smaller portfolios. Venture capital funds with more venture capital fund managers also have larger portfolios. Second, portfolio size is affected by the composition of the portfolio in terms of high-tech and early-stage investments. Third, portfolio size is significantly affected by the nature of the financing arrangements, including capital structure, staging, syndication, and the amount of venture capital fund capital invested in the entrepreneurial firm relative to the capital provided by other investors. Fourth, portfolio sizes are larger when formed during boom periods.

Interestingly, both the theory and evidence indicate the existence of a nonlinear relation in these factors that determine portfolio size. The evidence indicates that returns to scale are diminishing in the number of entrepreneurial firms in venture capital fund portfolios, and there are differences in the degree of nonlinearities depending on the type of venture capital fund.

The data indicated a few effects that were different among the subsample of 104 limited partnerships relative to the full sample of all 214 funds. Most notably, the data suggest that limited partnerships provide more value-added to earlier-stage entrepreneurial firms, are more constrained in their investment choices (likely due to their being bound by restrictive covenants), make better use of complementarities and experience from operating more than one venture capital fund per venture capital organization, but benefit less from the use of convertible securities. Limited partnerships also have less pronounced diminishing returns to scale for overall portfolio size but more pronounced diminishing returns to scale for the rate of portfolio expansion (portfolio size per manager per investment years). The heterogeneity across different venture capital fund types could provide a fruitful avenue for future theoretical and empirical research on many issues in venture finance, such as capital structure, venture capital value-added, rates of innovation among venture-backed companies, and the returns to venture capital investment. It would also be worthwhile to explore international differences in returns to scale and the determinants of venture capital portfolio size among venture capital funds across countries.

Appendix

This Appendix discusses the intuition underlying the nonlinearities in the factors that affect efficient venture capital fund portfolio size. Consider the shape of the PMB and PMC curves (Figure 18.1). The PMB curve may slope upward over a small number of portfolio firms if, for example, there exists complementarities across different entrepreneurial firms in a portfolio.[19] These benefits, however, do not exist over all ranges of portfolio expansion. That the PMB function will eventually slope downward is based on multitask principal agent theory (Holmström and Milgrom, 1991) and the law of diminishing returns (see, e.g., Gwartney and Stroup, 1997). For a given level of venture capital fund resources (including the number of venture capital fund managers), the value-added provided to all the entrepreneurial firms in the portfolio decreases as portfolio size increases. Further, multitask principal agency theory and the traditional microeconomic principle of diminishing marginal productivity (Gwartney and Stroup, 1997) suggest a concave PMB function. The addition of each entrepreneurial firm to a venture capital fund portfolio will decrease the marginal value of active venture capital investment at an increasing rate as the number of portfolio firms increases.[20] As with PMB, the slope and convex

[19]For example, there may be benefits from overlapping venture capital effort and strategic alliances across investee firms with related technologies.

[20]The concave shape of the PMB curve is analogous to the concave MP curve in standard microeconomic theory; similarly, the convex shape of the PMC curve (discussed following) is also analogous to convex MC curves in standard microeconomic theory (see, e.g., Gwartney and Stroup, 1997, Chapter 8).

shape of the PMC function also follows from basic microeconomic cost function theory. The marginal cost of financing an additional firm may decrease for a small number of entrepreneurial firms in a venture capital fund portfolio where similar value-added activities overlap across firms. Marginal costs, however, do not fall to zero; rather, marginal costs fall at a decreasing rate, and eventually increase. Given a fixed level of resources in a venture capital fund, for every additional entrepreneurial firm added to a venture capital fund portfolio, there are not only direct costs of financing and assisting the firm, but also opportunity costs of reduced assistance to the other firms in the portfolio.[21] Consistent with the law of diminishing returns, the marginal costs of increasing portfolio size will in fact increase at an increasing rate as the portfolio expands; therefore, we may expect the PMC curve to be convex.

If PMB is concave and PMC is convex, as depicted in Figure 18.1, then the relations between the variables that shift the PMC and PMB function and portfolio size will be concave.[22] A percentage increase in the "shift" variables will have a smaller effect on portfolio size than an identical percentage decrease in the variables. The intuition is straightforward from the geometry of concave and convex functions, as depicted in Figures 18.A1a and 18.A1b. In Figure 18.A1a, notice that, relative to a linear function, a concave PMB function gives rise to a smaller portfolio of entrepreneurial firms for a shift up in the PMC function from PMC_0 to PMC_1 (the size of the fund falls from EF_0 to EF_1, where "EF" refers to entrepreneurial firms). The same shift in the PMC function would give rise to a smaller change in the portfolio for a linear PMB function (the size of the fund falls from EF_0 to EF_3). The situation is different for a fall in the PMC function from PMC_0 to PMC_2: The increase in the portfolio is larger for a linear PMB function (portfolio size increases to EF_4) than for a concave function (portfolio size increases to EF_2).

The effect of the convex PMC function relative to a linear PMC function is depicted in Figure 18.A1b. Analogous to Figure 18.A1a, a decrease in PMB has a larger impact on portfolio size where PMC is concave (EF_0 to EF_1) relative to the case where PMC is linear (EF_0 to EF_3); an increase in PMB has a smaller impact on portfolio size where PMC is concave (EF_0 to EF_2) relative to the case where PMC is linear (EF_0 to EF_4).

The curvature of the PMB and PMC functions has implications for the econometric tests carried out in the chapter. The implications are depicted in Figure 18.A2 where changes in the factors that shift the PMC and PMB functions are plotted against expected changes in the number of entrepreneurial firms in a venture capital fund portfolio. The relationship is concave. Decreases in the variables measured on the horizontal axis in Figure 18.A2 have a greater

[21]For example, if there are five firms in the original portfolio, the opportunity costs of adding a sixth firm are the assistance and resources allocated to the sixth firm that would have been allocated to the original five firms; the opportunity costs of adding a seventh firm are the resources allocated to firm seven that would have been allocated to firms one through six, and so on.

[22]This statement presumes the PMC curve is upward sloping and the PMB curve is downward sloping, as would be expected for most ranges in portfolio size.

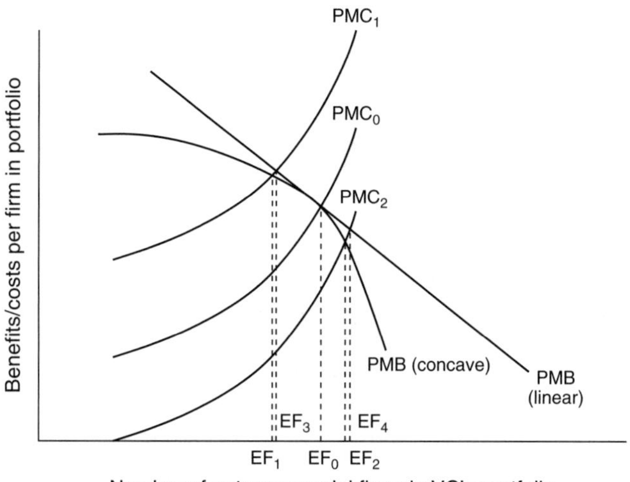

Figure 18.A1a Comparative Statistics and Nonlinearities

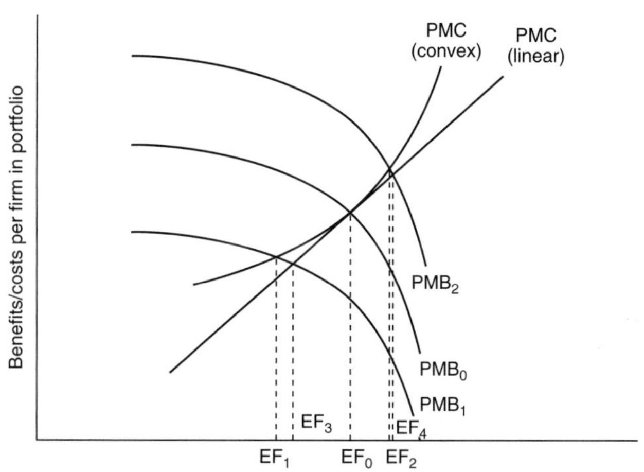

Figure 18.A1b Comparative Statistics and Nonlinearities

impact on the number of entrepreneurial firms in the venture capital fund portfolio. This is consistent with the depiction of EF_0 to EF_1 relative to EF_3 in Figures 18.A1a and 18.A1b given the concave shape of the PMB curve and convex shape of the PMC curve. Similarly, increases in the variables measured on the horizontal axis in Figure 18.A2 have a smaller impact on portfolio size (compare the smaller move from EF_0 to EF_2 to the larger move from EF_0 to EF_4 in Figures 18.A1a and 18.A1b).

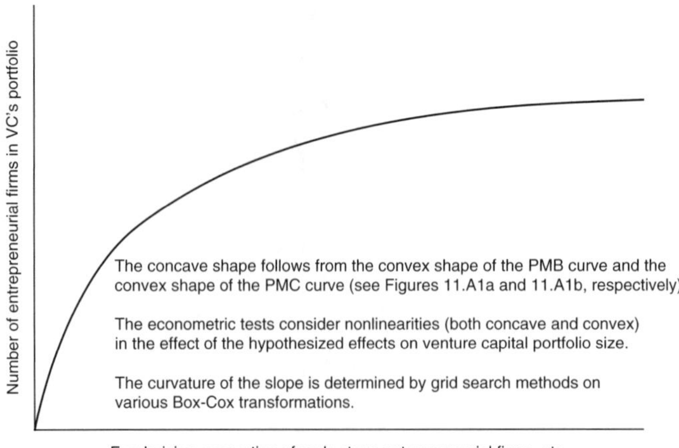

Number of entrepreneurial firms in VC's portfolio
The concave shape follows from the convex shape of the PMB curve and the convex shape of the PMC curve (see Figures 11.A1a and 11.A1b, respectively)
The econometric tests consider nonlinearities (both concave and convex) in the effect of the hypothesized effects on venture capital portfolio size.
The curvature of the slope is determined by grid search methods on various Box-Cox transformations.
Fundraising, proportion of early stage entrepreneurial firms, etc.

Figure 18.A2 Nonlinearities in Hypothesis Tests

The convex shape of the cost function and concave shape of the PMC function imply diminishing returns to scale, as depicted in Figure 18.A2. In particular, we consider outputs of a venture capital fund as the number of entrepreneurial firms that are financed by the fund, and inputs as the characteristics of the venture capital fund, characteristics of the entrepreneurial firm, the nature of the financing transaction, and market conditions.[23] The issue of returns to scale involves the question of how much outputs are changed when all the inputs are increased proportionately. If outputs rise by a smaller proportion than the increase in inputs, then returns to scale are diminishing, as depicted in Figure 18.A2. That is, there are decreasing returns to scale if doubling inputs leads to less than a doubling of outputs. Conversely, if outputs rise by a larger [the same] proportion than the increase in inputs, then returns to scale are increasing [constant]. Whether or not returns to scale are increasing or decreasing is an empirical question. Notice that the theory and evidence herein consider returns to scale in venture capital output production, not economies of scale in average costs.

It is impossible to predict a priori the precise extent to which nonlinearities may exist in the relation between proxies for costs and benefits to increasing portfolio size depicted in Figure 18.A2.[24] Indeed, the relations could even be convex. The empirical analysis therefore explores nonlinearities in the relation

[23]The definition of an input and an output in the venture capital context is rather new and probably not free from debate. Similarly, the definition of inputs and outputs in the banking literature has been debated extensively (see Molyneux et al., 1996, and Berger and Humphrey, 1997, for surveys).
[24]In the related banking literature, for example, there is little consensus in both theory and empirical evidence as to the extent of scale economies among banks (see Molyneux et al., 1996, and Berger and Humphrey, 1997, for surveys).

between the cost and benefit proxies just discussed and the size of the venture capital portfolio through the use of grid search and maximum likelihood optimization methods. To this end, we employ Box-Cox regression methods (Box and Cox, 1964), which is a standard and well-accepted methodology for accounting for the nonlinearities predicted by the theory and described in this Appendix (and as discussed in, for example, Davidson and MacKinnon, 1993, and Abrevaya, 2002).

Key Terms

Portfolio size
Projected marginal benefit
Projected marginal cost
Box-Cox

Discussion Questions

18.1. How many entrepreneurial firms do venture capital funds usually finance? How many entrepreneurial firms are typically financed per fund manager per year? How would you assess the trade-off between diversification and investor value-added? As an institutional investor in a private limited partnership, how many investees per fund manager per year would you like to see among the funds in which you invested?

18.2. In what ways do fund manager characteristics influence your response to question 18.1.? Would you attribute these differences to fund covenants, fund structure, fund compensation, or fund manager skill?

18.3. In what ways do entrepreneurial firm characteristics influence your response to question 18.1? To what extent would you expect complementarities to exist across entrepreneurial firms? Or would you expect different entrepreneurial firms of the same fund to be in competition with one another?

18.4. How are transaction-specific characteristics such as staging, syndication, and securities related to portfolio size? Why?

18.5. How do market conditions affect venture capital fund portfolio size? Why?

18.6. How would you expect portfolio size per fund manager to be related to investment returns? What does this imply for entrepreneurs seeking venture capital investment?

Part Five

Divestment

19 The Divestment Process

19.1 Introduction and Learning Objectives

Part IV consists of Chapters 19 to 22, and it considers the divestment of venture capital and private equity investments. The term *divestment* in this case refers to the sale of venture capital fund investments, otherwise known as "exits." This chapter provides an overview of the issues to consider during the divestment or exit process.

Exits are central to the entire venture capital and private equity investing process. Investee entrepreneurial firms typically lack cash flows to pay interest on debt and dividends on equity. Venture capital funds therefore really only profit from capital gains upon exit from investee entrepreneurial firms approximately two to seven years from initial investment. There are five ways in which a venture capital or private equity fund may exit an investment (Cumming and MacIntosh, 2003a,b):

1. Initial public offering (IPO): a new listing on a stock exchange.
2. Acquisition (merger): a sale to a firm larger than the one being acquired.[1] Both the entrepreneur and the venture capital fund sell their stake in the firm in the case of an acquisition exit.
3. Secondary sale: a sale to another firm or another investor. The venture capital fund sells its interest, but the entrepreneur does not sell his interest.
4. Buyback: The entrepreneur repurchases the stake held by the venture capital fund.
5. Write-off: a liquidation of the investment.

Often, exits are partial. Generally speaking, a partial exit means that the investor keeps some "skin in the game." For IPOs, acquisitions, and secondary sales, this is done to help the new owner have greater confidence in the entrepreneurial firm that is being purchased. A partial exit is defined somewhat differently depending on the mode of exit, and common definitions used

[1]The term *merger* is more often used where the acquiring firm is approximately the same size or smaller than the one being acquired. Mergers are very rare relative to acquisitions, so only the term *acquisition* is used hereafter.

by industry associations such as the Canadian Venture Capital Association are as follows (see Cumming and MacIntosh, 2003a):

1. Partial IPO: The venture capital fund does not sell its interest for at least one year after the first date of the IPO.[2]
2. Partial acquisition: The venture capital fund is paid in shares (of the acquirer firm) instead of cash for its interest.
3. Partial secondary sale: The venture capital fund does not sell its interest in full for at least one year after the first date of the sale.
4. Partial buyback: The venture capital fund is not paid for its interest in full from the entrepreneur for at least one year after the date of first exit.
5. Partial write-off: The venture capital fund writes down the book value of its investment in the entrepreneurial firm.

The divestment process includes the following primary issues:

- Choice of mode of exit, and allocation of decision rights among the venture capital fund and entrepreneur
- Choice of time of exit
- Choice of full versus partial exits
- Ensuring the performance of the investee entrepreneurial firm post exit in the case of IPOs and the performance of the acquirer firm post exit in the case of an acquisition exit
- Anticipating the exit value (and in turn deciding the value to place on the investee entrepreneurial firm at the time of initial investment) and reporting valuations of unexited investments to institutional investors of limited partnership funds

In this brief overview chapter we will do the following:

- Review the economics of initial public offering markets
- Discuss factors that influence the duration of venture capital fund investment, based on theory and evidence from Cumming and MacIntosh (2001), Giot and Schwienbacher (2007), and Cumming and Johan (2007d)
- Discuss a general theory of exits and why we observe different exit outcomes and full versus partial exits, based on theory and evidence from Cumming and MacIntosh (2003a,b)
- Describe the performance of venture capital–backed IPO and acquisition exits

Also in this chapter we provide an overview of issues to be considered in more detail in Chapters 20 to 22, including theory and evidence on factors that influence the mode of exit (Chapters 20 and 21) and the returns and the valuation of venture capital fund investments (Chapter 22).

[2]Venture capital funds are deemed insiders at the time of exit and thus are subject to lock-in periods at securities laws so they cannot exit for a period of time (in many countries this lock-in period is six months). See Ritter (1998) and Brav and Gompers (2003).

19.2 The Economics of Initial Public Offerings

This section briefly reviews the literature on short- and long-run performances of IPOs.[3] More detailed surveys of the IPO literature are provided by Loughran et al. (1994), Jenkinson and Ljungqvist (2001), and Ritter (1994, 1998, 2003a,b).

It is important to review the economics of IPOs to understand what types of venture capital– and private equity–backed firms will be suitable candidates for IPOs relative to the other exit vehicles. This issue of exit choice is central to the investment process, as reviewed here and studied further in Chapters 20 and 21.

19.2.1 Short-run Performance

It is widely regarded that IPOs are "underpriced" in the short run. In other words, the first-day return on new issues is on the average positive, regardless of the country and time period considered. Ritter (2003) summarizes average IPO underpricing found in different countries around the world. Underpricing ranges from a low of 5.4% in Denmark for 1984–1998 to 256.9% in China for 1990–2000. Average underpricing was 17.4% in the United Kingdom for 1959–2001 and 19.4% in the United States for 1960–2001, while underpricing was only 6.3% in Canada for 1971–1979 and 12.1% in Australia for 1976–1995. There is evidence that exchanges with lower listing standards (e.g., by size, revenues, etc.) tend to have higher underpricing.

A number of explanations for the phenomenon have been offered in the literature, including the following (Ritter, 1998, 2003a):

- *The winner's curse hypothesis:* Uninformed investors tend to overpay for new issues relative to informed investors (Rock, 1986). Hence, if you own an IPO stock at the end of the first day of trading, then you might have made a mistake in the sense that you overvalued the firm relative to what other investors think it is worth.
- *The market feedback hypothesis:* In the bookbuilding process,[4] investment bankers ask institutional investors for their views as to the appropriate valuation for the firm. In exchange for truthful revelation for their views, Benveniste and Spindt (1989) have conjectured that the investment banker must underprice.
- *The bandwagon hypothesis [information cascades]:* Investors pay attention to the actions of other investors, thereby introducing a bandwagon in which subsequent investors want to buy regardless of the quality of the issue (Welch, 1992).
- *The lawsuit avoidance hypothesis:* An issuer (investment banker) is subject to an absolute (negligence) standard for material omissions in a prospectus. A way to mitigate the possibility of being sued is to underprice the issue (Hughes and Thakor, 1992).

[3]This section is primarily based on Ritter (1998, 2003a).

[4]Bookbuilding involves investment bankers collecting bids from investors prior to the IPO date to help determine the price and demand for the IPO.

- *The signaling hypothesis:* Issuers may underprice to gain favor with investors so when they come back to the market for subsequent equity offerings, they are able to attract more investors at a more favorable (i.e., nondiscounted) price (Allen and Faulhaber, 1989; Cao and Shi, 2006; Grinblatt and Hwang, 1989; Welch, 1989).
- *Marketing hypothesis:* Further to the signaling hypothesis, publicity is generated by a high first-day return, which could generate additional investor interest (Aggarwal et al., 2002; Chemmanur, 1993) and/or additional product market revenue from greater brand awareness (Demers and Lewellen, 2003).
- *The ownership dispersion hypothesis:* Underpricing increases demand for the stock, which in turn increases the liquidity of the stock by having a large number of small shareholders. This reduces the ability for outside blockholders to challenge management, so managers are better off by underpricing by not having large blockholders (Ritter, 2003a).
- *Prospect theory:* Prospect theory asserts that people tend to focus on changes in their wealth rather than their absolute level of wealth (Kahneman and Tversky, 1979). Loughran and Ritter (2002) apply this idea to IPO underpricing and find supporting evidence in that underpricing is higher where, during the bookbuilding process, the offer price is revised upward.
- *The investment banker's monopsony hypothesis:* Investment bankers may ingrate themselves with buy-side clients by underpricing, thereby permitting them to spend less on marketing efforts (Ritter, 1998, 2003a).[5]
- *Corruption/spinning:* Issuing firms and their venture capital fund managers might have an interest in hiring underwriters that underprice so the underwriter will make side payments in the form of allocating other underpriced IPO shares to discretionary accounts. Ritter (2003a) notes that this practice of "spinning" may in part explain the fact that underpricing is higher for bookbuilding IPOs than IPOs sold by way of a Dutch auction.[6]

It is noteworthy that two theories of IPO underpricing suggest that underpricing is actually illusory:

- *Price stabilization:* Underwriters are allowed to purchase shares of IPOs where prices fall below their desired level. As such, the distribution of prices is truncated in the left tail. On average, therefore, prices across different IPOs will be greater than the offer price at the end of the first day of trading by virtue of the fact that low prices will not be observed. Ruud (1993), among others, finds empirical evidence that is highly consistent with the idea that price support truncates the distribution of observed prices and thereby inflates the observed average end-of-day prices.
- *Industry peer multiples:* Purnanandam and Swaminathan (2004) show, based on a sample of over 2,000 IPOs from 1980 to 1997, that IPOs are overvalued when they are compared against valuations based on industry peer price multiples. Depending on the matching criteria, IPO overvaluation ranges from 14 to 50%. Their evidence suggests that IPO investors are overoptimistic about growth forecasts and pay insufficient attention to IPO firm profitability.

[5]There is less empirical support for this prediction, as investment banks underprice IPOs of their own stock as much as they do for other firms.

[6]See Ritter (2003a); see also http://en.wikipedia.org/wiki/Initial_public_offering, and http://en.wikipedia.org/wiki/Dutch_auction.

There is mixed evidence as to whether venture capital–backed IPOs are more or less underpriced. Early evidence (Barry et al., 1990; Megginson and Weiss, 1991) has found that venture capital–backed IPOs were less underpriced and interpreted this evidence as venture capitalists certifying the quality of the companies that they back, which lowers the uncertainty faced by the new investors at the time of the IPO.[7] Subsequent evidence from Smart and Zutter (2003) and others showed that venture capital–backed IPOs were more underpriced, particularly in the late 1990s in the peak of the Internet bubble. Lee and Wahal (2004) find consistent evidence that venture capital–backed IPOs are more underpriced by approximately 5 to 10%, even after controlling for endogeneity in the receipt of venture capital funding. Underpricing positively affects capital flows to venture funds, similar to venture capital grandstanding (Gompers, 1996).

19.2.2 Long-run Performance

The long-run returns to IPOs (as measured from the end of their first day price to periods of one year or longer) are on average negative and are negative relative to market performance. Ritter (2003) summarizes evidence on long-run underperformance for a number of countries around the world. Average underperformance was lowest in Brazil at −47.0% for the years 1980–1990, closely followed by Australia at −46.5% for the years 1976–1989. Average underperformance was −20.00% in the United States for the years 1970–1990, −17.90% in Canada for the years 1972–1992, and −8.10% in the United Kingdom for the years 1980–1988. Sweden and Korea were the only two countries that did not show underperformance, with average returns 1.2% (1980–1990) and 2.0% (1985–1988), respectively.

There are various explanations for the long-run underperformance of IPOs, as surveyed by Ritter (1998, 2003a,b):

- *The divergence of opinion hypothesis:* Large differences between optimistic and pessimistic investors can dampen long-run performance, since the divergence of opinions narrows over time (which in turn lowers market prices if optimistic owners find less optimistic potential buyers; see Miller, 1977; Morris, 1996).
- *The impresario hypothesis:* IPOs are often subject to fads and market swings. Only 25% of investors do any fundamental analysis of the firm before investing in an IPO (Ritter, 1998).
- *The windows of opportunity hypothesis:* Firms go public in "hot markets," which in turn creates the appearance of overpricing in the long run as market levels taper off. As newly listed firms are typically more sensitive to market swings, the decline in market activity tends to have a more pronounced effect on newly listed firms relative to the market (Schultz, 2003). The highly volatile nature of the IPO market in the United States is examined in Riffer (1998) and Lowry (2003).

[7]Similarly, higher-quality investment banks backing the new issue should also be associated with lower IPO underpricing; see Carter and Manaster (1990) and Carter et al. (1998).

- *IPO issuer costs:* The costs of going public in terms of the underwriter commission (typically 7% of the offer size; see Chen and Ritter, 2000) and indirect costs of underpricing might be viewed as costs that hurt the long-run performance of the issuing firm. As well, IPO firms almost always commit to a lock-up period of six months during which insiders cannot sell shares without written permission from the lead underwriter. Bradley et al. (2001) and Brav and Gompers (2003) find evidence that share prices fall approximately 2% around the expiration of the lock-up period.[8]

Long-run underperformance is not observed for U.S. venture capital–backed IPOs, which has been explained by the value-added that venture capitalists provide to their investee firm prior to the IPO (Brav and Gompers, 1997; Gompers and Lerner, 2003). The relatively better performance of venture capital–backed IPOs is consistent with the certification, governance, and value-added provided by venture capitalists, as discussed throughout this book.

Similar to the evidence on the performance of venture capital–backed IPOs, there is evidence on the performance of firms that acquire venture capital–backed firms versus nonventure capital–backed firms. Most notably, Gompers and Xuan (2007) examine the characteristics of acquisition of private firms by public firms. They find that compared to the acquirers of other nonventure-backed private firms, those public firms that acquire private venture capital–backed firms tend to be larger and have better long-run performance.

19.3 Investment Duration and Time to Exit

How long should a venture capital fund invest in a start-up before it initiates an exit? This question is best addressed by considering what makes venture capital distinct from other sources of capital. Venture capital funds are value-added active investors that provide financial, strategic, marketing, human resource, and other types of advice to their investee entrepreneurial firms. The venture capital fund is thus not only a financial resource but also a strategic resource to the entrepreneurial firm. Venture capital funds therefore generally maintain their investments for as long as the projected marginal value-added that they provide to the firm exceeds the projected marginal cost of providing such value-added resources.

Cumming and MacIntosh (2001) depicted this relationship between the projected marginal value-added (PMVA) and projected marginal cost (PMC; see Figure 19.1). PMVA refers to the additional value-added provided by the venture capital fund to the entrepreneurial, which varies over

[8]By contrast, notice that there is a quiet period of 40 days after the IPO date where underwriters are not permitted to release analysts' recommendations. When this period ends, for investment banks that initiate analyst recommendations, IPO share prices tend to rise by approximately 4% (Bradley et al., 2003).

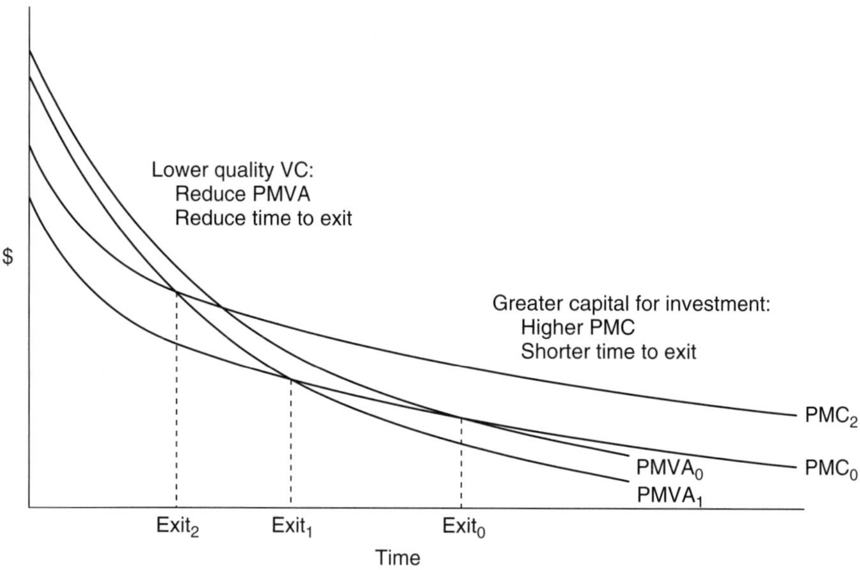

Figure 19.1 Time to Venture Capital Exit

the life of the investment. PMVA is somewhat larger at the start of the investment and diminishes over time as the firm matures. Effort carried out initially during the investment life is associated with large potential benefits as key strategic decisions are made, such as the selection of senior managers, the identification of product development, and marketing strategies. As well, a nascent firm typically has little access to professional advisors and other business contacts, and it is the venture capital fund that makes these networks accessible to the entrepreneurs and the firm early in the life of the investment. Initial PMVA therefore is quite high but diminishes as the entrepreneurial team progresses with experience and the management team itself builds its own network, which in turn becomes relatively more involved in the firm. The PMC function also declines over the course of the investment as the venture capital fund managers' intensity of effort, which is greatest at the initial stages, diminishes over time. At some point, however, the PMC will begin to decline more slowly than the PMVA as carrying costs comprise fixed elements while venture capital fund manager effort continues to decline (Cumming and MacIntosh, 2001).

Cumming and MacIntosh (2001) and Cumming and Johan (2007d) conjecture that various factors give rise to shifts in the PMC and PMVA functions that lead to changes in investment duration. Shifts in the functions may differ for different types of entrepreneurial firms, different types of venture capital funds, and different market and legal conditions. For example, PMVA is larger for investments in earlier-stage firms, which is represented by a shift up in the PMVA function and a longer investment duration. PMVA, however, shifts inward for lower-quality venture capital funds, since they provide less value-added to the investee entrepreneurial firms. PMC also shifts inward when there is an overabundance of available capital (or capital overhang) in the venture capital market, as the opportunity cost of providing value-added to an existing entrepreneurial firm is higher, and thus investment duration is shorter. This latter point is consistent with the observation that around the time of the Internet bubble in late 1999 and early 2000, venture capital investments were extremely short (Cumming and Johan, 2007d; Giot and Schwienbacher, 2007).

More generally, empirical predictions based on shifts of PMVA and PMC are very consistent with large datasets on factors that influence investment duration. Cumming and Johan (2007d) test this proposition with extensive data on the duration of venture capital fund investments in Canada and the United States. The data analyzed by Cumming and Johan (2007d) contain a sample of 557 Canadian and 1,607 U.S. venture capital–backed firms over the period 1991 to 2004. The data are consistent with the view that investment duration varies according to the ability of the venture capital fund to provide a sustained competitive advantage to the entrepreneurial firm. For example, investment duration is significantly longer for earlier-stage firms where the strategic, marketing, and advice provided by venture capital funds is comparatively more important to the entrepreneurial firm's development. By contrast, investment duration is notably shorter for labor-sponsored venture capital funds (LSVCCs) and corporate venture capital funds, both of which are regarded as providing less value-added assistance to their investee firms (see Chapter 9 for a discussion of LSVCCs and Chapter 13 for corporate venture capital funds). Similarly, where the venture capital fund's opportunity costs of maintaining an investment are greater, or rather the venture capital fund's resources allotted to the entrepreneurial firm become more valuable (such as during financial booms where new investments in entrepreneurial firms can easily be made, and periods of high capital overhang where venture capital funds engage in grandstanding to take advantage of the overabundance in capital that needs to be invested),[9] investment duration is significantly shorter. Overall, therefore, the data strongly support the view that venture capital fund manager effort, other than the capital provided, is a valuable resource for entrepreneurial firms.

It is noteworthy that investment duration is shorter in Canada than that in the United States, which is consistent with the view that greater value-added is provided to investee entrepreneurial firms by U.S. venture capital funds than their Canadian counterparts (Figures 19.2 and 19.3). In other words, the data are very supportive of the view that the institutional (or jurisdictional) context

[9]Grandstanding refers to making one's appearance look better to impress an audience. In the context of venture capital investment, empirical evidence from Gompers (1996) is highly consistent with the view that younger venture capital funds engage in grandstanding by taking investee entrepreneurial firms public earlier than that which would otherwise be optimal for the firm to enhance the venture capital fund's prominence in the eyes of institutional investors and accordingly facilitate future fundraising efforts.

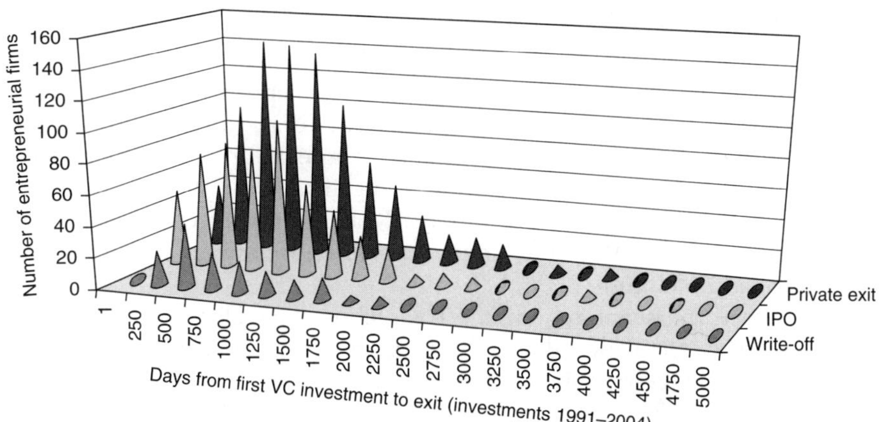

Figure 19.2 U.S. Venture Capital Investment Duration
Source: Cumming and Johan (2007d).

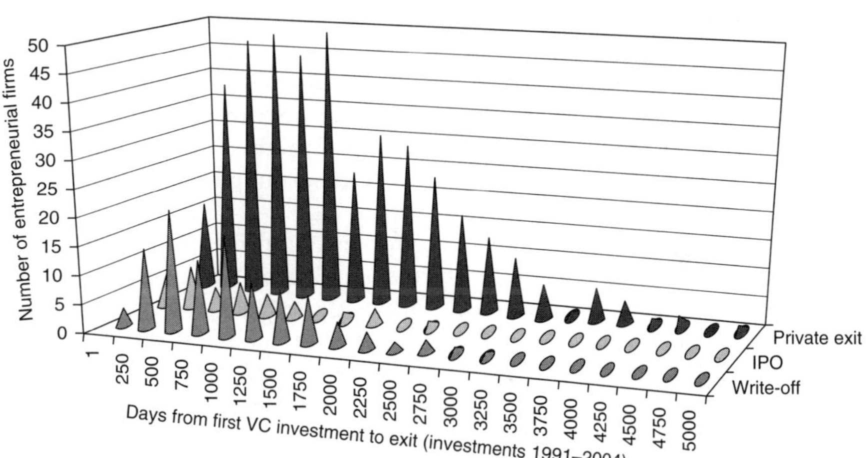

Figure 19.3 Canadian Venture Capital Investment Duration
Source: Cumming and Johan (2007d).

in which an entrepreneurial firm is based significantly affects the extent to which a venture capital fund can be considered a strategic resource for the firm. As well, it is noteworthy that investment duration is shorter in Canada than in Europe and Australasia, and that the proportion of exits as IPO exits is lower in Canada than in other countries. In prior work (e.g., Cumming and Johan, 2007d, among others), it has been argued that the shorter duration of investment in Canada and comparatively fewer IPO exits are attributable to the dominance of LSVCCs in Canada (see Chapter 9 and in particular Figures 9.1 and 9.3).

19.4 The Mode of Exit

Cumming and MacIntosh (2003a,b) provide a general theory about factors that influence the mode of exit and full versus partial exits. At a broad level of generality, Cumming and MacIntosh (2003a,b) posit a pecking order of exit outcomes for entrepreneurial firms of higher quality: IPOs, acquisitions, secondary sales, buybacks, and write-offs. Reasons for this rank ordering are summarized in Table 19.1 and briefly explained following (for details, see Cumming and MacIntosh, 2003b).

New owners pursuant to an exit transaction generally face information problems associated with valuing the firm and monitoring its management. These problems are typically most pronounced for IPO exits relative to the other exit vehicles. The new investors during an IPO are disparate retail shareholders that do not take the time nor have the inclination to accurately value the entrepreneurial firm and monitor other shareholders. As well, there is the agency problem of running a publicly listed firm whereby managerial interests diverge from that of the firm's owners. Hence, only the very best firms that are able to overcome these problems of information asymmetries and agency costs faced by new shareholders end up listing on a stock exchange. Further, it is more expensive to go public than to exit via other vehicles due to the obligatory legal, financial, and other professional advisors required to initiate the process, the transaction costs of preparing a prospectus, and the underpricing of IPOs, not to mention the ongoing costs of reporting requirements for publicly listed firms (Ritter, 1998, 2003a).

Entrepreneurs have a strong preference for having their entrepreneurial firms listed as a public firm. As discussed further in Chapters 20 and 21, entrepreneurs have a nonpecuniary preference for being the CEO of a publicly traded firm. The allocation of decision rights to venture capital funds versus entrepreneurs can therefore strongly influence the eventual exit outcomes as between IPOs and acquisitions. Due to the nonpecuniary benefits to the entrepreneur from going public, the allocation of more control rights to entrepreneurs is more often associated with entrepreneurial firms going public than being acquired (Chapters 14, 20, and 21).

Additional benefits of exits by IPO include transaction synergies such as efficiency of risk bearing across a large number of diverse shareholders and the added amount of new capital that the entrepreneurial firm can raise upon IPO. Further, venture capital fund managers derive substantial reputation benefit from taking an investee firm public. In fact, younger venture capital funds often engage in grandstanding by rushing their investee firms public sooner than that which would otherwise be optimal for the investees to attract additional funds from their institutional investors (see footnote 3). From the shareholder perspective, significant efficiency gains include increased liquidity of their investment and being part of an active, regulated, takeover market that will mitigate the risk of the management acting against their interest.

Table 19.1 Factors Influencing Exit Vehicles

	IPO	Acquisition	Secondary Sale	Buyback
Ability of New Owners to Resolve Information Asymmetry and Value of the Firm	4	1–2 1 For high-tech	2	1 For equity 5 For debt
Ability of New Owners to Monitor and Discipline the Managers	4–5 5 For high-tech	1–2 1 For high-tech	4	1 For equity 5 For debt
Entrepreneur's Preferences to Go Public	1	5	Indeterminate	1
Transaction Costs of Effecting a Sale	4	2	2	2
Ongoing Costs of Operating as a Public versus a Private Firm	5	1	1	1
Liquidity of Investment to the Buyer	1	Indeterminate	5	5
Liquidity of Exit to Seller: Cash or Cash Equivalent*	1	Indeterminate	Indeterminate	2
Managerial Incentives Post Exit	1	4–5	3	1, With variation
Transaction Synergies	1		2–4	5
Must New Capital Be Raised?	Yes	No	No	No
High-growth Firms	1	1–2	3	5
Efficiency of Risk Bearing	1	1, With variation	Indeterminate	5
Common Form of Exit	Yes	Yes	No	No
Common Exit Strategy	Usually	Usually	Ad hoc	Ad hoc
Cyclicality of Valuations in IPO Markets	Time dependent	Time dependent	3	3
Fund Termination Date Looms	1, If IPO hurdle cleared; 5 otherwise	2	2	2
The VC's Reputational Incentives	1	2	4	5
Agency Costs of Debt	1	Indeterminate	3	5
Public Profile of Firm	1	Indeterminate	5	5

*For IPOs, the ability to convert to cash within one year is considered a cash (full) exit.
Legend: 1 = strongly favors, 2 = favors, 3 = neutral, 4 = disfavors, 5 = strongly disfavors.
Source: Cumming and MacIntosh (2003b).

Acquisition exits typically involve significant transaction synergies that are more direct than that which is otherwise possible with an IPO. However, acquisitions typically involve the ousting of the founding entrepreneur as the CEO, which can be an emotional event for the entrepreneur (Petty et al., 1999).

A similarity between IPOs and acquisitions is that both the venture capital fund and the entrepreneur are on the same team in that they are both divesting their interests. Secondary sales and buybacks, by contrast, involve only the exit of the venture capital fund and not the entrepreneur from the entrepreneurial firm. Secondary sales in fact often signal a breakdown in the relationship between the venture capital fund and entrepreneurial firm (Cumming and MacIntosh, 2003b). Secondary sales are rarer forms of exit, as new owners worry about the quality of the investment (if it was a good investment, then the current investor would not want to sell to another investor). As well, the existing investor in a secondary sale will be concerned that the potential new investor will in turn prosper with the investment (if this happens, the original investor will suffer a reputation cost). An additional disadvantage of a secondary sale is that it typically involves less capital being raised for the entrepreneurial firm relative to that which is possible with IPOs and acquisitions.

Buybacks are a repurchase of the venture capital fund's interest by the entrepreneur. Buybacks do not bring in new capital to the firm, and as such, this form of exit is not the most suitable exit method for high-growth firms. Venture capital funds do not invest in a firm with the view toward a buyback exit, as they typically involve the lowest financial return for the venture capital fund upon exit. Buybacks are, however, a better option than the least-suited form of exit: the write-off.

Write-offs are understandably the least-desired form of exit, as it signals failure on the part of the venture capital fund. Sometimes, a venture capital fund will alleviate this loss by writing down the book value of an investment to avoid writing it off completely, but such write-downs (partial write-offs) are rare because they signal to potential new owners (if any) that there are troubles with the rest of the venture capital fund's portfolio (see also Cumming and Walz, 2004, on reporting investments at less than cost valuations).

Partial exits are more often observed where the new owner(s) face more pronounced information asymmetries in valuing the firm being sold and thereafter monitoring management (Cumming and MacIntosh, 2003a). For example, high-tech firms are more likely to be sold as a partial exit due to the greater information asymmetries in valuing intangible assets. Partial exits for buybacks are of course brought about for reasons other than information asymmetry (the new owner is the old owner). Partial buybacks enable the entrepreneur to acquire enough resources to repurchase the venture capital fund's stake in the firm.

19.5 International Exit Statistics

Table 19.2 presents some general exit statistics for Australasia, Canada, Europe, and the United States. Generally speaking, evidence from Cumming

Table 19.2 Exit Frequency and Time to Venture Capital Exit: Comparisons across Australasia, Canada, Europe, and the United States

This table presents the average number of years to venture capital exit for IPOs, acquisitions, secondary sales, buybacks, and write-offs. The percentages of observations that comprise each exit type are also indicated. All samples primarily comprise venture capital investments in that the investments are from venture capital funds, but some of the investments comprise investments by these funds into later-stage private equity investments. The Australasian data were assembled by Cumming et al. (2006) with the assistance of Wilshire and Associates. The Canadian data are from Macdonald and Associates, Limited, for the Canadian Venture Capital Association (CVCA) (http://www.cvca.ca). The European data were assembled by surveys and interviews by Schwienbacher (2003) and Cumming (2008). The United Kingdom data are from the Center for Management Buyout Research at the University of Nottingham and this sample comprises leveraged buyouts only. The United States data are from Venture Economics, Inc. Private exits comprise acquisitions, secondary sales, and buybacks (each type of private exit is not separately available for each country in each of these datasets).

	IPO	Private Exits	Write-off
Australasia (Cumming et al., 2006) 1989–2001	Average = 2.84 years (34% Exits)	Average = 3.43 years (60% Exits)	Average = 4.58 years (16% Exits)
Canada (Cumming and Johan, 2007) 1991–2004	Average = 2.45 years (5.85% Exits)	Average = 4.11 years (74.22% Exits)	Average = 3.18 years (19.93% Exits)
Continental Europe (Cumming, 2008) 1995–2005	Average = 3.33 years (17.02% Exits)	Average = 3.38 years (48.94% Exits)	Average = 3.58 years (34.04% Exits)
Europe (Schwienbacher, 2003) 1990–2001	Average = 3.7 years for all exit types (25.3% Exits)	(53.9% Exits)	(20.8% Exits)
United Kingdom (Nikoskelainen and Wright, 2007) 1995–2004	Average = 2.6 years (16.2% Exits)	Average = 3.56 years (46.1% Exits)	Average = 3.9 years (37.7% Exits)
United States (Cumming and Johan, 2007) 1991–2004	Average = 2.95 years (35.65% Exits)	Average = 3.16 years (54.64% Exits)	Average = 2.88 years (9.71% Exits)
United States (Giot & Schwienbacher, 2007) 1980–2003	Average = 3.34 years (16% Exits)	Average = 4.56 years (49.8% Exits)	Average = 3.30 years (32.8% Exits)

and MacIntosh (2001, 2003a,b), Schwienbacher (2003), Cumming et al. (2006), Cumming and Johan (2007), Nikoskelainen and Wright (2007), and Cumming (2008) show consistent factors that influence exit outcomes and the duration of venture capital fund investment. The primary factors include market conditions, venture capital fund characteristics (such as fund type, size, and reputation), entrepreneurial firm characteristics (such as stage of development at first investment and industry), transaction-specific characteristics (such as financial contracts and syndication), and legal conditions (such as the quality of investor protection for shareholders of publicly traded firms).

It is noteworthy that Canada shows the worst exit performance of any country listed in Table 19.2 in terms of the frequency of IPO exits and the time to IPO exit. Cumming and MacIntosh (2001, 2003a,b) argue that this poor performance is attributable to the dominance of LSVCCs in Canada. Cumming and Johan (2007, 2008) provide specific information on exits related to fund type (that type of detail was not available in the data in Cumming and MacIntosh, 2001, 2003a,b) and confirm that LSVCCs show worse exit performance than other types of venture capital funds. These details are provided in Chapter 20.

As would be expected, returns have been shown to systematically vary depending on the different exit routes. For example, Cochrane (2005, Table 6) shows average log returns are 81% for IPOs and 50% for acquisitions based on a sample of U.S. venture capital fund investments from 1987 to 2000. Nikoskelainen and Wright (2007) find from a sample of 321 U.K. private equity exits from 1995 to 2004 that IPOs had an average IRR of 136.9%, trade sales yielded 23.0%, secondary sales yielded 10.4%, and write-offs were associated with a return −21.5% (not 100% due to partial recovery of the investment). Based on a smaller sample of Canadian and U.S. investments, Cumming and MacIntosh (2003a,b) generally find that returns follow their posited pecking order of exits; that is, higher-quality entrepreneurial firms will rank order exits in the following way: IPOs, acquisitions, secondary sales, buybacks, and write-offs. Notice that exits do not cause returns; rather, underlying factors associated with quality and market conditions drive both exit outcomes and returns. Chapters 20 and 21 consider factors that lead to differences in exit outcomes, and Chapter 22 considers differences in returns.

19.6 Summary

This chapter briefly reviewed the issues involved in the divestment (exit) of venture capital and private equity investments in entrepreneurial firms. Exits are central to the venture capital and private equity process because financial returns are primarily derived from capital gains upon sale and not dividends on equity or interest on debt. It is therefore extremely worthwhile to consider factors that drive different exit outcomes, the allocation of control rights that allow selection of different exit vehicles by either the venture capital fund or entrepreneur, as well as the extent of exit and investment duration prior to exit.

The remaining chapters in Part V examine in further detail some of the more important issues in the divestment process. Chapters 20 and 21 consider drivers of exit outcomes. Chapter 22 examines returns performance and associated issues with valuation and disclosure of performance to institutional investors.

Key Terms

Initial public offering (IPO)
Acquisition
Merger
Secondary sale
Buyback
Write-off
Private exit
Investment duration
Grandstanding
Underpricing
Bookbuilding
Dutch auction
Certification
Listing standards
Explanations for IPO underpricing
The winner's curse hypothesis
The market feedback hypothesis
The bandwagon hypothesis (information cascades)
The lawsuit avoidance hypothesis
The signaling hypothesis
Marketing hypothesis
The ownership dispersion hypothesis
Prospect theory
The investment banker's monopsony hypothesis
Corruption/spinning
Price stabilization
Industry/peer multiples
Explanations for IPO overperformance
Divergence of opinion hypothesis
The impresario hypothesis
Window of opportunity hypothesis
IPO issuer costs

Discussion Questions

19.1. True/False/Uncertain and explain why: "Information asymmetries faced by new owners are more pronounced in an IPO exit than in a secondary sale exit."
19.2. True/False/Uncertain and explain why: "Information asymmetries faced by new owners are very pronounced in a buyback exit." [This is a trick question!]
19.3. Why are IPOs underpriced in the short run and overpriced in the long run?
19.4. True/False/Uncertain and explain why: "Entrepreneurial control over exit is less likely to result in acquisition exits."
19.5. What is the pecking order of exit outcomes? Explain why there is a pecking order of exit outcomes.
19.6. What might cause a buyback exit? Why might a buyback be more commonly observed than a secondary sale in venture capital and private equity finance?
19.7. How long do venture capital funds usually maintain their investments? What factors influence investment duration?

19.8. What is "grandstanding" in the context of venture capital finance? Which types of funds are more likely to engage in grandstanding? Why might entrepreneurs accept capital from an investor that has a pronounced incentive to grandstand?

19.9. What is a partial exit? Why do venture capital funds exit by way of partial exit? (Warning: Pay attention to the exit type. Your answer should vary for each exit vehicle.)

19.10. What factors might explain international differences in exit frequency and investment duration?

20 Exit Outcomes

20.1 Introduction and Learning Objectives

Early-stage high-tech firms generally do not have sufficient cash flow to pay interest on debt and/or dividends on equity investments; hence, venture capital fund returns are derived from capital gains upon exit transactions. Venture capital fund managers are widely regarded as being experts at due diligence in screening potential investments and adding value to their investee entrepreneurial firms through sitting on boards of directors and providing financial, strategic, marketing, and managerial advice, as well as facilitating a network of contacts for investee firms with suppliers, accountants, lawyers, and investment banks (Bascha and Walz, 2001; Bergmann and Hege, 1998; Gompers and Lerner, 1999; Kanniainen and Keuschnigg, 2003, 2004; Mayer et al., 2005; Megginson, 2004; Neus and Walz, 2005; Wright and Lockett, 2003). Venture capital funds typically invest for two to seven years prior to exit events.

There are five primary types of venture capital fund exits: initial public offerings (IPOs, or new listings on a stock exchange for sale to the general public), acquisitions (in which the venture capital fund and entrepreneur sell to a larger firm), secondary sales (in which the venture capital fund sells to another firm or another investor, but the entrepreneur does not sell), buybacks (in which the entrepreneur repurchases the interest of the venture capital fund), and write-offs (liquidations). Prior work (e.g., Petty et al., 1999) is consistent with the view that the best investee entrepreneurial firms are exited by means of IPOs or acquisitions, while secondary sales and buybacks are less desirable forms of exit. Briefly stated, the main intuition is that IPOs and acquisitions bring the most new capital to the entrepreneurial firm and the highest returns to the venture capital fund. As secondary sales only involve the current venture capital fund exiting (either to a firm or another investor) without the entrepreneur exiting (unlike acquisitions), the extent to which the new investor will pay a premium for the investment is diminished. Secondary sale exits are often indicative of a conflict of interest between the initial venture capital fund and the entrepreneur, and the entrepreneur and venture capital fund do not have a similar exit strategy in mind. Buybacks bring in no new capital; rather, the entrepreneur merely repurchases the shares of the venture capital fund. Hence, firms with high-growth options are not likely to be exited by a buyback. Write-offs are of course the least desirable form of exit.

In this chapter we will do the following:

- Consider why different types of venture capital funds are more likely to have different exit outcomes for their investee entrepreneurial firms
- Consider why investment in different entrepreneurial firms is more likely to result in different exit outcomes
- Consider how the structure of the financing arrangement influences the eventual exit outcome, particularly in reference to security design[1]
- Consider a new comprehensive dataset for all exited venture capital–backed firms in Canada over the period 1991 to 2004 to assess the validity of the conjectured relations discussed herein.

This chapter first discusses factors that give rise to venture capital–backed IPOs versus acquisitions, secondary sales, buybacks, and write-offs. It then introduces the exit data and describes the profile of exited firms in Canada. Multivariate empirical analyses are also provided.

20.2 Hypotheses

A number of potential factors might affect venture capital exit outcomes in terms of IPOs, acquisitions, secondary sales, buybacks, and write-offs.[2] At a general level, successful exits depend on the ability of new owners to resolve information asymmetry and value the firm and the allocation of control rights among the venture capital fund and entrepreneur,[3] among other things.[4]

[1]In the United States, venture capital funds invariably use convertible preferred equity securities, and there is a unique tax bias in favor of convertible preferred equity in the United States (Gilson and Schizer, 2003; see Chapters 10–14). However, in Canada (Cumming, 2005a,b; Chapters 11–13) and Europe (Schwienbacher, 2003; Cumming, 2008; Chapter 14), as well as all other non-U.S. countries from which venture capital data are available (Lerner and Schoar, 2005), venture capital funds use a variety of securities. Hence, an analysis of security choice relative to exit outcomes is more relevant for non-U.S. contexts. Nevertheless, in the U.S. context it is possible to study the relation between different veto and control rights and exit outcomes (see Broughman and Fried, 2008, for related work on topic). That issue is addressed with a European dataset in Chapter 21.

[2]A survey is provided by Cumming and MacIntosh (2003b), which largely builds on Black and Gilson (1998) and Gompers and Lerner (1999). See also Schwienbacher (2003). See also Goergen et al. (2006) on strategies for going public.

[3]This area has been a focus in the entrepreneurship literature. See Lockett and Wright (2001), Wright and Lockett (2003), Manigart et al. (2002a,b), Mason and Harrison (2002), Sapienza (1992), and Sapienza et al. (1996).

[4]Cumming and MacIntosh (2003b) survey a variety of other factors, including the ability of new owners to monitor and discipline the managers and add value to the venture, the growth of the entrepreneurial firm and the demand for funds, the transaction costs of effecting a sale, firm size, the ongoing costs of operating as a public versus a private firm including the reporting requirements and public profile of a firm that goes public, the liquidity of the investment to the buyer, the liquidity of exit to the seller, insider ownership and managerial incentives post-exit, transaction synergies, and the cyclicality of valuations in IPO markets. On this latter point, market timing matters to a significant degree; see Ritter (1984), Barry et al. (1990), Megginson and Weiss (1991), Lerner (1994b), Brav and Gompers (1997, 2003), and Gompers and Lerner (1999a).

In this section we develop hypotheses that relate a venture capital fund managers' ability to mitigate information asymmetries faced by the new owner(s) to different exit outcomes. Where venture capital fund managers are able to provide more governance to their investee entrepreneurial firms (such as financial, human resource, marketing, and administrative advice to professionalize the firm and facilitate greater transparency upon going public), the entrepreneur's ability to achieve a more successful exit outcome is higher. The theoretical development in this section is in the ways in which agency costs and information asymmetries are mitigated across different fund characteristics, entrepreneurial firm characteristics, and transactions characteristics. Later we summarize the testable hypotheses in Table 20.1. Empirical analyses follow in the subsequent sections.

20.2.1 Venture Capitalist Characteristics

A venture capital fund manager is a financial intermediary between the entrepreneurial firm and the new owners (public shareholders in the event of an IPO and the acquiring firm in the event of an acquisition). A venture capital fund manager can facilitate two primary roles: (1) add value through active assistance provided to the entrepreneurial firm (including strategic, financial, and marketing advice, as well as facilitate a network of contacts with legal and accounting advisors, investment banks, and suppliers; see Gompers and Lerner, 1999a; Lockett and Wright, 2001; Sahlman, 1990; Sapienza et al., 1996; and these aspects are typically enhanced by geographic proximity; see Gompers and Lerner, 1999a, 2001a); and (2) certify the quality of the entrepreneurial firm (Baker and Gompers, 2003; Barry et al., 1990; Gompers and Lerner, 1999a; Hochberg, 2005; Hochberg et al., 2007; Lerner, 1994b; Megginson and Weiss, 1991) so information asymmetries between the entrepreneurial firm and the new owners are lower than that which they otherwise would have been at the time of exit. Through both roles, the sale price of the entrepreneurial firm is higher by virtue of the presence of the venture capital fund.

The certification role of a venture capital fund differs for an IPO and acquisition because the new owners in an IPO (disparate retail-based shareholders) are unlike the new owners in an acquisition (a large corporation). We may conjecture that a large firm acquiring the entrepreneurial firm is better able to resolve information problems and monitor the entrepreneurial firm relative to a group of disparate shareholders in the case of an IPO. In an IPO, greater information asymmetry (all else being equal) is associated with more underpricing. As such, the roles played by a venture capital fund, particularly the role in certifying quality, matter to a much greater degree for IPOs than they do for acquisitions. Information asymmetries matter to a significant degree in sale transactions, as they are inversely correlated with the sale price. All else being equal, the certification provided by the venture capital fund lowers the indirect costs of an IPO (underpricing) and increases the probability of an IPO relative to an acquisition (Barry et al., 1990; Gompers and Lerner, 1999a;

Lerner, 1994b; Megginson and Weiss, 1991; Nahata, 2008). Both the value-added and certification roles of a venture capital fund of course depend on venture capital fund characteristics.

The certification role of a venture capital fund differs according to the characteristics of the particular venture capital fund, and the most notable differences are between limited partnerships, corporate, and government venture capital funds. Prior research is consistent with the proposition that limited partnership funds provide greater value-added and quality certification relative to other venture capital funds (Gompers and Lerner, 1999a).[5] The primary reason is that limited partnership venture capital fund managers are bound by contractual covenants that minimize agency costs associated with operating and managing the fund and incentive compensation arrangements that incentivize the fund managers to maximize the value of the fund's investments (Chapter 5). In contrast to limited partnership funds, corporate venture capital funds tend to have less efficient compensation arrangements and lack autonomy in decision making from their larger corporate headquarters (Chapter 13). Also, corporate venture capital funds have overriding strategic reasons for investment (Dushnitsky and Lennox, 2006; Riyanto and Schwienbacher, 2006) that often lead to preferences for acquisitions over IPOs so the technology developed by the investee entrepreneurial firm can be acquired by the corporation. Government venture capital funds are often structured with inefficient statutory covenants that diminish the value-added that funds provide to their investees and thereby limit the success potential of the investee entrepreneurial firms (Chapter 9; Cumming and MacIntosh, 2003a,b, 2006, 2007).

In sum, limited partnership venture capital funds are expected to have a greater proportion of successful exits and IPO exits in particular, as limited partnership venture capital funds certify quality in IPOs. Corporate venture capital funds are more inclined to acquisition exits given their strategic reasons for investment. Government venture capital funds are less likely to achieve successful exits due to their inefficient statutory contracts governing their organizational structure.

Hypothesis 20.1: *Limited partnership venture capital funds are more likely to have successful exits in terms of both IPOs and acquisitions due to their ability to mitigate information asymmetries and agency costs.*

[5]See also Santhanakrishnan (2005) and Riyanto and Schwienbacher (2006) for more detailed theory and evidence on corporate venture capital funds. In our empirical tests, other control variables related to venture capital fund characteristics and various interaction terms were considered but did not materially impact the variables of interest. The disaggregated Canadian venture capital data (described following) do not have complete details regarding capital under management for each venture capital fund. Portfolio size per venture capital fund manager is highly correlated with the type of venture capital fund in Canada: LSVCCs have substantially larger portfolio sizes per venture capital fund manager. This is consistent with Keuschnigg (2004; see also Keuschnigg, 2003; Keuschnigg and Nielsen, 2001, 2003a,b, 2004). Given the high correlation, we do not simultaneously include this control variable but rather simply control for the type of venture capital fund.

Hypothesis 20.2: *Corporate venture capital funds are more likely to have acquisition exits due to their strategic incentives for investment.*

Hypothesis 20.3: *Government venture capital funds are more likely to have unsuccessful exits (secondary sales, buybacks and write-offs) insofar as they have inefficient organization structures.*

Further to the type of venture capital fund, it is equally important to consider the number of syndicated venture capital funds (De Clercq and Dimov, 2004; Lockett and Wright, 2001; Manigart et al., 2006; Wright and Lockett, 2003). Syndication enhances due diligence with the initial investment and facilitates value-added provided to the entrepreneurial firm. We therefore expect a greater number of syndicated investors to be associated with more successful exit outcomes and particular IPO exits as the syndicated venture capital funds can better certify entrepreneurial firm quality to a group of diverse public shareholders.

Hypothesis 20.4: *A greater number of syndicated venture capital funds mitigates adverse selection and more hazard costs and enhance value-added post investment, as well as certify the quality of the firm to the new owners upon exit, thereby improving the probability of an IPO.*

20.2.2 Entrepreneurial Firm Characteristics

A number of different entrepreneurial firm characteristics can affect IPOs versus acquisitions; examples include the size of a firm's assets (minimum listing requirements for IPOs include minimum asset size) and the primary industry in which it operates. Generally, these characteristics affect the ability of the new owners to value the entrepreneurial firm's technology and monitor the firm. All else being equal, the cost of an IPO is lower when a firm's information problems attributable to its own characteristics are less pronounced. Younger firms without a track record in high-tech industries have more pronounced information problems; therefore, all else being equal, smaller high-tech firms face greater costs associated with going public than being taken over. Industry characteristics can also be related to transaction synergies, which could favor acquisitions relative to IPOs for certain high-tech firms, subject to investor preferences in different market conditions. In addition, because IPOs and acquisitions may generate different proceeds in the sale of the firm, an entrepreneurial firm's growth potential and capital needs may also be relevant for the choice between an IPO and acquisition. Firms in high-tech industries have higher market/book ratios and greater growth options and therefore may be more likely to go public (Gompers and Lerner, 1999a).

Hypothesis 20.5: *Life science and other high-tech firms are more likely to go public, as IPO investors have a greater appetite for technology firms.*

Hypothesis 20.6: *Venture capital investments in the seed or early stages of development are more likely to be write-off exits due to the greater risks at the earlier stage of investment, while expansion-stage investments are less likely to be written off.*

Hypothesis 20.7: *Larger investments are more likely to go public, as there are minimum capital requirements for listing.*

Further, we may expect entrepreneurs residing in the same province as their venture capital fund to be more likely to have better exit success (in terms of an IPO or acquisition). Lerner (1995), for example, shows that venture capital funds that are geographically closer to their investee entrepreneurial firms are more likely to serve on the firm's board of directors. Geographic proximity gives rise to improved due diligence (lower adverse selection costs) and greater value-added facilitated by regional proximity (lower moral hazard costs). Geographic proximity therefore should be positively correlated with exit success.[6]

Hypothesis 20.8: *Investors and entrepreneurs residing in the same province are less likely to have secondary sale, buyback, and write-off exits, since proximity enhances due diligence and adverse selection problems, and venture capital fund value-added is facilitated by regional proximity.*

20.2.3 Venture Capitalist-Entrepreneur Contracts

An important difference between IPOs and acquisitions arises from the fact that an entrepreneur may have a nonpecuniary preference for an IPO over an acquisition if the entrepreneur seeks to be the CEO of a publicly traded firm. The entrepreneur's nonpecuniary preference for an IPO may be viewed as an agency cost, since at times of poorly performing IPO markets, the entrepreneur may not always be interested in maximizing the financial return to the venture. In an acquisition exit, the founding entrepreneur often leaves the merged organization, which is frequently viewed as a negative and emotional event for the entrepreneur (Petty et al., 1999; see also Black and Gilson, 1998). Hence, exit outcomes may be influenced by the allocation of control rights between the venture capital fund and entrepreneur. When IPO markets are in a slump and an acquisition is comparatively more profitable but the entrepreneur still prefers an IPO due to the nonpecuniary benefits, then IPOs are more likely when the entrepreneur has control rights over exit but acquisitions are more likely when the venture capital funds have control rights. When IPO markets are "hot" and both the entrepreneur and venture capital fund prefer an IPO exit, then the allocation of control rights would not affect the exit outcome.

[6]Location choice is not random. For example, Sorenson and Stuart (2001) show the likelihood of a venture capital fund investing in an entrepreneurial firm increases the greater degree of proximity between the investor and entrepreneurial firm. Location is therefore not completely exogenous to exit outcomes. We consider endogeneity for this variable, among others, in the empirical assessment in this chapter.

We conjecture that venture capital fund-entrepreneur contracts are related to exit outcomes. Counter to the conventional wisdom put forth by more than 20 years of academic study (see, e.g., Bascha and Walz, 2001; Berglöf, 1994; Bergmann and Hege, 1998; Casmatta, 2003; Cornelli and Yosha, 2003; Gompers, 1998; Gompers and Lerner, 2001; Hellmann, 2006; Kaplan and Strömberg, 2003; Marx, 1998; Sahlman, 1990; Schmidt, 2003; Trester, 1998, and others), venture capital funds do not always use convertible preferred equity securities (see Chapters 10–14). More recent research from Canada (Cumming, 2005a,b), Germany (Bascha and Walz, 2007), Europe (Cumming, 2008; Cumming and Johan, 2008b; Hege et al., 2003; Schwienbacher, 2003), developing countries (Lerner and Schoar, 2005), Australia (Cumming et al., 2005b), and Taiwan (Songtao, 2001) shows that venture capital funds use a variety of securities, including warrants, common equity, debt, convertible debt, preferred equity, and convertible preferred equity, and convertible preferred equity is not the most frequently used security. The United States is the only country in the world (where data have been collected) where convertible preferred equity is the most frequently used security (hence the 20 years of academic work indicating convertible preferred shares are optimal), and Gilson and Schizer (2003) show that there is a unique tax bias in favor of convertible preferred securities in the United States.

Security design involves the allocation of both control and cash flow rights (Aghion and Berglöf, 1994; Bolton, 1994; Hart, 2001). Common equity holders are residual claimants whose payoff increases in proportion to the value of the firm. Equity holders also have voting rights to choose the members of the board of directors, which in turn has the right to make specific decisions. Prior work has also shown that common equity typically carries with it fewer contractual veto and control rights apart from the security itself (for theoretical work, see Bergmann and Hege, 1998; Casamatta, 2003; Cestone, 2002; Schmidt, 2003; Elitzur and Gavious, 2003; Hellmann, 2006; Trester, 1998; for empirical evidence, see Chapter 14, as well as Cumming, 2008; Gompers, 1998; and Kaplan and Strömberg, 2003). Debt holders, by contrast, are fixed claimants whose payoff does not depend on the value of the firm as long as the firm is able to repay the principal and interest payments on the debt. If the firm is unable to repay its debt, then debt holders have the ability to force the firm into bankruptcy and acquire the rights normally held by equity holders in regards to decision rights. Debt contracts can be written with convertibility clauses that enable the debt holder to convert the debt contract into common equity at prespecified (that is, specified at the time of initial contract) rates and terms of conversion.

Preferred equity holders are also fixed claimants in that the value of preferred equity depends on the present discounted value of preferred dividends associated with preferred equity. Preferred equity does not by itself provide voting rights, and a firm is not obligated to pay preferred equity dividends in the same way as it is obligated to meet interest payments on debt. A firm that does not pay its prespecified preferred equity dividends on a timely basis cannot be forced into bankruptcy, unlike in the instance of failure to pay interest payments on debt. Preferred equity holders have priority over common equity holders in bankruptcy, but preferred equity holders rank behind debt holders in bankruptcy. Preferred equity contracts can have convertibility options which enable the contract to be converted into common equity at prespecified rates and terms of conversion.

Generally speaking, debt is more suited toward high positive cash flow businesses that can meet the ongoing interest payment obligations on debt, whereas equity is more suited toward high-growth businesses (Hart, 2001). In the context of venture capital contracts, seminal papers examined the U.S. market, which indicated that U.S. venture capital funds finance their entrepreneurial investee firms with convertible preferred equity. This work also made clear the fact that venture capital contracts separate cash flow and control rights to appropriately allocate incentives that best maximize the expected value of the venture. Venture capitalists invariably use convertible preferred equity securities in the United States, and there is a unique tax bias in favor of convertible preferred equity in the United States (Gilson and Schizer, 2003). However, in Canada (Cumming, 2005a,b) and Europe (Schwienbacher, 2003), as well as countries other than the United States from which venture capital data are available (Lerner and Schoar, 2005), venture capital funds use a variety of securities. Hence, it is interesting to contemplate the relation between security design and exit outcomes for venture capital funds, as this issue is very relevant for all non-U.S. venture capital markets where venture capital funds use a variety of securities.[7]

In theory, it is natural to expect the allocation of control and decision rights between a venture capital fund and entrepreneur to affect the choice between an IPO and acquisition (Aghion, Bascha, and Walz, 2001; Bolton, 1992; Berglöf, 1994). Security design can (1) mitigate agency problems between the venture capital fund and entrepreneur (bilateral and/or trilateral moral hazard problems)[8] and (2) facilitate quality signals to the new owners. There is a

[7]For related work, see Cressy et al. (2007) and Nikoskelainen and Wright (2007) on the relation between governance mechanisms and performance of buyouts in European contexts.

[8]In the presence of entrepreneurial moral hazard (entrepreneur qua agent, venture capital fund(s) qua principal), and in the absence of bilateral moral hazard, it is efficient for the residual claim to be in the hands of the entrepreneur (i.e., straight debt or straight preferred equity) to get the maximum work from the entrepreneur. If the effort of the venture capital fund(s) also matters to the success of the entrepreneurial firm (that is, there is bilateral moral hazard), the investor will be efficiently allocated a residual claim (e.g., possibly in the form of common equity, mixes of debt and common equity, and especially option contracts such as convertible preferred equity, etc.). Trilateral moral hazard refers to situations in which to lower the cost of capital, an entrepreneur may give up control of the firm to an outside third party after the original venture capital fund provides capital. This entrepreneurial incentive is particularly pronounced around times of bankruptcy. An efficient solution to this problem is the use of convertible preferred equity or convertible debt (Berglöf, 1994), since it provides a state-contingent allocation of control rights. The venture capital fund has control in bad states where the entrepreneur may otherwise want to give up control to an outside third investor but exchanges control for upside potential in good states of nature.

trade-off between these two factors. On the one hand, theoretical research has established that convertible securities optimally mitigate agency problems in venture capital finance (Berglöf, 1994). As such, convertible securities could be associated with lower moral hazard problems, higher valuations, and a greater probability of an IPO (Bascha and Walz, 2001; Bayar and Chemmanur, 2007). On the other hand, capital structure can signal information to the new owners upon exit. Entrepreneurs make decisions during the early life of the enterprise that have effects that do not manifest until much later in the life of the enterprise, after the IPO or acquisition. The implications of the decisions for future cash flows will not be observable at the time of exit. Because an acquisition involves the entrepreneur being effectively ousted from the firm, the degree to which the entrepreneur's decisions early in the life of a firm are in conflict with the long-term eventual new owners of the firm will be more pronounced in acquisitions than in IPOs. The new owners in an acquisition will be more sanguine about the long-term value-enhancing nature of past decisions where such decisions were made under strong venture capital fund control rights. A strategic acquirer will therefore discount the value of the residual claim accordingly to the extent that past decisions were under the control of the entrepreneur. Conversely, if the venture capital fund employs a weak contract with few control rights and securities without downside protection, public shareholders contemplating an IPO may view the lack of strong venture capital fund governance and the entrepreneur's ability to negotiate control away from the venture capital fund as a favorable signal of entrepreneurial skill and firm quality.[9] Recent legal scholarship is consistent with this prediction (Fried and Gaynor, 2006; see also Broughman and Fried, 2006). As such, weak venture capital fund contracts with the use of common equity could be associated with a greater probability of an IPO.[10]

It is important to note that weak venture capital fund contracts through the use of common equity may also be associated with a greater probability of an IPO for reasons of bargaining power. Higher-quality entrepreneurs (in terms of skill and experience) may be able to negotiate control rights away from the

[9]The signaling conjecture is somewhat consistent with Garmaise's (2000), which is an exact reversal of Myers and Majluf (1984) (see also Leland and Pyle, 1977). Garmaise's result that common equity signals that high quality is attributable to the venture capital funds being more skilled and informed than the entrepreneur about the market value of the technology being financed, while in Myers and Majluf's model the investors are not as well informed as the entrepreneur.

[10]Predictions in respect of signaling are conditional on observable quality. Even if a signaling model would predict that common equity is correlated with favorable information about a firm, this does not necessarily imply that we expect to see common equity correlated with better outcomes unconditionally. If signaling is costly, it might be used among firms where uncertainty regarding the true type is more of a concern, which may well be among the firms in the lowest observable quality distribution (but in such cases, common equity would be much less attractive for the venture capitalist).

venture capital fund (and venture capital funds are more willing to acquiesce control to higher-quality entrepreneurs) and are more likely to go public.[11]

In sum, investments with common equity securities are associated with fewer venture capital fund rights of control, such as drag-along, redemption, and antidilution rights.[12] If the venture capital fund holds common equity, then the venture capital fund is less able to bring about a successful acquisition exit when the entrepreneur would otherwise prefer an IPO. As well, higher-quality entrepreneurs that are more likely to be able to reach an IPO are more likely to negotiate better deal terms (including common equity and not convertible securities), which afford the venture capital fund fewer rights of control. Convertible securities provide venture capital funds with added incentives to provide value-added advice to entrepreneurs and thereby increase the probability of an IPO or acquisition relative to secondary sales, buybacks, and write-offs. Straight debt and straight preferred equity securities do not provide incentives for venture capital funds and thereby are more likely to be associated with IPOs or acquisitions.

Hypothesis 20.9: *Venture capital investments made with common equity are more likely to be associated with IPO exits, as common equity allocates greater control rights to entrepreneurs and entrepreneurs have a nonpecuniary preference for IPOs over acquisitions. Further, higher-quality entrepreneurs that are more likely to go public are also more likely to negotiate control rights away from venture capital funds and obtain common equity financing as opposed to other securities such as convertible preferred equity or convertible debt.*

[11]It is also important to note that there is potential endogeneity of contract choices to expected exit outcomes, as well as changes in contracts at different rounds of venture capitalist investment, and different contracts held by different syndicated venture capitalists. Regarding potential endogeneity, we provide three robustness checks in the regression analyses below that exclude investments in the data for which investment duration from first investment to exit is less than two, three, and four years. The greater the time to exit from first investment, the less likely that initial contracts are endogenous to exit outcomes. As well, note that, our analyses focus on the financing terms at the first round investment and how the initial investment terms impact eventual exit. Initial investment terms dictate the trajectory in which the venture progresses toward exit. In some cases there are changes in contract terms and/or different terms used by follow-on venture capital funds at later financing rounds, but those changes are more likely to be endogenous to expected exit outcomes. Our empirical strategy relates initial deal terms to exit outcomes to mitigate endogeneity and focus on how deal origination influences the trajectory toward exit. We did consider the form of finance used in later financing rounds. Our empirical findings are quite robust to either specification. Alternative specifications are available upon request.

[12]We do not have details on these specific rights in this dataset. Nevertheless, prior work is consistent with this view. Cestone (2002) argues that common equity with strong investor veto and control rights would give the investor too great an incentive to intervene in the entrepreneurial firm. Casamatta (2003) argues that common equity is used to encourage advice, whereas convertible claims and contractual control rights tend to be used to facilitate monitoring. Cumming (2008) finds evidence consistent with this theoretical work that common equity is associated with fewer venture capital fund control rights (see Chapters 14 and 21).

Hypothesis 20.10: *Venture capital investments made with convertible preferred equity or convertible debt provide incentives for the venture capital fund to add value and thereby increase the probability of both IPOs and acquisitions over secondary sales, buybacks, and write-offs. Note that in our empirical analyses, we control for different types of securities as well as combinations of securities.*

20.2.4 Market and Regulatory Control Variables

IPO markets are subject to swings (see references in footnote 4). We control for the returns in the public market (with the country-specific Morgan Stanley Capital International [MSCI] data) in the year prior to exit (as well as other possibly relevant periods). We also use investment year and exit year dummy variables. There may also be regional differences related to economic regulatory factors. The data are from Canada, which contains 10 provinces and 3 northern territories. Each province's regulatory system is based on the common law system, with the exception of Quebec. To offer securities for sale throughout Canada, however, regulatory standards of each of the provincial securities commissions must be met. Hence, regulatory issues are not expected to generate regional differences. Regional differences may nevertheless exist due to economic conditions in different provinces. We control for regional differences in the empirical analyses with the use of provincial dummy variables.

20.2.5 Summary

The central theme in this section was to point out a potentially pivotal role for venture capital funds in an entrepreneurial firm's IPO or acquisition outcome. This section also discussed the importance of market and institutional conditions, as well as venture capital fund and entrepreneurial firm specific characteristics. Table 20.1 summarizes the testable hypotheses just discussed. The following sections of this chapter introduce a new dataset to test the hypotheses outlined in this section.

20.3 Data

In this section we introduce a dataset from 518 exited venture capital–backed firms in Canada over the 1991 to 2004 period. The data are first graphically presented in Figures 20.1 to 20.4. Statistical comparison tests and a correlation matrix are also presented in Tables 20.2 and 20.3, respectively. The data are from Macdonald and Associates, Ltd., Toronto. Additional data on IPOs from the Toronto Stock Exchange and firm prospectuses were matched with the Macdonald and Associates data. Macdonald and Associates believe their data are close to being 100% comprehensive for the entire Canadian venture capital industry. There do not exist comprehensive industry-wide data from any other country whereby contractual details such as security design can be

Table 20.1 Summary Testable Hypotheses

This table summarizes the central hypotheses and describes the variables used to test the hypotheses.

	Hypothesis #	Variable Description	Hypothesized Effect on Exit Outcomes
Venture Capital Characteristics			
Limited Partnership Venture Capitalist	20.1	The fraction of the number of limited partnership venture capital funds that were syndicated venture capital funds at the first round investment.	IPOs and acquisitions are more likely than secondary sales, buybacks, and write-offs for limited partnership venture capital funds.
Corporate Venture	20.2	The fraction of the number of corporate venture capital funds that were syndicated venture capital funds at the first round investment.	Acquisitions are more likely than IPOs as the corporate venture capital has strategic incentives to invest.
Government Venture Capital Fund	20.3	The fraction of the number of government venture capital funds that were syndicated venture capital funds at the first round investment.	Weaker governance structure associated with government funds, and therefore a greater probability of secondary sales, buybacks, and write-offs.
Number of Syndicated Venture Capital Funds	20.4	The number of syndicated venture capital funds in the first round of investment.	A greater number of syndicate venture capital funds will reduce adverse selection problems and facilitate value-added, thereby increasing the probability of an IPO.
Entrepreneurial Firm Characteristics			
Life Science Industry	20.5	A dummy variable equal to one for firms in one of the life sciences industries (biotechnology or medical).	Increases the probability of an IPO, as IPO investors often have an appetite for technology companies.

Other High-tech Industry	20.5	A dummy variable equal to one for firms in one of the high-tech industries other than the life sciences industries.	Increases the probability of an IPO, as IPO investors often have an appetite for technology companies.
Seed or Early Stage	20.6	A dummy variable equal to one for seed or early-stage investments in the first round of investment.	Higher probability of a write-off as risks are greater the earlier the stage of investment.
Expansion Stage	20.6	A dummy variable equal to one for expansion stage investments in the first round of investment.	Lower risks relative to seed and early-stage investments, and therefore a lower probability of a write-off.
Entrepreneur Capital Requirements [Log (Deal Size)]	20.7	The log of the amount invested in the first round investment across all syndicated venture capital funds, in thousands of 2004 Canadian dollars.	Larger investments are more likely to go public as there are minimum capital requirements for listing.
Venture Capital Fund and Entrepreneur in Same Province	20.8	A dummy variable equal to one if the venture capital fund and the entrepreneur were located within the same province at the time of first round investment.	Higher probability of an IPO and acquisition as adverse selection problems are mitigated and value-added facilitated by regional proximity.
Transaction Characteristics			
Common Equity and/or Warrants	20.9	The fraction of the number of first-round investment securities in the form of common equity and/or warrants. If only common equity was used then the variable equals 1, and if common equity was not used then the variable equals 0.	Increases the probability of an IPO over an acquisition, as common equity signals favorable information to the public market. As well, higher-quality entrepreneurs are more likely to negotiate common equity contracts. Further, entrepreneurs typically have stronger control rights when the venture capital fund uses common equity, and therefore entrepreneurs with a nonpecuniary preference for an IPO are less likely to be acquired than go public.

(*continued*)

Table 20.1 *(continued)*

	Hypothesis #	Variable Description	Hypothesized Effect on Exit Outcomes
Convertible Securities	20.10	The fraction of the number of first-round investment securities in the form of convertible preferred equity and/or convertible debt. If only convertible securities were used then the variable equals 1, and if convertible securities were not used then the variable equals 0.	Provides incentives for the venture capital fund to add value and thereby increase the probability of both IPOs and acquisitions over secondary sales, buybacks, and write-offs.
Control Variables: Institutional and Economic Conditions			
Ontario Entrepreneur		A dummy variable equal to one for an entrepreneur based in Ontario	Higher probability of an IPO and acquisition as economic activity is greater in the Province of Ontario and Quebec than other provinces.
Quebec Entrepreneur		A dummy variable equal to one for an entrepreneur based in Quebec	Higher probability of an IPO and acquisition as economic activity is greater in the Province of Ontario and Quebec than other provinces.
Log (1 + MSCI Index in Year of Exit)		The log of 1 + the Morgan Stanley Capital International stock index return for Canada in the year of exit	Higher probability of an IPO or acquisition in boom market conditions; greater probability of secondary sales, buybacks, and write-offs in bad market conditions.
Log (1 + MSCI Index in Year Prior to Exit)		The log of 1 + the Morgan Stanley Capital International stock index return for Canada in the year prior to exit	Higher probability of an IPO or acquisition in boom market conditions; greater probability of secondary sales, buybacks, and write-offs in bad market conditions.
Dummy for Exit in 1999		A dummy variable equal to one for exits in 1999	Higher probability of an IPO or acquisition in boom market conditions; greater probability of secondary sales, buybacks, and write-offs in bad market conditions.
Dummy for Exit in 2000		A dummy variable equal to one for exits in 2000	Higher probability of an IPO or acquisition in boom market conditions; greater probability of secondary sales, buybacks, and write-offs in bad market conditions.

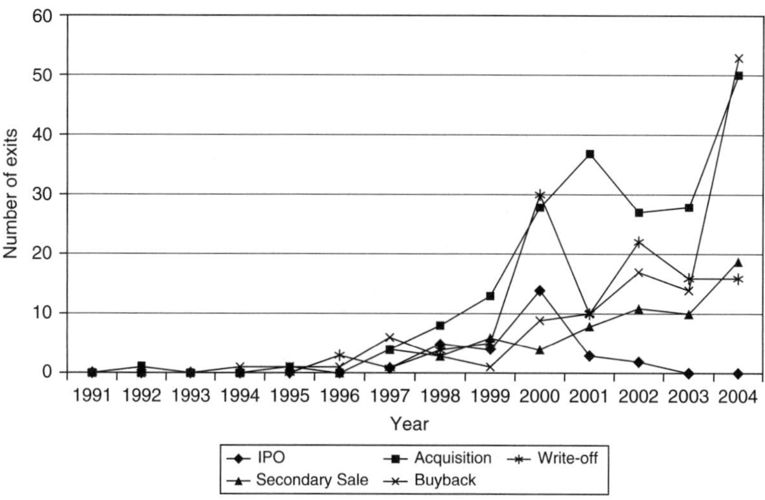

Figure 20.1 Number of Venture Capital–backed Exits by Year, 1991–1994

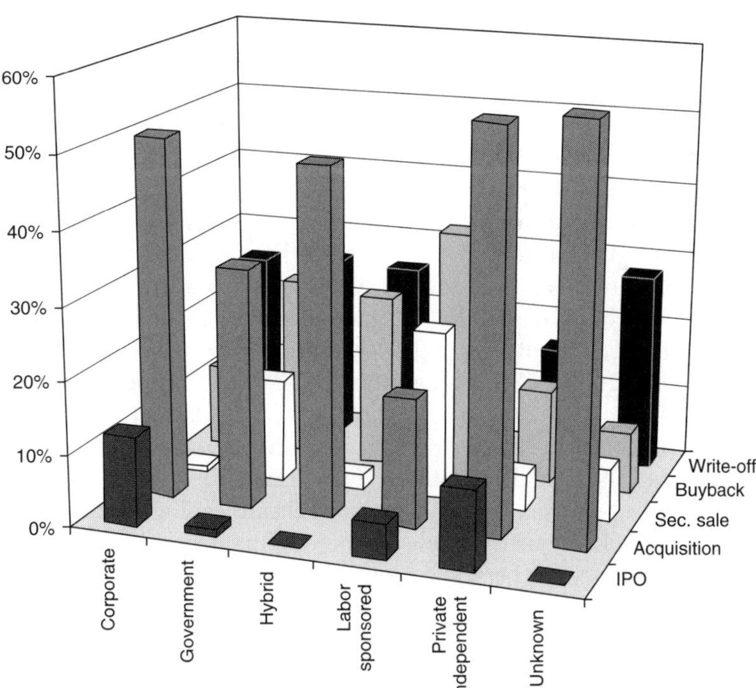

Figure 20.2 Percentage of Exit Outcomes for Each Type of Investor

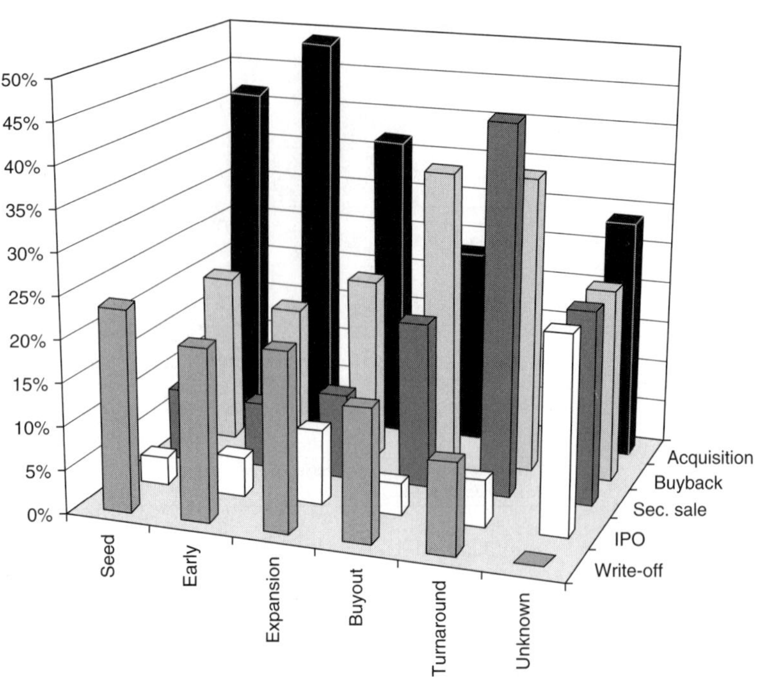

Figure 20.3 Percentage of Exit Outcomes for Each Stage of First Investment

matched to exit outcomes. Hence, the Macdonald and Associates data provide a useful source of information for the examination of venture capital contracts and exits.

Figure 20.1 depicts the percentage of exits by exit type and over time. There are 32 IPOs, 197 acquisitions, 66 secondary sales, 116 buybacks, and 107 write-offs. In total there were 518 exited firms between 1991 and 2004. The percentage of venture capital–backed IPOs relative to other exit types (6.2%) is extremely low in Canada, lower than in other countries. Venture capital funds achieved 34% of their exits as IPOs in Australasia in 1989 to 2001 (Cumming et al., 2006), 17% of their exits as IPOs in Europe in 1995 to 2005 (Cumming, 2008), 25% of their exits as IPOs in the 1990 to 2001 period in Europe (Schwienbacher, 2002), and U.S. venture capital funds achieved 16% of their exits as IPOs in the 1980 to 2003 period (Giot and Schwienbacher, 2007). The poor performance of Canadian venture capital funds in achieving IPO exits is most likely attributable to the dominant presence of LSVCCs in Canada.[13] Buybacks have been the most frequently used type of exit in 2004, followed by acquisitions, and then an equal number of secondary sales and write-offs. There were no venture capital–backed IPOs in Canada in 2003 or

[13]The low number of IPOs is not related to listing standards; IPO listing standards in Canada are much lower than that for NASDAQ and the NYSE. See Harris (2006).

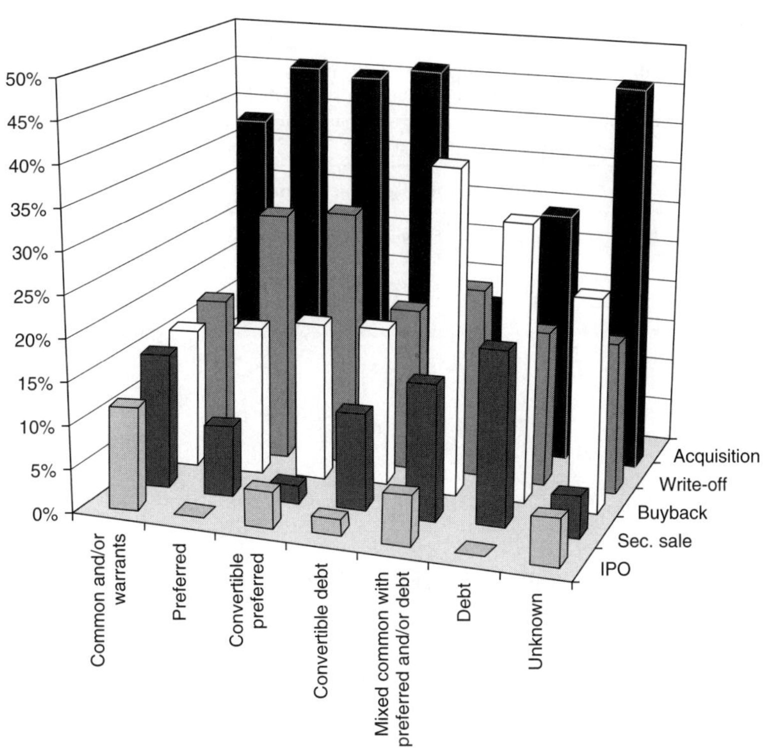

Figure 20.4 Percentage of Exit Outcomes for Each Type of Security

2004. Venture capital–backed IPOs reached their peak in 2000 in conjunction with the peak of the Internet bubble.

There are six types of venture capital funds in Canada (see also Amit et al., 1998; Macdonald, 1992; MacIntosh, 1994): limited partnership, corporate, government, institutional direct (formerly known as hybrid funds), foreign, and Labor-sponsored venture capital corporations (LSVCCs). Limited partnership venture capital funds are similar to U.S. private funds (described by Gompers and Lerner, 1999, and Sahlman, 1990) and are organized as limited partnerships. They tend, however, toward a lower degree of specialization in investment activity than their U.S. counterparts (Amit et al., 1998; MacIntosh, 1994). Canadian corporate venture capital funds are analogous to U.S. corporate venture capital funds (as described by Gompers and Lerner, 1999) but tend to finance a somewhat more heterogeneous group of entrepreneurial firms (Chapter 11; Cumming, 2005a,b). Government funds are government-funded funds that are managed by independent professional venture capital managers and also finance a wide variety of different entrepreneurial firms. The "hybrid" category consists of public pension funds that invest money directly in entrepreneurial firms, rather than investing through the medium of a private

Table 20.2 The Profile of Venture

This table summarizes the characteristics of exited venture capital investments in Canada from 1991–1994. There 518 firms exited. The data are summarized for the characteristics of the investee and the venture capital funds. of development, security choice) are provided for the first round investment only and not subsequent financing for each exit outcome versus the others. N/A = not applicable. *, **, *** Statistically significant at the 10%, 5%,

Variable	Mean Values for Each Type of Exit					Comparisons of	
	IPOs	Acquisitions	Secondary Sales	Buyback	Write-off	IPO vs. Acquisition	IPO vs. Secondary Sale
Limited Partnership Venture Capital Fund	0.476	0.392	0.106	0.159	0.208	0.900	4.103***
Corporate Venture Capital Fund	0.203	0.134	0.005	0.054	0.125	1.026	3.610***
Government Venture Capital Fund	0.016	0.078	0.101	0.102	0.113	−1.292	−1.523
Hybrid Venture Capital Fund	0.000	0.055	0.008	0.048	0.055	−1.366	−0.494
LSVCC	0.305	0.182	0.720	0.598	0.358	1.611	−3.906***
Other/Unknown Venture Capital Fund	0.000	0.157	0.061	0.040	0.142	−2.414**	−1.422
Number of Syndicated Venture Capital Funds	2.000	1.893	1.515	1.397	1.720	0.308	1.379
Amount Invested (Thousands $Can 2004)	$5,519	$2,256	$1,730	$1,640	$1,443	1.810*	2.061**
Deal Size All Syndicated Venture Capital Funds (Thousands $Can 2004)	$8,400	$4,275	$3,227	$2,418	$2,996	1.797*	1.961**
Life Science Firm Dummy Variable	0.406	0.157	0.076	0.078	0.131	3.315***	3.962***
Other High-tech Dummy Variable	0.406	0.721	0.288	0.310	0.523	−3.529***	1.172
Seed Dummy Variable	0.219	0.426	0.273	0.353	0.449	−2.226**	−0.575
Early-stage Dummy Variable	0.125	0.218	0.106	0.129	0.168	−1.212	0.279
Expansion Dummy Variable	0.438	0.294	0.242	0.293	0.308	1.617	1.965**
Buyout Dummy Variable	0.031	0.030	0.076	0.078	0.037	0.024	−0.862

Capital Exits in Canada, 1991–2004

were 32 IPOs, 197 acquisitions, 66 secondary sales, 116 buybacks, and 107 write-offs, and in total there were
Transaction characteristics (number of syndicated venture capital funds, amounts invested, deal size, stage
rounds. Comparisons of means tests (comparisons of proportions tests for dummy variables) are provided
and 1% levels, respectively.

Means and Proportions Test Statistics							
IPO vs. Buyback	IPO vs. Write-off	Acquisition vs. Secondary Sale	Acquisition vs. Buyback	Acquisition vs. Write-off	Secondary Sale vs. Buyback	Secondary Sale vs. Write-off	Buyback vs. Write-off
3.793***	3.004***	4.310***	4.328***	3.273***	−0.986	−1.733*	−0.946
2.674***	1.115	3.006***	2.261**	0.244	−1.689*	−2.831***	−1.874*
−1.563	−1.686*	−0.578	−0.715	−1.014	−0.017	−0.250	−0.274
−1.257	−1.349	1.652*	0.304	0.036	−1.451	−1.597	−0.236
−2.941***	−0.551	−8.119***	−7.517***	−3.401***	1.647*	4.625***	3.586***
−1.155	−2.261***	2.004***	3.146***	0.351	0.615	−1.661*	−2.666***
1.743*	0.797	2.591***	3.746***	1.186	0.806	−1.280	−2.187**
2.178**	2.277**	0.894	1.643	1.960*	0.174	0.524	0.638
2.640***	2.318**	0.709	3.072***	1.569	0.565	0.150	−0.794
4.627***	3.455***	1.669*	2.042**	0.622	−0.045	−1.126	−1.306
1.021	−1.163	6.247***	7.082***	3.450***	−0.317	−3.036***	−3.228***
−1.441	−2.333**	2.217**	1.273	−0.373	−1.119	−2.313**	−1.450
−0.065	−0.588	2.011**	1.956**	1.041	−0.463	−1.130	−0.818
1.545	1.354	0.813	0.025	−0.254	−0.736	−0.936	−0.249
−0.925	−0.163	−1.591	−1.885*	−0.323	−0.045	1.104	1.280

(*continued*)

Table 20.2

Variable	Mean Values for Each Type of Exit					Comparisons of	
	IPOs	Acquisitions	Secondary Sales	Buyback	Write-off	IPO vs. Acquisition	IPO vs. Secondary Sale
Turnaround Dummy Variable	0.063	0.005	0.242	0.112	0.037	2.650***	−2.157**
Other/Unknown Stage Dummy Variable	0.125	0.025	0.061	0.034	0.000	2.690***	1.092
Common Equity or Warrants	0.688	0.393	0.465	0.289	0.343	3.114***	2.075**
Preferred Equity	0.000	0.077	0.043	0.051	0.090	−1.624	−1.189
Convertible Preferred Equity	0.063	0.099	0.015	0.072	0.121	−0.652	1.276
Debt	0.000	0.099	0.210	0.182	0.117	−1.860*	−2.795***
Convertible Debt	0.031	0.114	0.086	0.080	0.092	−1.432	−1.007
Common and Preferred and/or Debt	0.094	0.045	0.124	0.163	0.110	1.145	−0.438
Other/Unknown Securities	0.125	0.172	0.058	0.163	0.127	−0.661	1.146
British Columbia Investee Firm	0.125	0.122	0.061	0.026	0.140	0.051	1.092
Alberta Investee Firm	0.031	0.051	0.000	0.026	0.009	−0.479	1.444
Saskatchewan Investee Firm	0.000	0.000	0.000	0.000	0.000	N/A	N/A
Manitoba Investee Firm	0.031	0.015	0.076	0.026	0.000	0.642	−0.862
Ontario Investee Firm	0.344	0.492	0.076	0.190	0.262	−1.562	3.366***
Quebec Investee Firm	0.438	0.289	0.788	0.724	0.589	1.681*	−3.469***
Newfoundland Investee Firm	0.000	0.000	0.000	0.000	0.000	N/A	N/A
New Brunswick Investee Firm	0.031	0.000	0.000	0.000	0.000	2.487**	1.444
Nova Scotia Investee Firm	0.000	0.030	0.000	0.009	0.000	−1.000	N/A
Prince Edward Island Investee Firm	0.000	0.000	0.000	0.000	0.000	N/A	N/A
Northern Territories Investee Firm	0.000	0.000	0.000	0.000	0.000	N/A	N/A

(*continued*)

Means and Proportions Test Statistics

IPO vs. Buyback	IPO vs. Write-off	Acquisition vs. Secondary Sale	Acquisition vs. Buyback	Acquisition vs. Write-off	Secondary Sale vs. Buyback	Secondary Sale vs. Write-off	Buyback vs. Write-off
−0.823	0.613	−6.787***	−4.423***	−2.115**	2.310**	4.097***	2.100**
2.005**	3.711***	−1.362	−0.465	1.662*	0.827	2.576**	1.938*
4.127***	3.465***	−1.020	1.870*	0.870	2.390**	1.598	−0.869
−1.301	−1.759*	0.948	0.892	−0.396	−0.239	−1.162	−1.148
−0.192	−0.938	2.194**	0.793	−0.602	−1.676*	−2.484**	−1.236
−2.609***	−2.033**	−2.340**	−2.120**	−0.503	0.450	1.637	1.350
−0.964	−1.127	0.641	0.956	0.590	0.132	−0.142	−0.318
−0.977	−0.261	−2.239**	−3.537***	−2.140**	−0.717	0.276	1.150
−0.523	−0.026	2.283**	0.208	1.035	−2.054**	−1.458	0.762
2.339**	−0.219	1.396	2.921***	−0.457	1.172	−1.626	−3.131***
0.166	0.913	1.866*	1.066	1.847*	−1.317	−0.788	0.928
N/A	N/A	N/A	N/A	N/A	N/A	N/A	N/A
0.166	1.835*	−2.478**	−0.663	1.283	1.579	2.889***	1.675*
1.854*	0.907	6.012***	5.329***	3.904***	−2.078**	−3.023***	−1.288
−3.035***	−1.511	−7.116***	−7.467***	−5.101***	0.951	2.695***	2.130**
N/A	N/A	N/A	N/A	N/A	N/A	N/A	N/A
1.910*	1.835	N/A	N/A	N/A	N/A	N/A	N/A
−0.527	N/A	1.434	1.262	1.823*	−0.756	N/A	0.963
N/A	N/A	N/A	N/A	N/A	N/A	N/A	N/A
N/A	N/A	N/A	N/A	N/A	N/A	N/A	N/A

(*continued*)

Table 20.2

Variable	Mean Values for Each Type of Exit					Comparisons of	
	IPOs	Acquisitions	Secondary Sales	Buyback	Write-off	IPO vs. Acquisition	IPO vs. Secondary Sale
British Columbia Venture Capital Fund	0.125	0.217	0.058	0.065	0.197	−1.203	1.146
Alberta Venture Capital Fund	0.016	0.055	0.025	0.040	0.011	−0.945	−0.304
Saskatchewan Venture Capital Fund	0.000	0.054	0.013	0.046	0.126	−1.341	−0.638
Manitoba Venture Capital Fund	0.042	0.045	0.096	0.048	0.017	−0.093	−0.941
Ontario Venture Capital Fund	0.365	0.591	0.144	0.218	0.322	−2.387**	2.490**
Quebec Venture Capital Fund	0.422	0.444	0.773	0.736	0.623	−0.232	−3.434***
Newfoundland Venture Capital Fund	0.000	0.000	0.000	0.000	0.000	N/A	N/A
New Brunswick Venture capital fund	0.000	0.000	0.000	0.000	0.000	N/A	N/A
Nova Scotia Venture Capital Fund	0.000	0.089	0.038	0.051	0.133	−1.758*	−1.115
Prince Edward Island Venture Capital Fund	0.000	0.000	0.000	0.000	0.000	N/A	N/A
Foreign Venture Capital Fund	0.031	0.166	0.033	0.012	0.059	−1.991**	−0.041
Investee Firm and Investor in Same Province	0.969	0.853	0.970	0.966	0.916	1.803*	−0.026
Year of First Investment	1,996.844	1,997.914	1,997.258	1,997.750	1,998.122	−2.438**	−0.787
Year of Exit	1,999.313	2,001.629	2,001.621	2,002.224	2,001.290	−7.351***	−5.782***
Duration in Years from Investment to Exit	2.469	3.716	4.364	4.474	3.168	−3.363***	−4.267***

(*continued*)

Means and Proportions Test Statistics							
IPO vs. Buyback	IPO vs. Write-off	Acquisition vs. Secondary Sale	Acquisition vs. Buyback	Acquisition vs. Write-off	Secondary Sale vs. Buyback	Secondary Sale vs. Write-off	Buyback vs. Write-off
1.117	−0.926	2.933***	3.541***	0.424	−0.190	−2.524**	−2.935***
−0.660	0.199	0.971	0.588	1.857*	−0.513	0.703	1.333
−1.235	−2.115**	1.416	0.298	−2.237**	−1.196	−2.632***	−2.152**
−0.159	0.835	−1.527	−0.124	1.291	1.249	2.396**	1.318
1.701*	0.445	6.287***	6.401***	4.466***	−1.217	−2.619***	−1.764*
−3.345***	−2.023**	−4.632***	−5.026***	−2.988***	0.545	2.048**	1.812*
N/A	N/A	N/A	N/A	N/A	N/A	N/A	N/A
N/A	N/A	N/A	N/A	N/A	N/A	N/A	N/A
−1.306	−2.182**	1.358	1.231	−1.206	−0.410	−2.064**	−2.139**
N/A	N/A	N/A	N/A	N/A	N/A	N/A	N/A
0.755	−0.612	2.755***	4.211***	2.664***	0.966	−0.768	−1.903*
0.090	1.015	−2.549**	−3.136***	−1.589	0.152	1.409	1.580
−1.831*	−2.769***	1.696*	0.476	−0.707	−1.095	−2.095**	−0.997
−8.264***	−5.893***	0.026	−2.272**	1.424	−1.681*	0.969	3.268***
−4.759***	−1.824*	−1.894*	−2.430**	2.118**	−0.279	3.360***	3.994***

Table 20.3 Correlation

This table presents correlations across selected variables in the dataset. Correlations significant at the 5% level are

		(1)	(2)	(3)	(4)	(5)	(6)	(7)	(8)	(9)	(10)	(11)	(12)
(1)	IPO	1.00											
(2)	Acquisition	−0.20	1.00										
(3)	Secondary Sale	−0.10	−0.30	1.00									
(4)	Buyback	−0.14	−0.42	−0.21	1.00								
(5)	Write-off	−0.13	−0.40	−0.19	−0.27	1.00							
(6)	Log (Deal Size)	0.17	0.15	−0.09	−0.07	−0.14	1.00						
(7)	Number of Syndicated Investors	0.06	0.12	−0.06	−0.13	0.01	0.42	1.00					
(8)	Life Science Industry	0.20	0.04	−0.07	−0.10	−0.01	−0.07	0.06	1.00				
(9)	Other High-tech Industry	−0.06	0.32	−0.17	−0.22	0.01	0.16	0.15	−0.41	1.00			
(10)	Common Equity and/or Warrants	0.17	0.01	0.07	−0.12	−0.05	0.05	−0.09	0.06	0.02	1.00		
(11)	Preferred Equity	−0.08	0.04	−0.04	−0.03	0.06	0.08	0.06	−0.03	0.06	−0.21	1.00	

Matrix

highlighted in underline font.

(13)	(14)	(15)	(16)	(17)	(18)	(19)	(20)	(21)	(22)	(23)	(24)	(25)	(26)

(continued)

Table 20.3

		(1)	(2)	(3)	(4)	(5)	(6)	(7)	(8)	(9)	(10)	(11)	(12)
(12)	Convertible Preferred Equity	−0.02	0.04	−0.10	−0.03	0.07	0.02	0.04	−0.06	0.12	−0.23	−0.07	1.00
(13)	Debt	−0.10	−0.08	0.10	0.09	−0.02	−0.13	−0.14	−0.07	−0.13	−0.32	−0.11	−0.13
(14)	Convertible Debt	−0.06	0.06	−0.01	−0.03	0.00	−0.10	0.07	0.19	−0.03	−0.23	−0.08	−0.10
(15)	Common and Debt and/or Preferred Equity	0.00	−0.15	0.04	0.13	0.02	−0.10	−0.08	−0.04	−0.17	−0.27	−0.10	−0.11
(16)	Seed or Early Stage	−0.11	0.15	−0.13	−0.07	0.07	−0.16	0.14	0.17	0.13	0.01	0.05	0.06
(17)	Expansion	0.08	−0.01	−0.05	−0.01	0.01	0.17	−0.07	−0.12	0.08	0.00	−0.03	0.03
(18)	Limited Partnership Venture Capital Fund	0.13	0.24	−0.16	−0.15	−0.08	0.02	0.03	0.12	0.24	0.07	0.00	0.07
(19)	Corporate Venture Capital Fund	0.10	0.10	−0.14	−0.10	0.04	0.02	0.00	−0.03	0.08	−0.01	0.05	0.08
(20)	Government or LSVCC	−0.12	−0.36	0.27	0.28	0.00	−0.15	−0.17	−0.06	−0.37	−0.05	−0.01	−0.13

(continued)

(13)	(14)	(15)	(16)	(17)	(18)	(19)	(20)	(21)	(22)	(23)	(24)	(25)	(26)
1.00													
−0.13	1.00												
−0.11	−0.10	1.00											
−0.11	0.11	−0.13	1.00										
0.03	−0.05	0.01	−0.72	1.00									
−0.12	0.13	−0.17	0.12	−0.02	1.00								
−0.01	−0.03	−0.04	−0.08	0.13	−0.21	1.00							
0.16	−0.09	0.20	−0.14	−0.01	−0.68	−0.37	1.00						

(continued)

Table 20.3

		(1)	(2)	(3)	(4)	(5)	(6)	(7)	(8)	(9)	(10)	(11)	(12)
(21)	Investor and Investee in Same Province	0.05	−0.17	0.08	0.10	0.01	−0.16	0.05	−0.01	−0.09	−0.08	−0.02	−0.02
(22)	Ontario Entrepreneur	0.02	0.30	−0.20	−0.14	−0.06	0.29	0.06	−0.14	0.39	0.06	0.06	−0.01
(23)	Quebec Entrepreneur	−0.04	−0.36	0.20	0.22	0.07	−0.34	−0.10	0.09	−0.32	−0.07	−0.03	−0.10
(24)	Log (1 + MSCI Returns in Year of Exit)	−0.04	−0.04	0.04	0.05	−0.03	0.02	0.08	−0.04	−0.04	−0.05	0.04	−0.04
(25)	Log (1 + MSCI Returns in Year Prior to Exit)	0.06	−0.07	−0.05	0.11	−0.03	−0.01	−0.02	0.00	−0.11	−0.06	−0.06	0.07
(26)	Dummy for Exit in 1999	0.08	0.03	0.06	−0.11	−0.02	0.03	0.09	0.00	−0.03	0.02	−0.01	−0.03
(27)	Dummy for Exit in 2000	0.19	−0.05	−0.11	−0.13	0.16	−0.02	0.00	0.06	−0.03	0.00	−0.01	0.01

(continued)

(13)	(14)	(15)	(16)	(17)	(18)	(19)	(20)	(21)	(22)	(23)	(24)	(25)	(26)
0.07	−0.03	0.11	−0.06	−0.01	−0.11	0.05	0.21	1.00					
−0.06	−0.05	−0.14	0.04	0.04	0.19	0.03	−0.29	−0.04	1.00				
0.14	0.03	0.19	−0.02	−0.11	−0.22	0.00	0.33	0.25	−0.71	1.00			
−0.05	0.05	0.03	0.00	0.02	0.01	−0.03	0.02	0.08	−0.08	0.08	1.00		
0.01	−0.02	0.12	−0.12	0.04	−0.05	0.01	0.07	0.07	−0.11	0.12	0.11	1.00	
−0.01	0.04	0.03	−0.07	0.12	0.07	−0.04	−0.02	0.05	−0.02	0.00	0.37	−0.19	1.00
−0.03	0.00	0.03	−0.02	0.09	−0.02	0.03	0.03	0.06	−0.03	0.05	−0.08	0.48	−0.11

intermediary fund. As of 2004, all institutional actors that make direct investments are reported as "institutional direct" funds, although this category largely corresponds with funds previously reported as hybrid funds (i.e., most are public pension funds). Foreign funds are mostly U.S.-based limited partnership funds operating in Canada.

LSVCCs are the largest category of funds in Canada that consist of roughly 50% of all venture capital under management as at 2004 (Cumming and MacIntosh, 2007).[14] LSVCCs are governed by statute, and their statutory covenants are arguably much less efficient than that of limited partnership venture capital funds (Cumming and MacIntosh, 2007; Osbourne and Sandler, 1998). LSVCC constraints include (1) all LSVCCs are constrained to invest only in the sponsoring jurisdiction (as determined by the location of the investee firm's assets, employment, or other similar factors); (2) an eight-year investor lock-in period; (3) restrictions on the number of allowable funds in certain jurisdictions; (4) statutory penalties for failure to reinvest fixed percentages of contributed capital in private entrepreneurial firms within a stated period of time (typically one to three years); and (5) constraints on the size and nature of investment in any given entrepreneurial firm. These constraints can have the effect of forcing investments to be made in inferior firms and/or without adequate due diligence, limiting competition across LSVCCs and limiting investor discipline through threat of withdrawal of capital contributions. Many covenants suitably designed to mitigate opportunistic behavior among limited partnership venture capital funds are *completely absent* among LSVCCs, including restrictions on the use of debt, restrictions on co-investment by the organization's earlier or latter funds, restrictions on co-investment by venture capital fund managers, restrictions on fundraising by venture capital fund managers, and restrictions on other actions of venture capital fund managers, among other things (Chapter 5; see also Gompers and Lerner, 1996). In Chapter 5, Gompers and Lerner (1999), showed that the use of these covenants varies depending on the characteristics of fund managers and economic conditions, and attribute this flexibility to one of the major factors leading to the success of the U.S. venture capital industry. By contrast, LSVCC covenants are inflexible across fund managers and invariant over time (subject to statutory changes). Given the inefficient governance of LSVCCs through poorly designed statutes, we may expect LSVCCs to provide less governance to their investee entrepreneurial firms. This reduces the probability of IPO and acquisition exits for LSVCC-backed firms. Furthermore, the inefficient LSVCC governance also means that LSVCCs have a diminished capacity to certify the quality of their investee entrepreneurial firms to IPO investors. This further reduces the probability of IPO exits for LSVCC-backed firms.

Figure 20.2 and Table 20.2 categorize the percentage of exit outcomes for each of the different venture capital funds. Most important, notice that the

[14]Some of the western European countries in the 1990 to 2005 period also experienced periods with a significant increase in the extent of government participation in venture capital funds; see the EVCA yearbooks (www.evca.com) as well as Armour and Cumming (2006).

data in Figure 20.2 are presented for the venture capital fund(s) that invested in the first round (i.e., the deal originators). Corporate venture capital funds and limited partnership venture capital funds have had much greater success at picking firms that eventually achieved an IPO than government venture capital funds, hybrid venture capital funds, and LSVCCs, which have had a much higher proportion of buyback exits. LSVCCs have had the greatest proportion of both buybacks and secondary sales, which are inferior exit outcomes. This is consistent with evidence of poor governance provided by LSVCCs (Cumming and MacIntosh, 2006, 2007). Table 20.2 also shows LSVCCs are statistically most likely to exit by secondary sales, followed by buybacks, write-offs, IPOs, and acquisitions. Corporate venture capital funds and limited partnership venture capital funds, by contrast, are statistically more likely to exit with IPOs and acquisitions than secondary sales, buybacks, and write-offs.

The percentage of exits by the stage of first investment is depicted in Figure 20.3 and Table 20.2. Write-offs are more often seen at the seed investment stage and are least likely to have been pursuant to buyouts and turnaround investments. IPOs are more likely for later-stage investments such as buyouts. Secondary sales and buybacks were most often a result of turnaround investments. Acquisitions were more often seen in early-stage and seed investments than later-stage investments.

The percentage of exit outcomes by type of security used at the initial investment round is depicted in Figure 20.4 and Table 20.2. For most IPOs, the security used at the initial investment is unknown; however, for those which are known, common equity was used for investments that went public. Securities for which the venture capital fund has downside protection are more likely to be divested through acquisitions than IPOs. These findings are consistent with the prediction that strong venture capital fund control rights are associated with acquisitions and weak venture capital fund control rights are associated with IPOs. Table 20.1 is consistent in that it shows that IPOs are also less likely than acquisitions when the security used has downside protection for the venture capital fund (although these differences between IPOs and acquisitions are significant and at the 10% level for debt only). As well, the data indicate buyback exits are more likely for investments that involved some debt, which is also expected as debt does not afford ownership to the venture capital fund and the entrepreneurial firm repays the principal upon expiration of the debt investment.

Table 20.2 shows the percentage of exit outcomes for firms in the life science industries (medical, environmental, and biotechnology), other types of high-tech (computers, electronics, Internet), and non-high-tech (such as manufacturing). Life science firms were more likely to go public than other types of high-tech and non-high-tech firms. Non-high-tech firms are more likely to be exited as buybacks, which is expected as such firms typically have cash flows that may enable the entrepreneur to repurchase the interests of the venture capital funds.

Table 20.2 presents the exit data for transactions for which the venture capital fund and the entrepreneurial firm were and were not resident in the same province at the time of first investment. Exits via acquisitions are more likely where the venture capital fund and the entrepreneurial firm are not residing in the same province, and more likely to be IPOs where the venture capital fund and the entrepreneurial firm are residing in the same province. Note that secondary sales and write-offs are more likely for investments within the same province. Figure 20.2 indicated that LSVCCs are more likely to experience buybacks and secondary sales. LSVCCs are also bound by statute to invest in the same province; hence, it is not surprising that buybacks and secondary sales are observed where the venture capital fund and the entrepreneurial firm are residing in the same province.

Table 20.2 shows the exit outcomes for the actual province in which the entrepreneurial firm is based. Canada comprises 10 provinces: British Columbia (BC), Alberta (AB), Saskatchewan (SK), Manitoba (MB), Ontario (ON), Quebec (QC), Newfoundland (NF), New Brunswick (NB), Nova Scotia (NS), and Prince Edward Island (PEI). As well, there are the Northern Territories (NT). Very few exits are from firms based in the Maritime Provinces (NF, NB, NS, and PEI). There was only one exit from NB (which was an IPO). The majority of activity is from BC, ON, and QC. Venture capital–backed firms in BC, ON, and QC have had a greater number of IPOs and acquisitions than firms in the other provinces (Table 20.1), although the IPO and acquisition exit outcomes as a fraction of total exits within the province are high in AB, SK, NS, and NB.

Table 20.2 also presents evidence showing the exit outcomes in relation to the location of the venture capital fund. We may expect regional differences that are in part associated with different skill levels among venture capital funds in different provinces, as well as proximity to greater levels of economic activity. The data indicate IPOs are more likely to have been financed by venture capital funds based in ON. Write-offs are more likely to have resulted among venture capital funds in SK and NS. Foreign venture capital funds are more likely to have exited by acquisitions.

Table 20.2 further depicts the exit outcomes by the duration of investment (time in years from first investment to exit) and the number of syndicated venture capital funds at the time of first investment. IPOs and acquisitions have a slightly higher average number of syndicated venture capital funds relative to secondary sales and buybacks. This is in part consistent with the idea that syndication facilitates screening and value-added. In Chapter 12 we showed that LSVCCs are less likely to syndicate, and this is consistent with the greater proportion of LSVCC exits as secondary sales buybacks (Figure 20.2). Write-offs also have a slightly higher average number of syndicated venture capital funds for the first investment round.

The shortest time to exit is experienced for IPOs, followed by write-offs and acquisitions (Table 20.2). Buybacks and secondary sales have the longest investment duration. The data indicate that venture capital funds rush to IPO to take advantage of stronger market conditions, consistent with the U.S. evidence in Giot and Schwienbacher (2007). Table 20.2 also presents the size of the average venture capital investment and deal size (including syndicated venture capital fund investments) for the first round investment for each exit type.

IPOs and acquisitions were much larger initial investments. Secondary sales, buybacks, and write-offs were much smaller initial investments and thereby possibly riskier investments resulting in worse outcomes. These differences are statistically significant, as indicated in Table 20.1.

The univariate relationships across the variables are further described by the correlation matrix in Table 20.3. The correlations provide similar empirical support for the view that IPOs are more often related to common equity transactions, larger deal sizes, and nongovernment venture capital funds, among the other things just discussed. The correlations also provide guidance regarding areas of concern for collinearity problems in the regression analyses, as provided following. Notice that each type of security is used by each type of venture capital fund (see Chapters 11–14 for additional evidence on security design by venture capital fund type), and thus it is possible to isolate the effect of venture capital fund type and security design on exit outcomes in the regression analyses following.

20.4 Regression Analyses

The regression analyses in this section consider the factors that give rise to each of the five alternative exit outcomes: IPOs, acquisitions, secondary sales, buybacks, and write-offs. Multinomial logit regressions are used to simultaneously capture these alternative exit routes. Five alternative regressions are presented in Table 20.4, Panels A to E, to show robustness to alternative specifications. Alternative specifications are available upon request. The first regression presented in Panel A of Table 20.4 considers the full sample of 518 exits and a rather complete set of explanatory variables. The second and third regressions (Table 20.4, Panels B and C, respectively) also use the full sample but with a different set of explanatory variables to assess robustness. The fourth regression (Panel D) considers the subsample of exits for which the duration of investment from date of first investment to exit was not less than two years. Panels E and F present regressions whereby the subsamples considered are exits for which investment duration was not less than three and four years, respectively. Panels D, E, and F consider more parsimonious specifications given the reduction in the sample size of exited investments. The full sample consists of 518 exits but only 32 IPOs. For instance, the reduction in the sample size gives rise to 8 IPO exits in Panel E, so it is appropriate to reduce the set of right-hand-side variables. The regressions in Panels D, E, and F are important robustness checks to ascertain the robustness of the results in regards to financing structures to potential endogeneity.[15] Deals completed a greater number of

[15]Additional robustness checks with different explanatory variables and differently defined samples (excluding bubble periods, including nonexits, excluding different types of investors, etc.) are available upon request. A wide variety of alternative specifications (not presented for reasons of conciseness) were considered and yielded similar results.

Table 20.4 Multinomial

This table presents multinomial logit regressions of the probability of each exit outcome. Panel A variables with the full sample. Panels D, E, and F present subsamples of the data whereby investment respectively. Ordinary multinomial logit coefficients are not presented; rather, marginal effects are economic significance. White's (1980) robust standard errors are used in all regressions. *, **, ***

Panel A. Full

	IPO		Acquisition	
	Marginal Effect	t-Statistic	Marginal Effect	t-Statistic
Constant	−0.127	−2.476**	−0.146	−0.622
Venture Capital Fund Characteristics				
Limited Partnership Venture Capital Fund	0.024	2.081**	0.161	2.394**
Number of Syndicated Venture Capital Funds	1.202E-05	0.004	0.016	0.639
Entrepreneurial Firm Characteristics				
Life Science Industry	0.036	2.349***	0.399	4.231***
Other High-tech Industry	0.005	0.504	0.356	4.938***
Seed or Early Stage	−0.032	−2.172**	0.068	0.659
Expansion Stage	−0.016	−1.465	−0.005	−0.049
Log (Deal Size)	0.009	2.030**	0.031	1.219
Venture Capital Fund and Entrepreneur in Same Province	0.036	1.785*	−0.112	−1.148
Transaction Characteristics				
Common Equity and/or Warrants	0.022	1.966**	−0.004	−0.062
Convertible Securities	−0.008	−0.601	−0.007	−0.080
Economic Conditions				
Ontario Entrepreneur	−0.015	−1.354	0.012	0.155
Quebec Entrepreneur	−0.014	−1.472	−0.309	−3.935***
Log (1 + MSCI Index in Year of Exit)	−0.049	−1.847*	−0.118	−0.924
Log (1 + MSCI Index in Year Prior to Exit)	0.007	0.296	0.137	1.135
Dummy for Exit in 1999	0.049	2.211**	0.358	2.337**
Dummy for Exit in 2000	0.028	1.954*	0.028	0.326
Model Diagnostics				
Number of Observations	518			
Log Likehood	−579.5458			
Pseudo R^2	0.235			
Chi-square	356.641***			

Regression Analyses

considers the full sample. Panels B and C consider different sets of explanatory
duration from first investment to exit is not less than 2, 3, and 4 years,
presented to explicitly highlight the statistical significance alongside the
Significant at the 10%, 5%, and 1% levels, respectively.

Sample

Secondary Sale		**Buyback**		**Write-off**	
Marginal Effect	**t-Statistic**	**Marginal Effect**	**t-Statistic**	**Marginal Effect**	**t-Statistic**
0.062	0.512	−0.131	−0.704	0.342	1.777*
−0.071	−1.524	−0.013	−0.216	−0.101	−1.630
0.003	0.221	−0.057	−2.413**	0.038	1.800*
−0.104	−2.039**	−0.259	−3.404***	−0.072	−0.929
−0.071	−2.032**	−0.243	−4.635***	−0.046	−0.822
−0.122	−3.021***	0.009	0.139	0.076	0.880
−0.107	−2.547**	0.027	0.388	0.101	1.127
−0.007	−0.603	0.023	1.261	−0.055	−2.757***
0.069	0.899	0.104	1.028	−0.097	−1.127
0.061	1.870*	−0.074	−1.464	−0.005	−0.092
−0.019	−0.370	−0.017	−0.259	0.050	0.749
−0.112	−2.103**	0.084	1.079	0.030	0.410
0.049	1.170	0.219	3.081***	0.055	0.801
0.034	0.506	0.098	0.953	0.034	0.325
−0.062	−1.019	0.196	2.197**	−0.278	−2.665***
0.024	0.391	−0.452	−2.551**	0.021	0.175
−0.081	−1.498	−0.265	−3.638***	0.290	4.291***

(*continued*)

Table 20.4

Panel B. Robustness Check with

	IPO		Acquisition	
	Marginal Effect	t-Statistic	Marginal Effect	t-Statistic
Constant	−0.107	−2.296**	0.055	0.232
Venture Capital Fund Characteristics				
Corporate Venture Capital Fund	0.015	1.202	0.282	2.362**
Government Venture Capital Fund or LSVCC	−0.021	−1.841*	−0.229	−3.137**
Number of Syndicated Venture Capital Funds	0.000	0.082	0.006	0.212
Entrepreneurial Firm Characteristics				
Life Science Industry	0.039	2.312**	0.410	4.185***
Other High-tech Industry	0.007	0.702	0.332	4.389***
Seed or Early Stage	−0.036	−2.254**	0.042	0.384
Expansion Stage	−0.021	−1.720*	−0.040	−0.360
Log (Deal Size)	0.008	1.951*	0.026	1.013
Venture Capital Fund and Entrepreneur in Same Province	0.032	1.591	−0.064	−0.626
Transaction Characteristics				
Common Equity and/or Warrants	0.025	2.039**	0.014	0.206
Convertible Securities	−0.007	−0.478	−0.027	−0.321
Economic Conditions				
Ontario Entrepreneur	−0.014	−1.274	−0.032	−0.387
Quebec Entrepreneur	−0.013	−1.265	−0.336	−4.070***
Log (1 + MSCI Index in Year of Exit)	−0.050	−1.801*	−0.103	−0.781
Log (1 + MSCI Index in Year Prior to Exit)	0.000	0.014	0.130	1.045
Dummy for Exit in 1999	0.053	2.257**	0.388	2.455**
Dummy for Exit in 2000	0.031	2.004**	0.042	0.462
Model Diagnostics				
Number of Observations	518			
Log Likehood	−559.658			
Pseudo R^2	0.262			
Chi-square	396.420***			

(*continued*)

Alternative Variables and Full Sample					
Secondary Sale		Buyback		Write-off	
Marginal Effect	t-Statistic	Marginal Effect	t-Statistic	Marginal Effect	t-Statistic
−0.028	−0.348	−0.241	−1.229	0.321	1.570
−0.351	−3.102***	−0.136	−1.236	0.191	1.902*
0.071	2.047**	0.146	2.309**	0.034	0.503
0.014	1.562	−0.053	−2.142**	0.034	1.503
−0.071	−1.882*	−0.268	−3.405***	−0.110	−1.305
−0.040	−1.630	−0.229	−4.165***	−0.070	−1.126
−0.078	−2.337**	−0.006	−0.079	0.078	0.834
−0.060	−1.918*	0.029	0.393	0.093	0.963
−0.004	−0.515	0.026	1.361	−0.056	−2.660***
0.038	0.771	0.087	0.821	−0.094	−1.002
0.035	1.522	−0.071	−1.331	−0.003	−0.051
−0.008	−0.262	0.010	0.148	0.032	0.448
−0.063	−1.694*	0.102	1.270	0.008	0.105
0.038	1.297	0.252	3.325***	0.060	0.806
0.018	0.414	0.099	0.919	0.036	0.320
−0.033	−0.846	0.211	2.251**	−0.309	−2.759***
0.004	0.093	−0.462	−2.562**	0.017	0.138
−0.070	−1.768*	−0.318	−4.120***	0.315	4.361***

(*continued*)

Table 20.4

Panel C. Additional Robustness Check with

	IPO		Acquisition	
	Marginal Effect	t-Statistic	Marginal Effect	t-Statistic
Constant	−0.144	−3.029***	−0.377	−2.204**
Venture Capital Fund Characteristics				
Government Venture Capital Fund or LSVCC	−0.036	−2.262**	−0.331	−5.321***
Number of Syndicated Venture Capital Funds	0.003	0.700	−0.020	−0.869
Entrepreneurial Firm Characteristics				
Life Science Industry or Other High-tech Industry	0.015	1.010	0.347	5.274***
Seed or Early Stage	−0.026	−1.926*	0.078	1.383
Log (Deal Size)	0.010	1.871*	0.068	3.114***
Transaction Characteristics				
Common Equity and/or Warrants	0.050	3.148***	0.003	0.049
Economic Conditions				
Log (1 + MSCI Index in Year of Exit)	−0.070	−1.755*	−0.130	−1.040
Log (1 + MSCI Index in Year Prior to Exit)	0.018	0.487	0.078	0.673
Dummy for Exit in 1999	0.079	2.558**	0.313	2.166**
Dummy for Exit in 2000	0.047	2.258**	0.034	0.401
Model Diagnostics				
Number of Observations	518			
Log Likehood	−603.762			
Pseudo R^2	0.203			
Chi-square	308.209***			

years prior to exit are less likely prone to endogeneity (potentially endogenous variables include the choice of security and location). Where the regressions provide stable estimated effects for different subsamples with different investment duration, we would be less concerned that estimates are biased by endogeneity. Table 20.4 presents the marginal effects, not the standard multinomial logit estimates, to highlight the economic significance of the results alongside the statistical significance.

Table 20.4, Panel A, presents the first multinomial regression with the full sample and a large number of explanatory variables. The first set of explanatory

(*continued*)

Alternative Variables and Full Sample					
Secondary Sale		Buyback		Write-off	
Marginal Effect	t-Statistic	Marginal Effect	t-Statistic	Marginal Effect	t-Statistic
0.023	0.270	0.102	0.797	0.397	2.832***
0.187	5.236***	0.205	4.045***	−0.026	−0.484
0.023	1.830*	−0.034	−1.509	0.028	1.401
−0.092	−3.112***	−0.203	−4.510***	−0.067	−1.268
−0.058	−2.081**	−0.001	−0.026	0.008	0.157
−0.023	−2.176**	0.000	−0.017	−0.055	−3.043***
0.053	1.893*	−0.078	−1.694*	−0.029	−0.576
0.046	0.727	0.121	1.205	0.034	0.327
−0.018	−0.318	0.213	2.476**	−0.291	−2.838***
0.017	0.292	−0.411	−2.401**	0.002	0.019
−0.118	−2.317**	−0.269	−3.809***	0.305	4.629***

variables comprises a variable for limited partnership venture capital funds and the number of syndicated investors. Panel B considers variables for corporate venture capital funds and government venture capital funds. These variables are not all simultaneously included in the same regression to avoid collinearity problems. These variables are used to test Hypotheses 20.1 to 20.4. The second set of explanatory variables comprises variables for entrepreneurial firm characteristics, including dummy variables for firms in life science and other types of high-tech industries and dummy variables for the seed/early and expansion stage of development at first investment (a single variable for seed

Table 20.4

Panel D. Robustness Check Excluding

	IPO		Acquisition	
	Marginal Effect	t-Statistic	Marginal Effect	t-Statistic
Constant	−0.068	−1.933*	−0.511	−2.597***
Venture Capital Fund Characteristics				
Government Venture Capital Fund or LSVCC	−0.016	−1.571	−0.348	−5.090***
Number of Syndicated Venture Capital Funds	0.005	1.472	−0.020	−0.683
Entrepreneurial Firm Characteristics				
Life Science Industry or Other High-tech Industry	0.020	1.749*	0.402	5.559***
Seed or Early Stage	−0.010	−1.146	0.066	1.030
Log (Deal Size)	0.001	0.248	0.082	3.183***
Transaction Characteristics				
Common Equity and/or Warrants	0.037	2.329**	0.009	0.131
Economic Conditions				
Log (1 + MSCI Index in Year of Exit)	−0.030	−1.237	−0.169	−1.239
Log (1 + MSCI Index in Year Prior to Exit)	0.009	0.461	0.042	0.343
Dummy for Exit in 1999	0.038	1.736*	0.327	2.020**
Dummy for Exit in 2000	0.024	1.616	0.061	0.633
Model Diagnostics				
Number of Observations	430			
Log Likehood	−490.663			
Pseudo R^2	0.210			
Chi-square	261.578***			

and early stages is used to avoid collinearity). Dummy variables for non-high-tech firms and other stages of development are suppressed to avoid collinearity. As well, a dummy variable is used to indicate whether the venture capital fund and entrepreneurial firm are based in the same province, and a variable for the log of deal size is included. These variables are used to test Hypotheses 20.5 to 20.8. The third set of explanatory variables includes transaction characteristics variables for the proportional use of common equity and convertible securities. Variables for straight debt, straight preferred equity, and/or mixes of straight debt and equity are suppressed to avoid collinearity problems. These variables

(*continued*)

Investment Duration <2 Years					
Secondary Sale		Buyback		Write-off	
Marginal Effect	t-Statistic	Marginal Effect	t-Statistic	Marginal Effect	t-Statistic
0.012	0.116	0.214	1.404	0.353	2.278**
0.207	4.959***	0.204	3.487***	−0.048	−0.820
0.032	1.999**	−0.041	−1.405	0.024	0.944
−0.104	−2.956**	−0.245	−4.672***	−0.074	−1.305
−0.061	−1.811*	−0.011	−0.209	0.016	0.290
−0.025	−1.925*	−0.007	−0.360	−0.050	−2.448**
0.069	2.044**	−0.087	−1.643	−0.027	−0.495
0.049	0.671	0.064	0.553	0.086	0.758
−0.031	−0.474	0.217	2.236**	−0.237	−2.214**
0.025	0.368	−0.408	−2.123**	0.018	0.143
−0.110	−1.831*	−0.284	−3.390***	0.308	4.310***

are included to test Hypotheses 20.9 and 20.10. Finally, four control variables are used for economic conditions: dummies for the year of exit for 1999 and 2000 (for the Internet bubble) and the returns to the MSCI index in the year of exit as well as the year prior to exit.

The data indicate venture capital fund characteristics strongly influence the exit outcomes. Panel A of Table 20.4 shows strong evidence in support of Hypothesis 20.1 that limited partnership venture capital funds achieve better exit outcomes than their counterparts. The regressions indicate limited partnership venture capital funds are 2.4% more likely to achieve an IPO and

Table 20.4

Panel E. Robustness Check Excluding

	IPO		Acquisition	
	Marginal Effect	t-Statistic	Marginal Effect	t-Statistic
Constant	−0.073	−1.774*	−0.267	−1.320
Venture Capital Fund Characteristics				
Government Venture Capital Fund or LSVCC	−0.019	−1.481	−0.450	−6.211***
Number of Syndicated Venture Capital Funds	0.006	1.471	−0.004	−0.130
Entrepreneurial Firm Characteristics				
Seed or Early Stage	0.003	0.279	0.166	2.488**
Log (Deal Size)	0.002	0.490	0.093	3.266***
Transaction Characteristics				
Common Equity and/or Warrants	0.034	2.097**	−0.037	−0.515
Economic Conditions				
Log (1 + MSCI Index in Year of Exit)	0.006	0.237	−0.318	−2.189**
Log (1 + MSCI Index in Year Prior to Exit)	−0.030	−1.137	−0.121	−0.938
Dummy for Exit in 2000	0.048	1.983**	0.119	1.083
Model Diagnostics				
Number of Observations	325			
Log Likehood	−390.739			
Pseudo R^2	0.167			
Chi-square	157.077***			

16.1% more likely to achieve an acquisition than the other types of venture capital funds. In Panel B, notice that, consistent with Hypothesis 20.2, corporate venture capital funds are 28.2% more likely to have an acquisition exit than limited partnership venture capital funds and other types of venture capital funds (the comparison is in reference to dummy variables for other types of venture capital funds that were suppressed to avoid collinearity). This is consistent with Gompers and Lerner (1999a) and Riyanto and Schwienbacher (2006), who show that corporate venture capital funds are strategic venture capital funds and not just primarily interested in financial profits (see Chapter 13). Acquisitions facilitate the merging of interests with regard to transaction synergies for certain technologies. Similarly, secondary sales are 25.1% less likely for corporate venture capital funds, as corporate venture capital funds

(*continued*)

Investment Duration <3 Years

Secondary Sale		Buyback		Write-off	
Marginal Effect	t-Statistic	Marginal Effect	t-Statistic	Marginal Effect	t-Statistic
0.032	0.278	0.053	0.315	0.255	1.608
0.226	4.898***	0.274	4.290***	−0.030	−0.526
0.021	1.023	−0.038	−1.123	0.016	0.557
−0.109	−2.872***	−0.064	−1.147	0.004	0.076
−0.035	−2.197**	−0.012	−0.516	−0.048	−2.158**
0.070	1.783*	−0.080	−1.338	0.013	0.229
0.125	1.578	0.037	0.291	0.151	1.296
−0.034	−0.475	0.343	3.251***	−0.158	−1.475
−0.095	−1.315	−0.352	−3.311***	0.280	3.665***

are less interested in selling to other competing investors technology for which they have invested and not [yet, possibly] brought to fruition. Corporate venture capital funds are also 20.1% more likely to have a write-off than limited partnership venture capital funds; possibly suggesting they are comparatively less skilled than limited partnership venture capital funds (as also suggested by Gompers and Lerner, 1999a).

In Panel B notice as well that government venture capital funds (predominantly LSVCCs) are 2.1% less likely to achieve an IPO than limited partnership venture capital funds, 22.9% less likely to achieve an acquisition, 7.1% more likely to achieve a secondary sale, and 14.6% more likely to achieve a buyback. This is consistent with our expectations (Hypothesis 20.3) that

Table 20.4

Panel F. Robustness Check Excluding

	IPO		Acquisition	
	Marginal Effect	t-Statistic	Marginal Effect	t-Statistic
Constant	−0.105	−1.915*	−0.052	−0.255
Venture Capital Fund Characteristics				
Government Venture Capital Fund or LSVCC	−0.008	−0.393	−0.464	−5.693***
Number of Syndicated Venture Capital Funds	0.000	0.043	0.044	1.085
Entrepreneurial Firm Characteristics				
Log (Deal Size)	0.004	0.559	0.072	2.406**
Transaction Characteristics				
Common Equity and/or Warrants	0.044	2.201**	−0.038	−0.489
Economic Conditions				
Log (1 + MSCI Index in Year of Exit)	−0.029	−0.563	−0.379	−2.257**
Log (1 + MSCI Index in Year Prior to Exit)	0.039	1.070	−0.160	−1.215
Model Diagnostics				
Number of Observations	250			
Log Likehood	−307.538			
Pseudo R^2	0.123			
Chi-square	86.152***			

LSVCCs have inferior statutory governance mechanisms that lower the quality of their investments and thus have a worse exit track record.

The evidence on syndication is for the most part insignificant, or not robust. Panels A and B indicate a greater number of syndicated investors gives rise to a smaller probability of a buyback. An extra syndicated venture capital fund reduces the probability of a buyback by 5.7% in Panel A (and 5.3% in Panel B), and this effect is significant at the 5% level. This is intuitive, as buybacks are an undesirable exit outcome and syndicated venture capital funds are more likely to more effectively screen potential investee entrepreneurial firms via due diligence, as well as add value in order to reduce the probability of a buyback. However, this effect is not robust in Panels C to F. As well, notice that Panel A suggests syndicates are more likely to achieve a write-off, but this effect is only significant at the 10% level and not robust in the other panels of Table 20.4. Overall, the data do not offer very strong support for Hypothesis 20.4.

(*continued*)

Investment Duration <4 Years

Secondary Sale		Buyback		Write-off	
Marginal Effect	t-Statistic	Marginal Effect	t-Statistic	Marginal Effect	t-Statistic
−0.087	−0.668	0.089	0.497	0.155	1.079
0.258	4.757***	0.246	3.451***	−0.032	−0.556
0.021	0.805	−0.071	−1.557	0.006	0.177
−0.029	−1.575	−0.014	−0.569	−0.033	−1.561
0.069	1.497	−0.097	−1.440	0.022	0.385
0.216	2.273**	0.165	1.084	0.027	0.214
−0.121	−1.566	0.200	1.745*	0.041	0.436

Table 20.4 also indicates that a variety of entrepreneurial firm characteristics are significant determinants of exit outcomes. Panel A shows life science firms are 3.6% more likely to go public and 39.9% more likely to be acquired than non-high-tech firms, and 10.4% less likely to be sold as a secondary sale and 25.9% less likely to be bought back than non-high-tech firms. Other types of high-tech firms (electronics, computer, etc.) are 35.6% more likely to be acquired, 7.1% less likely to be secondary sales, and 24.3% less likely to be bought back than non-high-tech firms. These results are expected as positive cash-flow nontech businesses (e.g., manufacturing) are more likely to be able to repurchase the venture capital fund's interests, unlike high-tech firms. The statistical and economic significance of these effects is very similar in the other panels in Table 20.4. Overall, this is very strong evidence in support of Hypothesis 20.5. Early-stage firms are 3.2% less likely to go public than late-stage investments, which is consistent with Hypothesis 20.6.

The estimated regression coefficients in Table 20.4, Panel A, indicate deal size is a relevant factor indicating the probability of an IPO exit outcome, consistent with Hypothesis 20.7. Larger initial investments are more likely to go public, but the economic significance is not large and the statistical significance is only at the 10% level. In particular, a Can$10,000,000 initial investment is 0.9% more likely to go public than a Can$1,000,000 initial investment. Given the log specification, increasing the size of the initial investment increases the probability of an IPO at a diminishing rate. A Can$20,000,000 investment is 0.2% more likely to go public than a Can$11,000,000 investment. First-round deal size is also an important determinant of write-offs, and this effect is statistically significant at the 1% level of significance. Write-offs are 5.6% less likely for Can$10,000,000 initial investments than a Can$1,000,000 initial investment, while a Can$20,000,000 initial investment is 1.5% less likely to be written off than a Can$11,000,000 investment.

Notice, however, that larger initial deal sizes are not more likely to go public in Panels C to E, unlike that for the full sample estimates in Panels A to C. One explanation for these different results is that size is more important in terms of meeting IPO listing standards in Canada for firms that have shorter track records, while length of operating history may be considered in lieu of size for smaller firms (Harris, 2006).

Hypothesis 20.8 conjectured that entrepreneur firms that are resident in the same province as their venture capital fund investor(s) are more likely to have better exit outcomes due to better screening and value-added. There is some support for this in Panel A of Table 20.4, which shows entrepreneurial firms in the same province as their investors are 3.6% more likely to go public. That effect, however, is statistically significant only at the 10% level of significance and not robust in the other Panels in Table 20.4.[16]

The data indicate that an IPO is 2.2% more likely when common equity is used in the transaction, and this effect is statistically significant at the 5% level. This supports the prediction (Hypothesis 20.9) that security design is important for IPO exits. We have already noted two alternative explanations for this effect: First, where both the entrepreneur and venture capital fund prefer an IPO exit, there is no conflict of interest between the entrepreneur and venture capital fund. However, in times of poor IPO markets when acquisitions may be relatively more attractive, entrepreneurs may prefer an IPO due to non-pecuniary benefits to the entrepreneur while venture capital funds prefer an acquisition. As such, common equity is more likely to be associated with an IPO because entrepreneurs have greater control rights and prefer IPO exits. Second, we may infer common equity is used for higher-quality entrepreneurs that seek and obtain greater control rights, and by venture capital funds that wish to signal to the investment bank(s) taking the firm public and the new

[16]Notice as well that, as discussed in Chapter 17, other evidence from the United States shows a positive association between geographic proximity and performance (Cumming and Dai, 2007).

public shareholders that the entrepreneur is of high quality (see Hypothesis 20.9 and accompanying text).[17]

Recall Panel C comprises a more parsimonious specification of right-hand-side variables than Panels A and B. The main difference with the regression results in Table 20.4, Panel C, is that the economic significance is larger for some of the key variables. Most notably, by not including the variable for convertible securities in Panel C (unlike Panels A and B), the economic significance of the common equity variable is twice as large for IPOs. IPOs are 5.0% more likely with common equity investments, and this effect is significant at the 1% level. Note as well that common equity is also 5.3% more likely to be associated with a secondary sale and 7.8% less likely to be associated with buybacks, and both of these effects are statistically significant at the 10% level. Hence, the support for Hypothesis 20.9 is quite robust to alternative specifications.

Table 20.4, Panels D, E, and F, provide specifications for which the sample excludes investments for which investment duration is less than two, three, and four years, respectively, from date of first investment to date of exit. These robustness checks are important to ascertain whether the estimates in Panels A, B, and C were subject to endogeneity biases in regards to transaction structures. Longer duration investments are less likely to have exited in the way contemplated at the time of first investment (that is, assuming the venture capital fund and entrepreneur contemplated the likely exit route at the time of first investment). The estimates do not appear to be significantly affected by endogeneity. For example, the statistical significance of the common equity variable in relation to IPO exits does not deviate from the 5% level of significance in Panels D to F, and the economic significance continues to remain at around the same level as in Panels A to C. The economic significance of the relation between common equity and IPOs is 3.7% in Panel D, 3.4% in Panel E, and 4.4% in Panel F (and it was 5.0% in Panel C, 2.5% in Panel B, and 2.2% in Panel A).

We do not find evidence of a relation between convertible securities and different exit outcomes. As such, while the data do support Hypothesis 20.9, the data do not support Hypothesis 20.10.

Finally, notice that many control variables are significant in the way that we would expect. The data provide support for the view that exit outcomes over the 1991 to 2004 period are affected by economic conditions. For example, in Panel A, IPOs are 4.9% more likely in 1999 and 2.8% more likely in 2000. Acquisitions are 35.8% more likely in 1999. Write-offs are also 29.0% more likely in 2000 (the date of the Internet bubble crash was April 14, 2000, and we may infer that the write-offs were likely in the latter part of 2000). The MSCI index variables are less informative than the Internet bubble dummy

[17]It is noteworthy that similar evidence of a correspondence between common equity and IPOs has been reported in the European venture capital market (see Chapter 21). Given similar results are observed in different institutional settings, this provides strong support for Hypothesis 20.9.

variables. The controls for regional differences, particularly for ON and QC, show some differences in that acquisitions are 30.9% less likely and buybacks 21.9% more likely in QC, while secondary sales are 11.2% less likely in ON.

Overall, the specification in Panel A of Table 20.4 provides a reasonable fit for the data with a pseudo R^2 of 23.5%. We also provide additional specifications in Panels B to F as robustness checks, as described above. The pseudo R^2 values for the robustness checks range from a low of 12.3% in Panel F (with the smallest subsample of the data) to 26.2% in Panel B.

20.4.1 *Additional Robustness Checks*

The regression results are in the main very robust to alternative specifications, with a few exceptions that were explicitly noted above. Alternative specifications not explicitly presented are available upon request. For instance, we dropped all turnaround and buyout transactions to see if the results were robust. Turnarounds and buyouts comprise 61 of the 518 exits in the sample. Dropping those observations did not materially impact the reported results.

Also, we had considered specifications that considered non-exited investments as well (e.g., to capture potentially "living dead" investments that have not yet been written off; see Ruhnka et al., 1992), but this did not materially affect the results (Cumming et al., 2006, adopt a similar procedure in estimates of the effect of legality on exit outcomes). The data are very comprehensive for the venture capital market in Canada, and comprise unique details regarding security design by venture capital funds, among other things described herein. Further research may consider other transaction and firm-specific details by hand-collecting information that is not in the Macdonald and Associates data, although this issue is beyond the scope of this chapter.

20.5 Conclusions

This chapter presented hypotheses based on the central theme that conditions of information asymmetries and agency costs are central to venture capital fund exit outcomes. Where venture capital funds are able to mitigate information asymmetries faced by the new owner(s) of the firm, and mitigate agency costs associated with entrepreneurial investment, better exit outcomes result. To this end, we conjectured IPOs and acquisitions would be more often associated with limited partnership venture capital funds, corporate venture capital funds would be more often associated with acquisitions and government venture capital funds more often associated with inferior exits (secondary sales, buybacks, and write-offs). We further conjectured that common equity investments which allocate relatively greater control rights to entrepreneurs would be more often associated with IPO exits, as well as developed other hypotheses pertaining to information asymmetries and agency costs.

We tested these hypotheses in this chapter with a comprehensive dataset comprising all venture capital–backed IPOs, acquisitions, secondary sales, buybacks, and write-offs in Canada over the period 1991 to 2004. We found evidence that venture capital–backed IPOs are statistically associated with larger deal sizes and high-tech and life sciences firms, and investments structured with the use of common equity. The significant and robust relation between common equity and IPOs highlights the importance of contractual corporate governance in facilitating exit outcomes, consistent with our theoretical expectations. Acquisitions are more likely for corporate venture capital funds, life science, and other high-tech firms. This evidence is consistent with prior work indicating corporate venture capital funds are unique with their strategic incentives for investment and not merely financial incentives. The data also indicate write-offs are more likely for smaller investments.

More important, the data show a strong influence of government subsidized LSVCCs on exit outcomes in Canada. As of 2004, LSVCCs comprise approximately 50% of capital under management in Canada and are an inferior government-sponsored organizational structure with inefficient statutory contractual corporate governance covenants. As summarized in this chapter, venture capital funds in Canada have had less success in achieving IPOs than venture capital funds in Australasia, Europe, and the United States. The Canadian data introduced in this chapter are consistent with the view that the dominant presence of LSVCCs in Canada has given rise to a high proportion of less successful exits by means of buybacks and secondary sales. The data in this chapter suggest that the policy objective associated with LSVCCs in terms of creating sustainable firms that will enhance entrepreneurial firm outcomes does not appear to have been successful.

Further research in the future could explore the role of governance structures and different types of venture capital funds in other countries, as well as IPO performance (see Chapter 21 for evidence from Europe). Exiting investments is a central part of the venture capital investment process, and rich detailed data on exits can always further our understanding of how venture capital investments are harvested.

Key Terms

IPO
Acquisition
Secondary sale
Buyback
Write-off
Pecking order of exits
Common equity
Warrants
Preferred equity
Convertible preferred equity
Debt
Convertible debt
Information asymmetries
Agency costs
Labour sponsored venture capital fund
Corporate venture capital fund
Limited partnership venture capital fund

Discussion Questions

20.1. True/False/Uncertain and explain why: "IPO exits generate higher returns than acquisition exits."

20.2. What is the pecking order of exit outcomes? Why is the ranking done in this way?

20.3. True/False/Uncertain and explain why: "Corporate venture capital–backed firms are most likely to exit by acquisitions, and this is potentially problematic for these entrepreneurial firms."

20.4. True/False/Uncertain and explain why: "Government venture capital–backed entrepreneurial firms are most likely to have unsuccessful exit outcomes."

20.5. Why might entrepreneurs prefer IPOs to acquisitions? What control rights might venture capital funds use to ensure that they have control over exit outcomes?

20.6. True/False/Uncertain and explain why: "The use of common equity and syndication facilitates IPO exits."

21 Contracts and Exits

21.1 Introduction and Learning Objectives

Venture capital (VC) financial contracts separately allocate cash flow and control rights (Chapters 10–14). In these contracts, the control rights might include the right to replace the CEO, among various other specific veto and control rights. Because entrepreneurs are likely to enjoy the private benefits of being the CEO of a publicly listed firm (Chapters 10–14), even when an acquisition is financially superior to an IPO, an entrepreneur might prefer the IPO because of the private benefits. Therefore, the structure of entrepreneurial private benefits leads to two empirical predictions. First, if a venture is less promising and/or the likelihood of a conflict in exit choice is high, then in exchange for getting the venture financed, venture capitalists will receive more control rights. Second, strong VC control should be associated with a greater probability of an acquisition. In this chapter we address the first prediction by controlling for the endogeneity of contracts vis-à-vis exits. We focus on the second empirical prediction through empirical testing.

In this chapter we will do the following:

- Consider how the allocation of cash flow, veto, and control rights influences the probability of achieving different exit outcomes
- Consider a detailed European dataset to assess the hypothesized relations between contracts and actual exits discussed herein

In this chapter we use a new dataset to produce results that relate the characteristics of VC contracts to the means by which a VC exits. The VC IPO-and-acquisition transactions span the years 1996 to 2005 and 11 European countries (Austria, Belgium, the Czech Republic, Denmark, France, Germany, Italy, the Netherlands, Poland, Portugal, and Switzerland). The data include detailed and confidential information on 223 investments. Of these investments, there are 187 actual dispositions (32 IPOs, 74 acquisitions, 17 buy-backs, and 64 write-offs) and 36 investments that had not exited by December 2005, the time of this study. In ascertaining the role of VC control rights in an IPO or acquisition, we control for a number of potentially relevant factors, including investor characteristics, entrepreneurial firm characteristics, transaction-specific characteristics, market sentiment, and institutional variables, among other control factors.

This chapter first develops testable hypotheses in the context of prior research and then summarizes and explains the variables used to test the theory. The data are presented, and multivariate empirical tests with a number of robustness checks are discussed.

21.2 Hypotheses

In the literature, related work has well established that VCs contribute significantly to innovation and economic growth (Gompers and Lerner, 1999, 2001a,b; Gompers et al., 2003, 2005; Kortum and Lerner, 2000; Lerner, 2002). The success of VC-backed companies has been attributed to the certification and the professional governance provided by VCs (Bakers and Gompers, 2003; Hochberg, 2005). Thus, VCs play an important role in the going-public process, and VC-backed IPOs tend to perform better than non-VC-backed IPOs. In recent years, research such as Sahlman (1990), Gompers (1998), Kaplan and Strömberg (2003, 2004), and Cumming and Johan (2007b) has shown that good VC governance is facilitated by strong VC contracts and that the allocation of control rights between VCs and entrepreneurs is consistent with the incomplete contracting theory of Aghion and Bolton (1992). However, with the exception of Lerner's (1995) paper relating board rights to executive turnover, no empirical study has actually tied investor control rights to investment outcomes.[1] This chapter provides such a link by examining VC control rights in relation to the acquisition versus IPO choice.

21.2.1 *VC Control Rights*

Aghion and Bolton (1992) analyze the contracting problem associated with the entrepreneur who derives private benefits (as distinct from monetary benefits from the venture) from running the firm. Obviously, such private benefits cannot be transferred or pledged to investors. Aghion and Bolton show any action that maximizes monetary benefits does not necessarily maximize private benefits and might be different from the first-best action that maximizes total surplus. Hence, if the entrepreneur has control and has pledged monetary benefits to investors, she has an incentive to act so as to maximize private benefits. If investors have control, then they will try to maximize monetary benefits. But given that investors have deep pockets, they can always bribe the entrepreneur into taking the efficient action; however, the opposite is not true. As a result, the entrepreneur's control is always ex post efficient, but investor control can

[1]Lerner (1995) studies CEO replacement, not exit outcomes. For legal scholarship on contracts and VC exits, see Smith (2005) and Broughman and Fried (2006, 2007).

lead to ex post inefficiencies. Ex ante control might have to be transferred to investors so they can break even, especially in ventures for which the expected monetary benefits are relatively low.

In the VC setting, Berglöf (1994), Black and Gilson (1998), Bascha and Walz (2001), Hellmann (2006), De Bettignies (2008), and others hypothesize that entrepreneurs' private benefits are higher when the firm is taken public compared to when it is acquired (see Petty et al., 1999, for case studies). VC control rights are relevant in the acquisition-versus-IPO exit decision because of the private benefits that the entrepreneur enjoys, which might go beyond the financial rewards he obtains from the entrepreneurial venture. Entrepreneurs are likely to obtain private benefits in an IPO through the reputational gain associated with being the CEO of a publicly listed firm. In contrast, VCs are not likely to enjoy private benefits. VCs are less actively involved in an investee firm that has been taken public, and either they exit within six months to two years and/or they transfer their shares to their institutional limited partners (Gompers and Lerner, 1999). In an acquisition exit, both the VC and the entrepreneur sell their shares to the acquiring firm and the entrepreneur is no longer the CEO. Thus, the scope of an entrepreneur's private benefits in an acquisition exit is likely to be smaller than if the firm had exited through an IPO.

Situations in which entrepreneurs enjoy private benefits lead us to make two empirical hypotheses. First, that in the original contract, higher NPV ventures will be associated with a higher degree of entrepreneur control, since investors will likely break even despite not having control. This result has been tested in previous VC contracting studies (Chapters 10–14; see also Cumming, 2005a,b; Cumming and Johan, 2007c; Kaplan and Strömberg, 2003). When the venture is extremely promising, VCs will seek and receive fewer control rights. If the venture is less valuable to begin with, and/or the likelihood of a conflict in exit choice is higher, then the VC will seek and receive more control rights, which the entrepreneur will grant to get the venture financed. We address this issue in this chapter by controlling for the endogeneity of contracts vis-à-vis exits.

Second, those ventures in which the VCs are in control are more likely to result in actions—that is, acquisitions—that hurt the entrepreneur's private benefits rather than ventures in which the entrepreneur is in control (Fried and Ganor, 2006). In an acquisition exit, the entrepreneur is, in effect, ousted as the CEO from the firm. Entrepreneurs most often find this permanent removal from their firms to be an emotionally upsetting event. Some entrepreneurs even describe it as equivalent to a divorce (Petty et al., 1999), which explains why many entrepreneurs are reluctant to agree to an acquisition exit. VCs with stronger control rights are better able to force the entrepreneur to agree to an acquisition. Therefore, in our second hypothesis we predict a positive association between VC control rights and the likelihood of acquisition. This hypothesis is the central prediction that is tested in this chapter.

There are offsetting advantages to assigning rights to the VC that result from the entrepreneur's informational advantage over the VC in the day-to-day operations of the enterprise. Whenever a manager assigns rights to agents who are within an organization but who are not in a position to have the best information, the manager incurs an efficiency cost. Allocating control rights trades off between the benefit of enhanced credibility in the market that the firm gains by assigning the rights to the VC and the benefit to the VC of using the entrepreneur's superior information, which is associated with assigning rights to the entrepreneur. An exit conflict makes it harder for the VC to break even, thus necessitating the transfer of control to the VC, even though it is inefficient.

Weak VC control rights might be associated with a greater probability of either an IPO or with a write-off exit. If a successful entrepreneurial firm is ready for an exit during a robust IPO market, then a conflict of interest in exit choice between a VC and the entrepreneur is unlikely. An IPO is most likely to result, regardless of VC control rights. However, for problematic ventures in which VCs have weak control rights and cannot bring about needed managerial decisions or changes in the entrepreneurial firm (for example, replacing the founding entrepreneur as CEO, or making control decisions regarding asset purchases and sales), there is a greater probability that the lack of VC control will lead to less VC assistance, which will produce a higher likelihood of a write-off. This latter prediction is consistent with the empirical work of Hege et al. (2003), Kaplan and Strömberg (2004), Kaplan et al. (2007), and Nikoskelainen and Wright (2007).

Another hypothesis is that if a VC uses strong control rights (e.g., in a world in which some investors make mistakes in contracting), doing so will improve the entrepreneurial firm's governance and increases the likelihood of better performance. Better performance could lead to a higher likelihood of a successful exit, whether by IPO or acquisition, and a lower likelihood of a complete write-off.

One of the most important empirical challenges in studying contract choices in conjunction with exit outcomes is accounting for endogeneity. Our dataset has information on whether the VC contracts are designed with a primary view toward an IPO or acquisition prior to signing the first-round investment. We test for robustness to the inclusion or exclusion of these preplanned exits, and to situations in which the VC has a clear exit strategy, in terms of an IPO or acquisition, at the time of first investment. We also use other robustness checks, such as the use of instrumental variables.

Nevertheless, there might be other factors that explain the relation between control rights and exit outcomes. More highly skilled and experienced entrepreneurs might be able to negotiate control rights away from the VC and could be more likely to go public. In that case, there is not direct causal link from contracts to exits. Instead, entrepreneurial quality independently drives contracts and exits. We control for entrepreneurial quality at the time of VC investment by using a variable that measures the investor's ranking of the entrepreneur's experience and ability.

21.2.2 Other Factors Relevant to the Choice between IPOs versus Acquisitions

Prior theoretical work identifies a number of factors that could affect IPOs versus acquisitions,[2] such as VC characteristics. VCs can take on two roles in exit outcomes: They can add value through active assistance provided to the entrepreneurial firm,[3] and they can certify the quality of the entrepreneurial firm so information asymmetries between it and the new owners are lower than what they otherwise would have been at the time of exit.[4] Both of these roles are consistent with the view that higher-quality and more reputable VCs facilitate IPO exits more often. Our empirical tests use proxies for VC quality and value-added. Our tests also control for captive VCs, which we define as funds that are part of a larger corporation or bank. Captive VCs might have nonfinancial strategic motives for wanting an acquisition rather than an IPO (Gompers and Lerner, 1999; Hellmann, 2002; Riyanto and Schwienbacher, 2006).

Several entrepreneurial firm characteristics, such as the size of a firm's assets, which for IPOs must meet minimum listing requirements, and the primary industry in which it operates, can also affect the choice of an IPO rather than an acquisition. In addition, because IPOs and acquisitions generate different proceeds in the sale of the firm, an entrepreneurial firm's growth potential and capital needs could be relevant for the choice between an IPO and an acquisition. Firms in industries with high market/book ratios have greater growth options and thus could be more likely to go public (Gompers and Lerner, 1999).

Market conditions and regulations also play an important role in VC exit outcomes. IPO markets are subject to massive swings (Ritter, 1984). We control for the returns in the public market by using the country-specific Morgan Stanley Capital International (MSCI) data for various periods in the year prior to exit. We also use investment-exit-year dummy variables; country differences, which we examine through the use of a variable for legality (La Porta et al., 1998; Berkowitz et al., 2003); stock market capitalization; and country dummy variables. We expect countries with larger stock markets to have more IPOs than acquisitions (Black and Gilson, 1998). Legal certainty and investor protection also are more valuable in the context of an IPO, because information asymmetry is more pronounced for a disparate group of new shareholders in an IPO than for new owners in an acquisition. Thus, the cost of going pub-

[2]A detailed survey is provided by Cumming and MacIntosh (2003b). See also Zingales (1995), Yosha (1995), Black and Gilson (1998), Gompers and Lerner (1999a), Cumming and MacIntosh (2003a), Das et al. (2003), Hege et al. (2003), Boot et al. (2006), and Schwienbacher (2003, 2007).

[3]See Sahlman (1990), Amit et al. (1998), Gompers and Lerner (1999a), Hellmann and Puri (2000, 2002), Kanniainen and Keuschnigg (2003, 2004), Keuschnigg (2004), Ueda (2004), Hsu (2004), Hochberg et al. (2005), and Sorensen (2008).

[4]See Barry et al. (1990), Megginson and Weiss (1991), Lerner (1994), Lin and Smith (1997), Gompers and Lerner (1999, 2003), Brav and Gompers (1997, 2003), Baker and Gompers (2003), Li and Masulis (2004), Neus and Walz (2005), Hand (2005), Armstrong et al. (2005), and Chemmanur and Chen (2006).

lic (e.g., in terms of underpricing) is lower among countries with more legal certainty and protection (Cumming et al., 2006; Shleifer and Wolfenzon, 2002).

21.3 Variables in the Econometric Specifications

Table 21.1 displays the primary variables used in our empirical analyses. There are five main categories of variables: VC control rights, investor characteristics, investee characteristics, market conditions, and legal and institutional factors.

The security of choice in the United States is typically convertible preferred equity (Gompers, 1998; Kaplan and Strömberg, 2003), but outside the United States many countries use a wide range of securities (Cumming, 2005a,b; Kaplan et al., 2007; Lerner and Schoar, 2005). In addition to voting and board rights, commonly allocated rights in VC contracts that are particularly important in the IPO-versus-acquisition decision (Hellmann, 2006; Kaplan and Strömberg, 2003) include a drag-along right in which the VC has the right to force the entrepreneur to sell at the same terms to a third party; a redemption right, which gives the VC the right to sell interest in the firm back to the entrepreneur at prespecified terms and after a specific point in time, which is typically three years after the initial investment; and an antidilution right that protects the VC against future financings at lower than the protected valuation. Other rights include a right of first refusal in a sale—in other words, the VC must be offered sale terms that are at least as good as, and in advance of, those offered to a third party—a co-sale right, which allows the VC to sell to a third party on the same terms as the third party offers the entrepreneur; and a protection right against new issues. There are also veto rights over asset sales, asset purchases, changes in control, issuances of equity, and many other decisions. In some cases, the VCs have the right to replace the founding entrepreneur as CEO. We do not expect all of the various control rights to have an equal effect on exit outcomes.

Perhaps closest to the notion of entrepreneurial control in incomplete contracting theories is the right to replace the CEO. That is, as a residual control right, it gives the investors the right to take this particular action. Investors can also force an acquisition through other measures of residual control rights, such as whether they control a majority of the board, a majority of the votes, or whether there are other terms in the contract that give the VCs the power to force an exit, for example, by using a redemption right or a drag-along clause. A redemption right can be used to force an acquisition if it is difficult or undesirable for the entrepreneur to repurchase the VC's interest. An antidilution right gives VCs more bargaining power in subsequent financing rounds, and if the firm needs further financing, this right is likely to lead to a larger dilution of entrepreneurial control. Rights to veto asset sales, purchases, and new equity issues could be used as threats in negotiations and might indirectly affect the exit outcome, although it is less clear that such rights could be used to force an acquisition or buyback.

Table 21.1 Variable Definitions

This table defines each of the variables. The data are from 223 venture capital fund investments in Austria, Belgium, Czech Republic, Denmark, France, Germany, Italy, the Netherlands, Poland, Portugal, and Switzerland over the period 1995–2002, and exits over the period 1996–2005. To ensure that we do not double-count observations, we use the entrepreneurial firm, not the investment round as the unit of observation, and base contract terms on the initial investment of the respondent VC investor.

Variable	Definition
Investor Fund Characteristics	
Noncaptive Fund	A dummy variable equal to 1 if the fund is not a captive fund (a limited partnership). We define a captive fund as one that is affiliated with a bank or corporation. Separate variables to distinguish corporate VCs and bank-affiliated VCs are also used as robustness checks.
Investor Capital (All Funds)	The real (thousands of €2003) total amount of capital for all affiliated funds that are part of the investor's organization.
Fund Capital	The real (thousands of €2003) total amount of capital for the specific fund within the investor's organization that provided data for this study.
Entrepreneurial Firm Characteristics	
Early/Expansion	A dummy variable equal to 1 if the entrepreneurial firm was an early- or expansion-stage transaction at the time of investment of the respondent VC fund, and 0 if the firm was a late- or buyout-stage firm. We do not use more specific categories because the unit of observation is the entrepreneurial firm, not the transaction round where more than one round is provided by the investor, and because firms may progress from one stage to the next. There are also differences in definitions of investment stages across countries. Alternative variables that separate out the early (69 companies), expansion (82 companies), late (32 companies), and buyout stage (40 companies) are used as robustness checks.
Foreign Firm	A dummy variable equal to 1 when the entrepreneurial firm is in a different country than the investor at the time of first VC investment.
Experience Rank	This is a subjective ranking provided by the respondent investor about the entrepreneur's quality, ability, and experience, and intended for the date of investment. The investor provided the ranking during the initial data collection in 2002 and follow-up interviews, not at the time of actual investment. Therefore, it is a proxy, since the investors were asked to rank the entrepreneur's ability going back to the time of initial investment. The ranking is on a scale of 1–10. An alternative variable equal to 1 for ranks greater than 7 is used as a robustness check.

(*continued*)

Table 21.1 (*continued*)

Variable	Definition
Industry Market/Book	The industry market/book ratio for the industry in which the entrepreneurial firm operates at the time of exit. We suppress the dummy variables for specific industries (e.g., medical/biotech, computers/electronic, Internet/ communications, and nontech industries) for reasons of collinearity.
Transaction Characteristics	
Common Equity	A dummy variable equal to 1 for common equity investments. We exclude dummy variables for other securities (convertible preferred equity, or mixes of debt or preferred and common equity) for reasons of collinearity. Special control rights, veto rights, contingencies, board seats, and so on, associated with the investment are considered separately.
Right to Replace CEO	A dummy variable equal to 1 if the investor(s) has the right to replace the CEO. This right is typically not a contractual right per se, but effectively a right in the hands of the investor by virtue of the voting power provided via the investor's shares in the firm and/or board seats. This is not our interpretation of the contracts. The investors themselves provided us with the information on whether or not the investor had such power.
Majority Board Seats	A dummy variable equal to 1 if the VC investor(s) has a majority of the board seats at the investee firm.
Majority Voting	A dummy variable equal to 1 if the VC investor(s) has a majority of the voting rights at the investee firm.
Drag-along	A dummy variable equal to 1 if the VC investor(s) has a drag-along right that obligates the entrepreneur to sell shares along with the offer that the VC initiates.
Redemption	A dummy variable equal to 1 if the VC investor(s) has a redemption right that enables the VC to sell shares back to the entrepreneur at prespecified terms.
Antidilution	A dummy variable equal to 1 if the VC investor(s) has an antidilution right that entitles the investors to additional shares to maintain their ownership percentage.
Control Rights Index	Sum of the following investor(s) control right dummy variables (dummy takes the value of 1 if investor has the right): drag-along, redemption, and antidilution. (I do not include other control rights in the index, as they do not directly relate to acquisition exits; however, these rights are available on request.)

Table 21.1 (*continued*)

Variable	Definition
Veto Rights Index	Sum of the following investor(s) veto right dummy variables (dummy takes the value of 1 if investor has the right): asset sales, asset purchases, changes in control, issuance of equity, any other decisions.
Syndication	The number of syndicated investors.
Prior Rounds	A dummy variable equal to 1 if there was a prior VC before the respondent VC had invested in the entrepreneur. (The precise number of prior rounds is not known for all the exited investments in the data, but in all cases it is known whether or not the other VC(s) used the same securities.)
Lead Investor	A dummy variable equal to 1 if the respondent investor was the lead investor in the syndicate.
Private Investment Value	The real (thousands of €2003) value of the respondent investors' initial investments in the entrepreneurial firm.
Total Investor Ownership %	Ownership % for all of the investors in the best-case scenario for the value of the entrepreneurial firm.
Exit Variables	
IPO	A dummy variable equal to 1 if the VC exits the investment by means of an IPO.
Acquisition	A dummy variable equal to 1 if the VC exits the investment by means of an acquisition (trade sale). The IRRs of the investment *were considered* to avoid misclassification of write-offs as acquisitions.
Buyback	A dummy variable equal to 1 if the VC exits the investment by means of a buyback whereby the entrepreneur repurchases the investors' interest.
Write-off	A dummy variable equal to 1 if the investor exits the investment by a write-off.
No Exit	A dummy variable equal to 1 if the investor does not exit the investment by the time of final data collection (December 2005).
IRR	The internal rate of return for the investor that provided the data. Calculated by the investor, and based on all of the actual cash flows.
Market Conditions and Institutional Variables	
Legality Index	Weighted average of the following factors (based on Berkowitz et al., 2003, and La Porta et al., 1998): efficiency of judicial system, rule of law, corruption, risk of expropriation, and risk of contract repudiation. Higher numbers indicate "better" legal systems. The Legality index is for the country in which the entrepreneur is based.

(*continued*)

Table 21.1 *(continued)*

Variable	Definition
Creditor Rights	An index aggregating different creditor rights from La Porta et al. (1998). Higher numbers indicate more creditor-friendly legal systems.
Antidirector Rights	An index aggregating the shareholder rights labeled as "antidirector rights" (shareholder rights) as defined in La Porta et al. (1998). Higher numbers indicate more shareholder-friendly (and minority shareholder-friendly) legal systems.
MSCI Returns 1 Year Prior to Exit	The country-specific monthly MSCI index in the 0–12 months prior to first exit (i.e., IPO date, or date of acquisition or write-off).
MSCI Returns 3–6 Months Prior to Exit	The country-specific monthly MSCI index in the 3–6 months prior to first exit (i.e., IPO date, or date of acquisition or write-off).
MSCI Returns 0–3 Months Prior to Exit	The country-specific monthly MSCI index in the 0–3 months prior to first exit (i.e., IPO date, or date of acquisition or write-off).
Market Capitalization	The real (billions of €2003) market capitalization of the domestic stock market of the country in which the investee resided in the year of exit.
Country Dummy Variables	Dummy variables for specific countries of the investee.
Year Dummy Variables	Dummy variables for the initial investment year (of the respondent investor) and exit years (same for all investors). The summary statistics (Table 21.3) also present a variable for the number of investment months of the respondent investor.

Other rights play a smaller role in the IPO versus acquisition decision. The automatic conversion provision usually only applies in an IPO (Hellmann, 2006) and is a precommitment to give up control rights when the firm is offered a sufficiently valuable exit (as in Black and Gilson, 1998). An IPO registration right can be viewed as the right of investors to force an IPO. Similarly, a piggyback right applies only in an IPO. A co-sale right, a right of first refusal, and a veto against change in control all give investors protection if the entrepreneur tries to sell the firm in part or whole to a new owner (Chemla et al., 2007, analyze some of these provisions). Information rights typically call for the firm to supply timely financial statements and related materials. These rights have no direct bearing on the exit decision. So, in the remainder of the chapter, we use the term "strong VC control rights" to refer to contractual control rights that are relevant to IPOs-versus-acquisitions, including the drag-along, redemption, and antidilution rights, as well as the right to replace the CEO, majority votes, and majority boards.

Written contracts include many of these contractual terms. However, we note that the right to replace the CEO is almost never an explicit contractual clause between the investor and the entrepreneur (in Italy, for example, Cumming and Zambelli, 2007, document that an explicit clause to replace the CEO would be illegal in the period considered by our dataset). Rather, the right to replace the CEO comes from the voting power (and, in some cases, special voting rights) of the investor with respect to board seats and ownership interest in the firm. For some investments, this right to replace the CEO becomes effective only in the event of nonperformance by the entrepreneur. (Performance hurdles are set up as conditions for the initial investment.) However, in our empirical analyses with limited degrees of freedom, controls for different standards are not tractable. Therefore, our variable for the right to replace the CEO is a dummy variable equal to one if the investor informed us that there was some mechanism in the contract whereby the investor(s) could bring about such a change.

We note that across financing rounds, the European investors did not indicate significant alterations to their contract structures, such as a change in the use of one security or another across rounds or the inclusion/exclusion of terms such as veto rights and the right to replace the founding entrepreneur as CEO. Over the course of interviews with the fund managers who provided the data, we learned that generally an extreme event would be needed to warrant alteration of specific terms across rounds. The investors indicated that such extreme changes would lead to a breakdown in the relationship between the investor and entrepreneur and would be unduly costly to renegotiate.

However, founder ownership and control do tend to get diluted in each financing round, particularly when more syndicated investors are added in a new round. In such cases, the basis for coding is the first-round investment data because there are differing numbers of rounds prior to exit and a number of nonexits in the data so the final round ownership and control data are not directly comparable; also, by the last investment round, ownership and control rights are likely to be more endogenous to exit outcomes than are those at the initial investment round. Regardless, we find that the primary results are robust to the use of different periods of measurement for terms that vary across rounds. Obviously, there are also contingencies in certain contractual terms, such as contingencies pertaining to ownership percentages. We use the ownership percentages in the event of successful outcomes, not write-offs. In a few cases, the common stock has limited redemption rights (jointly with liquidation rights) attached to them, and other veto and control rights. We do not find that attributes of the common stock variables make a material difference to the exit results, other than what is recorded separately in the other variables. Table 21.1 lists the veto rights, control rights, and so on.

Other variables for transaction characteristics include a dummy for whether there are VCs invested in the entrepreneurial firm prior to the respondent investor. This dummy controls for differences across VCs that originate the deal. To control for size effects we also include a variable for the book value of the initial investment of the respondent VC. Due to data limitations, we do not control for other VC investment amounts, because we could not determine all amounts of other investors. Nor do we include the amount invested in all financing rounds, since that amount would be endogenous (Gompers, 1995).

Table 21.1 also shows the variables for investor characteristics. We consider dummy variables equal to one for noncaptive VCs. Captives often behave differently than noncaptives because they have strategic reasons for investing in firms that are developing technologies relevant to the larger organization. Hence, they might be more likely to exit by acquisition when the acquirer is the affiliated company of the captive (Hellmann, 2002). Noncaptives often have pay incentives that attract superior VC talent (Gompers and Lerner, 1999), which could lead to an association between noncaptives and IPOs. VCs with more capital might also have superior talent, which could result in an association with IPOs. We also consider dummy variables for different funds.

Table 21.1 also defines various investee characteristics that we use in our specifications. We use dummy variables for different stages of development at the time of first investment because later-stage investments could be connected to different exit outcomes, regardless of contract terms and other factors. And we use the ranking of the entrepreneur by the VC as a variable to control for entrepreneurial quality. The rank is on a scale of 1 (lowest) to 10 (highest). We note that this ranking was made in 2002 when, although there had been many IPOs by this time, many investments had not yet exited. Hence, there is some degree of look-back bias that cannot be avoided for the pre-2002 exits. But this look-back bias overcompensates for this factor in the direction of IPOs, and thus this control variable is quite appropriate. We also control for industry market/book values at the time of exit because higher market/book industries are more likely to be associated with IPOs (Gompers and Lerner, 1999a).

As in Gompers and Lerner (1999a), we use MSCI returns in the three months prior to exit and in the six- to three-month period prior to exit to control for market conditions. We use the year of investment and year of exit dummy variables to control for market conditions and hot-issue markets. We use variables for country-specific market capitalization and the Legality index of the country of domicile of the entrepreneur, and country dummy variables, since law quality can influence the development of venture capital and stock markets and the likelihood of an IPO exit (Armour and Cumming, 2006; Cumming et al., 2006; La Porta et al., 1998; Schliefer and Wolfenzon, 2002).

21.4 Data

In this section we describe the data and provide summary statistics and comparison of means and medians tests.

21.4.1 Sample Description

The data come from 223 entrepreneurial firms financed by 35 VC funds from 11 continental European countries: Austria, Belgium, the Czech Republic, Denmark, France, Germany, Italy, the Netherlands, Poland, Portugal, and Switzerland. The VCs financed these firms between 1995 and 2002. There are 32 IPOs, 74 acquisitions, 17 buybacks, and 64 write-offs between 1996 and 2003, comprising a total of 187 VC financings. There were 36 unexited investments as at 2005, the time of this study. The unit of analysis is the entrepreneurial firm, not an investment round, or the syndicated investor (staging and/or syndication is not double counted in the data).

To collect the data, we first sent surveys to all continental European funds that were members of the European Venture Capital Association (EVCA) between January 2002 and January 2003. Then we carried out follow-up interviews in person for most Dutch, Belgian, and German funds, and by phone for funds in other countries. Some of the funds did not provide details on all of their investments; rather, the manager(s) only provided data for specific investments or deals on which the manager(s) worked. We studied and analyzed actual contracts, with the assistance of the VC managers alongside a Ph.D. student in law, in 2004 and 2005. The survey and interview method also revealed other information that is not found in a written contract.

To ensure the integrity of the data collected, we promised the respondents that the information collected from the 35 funds would remain strictly confidential and would not be made publicly available. The data were disclosed on a completely voluntary basis. Given the type of confidential information collected, we cannot refer to an aggregate industry database for comparison. However, we can point out that in terms of the frequency of IPOs, acquisitions, and write-offs, our sample is similar to prior data sets on private equity exits (Cochrane, 2005; Cumming and MacIntosh, 2003a,b; Schwienbacher, 2003).

The scope of other VC data sets (Cumming and MacIntosh, 2003a,b; Kaplan and Strömberg, 2003; Lerner and Schoar, 2005; Schwienbacher, 2003) is also similar to mine in terms of detail and number of observations. Further, the frequency of use of particular contracts is similar to that reported in this study, thus accounting for institutional differences between the United States and Europe. The most notable institutional difference between Europe and the United States is in the use of convertible securities in the United States (Bergmann and Hege, 1998; Gompers, 1998; Kaplan and Strömberg, 2003; Sahlman, 1990; Schwienbacher, 2003). Tax considerations are one explanation for the dominant use of convertible securities for VC-backed firms in the United States (Gilson and Schizer, 2003). We do not exclude investments in the sample based on the security used. For instance, we report the use of straight preferred investments, because this security is also occasionally used by Canadian and U.S. VCs that invest in Canada (Cumming, 2005a,b) and by VCs in developing countries (Lerner and Schoar, 2005). Regardless, in our data the results are robust to the inclusion/exclusion of this subsample.

21.4.2 Summary Statistics

Table 21.2 shows the total number of investments each year, with breakdowns by the type of security used in each year of first investment. The time variations in the contracts are consistent with other international datasets (see, e.g., Kaplan et al., 2007). The data indicate that the greatest number of investments occurred in 2000. This finding is consistent with the aggregate EVCA data (http://www.evca.com). The EVCA does not record details on contracts.

One important aspect of the data is that syndicated investors almost invariably used the same securities as the investors who provided these data. We observe differences in only six of 223 cases. These are the cases in which the syndicated investor used common equity or warrants while the respondent investor used a security involving debt and/or preferred equity.

Due to considerations of confidentiality, we do not provide details for each of the 35 funds. We can best describe the funds as "generalist" funds that have a broad focus on entrepreneurs at different stages of development, from very early to very late. The lack of specialization of VCs in Europe is a function of the depth of the market, particularly in continental Europe. (I note that the U.S. market has funds with a much greater degree of specialization; see Gompers and Lerner, 1999a, 2001a,b.) Some funds in our sample are part of a larger corporation or bank (captive funds); some are noncaptive VCs (limited partnerships). We examine country (and fund) effects in our multivariate tests and focus on the countries that involve a majority of the exits. No single fund provides more than 20 investments, and no single fund or country accounts for a majority of the exits.

Table 21.3 provides summary statistics across columns 1–12 and differences tests across columns 13–18. The table summarizes the data for all observations, as well as for the subsample of IPOs, acquisitions, and write-off exits. The subsamples of buybacks and nonexits are not summarized in Table 21.3 for reasons of conciseness. Because Table 21.3 does not summarize the data for any particular fund, greater details are possible without compromising the confidentiality of any single fund. The funds from the Eastern European countries are small; others funds from elsewhere in Europe are large. We control for fund size in the multivariate empirical analyses.

The results of comparison tests in Table 21.3 (columns 13–18) provide a number of insights into the role of VCs in IPOs compared to acquisitions. The most important results appear in column 13 (for comparison of medians tests) and column 16 (comparison of means and proportions tests). The data indicate that IPOs are more likely than acquisitions for common equity investments when the mean and median public market returns have been greater in the months prior to exit (consistent with Gompers and Lerner, 1999) and among countries with greater stock market capitalization (consistent with Black and Gilson, 1998).

A higher ranking of the entrepreneur by the VC (on a scale of one to ten) is associated with a greater probability of an IPO (column 16), and median IRRs are higher for IPOs than acquisitions (column 13). There are other differences, depending on the industry and the stage of first investment. The table shows that a greater proportion of high-tech firms (with high market/book ratios) and early-stage firms are more likely to go public (column 16) and more likely to be written off (column 18).

The summary statistics in Table 21.3 support our central hypothesis in this chapter by indicating that acquisitions are more likely when the investor has greater control rights. Investments in which the investor has the right to replace the CEO are more often associated with acquisitions than with IPOs. Write-offs also are less common among investments in which the investor has the right to replace the founding entrepreneur as CEO. Acquisitions are more likely for investments with convertible debt and convertible preferred equity, with mixes of debt or preferred equity with common equity, and for investments with a greater proportion of investor veto rights and control rights.

Table 21.4, Panels A and B, show two correlation matrices. Panel A presents correlations across exit outcomes, and investor, entrepreneur, transaction, market, and institutional variables. Panel B presents correlations across exit outcomes and transaction characteristics, and the country dummy variables. Significant correlations at the 5% level appear in boldface and are consistent with the comparison tests in Table 21.3.

One implication of Table 21.4, Panel A, is that common equity is a proxy for weak VC control rights. The table shows that investors are less likely to use veto and control rights when the VC uses common equity. This finding is consistent with related theoretical work on the topic.[5]

Table 21.4, Panel B, presents correlations across country-specific dummy variables. We find statistically significant values in certain cases. Therefore, we use country dummy variables for these countries to check the robustness in our empirical tests. However, we note that the country dummies might reflect fund-specific factors, as there are not many funds in the data for each of the specific countries. We also examine fund dummy variables, but due to collinearity and a loss of degrees of freedom, not all such dummy variables can be included simultaneously with the country dummy variables.

21.5 Multivariate Regressions

Here we describe our regression model specifications, robustness checks, and extensions.

21.5.1 Base Regression Models

Table 21.5 reports two multinomial logit regression models of the impact of VC fund, entrepreneurial firm, transaction details, and market and institutional

[5]Cestone (2002) argues that common equity with strong investor veto and control rights would give the investor too great an incentive to intervene in the entrepreneurial firm. Casamatta (2003) argues that common equity is used to encourage advice, whereas convertible claims and contractual control rights tend to be used to facilitate monitoring.

Table 21.2 Summary

This table presents, for each year of investment covered by the dataset, the number of investments in not exited as at 2005), the type of security (common equity, convertible preferred equity, mixes of debt and defined in Table 21.1). The table also shows the values for the periods 1995–1998, 1999–2000, 2001–2002,

Panel A. Summary of the

Year of Investment	Sample Size		Exit Type by Year of Investment				
	# Investments by Year of Investment	# Exits by Year of Investment	IPOs	Acquisitions	Buybacks	Write-offs	Not Exited
Numbers:							
1995	6	6	1	4	0	1	0
1996	8	8	6	1	0	1	0
1997	17	17	7	5	0	5	0
1998	22	21	5	12	0	4	1
1999	34	30	5	11	5	9	4
2000	74	55	4	18	7	26	19
2001	51	39	3	19	4	13	12
2002	11	11	1	4	1	5	0
Whole Sample	223	187	32	74	17	64	36
Percentages:							
1995–1998	53	52	35.85%	41.51%	0.00%	20.75%	1.89%
1999–2000	108	85	8.33%	26.85%	11.11%	32.41%	21.30%
2001–2002	62	50	5.60%	29.60%	8.80%	31.20%	24.80%
Whole Sample	223	187	14.35%	33.18%	7.62%	28.70%	16.14%

conditions on exit outcomes. We present the marginal effects from the multinomial logit estimates to explicitly illustrate economic significance as well as statistical significance. The marginal effects indicate the probability of each exit outcome that is associated with the particular right-hand-side variable. The explanatory variables are as defined in Table 21.1. We do not use year-of-exit dummy variables because buybacks and nonexits are both possible outcomes (besides IPOs, acquisitions, and write-offs). There were buybacks only in 2004 and 2005 and nonexits are as of 2005, so the year-of-exit dummies would give rise to problems of perfect collinearity. Model 2 is presented alongside Model 1 to show different explanatory variables.

The strongest finding in Table 21.5 is the relation between transaction characteristics and exit outcomes. There is a positive association between acquisitions,

of the Data by Year

different investee companies, the number of exits, the type of exit (IPO, acquisition, write-off, or preferred with common, and straight [nonconvertible] debt or preferred), and control rights (as and the whole sample.

Data by Year of Investment

Security by Year of Investment				Control Rights by Year of Investment		
Common	**Convertible Preferred**	**Mixed Debt/ Preferred/ Common**	**Straight Debt or Straight Preferred**	**Right to Replace CEO**	**Majority Board Seats**	**Average Control + Veto Rights Index**
3	1	2	0	5	4	7.5
6	z0	2	0	5	5	6.3
9	2	6	0	12	10	6.6
12	3	7	0	8	10	5.6
13	11	10	0	12	14	4.7
31	34	7	2	23	30	4.6
23	17	6	5	16	14	5.0
3	4	3	1	9	7	5.4
100	72	43	8	90	94	5.1
56.60%	11.32%	32.08%	0.00%	56.60%	54.72%	78.02%
40.74%	41.67%	15.74%	1.85%	32.41%	40.74%	57.89%
43.20%	40.80%	10.40%	5.60%	31.20%	35.20%	63.39%
44.84%	32.29%	19.28%	3.59%	40.36%	42.15%	64.20%

strong VC control rights, and the right to replace the founding entrepreneur as CEO. There is a negative association between IPOs and VC control rights. Further, the data indicate a negative association between write-offs and VC control rights.

Model 1 indicates that the right to replace the CEO is associated with a 38.6% greater probability of an acquisition. The economic significance is lower, at 23.6%, in Model 2 when we add correlated variables—including majority boards, majority votes, veto rights and the sum of drag-along, redemption, and antidilution rights—on the right-hand side. Majority boards are associated with a 23.7% increase in the probability of an acquisition in Model 1 and an 18.4% increase in Model 2. Model 2 shows each additional control right (drag-along, redemption, and antidilution rights) results in an

Table 21.2

This table presents, for each year of exit covered by the dataset, the number of investments in different exited as at 2005), the type of security (common equity, convertible preferred equity, mixes of debt and defined in Table 21.1). We note that the table shows the number of securities and control rights for the presented for the periods 1995–1998, 1999–2000, 2001–2005, and the whole sample.

Panel B. Summary of the

Year of Exit	Sample Size		Exit Type by Year of Exit				
	# Investments by Year of Investment	# Exits by Year of Exit	IPOs	Acquisitions	Buyback	Write-offs	Not Exited
Numbers:							
1995	6	0	0	0	0	0	6
1996	8	1	0	0	0	1	13
1997	17	0	0	0	0	0	30
1998	22	1	0	0	0	1	51
1999	34	2	2	0	0	0	83
2000	74	30	16	13	0	1	127
2001	51	19	2	10	0	7	159
2002	11	20	1	11	0	8	150
2003	0	19	0	10	0	9	131
2004	0	41	5	13	3	20	90
2005	0	54	6	17	14	17	36
Whole Sample	223	187	32	74	17	64	36
Percentages:							
1995–1998	53	2	0.00%	0.00%	0.00%	100.00%	96.23%
1999–2000	108	32	56.25%	40.63%	0.00%	3.13%	78.88%
2001–2005	62	153	9.15%	39.87%	11.11%	39.87%	16.14%
Whole Sample	223	187	17.11%	39.57%	9.09%	34.22%	16.14%

additional 12.2% increase in the probability of an acquisition exit. The evidence on majority boards, right to replace the CEO, and VC control rights is consistent with the notion that entrepreneurs derive a nonpecuniary benefit associated with being the CEO of a publicly listed firm, and that investor control is valuable in effecting acquisitions when entrepreneurs would otherwise prefer an IPO for nonpecuniary reasons.

In Table 21.5, the most important variable for IPO exits is that of market conditions. Public market returns in the three months prior to exit are closely

(*continued*)

investee companies, the number of exits, the type of exit (IPO, acquisition, write-off, or not preferred with common, and straight [nonconvertible] debt or preferred), and control rights (as years in which exit occurred, and not the years for which investment occurred. Values are also

Data by Year of Exit

Security by Year of Exit				Control Rights by Year of Exit		
Common	Convertible Preferred	Mixed Debt/ Preferred/ Common	Straight Debt or Straight Preferred	Right to Replace CEO	Majority Board Seats	Average Control + Veto Rights Index
0	0	1	0	1	0	8
0	0	0	0	0	0	0
1	0	0	0	1	0	8
2	0	0	0	0	0	4
20	3	7	0	16	19	5.8
8	7	4	0	9	12	5.5
7	3	10	0	12	6	6.5
9	5	5	0	6	9	4.8
16	18	5	2	14	22	5.1
13	28	8	5	25	19	5.2
76	64	40	7	84	87	5.4
50.00%	0.00%	50.00%	0.00%	100.00%	0.00%	100.00%
68.75%	9.38%	21.88%	0.00%	50.00%	59.38%	71.09%
34.64%	39.87%	20.92%	4.58%	43.14%	44.44%	66.63%
40.64%	34.22%	21.39%	3.74%	44.92%	39.01%	67.76%

related to IPOs. In terms of economic significance, the regression models indicate that an increase in public market returns from 1 to 4% increases the probability of an IPO by approximately 1%. The role of public market returns in the three-month period prior to the IPO very strongly supports the evidence for the U.S. market presented by Gompers and Lerner (1999). The variable for the three- to six-month MSCI return is not significant, nor is a variable for the MSCI return in the year prior to the IPO date. We do not use this variable in the regressions, but the results are available on request.

Table 21.3 Summary Statistics and Difference Tests

This table presents a summary of the data by (columns 1–3) the total sample, (columns 4–6) IPOs, (columns 7–9) acquisitions, and (columns 10–12) write-offs. The table shows median values are presented. (Means are not presented for reasons of conciseness.) Proportions represent the fraction of the number of observations on the top row for each column. The table does not show minimum and maximum values for proportions, because the minimum is always 0 and the maximum is always 1. Investment years span 1995–2002. Exit years span 1996–2005. Variables are as defined in Table 21.1. The table shows comparison tests for differences in medians, means, and proportions of various characteristics of the investors and entrepreneurs for the different exit outcomes. The mean test is the standard test for two samples and based on the t-distribution, under the assumption that population distributions are normal. The median test is the two-sample equivalent of the one-sample sign test, and does not have any distributional assumptions and/or any assumptions about the population variance. See http://www.fon.hum.uva.nl/Service/Statistics.html for a summary of these different test statistics. *, **, *** indicate statistical significance at the 10%, 5%, and 1% levels, respectively.

	Full Sample of All Exits and Nonexits			IPO Exits		
	(1)	(2)	(3)	(4)	(5)	(6)
	Proportion or Median	**Minimum**	**Maximum**	**Proportion or Median**	**Minimum**	**Maximum**
Total Number of Observations (# Entrepreneurial Firms)	223			32		
Proportion of Noncaptive Investors	0.65	0.00	1.00	0.78	0.00	1.00
Proportion of Captive Investors	0.35	0.00	1.00	0.22	0.00	1.00
Median Total Capital Managed by Investor ('000) (This Fund Only)	€160,000.00	€9,400	€760,000	€150,000	€27,250	€760,000
Median Total Capital Managed by Investor ('000) (All Affiliated Funds)	€190,000.00	€9,400	€4,000,000	€150,000	€27,250	€4,000,000
Median IRR	15.00%	−100.00%	900.00%	64.00%	30.00%	900.00%
Median Private Investment Value ('000)	€3,607.00	€50.00	€108,000	€4,449	€500	€108,000

Proportion of All Types of High-tech Firms	0.54	0.00	1.00	0.53	0.00	1.00
Proportion of Biotech/Medical Firms	0.12	0.00	1.00	0.16	0.00	1.00
Proportion of Computer/Electronics Firms	0.20	0.00	1.00	0.19	0.00	1.00
Proportion of Communications/ Internet Firms	0.22	0.00	1.00	0.19	0.00	1.00
Median Industry Market/Book	5.61	4.05	6.77	5.61	4.05	6.77
Median Investor Rank of Entrepreneur	6.00	1.00	10.00	7.00	3.00	10.00
Proportion of Early-/Expansion-stage Firms	0.68	0.00	1.00	0.63	0.00	1.00
Proportion of Common Equity Investments	0.45	0.00	1.00	0.75	0.00	1.00
Proportion of Convertible Securities	0.32	0.00	1.00	0.16	0.00	1.00
Proportion of Debt or Preferred and Common Securities	0.19	0.00	1.00	0.09	0.00	1.00
Proportion of Prior Round(s) of Other Investors	0.11	0.00	1.00	0.19	0.00	1.00
Median # Syndicated Investors	1.00	0.00	5.00	1.00	0.00	3.00
Median Ownership % of All Investors	51.00%	20.00%	96.00%	55.50%	4.16%	92.00%
Proportion of Investments with Majority VC Voting	0.54	0.00	1.00	0.59	0.00	1.00

(continued)

Table 21.3 *(continued)*

	Full Sample of All Exits and Nonexits			IPO Exits		
	(1)	(2)	(3)	(4)	(5)	(6)
	Proportion or Median	Minimum	Maximum	Proportion or Median	Minimum	Maximum
Median All Investor Board Seats/ Total Board Seats	0.40	0.00	1.00	0.40	0.00	0.80
Proportion of Investments with Right to Replace CEO	0.40	0.00	1.00	0.34	0.00	1.00
Proportion of Investments with Drag-along Rights	0.23	0.00	1.00	0.13	0.00	1.00
Proportion of Investments with Redemption Rights	0.37	0.00	1.00	0.31	0.00	1.00
Proportion of Investments with Antidilution Rights	0.57	0.00	1.00	0.41	0.00	1.00
Median Total # Types of Veto Rights	5.00	0.00	5.00	4.50	0.00	5.00
Median Number of Investment Months of Respondent Investor	46	6	96	40	12	75
Median MSCI Return 1 Year Prior to Exit	0.07	−0.56	1.88	0.24	−0.56	1.88
Median MSCI Return 0–3 Months Prior to Exit	0.01	−0.43	0.77	0.06	−0.16	0.77
Median Legality Index	20.76	15.00	21.91	20.84	15.00	21.91
Median Market Capitalization (Billions)	€695,210	€11,002	€1,475,457	€695,210	€31,279	€1,475,457

Table 21.3 *(continued)*

	Acquisitions			Write-offs		
	(7)	(8)	(9)	(10)	(11)	(12)
	Proportion or Median	Minimum	Maximum	Proportion or Median	Minimum	Maximum
Total Number of Observations (# Entrepreneurial Firms)	74			64		
Proportion of Noncaptive Investors	0.64	0.00	1.00	0.56	0.00	1.00
Proportion of Captive Investors	0.36	0.00	1.00	0.44	0.00	1.00
Median Total Capital Managed by Investor ('000) (This Fund Only)	€210,000.00	€9,400	€760,000	€150,000	€27,250	€760,000
Median Total Capital Managed by Investor ('000) (All Affiliated Funds)	€500,000.00	€9,400	€4,000,000	€160,000	€15,000	€4,000,000
Median IRR	25.90%	8%	900%	−100%	−100%	−10.29%
Median Private Investment Value ('000)	€4,000	€150	€108,000	€3,500	€50.00	€33,625
Proportion of All Types of High-tech Firms	0.47	0.00	1.00	0.61	0.00	1.00
Proportion of Biotech/Medical Firms	0.12	0.00	1.00	0.13	0.00	1.00
Proportion of Computer/Electronics Firms	0.19	0.00	1.00	0.19	0.00	1.00
Proportion of Communications/ Internet Firms	0.16	0.00	1.00	0.30	0.00	1.00
Median Industry Market/Book	4.05	4.05	6.77	5.61	4.05	6.77

(continued)

Table 21.3 (*continued*)

	Acquisitions			Write-offs		
	(7)	(8)	(9)	(10)	(11)	(12)
	Proportion or Median	Minimum	Maximum	Proportion or Median	Minimum	Maximum
Median Investor Rank of Entrepreneur	6.00	2.00	10.00	6.00	1.00	10.00
Proportion of Early- and Expansion-stage Firms	0.55	0.00	1.00	0.77	0.00	1.00
Proportion of Common Equity Investments	0.27	0.00	1.00	0.47	0.00	1.00
Proportion of Convertible Securities	0.42	0.00	1.00	0.25	0.00	1.00
Proportion of Debt or Preferred and Common Securities	0.24	0.00	1.00	0.25	0.00	1.00
Proportion of Prior Round(s) of Other Investors	0.15	0.00	1.00	0.06	0.00	1.00
Median # Syndicated Investors	1.00	0.00	3.00	1.00	0.00	4.00
Median Ownership % of All Investors	55.00%	2.00%	92.00%	44.85%	9.00%	99.60%
Proportion of Investments with Majority VC Voting	0.59	0.00	1.00	0.44	0.00	1.00

Median All Investor Board Seats/ Total Board Seats	0.50	0.00	0.80	0.40	0.00	1.00
Proportion of Investments with Right to Replace CEO	0.65	0.00	1.00	0.30	0.00	1.00
Proportion of Investments with Drag-along Rights	0.42	0.00	1.00	0.22	0.00	1.00
Proportion of Investments with Redemption Rights	0.54	0.00	1.00	0.30	0.00	1.00
Proportion of Investments with Antidilution Rights	0.69	0.00	1.00	0.52	0.00	1.00
Median Total # Types of Veto Rights	5.00	0.00	5.00	5.00	0.00	5.00
Median Number of Investment Months of Respondent Investor	40	12	60	43	6	96
Median MSCI Return in 1 Year Prior to Exit	0.07	−0.56	1.88	0.07	−0.33	0.56
Median MSCI Return in 0–3 Months Prior to Exit	0.00	−0.43	0.77	0.01	−0.24	0.16
Median Legality Index	20.60	15.00	21.91	20.76	15.00	21.91
Median Market Capitalization (Billions)	€695,210	€11,002	€1,475,457	€695,210	€11,002	€1,432,190

Table 21.3 *(continued)*

	Median Tests			Mean Tests and Comparison of Proportions Tests		
	(13)	(14)	(15)	(16)	(17)	(18)
	Test of IPOs (4) vs. Acquisitions (7)	Test of IPOs (4) vs. Write-offs (10)	Test of Acquisitions (7) vs. Write-offs (10)	Test of IPOs (4) vs. Acquisitions (7)	Test of IPOs (4) vs. Write-offs (10)	Test of Acquisitions (7) vs. Write-offs (10)
Total Number of Observations (# Entrepreneurial Firms)				−3.79***	−3.10	0.85
Proportion of Noncaptive Investors				1.48	2.10**	0.87
Proportion of Captive Investors				−1.48	−2.10**	−0.87
Total Capital Managed by Investor ('000) (This Fund Only)	$p \leq 0.395$	$p \leq 0.717$	$p \leq 0.091$*	−1.07	0.00	1.75*
Total Capital Managed by Investor ('000) (All Affiliated Funds)	$p \leq 0.151$	$p \leq 0.719$	$p \leq 0.061$*	−0.98	−0.03	1.93*
IRR	$p \leq 0.000$***	$p \leq 0.000$***	$P \leq 0.000$***	1.01	4.62***	11.82***
Private Investment Value ('000)	$p \leq 0.528$	$p \leq 0.282$	$p \leq 0.610$	0.10	0.21	−0.12
Proportion of All Types of High-tech Firms				0.55	−0.73	−1.60
Proportion of Biotech/Medical Firms				0.48	0.42	−0.06
Proportion of Computer/Electronics Firms				−0.02	0.00	0.03
Proportion of Communications/ Internet Firms				0.32	−1.15	−1.89*

Industry Market/Book	$p \leq 0.664$	$p \leq 0.334$	$p \leq 0.154$	5.66***	0.00	−6.99***
Investor Rank of Entrepreneur	$p \leq 0.103$	$p \leq 0.349$	$p \leq 0.748$	3.04***	2.85***	−1.17
Proportion of Early and Expansion Stage Firms				0.68	−1.44	−2.60***
Proportion of Common Equity Investments				4.60***	2.62***	−2.42**
Proportion of Convertible Securities				−2.62***	−1.05	2.09**
Proportion of Debt or Preferred and Common Securities				−1.77*	−1.81*	−0.09
Proportion of Prior Round(s) of Other Investors				0.50	1.89*	1.62
# Syndicated Investors	$p \leq 0.062$*	$p \leq 0.309$	$p \leq 0.375$	0.00	0.00	1.03
Ownership % of All Investors	$p \leq 0.015$**	$p \leq 0.282$	$p \leq 0.126$	0.00	0.02	1.23
Proportion of Investments with Majority VC Voting				−0.01	1.44	1.84*
All Investor Board Seats/Total Board Seats	$p \leq 0.528$	$p \leq 0.719$	$p \leq 0.860$	−2.17**	0.00	0.67
Proportion of Investments with Right to Replace CEO				−2.90***	0.47	4.12***
Proportion of Investments with Drag-along Rights				−2.91***	−1.06	2.50**
Proportion of Investments with Redemption Rights				−2.18**	0.10	2.84***

(*continued*)

Table 21.3 *(continued)*

	Median Tests			Mean Tests and Comparison of Proportions Tests		
	(13)	(14)	(15)	(16)	(17)	(18)
	Test of IPOs (4) vs. Acquisitions (7)	Test of IPOs (4) vs. Write-offs (10)	Test of Acquisitions (7) vs. Write-offs (10)	Test of IPOs (4) vs. Acquisitions (7)	Test of IPOs (4) vs. Write-offs (10)	Test of Acquisitions (7) vs. Write-offs (10)
Proportion of Investments with Antidilution Rights				−2.71***	−1.02	2.04**
Total # Types of Veto Rights	$p \leq 0.008$***	$p \leq 0.720$	$p \leq 0.003$***	−1.16	−1.04	3.41***
Number of Investment Months of Respondent Investor	$p \leq 0.426$	$p \leq 0.829$	$p \leq 0.849$	0.00	−0.80	−0.79
MSCI Return 1 Year Prior to Exit	$p \leq 0.006$***	$p \leq 0.003$***	$p \leq 0.856$	0.62	0.60	0.11
MSCI Return 0–3 Months Prior to Exit	$p \leq 0.004$***	$p \leq 0.456$	$p \leq 0.845$	1.37	1.14	−2.56***
Legality Index	$p \leq 0.375$	$p \leq 0.615$	$p \leq 0.860$	0.56	0.18	0.47
Market Capitalization (Billions)	$p \leq 0.008$***	$p \leq 0.017$**	$p \leq 0.839$	0.00	0.00	−0.28

21.5.2 Endogeneity

Table 21.6 presents regression models on the determinants of exit outcomes that are similar to those in Table 21.5 but with one major exception. In Table 21.6, we examine the effect of endogeneity of control rights on exits. We use two-step instrumental variable estimates. Step 1 of Models 3 and 4 accounts for the factors that affect the extent of VC control. Step 1 of Model 3 considers binomial logit estimates for majority board seats and the right to replace the CEO. Step 1 of Model 4 considers ordered logit estimates of the control rights index for the sum of dummy variables for drag-along, redemption, and antidilution rights. Step 2 of Models 3 and 4 estimates the multinomial logit model of exit outcomes.

In Table 21.6, we use the exogenous variables that are included in step 1 and excluded in step 2 of Models 3 and 4. These variables are the La Porta et al. (1998) indexes for creditor rights and antidirector (shareholder) rights. These instruments are intuitively related to contract terms, as confirmed by all of the correlations that are reported in Table 21.7. We do not expect to find a relation between creditor rights and exit outcomes, unless the efficiency of bankruptcy law is related to write-offs. Table 21.7 indicates that creditor rights are not statistically related to any of the exit outcomes, which confirms the suitability of that instrument for the data. Antidirector rights may be positively related to the probability of an IPO (La Porta et al., 1998), but the data here indicate the opposite. The correlation between antidirector rights and IPO exits is −0.18. This negative correlation can only be explained by independent factors driving the IPO exits, and by little or no direct relation between IPOs and antidirector rights. In contrast, the antidirector rights index is significant and negatively related to the contract terms. This finding is consistent with the view that as shareholders, VCs use contracts as substitutes for the absence of strong legal protection (Lerner and Schoar, 2005). Creditor rights are positively and significantly related to contract terms, which is intuitive, because when decisions have be made in times of financial distress, VCs as shareholders want priority over and above creditors. Also, we use the industry market/book value at the time of first investment as an instrumental variable. This is a valid instrument because the second-step regressions use the industry market/book value at the time of exit. The results of the second step regressions are similar when we use the different instruments and different specifications for the first-step regressions and are available on request.

In Table 21.6, the step 1 evidence in Models 3 and 4 indicates that creditor rights are statistically and positively related to the extent of VC control and to the right to replace the CEO, but not statistically related to majority board seats. A one-point increase in the creditor rights index (on the scale of zero to four) increases the probability of the VC acquiring the right to replace the CEO by 31.6%. We note that although the creditor and antidirector rights are negatively correlated (−0.42 for this sample), the statistical and economic significance of the regressions is not materially affected by the inclusion or exclusion of these variables. For instance, excluding antidirector rights in step 1 of Model 3 in

Table 21.4

This table presents correlation coefficients across various contractual variables, exit outcomes, market variables, and legal of 187 exited companies for the following variables: IPO, acquisition, write-off, IRR, MSCI prior year, and market variables are as defined in Table 21.1. Correlations highlighted in boldface are statistically significant at the 5% level.

Panel A. Correlations across

		(1)	(2)	(3)	(4)	(5)	(6)	(7)	(8)	(9)
(1)	IPO	1.00								
(2)	Acquisition	**−0.37**	1.00							
(3)	Buyback	**−0.14**	**−0.26**	1.00						
(4)	Write-off	**−0.33**	**−0.58**	**−0.23**	1.00					
(5)	IRR	**0.36**	**0.30**	0.03	**−0.61**	1.00				
(6)	Noncaptive	0.11	−0.05	**0.19**	**−0.15**	0.11	1.00			
(7)	Investor Fund Capital	**0.15**	0.08	**−0.14**	−0.12	0.05	0.11	1.00		
(8)	Private Investment Value	**0.17**	−0.07	0.00	−0.06	0.07	0.13	0.12	1.00	
(9)	Industry Market/Book	0.00	−0.10	−0.06	**0.15**	0.02	**−0.16**	0.04	**−0.21**	1.00
(10)	Entrepreneur Experience	0.13	−0.12	−0.03	0.04	0.08	−0.04	−0.07	0.01	−0.13
(11)	Early/ Expansion Stage	−0.03	**−0.17**	0.04	**0.17**	−0.07	**−0.33**	**−0.16**	**−0.36**	**0.48**
(12)	Common Equity	**0.32**	**−0.22**	**−0.19**	0.09	0.15	−0.03	0.09	0.04	0.04
(13)	Convertible Security	**−0.18**	0.13	**0.24**	**−0.14**	−0.04	−0.03	**−0.26**	−0.06	0.07
(14)	Prior Round(s)	0.10	0.08	−0.06	−0.12	**0.24**	0.01	0.05	0.12	**0.20**
(15)	Number of Syndicated Investors	0.00	0.11	−0.12	−0.04	0.03	**−0.17**	0.00	0.03	**0.17**
(16)	Replace CEO	−0.10	**0.32**	−0.06	**−0.22**	−0.01	**0.19**	**0.47**	0.11	**−0.24**
(17)	Majority Board	−0.03	0.10	−0.11	−0.02	0.02	0.05	**0.23**	**0.18**	0.05
(18)	Majority Voting	0.06	0.11	−0.04	−0.13	0.04	**0.17**	**0.23**	**0.18**	**−0.21**
(19)	Drag-along	**−0.15**	**0.27**	−0.11	−0.09	0.04	0.03	0.11	0.00	0.05
(20)	Redemption	−0.07	**0.25**	−0.10	**−0.14**	0.03	0.06	**0.55**	0.06	−0.05
(21)	Antidilution	**−0.16**	**0.18**	0.04	−0.09	0.05	0.03	**0.39**	−0.02	0.08
(22)	Veto Rights	−0.07	**0.28**	**−0.14**	**−0.14**	−0.02	**−0.18**	**0.35**	0.07	**−0.18**
(23)	MSCI 0–3 Months	**0.39**	**−0.28**	0.01	−0.02	0.04	−0.07	**0.17**	0.09	0.06
(24)	Legality	−0.07	0.11	**−0.16**	0.04	−0.10	**−0.23**	**0.47**	0.06	−0.07
(25)	Market Capitalization	−0.13	0.06	−0.07	0.09	−0.06	−0.01	0.08	0.01	**0.27**

Correlation Matrix

variables. Because the following variables are contingent on exit and the exit year, the sample comprises only the exit sample capitalization. For all other variables, the sample represents the full sample of all 223 exited and unexited investments. The

Contracts, Exits, Market Variables, and Legal Variables

(10)	(11)	(12)	(13)	(14)	(15)	(16)	(17)	(18)	(19)	(20)	(21)	(22)	(23)	(24)
1.00														
0.03	1.00													
0.28	0.08	1.00												
−0.13	**0.22**	**−0.60**	1.00											
0.08	0.09	0.07	0.05	1.00										
−0.05	0.13	0.02	0.04	**0.29**	1.00									
−0.22	**−0.40**	**−0.22**	−0.04	−0.03	0.03	1.00								
0.04	−0.11	0.08	0.03	0.13	**0.19**	0.13	1.00							
−0.15	**−0.40**	−0.07	−0.02	−0.09	**0.22**	**0.42**	**0.26**	1.00						
−0.27	−0.08	−0.12	0.12	−0.04	−0.07	**0.20**	**0.39**	**0.19**	1.00					
−0.14	**−0.22**	−0.13	**−0.18**	−0.09	0.06	**0.60**	0.06	**0.23**	0.05	1.00				
−0.17	**−0.15**	**−0.20**	0.00	**−0.16**	0.09	**0.45**	0.08	**0.32**	0.09	**0.68**	1.00			
−0.14	**−0.26**	**−0.28**	0.06	**−0.17**	−0.04	**0.52**	**0.19**	**0.21**	**0.25**	**0.40**	**0.35**	1.00		
0.03	0.09	**0.22**	0.02	−0.01	0.07	−0.10	**0.17**	**0.19**	0.04	−0.08	−0.06	−0.04	1.00	
−0.10	**−0.14**	−0.08	**−0.20**	−0.01	−0.02	**0.37**	−0.01	0.11	0.01	**0.33**	**0.38**	**0.23**	0.03	1.00
−0.18	0.01	−0.07	0.05	**0.18**	0.06	0.05	0.08	0.05	0.14	−0.10	0.08	0.03	−0.02	**0.31**

(continued)

Table 21.4 *(continued)*

This table presents correlation coefficients across country dummy variables and various contractual variables and the exit outcomes. Because the following variables are contingent on exit and the exit year, the sample comprises only the exit sample of 187 exited companies. The number of exits from each country is summarized at the bottom of this table. The variables are defined in Table 21.1. Correlations highlighted in boldface are statistically significant at the 5% level of significance.

Panel B. Correlations across Country Dummy Variables and Contracts and Exits											
	Austria	Belgium	Czech Rep.	Denmark	France	Germany	Italy	Netherlands	Poland	Portugal	Switzerland
IPO	0.00	0.03	−0.06	0.06	0.00	**−0.19**	**0.23**	**−0.16**	0.00	0.03	**0.23**
Acquisition	−0.02	−0.08	−0.02	0.01	0.04	−0.02	−0.09	**0.18**	−0.08	−0.04	−0.04
Buyback	−0.06	**0.19**	−0.04	−0.06	**0.15**	−0.02	−0.12	−0.08	**0.30**	−0.05	−0.09
Write-off	0.06	−0.06	0.09	−0.02	−0.13	**0.18**	−0.02	−0.01	−0.10	0.05	−0.09
IRR	−0.06	0.02	0.11	−0.01	0.04	−0.11	**0.15**	−0.06	−0.01	0.00	0.05
Common Equity	0.16	−0.08	**0.15**	−0.05	−0.09	−0.08	**0.24**	**−0.16**	**−0.22**	**0.18**	**0.20**
Convertible Security	−0.07	0.10	−0.09	**0.15**	**0.19**	**0.21**	**−0.16**	**−0.23**	**0.36**	−0.11	**−0.21**
Prior Round(s)	−0.07	0.00	−0.05	0.02	**0.31**	0.03	0.12	**−0.17**	−0.10	−0.05	0.08
Number of Syndicated Investors	0.04	0.11	−0.04	0.12	**0.16**	0.03	0.13	**−0.22**	**−0.16**	0.08	0.01
Right to Replace CEO	−0.10	−0.10	−0.12	0.05	**0.20**	**−0.21**	**−0.23**	**0.26**	**−0.24**	0.09	**0.33**
Majority Board	−0.11	−0.11	0.14	0.04	**0.20**	−0.06	0.09	−0.13	−0.07	−0.06	**0.24**
Majority Voting	−0.13	0.01	0.04	0.02	0.11	−0.12	**0.14**	0.00	**−0.28**	**0.14**	**0.16**
Drag-along	−0.11	−0.08	0.02	−0.12	−0.04	0.15	−0.04	−0.03	0.04	−0.01	0.08
Redemption	**−0.15**	−0.03	−0.10	0.07	**−0.15**	**−0.20**	**−0.19**	**0.26**	**−0.21**	**0.18**	**0.37**
Antidilution	**−0.15**	**0.14**	**−0.15**	0.05	**−0.15**	0.04	**−0.16**	0.11	**−0.31**	0.13	**0.25**
Veto Rights	−0.02	**−0.30**	**−0.25**	−0.05	0.09	**−0.17**	**−0.20**	**0.34**	0.04	0.02	**0.20**
Summary of # Exits from Each Country											
# IPOs	1	2	0	2	1	2	7	7	2	1	7
# Acquisitions	2	2	1	3	3	14	6	34	3	1	5
# Buyback	0	3	0	0	2	3	0	4	5	0	0
# Write-offs	3	2	2	2	0	19	7	22	2	2	3
# Unexited Investments as at 2005	4	1	2	4	0	13	1	7	0	2	0

Table 21.5 Multinomial Logit Regressions

This table presents multinomial logit estimates of the impact of investor characteristics, investee characteristics, transaction characteristics, market conditions, and institutional and legal factors on the various venture capital exit outcomes IPOs, acquisitions, buybacks, and write-offs. Models 1 and 2 examine all 223 exits and nonexits. The variables are as defined in Table 21.1. We use investment-year dummy variables for 2000 and 2001, and country dummy variables for the Netherlands and Germany. We do not use additional year and country dummy variables due to perfect collinearity problems—that is, where there is no variation for any one of the exit outcomes associated with a year and/or a country. We use the MSCI returns prior to exit for 2005 for the no-exit observations. The table presents values for the marginal effects, not the standard multinomial logit coefficients in order to explicitly highlight economic significance alongside statistical significance. The marginal effects are not presented for the no-exit outcomes for reasons of conciseness. Standard errors are clustered by VC fund following the procedure in Greene (2002; see also Petersen, 2006). White's (1980) HCCME is used in all models. *, **, *** indicate statistical significance at the 10%, 5%, and 1% levels, respectively.

	Model 1: Basic Specification				Model 2: Alternate Basic Specification			
	IPO	**Acquisition**	**Buyback**	**Write-off**	**IPO**	**Acquisition**	**Buyback**	**Write-off**
Constant	−0.613	3.173*	−0.013	−1.260	−1.056	3.259*	0.226	−0.984
Investor Characteristics								
Log (Fund Capital)	−0.011	−0.036	−0.047**	−0.001	0.030	−0.108	−0.050*	0.037
Noncaptive VC Fund	−0.004	−0.221*	0.103**	0.048	0.058	−0.214*	0.084*	0.012
Investee Characteristics								
Early or Expansion Stage	−0.026	−0.097	0.003	0.121	−0.005	−0.120	−0.001	0.094
Entrepreneur Experience Rank	0.007	−0.034	−0.004	0.015	0.011	−0.029	−0.003	0.006
Log (Industry Market/Book)	0.058	−0.235	−0.051	0.167	0.096	−0.295	−0.062	0.178

(*continued*)

Table 21.5 *(continued)*

	Model 1: Basic Specification				Model 2: Alternate Basic Specification			
	IPO	Acquisition	Buyback	Write-off	IPO	Acquisition	Buyback	Write-off
Transaction Characteristics								
Log (Private Investment Value)	0.019	−0.043	0.005	0.039	0.014	−0.031	0.004	0.023
Prior Rounds	0.029	0.282**	−0.019	−0.301**	0.030	0.395**	−0.019	−0.413**
Replace CEO	−0.068	0.386***	0.024	−0.159	−0.068	0.236*	0.036	−0.028
Majority Board	−0.106**	0.237***	−0.039	0.035	−0.092*	0.184*	−0.043	0.082
Majority Vote					0.040	−0.059	0.006	−0.085
Control Rights Index					−0.066**	0.122**	0.014	−0.072
Veto Rights					0.011	0.056	0.008	−0.052
Market Characteristics								
Log (MSCI 3–6 Months)	0.122	−0.056	0.123	−1.199	0.058	0.251	0.123	−1.323
Log (MSCI 0–3 Months)	1.007***	−1.668***	0.290	0.366	0.916***	−1.682***	0.254	0.603
Investment Year Dummies?	Yes	Yes	Yes	Yes	Yes	Yes	Yes	Yes

Institutional and Legal Variables								
Log (Legality)	−0.026	−0.833	0.110	0.203	0.046	−0.787	0.060	0.116
Log (Market Capitalization)	0.052*	0.063	0.014	0.003	0.022	0.093	0.013	0.005
Country Dummies?	Yes	Yes	Yes	Yes	Yes	Yes	Yes	Yes
Model Diagnostics								
Number of Observations	223				223			
Chi-squared	191.197***				215.221***			
Log Likelihood	−237.457				−225.445			
Pseudo R^2	0.287				0.323			

Table 21.6 Instrumental Variable Multinomial Logit Regressions

This table presents instrumental multinomial logit estimates of the impact of investor characteristics, investee characteristics, transaction characteristics, market conditions, and institutional and legal factors on the various venture capital exit outcomes IPOs, acquisitions, buybacks, and write-offs. Models 3 and 4 examine all 223 exits and nonexits. The variables are as defined in Table 21.1. We use investment-year dummy variables for 2000 and 2001, and country dummy variables for the Netherlands and Germany. We do not use additional year and country dummy variables due to perfect collinearity problems—that is, where there is no variation for any one of the exit outcomes associated with a year and/or a country. We use the MSCI returns prior to exit for 2005 for the no-exit observations. In Model 3, step 1 we first regress the binary, dependent variables for the right to replace the CEO and majority board seats on investee characteristics, investment dummies, and the legal indexes for anti-director and creditor rights. Panel B presents the correlations between endogenous variables, instruments, and exit outcomes. Step 2 of Model 3 then uses the fitted values of the step 1 regressions for the right to replace the CEO and majority board seats variables. Model 4 is identical to Model 3, except that Model 3's step 1 uses an ordered logit estimate of the number of control rights for the sum of drag-along, redemption, and antidilution rights and then the fitted values of that estimated variable for step 2. For step 1 in Model 3 and step 2 in Models 3 and 4, to explicitly highlight economic significance alongside statistical significance, the values are the marginal effects, not the standard multinomial logit coefficients. Step 1 in Model 4 presents values of the standard ordered logit coefficients, not the marginal effects for each ranked outcome for reasons of conciseness. The step 2 in Models 3 and 4 does not show the marginal effects the buyback and no-exit outcomes for reasons of conciseness. Standard errors are clustered by VC fund following the procedure in Greene (2002). White's (1980) HCCME is used in all models. *, **, *** indicate statistical significance at the 10%, 5%, and 1% levels, respectively.

	Model 3: Instrumental Variables					Model 4: Alternate Instrumental Variables			
	Step (1): Determinants of Choice Variables		Step (2): Determinants of Exit Outcomes			Step (1): Determinants of Choice Variables	Step (2) Model (b): Determinants of Exit Outcomes		
	Binary Logit: Replace CEO	Binary Logit: Majority Board	IPO	Acquisition	Write-off	Ordered Logit: Control Index	IPO	Acquisition	Write-off
Constant	0.412	0.005	−0.530	2.096	−0.581	1.777***	−0.258	1.882	−0.444

Investor Characteristics									
Log (Fund Capital)			−0.027	0.036	−0.029		−0.033	0.012	0.004
Noncaptive VC Fund			0.005	−0.201*	0.010		−0.009	−0.233**	0.048
Investee Characteristics									
Early or Expansion Stage	−0.324***	−0.187**	0.014	−0.219*	0.173	−0.453**	0.045	−0.128	0.040
Entrepreneur Experience Rank	−0.063**	0.012	0.016	−0.060**	0.019	−0.158***	0.029*	−0.002	−0.035
Log (Industry Market/Book) (Time of Investment for Step 1 and Time of Exit for Step 2)	−0.016	0.230**	0.121	−0.426*	0.181	0.417*	0.018	−0.385	0.327
Transaction Characteristics									
Log (Private Investment Value)			0.015	−0.044	0.050		0.016	−0.042	0.049
Prior Rounds			0.014	0.285**	−0.259*		0.019	0.301**	−0.278*
Replace CEO (Fitted Value from Step 1)			0.051	−0.176	0.041				

(continued)

Table 21.6 *(continued)*

	Model 3: Instrumental Variables					Model 4: Alternate Instrumental Variables			
	Step (1): Determinants of Choice Variables		Step (2): Determinants of Exit Outcomes			Step (1): Determinants of Choice Variables	Step (2) Model (b): Determinants of Exit Outcomes		
	Binary Logit: Replace CEO	Binary Logit: Majority Board	IPO	Acquisition	Write-off	Ordered Logit: Control Index	IPO	Acquisition	Write-off
Majority Board (Fitted Value from Step 1)			−0.073	0.223*	0.039				
Control Index (Fitted Value from Step 1)							0.041	0.145**	−0.155***
Market Characteristics									
Log (MSCI 3–6 Months)			0.158	−0.176	−1.382*		0.157	0.166	−1.628**
Log (MSCI 0–3 Months)			0.974***	−1.757***	0.377		0.961***	−1.660***	0.357
Investment Year Dummies?	Yes	Yes	Yes	Yes	Yes	Yes	Yes	Yes	Yes

Institutional and Legal Variables									
Antidirector Rights	−0.058	−0.126**				−0.096			
Creditor Rights	0.316***	0.055				0.192*			
Log (Legality)			−0.067	−0.413	−0.093		−0.140	−0.510	−0.120
Log (Market Capitalization)			0.050*	0.051	0.024		0.053**	0.063	0.020
Country Dummies?	No	No	Yes	Yes	Yes	No	Yes	Yes	Yes
Ordered Logit Parameters									
Mu(1)						0.679***			
Mu(2)						1.951***			
Model Diagnostics									
Number of Observations	223	223	223			223	223		
Chi-squared	85.450***	26.371***	154.568***			41.057***	155.232		
Log Likelihood	−107.675	−138.629	−255.771			−270.077	−255.439		
Pseudo R^2	0.284	0.087	0.232			0.071	0.233		

Table 21.6 increases the economic significance of creditor rights from 31.6 to 34.3% for the right to replace the CEO without changing the statistical significance.

A one-point increase in the creditor rights index also increases the probability of an extra control right (drag-along, redemption, or antidilution) by on average approximately 3%. The economic significance of a one-point increase in creditor rights is 4.9% to move from two to three, and 2.6% to move from three to four in step 1 of Model 4.

In contrast, antidirector rights are more closely tied to majority board seats. An increase of one point in the index (on the scale of 0 to 6) reduces the probability of VC majority board seats by 12.6%. The step 1 regressions in Table 21.6 further indicate that VCs are more likely to have a majority on the board and to have greater control rights for those firms in industries with higher market/book ratios (high-tech industries). VCs are less likely to take majority board seats, have the right to replace the CEO, and to have other control rights for earlier-stage investments. VCs are also less likely to have the right to replace the CEO and other control rights when the entrepreneur has a higher experience ranking.

The step 2 regressions in Models 3 and 4 in Table 21.6 are consistent with those reported for Models 1 and 2 in Table 21.5. Majority board seats lead to a 22.3% increase in the probability of an acquisition exit (Model 3), and each additional control right increases the probability of an acquisition by 14.5% (Model 4). The one result that differs from Models 1 and 2 is that the right to replace the CEO is statistically insignificant in Model 3.

In general, the alternative specifications for the step 1 and 2 regressions in Table 21.6 invariably support at least one of the VC control right variables as being significantly related to acquisition exits. The instrumental variables regressions are not completely robust to alternative specifications, but nevertheless indicate support for the central proposition in the chapter that VC control influences the IPO versus acquisition choice, even after controlling for endogeneity.

21.5.3 Additional Robustness Checks

In this subsection we describe the results from six additional robustness checks (Models 5–10) that are presented in Table 21.8. As well, we discuss a number of additional robustness checks that were carried out but not explicitly reported.

So that we can include dummy variables for exit years, Models 5–10 exclude buyback and non exits from the sample. Model 5 presents a standard specification without buybacks and nonexits that is comparable to Model 1 without such exclusions. The regression results are similar and continue to support our central hypothesis.

Model 6 provides a similar regression, but excludes investment years 1995 to 1998, because we want to check if contracts are related to exits in a way that is driven by the time period spanned by the data. For instance, if VCs in Europe

Table 21.7 Correlations between Instruments, Endogenous Variables, and Exit Outcomes

This table presents correlations between the instruments (creditor rights, antidirector rights, and industry market/book at first investment), the endogenous variables (right to replace CEO, majority board seats, and the control rights index), and the second step exit outcome variables (IPOs, acquisitions, and write-offs). Correlations are for the full sample for the contract terms, and for the subsample of 187 exits for the exit variables. Correlations that are statistically significant at the 5% level are highlighted in boldface.

		(1)	(2)	(3)	(4)	(5)	(6)	(7)	(8)
(1)	Creditor Rights	1.00							
(2)	Antidirector Rights	**−0.42**	1.00						
(3)	Log (Industry Market/Book) at 1st Investment	**−0.30**	0.13	1.00					
(4)	IPO Exit	0.00	**−0.18**	0.00	1.00				
(5)	Acquisition Exit	0.14	0.02	−0.10	**−0.37**	1.00			
(6)	Write-off Exit	−0.07	**0.23**	0.13	**−0.33**	**−0.58**	1.00		
(7)	Right to Replace CEO	**0.43**	**−0.28**	**−0.21**	−0.05	**0.35**	−0.14	1.00	
(8)	Majority Board Seats	**0.16**	**−0.23**	0.04	0.01	**0.15**	0.04	0.13	1.00
(9)	Control Rights Index	**0.19**	**−0.15**	0.04	−0.13	**0.33**	−0.09	**0.54**	**0.25**

were less sophisticated in the mid-1990s, and thus wrote less detailed contracts, and since market conditions enabled different exit opportunities in the Internet bubble period, then contracts might be connected to exits for reasons unrelated to the hypotheses discussed in subsection 21.2.1. However, the estimates in Model 6 indicate that the data do not support this alternative explanation for the results. The relation between VC control rights and acquisitions continues to hold for the subsample that excludes investment years 1995 to 1998. The results also hold for other subsamples that exclude other periods that are not explicitly presented here. These results are available on request.

Regression Models 5–8 in Table 21.8 indicate a negative relation between the right to replace the CEO and write-offs. That is, detailed VC contracts tend to enable the VC to prevent "bad" outcomes. In Model 7, for example, the right to replace the founding entrepreneur specifically reduces the probability of a write-off by 31.7%, and each additional control right studied (drag-along, redemption, and antidilution) reduces the probability of a write-off by 18.2%. This finding is consistent with Lerner (1995) and Gompers and Lerner (1999a). It is also consistent with the Kaplan et al. (2007) result that international VC funds that do use contracts with strong VC control rights are more likely to survive the Internet bubble crash after 2000.

Our results suggest that strong VC rights are more likely to protect a VCs interest and force an acquisition. Weak control rights are more often associated with IPOs, but are also associated with write-offs and a non-covered investment. For instance, there were 15 pure common equity investments in the data with absolutely no control rights above and beyond those held by the entrepreneur. Among those, six were IPOs, six were write-offs, and three were not yet exited in 2005. We also note that the trend in the European data is more often toward using convertible securities, both in the data introduced in this chapter (Table 21.2) and in the Kaplan et al. (2007) data. These trends also are consistent with the use of greater downside protection after the crash of the Internet bubble on April 14, 2000, which caused a major downturn in the market.

To control for the possibility of endogeneity of contracts vis-à-vis exits, Model 7 excludes the preplanned exits in the data. In the full sample of 223 investments, 70 of the investments (31.4%) indicate a degree of preplanned exit behavior at the time of investment (and do not necessarily indicate such plans to the investee); 55 of the 70 (79%) are exited investments in our sample as of 2005. This evidence on preplanning behavior suggests the possibility of endogeneity vis-à-vis contracts and exits, although the VCs indicate that the preplanned exit outcome was by no means certain at the time of investment. Among the preplanned exits, the investors indicate that their (preplanned) strategy turned out to have the desired result only 53% of the time. Regression Model 7 in Table 21.8 indicates that the results are robust to excluding preplanned exits. This finding is strongly consistent with alternative controls for endogeneity in Table 21.6.

In Models 8 and 9, we examine the subsample of only seed investments i.e., start-ups at the time of first VC investment, and seed and expansion

Table 21.8 Robustness Checks

This table presents additional robustness checks on the multinomial logit estimates of the impact of investor characteristics, investee characteristics, transaction characteristics, market conditions, and institutional and legal factors on the venture capital exit outcomes IPOs, acquisitions, buybacks, and write-offs. To use dummy variables for exit years (2000–2005), investment years (1997–2002), and countries (Germany, Italy, the Netherlands, and Switzerland), Models 5–10 present estimates excluding buybacks and nonexits. Model 6 excludes the subsample of investments in 1995–1998. Model 7 excludes the subsample of preplanned exits. Models 8 and 9 examine the subsample of investments at the seed-money and expansion stages, and only the seed stage, respectively. Model 10 examines the subsample of funds that provided all of their investments as at 2002. To explicitly highlight economic significance alongside statistical significance, the values are the marginal effects, not the standard multinomial logit coefficients. Standard errors are clustered by VC fund following the procedure in Greene (2002). White's (1980) HCCME is used in all models. *, **, *** indicate statistical significance at the 10%, 5%, and 1% levels, respectively.

	Model 5: Excluding Buybacks and Nonexits			Model 6: Excluding Investment Years 1995–1998			Model 7: Excluding Preplanned Exits		
	IPO	Acquisition	Write-off	IPO	Acquisition	Write-off	IPO	Acquisition	Write-off
Constant	−0.389	2.959	−2.570	0.084	2.191	−2.275	0.015	10.561***	−10.576***
Investor Characteristics									
Log (Fund Capital)	−0.044	−0.151	0.195*	−0.002	−0.173	0.175	−0.006	−0.092	0.099
Noncaptive VC Fund	−0.005	−0.299*	0.305*	0.011	−0.161	0.150	0.013	−0.205	0.192
Investee Characteristics									
Early or Expansion Stage	0.041	−0.225	0.185	−0.030	−0.239	0.269	0.033	−0.102	0.069
Entrepreneur Experience Rank	0.017	−0.033	0.016	0.004	−0.007	0.002	0.004	0.019	−0.023
Log (Industry Market/Book)	0.122	−0.441	0.319	0.061	−0.332	0.271	−0.051	−0.137	0.187
Transaction Characteristics									
Log (Private Investment Value)	0.018	−0.085	0.067	0.004	−0.044	0.040	0.022	−0.162**	0.141
Prior Rounds	−0.001	0.405**	−0.404**	−0.011	0.610***	−0.599**	0.009	0.481*	−0.490*

(continued)

Table 21.8 *(continued)*

	Model 5: Excluding Buybacks and Nonexits			Model 6: Excluding Investment Years 1995–1998			Model 7: Excluding Preplanned Exits		
	IPO	Acquisition	Write-off	IPO	Acquisition	Write-off	IPO	Acquisition	Write-off
Replace CEO	−0.019	0.374**	−0.355**	−0.021	0.334*	−0.313*	−0.003	0.321*	−0.317*
Majority Board	−0.089	0.217*	−0.128	−0.022	0.128	−0.106	−0.056	0.163	−0.107
Control Rights Index	−0.048	0.121*	–0.073	−0.007	0.184**	−0.177**	0.002	0.181**	−0.182**
Market Characteristics									
Log (MSCI 3–6 Months)	−0.171	−1.698	1.868	0.455	−0.035	−0.421	0.715	−7.980***	7.265
Log (MSCI 0–3 Months)	0.561	−2.818***	2.257**	0.167	−1.371	1.204	0.282	−5.345***	5.063**
Exit Year Dummies?	Yes	Yes	Yes	Yes	Yes	Yes	Yes	Yes	Yes
Investment Year Dummies?	Yes	Yes	Yes	Yes	Yes	Yes	Yes	Yes	Yes
Institutional and Legal Variables									
Log (Legality)	−0.063	−0.947	1.011	0.013	−0.142	0.129	0.082	−4.369***	4.287***
Log (Market Capitalization)	0.061	0.311	−0.372*	−0.023	0.063	−0.040	−0.023	0.329**	−0.306
Country Dummies?	Yes	Yes	Yes	Yes	Yes	Yes	Yes	Yes	Yes
Model Diagnostics									
Number of Observations	170			118			117		
Chi-squared	145.158***			69.347***			127.876***		
Log Likelihood	−104.934			−79.033			−60.181		
Pseudo R^2	0.409			0.305			0.515		

Table 21.8 (*continued*)

	Model 8: Early and Expansion Stage			Model 9: Early Stage			Model 10: Subsample of Funds That Provided All Investments		
	IPO	Acquisition	Write-off	IPO	Acquisition	Write-off	IPO	Acquisition	Write-off
Constant	0.105	0.668	−0.773	0.041	−1.235	1.193	−1.148	5.233	−4.086
Investor Characteristics									
Log (Fund Capital)	0.062	−0.198*	0.136	−0.002	−0.263	0.265	−0.021	−0.050	0.071
Noncaptive VC Fund							0.090	−0.395**	0.305*
Investee Characteristics									
Early or Expansion Stage							−0.001	−0.206	0.206
Entrepreneur Experience Rank	0.018	−0.024	0.005	0.002	−0.042	0.040	0.017	−0.052	0.035
Log (Industry Market/Book)	−0.034	−0.150	0.184	−0.003	−0.723	0.726	0.150	−0.624*	0.474
Transaction Characteristics									
Log (Private Investment Value)	0.009	0.060	−0.069	0.006	0.245	−0.251	−0.003	−0.042	0.045
Prior Rounds							−0.025	0.519***	−0.494**
Replace CEO	0.018	0.270	−0.288*	0.002	0.449	−0.451	−0.013	0.109	−0.096
Majority Board	−0.111*	0.293**	−0.181	−0.009	0.457	−0.448	−0.057	0.069	−0.012
Control Rights Index	−0.100**	0.223***	−0.123	−0.006	0.405**	−0.399**	−0.056*	0.172**	−0.116
Market Characteristics									
Log (MSCI 3–6 Months)							0.098	0.063	−0.161
Log (MSCI 0–3 Months)	1.017**	−1.539**	0.523	0.066	−1.506	1.440	0.902**	−1.830**	0.928

(*continued*)

Table 21.8 *(continued)*

	Model 8: Early and Expansion Stage			Model 9: Early Stage			Model 10: Subsample of Funds That Provided All Investments		
	IPO	Acquisition	Write-off	IPO	Acquisition	Write-off	IPO	Acquisition	Write-off
Exit Year Dummies?	Yes	Yes	Yes	Yes	Yes	Yes	Yes	Yes	Yes
Investment Year Dummies?	Yes	Yes	Yes	Yes	Yes	Yes	Yes	Yes	Yes
Institutional and Legal Variables									
Log (Legality)	−0.230	0.099	0.131	−0.017	−0.097	0.113	0.238	−1.113	0.875
Log (Market Capitalization)	−0.016	0.061	−0.045	−0.001	0.244	−0.243	0.029	0.045	−0.075
Country Dummies?	Yes	Yes	Yes	Yes	Yes	Yes	Yes	Yes	Yes
Model Diagnostics									
Number of Observations	110			49			127		
Chi-squared	66.861***			42.305***			82.122***		
Log Likelihood	−80.752			−26.765			−90.160		
Pseudo R^2	0.293			0.441			0.313		

investments, respectively. These are important to show that the results are not driven by investments that were close to exiting at the time of first investment.[6] Model 10 examines only the funds that provided all of their investments as of 2002, which means we had to reject the observations of 15 funds. This robustness check is important to show that the results are not affected by VCs withholding information on some of their investments, such as the poorer performing ones.

All of the estimates consistently support the central propositions that relate contracts to exits. In other models (not reported but available on request), we consider dummy variables for funds, rather than countries. The results show that fund effects are not driving the results. However, we note that we could not use dummy variables for 12 funds because of collinearity problems. Further, in other models, which are available on request, we consider different definitions of certain variables to show that the results are not driven by the model specifications. These models use dummy variables for seed, expansion, and late stages. At the time of the first VC investment, there are 69 seed investments, 82 expansion investments, 32 late investments, and 40 buyouts in the data. The models also use a dummy variable for entrepreneurs with rankings of seven or more (as an alternative to the other models with the ranking variable on the one-to-ten scale) and a second VC dummy for both captive and non-captive VCs. (We suppress the captive bank VC dummy for reasons of collinearity). Because there are 28 exits of foreign investments and nine unexited foreign investments, we also include a variable for the exits in which the investment is initially in a foreign firm. Also, we consider the use of different contract terms, which we include as right-hand-side variables. When we use common equity as a proxy for weak VC control rights, we find that it is associated with a 12.3% greater chance of an IPO and a 30.1% smaller chance of an acquisition. These findings are consistent with the comparison tests in Table 21.3. In a similar specification, we find that drag-along rights are more important in effecting an acquisition than are redemption or antidilution rights. Drag-along rights are associated with a 15.8% reduction in the probability of an IPO and a 31.5% increase in the probability of an acquisition.

We also considered other robustness checks, such as Heckman (1976, 1979) sample selection corrections to control for the non-random selection of an exit event versus an ongoing investment in the portfolio.[7] The results are robust. These checks are not reported here but are available on request.

[6]Most of the econometric specifications in Tables 21.5, 21.6, and 21.8 use a dummy variable for early/expansion stages. One difficulty with using more specific definitions of stages of development is that such terms are sometimes interpreted differently in different countries. However, we attempted as best as possible to mitigate such definitional problems in recording the data.

[7]Unexited investments tend to be poorer performing ones and VCs on average inflate valuations of unexited investments to their institutional investors (Chapters 7 and 22; see also Cochrane, 2005; Cumming and Johan, 2007b; Cumming and Walz, 2004). There are fewer unexited investments in our sample relative to other datasets.

21.6 Conclusions

In this chapter we introduce a new dataset that is based on 35 European VC funds and 223 entrepreneurial firms in 11 continental European countries. Our sample covers the years 1995 to 2005. Detailed contract data indicate a wide range of cash flow and control rights. Among the 223 entrepreneurial firms, there are 187 IPO, acquisition, and write-off exits. Controlling for market conditions, legal and institutional factors, and a variety of entrepreneurial firm and VC characteristics, the data highlight a statistically and economically significant positive association between acquisitions and the use of VC veto and control rights, particularly for the right to replace the founding entrepreneur as CEO. The relation between strong VC rights and acquisitions is robust to controls for endogeneity and the exclusion of preplanned exit transactions.

Although many regressions presented in this chapter show some differences in economic significance, the data indicate that the probability of an acquisition is approximately 30% more likely when VCs have effective contractual control rights, such as drag-along rights and/or board control to replace the founding entrepreneur as CEO. The data further show that weak VC control rights are associated with a greater probability of IPO exits and a greater probability of write-off exits. The new evidence in this chapter supports a growing body of theoretical work on the proposition that VC control rights are correlated with and facilitate exit outcomes.

Key Terms

Common equity
Convertible preferred equity
Veto rights
Control rights
The right to replace the CEO
Drag-along rights
Redemption rights
Antidilution rights
Creditor rights index
Antidirector rights index
Legality index
Market capitalization
Industry market/book
Captive fund

Discussion Questions

21.1. In what ways do contracts matter in terms of influencing eventual exit outcomes of venture capital–backed companies? Do cash flow or control rights matter more in terms of influencing exit outcomes? Why?

21.2. What specific contractual rights matter the most for an investor who wants to force an acquisition exit and the entrepreneur who otherwise prefers an IPO exit?

21.3. What specific contractual rights matter the most for an investor who wants to force an IPO exit and the entrepreneur otherwise prefers an acquisition exit?

21.4. True/False/Uncertain and explain why: "Entrepreneurs typically prefer IPOs to acquisitions for non-pecuniary reasons."
21.5. Do contracts affect exits or do exits affect contracts? Why?
21.6. What is more important in influencing exit outcomes of entrepreneurial firms across countries: legal conditions or market capitalization? Does your response depend on the countries considered? Why?
21.7. What specific contractual rights are important for influencing exit outcomes? What rights are comparatively less important for influencing exits? Why?
21.8. In what ways (i.e., through what channels) does entrepreneurial experience (or quality) influence exit outcomes? In what ways does investor experience influence exit outcomes? Is entrepreneurial experience more or less important than investor experience? Why?
21.9. Are different contractual rights complements or substitutes? Why?
21.10. How and why are venture capital contracts related to write-off exits?

22 Valuation, Returns, and Disclosure

22.1 Introduction and Learning Objectives

Entrepreneurial firms typically do not have significant cash flow to pay dividends on equity or interest on debt. Therefore, venture capital fund investments are valued primarily on the basis of a capital gain upon an exit event. Exits typically occur two to seven years after the initial investment, so it is crucial that venture capital fund managers accurately value a firm, or its potential, prior to initial investment in view of the resources to be expanded by the venture capital fund manager over the investment life. Unlike more traditional investments, the valuation of the initial investment depends primarily on an expected exit value, which is rather challenging to predict in view of information asymmetries and potential agency costs. The purpose of this chapter is to shed light on a typical methodology used in valuing venture capital investments by venture capital fund managers. As well, we present evidence on how returns to venture capital investment vary depending on the structure of the investment, with consideration to the characteristics of the venture capital fund, the characteristics of the entrepreneurial firm, the contractual relation between the venture capital fund and entrepreneurial firm, market conditions, and different legal settings across countries.

It is noteworthy that over the life of the venture capital fund, venture capital fund managers are required to regularly report valuations of unexited investments, and returns of exited investments, to their limited partner institutional investors. As shown by Cumming and Walz (2004), the reported returns on unexited investments, however, tend to be biased upward (Phalippou and Zullo, 2005, confirm this finding). In this chapter we explain factors that lead to reports being biased upward with reference to an international dataset from Cumming and Walz (2004) from 39 countries around the world. The valuation of unexited investments has been a frequently debated issue in the media since the CalPERS lawsuit in 2002 (see Chapter 7) and an issue that has negatively influenced venture capital fund-raising on an industry-wide level.

In this chapter we will do the following:

- Review the mechanics underlying the venture capital valuation method
- Present evidence on venture capital fund returns to show ways in which the discount rate or cash flows considered in valuations might be adjusted depending on

the characteristics of the venture capital fund, characteristics of the entrepreneurial firm, structure of investment, market conditions, and legal conditions

- Present evidence that shows how returns are disclosed to institutional investors prior to an exit event

22.2 Venture Capital Valuation Method

There are numerous ways to value a firm. There are even more books written on how to value a firm than there are valuation methods.[1] A review of different valuation methods is therefore understandably beyond the scope of this book. We will, in this section, describe the venture capital valuation method only.[2] Normally, when carrying out a business valuation, it is appropriate to use a few different methods to assess robustness of the valuation figure to different methods.[3] As well, within any given valuation method, it is normal to consider the robustness of the valuation result to assumptions underlying the method. In the end, it is important to be transparent about the sensitivity of the valuation results to alternative assumptions used in arriving at the valuation and to different valuation methods.

The difficulty with valuing venture capital–backed entrepreneurial firms lies in the variability of the returns associated with venture capital investments. As shown in Chapters 19–21, for example (see also Cumming and MacIntosh, 2003a,b; Cumming and Walz, 2004; Cochrane, 2005; Cumming et al., 2006; Cumming, 2008), a significant percentage (often 20 to 30%) of investments are written off. Hence, there is huge variability in returns and a massive scope for valuation error. At best, therefore, valuation of venture capital investments is an art and not a science.

One valuation method commonly used by venture capital fund managers is known as the venture capital method. This method involves assumptions that may on the surface seem rather arbitrary. A typical successful venture capital–backed entrepreneurial firm has negative cash flows in the early years of the life of the firm and thereafter positive cash flows (Chapter 1, Figure 1.2). The venture capital fund manager first determines the life of the investment before the exit event and the price at which the investment will be sold at that future exit date. For example, if there is a projection about the firm's earnings in the exit year, then the sale price might be determined in reference to the price earnings multiple of a typical firm in the same industry. The sale price or "terminal value" is then discounted back to the day of first investment with the formula in equation 22.1.

[1]Some useful books devoted entirely to valuation include Abrams (2000), Arzac (2008), Damodaran (2006), and McKinsey and Company (2000).

[2]This section is based on the discussion of the venture capital valuation method in the casebook of Lerner et al. (2005).

[3]Other methods include, for example, net present value, comparables based on financial rations, and various real options approaches.

$$\text{Discounted Terminal Value} = \frac{\text{Terminal Value}}{(1 + \text{Target Rate})^{\text{Years}}} \tag{22.1}$$

The target rate is the discount rate required by the venture capital fund. This discount rate is critical to the valuation of the investment and varies depending on various factors that are explained following. In practice, the discount rate can be as large as 75%.

Venture capital funds do not own 100% of the firms in which they invest. The venture capital fund's valuation of the entrepreneurial firm must therefore be adjusted to account for the fact that it will hold less than 100% ownership. In the first step in making this adjustment, the venture capital fund calculates the eventual ownership percentage that it will have at the time of exit, or the "Required Final Percent Ownership," as in equation 22.2.

$$\text{Required Final Percent Ownership} = \frac{\text{Investment}}{\text{Discounted Terminal Value}} \tag{22.2}$$

The second step in this adjustment accounts for the fact that over successive financing rounds, investment syndication, and changes in the entrepreneurial firm's management team's ownership percentage (e.g., through the issuance of stock options), and so on, the venture capital fund's ownership will get diluted. The required current percentage ownership depends on the venture capital fund's retention ratio, or percentage of the investment that will be retained from first investment round to final investment round. Consideration of the retention ratio enables the venture capital fund to figure out what percentage of the firm the venture capital fund must own at the date of initial investment to maintain the required final ownership percentage at the date of exit so the venture capital fund maintains enough equity in the firm to achieve the desired rate of return. The calculation for the required current ownership is given by equation 22.3.

$$\begin{matrix}\text{Required Current} \\ \text{Ownership Percent}\end{matrix} = \frac{\text{Required Final Percent Ownership}}{\text{Retention Ratio}} \tag{22.3}$$

Consider the following example. Suppose you are employed at the Soprano Venture Capital Fund, a hypothetical venture capital fund in New Jersey. Your first assignment is to value the price per share for a \$10 million investment in a start-up green technology venture and to decide on what share of the firm you should demand. You project the firm will have net income in Year 6 of \$40 million. Similar profitable green ventures listed on stock exchanges are trading at an average price-earning ratio of 15. The firm currently has 400,000 shares outstanding. Tony, your boss, tells you that the Soprano Venture Capital Fund requires a target rate of return of 80%. What is the appropriate price per share, and how many shares do you require? The answer is obtained by following the steps in equation 22.3.

$$\text{Discounted Terminal Value} = \frac{\text{Terminal Value}}{(1 + \text{Target Rate})^{\text{Years}}}$$
$$= \frac{40 * 15}{(1 + 80\%)^{6}} = \$17.64 \text{ million}$$

$$\text{Required Percent Ownership} = \frac{\text{Investment}}{\text{Discounted Terminal Value}}$$
$$= \frac{\$10 \text{ million}}{\$17.64 \text{ million}} = 56.7\%$$

$$\text{Number of New Shares} = \frac{400{,}000}{(1 - 56.7\%)} - 400{,}000$$
$$= 523{,}511 \text{ new shares}$$

$$\text{Price per New Share} = \frac{\$10 \text{ million}}{523{,}511 \text{ shares}} = \$19.10 \text{ per share}$$

$$\text{Implied Pre-Money Valuation} = 400{,}000 \text{ shares} * \$19.10 \text{ per share}$$
$$= \$7{,}640{,}716$$

$$\text{Implied Post-Money Valuation} = 923{,}511 \text{ shares} * \$19.10 \text{ per share}$$
$$= \$17{,}640{,}716$$

Suppose further that you are of the opinion that three more senior staff will need to be hired by this green technology venture, and this number of top caliber recruits will probably require options amounting to 15% of this venture's common stock outstanding. Additionally, you believe that, at the time the venture goes public, additional shares equivalent to 20% of the common stock will be sold to the public. As such, you would perform the following adjustments to your calculations:

$$\text{Retention Ratio} = \frac{\frac{1}{1 + 0.15}}{1 + 0.2} = 72.5\%$$

$$\text{Required Current Percent Ownership} = \frac{\text{Required Final Percent Ownership}}{\text{Retention Ratio}}$$
$$= \frac{56.7\%}{72.5\%} = 78.2\%$$

$$\text{Number of New Shares} = \frac{400{,}000}{(1 - 78.2\%)} - 400{,}000$$
$$= 1{,}435{,}443 \text{ new shares}$$

$$\text{Price per New Share} = \frac{\$10 \text{ million}}{1{,}435{,}443 \text{ shares}}$$
$$= \$6.97 \text{ per share}$$

Notice in the preceding example that there is a problem associated with using the average price-earnings ratios of existing publicly trading green technology firms. Private firms are illiquid relative to publicly listed firms on stock exchanges, and typically an adjustment needs to be made downward (e.g., possibly by 20%) depending on the expected illiquidity of the private firm.

More generally, the main difficulty in this venture capital valuation method involves the choice of discount rate. One justification for placing an arbitrarily high discount rate is the value-added advice provided by the venture capital fund manager. Empirical evidence has shown that more prestigious venture capital funds in fact charge higher discount rates (Hsu, 2004). Entrepreneurs are typically more than willing to accept inferior valuations from more prestigious venture capital funds because of the better advice they expect to receive, as well as the access to better networks of legal and accounting advisors, investments bankers, and other individuals and firms that will help the firm succeed. Therefore, in the next section we present evidence on returns and discuss how returns to venture capital fund investment vary systematically depending on the characteristics of the venture capital fund, entrepreneurial firm, transaction-specific issues, and legal and market conditions.

22.3 Factors That Affect Venture Capital Realized Returns and Reported Unrealized Returns

In this section we examine returns because an ex-post analysis of returns provides guidance as to how discount factors in valuations might vary depending on the characteristics of the investment. To begin, it is important to point out that performance statistics vary widely in terms of data quality. Performance indicators are generally not made available to the public, and therefore large representative samples are hard to obtain. Details vary depending on the number of transactions, the years of the transactions, and the different variables in the dataset examined.

Cochrane (2005) examines the VentureOne database from its beginning in 1987 to June 2000, which consists of 16,613 financing rounds, with 7,765 investee firms. That data enable one to compare market returns to venture capital fund returns while controlling for selection biases in terms of which realized returns are observed. Cochrane estimates that the average log return is 15% per year and finds a beta (the covariance between market returns and venture capital fund returns divided by the variable of market returns) to be 1.7 and the alpha (the performance of venture capital fund returns above that which would otherwise be predicted by the Capital Asset Pricing Model [CAPM], which accounts for systematic risk) to be 32%.

The statistics in reference to venture capital fund returns presented by Cochrane are interesting, but the dataset used cannot account for features of venture capital that are central to what it is that makes venture capital fund investment distinct from other types of investment. That is, the dataset used provides scant details in terms of venture capital fund characteristics, entrepreneurial firm characteristics, and investment structure characteristics. To be able to value a venture capital fund investment, ideally we would like to analyze more than alphas and betas in a CAPM framework. Venture capital funds hold a small nondiversified portfolio of entrepreneurial firms and pay great attention to the structure of their investment by writing detailed contracts to mitigate agency costs and idiosyncratic risks. It is worthwhile to assess how returns vary pursuant to evaluating these details to come up with a more accurate portrayal of value drivers.

Arguably the most comprehensive and detailed venture capital and private equity dataset collected to date is the CEPRES (Center for Private Equity Research) dataset, which is based out of Goethe University of Frankfurt, Germany. The dataset has been described in prior work, including Cumming et al. (2004), Cumming and Walz (2004), and Nowak et al. (2004). The sample contains cash flow information at the level of the individual investment for 5,038 portfolio firms in 221 private equity funds spanning a time period of 33 years (1971 to 2003). The data indicate very detailed information including all cash flow between venture capital funds and entrepreneurial firms,[4] fund characteristics (such as age, fund number, portfolio size per fund manager), entrepreneurial firm characteristics (such as stage of development at the time of first investment and industry), and investment characteristics, such as whether the fund returns are observed by the lead venture capital fund investor in a syndicate, the presence of syndicated investors, co-investment from the same fund managers operating a different fund, board seats, the use of convertible securities, amounts invested, and the standard deviation of cash flows.

Based on the CEPRES data, Cumming and Walz (2004) identified a number of factors that potentially influence the performance of venture capital and private equity investments. The data are presented for internal rates of return (IRRs) that are fully realized versus IRRs that are yet to be realized but reported to institutional investors, are summarized in Table 22.1.[5] Table 22.1 further indicates differences in mean and median IRRs for realized and unrealized IRRs for different funds, entrepreneurial firm and investment characteristics, and differences across countries and in different economic conditions. Part A summarizes all of the investments in the dataset. Part B considers differences for across different market conditions and legal standards in different countries. Part C considers fund-specific characteristics, Part D considers entrepreneurial firm characteristics, Part E considers investment characteristics, and Part F considers country differences.

[4]This cash flow information is important so returns can be precisely calculated. By contrast, the dataset used by Cochrane (2005) only enables estimates of returns on the bases of initial and final cash flows and does not indicate partial exits, among other things (unlike the CEPRES dataset).

[5]IRR satisfies the following equation:

$$NPV = 0 = \text{Initial Investment} + \sum_{t=1}^{N} \frac{C_t}{(1 + \text{IRR})^t}$$

Table 22.1 Summary Statistics

Table 22.1 presents summary statistics according to various characteristics of the private equity ("PE") funds: (A) all portfolio firms in the dataset, (B) market and legal factors, (C) PE fund characteristics, (D) portfolio firm characteristics, (E) transaction-specific characteristics, and (F) country and legal origin. The data summary for the average and median internal rates of return for number of realized and unrealized transactions are presented. The unit of observation is the portfolio firm ("Ent Firm"). Difference tests: *, **, *** Significant at the 10%, 5%, and 1% levels, respectively. Dollar values expressed in real 2003 U.S. dollars. Variables are described in the text. *Source:* Cumming and Walz (2004).

PE Fund Characteristics		Unrealized/Partially Realized Portfolio Firm Investments			Fully Realized Portfolio Firm Investments			Difference Tests	
		# Firms	Average IRR	Median IRR	# Firms	Average IRR	Median IRR	Means	Medians
Part A All Funds									
1	All Funds in the Data	2619	63.23	0.00	2419	68.67	16.99	0.22	$p <= 0.00^{***}$
Part B Market and Legal Factors									
2	MSCI Return >3.5%	611	76.88	9.32	1908	58.07	20.21	−1.14	$p <= 0.000^{***}$
3	MSCI Return <3.5%	2008	59.07	0.00	511	108.24	−10.99	0.64	$p <= 0.000^{***}$
6	Legality Index >20	1874	60.01	2.16	1631	47.23	19.26	−0.87	$p <= 0.000^{***}$
7	Legality Index <20	745	71.30	0.00	788	113.04	14.21	0.54	$p <= 0.000^{***}$

(continued)

Table 22.1 (*continued*)

PE Fund Characteristics		Unrealized/Partially Realized Portfolio Firm Investments			Fully Realized Portfolio Firm Investments			Difference Tests	
		# Firms	Average IRR	Median IRR	# Firms	Average IRR	Median IRR	Means	Medians
Part C Fund Characteristics									
8	Fund Number in the PE Firm >3	1603	69.37	0.00	781	88.72	1.51	0.34	p <= 0.000***
9	Fund Number in the PE Firm <3	1018	53.55	10.30	1638	59.11	20.27	0.29	p <= 0.000***
10	Age of Specific PE Fund >1795 Days	1230	54.15	9.23	2233	57.48	18.73	0.19	p <= 0.000***
11	Age of Specific PE Fund <1795 Days	1391	71.25	0.00	186	202.96	−91.74	0.67	p <= 0.000***
12	Portfolio Size (# Portfolio Firms)/# General Partners >20	1035	59.58	0.00	988	21.29	12.34	**−2.52****	p <= 0.000***
13	Portfolio Size (# Portfolio Firms)/# General Partners <20	1586	65.61	1.70	1431	101.38	22.07	0.87	p <= 0.000***

Part D Portfolio Firm Characteristics									
14	Seed Stage	146	8.88	0.00	71	520.37	−2.92	1.01	**p <= 0.097***
15	Start-up Stage	56	126.72	18.97	34	48.58	−11.45	**−1.65***	p <= 0.127
16	Early Stage	670	39.55	0.00	424	−1.52	−29.14	**−2.93*****	**p <= 0.000*****
17	Expansion Stage	240	36.40	0.00	226	28.91	14.54	−0.56	**p <= 0.000*****
18	Unknown Seed, Early, or Expansion Stage	838	91.80	5.09	1119	71.69	20.00	−0.36	**p <= 0.000*****
19	Late Stage	168	55.77	0.00	116	121.20	25.34	1.50	**p <= 0.000*****
20	MBO/MBI	309	43.79	8.53	266	33.33	28.27	−0.35	**p <= 0.000*****
21	LBO	30	27.43	13.55	17	32.73	44.72	0.37	**p <= 0.052***
22	Other Type of Private Equity	153	144.32	17.14	132	69.11	25.52	−0.69	**p <= 0.006*****
23	Publicly Listed Firm	9	31.41	0.00	14	649.54	29.45	1.29	p <= 0.680
24	Industry Market/Book >5	1448	101.95	0.00	816	80.27	6.08	−0.55	**p <= 0.000*****
25	Industry Market/Book <5	1173	15.42	7.92	1603	62.76	20.28	**2.01****	**p <= 0.000*****

(continued)

Table 22.1 *(continued)*

PE Fund Characteristics		Unrealized/Partially Realized Portfolio Firm Investments			Fully Realized Portfolio Firm Investments			Difference Tests	
		# Firms	Average IRR	Median IRR	# Firms	Average IRR	Median IRR	Means	Medians
Part E Investment Characteristics									
26	Syndicated investment	729	68.11	0.00	449	151.27	15.88	1.01	p <= 0.000***
27	Co-Investment	526	44.51	0.00	313	48.02	13.27	0.13	p <= 0.000***
28	PE Board Seat(s)	743	42.84	0.00	447	112.40	0.26	0.84	p <= 0.000***
29	Convertible Security with Actual Periodic Cash Flows	967	123.03	12.77	1162	73.62	25.99	−0.95	p <= 0.000***
30	Initial Amount Invested > $US 2,500,000	1310	34.62	5.04	1040	75.58	25.22	1.09	p <= 0.000***
31	Initial Amount Invested < $US 2,500,000	1311	91.80	0.00	1379	63.46	8.60	−0.75	p <= 0.000***
Part F									
39	Canada	13	501.36	0.00	10	40.83	54.16	−1.29	p <= 0.547
40	Hong Kong	12	18.16	0.00	0				
41	India	33	10.32	0.00	0				

42	Ireland	9	1.05	0.00	3	−6.05	0.00		
43	Israel	46	20.76	0.00	7	16.41	8.45		
44	Malaysia	1	−7.99	−7.99	0				
45	Singapore	6	−10.92	0.00	2	14.67	14.67		
46	U.K.	305	22.04	6.25	304	40.81	24.10	1.36	$p <= 0.00$***
47	USA	1273	60.89	0.19	1162	43.62	13.84	−0.95	$p <= 0.00$***
48	USA/Israel	1	−31.86	−31.86	5	43.84	33.77		
49	All English Legal Origin	1699	54.25	1.16	1493	42.76	17.49	−0.80	$p <= 0.00$***
50	Argentina	0			2	−100.00	−100.00		
51	Belgium	10	−4.52	0.00	6	−31.93	−20.43		
52	Benelux	4	−17.45	0.02	2	112.14	112.14		
53	Brazil	10	27.74	0.00	2	−100.00	−100.00		
54	France	226	17.94	3.82	259	149.53	12.35	0.88	$p <= 0.00$***
55	Greece	3	107.79	165.68	0				
56	Guatemala	1	0.00	0.00	0				
57	Indonesia	0			1	−64.81	−64.81		
58	Italy	21	2.93	0.00	18	89.87	22.12	1.66*	$p <= 0.08$*
59	Netherlands	18	49.75	16.30	6	−7.80	7.26		
60	Philippines	2	−78.66	−78.66	3	−100.00	−100.00		
61	Portugal	1	180.45	180.45	3	49.42	52.05		
62	Puerto Rico	0			2	−100.00	−100.00		

(continued)

Table 22.1 *(continued)*

PE Fund Characteristics		Unrealized/Partially Realized Portfolio Firm Investments			Fully Realized Portfolio Firm Investments			Difference Tests	
		# Firms	Average IRR	Median IRR	# Firms	Average IRR	Median IRR	Means	Medians
63	Romania	1	0.00	0.00	0				
64	Spain	21	26.35	4.82	8	25.01	21.96		
65	All French Legal Origin	318	19.10	3.82	312	127.30	12.76	0.95	p <= 0.00***
66	Austria	8	3.35	4.28	7	−95.93	−100.00		
67	China	15	8.90	0.00	2	−82.62	−82.62		
68	Czech Republic	8	0.83	7.61	0				
69	Germany	126	142.74	0.00	109	105.31	15.39	−0.35	p <= 0.04**
70	Japan	5	0.00	0.00	4	−40.23	−44.60		
71	Korea	15	12.22	0.00	0				
72	Poland	2	−10.07	−10.07	0				
73	Switzerland	19	11.48	3.84	12	60.51	35.51	1.48	p <= 0.21
74	Taiwan	8	0.00	0.00	0				
75	All German Legal Origin	206	89.97	0.00	134	83.64	10.95	−0.08	p <= 0.00***
76	Denmark	10	11.37	0.00	3	31.09	41.77		
77	Finland	6	46.59	10.08	4	10.26	15.68		

78	Iceland	0			1	−100.00	−100.00		
79	Norway	7	16.58	7.72	12	−0.80	3.82		
80	Pan-Scandinavian	4	10.87	9.71	2	625.69	625.69		
81	Sweden	27	7.73	0.00	27	44.99	21.44	1.41	p <= 0.11
82	All Scandinavian Legal Origin	54	14.10	3.27	49	50.84	19.29	1.33	p <= 0.02**
83	Continental European	2	21.92	21.92	4	39.12	38.46		
84	Germany/Netherlands	1	33.99	33.99	0				
85	Germany/Israel	1	−9.55	−9.55	0				
86	Germany/Luxembourg	1	0.00	0.00	3	44.85	19.36		
87	Germany/U.K.	8	120.58	0.02	1	66.61	66.61		
88	Pan European	8	34.10	13.27	3	55.65	25.45		
89	Unknown	302	154.32	0.00	491	98.21	12.54	−0.47	p <= 0.00***
90	Russian	2	0.00	0.00	1	25.83	25.83		
91	U.S./Europe	4	9.85	19.66	3	−60.55	−58.59		
92	U.S./France	2	27.22	27.22	0				
93	U.S./Germany	11	23.86	25.54	3	26.40	53.06		

(*continued*)

Table 22.1 *(continued)*

PE Fund Characteristics		Unrealized/Partially Realized Portfolio Firm Investments			Fully Realized Portfolio Firm Investments			Difference Tests	
		# Firms	Average IRR	Median IRR	# Firms	Average IRR	Median IRR	Means	Medians
94	U.S./ Netherlands	0			1	97.91	97.91		
95	All Other/ Mixed/ Unknown Legal Origin	342	141.13	0	510	95.62	14.52	−0.41	p <= 0.00***
			Mean Test	**Median Test**		**Mean Test**	**Median Test**		
96	English versus French		2.84***	p <= 0.63		−0.73	p <= 0.02**		
97	English versus German		−0.73	p <= 0.14		−0.68	p <= 0.48		
98	English versus Scandinavian		3.22***	p <= 0.99		−0.27	p <= 0.93		
99	French versus German		−1.48	p <= 0.43		0.34	p <= 0.92		
100	French versus Scandinavian		0.70	p <= 0.88		0.64	p <= 0.50		
101	German versus Scandinavian		1.58	p <= 0.75		0.49	p <= 0.48		

Although venture capital fund managers are obliged to periodically provide reports of the value of the unexited investments to their institutional investors, it has to be noted that by the very fact that the investments that are to be valued as "unrealized," their valuation by the venture capital fund managers are by all accounts subjective and extremely difficult to corroborate. Venture capital fund managers therefore may have an incentive to misreport valuations to their institutional investors for various obvious reasons, most notable of which is to attract more capital for investment.

Hege et al. (2003), Cumming and Walz (2004), and others focus on IRRs in performance measurement of venture capital investments, despite the fact that IRRs are subject to manipulation (see, e.g., Damodaran, 2006),[6] for a number of reasons. Cumming and Walz explain that perhaps the most important reason is that the venture capital and private equity funds in the CEPRES sample do report IRR for realized and unrealized investments. As Cumming and Walz show, the fund managers do at times manipulate unrealized IRRs in their reports to institutional investors. Hence, it is appropriate to consider IRR because this is what is reported to the institutional investors. It is likewise particularly important to assess robust in regress estimates of factors that influence IRRs, by considering alternative adjusted metrics of performance and various causal mechanisms that influence performance, as well as multistep selection effects (Cumming and Walz, 2004). Herein we do not go into details beyond summarizing the CEPRES data, since we believe this is an area of evolving research. We do, however, summarize factors that plausibly influence performance that are present in the CEPRES data, as well as discuss in the next subsection other factors that could be considered in valuation and performance that are not present in any current dataset.

The data reported in Table 22.1 indicate that realized IRRs are significantly higher when the country-specific Morgan Stanley Capital International ("MSCI") index returns over the contemporaneous investment period have been higher. Accounting for selection biases as to which firms are fully exited, Cumming and Walz estimate the beta to be approximately 1.45 for all venture capital and private equity investments, which is slightly less than Cochrane's (2005) beta estimate of 1.7 for venture capital fund investments in the United States. The data in Table 22.1 indicate that the average (median) realized IRR is 58.07% (20.21%) when MSCI returns over the contemporaneous period have been greater than 3.5%. When MSCI returns are less than 3.5%, the average (median) realized IRR is 108.24% (–10.99%). For unrealized investments, the average (median) IRR is 76.88% (9.32%) when MSCI returns over

[6]One criticism of the use of IRR as a performance measurement, for example, is that investment duration can be manipulated (see, e.g., Phalippou and Zullo, 2005). To some extent this is true, but for most entrepreneurial firms the duration from first investment until actual exit (e.g., in an IPO or acquisition) will be determined by exogenous factors, such as market conditions and factors internal to the investee company itself that affect readiness of exit. As such, realized IRRs are much harder to manipulate than unrealized IRRs. Moreover, adjustments to IRRs give rise to inferences that are very similar in different academic studies.

the contemporaneous period have been above 3.5%. When MSCI returns are less than 3.5%, the average (median) realized IRR is 59.07% (0.00%). It is noteworthy that with the very high-standard deviations in IRRs, differences in average values are statistically insignificant. However, differences in medians are statistically significant. Median realized IRRs are higher in times of better market conditions, but median unrealized IRRs are higher in times of worse market conditions. In other words, venture capital fund managers tend to overreport the value of their unexited investments in times of worse market conditions relative to what one might otherwise expect given existing market conditions (Cumming and Walz, 2004).

It is interesting to note that a variety of fund characteristics are related to fund IRRs. Based on the Venture Economics data from 1980 to 2001, Kaplan and Schoar (2005) estimate that U.S. fund managers with better performance by 1% on a prior fund achieve a 77-basis-point better performance on the subsequent fund, demonstrating persistence in private equity performance over time. Given this persistence in performance, entrepreneurs tend to prefer financing from more reputable venture capital fund managers. Based on a hand-collected sample (from a dataset collected by MIT) of 148 entrepreneurs, Hsu (2004) estimates that entrepreneurs are three times more likely to accept a financing offer from a high-reputation venture capital fund manager, and these high-reputation venture capital fund managers acquire equity from the investee entrepreneurial firms at a 10 to 14% discount. As well, Lerner et al. (2007) find that different institutional investors tend to be systematically better at selecting fund managers that achieve superior performance results (or have better access to such fund managers).

In Table 22.1, Part C, we present the data from Cumming and Walz (2004) by fund characteristics. The data do not indicate specific trends in performance based on the age of the fund manager or the number of funds operated by the fund manager. The data do, however, indicate that the fund manager is much more likely to perform better where portfolio size in terms of the number of investee entrepreneurial firms per fund manager is smaller. The regression estimates in Cumming and Walz (2004) are consistent in showing portfolio size per manager as a very important factor in explaining realized IRRs. A change in portfolio size per manager from 10 to 20 investee entrepreneurial firms, for example, is associated with an expected reduction in realized IRRs by 10%. This evidence is consistent with the findings presented in Chapters 16 and 18 (as well as the theoretical work of Kanniainen and Keuschnigg, 2003, 2004; Keuschnigg, 2004b; and Bernile et al., 2007) that venture capital fund managers with larger portfolios provide less advice to the investee entrepreneurial firms.

Part D of Table 22.1 indicates differences in IRRs depending on stage of development and industry. Recall the development stages that were defined in Chapter 1.[7] Earlier-development stages are associated with lower median realized IRRs but higher average IRRs, which means that there is much greater variance in IRRs and higher potential upside with earlier stages of investment. Similarly, for high-tech investments (in industries with higher market/book values), average IRRs are higher but median IRRs are lower, which likewise reflects greater variance in IRRs and greater upside potential in high-tech industries. In the dataset there are 14 realized investments from firms that are publicly listed, and their IRRs are very high. The investments appear to be IPO allocations to venture capital funds for which the fund managers were able to flip the investment shortly after the IPO for a substantial capital gain (see Chapter 19 on IPO underpricing). Notice that start-up stage investments tend to have the greatest unrealized valuations. Valuation standards (Chapter 7) typically suggest that valuations not deviate from zero for recent investments, particularly at the seed stage.[8] But where it is possible to indicate an appreciation in investment values, this is often done at the start-up stage. Both average and median valuations of start-up and early-stage investments are significantly larger than the realized IRRs for those investment stages.

Part E of Table 22.1 indicates differences in IRRs depending on specific investment characteristics. IRRs of realized investments tend to be higher where unaffiliated funds syndicate, while co-investments by affiliated funds tend to show lower IRRs. Recall from Chapter 5 that funds often prohibit co-investment of fund capital in firms which have obtained prior funding from affiliated funds managed by the fund manager because fund managers may have an incentive to use new capital from recently raised funds to bail out the bad investments of prior affiliated funds (e.g., a low IRR buyback exit would look better than a write-off). Regression analyses in Cumming and Walz (2004) show that syndicated investments tend to yield 73% higher IRRs than nonsyndicated investments, while co-investments tend to yield 33% lower IRRs than non-co-investments. The relation between IRRs and board seats and

[7]The definitions are as follows:
Seed: financing provided to research, assess, and develop an initial concept.
Start-up: financing provided to firms for initial product development and marketing. Firms may be in the process of being set up or may have been in business for a short time but have not sold their product commercially.
Early: financing provided to firms with product in testing and/or pilot production. The firm may or may not be generating revenue and has usually been in business less than 30 months.
Expansion: financing provided to firms in need of development capital. The financing is provided for the growth and expansion of a firm, which may or may not break even or trade profitably. Capital may be used to: finance increased production capacity; market or product development; provide additional working capital.
Late: the firm has reached profitable operating levels.
MBO: a buyout in which external managers take over the firm. Financing is provided to enable a manager or group of managers from outside the target firm to buy into the firm with the support of private equity investors.
MBI: a buyout in which the target's management team acquires an existing product line or business from the vendor with the support of private equity investors.
LBO: a buyout in which the new firm's capital structure incorporates a particularly high level of debt, much of which is normally secured against the firm's assets.
Public: firms with a listing on a stock exchange.
[8]See, for example, http://www.evca.com/html/PE_industry/IS.asp.

convertible securities that enable periodic cash flow back to the venture capital fund prior to exit tends to be sensitive to the econometric specification in Cumming and Walz (2004). One explanation is that the use of the convertibles and board seats is endogenous to expected exit outcomes.[9] Convertible securities with periodic cash flow tend to be positively associated with IRRs, but only for positive IRRs; in other words, cash flows back to the venture capital fund periodically where the entrepreneur is expected to be able to pay back the investor. Board seats tend to be associated with IRRs that are less than zero; in other words, venture capital fund managers are more likely to sit on boards of firms that are performing poorly. Finally, smaller initial investment amounts tend to be associated with lower IRRs. The econometric evidence in Cumming and Walz (2004) shows that an increase in the initial investment from US$1 million to US$2 million tends to be associated with an increase in IRRs by 3%, while an increase in the initial investment from US$19 million to US$20 million tends to be associated with an increase in IRRs by 0.2%.

Part F of Table 22.1 reports the data by country and legal origin. IRRs may also vary depending on legal standards in different countries, although it is difficult to predict the relationship between IRRs and legal conditions.[10] On one hand, given risks are more pronounced in countries with inferior legal standards, IRRs may be greater in countries with inferior legal standards in order to compensate for such risks. On the other hand, higher legal standards are associated with lower information asymmetry and lower agency costs that enhance the efficiency of advice provided by venture capital fund managers to entrepreneurs and mitigate venture capital fund-entrepreneur conflicts (see also Chapter 16). As such, we might expect a positive relation between legal standards and IRRs. The data indicate that English legal origin countries have experienced the highest median realized IRRs (17.49%), while German legal origin countries experienced the lowest median realized IRRs (10.95%). Tests for differences in medians (rows 96–101), however, are statistically significant for differences in medians between English and French legal origin. There are no statistically significant differences in means across legal origins, and this finding is explained by the high variability in returns, consistent with Cochrane's (2005) evidence for the United States. There are no statistically

[9]Empirically, it is very difficult to assess this endogeneity problem, as there are very few instruments that are correlated with the use of different securities and not correlated with returns. Cumming and Walz (2004) conjecture that not considering these variables, however, might give rise to a more pronounced missing variables problem than an endogeneity problem.

[10]There are a variety of ways one might measure legal standards in different countries. One well-accepted approach is to use the indices reported in La Porta et al. (1998), which include the efficiency of judicial system, rule of law, corruption, risk of expropriation, risk of contract repudiation, and shareholder rights (see Chapter 3, Table 3.1). Berkowitz et al. (2003) use a weighted average of these factors, which is practical given the fact that many of these indices are highly positively correlated. Values of the Berkowitz et al. "Legality Index" range from approximately 8.51 for the Philippines to 21.55 for New Zealand (where the United States is at 20.85 and Canada is at 21.13) (see Table 3.1 for details).

significant differences in medians across legal origins for unrealized returns. Mean unrealized returns are highest in German legal origin countries (89.97%), but differences in mean unrealized returns are not significant for German legal origin relative to other legal origin countries (and again, this is due to the high variance). Mean English legal origin unrealized returns are 54.25%, and significantly higher than mean French legal origin unrealized returns (19.10%) and mean Scandinavian legal origin unrealized returns (14.10%). Further, it is noteworthy that for all legal origins, median unrealized returns are lower than median realized returns. Overall, therefore, Part F of Table 22.1 indicates legal origins and country-specific factors do not appear to play as great a role in driving differences in means and medians, at least relative to market and legal factors (Part B of Table 22.1), fund characteristics (Part C), portfolio firm characteristics (Part D), and investment characteristics (Part E). In particular, it is noteworthy that the differences in Legality and accounting standards (Part B, rows 6–11) appear to be stronger drivers of differences in realized and unrealized returns than the legal origins variables in Part F of Table 22.1.

The available evidence to date in fact indicates that IRRs are positively correlated with legal conditions. Cumming and Walz (2004) show that median realized IRRs are higher in countries with Legality indices above 20, but mean IRRs are higher in countries with Legality indices below 20. In other words, there is greater variability in IRRs in countries with lower legal standards. Cumming and Walz (2004) show a positive relation between IRRs and legal standards with a dataset from 39 countries and over 5,000 transactions, even after controlling for selection effects and other factors in multistep multivariate regression analyses. Similarly, Lerner and Schoar (2005) analyze 210 investments in 25 developing countries and show a positive relation between post money valuation and legal conditions. Cumming et al. (2006) show a positive relation between legal conditions and the probability that a venture capital–backed firm will exit via an IPO rather than a private sale or write-off, and this effect is robust to statistical selection effects.

It is also noteworthy in Table 22.1 that the mean unrealized IRRs are higher in countries with lower legal standards (while the median unrealized IRR is slightly higher in countries with Legality indices above 20). Cumming and Walz (2004) show that unrealized IRRs tend to be higher than what we would otherwise expect based on factors that drive realized IRRs. As well, for a subsample of their data, Cumming and Walz (2004) can compare actual realized IRRs with previously reported unrealized IRRs and find legal conditions are a key factor in explaining venture capital fund managers' tendency to overvalue unrealized IRRs when reporting to their institutional investors.

It is also noteworthy that Cumming and Walz (2004) find evidence that the structure of the investment tends to influence the propensity to overreport valuations on unexited investments. Valuations tend to be overreported for nonsyndicated investments and for co-investments. The intuition is that fund managers are less prone to exaggerate unexited investments when there is a syndicated investor that is potentially independently valuing the investment. By contrast, co-investments involve the same venture capital fund manager and, as discussed, there are agency problems with co-investment that would be consistent with a tendency to overvalue the investment. Convertible securities with periodic cash flows are less likely to be overvalued because the stream of cash flow does in fact make it easier to value the investment (since the valuation does not strictly rest on the estimate of the exit value). Finally, larger investments tend to have a shorter investment horizon until exit and valuations are less opaque. In Table 22.1 we note that the valuation average IRRs of unexited investments of less than US$2,500,000 are 91.8%, while average realized IRRs of exited investments of less than US$2,500,000 are 63.5%, and average IRRs of unexited investments of more than US$2,500,000 are only 34.6%, while average realized IRRs of exited investments of more than US$2,500,000 are 75.6%.

22.4 Conclusions and Remarks

This chapter presented evidence that venture capital fund valuation methods might be viewed as being rather arbitrary insofar as discount rates are arbitrarily selected. We noted from empirical studies that discount rates depended on the reputation of the venture capital fund (and its fund manager), for example. We presented some summary statistics and discussed related empirical evidence that showed IRRs varied depending on market conditions, legal conditions, fund characteristics, entrepreneurial firm characteristics, and investment characteristics. The range of factors within each of the categories enumerated in Table 22.1 and discussed in the text is very detailed, but there are always additional items one might consider.

Other things one might consider can become very case specific. Additional items pursuant to valuation are beyond the scope of this book but are considered in other books.[11] Other things one might consider include specific investee entrepreneurial firm details in the business plan, such as its strategy, history, trends, and product specifications. Michael Porter's five factors are very well accepted drivers of value;[12] they include rivalry,[13] the threat of substitutes,[14] buyer power,[15] supplier power,[16] and barriers to entry.[17] As well, an important

[11]See footnote 1.

[12]http://www.isc.hbs.edu/.

[13]For example, number, strength, characterization, product differences, concentration, diversity, management, industry capacity, and competitive advantages.

[14]For example, relative price/performance of substitutes, switching cost, and buyer propensity to substitute.

[15]For example, bargaining leverage, buying patterns, concentration, volume, switching cost, ability to backward integrate, substitute products, price sensitivity, price/total purchases, product differences, brand identity, impact on quality/performance, buyer profitability, decision-making units' incentives, and complexity.

[16]For example, relationship, concentration, manufacturing/marketing process, presence of substitute inputs, importance of volume to supplier, switching cost of supplier, cost relative to total purchases, impact of inputs on cost or differentiation, threat of forward integration, and supplier profitability.

[17]For example, economies of scale, proprietary technology, switching costs, capital requirements, access to distribution, cost advantages, government policy, expected retaliation, brand identity, and exit cost.

factor is the entrepreneurial management team. Venture capital fund managers almost always claim that they would prefer to invest in a great management team and an average business plan than an average management team and a great business plan. However, systematic large-scale empirical data matching venture capital and private equity returns to each of these factors are limited or non-existent at this stage. Further research is warranted.

Generally speaking, the theme in this book has been that valuation is enhanced when agency problems are mitigated. Different agency problems are more pronounced depending on market and legal conditions, fund characteristics, and entrepreneurial firm characteristics. Supporting empirical evidence on topic was presented throughout this book. In this chapter, we specifically focused on valuation and showed how returns varied depending on investment structures. Investment structures and financial contracts help mitigate agency problems and maximize expected values.

Key Terms

Valuation
Retention ratio
Required current ownership %
Required final ownership %
Discounted terminal value
Dilution
Premoney valuation
Postmoney valuation
Internal rate of return
Unexited investment
Seed
Start-up
Expansion
Late
MBO
MBI
LBO
Market/book value
CalPERS lawsuit
Legality index

Discussion Questions

22.1. True/False/Uncertain and explain why: "Syndicated investments should be valued higher than co-investments."

22.2. True/False/Uncertain and explain why: "It is better to be financed by a more reputable venture capital fund because you will obtain more favorable valuations and contractual terms."

22.3. Describe the CalPERs legal case and how it relates to the venture capital markets around the world. What are the five things that affect the valuation of unexited investments in venture capital, as they are reported to their institutional investors?

22.4. True/False/Uncertain and explain why: "Funds with a higher beta should have higher returns."

22.5. True/False/Uncertain and explain why: "There is significant persistence in the performance of venture capital and private equity fund returns."

22.6. True/False/Uncertain and explain why: "Venture capital and private equity returns should be higher in countries with lower legal standards to compensate investors for the increased risk."

22.7. True/False/Uncertain and explain why: "Venture capital returns are largely explained by portfolio size per manager."

22.8. True/False/Uncertain and explain why: "Diversified venture capital funds perform better than nondiversified venture capital funds."

22.9. True/False/Uncertain and explain why: "The use of convertible securities causes higher venture capital returns."

22.10. True/False/Uncertain and explain why: "Venture capital investments should be valued higher where fund managers sit on the board of directors of the investee entrepreneurial firm."

22.11. Suppose you are employed at the GreenWorld Venture Capital Fund, a hypothetical venture capital fund in Seattle. Your first assignment is to value the price per share for a $5 million investment in a start-up green technology venture and to decide on what share of the firm you should demand. You project the firm will have net income in Year 5 of $15 million. Similar profitable green ventures listed on stock exchanges are trading at an average price-earning ratio of 5. The firm currently has 400,000 shares outstanding. The GreenWorld Venture Capital Fund requires a target rate of return of 50%. What is the appropriate price per share, and how many shares do you require? Suppose further that you are of the opinion that three more senior staff will need to be hired by this green technology venture, and this number of top-caliber recruits will probably require options amounting to 10% of this venture's common stock outstanding. At the time the venture goes public, you expect additional shares equivalent to 10% of the common stock will be sold to the public.

Part Six

Conclusion

23 Summary and Concluding Remarks

Venture capital and private equity funds hold small portfolios of entrepreneurial firms that are not well diversified, although this enables fund managers to take their time carrying out extensive due diligence before investments are made and to sit on boards of directors, monitor management, and add value to the enterprise by providing strategic, financial, marketing, human resource, and other advice during the investment life. However, because such funds are not diversified, idiosyncratic risk matters; because idiosyncratic risk matters, agency costs matter, and thus the design of financial contracts matters.

This book is the first of its kind in the literature on venture capital and private equity to focus its theme specifically on the financial contracting between parties in venture capital and private equity. One of the primary reasons for the existence of specialized venture capital and private equity funds is the occurrence of information asymmetries and agency costs. If idiosyncratic risks could be diversified away and/or information asymmetries and agency costs were not present, there would be little scope for venture capital and private equity fund managers to provide value in ways that extend beyond that which banks or other sources of capital do for private and entrepreneurial firms. Part I, Chapter 2 provided an extended review of agency theory in the context of financial contracting with a focus on security design. With the empirical and international focus of this book, Chapter 3 reviewed institutional and legal differences across the countries considered and reviewed the empirical methods used in the data analyses in each of the chapters of this book.

In Part II we showed that contracts are extremely important for limited partnership funds that act as financial intermediaries between institutional investors and their investee entrepreneurial firms (Chapter 5). As well, public policy that gives rise to "statutory contracts" matters a great deal for venture capital and private equity fund-raising efforts (Chapters 7 and 9) and the performance of government-created funds (Chapter 9). Further, we showed that compensation is a significant element in venture capital and private equity fund structure and explained the ways in which compensation varied across different countries (Chapter 6). We also addressed related issues of specialized fund mandates and style drift (Chapter 8) and considered the factors that are important to institutional investors when they invest in venture capital and private equity funds (Chapter 4).

Part III focused on the relationship between fund managers and investee entrepreneurial firms. We addressed in detail issues relating to financial contracts design in terms of security choice (Chapters 10 and 11), adverse selection (Chapter 12), corporate venture capital contracts (Chapters 11 and 13), and the use of specific veto and control rights in venture capital contracts (Chapter 14).

Part IV started with Chapter 15 with an overview of factors that affect the extent of value-added provided by the investor and the impact of venture capital and private equity investment on innovative activity. We specifically considered the impact of financial contracts on the advice and monitoring provided by venture capital fund managers, as well as scope of disagreement with the investee (Chapter 16). Financial contracts by themselves are incomplete, and as such other factors matter for investor value-added, including location (Chapter 17) and portfolio size (Chapter 18).

Finally, in Part V we explained the central role of divestment or "exit" to the venture capital and private equity investment process. We overviewed factors that affect the extent of exit and duration of investment in Chapter 19. Contracts that inefficiently govern the structure of funds have negative consequences for the exit performance of the fund (Chapters 20 and 21). Contractual structures affect the returns to venture capital and private equity investments, which in turn impacts investment valuations (Chapter 22). We also reviewed evidence (Chapter 22; see also Chapter 7), which showed that the ways in which valuations of unexited investments are reported to institutional investors depend significantly on contractual structures between the fund and its investee entrepreneurial firms. In short, all aspects of venture capital and private equity investment involve idiosyncratic risks and a central role for financial contracts.

A striking feature about the venture capital and private equity market is the international differences in the size of markets around the world (Chapter 1; see also Armour and Cumming, 2006; Jeng and Wells, 2000). We had documented international differences in fund structures (Part II), contracts between funds and entrepreneurs (Part III), differences in value-added (Part IV), and differences in exit performance (Part V). International differences in venture capital markets are largely consistent insofar as poor legal conditions are associated with less efficient limited partnership contracts, less efficient managerial compensation, less efficient financial contracts with entrepreneurs, and less successful exit outcomes and financial returns. We may expect that countries with weaker venture capital and private equity markets will continue to lag behind with a poor supply of capital as long as poor legal conditions with weak shareholder rights and enforcement conditions persist in those countries. As well, there is evidence that law impacts the demand for venture capital: Countries with entrepreneur-friendly bankruptcy laws are more likely to have a greater demand for venture capital (Armour and Cumming, 2006) and a greater rate of self-employment (Armour and Cumming, 2008). (For more generally on public policy toward venture capital, see Chapter 9; see also Kanniainen and Keuschnigg, 2003, 2004; Keuschnigg, 2003, 2004a,b; Keuschnigg and Nielsen, 2001, 2003a,b, 2004a,b,c.)

There has been some work on the real effects of venture capital and private equity, which we had reviewed in Chapter 15 (for a more detailed survey, see Cumming et al., 2007). Further research could consider international differences in the real effects in relation to contractual structures employed in different countries.

International differences in venture capital may become blurred over time as markets become increasingly integrated. As we showed in Chapters 4 and 7, many institutional investors invest internationally in venture capital and private equity funds. Evidence on international contract structures, such as U.S. venture capital investment in Canadian entrepreneurial firms (Chapter 11) and cross-border European venture capital investment (Chapter 14) shows contracts are written in ways that are very similar to those between entrepreneurs resident in those countries and domestic investors. Additional data on topic across other countries might, however, shed further light on topic.

Finally, it is noteworthy that there is evidence that venture capital and private equity funds relocate their investee entrepreneurial firms to other countries after investment. For instance, Cumming et al. (2004a) show that Asia-Pacific venture capital funds often relocate their investee entrepreneurial firms to the United States after they invest but before they exit. Relocations yield higher returns than keeping the investee entrepreneurial firms in their respective country of origin. These differences can be explained by the improvement in legal conditions in the United States relative to the country of origin, as well as the increased size of the product market. Further work on transnationals in entrepreneurial, venture capital, and private equity markets would be a fruitful avenue for future work, particularly in relation to contract structures. As Meggingson (2004) predicts, it appears likely that there will be a growing trend toward a more global venture capital and private equity market around the world and greater internationalization of entrepreneurial ventures in the coming years. How and why venture capital and private equity contracts evolve in different countries will likely have significant implications for the performance and growth of venture capital and private equity markets.

Online Appendices

Please visit http://venturecapitalprivateequitycontracting.com for the following appendices:

Appendix 1: Sample Limited Partnership Fund Agrrement
Appendix 2: Sample Term Sheet
Appendix 3: Sample Shareholder Agreement
Appendix 4: Sample Subscription Agreement

References

Abrams, J. B. (2000). *Quantitative business valuation.* New York: McGraw-Hill.

Abrevaya, J. (2002). Computing marginal effects in the Box-Cox model. *Econometric Reviews, 21*(3), 383–393.

Acemoglu, D., & Zilibotti, F. (1999). Information accumulation in development. *Journal of Economic Growth, 4*, 5–38.

Admati, A. R., & Pfleiderer, P. (1994). Robust financial contracting and the role for venture capitalists. *Journal of Finance, 49*, 371–402.

Aggarwal, R., Krigman, L., & Womack, K. (2002). Strategic IPO underpricing, information momentum, and lockup expiration selling. *Journal of Financial Economics, 66*, 105–137.

Aghion, P., & Bolton, P. (1992). An incomplete contracts approach to financial contracting. *Review of Economic Studies, 59*, 473–494.

Aghion, P., & Howitt, P. (2006). Appropriate growth policy: A unifying framework. *Journal of European Economics Association, 4*(2–3), 269–314.

Akerlof, G. (1970). The market for lemons: quality uncertainty and the market mechanism. *Quarterly Journal of Economics, 84*, 488–500.

Ali, P. U., & Gold, M. L. (2002). An appraisal of socially responsible investments and implications for trustees and other investment fiduciaries, Working Paper, Centre For Corporate Law and Securities Regulation, University of Melbourne, 1–32.

Allen, F., & Faulhaber, G. (1989). Signalling by underpricing in the IPO market. *Journal of Financial Economics, 23*, 303–323.

Allen, F., & Song, W. L. (2003). Venture capital and corporate governance. In P. K. Cornelius & B. Kogut (Eds.), *Corporate Governance and Capital Flows in a Global Economy* (pp. 133–156). New York: Oxford University Press.

Amess, K., & Wright, M. (2007). The wage and employment effects of leveraged buyouts in the UK. *International Journal of the Economics of Business, 14*(2), 179–195.

Amit, R., Brander, J., & Zott, C. (1998). Why do venture capital firms exist? Theory and Canadian evidence. *Journal of Business Venturing, 13*, 441–466.

Amit, R. J., Glosten, L., & Muller, E. (1990). Entrepreneurial ability, venture investments, and risk sharing. *Management Science, 36*, 1232–1245.

Ammann, M. (2003). Return guarantees and portfolio allocation of pension funds. *Financial Markets and Portfolio Management, 17*, 277–283.

Ammann, M., & Siez, R. (2005). An IFRS and FASB 123 (R) compatible model for valuation of employee stock options. *Financial Markets and Portfolio Management, 19*, 391–396.

Anand, A. L., Johnston, D., & Peterson, G. (1999). *Canadian Securities Regulation—Cases, Notes and Materials*. Markham, Ontario: Butterworths Canada Ltd.

Anderson, S., & Tian, Y. S. (2003). Incentive fees, valuation and performance of Labour Sponsored Investment Funds, *Canadian Investment Review, 16*(3) Fall, 20–27.

Angel, D. P., & Rock, M. T. (2005). Global standards and the environmental performance of industry. *Environment and Planning A, 37*, 1903–1918.

Angrist, J. D. (2001). Estimation of limited-dependent variable models with dummy endogenous regressors: Simple Strategies for Empirical Practice. *Journal of Business and Economic Statistics, 19*, 2–28.

Armour, J. (2004). Law, innovation and finance. In J. A. McCahery & Luc Renneboog (Eds.), *Venture Capital Contracting and the Valuation of High Technology Firms* (pp. 131–161): Oxford University Press.

Armour, J., & Cumming, D. J. (2006). The legislative road to Silicon Valley. *Oxford Economic Papers, 58*, 596–635.

Armour, J., & Cumming, D. J. (2008). Bankruptcy law and entrepreneurship, *American Law and Economics Review*, forthcoming.

Armstrong, C., Davila, A., & Foster, G. (2005). Venture-backed private equity valuation and financial statement information. *Review of Accounting Studies, 11*, 119–135.

Arzac, E. R. (2008). *Valuation for mergers, buyouts and restructuring*. New York: Wiley.

Atanasov, V., Ivanov, V., & Litvak, K. (2006). VCs and the expropriation of entrepreneurs, Working Paper, College of William and Mary, University of Kansas and University of Texas.

Baker, M., & Gompers, P. A. (2003). The determinants of board structure at the initial public offering. *Journal of Law and Economics, 46*, 569–598.

Barclay, M., & Holderness, C. (1999). The capital structure puzzle: Another look at the evidence. *Journal of Applied Corporate Finance, 12*, 8–20.

Barney, J. B., Busenitz, L. W., Fiet, J. O., & Moesel, D. D. (1994). The relationship between venture capitalists and managers in new firms: determinants of contractual covenants. *Managerial Finance, 20*, 19–30.

Barry, C. B., Muscarella, C. J., Peavy, J. W., III, & Vetsuypens, M. R. (1990). The role of venture capitalists in the creation of public companies: evidence from the going public process. *Journal of Financial Economics, 27*, 447–471.

Bascha, A., & Walz, U. (2001a). Convertible securities and optimal exit decisions in venture capital finance. *Journal of Corporate Finance, 7*, 285–306.

Bascha, A., & Walz, U. (2001b). Financing practices in the German venture capital industry: an empirical assessment, Working Paper No. 2002/08, Center for Financial Studies, University of Frankfurt.

Bascha, A., & Walz, U. (2007). Financing practices in the German venture capital industry: an empirical assessment. In G.N. Gregoriou, M. Kooli, & R. Kraeussl (Eds.), *Venture Capital in Europe,* Chapter 15, Elsevier.

Bates, T. (2002). Government as a venture capital catalyst: Pitfalls and promising approaches. *Economic Development Quarterly, 16*, 49–59.

Bayar, O., & Chemmanur, T. J. (2007). IPOs or acquisitions? A theory of the choice of exit strategy by entrepreneurs and venture capitalists, Working Paper, Boston College.

Bebchuk, L. A., & Fried, J. M. (2004). *Pay Without Performance: The Unfulfilled Promise of Executive Compensation*, Harvard University Press.

Beck, T., Demirguc-Kunt, A., Laeven, L., & Levine, R. (2005). Finance, firm size and growth, World Bank Policy Research Working Paper No. 3485.

Becker, R., & Hellmann, T. (2005). The genesis of venture capital: lessons from the German experience. In V. Kanniainen, & C. Keuschnigg (Eds.), *Venture Capital, Entrepreneurship, and Public Policy* (pp. 33–67), Chapter 2, MIT Press.

Beckman, C. M., Burton, M. D., & O'Reilly, C. (2007). Early teams: The impact of team demography on VC financing and going public. *Journal of Business Venturing, 22*, 147–173.

Bello, Z. Y. (2005). Socially responsible investing and portfolio diversification. *The Journal of Financial Research, 28*, 41–57.

Benveniste, L. M., & Spindt, P. A. (1989). How investment bankers determine the offer price and allocation of new issues. *Journal of Financial Economics, 24*, 343–361.

Berger, A. N., & Humphrey, D. B. (1997). Efficiency of financial institutions: international survey and directions for future research. *European Journal of Operational Research, 98*, 175–212.

Berger, A. N., De Young, R., & Udell, G. F. (2001). Efficiency barriers to the consolidation of the European financial services industry. *European Financial Management, 7*, 117–130.

Berger, A. N., & Udell, G. F. (1998). The economics of small business finance: the roles of private equity and debt markets in the financial growth cycles. *Journal of Banking and Finance, 22*, 613–673.

Berglöf, E. (1994). A control theory of venture capital finance. *Journal of Law, Economics, and Organization, 10*, 247–267.

Bergmann, D., & Hege, U. (1998). Venture capital financing, moral hazard, and learning. *Journal of Banking and Finance, 22*, 703–735.

Berkowitz, D., Pistor, K., & Richard, J. F. (2003). Economic development, legality, and the transplant effect. *European Economic Review, 47*, 165–195.

Bernile, G., Cumming, D. J., & Landres, E. (2007). The size of private equity fund portfolios: theory and international evidence. *Journal of Corporate Finance, 13*, 564–590.

Bessler, W., & Kurth, A. (2007). Agency problems and the performance of IPOs in Germany: exit strategies, lock-up periods, and bank ownership. *European Journal of Finance*, 29–63.

Bierens, H.J. (2003). Modeling fractions. Research note posted online, available at: http://econ.la.psu.edu/~hbierens/EasyRegTours/FRACTIONS.PDF

Bigus, J. (2002). Moral hazard by inside investors in the context of venture financing, Working Paper, Hamburg University Institute for Law and Economics.

Bigus, J. (2006). Staging of venture financing, investor opportunism, and patent law. *Journal of Business, Finance and Accounting, 33*, 939–960.

Birmingham, C., Busenitz, L., & Arthurs, J. (2003). The escalation of commitment by venture capital fund managers in reinvestment decisions. *Venture Capital: An International Journal of Entrepreneurial Finance, 5*, 218–230.

Black, B. S. (2001). The legal and institutional preconditions for strong securities markets. *UCLA Law Review, 48*, 781–849.

Black, B., Cheffins, B., & Klausner, M. (2005). Liability risk for outside directors: a cross-border analysis. *European Financial Management, 11*, 153–172.

Black, B. S., & Gilson, R. J. (1998). Venture capital and the structure of capital markets: banks versus stock markets. *Journal of Financial Economics, 47*, 243–277.

Blanchard, O. J., Lopez de Silanes, F., & Shleifer, A. (1994). What do firms do with cash windfalls? *Journal of Financial Economics, 36*, 337–360.

Blaydon, C., & Wainwright, F. (2005). Surprise! Valuation guidelines are being adopted. *Venture Capital Journal*, June 1. http://www.ventureeconomics.com/vcj/protected/1110466091014.html.

Bloom, N., Griffith, R., & Van Reenen, J. (2002). Do R&D tax credits work? Evidence from a panel of countries 1979–1997. *Journal of Public Economics, 85*, 1–31.

Boldrin, M. and D.K. Levine, 2002. The case against intellectual property, *The American Economic Review* (Papers and Proceedings) 92, 209–212.

Bonini, S., & Zullo, R. (2000). Venture capital and debt financing with costly default, Working Paper, Universita Commerciale "Luigi Bocconi", Milano, Italy.

Boot, A. W. A., Gopalan, R., & Thakor, A. V. (2006). The entrepreneur's choice between private and public ownership. *Journal of Finance, 61*, 803–836.

Booth, G. G., Dalgic O. M. & Kallunki, J. P. (2006). Cultural networks in an upstairs financial market. In Bessler, W. (Ed.) *Boersen, Banken, Kapitalmaerkte*, (pp. 187–204), Berlin.

Bottazzi, L., Da Rin, M., & Hellmann, T. (2005). What role of legal systems in financial intermediation? Theory and evidence, UBC Working Paper.

Box, G. E. P., & Cox, D. R. (1964). An analysis of transformations. *Journal of the Royal Statistical Society, Series B, 25*, 211–252.

Bradley, D., Jordan, B., Roten, I., & Yi, H. (2001). Venture capital and lockup expiration: an empirical analysis. *Journal of Financial Research, 24*, 465–493.

Bradley, D., Jordan, B., & Ritter, J. R. (2003). The quiet period goes out with a bang. *Journal of Finance, 58*, 1–36.

Brander, J., Amit, R., & Antweiler, W. (2002). Venture-capital syndication: Improved venture selection vs. the value-added hypothesis. *Journal of Economics and Management Strategy, 11*, 423–452.

Brau, C., & Fawcett, S. E. (2006). Initial public offerings: an analysis of theory and practice. *Journal of Finance, 61*, 399–436.

Brav, A., & Gompers, P. (1997). Myth or reality? The long-run underperformance of initial public offerings: evidence from venture and non-venture capital-backed companies. *Journal of Finance, 52*, 1791–1821.

Brav, A., & Gompers, P. (2003a). Insider trading subsequent to initial public offerings: evidence from expirations of lockup provisions. *Review of Financial Studies, 16*, 1–29.

Brav, A., & Gompers, P. A. (2003b). The role of lockups in initial public offerings. *Review of Financial Studies, 16*, 1–29.

Brav, A., Geczy, C., & Gompers, P. (2000). Is the abnormal return following equity issuances anomalous? *Journal of Financial Economics, 56*, 209–249.

Brennan, M. J., & Kraus, A. (1987). Efficient financing under asymmetric information. *Journal of Finance, 42*, 1225–1243.

Bris, A. (2005). Do insider trading laws work? *European Financial Management, 11*, 267–312.

Broughman, B., & Fried, J. (2006). Power and payouts in the sale of start-ups, Working Paper, Boalt Hall School of Law, U.C. Berkeley.

Broughman, B., & Fried, J. (2007). Deviations from contractual priority in the sale of VC-backed firms, *Journal of Financial Economics*, forthcoming.

Bruining, H., Boselie, P., Wright, M., & Bacon, N. (2004). The impact of business ownership change on employee relations: Buyouts in the U.K. and the Netherlands. *International Journal of Human Resource Management* 16:3, 345–365.

Bruining, H., Verwaal, E., Wright, M., Lockett, A., & Manigart, S. (2005). Firm size effects on venture capital syndication: The role of resources and transaction costs, Working Paper, ERIM Report Series Reference No. ERS-2005-077-STR.

Bührer, C., Hubli, I., & Marti, E. (2005). The regulatory burden of the Swiss wealth management industry. *Financial Markets and Portfolio Management, 19*, 99–108.

Burkart, M., Gromband, D., & Panunzi, F. (1997). Large shareholders, monitoring, and the value of the firm. *The Quarterly Journal of Economics, 112*, 693–728.

Busenitz, L. W., Fiet, J. O., & Moesel, D. M. (2004). Reconsidering the venture capitalists' "value added" proposition: an inter-organizational learning perspective. *Journal of Business Venturing, 19*, 787–807.

Canadian Venture Capital Association, Various years. *Venture Capital in Canada: Annual Statistical Review and Directory.* Toronto: Canadian Venture Capital Association.

Cao, M., & Shi, S. (2006). Signaling in the Internet craze of initial public offerings. *Journal of Corporate Finance, 12*, 818–833.

Carhart, M., Carpenter, J., Lynch, A., & Musto, D. (2002). Mutual fund survivorship. *Review of Financial Studies, 15*, 1439–1463.

Carpentier, C., Kooli, M., & Suret, J. M. (2003). Initial public offerings: status, flaws and dysfunctions, Research Paper Prepared for the Small Business Policy Branch, Industry Canada.

Carter, R. B., Dark, F., & Singh, A. (1998). Underwriter reputation, initial returns, and the long-run performance of IPO stocks. *Journal of Finance*, 285–311.

Carter, R. B., & Manaster, S. (1990). Initial public offerings and underwriter reputation. *Journal of Finance*, 1045–1068.

Casamatta, C. (2003). Financing and advising: optimal financial contracts with venture capitalists. *Journal of Finance, 58*, 2059–2086.

Casamatta, C., & Haritchabalet, C. (2007). Learning and syndication in venture capital investments, *Journal of Financial Intermediation.*

Cestone, G., (2002). Venture capital meets contract theory: risky claims or formal control? Working Paper, N. 480 University of Toulouse and Institut d'Analisi Economica, Barcelona.

Chan, Y-S., Siegel, D. R., & Thakor, A. V. (1990). Learning, corporate control and performance requirements in venture capital contracts. *International Economic Review, 31*, 365–382.

Charemza, W., & Majerowska, E. (2000). Regulation of the Warsaw Stock Exchange: The portfolio allocation problem. *Journal of Banking and Finance, 24*, 555–576.

Chemla, G., & De Bettignies, J. E. (2007). Corporate venturing, allocation of talent, and competition for star managers. *Management Science, 54*(3), 505–521.

Chemla, G., Habib, M. A., & Ljungqvist, A. (2007). An analysis of shareholder agreements. *Journal of the European Economic Association, 5*(1), 93–121.

Chemmanur, T. J. (1993). The pricing of initial public offerings: a dynamic model with information production. *Journal of Finance, 48*, 285–304.

Chemmanur, T. J., & Fulghieri, P. (1999). A theory of the going-public decision. *Review of Financial Studies, 12*, 249–279.

Chemmanur, T. J., & Chen, Z. (2006). Venture capitalists versus angels: The dynamics of private firm financing contracts, Working Paper, AFA 2003 Washington, DC Meetings and Boston College.

Chemmanur, T., Krishnan, K., & Nandy, D. (2007). How does venture capital financing improve efficiency in private firms? A look beneath the surface. Working Paper, CES-WP-08-16, Center for Economic Studies, U.S. Census Bureau.

Chemmanur, T. J., & Tian, X. (2008). Peer monitoring and venture capital expertise: Theory and evidence on syndicate formation and the dynamics of VC interactions, Working Paper, Boston College and Indiana University, Bloomington.

Chen, H.-C., & Ritter, J. R. (2000). The seven percent solution. *Journal of Finance, 55*, 1105–1131.

Chevalier, J., & Ellison, G. (1997). Risk taking by mutual funds as a response to incentives. *Journal of Political Economy, 114*, 389–432.

Chevalier, J., & Ellison, G. (1999a). Career concerns of mutual fund managers. *Quarterly Journal of Economics, 105*, 1167–1200.

Chevalier, J., & Ellison, G. (1999b). Are some mutual fund managers better than others? Cross-sectional patterns in behaviour and performance. *Journal of Finance, 54*, 875–899.

Citron, D., Wright, M., Ball, R., & Rippington, F. (2003). Secured creditor recovery rates from management buyouts in distress. *European Financial Management, 9*, 141–162.

Clark, D. (2002). A Study of the relationship between firm age-at-IPO and aftermarket stock performance. *Financial Markets, Institutions and Instruments, 11*, 385–400.

Clarkson, P. M., Dontoh, A., Richardson, G., & Sefcik, S. (1992). The voluntary inclusion of earnings forecasts in IPO prospectuses. *Contemporary Accounting Research*, 601–626.

Clarkson, P. M., & Merkley, J. (1994). Ex ante uncertainty and the underpricing of initial public offerings: further Canadian evidence. *Canadian Journal of Administrative Sciences II*(2), 54–67.

Clarkson, P. M., and D. Simunic, 1994. The association between audit quality, retained ownership, and firm-specific risk in *U.S. and Canadian IPO Markets Journal of Accounting and Economics* 17, 207–228.

Cochrane, J. (2005). The risk and return to venture capital. *Journal of Financial Economics, 75*, 3–52.

Connell, D. (2006). "Secrets" of the World's largest seed capital fund: How the United States Government uses its small business innovation research (SBIR) programme and procurement budgets to support small technology firms, Working Paper, ESRC Centre for Business Research, University of Cambridge.

Copeland, T. E., & Weston, J. F. (1988). *Financial Theory and Corporate Policy* (3rd ed.). New York: Addison-Wesley Publishing Company.

Cornelli, F., & Yosha, O. (2003). Stage financing and the role of convertible securities. *Review of Economic Studies, 70*, 1–32.

Cosh, A., Cumming, D. J., & Hughes, A. (2005). Outside entrepreneurial capital. *Economic Journal*, forthcoming.

Coval, J. D., & Moskowitz, T. J. (1999). Home bias at home: local equity preference in domestic portfolios. *Journal of Finance, 54*, 2045–2074.

Coval, J. D., & Moskowitz, T. J. (2001). The geography of investment: informed trading and asset prices. *Journal of Political Economy, 109*, 811–841.

Cowton, C. J. (2002). Integrity, responsibility and affinity: three aspects of ethics in banking. *Business Ethics: A European Review, 11*, 393–400.

Cowton, C. J. (2004). Managing financial performance at an ethical investment fund. *Accounting, Auditing and Accountability Journal, 17*, 249–275.

Cressy, R. (2002). Funding gaps: a symposium. *Economic Journal, 112*, F1–F16.

Cressy, R., Malipiero, A., & Munari, F. (2006). *The heterogeneity of private equity firms and its impact on post-buyout performance: evidence from the United Kingdom*: Cass Business School, Working Paper.

Cressy, R., Malipiero, A., & Munari, F. (2007a). Playing to their strengths? Evidence that specialization in the Private Equity industry confers competitive advantage. *Journal of Corporate Finance, 13*(4), 647–669.

Cressy, R., Munari, F., & Malipiero, A. (2007b). Creative destruction? UK evidence that buyouts cut jobs to raise returns, Working Paper, University of Birmingham Business School.

Cressy, R. C., & Toivanen, O. (2001). Is there adverse selection in the credit market? *Venture Capital: An International Journal of Entrepreneurial Finance, 3*, 215–238.

Cumming, D. J. (1999). Empirical Essays on Agency Costs in Law and Economics, Ph.D. Thesis, University of Toronto.

Cumming, D. J. (2003). The structure, governance and performance of U.K. venture capital trusts. *Journal of Corporate Law Studies, 3*, 401–427.

Cumming, D. J. (2005a). Capital structure in venture finance. *Journal of Corporate Finance, 11*, 550–585.

Cumming, D. J. (2005b). Agency costs, institutions, learning and taxation in venture capital contracting. *Journal of Business Venturing, 20*, 573–622.

Cumming, D. J. (2005c). A review of global venture capital transactions. *Venture Capital: An International Journal of Entrepreneurial Finance, 7*, 185–201.

Cumming, D. J. (2005d). Do companies go public too early in Canada? Report prepared for the Investment Dealers' Association of Canada Task Force to Modernize Securities Legislation, Canada.

Cumming, D. J. (2006a). The determinants of venture capital portfolio size: empirical evidence. *Journal of Business, 79*, 1083–1126.

Cumming, D. J. (2006b). R&D tax offsets, premium offsets and premium concessions: Australia 1998–01 versus 2001–04, Report Prepared for the Government of Australia.

Cumming, D. J. (2006c). Adverse selection and capital structure: Evidence from venture capital. *Entrepreneurship Theory and Practice, 30*, 155–184.

Cumming, D. J. (2007a). United States venture capital financial contracting: Foreign securities. In M. Hirschey, K. John, & A. Makhija (Eds.), *Advances in financial economics*, Vol. 12 (pp. 405–444). Elsevier.

Cumming, D. J. (2007b). Financing entrepreneurs: Better Canadian policy for venture capital, *CD Howe Institute Commentary* No. 247.

Cumming, D. J. (2007c). Government policy towards Entrepreneurial Finance: Innovation Investment Funds. *Journal of Business Venturing, 22*, 193–235.

Cumming, D. J. (2008). Contracts and exits in venture capital finance. *Review of Financial Studies, 21*, 1947–1982.

Cumming, D. J., & Dai, N. (2007). Local bias in venture capital investments, Working Paper, Schulich School of Business, York University, and University of New Mexico.

Cumming, D. J., Fleming, G., & Schwienbacher, A. (2004a). Corporate relocation in venture capital finance, *Entrepreneurship Theory and Practice*, forthcoming.

Cumming, D. J., Fleming, G., & Schwienbacher, A. (2004b). Style drift in private equity, *Journal of Business, Finance and Accounting*, forthcoming.

Cumming, D. J., Fleming, G., & Schwienbacher, A. (2005a). Liquidity risk and venture capital finance. *Financial Management, 34*, 77–105.

Cumming, D., Fleming, G., & Suchard, J. (2005b). Venture capitalist value added activities, fundraising and drawdowns. *Journal of Banking and Finance, 29*, 295–331.

Cumming, D. J., Fleming, G., & Schwienbacher, A. (2006). Legality and venture capital exits. *Journal of Corporate Finance, 12*, 214–245.

Cumming, D. J., & Johan, S. A. (2006a). Is it the law or the lawyers? Investment covenants around the World. *European Financial Management, 12*, 553–574.

Cumming, D. J., & Johan, S. A. (2006b). Provincial preferences in private equity. *Financial Markets and Portfolio Management, 20*, 369–398.

Cumming, D. J., & Johan, S. A. (2007a). Advice and monitoring in venture finance. *Financial Markets and Portfolio Management, 21*(1), 3–43.

Cumming, D. J., & Johan, S. A. (2007b). Regulatory harmonization and the development of private equity markets. *Journal of Banking and Finance, 31*, 3218–3250.

Cumming, D. J., & Johan, S. A. (2007c). "Socially Responsible Institutional Investment in Private Equity". *Journal of Business Ethics, 75*, 395–416.

Cumming, D. J., & Johan, S. A. (2007d). Venture capital investment duration. *Journal of Small Business Management*, forthcoming.

Cumming, D. J., & Johan, S. A. (2008a). Information asymmetries, agency costs and venture capital exit outcomes. *Venture Capital: An International Journal of Entrepreneurial Finance, 10*, 197–231.

Cumming, D. J., & Johan, S. A. (2008b). Pre-planned venture capital exits. *European Economic Review, 52*, 1209–1241.

Cumming, D. J., & Johan, S. A. (2009a). Legality and fund manager compensation, *Venture Capital: An International Journal of Entrepreneurial Finance*, forthcoming.

Cumming, D. J., & Johan, S. A. (2009b). Pre-seed government venture capital funds. *Journal of International Entrepreneurship*, forthcoming.

Cumming, D. J., & MacIntosh, J. (2000a). The determinants of R&D expenditures: A study of the Canadian biotechnology industry. *Review of Industrial Organization, 17*(4), 357–370.

Cumming, D. J., & MacIntosh, J. G. (2000b). The role of interjurisdictional competition in shaping Canadian corporate law. *International Review of Law and Economics, 20*, 141–186.

Cumming, D. J., & MacIntosh, J. G. (2001). Venture capital investment duration in Canada and the United States. *Journal of Multinational Financial Management, 11*, 445–463.

Cumming, D. J., & MacIntosh, J. G. (2002). The rationales underlying reincorporation and implications for Canadian corporations. *International Review of Law and Economics, 22*, 277–330.

Cumming, D. J., & MacIntosh, J. G. (2003a). A cross-country comparison of full and partial venture capital exits. *Journal of Banking and Finance, 27*, 511–548.

Cumming, D. J., & MacIntosh, J. G. (2003b). Venture capital exits in Canada and the United States. *University of Toronto Law Journal, 53*, 101–200.

Cumming, D. J., & MacIntosh, J. G. (2004). Canadian labour-sponsored venture capital corporations: bane or boon? In A. Ginsberg & I. Hasan (Eds.), *New Venture Investment: Choices and Consequences* (pp. 169–200). Elsevier Science Academic Press.

Cumming, D. J., & MacIntosh, J. G. (2006). Crowding out private equity: Canadian evidence. *Journal of Business Venturing, 21*, 569–609.

Cumming, D. J., & MacIntosh, J. G. (2007). Mutual Funds that invest in private equity? An analysis of labour sponsored investment funds. *Cambridge Journal of Economics, 31*, 445–487.

Cumming, D. J., Schmidt, D., & Walz, U. (2008). Legality and venture governance around the world, *Journal of Business Venturing*, forthcoming.

Cumming, D. J., Siegel, D., & Wright, M. (2007). Private equity, leveraged buyouts and governance. *Journal of Corporate Finance, 13*, 439–460.

Cumming, D. J. & Walz, U. (2004). Private equity returns and disclosure around the World, Presented at the 2004 European Finance Association Annual Conference.

Cumming, D. J., & Zambelli, S. (2007). Illegal buyouts, Working Paper, Schulich School of Business, York University and University of Bologna.

Dai, N. (2007). Does investor identity matter? An empirical examination of investments by venture capital funds and hedge funds in PIPEs. *Journal of Corporate Finance, 13*, 538–563.

Damodaran, A. (2006). *Damodaran on valuation: Security analysis for investment and corporate finance*. New York: Wiley. http://pages.stern.nyu.edu/~adamodar/

Daniels, R. J. (1991). Should the provinces compete? The case for a competitive corporate law market. *McGill Law Journal, 36*, 130–190.

Das, S., Jagannathan, M., & Sarin, A. (2003). Private equity returns: An empirical examination of the exit of venture-backed companies. *Journal of Investment Management, 1*, 152–177.

Davidson, R., & MacKinnon, J. G. (1993). *Estimation and inference in econometrics*. New York: Oxford University Press.

Davis, S. J., Haltiwanger, J., Jarmin, R., Lerner, J., & Miranda, J. (2007). Private equity's impact: productivity and labor markets, Working Paper, University of Chicago.

De Bettignies, J-E. (2008). Financing the entrepreneurial venture. *Management Science, 54*(1), 151–166.

De Clercq, D., & Dimov, D. P. (2004). Explaining venture capital firms' syndication behavior: A longitudinal study. *Venture Capital: An International Journal of Entrepreneurial Finance, 6*, 243–256.

De Clercq, D., & Sapienza, H. J. (2001). The creation of relational rents in venture capitalist-entrepreneur dyads. *Venture Capital: An International Journal of Entrepreneurial Finance, 3*(2), 107–127.

De Clercq, D., & Sapienza, H. J. (2005). When do venture capital firms learn from their investments? *Entrepreneurship Theory & Practice, 29*(4), 517–535.

Deloite Touche Tohmatsu (2006). Global venture capital: 2006 survey. Deloite Touche Tohmatsu. (available at http://www.evca.com/images/attachments/tmpl_8_art_204_att_1014.pdf).

Demers, E., & Lewellen, K. (2003). The marketing role of IPOs: evidence from internet stocks. *Journal of Financial Economics, 68*(3), 413–437.

DeMeza, D., & Webb, D. C. (1987). Too much investment: a problem of asymmetric information. *Quarterly Journal of Economics, 102*, 281–292.

DeMeza, D., & Webb, D. C. (1992). Efficient credit rationing. *European Economic Review, 36*, 1277–1290.

Denis, C., & Huizinga, H. (2004). Are foreign ownership and good institutions substitutes? The case of non-traded equity, Working Paper DP4339, CEPR.

Department of Industry, Tourism and Resources (2004). Aus Industry venture capital programs. September 21, 2004, document.

Derwall, J., & Koedijk, K. C. G. (2005). The performance of socially responsible bond funds, Working Paper, Erasmus University Rotterdam.

DeTienne, D. (2007). Entrepreneurial exit: Theory development and a research agenda, *Journal of Business Venturing*, forthcoming.

Dillenburg, S., Greene, T., & Erekson, O. H. (2003). Approaching socially responsible investment with a comprehensive ratings scheme: total social impact. *Journal of Business Ethics, 43*, 167–177.

Dimov, D. P., & De Clercq, D. (2004). Effects of venture capital investment strategy on new venture failure, Working Paper, London Business School and Vlerick Leuven Gent Management School.

Doh, J., Rodriguez, P., Uhlenbruck, K., & Eden, L. (2003). Coping with corruption in foreign markets. *Academy of Management Executive, 17*, 114–127.

Dowell, G., Hart, S., & Yeung, B. (2000). Do corporate global environmental standards create or destroy market value? *Management Science, 46*, 1059–1074.

Drobetz, W. (2002). Corporate governance—legal fiction or economic reality. *Financial Markets and Portfolio Management, 16*, 431–439.

Dunning, J. H. (2003). *Making Globalization Good. The Moral Challenges of Global Capitalism*. Oxford: Oxford University Press.

Dushnitsky, G., & Lenox, M. (2006). When does corporate venture capital create firm value? *Journal of Business Venturing, 21*(6), 753–772.

Eling, M. (2006). Performance measurement of hedge funds using data envelopment analysis. *Financial Markets and Portfolio Management, 20*(4), 442–471.

Elitzur, R., & Gavious, A. (2003). Contracting, signaling and moral hazard: a model of entrepreneurs, "angels," and venture capitalists. *Journal of Business Venturing, 18*, 709–725.

Elton, E. J., Gruber, J. M., & Blake, C. R. (2003). Incentive fees and mutual funds. *Journal of Finance, 58*, 779–804.

Errunza, V. (2001). Foreign portfolio equity investments, financial liberalization, and economic development. *Review of International Economics, 9*, 703–726.

EVCA (European Venture Capital Association)/PriceWaterhouseCoopers, 2005. IFRS and the Private Equity Industry, EVCA Discussion Paper No.1 (available at http://www.evca.com/images/attachments/tmpl_9_art_110_att_775.pdf).

Fama, E. F., & French, K. R. (1992). The cross-section of expected stock returns. *Journal of Finance, 47*, 427–465.

Farag, H., Hommel, U., Witt, P., & Wright, M. (2004). Contracting, monitoring and exiting venture capital investments in transition economies: a comparative analysis of Eastern European and German markets. *Venture Capital: An International Journal of Entrepreneurial Finance*, 6, 257–282.

Farmer, R. E. A., & Winter, R. A. (1986). The role of options in the resolution of agency problems. *Journal of Finance, 41*, 1157–1170.

Financial Times. (2005). South Korean tax probe into foreign private equity funds. *Financial Times*, 16/17 April 2005, 2.

Fisman, R., & Di Tella, R. (2004). Are Politicians Paid Like Bureaucrats? *Journal of Law and Economics XXVII*, 477–513.

Fleischer, V. (2005). The missing preferred return, Working Paper, Law-Econ Research Paper No. 05-8, UCLA School of Law.

Fleischer, V. (2008). Two and twenty: taxing partnership profits in private equity funds, New York. *University Law Review, 83*(1), 1–59.

Fleming, G. (2004). Venture capital returns in Australia, Venture Capital: An International. *Journal of Entrepreneurial Finance, 6*, 23–45.

Forbes, D. P., Borchert, P. S., Zellmer-Bruhn, M. E., & Sapienza, H. J. (2004). Entrepreneurial team formation: an exploration of new member addition. *Entrepreneurship Theory & Practice, 30*(2), 225–248.

Fried, J. M., & Ganor, M. (2006). Agency costs of venture capitalist control in startups, New York. *University Law Review, 81*, 967–1025.

Gallini, N. (2002). The economics of patents: Lessons from recent U.S. patent reform. *Journal of Economic Perspectives, 16*, 131–154.

Garmaise, M. (2001). Informed investors and the financing of entrepreneurial projects, Working Paper, EFMA 2001, Lugano Meetings.

Garmaise, M. (2007). Informed investors and the financing of entrepreneurial projects, Working Paper, UCLA Anderson School of Management.

Gatti, S. (2005). Corporate finance and corporate financial advisory for family business. In *Banking for Family Business* (pp. 115–135): Springer Berlin Heidelberg.

Geczy, C., Stambaugh, R. F., & Levin, D. (2003). Investing in socially responsible mutual funds, Working Paper, Wharton School Finance.

Gillen, M. (1998). *Securities Regulation in Canada* (2nd ed.). Toronto: Carswell.

Gilson, R.J., 1998. The lawyer as transactions cost engineer. In *Palgrave Encyclopedia of Law & Economics.*

Gilson, R. J. (2003). Engineering a venture capital market: lessons from the American experience. *Stanford Law Review, 55*, 1067–1103.

Gilson, R. J., & Schizer, D. M. (2003). Understanding venture capital structure: a tax explanation for convertible preferred stock. *Harvard Law Review, 116*, 874–916.

Giot, P., & Schwienbacher, A. (2007). IPOs, trade sales and liquidations: Modelling venture capital exits using survival analysis. *Journal of Banking and Finance, 31*, 679–702.

Giudici, G., & Roosenboom, P. (2004). Pricing initial public offerings on Europe's new stock markets. In Giudici, G. & P. Roosenboom, *The rise and fall of Europe's new stock markets*, Ch. 2, Elsevier.

Goergen, M., Khurshed, A., & Mudambi, R. (2006). The strategy of going public: how firms choose their listing contracts. *Journal of Business Finance & Accounting, 33*, 306–328.

Goergen, M., & Renneboog, L. (2007). Does ownership matter? A study of German and UK IPOs. *Managerial Finance, 33*(6), 368–387.

Gompers, P. A. (1995). Optimal investment, monitoring, and the staging of venture capital. *Journal of Finance, 50*, 1461–1489.

Gompers, P. A. (1996). Grandstanding in the venture capital industry. *Journal of Financial Economics, 42*, 133–156.

Gompers, P. A. (1998). Ownership and control in entrepreneurial firms: an examination of convertible securities in venture capital investments, Working Paper, Harvard University.

Gompers, P. A. (2002). Corporations and the financing of innovation: The corporate venturing experience. *Federal Reserve Bank of Atlanta Economic Review*, 1–17.

Gompers, P. A., Kovner, A., Lerner, J., & Scharfstein, D. (2008). Venture capital investment cycles: the impact of public markets. *Journal of Financial Economics, 87*(1), 1–23.

Gompers, P. A., & Lerner, J. (1996). The use of covenants: An empirical analysis of venture partnership agreements. *Journal of Law and Economics, 39*(2), 463–498.

Gompers, P. A., & Lerner, J. (1997). Venture capital distributions: short run and long run reactions. *Journal of Finance, 53*, 2161–2183.

Gompers, P. A., & Lerner, J. (1998a). Risk and reward in private equity investments: the challenge of performance assessment. *Journal of Private Equity, 1*, 5–12.

Gompers, P. A., & Lerner, J. (1998b). What drives venture capital fundraising? *Brookings Papers on Economic Activity: Microeconomics*, 149–204.

Gompers, P. A., & Lerner, J. (1999a). *The Venture Capital Cycle*. Cambridge, MA: MIT Press.

Gompers, P. A., & Lerner, J. (1999b). An Analysis of Compensation in the US venture capital partnership. *Journal of Financial Economics, 55*, 3.

Gompers, P. A., & Lerner, J. (1999c). The determinants of corporate venture capital success: organizational structure, incentives, and complementarities. In R. K. Morck (Ed.), *Concentrated Corporate Ownership* (pp. 17–50). Chicago: University of Chicago Press for the National Bureau of Economic Research.

Gompers, P. A., & Lerner, J. (2000). Money chasing deals? The impact of fund inflows on the valuation of private equity investments. *Journal of Financial Economics, 55*, 281–325.

Gompers, P. A., & Lerner, J. (2001a). The venture capital revolution. *Journal of Economic Perspectives, 15*, 145–168.

Gompers, P. A., & Lerner, J. (2001b). *The Money of Invention: How Venture Capital Creates New Wealth*. Boston: Harvard Business School Press.

Gompers, P. A., & Lerner, J. (2003). The really long-run performance of initial public offerings: the pre-Nasdaq evidence. *Journal of Finance, 58*, 1355–1392.

Gompers, P., Lerner, J., & Desai, M. (2003). The two faces of entrepreneurship: Evidence from eastern and western Europe, Working Paper, Harvard Business School.

Gompers, P. A., Lerner, J., & Scharfstein, D. (2005). Entrepreneurial spawning: public corporations and the genesis of new ventures, 1986–1999. *The Journal of Finance, 60*(2), 577–614.

Gompers, P. A., & Sahlman, W. (2001). *Entrepreneurial Finance: A Casebook*. New York: John Wiley & Sons.

Gompers, P. A., & Xuan, Y. (2007). The role of venture capitalists in the acquisition of private companies, Working Paper, Harvard Business School.

Gorman, M., & Sahlman, W. (1989). What do venture capitalists do? *Journal of Business Venturing, 4*, 231–248.

Graham, J. R., & Harvey, C. R. (2001). The theory and practice of corporate finance: Evidence from the field. *Journal of Financial Economics, 60*, 187–243.

Green, R. (1984). Investment incentives, debt, and warrants. *Journal of Financial Economics, 13*, 115–136.

Greene, W. H. (2002). *Limdep econometric modeling guide, version 8.0*: Econometric Software, Inc.

Greene, W. H. (2003). *Econometric Analysis* (5th ed.): Prentice-Hall, Inc.

Grinblatt, M., & Hwang, C. Y. (1989). Signalling and the pricing of new issues. *Journal of Finance, 44*, 393–420.

Guay, T., Doh, J. P., & Sinclair, G. (2004). Non-governmental organizations, shareholder activism, and socially responsible investments: ethics, strategic, and governance implications. *Journal of Business Ethics, 52*, 125–139.

Guiso, L., Sapienza, P., & Zingales, L. (2003). Does culture affect economic outcomes? *Journal of Economic Perspectives, 20*, 23–48.

Guyatt, D. (2005). A summary of the findings of a survey into: Investment beliefs relating to corporate governance and corporate responsibility, Working Paper, University of Bath.

Guyatt, D. (2006). Institutional investors and the promotion of CSR: The investor perspective, Working Paper, University of Bath.

Gwartney, J. D., & Stroup, R. L. (1997). *Economics: Private and public choice*. New York: The Dryden Press, Harcourt Brace College Publishers.

Gygax, A., & Griffiths, A. (2007). Do venture capital fund managers imitate portfolio size? *Financial Markets and Portfolio Management, 21*(1), 69–94.

Habib, M. A., & Ljungqvist, A. P. (2001). Underpricing and entrepreneurial wealth losses in IPOs: Theory and evidence. *Review of Financial Studies, 14*, 433–458.

Halpern, P. (1997). *Financing growth in Canada*, University of Calgary Press.

Hamao, Y., Packer, F., & Ritter, J. (2000). Institutional affiliation and the role of venture capital: Evidence from initial public offerings in Japan. *Pacific-Basin Finance Journal, 8*, 529–558.

Hand, J. R. M. (2005). The value relevance of financial statements in the venture capital market. *The Accounting Review, 80*, 613–648.

Hanna, J. (2004). How corporate responsibility is changing in Asia (February 23, 2004). *Harvard Business School Working Knowledge.*

Hannafey, F. T. (2003). Entrepreneurship and ethics: a literature review. *Journal of Business Ethics, 46*, 99–110.

Harris, A.D., 2002. A symposium on Canadian securities regulation: harmonization or nationalization? White Paper, Capital Markets Institute, University of Toronto.

Harris, A. D. (2006). The impact of hot issue markets and noise traders on stock exchange listing standards. *University of Toronto Law Journal, 56*, 223–280.

Harris, M., & Raviv, A. (1991). The theory of capital structure. *Journal of Finance, 46*, 297–356.

Harris, R., Siegel, D. S., & Wright, M. (2005). Assessing the impact of management buyouts on economic efficiency: Plant-level evidence from the United Kingdom. *The Review of Economics and Statistics, 87*, 148–153.

Hart, O. (2001). Financial contracting. *Journal of Economic Literature, 39*, 1070–1100.

Hart, O., & Moore, J. (1994). A theory of debt based on the alienability of human capital. *Quarterly Journal of Economics, 109*, 841–879.

Hart, O., & Moore, J. (1999). Foundations of incomplete contracts. *Review of Economics Studies, 66*, 115–138.

Heckman, J. (1976). The common structure of statistical models of truncation, sample selection, and limited dependent variables and a simple estimator for such models. *Annals of Economic and Social Measurement, 5*, 475–492.

Heckman, J. (1979). Sample selection bias as a specification error. *Econometrica, 47*, 153–161.

Hege, U., Palomino, F., & Schwienbacher, A. (2006). Venture Capital Performance: the Disparity between Europe and the United States, Working Paper, RICAFE Working Paper No. 001.

Hellmann, T. (1998). The allocation of control rights in venture capital contracts. *Rand Journal of Economics, 29*, 57–76.

Hellmann, T. (2002). A theory of strategic venture investing. *Journal of Financial Economics, 64*, 285–314.

Hellmann, T. (2006). IPOs, acquisitions and the use of convertible securities in venture capital. *Journal of Financial Economics, 81*, 649–679.

Hellmann, T., & Puri, M. (2000). The interaction between product market and financing strategy: The role of venture capital. *Review of Financial Studies, 13*, 959–984.

Hellmann, T., & Puri, M. (2002). Venture capital and the professionalization of start-up firms: empirical evidence. *Journal of Finance, 57*, 169–197.

Hillman, A. J., & Kleim, G. D. (2004). Corporate political activity: a review and research agenda. *Journal of Management, 30*, 837–857.

Hochberg, Y. A. (2005). Venture capital and corporate governance in the newly public firm, Working Paper, Northwestern University.

Hochberg, Y. A., Ljungqvist, A., & Lu, Y. (2007). Whom you know matters: venture capital networks and investment performance. *Journal of Finance, 62*(1), 251–302.

Holmstrom, B., & Milgrom, P. (1991). Multitask principal–agent analyses: Incentive contracts, asset ownership, and job design. *Journal of Law, Economics & Organization, 7*, 24–52.

Hopenhayn, H. A., & Vereshchagina, G. (2004). *Risk taking by entrepreneurs* Working Paper No. 500: University of Rochester—Center for Economic Research (RCER).

Hornstein, A., & Kruseel, P. (1996). Can technology improvements cause productivity slowdowns? *Macroeconomics Annual 1996 National Bureau of Economic Research*. Cambridge, MA: The Mitt Press.

Hsu, D. (2004). What do entrepreneurs pay for venture capital affiliation? *Journal of Finance, 59*, 1805–1844.

Hughes, J. P., Mester, J. L., & Moon, C. G. (2001). Are scale economies in banking elusive or illusive? Evidence obtained by incorporating capital structure and risk-taking into models of bank production. *Journal of Banking and Finance, 25*, 2169–2208.

Hughes, P., & Thakor, A. (1992). Litigation risk, intermediation, and the underpricing of initial public offerings. *Review of Financial Studies, 5*, 709–742.

Industry Canada (2002). *Gaps in SME financing: An analytical framework*: Small Business Policy Branch, Industry Canada.

Industry Canada (2006). *Financing global gazelles*: Small Business Policy Branch, Industry Canada.

Jääskeläinen, M., Maula, M., & Murray, G. (2007). Profit distribution and compensation structures in publicly and privately funded hybrid venture capital funds. *Research Policy, 36*, 913–919.

Jääskeläinen, M., Maula, M., & Seppä, T. (2006). Allocation of attention to portfolio companies and the performance of venture capital firms. *Entrepreneurship Theory and Practice, 30*(2), 185–206.

Jaffe, A., & Lerner, J. (2004). *Innovation and its discontents: How our broken patent Ssstem is endangering innovation and progress, and what to do about it*. Princeton: Princeton University Press.

Jeng, L. A., & Wells, P. C. (2000). The determinants of venture capital fundraising: evidence across countries. *Journal of Corporate Finance, 6*, 241–289.

Jenkinson, T., & Ljungqvist, A. (2001). *Going public: The theory and evidence on how companies raise equity finance* (2nd edition). Oxford University Press.

Jensen, M. C. (1986). Agency costs of free cash flow, corporate finance, and takeovers. *American Economic Review, 76*, 323–329.

Jensen, M. C. (2001). Value maximization, stakeholder theory, and the corporate objective function. *European Financial Management, 7*, 297–318.

Jensen, M. C. (2004). The agency costs of overvalued equity and the current state of corporate finance. *European Financial Management, 10*, 549–566.

Jensen, M. C., & Meckling, W. H. (1976). Theory of the firm: managerial behaviour, agency costs and ownership structure. *Journal of Financial Economics, 3*, 305–360.

Jog, V. M. (1997). The climate for Canadian initial public offerings. In P. Halpern (Ed.), *Financing growth in Canada* (pp. 357–401). University of Calgary Press.

Jog, V. M., & McConomy, B. (2003). Voluntary disclosure of management earnings forecasts in IPO prospectuses. *Journal of Business Finance and Accounting, 30*, 125–167.

Jog, V. M., & Wang, L. (2002). Aftermarket volatility and underpricing of Canadian initial public offerings. *Canadian Journal of Administrative Sciences, 19*, 231–248.

Jog, V. M., & Wang, L. (2004). Growth of income trusts in Canada and economic consequences. *Canadian Tax Journal, 52*, 1–30.

Judge, G. G., Hill, R. C., Griffiths, W. E., Lutkepohl, H., & Lee, T. (1982). *Introduction to the Theory and Practice of Econometrics*. New York: John Wiley.

Kahneman, D., & Tversky, A. (1979). Prospect theory: an analysis of decision under risk. *Econometrica, 47*, 263–291.

Kaiser, K. N. J., & Stouraitis, A. (2001). Agency costs, and strategic considerations behind sell-offs: the UK evidence. *European Financial Management, 7*, 319–350.

Kanniainen, V., & Keuschnigg, C. (2003). The optimal portfolio of start-up firms in venture capital finance. *Journal of Corporate Finance, 9*, 521–534.

Kanniainen, V., & Keuschnigg, C. (2004). Start-up investment with scarce venture capital support. *Journal of Banking and Finance, 28*, 1935–1959.

Kaplan, S.N., 2007. Private equity: past, present and future, Paper Presented at the American Enterprise Institute, Washington D.C., November.

Kaplan, S. N., Martel, F., & Strömberg, P. (2007). How do legal differences and experience affect financial contracts? *Journal of Financial Intermediation, 16*(3), 273–311.

Kaplan, S. N., & Schoar, A. (2005). Private equity performance: returns, persistence, and capital flows. *Journal of Finance, 60*, 1791–1823.

Kaplan, S. N., & Strömberg, P. (2003). Financial contracting theory meets the real world: an empirical analysis of venture capital contracts. *Review of Economic Studies, 70*, 281–315.

Kaplan, S. N., & Strömberg, P. (2004). Characteristics, contracts, and actions: Evidence from venture capitalist analyses. *Journal of Finance, 59*(5), 2177–2210.

Kassberger, S., & Kiesel, R. (2006). A fully parametric approach to return modeling and risk management of hedge funds. *Financial Markets and Portfolio Management, 4*, 472–491.

Kennedy, P. (1998). *A guide to econometrics*. Oxford: Blackwell.

Kenney, M., Haemmig, M., & Goe, W. G. (2007). The globalization of the venture capital industry, Working Paper, University of California, Davis.

Keuschnigg, C. (2003). *Optimal public policy for venture capital backed innovation* CEPR, Working Paper No. 3850, Centre for Economic Policy Research.

Keuschnigg, C. (2004a). Venture capital backed growth. *Journal of Economic Growth, 9*, 239–261.

Keuschnigg, C. (2004b). Taxation of a venture capitalist with a portfolio of firms. *Oxford Economic Papers, 56*, 285–306.

Keuschnigg, C., & Nielsen, S. B. (2001). Public policy for venture capital. *International Tax and Public Finance, 8*, 557–572.

Keuschnigg, C., & Nielsen, S. B. (2003a). Tax policy, venture capital and entrepreneurship. *Journal of Public Economics, 87*, 175–203.

Keuschnigg, C., & Nielsen, S. B. (2003b). Taxes and venture capital support. *Review of Finance, 7*, 515–538.

Keuschnigg, C., & Nielsen, S. B. (2004a). Progressive taxation, moral hazard, and entrepreneurship. *Journal of Public Economic Theory, 6*, 471–490.

Keuschnigg, C., & Nielsen, S. B. (2004b). Start-ups, venture capitalists and the capital gains tax. *Journal of Public Economics, 88*, 1011–1042.

Keuschnigg, C., & Nielsen, S. B. (2004c). Public policy for start-up entrepreneurship with venture capital and bank finance, Working Paper, University of St. Gallen and Copenhagen Business School.

Khorana, A., Servaes, H., & Tufano, P. (2008). Mutual funds fees around the world. *Review of Financial Studies*, forthcoming.

Kirilenko, A. A. (2001). Valuation and control in venture finance. *Journal of Finance, 56*, 565–587.

Klapper, L., Laeven, L., & Rajan, R. (2006). Entry regulation as a barrier to entrepreneurship. *Journal of Financial Economics, 82*(3), 591–629.

Klausner, M., & Litvak, K. (2001). What economists have taught us about venture capital contracting. In M. J. Whincop (Ed.), *Bridging the Entrepreneurial Finance Gap: Linking Governance with Regulatory Policy* (pp. 54–74). Aldershot: Ashgate.

Knauff, P., Roosenboom, P. G. J., & van der Goot, L. R. T. (2003). Is accounting information relevant to valuing European Internet IPOs? In I. Hasan, & A. Ginsberg (Eds.), *New venture investment: Choices and consequences* (pp. 257–280). Amsterdam: Elsevier.

Kolk, A. (2005). Corporate social responsibility in the coffee sector: the dynamics of MNC responses and code development. *European Financial Management, 23*, 228–236.

Kolk, A., & van Tulder, R. (2001). Multinationality and corporate ethics: Codes of conduct in the sporting goods industry. *Journal of International Business Studies, 32*, 267–283.

Kolk, A., van Tulder, R., & Welters, C. (1999). International codes of conduct and corporate social responsibility: can transnational corporations regulate themselves?. *Transnational Corporations, 8*, 143–180.

Kortum, S., & Lerner, J. (2000). Assessing the contribution of venture capital to innovation. *RAND Journal of Economics, 31*, 647.

Lakonishok, J., Shleifer, A., Thaler, R., & Vishny, R. (1991). Window dressing by pension fund managers. *American Economic Review Papers and Proceedings*, May.

Landier, A. (2003). Start-up financing: from banks to venture capital, Working Paper, Leonard N. Stern School of Business.

Landier, A., & Thesmar, D. (2008). Financial contracting with optimistic entrepreneurs: theory and evidence. *Review of Financial Studies*, forthcoming.

Landström, H., Manigart, S., Mason, C., & Sapienza, H. (1998). Contracts between entrepreneurs and investors: terms and negotiation process. In P. D. Reynolds, W. D. Bygrave, N. M. Carter, S. Manigart, C. M. Mason, G. D. Meyer, & K. G. Shaver (Eds.), *Frontiers of Entrepreneurship Research 1998* (pp. 571–585). Wellesley, MA: Babson College.

La Porta, R., Lopez-De-Silanes, F., Shleifer, A., & Vishny, R. (1997). Legal determinants of external finance. *Journal of Finance, 52*, 1131–1150.

La Porta, R., Lopez-De-Silanes, F., Shleifer, A., & Vishny, R. (1998). Law and finance. *Journal of Political Economy, 106*, 1113–1155.

Lauterbach, R., Welpe, I. M., & Fertig, J. (2007). Performance differentiation: cutting losses and maximizing profits of private equity and venture capital investments. *Financial Markets and Portfolio Management, 21*(1), 45–67.

Lee, S., & Wahal, S. (2004). Grandstanding, certification and the underpricing of venture capital backed IPOs. *Journal of Financial Economics, 73*, 375–407.

Leland, H., & Pyle, D. (1977). Informational asymmetries, financial structure, and financial intermediation. *Journal of Finance, 32*, 371–387.

Leleux, B., & Surlemont, B. (2003). Public versus private venture capital: seeding or crowding out? A pan-European analysis. *Journal of Business Venturing, 18*, 81–104.

Le Moigne, C., & Savaria, P. (2006). Relative importance of hedge fund characteristics. *Financial Markets and Portfolio Management, 20*(4), 419–441.

Lerner, J. (1994a). The syndication of venture capital investments. *Financial Management, 23*, 16–27.

Lerner, J. (1994b). Venture capitalists and the decision to go public. *Journal of Financial Economics, 35*, 293–316.

Lerner, J. (1995). Venture capitalists and the oversight of private firms. *Journal of Finance, 50*, 301–318.

Lerner, J. (1999). The government as a venture capitalist: the long-run effects of the SBIR program. *Journal of Business, 72*, 285–318.

Lerner, J. (2000). *Venture capital and private equity: A casebook*. New York: Wiley.

Lerner, J. (2002a). When bureaucrats meet entrepreneurs: The design of effective 'Public Venture Capital' programmes. *Economic Journal, 112*, F73–F84.

Lerner, J. (2002b). Boom and bust in the venture capital industry and the impact on innovation. *Federal Reserve Bank of Atlanta Economic Review, 4*, 25–39.

Lerner, J., Hardymon, F., & Leamon, A. (2005). *Venture capital and private equity: A casebook* (3rd ed.). New York: Wiley.

Lerner, J., & Schoar, A. (2004). The illiquidity puzzle: theory and evidence from private equity. *Journal of Financial Economics, 72*, 3–40.

Lerner, J., & Schoar, A. (2005). Does legal enforcement affect financial transactions? The contractual channel in private equity. *The Quarterly Journal Economics, 120*(1), 223–246.

Lerner, J., Schoar, A., & Wong, W. (2007). Smart institutions, foolish choices? The limited partner performance puzzle. *Journal of Finance, 62*(2), 731–764.

Li, X., & Masulis, R. (2005). Venture capital investments by IPO underwriters: certification, alignment of interest or moral hazard? Working Paper, Owen Graduate School of Management.

Lichtenberg, F. R., & Siegel, D. (1990). The effect of leveraged buyouts on productivity and related aspects of firm behavior. *Journal of Financial Economics, 27*, 165–194.

Lin, T. H., & Smith, R. L. (1997). Insider reputation and selling decisions: The unwinding of venture capital investments during equity IPOs. *Journal of Corporate Finance, 4*, 241–263.

Litvak, K. (2004a). Governance through exit: default penalties and walkaway options in venture capital partnership agreements. *Willamette Law Review, 40*, 771–812.

Litvak, K. (2004b). Venture capital limited partnership agreements: understanding compensation arrangements, Working Paper, U of Texas Law and Economics Research Paper No. 29; Columbia Law and Economics Research Paper No. 254.

Ljungqvist, A. P. (1999). IPO underpricing, wealth losses and the curious role of venture capitalists in the creation of public companies, Working Paper 1999fe04, Said School of Business, Oxford.

Ljungqvist, A.P. and M.P. Richardson, (2003). The investment behavior of private equity fund managers, Working Paper, RICAFE No 005.

Ljungqvist, A., & Wilhelm, W. J. (2003). IPO pricing in the dot-com bubble. *Journal of Finance, 58*, 723–752.

Lockett, A., Moon, J., & Visser, W. (2006). Corporate social responsibility in management research: focus, nature, salience and sources of influence. *Journal of Management Studies, 43*(1), 115–136.

Lockett, A., & Wright, M. (1999). The syndication of private equity: evidence from the U.K. *Venture Capital: International Journal of Entrepreneurial Finance, 1*, 303–324.

Lockett, A., & Wright, M. (2001). The syndication of venture capital investments. *Omega: The International Journal of Management Science, 29*, 375–390.

Lockett, A., Wright, M., Pruthi, S., & Sapienza, H. (2002). Venture capital investors, valuation and information: a comparative study of US, Hong Kong, India and Singapore. *Venture Capital: An International Journal of Entrepreneurial Finance, 4*, 237–252.

Loughran, T., & Ritter, J. R. (2002). Why don't issuers get upset about leaving money on the table in IPOs? *Review of Financial Studies, 15*, 413–443.

Loughran, T., & Ritter, J. R. (2004). Why has IPO underpricing changed over time? *Financial Management, 33*(3), 5–37.

Loughran, T., Ritter, J. R., & Rydqvist, K. (1994). Initial public offerings: International insights. *Pacific-Basin Finance Journal, 2*, 165–199.

Macdonald, M. (1992). *Venture Capital in Canada: A Guide and Sources*. Toronto: Canadian Venture Capital Association.

Macdonald & Associates. Various years. Limited. *Canadian Venture Capital Association annual reports*. Toronto: Canadian Venture Capital Association.

Macey, J. R., & O'Hara, M. (2002). The economics of stock exchange listing fees and listing requirements. *Journal of Financial Intermediation, 11*, 297–319.

MacIntosh, J. G. (1994). *Legal and institutional barriers to financing innovative enterprise in Canada, monograph prepared for the Government and Competitiveness Project*: School of Policy Studies Queen's University Discussion Paper 94–10.

MacIntosh, J. G. (1997). Venture capital exits in Canada and the United States. In P. Halpern (Ed.), *Financing Innovative Enterprise in Canada* (pp. 279–356): University of Calgary Press.

Maddala, G. S. (2001). *Introduction to Econometrics*. New York: Wiley.

Mallin, C. (2001). Institutional investors and voting practices: an international comparison. *Corporate Governance: An International Review, 9*, 118–126.

Mallin, C., Mullineux, A., & Wihlborg, C. (2005). The financial sector and corporate governance: the UK case. *Corporate Governance: An International Review, 13*, 532–541.

Manigart, S., Collewaert, V., Wright, M., Pruthi, S., Lockett, A., Bruining, H., Hommel, U., & Landström, H. (2007). Human capital and the internationalization of venture capital firms. *International Entrepreneurship and Management Journal, 3*, 109–125.

Manigart, S., De Waele, K., Wright, M., Robbie, K., Desbrières, P., Sapienza, H., & Beekman, A. (2000). Venture capitalists, investment appraisal and accounting information: a comparative study of the USA, UK, France, Belgium and Holland. *European Financial Management, 6*, 389–404.

Manigart, S., De Waele, K., Wright, M., Robbie, K., Desbrières, P., Sapienza, H., & Beekman, A. (2002a). The determinants of the required returns in venture capital investments: a five-country study. *Journal of Business Venturing, 17*, 291–312.

Manigart, S., Korsgaard, M. A., Folger, R., Sapienza, H., & Baeyens, K. (2002b). The impact of trust on private equity contracts, Working Paper, Vlerick Leuven Ghent Management School.

Manigart, S., Lockett, A., Meuleman, M., Wright, M., Landstrom, H., Bruining, H., Desbrieres, P., & Hommel, U. (2002c). Why do European venture capital compaies syndicate? Working Paper, Vlerick Leuven Gent Management School, ERIM Report Series Reference No. ERS-2002-98-ORG.

Manigart, S., Lockett, A., Meuleman, M., Wright, M., Landstrom, H., Bruining, H., Desbrieres, P., & Hommel, U. (2006). Venture capitalists decision to syndicate. *Entrepreneurship Theory and Practice, 30*, 131–153.

Manigart, S., Sapienza, H., & Vermeir, W. (1996). Venture capital governance and value-added in four countries. *Journal of Business Venturing, 11*, 439–469.

Manignan, I., & Ralston, D. A. (2002). Corporate social responsibility in Europe and the US: Insights from businesses' self-presentations. *Journal of International Business Studies, 33*, 497–514.

Marx, L. (1998). Efficient venture capital financing combining debt and equity. *Review of Economic Design, 4*, 371–387.

Mas-Colell, A., Whinston, M. D., & Green, J. R. (1995). *Microeconomic Theory*. New York: Oxford University Press.

Mason, C. M., & Harrison, R. T. (2002). Is it worth it? The rates of return from informal venture capital investments. *Journal of Business Venturing, 17*, 211–236.

Maula, M. V. J., Autio, E., & Murray, G. C. (2003). Prerequisites for the creation of social capital and subsequent knowledge acquisition in corporate venture capital. *Venture Capital: An International Journal of Entrepreneurial Finance, 5*, 117–134.

Maula, M., & Murray, G. (2001). Corporate venture capital and creation of US public companies: The impact of sources of venture capital on the performance of portfolio companies. In: *Strategy in the Entrepreneurial Millennium*: John Wiley and Sons.

Mayer, C. (2001). *Institutional investment and private equity in the UK*. OFRC Working Paper No. 2001fe10, Oxford Financial Research Centre, Oxford University.

Mayer, C., Schoors, K., & Yafeh, Y. (2005). Sources of funds and investment activities of venture capital funds: evidence from Germany, Israel, Japan and the UK. *Journal of Corporate Finance, 11*, 586–608.

McCahery, J., & Vermeulen, E. P. M. (2004). Business organization law and venture capital. In J. A. McCahery & L. Renneboog (Eds.), *Venture Capital Contracting and the Valuation of High Technology Firms* (pp. 162–187): Oxford University Press.

McConomy, B. J., & Jog, V. M. (2003). Voluntary disclosure of management earnings forecasts in IPO prospectuses. *Journal of Business, Finance & Accounting, 30*(1 and 2), 125–167.

McInerney, T. F. (2006). Putting regulation before responsibility: Towards binding norms of corporate social responsibility, Working Paper, Bepress Legal Series, 1029.

McKaskill, T., Mark Weaver, K., & Dickson, P. (2004). Developing and exit readiness index: a research note. *Venture Capital: An International Journal of Entrepreneurial Finance, 6*, 173–179.

McKinsey and Company Inc. (Copeland, T., Koller, T., & Murrin, J.), 2000. *Valuation: Measuring and managing the value of companies*, New York: Wiley.

Megginson, W. L. (2004). Towards a global model of venture capital. *Journal of Applied Corporate Finance, 16*, 8–26.

Megginson, W. L., Nash, R., Netter, J., & Poulsen, A. (2004). The Choice of public versus private markets: Evidence from privatizations. *Journal of Finance, 59*, 2835–2870.

Megginson, W. L., & Weiss, K. A. (1991). Venture capitalist certification in initial public offerings. *Journal of Finance, 46*, 879–903.

Merton, R. C. (1995). A Functional Perspective of Financial Intermediation. *Financial Management, 24*, 23–41.

Metrick, A. (2006). *Venture capital and the finance of innovation.* New York: Wiley.

Metrick, A., & Yasuda, A. (2006). Economics of private equity funds, Working Paper, Wharton School, University of Pennsylvania.

Meuleman, M., & Wright, M. (2006). Industry concentration, syndication networks and competition in the UK private equity market for management buy-outs, Working Paper, Nottingham University.

Miles, M. P., Munilla, L. S., & Covin, J. G. (2004). Innovation, ethics and entrepreneurship. *Journal of Business Ethics, 54*, 97–101.

Mill, G. A. (2006). The financial performance of a socially responsible investment over time and a possible link with corporate social responsibility. *Journal of Business Ethics, 63*, 131–148.

Miller, E. M. (1977). Risk, uncertainty, and divergence of opinion. *Journal of Finance, 32*, 1151–1168.

Miller, M., & Modigliani, F. (1963). Corporate income taxes and the cost of capital: a correction. *American Economic Review, 53*(3), 433–443.

Mintz, J. (1997). *Report of the Technical Committee on Business Taxation.* Ottawa: Department of Finance.

Modigliani, F., & Miller, M. (1958). The cost of capital, corporation finance and the theory of investment. *American Economic Review, 48*, 261–297.

Molyneux, P., Altunbas, Y., & Gardner, E. (1996). *Efficiency in European banking.* New York: John Wiley.

Montgomery, D. B., & Ramus, C. A. (2003). Corporate social responsibility reputation effects on MBA job choice, Working Paper No. 1805, Stanford GSB.

Morris, S. (1996). Speculative investor behavior and learning. *Quarterly Journal of Economics, 111*, 1111–1133.

Moskowitz, T., & Vissing-Jorgensen, A. (2002). The returns to entrepreneurial investment: a private equity premium puzzle? *American Economic Review, 92*, 745–778.

Myers, S. C. (2000). Outside equity. *Journal of Finance, 55*, 1005–1037.

Myers, S. C., & Majluf, N. (1984). Corporate financing and investment decisions when firms have information that investors do not have. *Journal of Financial Economics, 13*, 187–222.

Nahata, R. (2008). Venture capital reputation and investment performance. *Journal of Financial Economics*, forthcoming.

Neus, W., & Walz, U. (2005). Exit timing of venture capitalists in the course of an initial public offering. *Journal of Financial Intermediation, 14*, 253–277.

Nielsen, K. M. (2008). Institutional investors and private equity. *Review of Finance, 12*(1), 185–219.

Nikoskelainen, E., & Wright, M. (2007). The impact of corporate governance mechanisms on value increase in leveraged buyouts. *Journal of Corporate Finance, 13*(4), 511–537.

Noe, T. H., & Rebello, M. J. (1992). Adverse selection, contract design and investment distortion. *Journal of Financial Intermediation, 2*, 347–375.

Noe, T. H., & Rebello, M. J. (1996). Asymmetric information, managerial opportunism, financing and payout policies. *Journal of Finance, 51*, 637–660.

Nowak, E., Knigge, A., & Schmidt, D. (2004). *On the performance of private equity. Investments: Does market timing matter?* Working Paper. Frankfurt: CEPRES.

Organisation for Economic Co-operation and Development (OECD). (1996). *Government programmes for venture capital.* Paris: Organization for Economic Corporation and Development.

Osborne, D., & Sandler, D. (1998). A tax expenditure analysis of Labour-Sponsored Venture Capital Corporations. *Canadian Tax Journal, 46*, 499–574.

Otten, R., & Bams, D. (2002). European mutual fund performance. *European Financial Management, 8*, 75–102.

Pagano, M., Panetta, F., & Zingales, L. (1998). Why do companies go public? An empirical analysis. *Journal of Finance, 53*, 27–64.

Pagano, M., & Roell, A. (1998). The choice of stock ownership structure: agency costs, monitoring, and the decision to go public. *Quarterly Journal of Economics, 113*, 187–225.

Parhankangas, A., Landstrom, H., & Smith, G. D. (2005). Experience, contractual covenants and venture capitalists' responses to unmet expectations. *Venture Capital: An International Journal of Entrepreneurial Finance, 7*, 297–318.

Parhankangas, A., & Smith, G. (2000). Conflict management in the entrepreneur-venture capitalist relationship: an international comparative study, *Proceedings of the 20th Annual Entrepreneurship Research Conference*, Babson College.

Pawline, G., & Renneboog, L. (2005). Is investment-cash flow sensitivity caused by agency costs or asymmetric information? Evidence from the UK. *European Financial Management, 11*, 483–514.

Peasnell, K. V., Pope, P. F., & Young, S. (2005). Managerial ownership and the demand for outside directors. *European Financial Management, 11*, 231–250.

Peng, L. (2001). Building a venture capital index, Working Paper, Yale Center for International Finance.

Petersen, M. A. (2006). Estimating standard errors in finance panel data sets: Comparing approaches. *Review of Financial Studies*, forthcoming.

Petty, J. W., Martin, J. D., & Kensinger, J. W. (1999). *Harvesting investments in private companies.* Morristown, N.J.: Financial Services Research Foundation, Inc.

Phalippou, L., & Zollo, M. (2005). Performance of private equity funds: another puzzle? Wharton Financial Working Paper No. 05–42.

Plantinga, A., & Scholtens, B. (2001). Socially responsible investing and management style of mutual funds in the Euronext stock markets, Working Paper, Depaul University—Driehaus Center for Behavioral Finance.

Porter, M. E. (1998). *On competition*. Boston: Harvard Business School Press.

Poterba, J. (1989a). Capital gains tax policy towards entrepreneurship. *National Tax Journal, 42*, 375–389.

Poterba, J. (1989b). Venture capital and capital gains taxation. In L. H. Summers (Ed.), *Tax Policy and the Economy 3* (pp. 47–67). Cambridge, MA: MIT Press.

PriceWaterhouseCoopers', (2005). *Global Private Equity Report 2005*. PriceWaterhouse Coopers. Available at http://www.pwcmoneytree.com/exhibits/GPE_Report_2005.pdf#search=%22private%20equity%20fundraising%20the%20netherlands%202005%22.

Purnanandam, A. K., & Swaminathan, B. (2004). Are IPOs really underpriced? *The Review of Financial Studies, 17*(3), 811–848.

Rajan, R. G. (1992). Insiders and outsiders: the choice between informed and arm's length debt. *Journal of Finance, 47*, 1367–1400.

Rajan, R. G., & Zingales, L. (1995). What do we know about capital structure? Some evidence from international data. *Journal of Finance, 50*, 1421–1460.

Rebello, M. J. (1995). Adverse selection costs and the firm's financing and insurance decisions. *Journal of Financial Intermediation, 4*, 21–47.

Renneboog, L., Simons, T., & Wright, M. (2007). Why do public firms go private in the UK? The impact of private equity investors, incentive realignment and undervaluation. *Journal of Corporate Finance, 13*, 591–628.

Repullo, R., & Suarez, J. (2004). Venture capital finance: a security design approach. *Review of Finance, 8*, 75–108.

Ritter, J. R. (1984). The hot issue market of 1980. *Journal of Business, 32*, 215–240.

Ritter, J. R. (1991). The long-run performance of initial public offerings. *Journal of Finance, 42*, 365–394.

Ritter, J. R. (1998). Initial public offerings. In D. Logue, & J. Seward (Eds.), *Warren Gorham & Lamont Handbook of Modern Finance*. New York: WGL/RIA 1998.

Ritter, J.R. (2003a). Investment banking and securities issuance, in *Constantinides, Harris, and Stulz's Handbook of the Economics of Finance*, Ch. 5, Amsterdam: North-Holland.

Ritter, J. R. (2003b). Differences between European and American IPO markets. *European Financial Management, 9*, 421–434.

Rivers, D., & Vuong, Q. (1988). Limited information estimators and exogeneity tests for simultaneous probit model. *Journal of Econometrics, 39*, 347–366.

Riyanto, Y. E., & Schwienbacher, A. (2006). The strategic use of corporate venture capital for securing demand. *Journal of Banking and Finance, 30*, 2809–2833.

Rock, E. (2001). Greenhorns, Yankees and Cosmopolitans: venture capital, IPOs, foreign firms and US markets. *Theoretical Inquiries in Law 2*, Article 6, 1–35.

Rock, K. (1986). Why new issues are underpriced. *Journal of Financial Economics, 15*, 187–212.

Roosenboom, P., & van der Goot, T. (2003). Takeover defences and IPO firm value in the Netherlands. *European Financial Management, 9*, 485–512.

Roell, A. (1996). The decision to go public: an overview. *European Economic Review, 40*, 1071–1081.

Roosenboom, P., van der Goot, T., & Mertens, G. (1999). Earnings management and initial public offerings: Evidence from the Netherlands, Working Paper, Eramus University.

Ruckman, K. (2003). Expense ratios of North American mutual funds. *Canadian Journal of Economics, 36*, 192–223.

Ruef, M., Aldrich, H. E., & Carter, N. M. (2003). The structure of founding teams: homophily, strong ties and isolation among U.S. entrepreneurs. *American Sociological Review, 68*, 195–222.

Ruhnka, J. C., Feldman, H. D., & Dean, T. J. (1992). The "living dead" phenomenon in venture capital investments. *Journal of Business Venturing, 7*, 137–155.

Ruud, J. R. (1993). Underwriter price support and the IPO underpricing puzzle. *Journal of Financial Economics, 34*, 135–151.

Sah, R., & Stiglitz, J. (1986). The architecture of economic systems: Hierarchies and polyarchies. *American Economic Review, 76*, 716–727.

Sahlman, W. A. (1990). The structure and governance of venture capital organizations. *Journal of Financial Economics, 27*, 473–521.

Sandler, D. (2001). The tax treatment of employee stock options: Generous to a fault. *Canadian Tax Journal, 49*, 259–302.

Santhanakrishnan, M. (2005). The impact of complementarities on the performance of entrepreneurial companies, Working Paper, Arizona State University.

Sapienza, H. (1992). When do venture capitalists add value? *Journal of Business Venturing, 7*, 9–27.

Sapienza, H. J., De Clercq, D., & Sandberg, W. R. (2005). Antecedents of international and domestic learning effort. *Journal of Business Venturing, 20*(4), 437–457.

Sapienza, H., Manigart, S., & Vermeir, W. (1996). Venture capital governance and value-added in four countries. *Journal of Business Venturing, 11*, 439–469.

Schleifer, A. (2005). Understanding regulation. *European Financial Management, 11*, 439–452.

Shleifer, A., & Wolfenzon, D. (2002). Investor protection and equity markets. *Journal of Financial Economics, 66*, 3–27.

Schmidt, D., & Wahrenburg, M. (2004). Contractual relations between European VC funds and investors: The impact of bargaining power and reputation on contractual design, Working Paper, RICAFE Working Paper No. 008.

Schmidt, K. M. (2003). Convertible securities and venture capital finance. *Journal of Finance, 58*, 1139–1166.

Schroder, M. (2003). Socially responsible investments in Germany, Switzerland and the United States—An analysis of Invest Funds and Indices, ZEW Discussion Paper No. 03-10.

Schultz, P. (2003). Pseudo market timing and the long-run underperformance of IPOs. *Journal of Finance, 58*, 483–517.

Schuster, J. A. (2003). IPOs: Insights from seven European countries, Working Paper, London School of Economics.

Schwienbacher, A. (2003). Venture capital exits in Europe and the United States, Working Paper: University of Amsterdam.

Schwienbacher, A. (2005). An empirical analysis of venture capital exits in Europe and the United States, Working Paper, EFA 2002 Berlin Meetings Discussion Paper.

Schwienbacher, A. (2007). Innovation and venture capital exits. *Economic Journal*, forthcoming.

Schwienbacher, A. (2008). Venture capital investment practices in Europe and the United States, *Financial Markets and Portfolio Management, 22*, 195–217.

Shaffer, B. (1995). Firm level responses to government regulation: theoretical and research approaches. *Journal of Management, 21*, 495–514.

Shepherd, D. A., Armstrong, M. J., & Levesque, M. (2005). Allocation of attention within venture capital firms. *European Journal of Operational Research, 116*(2), 545–564.

Siegel, R., Siegel, E., & MacMillan, I. C. (1988). Corporate venture capitalists: Autonomy, obstacles and performance. *Journal of Business Venturing, 3*, 233–247.

Sorensen, M. (2008). How smart is smart money? An empirical two-sided matching model of venture capital. *Journal of Finance, 62*, 2725–2762.

Small III, A. A., & Zivin, J. G. (2005). A Modigliani-Miller theory of corporate social responsibility. *Topics in Economic Analysis & Policy, 5*, 1.

Smart, S., & Zutter, C. (2003). Control as a motivation for underpricing: A comparison of dual- and single-class IPOs. *Journal of Financial Economics, 69*, 85–110.

Smith, D. G. (2005). The exit structure of venture capital. *UCLA Law Review, 53*, 315–356.

Social Investment Forum (2003). 2003 Report on Socially Responsible Investing Trends in the United States. Social Investment Forum, Washington D.C., United States, http://www.socialinvest.org/areas/research/trends/sri_trends_report_2003.pdf.

Songtao, L. (2001). Venture capital development in Taiwan. Asia and Pacific Economics 3.

Sorenson, O., & Stuart, T. E. (1999). Syndication networks and the spatial distribution of venture capital investments. *American Journal of Sociology, 106*, 1546–1586.

Sparkes, R., & Cowton, C. J. (2004). The maturing of socially responsible investment: A review of the developing link with corporate social responsibility. *Journal of Business Ethics, 52*, 45–57.

Spence, L. J., Schmidpeter, R., & Habisch, A. (2003). Assessing social capital: small and medium sized enterprises in Germany and the UK. *Journal of Business Ethics, 47*, 17–29.

Spence, M. (1973). Job Market Signaling. *Quarterly Journal of Economics, 87*, 355–374.

Stiglitz, J., & Weiss, A. (1981). Credit rationing in markets with imperfect information. *American Economic Review, 73*, 393–409.

The Economist (2007). Tax breaks for private equity. *The Economist*, June 7, 2007.

Tian, X. (2007). Geography, staging and venture capital financing, Working Paper, Indiana University, Bloomington.

Tian, X. (2008). The role of venture capital syndication in value creation for entrepreneurial firms. Working Paper, Indiana University Bloomington.

Theil, H. (1969). A multinomial logit extension of the linear logit model. *International Economic Review, 10*, 251–259.

Tirole, J. (1988). *The Theory of Industrial Organization*. Cambridge: MIT Press.

Torstila, S. (2001). What determines IPO gross spreads in Europe? *European Financial Management, 7*, 523–542.

Trester, J. J. (1998). Venture capital contracting under asymmetric information. *Journal of Banking and Finance, 22*, 675–699.

Triantis, G. G. (2001). Financial contract design in the world of venture capital. *University of Chicago Law Review, 68*, 305–322.

Tykvova, T. (2006). How do investment patterns of independent and captive private equity funds differ? Evidence from Germany. *Financial Markets and Portfolio Management, 20*(4), 399–418.

Tykvova, T., & Walz, U. (2007). How important is participation of different VCs in German IPOs?. *Global Finance Journal, 17*, 350–378.

Ueda, M. (2004). Banks versus venture capital: Project evaluation, screening, and expropriation. *Journal of Finance, 59*, 601–621.

Ueda, M., & Hirukawa, M. (2003). Venture capital and productivity, Working Paper, University of Wisconsin, Madison.

Ursel, N. (2000). Priced to sell: The evolution of underpricing in Canadian initial public offerings. *Canadian Business Economics*, 15–20.

Vandemaele, S. (2003). Choice of selling mechanism at the IPO: The case of the French Seconde Marché. *European Financial Management, 9*, 435–455.

Van der Goot, T. (2003). Risk, the quality of intermediaries and legal liability in the Netherlands IPO market. *International Review of Law and Economics, 23*, 121–140.

Van der Goot, T., & Knauff, P. (2001). The relevance of reported financial information for valuing European internet IPOs, Working Paper, EFMA 2001 Lugano Meetings.

Wang, C. (2005). Ownership and operating performance of Chinese IPOs. *Journal of Banking and Finance, 29*, 1835–1856.

Waring, P., & Lewer, J. (2004). The impact of socially responsible investment on human resource management: a conceptual approach. *Journal of Business Ethics, 52*, 99–108.

Welch, I. (1989). Seasoned offerings, imitation costs, and the underpricing of initial public offerings. *Journal of Finance, 44*, 421–449.

Welch, I. (1992). Sequential sales, learning, and cascades. *Journal of Finance, 47*, 695–732.

Wempe, J. (2005). Ethical entrepreneurship and fair trade. *Journal of Business Ethics, 60*, 211–220.

White, H. (1980). A heteroskedasticity-consistent covariance matrix estimator and a direct test for heteroskedasticity. *Econometrica, 48*, 817–838.

Wilson, R. (1968). The theory of syndicates. *Econometrica, 36*, 119–132.

Witt, P., & Brachtendorf, G. (2006). Staged financing of start-ups'. *Financial Markets and Portfolio Management, 20*, 185–203.

Wong, A. (2002). Angel finance: the 'other' venture capital, Working Paper, University of Chicago.

Wooldridge, J. M. (2000). *Introduction to Econometrics: A Modern Approach*. Cincinnati, OH: South-Western College.

Wooldridge, J. M. (2002). *Econometric Analysis of Cross Section and Panel Data*. Cambridge, Mass: MIT Press.

World Bank. (1994). *Can intervention work? The role of Government in SME success*. Washington, DC: World Bank.

World Bank. (2002). *World Bank group review of small business activities*. Washington, DC: World Bank.

World Bank. (2004). *World Bank group support for small business*. Washington, DC: World Bank.

Wright, M., Hoskisson, R. E., Busenitz, L. W., & Dial, J. (2001). Finance and management buyouts: agency versus entrepreneurship perspectives. *Venture Capital: An International Journal of Entrepreneurial Finance, 3*, 239–262.

Wright, M., & Lockett, A. (2003). The structure and management of alliances: syndication in the venture capital industry. *Journal of Management Studies, 40*, 2073–2104.

Wright, M., Lockett, A., & Pruthi, S. (2002). Internationalization of western venture capitalists into emerging markets: risk assessment and information in India. *Small Business Economics, 19*, 13–29.

Yosha, O. (1995). Information disclosure costs and the choice of financing source. *Journal of Financial Intermediation, 4*, 3–20.

Yung, C. (2002). Security design in private markets, Working Paper, University of Colorado.

Zacharakis, A. L., & Shepherd, D. A. (2001). The nature of information and venture capital fund managers' overconfidence. *Journal of Business Venturing, 16*, 311–332.

Zacharakis, A. L., & Shepherd, D. A. (2005). A non-additive decision-aid for venture capital fund managers' investment decisions. *European Journal of Operational Research, 162*(3), 673–689.

Zimmermann, H. (2002). On patience, recovery, and market expectations. *Financial Markets and Portfolio Management, 16*, 299–302.

Zingales, L. (1995). Insider ownership and the decision to go public. *Review of Economic Studies, 62*, 425–448.

Index